THE MAN VERDI

FRANK WALKER

The Man VERDI

WITH A NEW INTRODUCTION BY
PHILIP GOSSETT

THE UNIVERSITY OF CHICAGO PRESS

For Anne

The University of Chicago Press, Chicago 60637

Paperback edition 1982
Published by arrangement with J. M. Dent & Sons, Ltd.

ISBN-13: 978-0-226-87132-5 (paper)

22 21 20 19 18 17 16 2 3 4 5 6

Library of Congress Cataloging-in-Publication Data

Walker, Frank, 1907–1962.
The Man Verdi.
Reprint. Originally published: New York: Knopf, 1962.
With new introd.
Includes index.
1. Verdi, Giuseppe, 1813–1901. 2. Composers—Italy—Biography. I. Title.
[ML410.V4W3 1982] 782.1′092′4 [B] 82-2755
ISBN 0-226-87132-0 (pbk.) AACR2

⊗ This paper meets the requirements of ANSI/NISO Z39.48-1992 (Permanence of Paper).

Contents

Introduction to the Paperback

IN Italy a portrait of Giuseppe Verdi is on the equivalent of the one dollar bill. He is more than a great musician and a great man: he is a legend, a symbol of Italian art, a hero of the Risorgimento. The events of Verdi's boyhood are as familiar to Italian schoolchildren as those of George Washington to American. His very name was appropriated by Italian patriots: "Viva Verdi" signified "Viva Vittorio Emanuele, Re D'Italia," an "Italia" that had yet to be called into being. He is the subject of countless biographical and musical studies of all qualities and persuasions. Most of them idealize the composer. None, even today, is wholly satisfactory.

Verdi is a notoriously difficult man to penetrate. He hated publicity, shunned contacts with journalists, avoided the theatrical world. The bitter experiences of the young composer in Milan, especially the complete failure of his second opera, *Un giorno di regno* (1840), shortly after the deaths of his wife and two children, created a fierce barrier between the man Verdi and his audience, a barrier that was never breached. After a mediocre revival of *Simon Boccanegra* in Milan in 1859, Verdi wrote to his publisher, Tito Ricordi:

> Since that period I have not seen the *Giorno di Regno* again, and it may certainly be a terrible opera, though who knows how many other operas no better than it have been tolerated or perhaps even applauded. Oh if then the public had not applauded, but supported in silence that opera, I would not have words enough to thank it! . . . I do not intend to condemn it: I allow its severity, I accept its whistles, on the condition that I do not have to be grateful for its applause. We poor gypsies, charlatans, and whatever you will, are constrained to sell our efforts, our thoughts, our ecstasies for gold—the public, for three lire, buys the right to whistle at us or to applaud us. Our destiny is to be resigned to it: that's all!

These sentiments echo again and again throughout his correspondence. Though the artist may acknowledge responsibilities to his public, they end decisively when the curtain falls. The man acknowledges none. From their retreat in the villa at Sant' Agata near Busseto, the town in whose environs he was raised, Verdi and his Giuseppina Strepponi lived together from the 1850s until their deaths half a century later, first as lovers, then as man and wife, in an isolation almost complete. Few were admitted to their private realm, and those friends who violated the intimacy of their ties with the composer by speaking openly of those ties were expelled mercilessly from Verdi's favor.

Yet, despite the ostensible wall he constructed around his private life, despite his oft repeated claims to take no notice of the gossip that surrounds men of genius, Verdi was singularly concerned with his public image. He gave far more credence to newspaper accounts about his friends than was warranted: indeed, the *Otello* project almost came to grief when some remarks that Boito was alleged to have made came to Verdi's attention. The composer insisted on certain facts about his life, his date of birth, his humble origins, the story of his rejection at the Milan Conservatory, the chronology of his early years in Milan, even when evidence of which he himself must have been aware proved them false. In his private correspondence he strove so hard to project an image of strength and independence that one cannot help but speculate about the psychological motivations impelling him to construct a persona with meticulous care even to his closest friends. He instructed correspondents to destroy his letters (an injunction most of them failed to follow), while amassing at Sant'Agata a truly awesome archive of documents. Is there another public figure who preserved so thoroughly his correspondence, while simultaneously professing indifference and even scorn for the biographer's art?

Access to this and other collections with documentation about Verdi's life and art, however, has frequently been difficult. The archives at Sant' Agata remain in the hands of the Verdi heirs, descendants of his adopted daughter. For several decades now, they have permitted selective entry to those in their favor and no entry to others. They have refused to admit that musical manuscripts, early drafts, sketches, are preserved, denying even the existence of documents in their possession which have been published previously in facsimile. There is hope that matters may soon improve dramatically. The American Institute of Verdi Studies has been granted permission to film the letters, draft libretti, copybooks, etc., at Sant' Agata. Work has already begun, and the films are to be deposited at Bobst Library of New York University. For the moment, however, musical manuscripts are excluded from this agreement.

Some private collectors have been very generous, offering copies of the treasures in their possession to the Istituto di Studi Verdiani in Parma, where an impressive archive is being amassed. The Istituto has announced as its highest priority the long-awaited publication of a complete edition of Verdi's correspondence. Other collectors have permitted a single writer glimpses of their documents, then removed them from public scrutiny. Thus, the letters from Verdi to Francesco Piave, whose librettos for Verdi include *Ernani, Rigoletto, La Traviata,* and *La forza del destino,* letters which illustrate in wondrous detail Verdi's working methods, remain unavailable to scholars. Their owner, the Milanese antiquarian Natale Gallini, showed them to Franco Abbiati for use in the preparation of his massive but irreparably flawed biography of Verdi (1959). Abbiati published extracts from them with so many errors in dating and transcription, with such a limited understanding of their content, that readers are often compelled to guess what the originals might contain.

A growing number of Verdi's own letters and those of Giuseppina are housed in public libraries. During the past few years, for example, two extremely important collections have been donated to cultural institutions in Parma. The surviving letters from Verdi to Boito were offered by Boito's heirs to the Istituto di Studi Verdiani and have since been published in a magnificent edition prepared by Marcello Conati and Mario Medici. An extraordinary group of letters written during the 1880s and 1890s by Verdi to his publisher were listed for sale in an antiquarian catalog in Germany during the 1970s. After long negotiations these letters, which had disappeared half a century earlier from the Ricordi archives in Milan, were finally acquired by the Italian government and given to the Biblioteca Palatina in Parma. An edition is now being prepared by Franca Cella and Pierluigi Petrobelli.

Given the formidable difficulties in controlling this vast documentation, it is not surprising that early Verdian biography was largely anecdotal. Most of it is without substance. Modern biographical study really begins only with Carlo Gatti's *Verdi,* first published in two volumes in 1931, reissued in a revised, one-volume edition in 1951. Gatti put Verdian biography on a sound scholarly basis, publishing for the first time innumerable authentic documents. Still, with so much material to sort through and with only limited access to the materials at Sant'Agata, Gatti was in no position to penetrate fully crucial aspects of Verdi's life and art. Indeed, many of his assertions were soon challenged by Alessandro Luzio, who had almost free rein at the Villa Verdi. Luzio's collection of essays and documents, *Carteggi Verdiani,* published in four volumes (two in 1935 and two in 1947), remains a fundamental source even today. Unfortunately his penetration into the material he published, his ability to draw objective conclusions from the documentation, was marred by an idealized, previously defined image of the composer. In Luzio's world, Verdi must have dominated Boito in their collaboration, while it was inconceivable that Verdi had a physical relationship with the singer Teresa Stolz. Contrary evidence could be ignored or denigrated. Luzio never attempted a complete biography. Franco Abbiati published his four-volume life, *Verdi,* in 1959, surely one of the most unsatisfying biographies ever prepared. And it is maddeningly so, for Abbiati had access to materials no one else has seen to this day. He published them incompletely, with errors of every description, incorporating spectacular documents into a narrative whose style often resembles a popular romance. In the absence of documentary evidence, he indulges in four-page flights of imagination. He will misdate a letter, then create a fairy-tale to justify his blatant error. Not a footnote graces the book, which means that readers must control the entire Verdi literature to know what Abbiati is inventing and what is supported by the facts.

It is against this background that Frank Walker's *The Man Verdi* must be understood. Published posthumously after Walker's tragic suicide in 1962, the book made an immediate sensation. It is not a complete biography. Rather, Walker focuses on some of the more significant people in Verdi's life and carefully scrutinizes his relationships with them. His wife, Giuseppina Strepponi; his student and amanuensis, Emanuele Muzio; the conductor who first fully understood Verdi's mature art, Angelo Mariani; the great prima donna, Teresa Stolz; the incomparable librettist and friend of his old age, Arrigo Boito—each passes before our eyes in Walker's meticulous reconstruction. As we learn more about them, we learn more about Verdi. We see him through the eyes of his closest friends, we watch his daily activities, his daily thoughts, his habits, his warmth, his domestic tyranny. The myth dissolves and a human being stands before us.

Nothing so captures the spirit of Frank Walker's work as a footnote on page 5. How many biographies have stressed the hardships faced by the young Verdi. Having been sent by his family to live in Busseto so that he could continue formal studies (Le Roncole was too small to support more than an elementary school), for example, Verdi returned to Le Roncole on Sundays and holidays to play the organ at the local church: "seven kilometers to go from Busseto to Le Roncole to play the organ, and seven kilometers to return from Le Roncole to Busseto," says Carlo Gatti (p. 16). Walker, with his characteristic mixture of common sense and exasperation, remarks: "A town-bred Italian of today would undoubtedly faint if it were suggested that he should do the same, but this walk of about three miles in each direction would be nothing to a peasant boy in ordinary circumstances" (p. 5). Then he adds in a footnote: "I have myself walked from Busseto to Le Roncole in forty-three minutes."

That walk puts the whole story into perspective. Whenever Frank Walker could verify for himself some fact or statement about the life of Giuseppe Verdi, he did so; in the process, one myth after another fell victim to his keen analytical intelligence.

There were many myths to destroy, some reaching back to the composer, some constructed by those who wanted to create an image of Verdi closer to an imaginary ideal than to the original article. In 1939 and 1942, to take a notorious case, one Lorenzo Alpino, who was brought up in the Institute of Little Artisans run by Don Francesco Montebruno, Giuseppina Strepponi's confessor during the latter part of her life, published a series of letters which he claimed had been sent by Giuseppina to Montebruno and to other figures in the church. With these letters, purportedly taken from a copybook in which Montebruno entered the texts of important letters he received, Alpino attempted "at all costs and in the face of all the evidence to the contrary . . . to represent Verdi as a Christian and a Catholic" (Walker, p. 280). It is easy enough to imagine why in a Catholic country an unbeliever makes an embarassing national hero. Walker meticulously dissects these letters. He compares their content with other available documents. He places them in their supposed chronological context, checking their veracity on each point of detail. When he has finished, the truth is inescapable: the letters are simple forgeries, forgeries accepted by every writer on Verdi from the time of their publication, even, in an unguarded moment, by Walker himself in his article about the composer in Grove's *Dictionary of Music and Musicians* (fifth edition, 1954).

Walker does not exclude from consideration personal reminiscences and anecdotes. Near the beginning of his book, indeed, he muses:

> Today the tendency is to look askance at 'anecdotal biography', distrusting every story that cannot be supported by documentary evidence. This is all to the good as long as it is not carried too far. The documents available are often insufficient to illuminate all phases of a great man's life, and where other evidence is lacking, even a legend is better than nothing. Everything depends on the number of the documents and the quality of the legends. (pp. 3–4)

In chapter 8, which treats the touchy and still disputed question of Verdi's feeling towards Teresa Stolz, he returns to the subject, providing some stunning examples of written reminiscences which falsify events: "Even in the cases of people not emotionally involved, self-importance, a love of tidying up or the pleasure of telling a good story may lead to misrepresentation" (p. 393). Where documents are unavailable, Walker may turn to anecdotes, but he always analyzes carefully their "quality," accepting what seems reasonable, rejecting the purely fanciful, differentiating unequivocally statements based on documents from those derived from legend. Much, he insists, depends on "the number of the documents," and the contributions of *The Man Verdi* in this sphere are overwhelming.

Only relentless pursuit can separate truth from fiction; resourcefulness, patience, and clarity of thought must be employed. Frank Walker explored every avenue known and discovered other paths that had not even been suspected. Biographers had squabbled relentlessly about the true relations between Teresa Stolz, Angelo Mariani, and Giuseppe Verdi. Much of the argument depended on the presumption that Stolz was in certain places at certain times in the company of Mariani or Verdi. Whole fictions were written about when she came to know the two men and how her feelings about them developed. But no biographer had made a concerted effort to gather facts. Walker turned to the theatrical and operatic journals of the time, studying the schedules of major theaters and lists of performers engaged by them. As a result he was able to reconstruct Stolz's professional itinerary (see pp. 326–327). It was as simple as that. Layers of conjecture fell in rubble before this evidence. He did a similar survey for Giuseppina Strepponi's career as a singer (see pp. 52–56), clarifying her early history and going far towards resolving the problem of the paternity of her illegitimate children.

The search for new letters and documents goes on. In the absence of a collected correspondence, a scholar who seeks to know Verdi must command an immense bibliography. Frank Walker had an unequaled control of previous publications and the determination to fill whatever gaps he could find. He was the first to recognize the true importance of the copybooks Strepponi kept of her letters, though Luzio had earlier published extracts. In his chapter concerning Boito, Walker published for the first time many of Verdi's letters to his librettist. Though these letters had been available to Boito's biographer, Pietro Nardi, Nardi included only short extracts in his book. Indeed, until the appearance of the Verdi-Boito correspondence, Walker's book marked the only publication of many letters in any language. But he did more than print the documents: he was the first fully to understand the role Boito played in the creation of Verdi's last operas. While Luzio insisted on Verdi's controlling hand in the creation of *Otello* and *Falstaff,* Walker demonstrated unequivocally that theirs was a collaboration between equals, that these operas would never have been possible without Boito's knowledge of Verdi's character, his subtle ability to lead Verdi towards new approaches and new solutions to musical and dramatic problems. Walker's account of their collaboration remains the finest available even today.

"Neither time nor biography stands still. New facts and documents are constantly coming to light which make, every generation or so, a new approach necessary" (p. 289). A modern biography of Verdi remains to be written. The work of many scholars during the past two decades fills in several uncertain points in Walker's account. Mary Jane Matz has probed further into the secrets of Verdi's youth. Ursula Gunther's discovery of a written "dialogue," a declaration of love between Verdi and Strepponi within the autograph score of *Jérusalem* reveals as nothing else could the true state of their feelings in 1847. The rediscovery by Gabriella Carrara-Verdi of a crucial letter from Boito to Verdi fills in our knowledge of the earliest part of their collaboration. The correspondence with the Ricordi firm, now being edited by Franca Cella, will provide a mine of new information for Verdi scholars. And Julian Budden's masterful study of the Verdi operas has biographical implications that cannot be ignored in future discussions of Verdi the man. Modern biographers, furthermore, may avoid the "objective" tone that Walker cultivates, preferring the model of Maynard Solomon's remarkable *Beethoven*, with its emphasis on psychological explanation. Certainly Walker's revelations frequently cry out for similar interpretations.

All these efforts will reach back to *The Man Verdi*. Walker succeeds in reconstructing Verdi the man, the human being. In the process he does not detract from Verdi's greatness. If Verdi is no longer the ignorant peasant boy overcoming all odds to succeed, he is instead a son of the lower middle class, able and willing to take advantage of the opportunities placed before him. Knowing the depths of Giuseppina Strepponi's misery in the 1840s, we appreciate Verdi's feelings for her even more. We cannot close our eyes to Verdi's jealousies and, in the case of Angelo Mariani, unreasoned ingratitude towards those close to him. But Walker has no interest in gossip. He seeks to penetrate the soul of Verdi in the decade of the 1870s, when the composer felt his artistic life was behind him. Even a national hero must face his own mortality.

This is a detective story of the highest order, a panorama of Italy in the Risorgimento, an entryway into nineteenth-century society. Walker tells his story in a way that holds our interest throughout. *The Man Verdi* is a classic of musical biography, and will remain so in the years to come.

Philip Gossett
The University of Chicago

Introduction

VERDI has a way of escaping his biographers. The known facts of his long and busy career have been told and retold, but the man himself remains a distant figure, protected still by his habitual reserve and mistrust. In all the vast mass of his published correspondence, highly characteristic and absorbingly interesting as much of it is, there are few really confidential revelations. The *Copialettere* tell us much about his business relations with publishers, impresarios and librettists, but very little about his intimate private life.

This book has been written in the belief that the material, nevertheless, *does* exist, from which Verdi and his times can be clearly evoked, if only the form be found in which to present it. In my view, the unimaginative 'Life and Works' scheme has failed; again and again Verdi has been buried under masses of facts and dates. A fresh approach to the problem is necessary.

In this biographical experiment I have tried to depict Verdi the man through the stories of his relationships with some of those who knew him best. Perhaps a living figure will emerge if we can see him as he was seen, at different periods of his life, by his benefactor and father-in-law Antonio Barezzi, by his adoring pupil Emanuele Muzio, by Giuseppina Strepponi, by Mariani, Teresa Stolz, Boito and others. The plan of the book takes us, on a broadly chronological basis, through the whole of his life, and permits full discussion of various controversial matters. One of the consequences of Verdi's reticence has been that, in Italy in recent years, the gaps in our knowledge have been filled by inventions, which, endlessly repeated and amplified by ignorant and unscrupulous journalists, and popularized by films, have come to be accepted almost as gospel. This book sticks to the documents and attempts to build up a true picture from them, and to destroy the false legends.

In Verdi's case the most revealing things are often letters written to him, or about him. An almost unhoped for glimpse of what went on behind the iron curtain that was the fence and poplar screen of Sant' Agata was given by Alessandro Luzio in 1937, when he published a number of Giuseppina Strepponi's letters to Verdi. More recently the rediscovery of Giuseppina's own correspondence with the impresario Alessandro Lanari has thrown new light on her early life and the antecedents of her relationship with Verdi. I offer no apology for devoting long sections of this book to this remarkable and most lovable woman, the most important person in Verdi's life.

Muzio's letters to Barezzi, published by Luigi Agostino Garibaldi in 1931, provide a unique picture of Verdi and Milan before the revolution of 1848; they are quoted here at much greater length than would be possible in the course of a straightforward biography. At the other end of the composer's life we have some wonderful letters of Boito.

Special attention has been given to the backgrounds against which Verdi moved and worked—from the parish pump of Busseto to the cathedral of Milan, from the shady theatrical underworld to the solitude and calm of Sant' Agata.

The whole Verdi literature, including the periodical literature, has been used in the preparation of this book, and all the unpublished material to which I have been able to obtain access. During the last fifteen years I have worked in many Italian libraries, and tried the patience of friends too numerous to mention. Unpublished material used here has been drawn chiefly from four sources: the Scala Museum at Milan, the archives of Villa Verdi at Sant' Agata, the Biblioteca Nazionale Centrale at Florence and the Boito archives at Parella. The Scala Museum has many visitors, but few people realize how rich it is—apart from the beautifully displayed exhibits in the show-cases—in letters and other documents of theatrical history of all periods. I must acknowledge here the great kindness of the director of the museum, Count Stefano Vittadini, in allowing me free access to the very numerous letters of Verdi, Giuseppina Strepponi, Moriani and others in this collection. On the other hand, everybody has long known what treasures Villa Verdi contains. Alessandro Luzio worked there for many years and published his findings in the *Carteggi verdiani*, but it is said to have been difficult for ordinary mortals to gain access to these archives. I can only record my own experience. The late Dr Angiolo Carrara Verdi always replied to my inquiries, and since his death his family has been wonderfully kind and helpful. Visiting Busseto, I have been able to study Giuseppina Strepponi's manuscript letter-books, the whole of Mariani's correspondence with Verdi, a large part of that of Teresa Stolz and various other documents that specially interested me. To the whole family, and in particular to Signorina Gabriella Carrara Verdi, I owe a great debt. At Florence I have been chiefly concerned with the vast and almost unexplored collection of the letters and papers of the impresario Alessandro Lanari. It consists of about fifteen thousand letters to and from composers, singers, impresarios and theatrical agents. Giuseppina Strepponi's letters to Lanari were photographed for me by courtesy of Dr Rodolfo Paoli, but my chief debt in this connection is to Dr Franco Schlitzer, who by an exchange arrangement read on my behalf at least two thousand letters and transcribed about a hundred passages concerning Giuseppina in the correspondence of Lanari with other people. My last chapter owes much to Piero Nardi's splendid *Vita di Arrigo Boito* of 1942. Verdi's letters to Boito are still largely unpublished. In order that I might be able to study them independently, Boito's biographer magnanimously presented me with his own copies; since at first only about half of the correspondence could be found, the rest was photographed for me by Dr Leonardo Albertini from the autographs at Parella. As a result I have been able to incorporate a number of unpublished or incompletely published letters from Verdi to Boito in this chapter.

My acknowledgments are due also to Professor Napoletano, of the library of the Monte di Credito su Pegno, at Busseto; to Arthur Hedley and Mlle Suzanne Chainaye, for material concerning Giuseppina Strepponi in Paris; to Dr Enrico Olmo and Claudio Sartori, for copies of that part of Verdi's and Giuseppina's correspondence with the Countess Maffei which remained in possession of her heirs; to Don Ferruccio Botti, Signora Cina Orlandi, Professor Gino Roncaglia, Senator Giovanni Treccani degli Alfieri, Dr Leonardo Lapiccirella, Maestro Guglielmo Barblan, Mr Edward Kravitt and finally to my friend Uberto Limentani of Cambridge, to whom over many years I have repeatedly submitted tricky problems of interpretation, translation, dialect, etc.

A version of my investigations into the relations between Verdi, Donizetti and Giuseppina Appiani appeared in *Music & Letters* for January 1951; a full discussion of the Verdian forgeries of Lorenzo Alpino is to be found in the *Music Review* for November 1958 and February 1959. I have to thank the editors of these periodicals for permission to reprint some of this material.

F. W.

CHAPTER I

Early Life at Busseto and Milan: Legends and Documents

THE REGISTERS of the parish church of Le Roncole, in the plain of Parma, show that Giuseppe Fortunino Francesco Verdi was born there at 8 p.m. on 10th October 1813, and baptized the next day. There was for a long time confusion about even this apparently simple matter, for Verdi himself believed what his mother had always told him—that he was born on 9th October 1814. When in 1876 he learned from the church registers of Le Roncole that he was a year older than he had thought, he accepted the fact, but nevertheless continued for the rest of his life to celebrate his birthday on the wrong day.

Since the composer whose name was afterwards to be so closely associated with the Risorgimento and unification of Italy came into the world while the Duchy of Parma was under French domination, his father had also to go into the neighbouring town of Busseto to register the birth there with the French civil authorities. Verdi thus appears in the books at Busseto as Joseph Fortunin François. A year or two later this entry would perhaps have been made out in German by the Austrians. But what is actually the earliest record of his birth and baptism is in the parish register of Le Roncole and is in Latin.

Le Roncole was, and is, the merest hamlet—a number of scattered houses, a church and, on a corner where two roads meet, the squalid building where Verdi's father kept a tavern of sorts and sold wine and groceries.

Very little is known about the composer's parents. In his case there are no family letters, such as those that reveal so much of the home life and family affections of Mozart, Mendelssohn, Chopin or Wolf. Verdi's parents could apparently neither read nor write: both are described as 'illiterate' in an official report on the family compiled at Busseto in 1832. The father could sign his name, but the few existing documents to which his signature is attached were drawn up for him by other people.

Carlo Verdi was born on 22nd August 1785, at Le Roncole, where his forbears had lived for at least six generations. His father died in the open street at Busseto when Carlo was thirteen years of age, and in 1804, when he was nineteen, he was endeavouring to support his widowed mother and a younger brother on the profits of his *osteria.* It was no easy task and he was desperately poor. In a surviving document,[1] dated 2nd October 1804, he petitions against the verdict of the district court at Busseto, which had found him guilty of permitting gambling in his establishment. Some youths had been surprised there with a pack of cards and had defended themselves by declaring that the cards did not belong to them but had been found on the premises. Carlo Verdi denied this, pleaded that he had himself been absent with his mother at the church of the Madonna dei Prati when the incident occurred, and supplied testimonials to his character from the parish priest and the four deputies of Le Roncole. The priest declared: 'He is poor in worldly goods, possessing nothing at all, but is nevertheless a youth of excellent habits, very conscientious, assiduously attentive to the Church, to Christian doctrine and to the Sacraments, not at all inclined to the taverns, an enemy of gaming, of dangerous companions and of everything that could obscure the good name and the high esteem he has always enjoyed and enjoys still among good people, not only in this village but in the whole district.' The deputies confirmed that Carlo was a youth of praiseworthy character, of good name and fame, pious and 'hostile to any sort of gaming and card-playing in particular, especially in his own inn'. A prodigy of virtue! But Dionigi Crescini, President of the Council of Criminal Justice, was not impressed by these testimonials: 'The contravention of the law was proved at the trial. Furthermore, the cards were found on the table of the inn when the players entered, which is a kind of invitation to gaming on the part of the host. The law is most sacred; rigorous examples are necessary; hence it is not deemed expedient to grant the requested remission of punishment.'

After that, although he lived until 1867, we hear little more of Verdi's father. About his mother, Luigia Uttini, we know almost nothing, except that, born on 29th September 1787 at Saliceto di Cadeo (Piacenza), where her parents kept an inn, she came to Busseto with one of her brothers in 1804, married Carlo Verdi on 30th January

[1] Giovanni Drei, 'Notizie e documenti verdiani' (*Aurea Parma, fasc.* 1–2, 1941).

1805[1] and died on 30th June 1851, having given birth to a musical genius and to a girl-child, Giuseppa Francesca, who, believedly as the result of meningitis, was mentally deficient. Giuseppa, born on 20th March 1816, died at Le Roncole on 9th August 1833, at the age of seventeen.

Italo Pizzi of Parma, who became one of Verdi's friends and also collected information about the composer from the Barezzi family, has some remarks on the characters of his parents.[2] Luigia was hard-working, courageous, sensible and dignified; it was from her that Verdi inherited his best qualities. Carlo, however, according to Pizzi, gave up his tavern and lived a life of ease at his son's expense, as soon as the latter began to win fame and to make money. From the papers of Ercolano Balestra,[3] notary of Busseto, we know that in 1846 Carlo sold a small field at Le Roncole for 1,000 lire and in 1849 sold his house and a piece of ground for 2,900 lire. And we know that in May 1849 the composer installed his parents in the house that was to become, after many alterations, the Villa Verdi, at Sant' Agata. There was certainly sometimes friction between father and son. A letter from Verdi to Balestra in 1851 states that he has heard that his father is going about saying that the administration of the Sant' Agata farms had been entrusted to him. Verdi denies this and adds: 'I can only repeat what I told you yesterday by word of mouth: to the world, Carlo Verdi must be one thing and Giuseppe Verdi another.'

Most of the current stories of Verdi's early life appeared first in Pougin's 'anecdotal biography', originally published serially in *Le Ménestrel* in French, and then in 1881 in book form in an Italian translation, with additional material by 'Folchetto' (Jacopo Caponi). This Italian edition is the most valuable as a source book.[4] Verdi was sceptical about the interest which an account of his own life could have for the public, but he told Ricordi that if he was publishing it he should see that it was as accurate as possible. He collaborated to the extent of giving Ricordi an account of his early years at Milan. He was sent the proofs, and returned them 'with corrections of various inaccuracies of some importance'. However, Verdi's own recollections, in this document and in some later letters, are often demonstrably inaccurate.

Today the tendency is to look askance at 'anecdotal biography', distrusting every story that cannot be supported by documentary evidence. This is all to the good as long as it is not carried too far.

[1] Emilio Ottolenghi, 'La Madre di Verdi' (*Bollettino storico piacentino*, July–Dec. 1940).

[2] *Per il primo centenario della nascita di Giuseppe Verdi*, (Turin, 1913).

[3] P. Luigi Ag. Grazzi, 'Documenti inediti della giovinezza di Verdi' (*Gazzetta di Parma*, 3rd July 1950).

[4] The English version of 1887 is translated from a revision by Pougin of his own material and that of 'Folchetto'.

The documents available are often insufficient to illuminate all phases of a great man's life, and where other evidence is lacking, even a legend is better than nothing. Everything depends on the number of the documents and the quality of the legends.

Carlo Gatti in his monumental biography [1] does not accept at its face value the earliest of all the stories of the composer's youth, which relates how in 1814, when the Austrian and Russian armies began to turn the French out of northern Italy, a group of Russians passed through Le Roncole, looting, raping and killing some of the inhabitants, including women who had taken refuge in the church, Verdi's mother saving herself and her child by hiding in the belfry. Gatti wants documentary evidence and says the episode is not mentioned in Verdi's letters nor in any of his recorded conversations. But it is worth noting that this story was among those told to Luisa Mancinelli-Cora by Giuseppina Strepponi, the composer's second wife.[2] If Giuseppina told the story, it may be taken that Verdi himself believed it to be true. And certainly no one who has had any experience of what it means to be 'liberated' by Russians could find anything improbable about it.

Verdi's first music master was the village organist of Le Roncole, old Pietro Baistrocchi. Before very long the pupil was taking his teacher's place. At the age of ten, on the death of the priest who taught him in the village elementary school, Giuseppe began to attend the *ginnasio* at Busseto and it was arranged that he should lodge there with a friend of his father's, a cobbler called 'Pugnatta' (this would be a nickname), who charged thirty *centesimi* a day. It can be imagined that this sum did not permit much luxury. A schoolfellow, Marco Boccelli, who became a priest, recalled later how he used to share his lunch with the young Verdi, who generally had nothing more than a slice of toasted polenta and some pickled onions. By this time Baistrocchi was dead and his former pupil engaged officially as organist of the church of Le Roncole, at a salary of thirty-six lire per annum, plus additional fees for weddings and funerals and the benefit of a collection at harvest-time. His basic salary was raised to forty lire after repeated appeals by his father. The job brought in the equivalent of four pounds a year and Verdi retained it until he left for Milan at the age of eighteen.

'I had a hard time of it in my youth,' the composer told Camille Bellaigue, and we can well believe it. Nevertheless mistaken emphasis has been laid by some of his biographers on the fact that on Sundays and feast days he used to go on foot from Busseto to Le Roncole and back, to fulfil his duties as organist. A town-bred Italian of today would undoubtedly faint if it were suggested that he should do the

[1] *Verdi* (first edition, Milan, 1931; second edition, Milan, 1951).
[2] Luisa Mancinelli-Cora, *Giuseppe Verdi* (*Ricordi personali*) (Genoa, 1936).

same, but this walk of about three miles in each direction would be nothing to a peasant boy in ordinary circumstances.[1] The story has more point in the version given by Giuseppina Strepponi to Luisa Mancinelli-Cora, according to which Verdi often walked this distance *barefoot*, carrying his boots so as not to wear them out. But presumably he did not do that in the winter.

One Christmas morning, before dawn, Verdi was making his way to Le Roncole for the early mass when he stumbled into a deep ditch and might have been drowned if his cries for help had not been heard by a passing peasant. This anecdote can be readily accepted as authentic by anyone who has visited this part of Italy. Great irrigation ditches, ten or more feet wide and very deep, are a feature of the country; one of them accompanies the road between Busseto and Le Roncole, with no hedge or fence to guard it, and at one point the road makes a sudden almost right-angled turn to the right. This was perhaps the scene of Verdi's accident. Anyone who in darkness or fog missed the turn would inevitably walk straight into the ditch.

It is not unfitting that Verdi's parents should have remained in the obscurity in which they lived, for there was another person who seems to us today to stand in relationship to him in the position normally occupied by a father. In everything except the actual physical fact Antonio Barezzi, a most attractive and lovable figure, *was* Verdi's father. Barezzi, born in 1787, was a prosperous merchant with a house on the *piazza* facing the Rocca di Busseto at the end of the arcaded main street of the sleepy little town. There he sold wine, groceries, and liqueurs of his own distillation, and Carlo Verdi was one of his customers, when he came in to Busseto each week to renew supplies for the tavern of Le Roncole. Barezzi was also an enthusiastic music lover, or, as a contemporary fellow townsman put it, a 'maniaco dilettante'. He was the founder and president of the local Philharmonic Society, which met for rehearsals and performances in a large room in his house. He himself played the flute well and could also take a hand with a clarinet, horn or ophicleide. It cannot be precisely determined when Barezzi first began to show interest in the young Verdi, but it seems almost certain that it was on his advice that the boy was sent to lodge at Busseto.

Gatti tells us that Verdi was admitted to the *ginnasio* at Busseto in November 1823. In a later document the priest Don Pietro Seletti attests that the composer attended his classes in Italian grammar, elementary and advanced, for two years, and Canon Giuseppe Demaldè, school inspector of Busseto, adds that Verdi also completed

[1] G. Pighini ('Giuseppe Verdi visto da un biologo', in *Archivio storico per le provincie parmensi*, 1941) says: 'Seven kilometres of road! *Three or four hours* just for the journey there and back!' I have myself walked from Busseto to Le Roncole in forty-three minutes.

the course in 'humanity and rhetoric' under Carlo Curotti and Don Giacinto Volpini.[1] The boy studied music under Ferdinando Provesi, *maestro di cappella* and organist of the collegiate church of San Bartolomeo,[2] and director of the municipal school of music and of the Philharmonic Society; but it is not established that he began his musical studies with Provesi at the same time as his lessons in grammar with Seletti. A familiar story tells of the rivalry of these two men. Seletti wished Verdi to become a priest; Provesi was sure he had before him a great future as a musician; Seletti capitulated after hearing Verdi improvise on an occasion when he was deputizing for a local organist, one Captain Soncini. Perhaps this was towards the close of 1825 and marked the beginning of his serious studies at the municipal school of music under Provesi. When Verdi made application for employment as organist of Soragna, a village not far from Le Roncole, at the end of October 1829, Provesi wrote him a letter of recommendation,[3] and in this he specifies four years of music study then completed. So the four years in the school of music only began in the autumn of 1825, after Verdi had been already for two years under Seletti at the *ginnasio*.

It is very frequently stated by biographers that Verdi became an apprentice in Barezzi's grocer's shop, but this seems not to be true. Pougin originally wrote that Verdi's father obtained for him a position with Barezzi and further remarked that 'without at all neglecting his duties he actively occupied himself with music'. To this 'Folchetto' in the Italian edition added the note: 'Verdi had no duties of any kind, except those arising from his position as organist.' This note was ignored by Pougin in his later revision of his Verdi biography, but 'Folchetto' probably had good reason for making the emendation. In an early biography, which is of some importance owing to the author's friendship with the Barezzi family and his use of material in their possession, Franco Temistocle Garibaldi refers to Verdi's 'life full of activity, in which the offices of shop assistant, or draper's boy, play little or no part—not to say they play no part at all—if the *Libro di casa* written day by day by the truthful pen of Signor Antonio has authority rather than the affirmations of hasty biographers *who say they have heard*'.[4] That is not an ideally clear statement, but suggests that Garibaldi too did not believe Verdi was ever employed by Barezzi. There is no mention of any such employment in the manuscript *Cenni biografici* compiled in 1856 by Giuseppe

[1] Gatti, first edition, I, pp. 37–8; second edition, p. 39.

[2] The biographers frequently refer to the 'cathedral' of Busseto, the contemporary documents to the 'Collegiata'. There was no cathedral of Busseto, the town being within the diocese of the Bishop of Borgo San Donnino, the modern Fidenza.

[3] Facsimiles of Verdi's application (the earliest surviving Verdi letter) and Provesi's letter of recommendation are given by Nullo Musini in his article 'Il primo sfortunato concorso di Giuseppe Verdi' (*Aurea Parma, fasc.* 1, 1937).

[4] *Giuseppe Verdi nella vita e nell'arte* (Florence, 1904).

Demaldè of Busseto, who was probably a relative of Barezzi's wife.[1] There is no mention if it, either, in Michele Lessona's *Volere è potere* (Florence, 1869), a book containing an account of the composer's early days for which he himself provided information.[2]

The application for employment as organist at Soragna was unsuccessful, and from this time forward Verdi began more and more to deputize for his master in all the manifold musical activities of Busseto as well as continuing his duties at Le Roncole. He taught younger pupils in the school of music, he played the organ in the church, he copied parts for the Philharmonic Society, directed their rehearsals and appeared frequently as pianist at the *accademie* held in Barezzi's house. He was accounted the best pianist in the district and was already composing a prodigious quantity of music for all the local functions. In a document in his own hand, dating from 1853, he declared:

> From my thirteenth to my eighteenth year (the age at which I went to Milan to study counterpoint) I wrote an assortment of pieces: marches for brass band by the hundred, perhaps as many little *sinfonie*,[3] that were used in church, in the theatre or at concerts, five or six concertos and sets of variations for pianoforte, which I played myself at concerts, many serenades, cantatas (arias, duets, very many trios) and various pieces of church music, of which I remember only a *Stabat Mater*.[4]

An overture to *The Barber of Seville* was performed in the Busseto theatre in 1828, and Gatti mentions several other works from the same period, of which Barezzi kept a record. Provesi had taught Verdi all he knew and regarded him as his own equal. This is shown by the fact that at the end of 1831, when Verdi applied for financial assistance from the Monte di Pietà of Busseto, Provesi supplied him with a second testimonial, and in this he still declared that he had taught Verdi for four years—the period he had already mentioned in his letter of recommendation of two years earlier. From the autumn of 1829 until 1832 Verdi was thus Provesi's assistant, and no longer his pupil. This points to very definite limitations in Provesi's equipment.

In Barezzi's house, where Verdi spent most of his time, he was treated like a beloved son, and from 14th May 1831 he abandoned his lodgings and lived there altogether. Barezzi had four daughters and two sons. The eldest daughter Margherita, born 4th May 1814, and

[1] The *Cenni biografici*, used and quoted by Gatti, were written for Carlo Viviani, editor of *Fuggilozio*, in which periodical Demaldè hoped they would be published. The manuscript, together with some of the relative correspondence, is in possession of the Monte di Credito su Pegno at Busseto.

[2] See the letter to Arrivabene of 7th March 1874, in A. Alberti's *Verdi intimo* (Milan, 1931).

[3] Probably single-movement works of the overture type.

[4] Facsimile in *Nel primo centenario di Giuseppe Verdi. Numero unico illustrato* (Milan, 1913).

thus seven months younger than Verdi, took singing and piano lessons from him. They fell in love. This was discovered by the mother and disclosed to Signor Antonio, who was not at all displeased. But it was time, if Verdi was to become his son-in-law, to look to the future. The possibilities of Busseto were exhausted. Verdi must complete his studies at Milan. So Carlo Verdi was persuaded by Barezzi to apply for one of the four monetary grants available to poor children of talent from the institution known as the Monte di Pietà e d'Abbondanza. These grants were normally of 300 lire a year for four years. As is well known, Verdi received financial assistance from the Monte di Pietà, but the facts of the matter have been very much misunderstood. The documents published by Gatti have not prevented later biographers from giving misleading accounts of what happened.

Carlo Verdi's first application to the administrators of the Monte di Pietà was made on 14th May 1831. Seven months later he appealed to the Duchess of Parma, Marie Louise. On 14th January 1832 the administrators met to consider the case, having before them testimonials provided by Provesi, by the schoolmaster Seletti and by a group of members of the Philharmonic Society headed by Barezzi. Barezzi had also guaranteed his financial support for a year. He knew, as well as the rest of Busseto, that none of the four scholarships was in fact vacant at this time, nor would be vacant until 1st November 1833—nearly two years later. The minutes of the meeting of 14th January show that two out of the six members of the council were against promising any pension in advance, while the other four were in favour of granting Verdi the first available pension, on condition of receiving regular good reports on his ability and progress. One Giovanni Bonatti specified 'one year of assiduous musical study in the Conservatorio at Milan, by means of Signor Antonio Barezzi's subvention' preliminary to the Monte di Pietà scholarship.

Verdi's passport for Milan was issued on 22nd May and he travelled some time in the second half of June. Lodgings had been arranged for him, on a temporary basis, with Giuseppe Seletti, a school-teacher—nephew of his old master in the *ginnasio* of Busseto and a close friend of Barezzi's. On 22nd June Verdi applied in writing for admission to the Conservatorio as a paying pupil, under article 10 of the regulations, which permitted the acceptance of pupils over the normal age limit if they were exceptionally gifted. As everybody knows, after a brief examination his application was rejected. With the important recent exception of Alessandro Luzio, writers on Verdi have long ceased abusing the registrar Basily and his colleagues for this unfortunate decision. It is recognized that the Conservatorio authorities acted reasonably enough in the circumstances. Verdi's own account of these events is given in a letter to Jacopo Caponi of 13th October 1880:

In 1832, in June (I was not yet nineteen), I applied in writing to be admitted to the Milan Conservatorio as a paying pupil. Moreover I underwent a kind of examination at the Conservatorio, submitting some of my compositions and playing a piano piece before Basily, Piantanida, Angeleri and others, including old Rolla, to whom I had been recommended by my teacher at Busseto, Ferdinando Provesi. About a week later I went to Rolla, who said to me: 'Give up all idea of the Conservatorio; choose a teacher in the city; I suggest either Lavigna or Negri.' I heard nothing more from the Conservatorio. Nobody replied to my application. Nobody spoke to me, either before or after the examination, of the Regulations.

This shows that the passage of nearly fifty years and the attainment of every conceivable ambition, material and artistic, did not suffice to wipe out the bitterness of that early setback, but Verdi's letter is not a trustworthy guide to what actually took place. His application *must* have been returned, for it was found among his papers after his death, and in it he specifically mentions the regulation concerning the age limit, upon which his only hope of entering the Conservatorio depended. The whole of this matter has been thrashed out in exemplary fashion by Carlo Gatti and need only be summarized here. Verdi failed to obtain admission because he was four years over the normal age limit, because he was, in Lombardo-Venetia, a 'foreigner', because the Conservatorio classrooms and dormitories were already overcrowded, and because the report on his piano-playing was unsatisfactory, so that it was not found expedient to make an exception in his case. Nobody has suggested that the compositions he was then producing were masterpieces, but the verdict on this side of his musical attainments was quite favourable. Basily's report to Count Sormoni, director of the Conservatorio, is correct and apparently unbiased:

> Signor Angeleri, teacher of the pianoforte, found that the said Verdi would have need to change the position of his hand, which, he said, at the age of eighteen would be difficult. As regards the compositions that he presented as his own, I am in complete agreement with Signor Piantanida, teacher of counterpoint and vice-registrar, that if he [Verdi] applies himself attentively and patiently to study the rules of counterpoint, he will be able to control the genuine imagination he shows himself to possess, and thus turn out creditably as a composer.[1]

Basily further remarked that he was receiving continual complaints about the difficulties created by so many students having to work in the restricted space available and in particular by the fact that there was only one instrument for the use of all the pianoforte pupils. Count Sormoni, in his turn, suppressed these latter remarks of Basily's in

[1] Ludovico Corio, *Ricerche storiche sul R. Conservatorio di Musica di Milano* (Milan, 1908).

passing on the report to the governing authorities, but added: 'As I have many times reported, restrictions of space in the dormitory make it impossible to accept him unless some other paying pupil leaves in the new school year.' With the use of the word 'impossible' by the director, Verdi's case was lost. It only remained for a civil servant to scribble underneath: 'Verdi is eighteen and is thus four years above the normal age; *he is a foreigner*; the pianoforte examination has shown he is not very talented [*non ha disposizioni favorevoli*]. It is proposed therefore to *return* the petition.'

Luzio has published some letters from Giuseppe Seletti, with whom Verdi was staying at Milan, to Antonio Barezzi, concerning the Conservatorio examination.[1] They do not really justify revival of the old campaign against Basily and the other authorities, but are nevertheless interesting as showing how things looked at the time to Verdi's supporters. Pending official notification of the result, Seletti did his best to pump the examiners, both personally and through an influential friend, Dr Frigeri. A letter of 4th July tells, apart from a lot of hearsay, how Angeleri had declared to Seletti himself that, asked by Basily for his honest opinion, he had replied that Verdi did not know how to play the piano and would never learn. Rolla and Carlo Coccia, another teacher, found this opinion of Angeleri's excessively derogatory and final, and Rolla promised to speak to Angeleri about it. But if he did so, he was already too late, for Seletti spoke to Rolla on 3rd July, and Basily's report is dated 2nd July.

Similarly the unfortunate quarrel between Basily and Rolla at a rehearsal, mentioned in this letter, occurred after the official report had gone in and cannot have affected the issue. When the result of the examination was made known Seletti wrote again to Barezzi, freely criticizing everyone concerned: Basily was a man without character, Count Sormoni had acted solely in his own interests, Rolla and Frigeri had deceived him, saying one thing to his face and doing another thing behind his back, and so on. It was all natural enough in the circumstances, but the official documents carry more weight than these peevish private expressions of disappointment, and there are no real grounds for questioning the integrity of the authorities. Luzio, who does so, refrains from quoting Basily's actual report.

Verdi's rejection by the Conservatorio completely upset Barezzi's plans. His idea clearly had been for Verdi, had he been accepted as a pupil, to have commenced his studies at the Conservatorio after the long vacation, which lasted from the beginning of July until November. The year for which Barezzi had guaranteed his expenses would then have come to an end just after the earliest date at which one of the Monte di Pietà pensions would have become available. Seletti

[1] 'Verdi e il Conservatorio di Milano' (*Nuova Antologia*, 1st March 1937). Reprinted in *Carteggi verdiani*, IV (Rome, 1947).

now told Barezzi he must make up his mind whether to recall Verdi to Busseto or not. One year's board, lodging and tuition in the Conservatorio would have cost 600 lire, but this sum would by no means suffice if Verdi was to remain in the city and study privately. Barezzi, to his eternal credit, his faith in his protégé undimmed, prepared himself for further sacrifices. Verdi was to stay at Milan and study under Lavigna. Some idea of the cost of this may be gathered from the first accounts rendered to Barezzi by Seletti, which are reproduced in facsimile in Carlo Gatti's *Verdi nelle immagini* (Milan, 1941). Twelve lessons a month with Lavigna cost 48 Austrian lire, hire of music cost 3 Austrian lire a month and Seletti charged 70 Milanese lire a month—equivalent to about 61 Austrian lire—for board and lodging. So on these accounts alone Barezzi had to pay 1,344 Austrian lire a year, or considerably more than twice as much as had been anticipated, and more than four times as much as the annual pension available from the Monte di Pietà after November 1833. There were doubtless additional expenses. It is by no means certain that Carlo Verdi was able to keep his son decently clothed. Seletti's account has a postscript: 'I wrote you before that Maestro Lavigna told Verdi to take a season ticket for the theatre. Now Verdi tells me he cannot do so unless you instruct me to let him have the necessary money. Besides this, he says he needs money for music paper.' Everything was paid for by Barezzi, who also gave Verdi a square piano, to be seen today in the Scala Museum at Milan, with inlaid inscription: 'To Giuseppe Verdi. Barezzi Antonio. 1832.'

What of the Monte di Pietà? How was the attitude of the administrators affected by Verdi's failure to enter the Conservatorio? Documents published by Gatti [1] show that in January 1836, after a total payment of only 650 lire, the Monte di Pietà suspended Verdi's pension, on the completion of his studies at Milan. Barezzi, in a letter to the president of the council of the Monte di Pietà, protested against this course of action. He claimed that the full four years' pension was due, as, in order to make the utmost use of his time, Verdi had worked twelve months in the year, whereas the Conservatorio year had only eight working months—from November to June. In the thirty-two months he had spent at Milan, Verdi had thus studied precisely as long as he would have done had he attended the Conservatorio for four full years. It seems that in the end, after Verdi's studies were completed and after prolonged haggling, Barezzi recovered the balance—550 lire—of the full four years' pension, 1,200 lire, towards the very much higher expenses in which he had involved himself; but this is a very different story from that told by most of the

[1] First edition, I, pp. 133–5 (second edition, pp. 115–16) and pp. 193–4 (omitted in second edition).

biographers. Francis Toye, for instance, writing of the Monte di Pietà pensions, says: 'Normally they were worth three hundred francs a year and were tenable for four years, but the administrators of the trust, *with rare intelligence*, managed to meet young Verdi's requirements by allotting him six hundred francs for two years.' But in justice to Antonio Barezzi it needs to be pointed out that he took on his own shoulders almost the whole burden, that the Monte di Pietà did little until the end had been achieved, and that the sums paid out from November 1833 to December 1835, together with that later repaid to Barezzi, amounted certainly to not more than one-third of what he had actually expended. Probably, in all, Barezzi paid three-quarters of the expenses of Verdi's musical education. These facts help to explain the intense resentment aroused in the composer in later years whenever he was reminded of what he owed to Busseto and the Bussetani. In 1865, for example, when claims to which he objected were made upon him in connection with the newly built municipal theatre, he reacted violently:

What? They dispose of me, of my will, of my means, without speaking to me, without consulting me? But this is more than unbecoming—it's an insult. *What need of speaking to him about it? Oh, he'll do it. He'll have to do it.* With what right do they act in this way? I know well that many of them, speaking about me, go about whispering a phrase I don't know whether more ridiculous or despicable—*We made him!*—words that reached my ear the last time I was at Busseto, eight or ten days ago. I repeat that that is ridiculous and despicable. Ridiculous because I can reply: 'Why don't you *make* the others then?' Despicable, because nothing more was done than execute the terms of a legacy. But if they throw this benefit in my face, I can still reply: 'Gentlemen, I received a pension for four years, 25 francs a month, 1,200 francs in all. That was thirty-two years ago. Let's draw up a bill of the capital and the interest, and I'll settle up.' The moral debt will always remain. Agreed. But I raise my head and I say with pride: 'Gentlemen, I have carried your name with honour all over the world. That's well worth 1,200 francs.'

We return now to the year 1832, to Milan, where Verdi has begun studying with Vincenzo Lavigna. On 8th August Seletti was able to tell Barezzi: 'He has already had five lessons, all of an hour and a half. Lavigna seems most attentive and in speaking both to me and to Dr Frigeri declared that Verdi is working hard and good results are promised.' Further: 'He has already made him write a *sinfonia*, which he will have performed later at a private gathering, held every Sunday, to which he has promised to introduce him. In short, everything is going well.' Verdi himself in later life gave some account of Lavigna and his studies with him, in a letter to Francesco Florimo:

I have seen on other occasions that you knew that Lavigna was my master. And do you know who Lavigna was? Lavigna was a pupil of

Fenaroli, who as an extremely old man still gave lessons in the College of . . . (I no longer know which), but at the same time Lavigna took private lessons from Valente. Valente's name is little known to us, but *you* should know him well. Lavigna had a very high opinion of him, and if one may judge from five or six original fugues that Lavigna preserved, and by many fugue subjects that served also for my own studies, Valente was a contrapuntist very much more assured and profound than Fenaroli. Lavigna was taken (I believe in 1801) to Milan by Paisiello who was going to Paris for I don't know what purpose. Recommended by Paisiello, he wrote an opera for La Scala and settled down as *maestro concertatore* at that theatre, where he remained until 1832. In that year I knew him and studied counterpoint under his direction until 1835. Lavigna was very strong in counterpoint, a bit of a pedant, and had no use for any other music than that of Paisiello. I remember that in a *sinfonia* that I wrote he corrected all the scoring in the manner of Paisiello. 'I should be in a fix,' I said to myself—and from that moment I did not show him any more of my original compositions, and in the three years spent with him I did not do anything but canons and fugues, fugues and canons of all sorts. No one taught me orchestration and how to treat dramatic music.

There you are, that's who Lavigna was.

I add that he wrote seven or eight operas for Milan and Turin, with varied fortune. I repeat: he was learned, and I wish all teachers were like him.

In the summary of his own early compositions, from which a quotation has already been given (page 7), Verdi says:

In the three years I was at Milan, I wrote very few original compositions: two *sinfonie*, that were performed at Milan at a private concert in the Contrada degli Orefici (I can't remember any more in which house), a cantata that was performed at the house of Count Renato Borromeo and various pieces, most of them comic, which my master made me do as exercises and which were not even scored.

It is fair to remember that Lavigna made Verdi hire scores each month from a music dealer, and that he advised him to take a season ticket for the opera house, where he would learn 'how to treat dramatic music' by practical example. The operas performed at La Scala in this winter season, 1832–3, were *Donna Caritea*, *Ismalia* and *Il conte d'Essex*—all by Mercadante, *Chiara di Rosemberg*, *Fernando Cortez* and *Il nuovo Figaro*—all by Luigi Ricci, *Fausta* by Donizetti, *Caterina di Guisa* by Carlos Coccia and *Elena e Malvina* by the Maltese composer Francesco Schira. It was on works like these, totally unfamiliar today, that Verdi was brought up.

Verdi had been studying at Milan for twelve months when the news arrived from Busseto that his old teacher Provesi was dead. Thus the associated posts of *maestro di cappella* and organist of the collegiate church and municipal music master fell vacant while Verdi, considered by Barezzi and his friends as Provesi's pre-ordained successor, was still incompletely equipped. He remained at Milan and went on working.

The position at Busseto was somewhat complicated. The ecclesiastical and municipal authorities had each contributed to Provesi's salary. The Philharmonic orchestra, or town band, which he trained and directed, participated also in the church festivals. We do not know how long Provesi had been incapacitated by illness, but three months before his death he had written in agony of mind to a friend at Parma, imploring his intervention to save the Philharmonic Society of Busseto. Provesi was apparently less concerned for the difficulties of the church authorities, with whom he had a long-standing feud. He was a liberal, anti-clerical, and the composer of many a barbed epigram about the priests on whom he depended for half his salary. After his death the ecclesiastics, headed by the Provost, Don Gian Bernardo Ballarini, determined that the post should be filled by a candidate of their own, Giovanni Ferrari, *maestro di cappella* at Guastalla. Ferrari and two other musicians applied for the position and in November 1833 an application from Verdi himself was in Barezzi's hands. It was not presented, as verbal assurances were given that a competitive examination would be held. While waiting for an official announcement to this effect Verdi remained at Milan, doing all he could to equip himself as Provesi's successor. According to a letter from Lavigna to the administrators of the Monte di Pietà, in December 1833 he still needed about another year's study.

It is extraordinary that the ecclesiastical authorities should have waited so long before showing their hand; while Verdi was away and, according to Lavigna himself, not yet qualified to call himself *maestro di musica*, Don Ballarini would seem to have had every right to appoint his own candidate as organist and music master of the church, and to have had an excellent opportunity to persuade the municipal authorities to accept his choice. Yet it was not until 18th June 1834, nearly a year after Provesi's death, that Ferrari was in fact appointed, without warning and without a competition, to the consternation of Barezzi and his friends of the Philharmonic Society. No small part of the general exasperation at Busseto is attributable to this delay, which left the musical side of the church services in the hands of incompetent substitutes and left the Philharmonic Society and the school of music without any leadership at all, so far as is known. Verdi, hastily recalled by Barezzi as soon as he learned what was happening, arrived at Busseto on the day of Ferrari's appointment. On 20th June he sent in his own application for the post; on the next day the administrators of the Monte di Pietà decided to accept the appointment of Ferrari, subject only to their being satisfied as to his qualifications, Verdi's application being set aside as having been received too late. On 28th June Verdi protested and appealed in a letter to the Duchess Marie Louise.

Barezzi was utterly disconcerted by these developments. The mayor of Busseto, Antonio Accarini, who had a place not only on the council of the Monte di Pietà but on that of the collegiate church, was an admirer of Verdi and should have been able to hold the church authorities to their promise of a competitive examination. He had been represented, however, by his deputy, the syndic Ferdinando Galluzzi; and this man, although an old friend of Barezzi's and another Verdian partisan, was held to have betrayed the cause. Passages in a letter from Galluzzi to Barezzi allow us a glimpse of the truth.

Galluzzi recalls in this letter [1] how he himself had proposed at an early meeting of the church council that Provesi's post should be filled by competitive examination. This was agreed upon, subject to the approval of the Monte di Pietà, but in point of fact no approach was made to that body in succeeding months:

Such was the position when the rumour arose from your house that Verdi no longer aspired to the vacant position, as he was dedicating himself wholly to the study of music for the theatre and had already more profitable and attractive offers. Knowing the gossiping proclivities of not a few of my fellow-citizens, I took no account of the common rumour, but rather considered this tittle-tattle a trick of some adversary of Verdi's. In this state of affairs the not infrequent mishaps that occurred during the musical functions of the church induced the president to convoke the council for 18th June 1834. I had been told in confidence by a member of the council that at this meeting the matter of the *maestro di cappella* would be finally dealt with, and out of friendly regard I hastened to confide to you the object of the meeting, to learn whether Verdi still wished to compete, and if so to suggest hurrying up with the application. In the uncertainty due to the unexpected resolution of the council, you hesitated somewhat and asked me to find some way of postponing the business, as Verdi's arrival at Busseto was expected daily. . . . Being in doubt meanwhile as to your real attitude, I wished for more certain information and questioned the betrothed of the candidate in question, by whom I was told frankly: 'Verdi will never, never settle at Busseto. First of all because by so doing he would interrupt his studies; and secondly because, having devoted himself to music for the theatre, he looks for success in that and not in church music.' She added: 'In the last analysis, any advantageous commission he has obtained would be invalidated and all his patrons let down.' (Your daughter's very words.) After such a decided reply, which I faithfully reported to you, I asked you once again what your decision was, and after brief reflection the only answer I got from you was: 'Let the council do what they like; I'm completely indifferent.'

Galluzzi explains further that he did not feel, after this, that it rested

[1] Giovanni Drei, 'Il concorso di Verdi a Busseto secondo nuovi documenti' (*Aurea Parma, fasc.* IV–V, 1939).

with *him* to fight Verdi's battles in the council, although he did point out that the proposed appointment of Ferrari was contrary to the decision of the earlier council meeting to fill the post by competitive examination. The reply to this was that one of the other two applicants had withdrawn and the other was ineligible, and 'as for Verdi, who it was formerly supposed would compete, it was known everywhere that he did not want to do so any longer, having already a proposed engagement worth 3,000 francs'.

This letter has the ring of truth, and indeed Barezzi himself afterwards recognized Galluzzi's loyalty and became reconciled with him. Clearly the house of Barezzi was at this time divided against itself. Verdi, who in November 1833 had aspired to Provesi's post at Busseto, had other things in view six months later. Margherita Barezzi, who was already spoken of as his *fiancée*, knew all about this, and took Verdi's part, naturally, wishing and hoping for his greater advancement and perhaps also dreaming herself of life in the great city of Milan. 'Verdi will never, never settle at Busseto. . . .' This passage of Galluzzi's letter is extraordinarily interesting, allowing us, as it does, almost to hear the actual voice of that shadowy figure, the girl who became Verdi's first wife. She speaks too in no uncertain terms.

We must now refer back to the account of his own early years given by Verdi to Giulio Ricordi, for use in Caponi's revision of Pougin's biography.

'In 1833 or 1834 there existed at Milan a Philharmonic Society composed of good vocalists: it was directed by Maestro Massini, a man who, if he had no great learning, was nevertheless painstaking and patient and thus of the sort required by a society of amateurs. A performance of Haydn's *Creation* was being prepared in the Teatro Filodrammatico and my master Lavigna asked me if, to gain experience, I would like to attend the rehearsals. I accepted with pleasure. Nobody paid any attention to the young man sitting modestly in a dark corner. Three *maestri*—Perelli, Bonoldi and Almasio—conducted the rehearsals, but one day by a strange chance all three *maestri concertatori* failed to attend a rehearsal. The ladies and gentlemen were beginning to get impatient when Massini, who did not himself feel equal to the task of accompanying at the pianoforte from the full score, turned and asked me to act as accompanist, and perhaps because he had little confidence in a young and unknown artist, said to me: "It will be quite sufficient to play just the bass." I was fresh from my studies and certainly not at all embarrassed by a full orchestral score. I therefore accepted and sat myself down at the pianoforte to begin the rehearsal. I remember very well the ironical smiles of some of the *signori dilettanti*, and it seems that my youthful figure, lean and not too tidily dressed, was not such as to inspire much confidence. In short, the rehearsal began and, little by little warming up and getting excited, instead of confining myself to accompanying, I began also to conduct with my right hand, playing with my left hand alone. I had a great success—all the greater for being unexpected. At the end of the rehearsal compliments and congratulations from all sides, and especially from Count Pompeo Belgiojoso and Count Renato Borromeo. Finally, either because the three *maestri* mentioned above were too busy to take on the job, or for some other reason, in the end they entrusted the whole concert to me. The public performance took place, with such success that it was repeated later in the large hall of the Casino de' Nobili, in the presence of the Archduke and Archduchess Ranieri and all the high society of that day. Shortly afterwards Count Renato Borromeo engaged me to compose the music of a cantata—for the marriage of some member of his family I believe. It should be noted, however, that I got nothing out of all that, my services being entirely gratuitous.'

The libretto of this performance of *The Creation*, in which Verdi's name appears as *maestro al cembalo*, shows that it took place in April 1834 [1]—two months before the crisis at Busseto. Here surely is the source of all those stories of 'profitable and attractive offers', 'commissions' and 'patrons'. The fact that he got nothing out of these commissions in the end does not mean to say that he did not at the time expect to get something out of them, or at least expect them to lead to more profitable engagements in the future. Verdi was beginning to spread his wings, and with the praises of his noble Milanese friends in his ears, the position of music master and organist at Busseto began to lose its attraction. Pietro Massini, the director of the Milanese Philharmonic Society, played an important role in the life of the young Verdi. He is referred to again in the postscript of a letter from Verdi to Lavigna, dated 5th August of this year: 'A few days after my arrival at Busseto I wrote to Massini, from whom I have not yet received a reply. So if you happen to see him remind him to reply about the libretto that Tasca was going to write for me.[2] A libretto! This was Verdi's first operatic project. It remained a project only, and nothing more is heard of the poet Tasca, but from this time forward Verdi knew where he was going. He was 'dedicating himself wholly to the study of music for the theatre', as reported by the gossips of Busseto. In Galluzzi's apologia we have heard the echo

[1] A critique in the *Gazzetta Privilegiata di Milano* of 20th April praises Massini and the singers, but does not mention Verdi.

[2] This letter was published by Giuseppe De Napoli in *La Lettura* for February 1928, and quoted, from this article, by Gatti (first edition, I. p. 83; second edition, p. 75). These writers have 'Nicolini' instead of 'Massini'. The name, however, is quite clear on the original in the Biblioteca Lucchesi-Palli, Naples. The mythical Nicolini has a separate entry on Gatti's index. He appears also in Franco Abbiati's *Giuseppe Verdi* (Milan, 1959), vol. i, p. 147.

of the hopes and the ambitions expressed in the young composer's lost letters to Margherita Barezzi.

We must suppose that Verdi bowed to the will of his benefactor in sending in his own belated application for the Busseto appointment and in appealing over the heads of the local authorities to Marie Louise. His appeal, however, remained unanswered for another whole year, during which time, and during the succeeding eight or nine months before the position was actually regularized, something like civil war raged at Busseto.

We read in the biographies of the almost incredible feuds which, in consequence of the appointment of Ferrari, divided this little town of two thousand inhabitants. The church was invaded by the members of the Philharmonic Society, who seized their music, refusing to allow it to be used by the priests or Ferrari. There were brawls in the streets, lampoons, arrests and prosecutions. And there has been no exaggeration here on the part of the biographers. The account in Pougin's book, taken from some articles by a resident of Busseto, is all substantially true; and there are enough documents concerning the wars of the 'Coccardini', the revolutionary Verdian party, and the 'Codini', the reactionary priestly set, supporters of Ferrari, to fill a volume.

Both sides tried to influence the governmental decision. Francesco Cocchi, Presidente dell' Interno—the Home Secretary of the little state of Parma—received long reports from Monsignore Luigi Sanvitale, Bishop of Borgo San Donnino (Fidenza), who of course supported his rural dean at Busseto, the Provost Don Ballarini, in his appointment of Ferrari. He made excuses for the priests and blamed the young hotheads of the Philharmonic Society for all the disturbances. The bishop admitted that he was more concerned with morality than musical ability. 'Ferrari, a grown man, with the guarantees he gives, seems to me more to be depended on than a beardless youth who learned music in a populous city where the young are apt to be more attracted by the scandalous goings-on that swarm there in public than by the great virtues which lie hidden.' [1] In another letter he expressed his fears that a revolution would break out: 'Let the civil and military authorities then be ordered to watch attentively, to crush the rebellion at its birth.'

The Verdi party hoped to influence Cocchi through one of his secretaries, Lorenzo Molossi, who was a friend of Barezzi's. The Mayor of Busseto, who tried hard to remain impartial, but whose sympathies were with Verdi, also sent in reports to Cocchi and himself received complaints from aggrieved citizens, such as Luigi Seletti, who declared that he had been insulted and threatened in the street by members of the Barezzi family. He had been accosted by

[1] Giovanni Drei, 'Il concorso di Verdi a Busseto secondo nuovi documenti', loc. cit.

Giovannino, Barezzi's elder son, and the following words were exchanged:

> 'You infamous old man—it's not enough to stare and walk away.'
> 'What business have you with me?'
> 'You spoke evil of Verdi with Don Ubaldo Neri. I've just heard you, you slanderer, you old fibber, you old hypocrite!'

Barezzi then threatened to thrash him and would have done so too, if he had not been restrained by the bystanders. The boy's mother then arrived and repeated what her son had said, adding: 'You infamous old man—it suffices to say that you hate even your own children.'

The wars of the 'Codini' and the 'Coccardini' were subsequently celebrated by a local writer in a poem, *Gli uccelli accademici*, in nine cantos, in which Marie Louise appeared as the royal eagle, Cocchi as an owl, Molossi as a falcon, Barezzi and Margherita as a pair of blackbirds, Verdi as a parrot and Ferrari as the cuckoo in the nest.

Verdi held aloof, as far as possible, from these unedifying squabbles. He stayed at Busseto from 18th June to 15th December, during which time he appeared at concerts with the Philharmonic band; then he returned to Milan and took up again his interrupted lessons with Lavigna. A well-known story, one of the additions of 'Folchetto' to Pougin, tells how Verdi scored off Basily, who had been one of his examiners for the Conservatorio in 1832. Basily called to see Lavigna and the two discussed the deplorable result of a recent competition for the post of *maestro di cappella* of Monza Cathedral, when not one of the applicants had been able to produce a decent fugue on the given subject. Lavigna suggested that his pupil Verdi should try his hand on the same subject, which he did, surprising Basily by his fluency and mastery and adding a double canon, as he found the subject 'a little thin'. The examination of the candidates for the position at Monza took place on 26th November 1834,[1] while Verdi was at Busseto. Lavigna, as well as Basily, was among the examiners. It is clear that it must have been shortly after his return to Milan on 15th December 1834 that Verdi showed what he could do with Basily's theme, and it is probable that out of this incident the suggestion arose that he should himself apply for the post, which none of the competitors had been found capable of filling. This was to have violent repercussions at Busseto, as we shall see.

In January 1835 the governmental decision was made known: Ferrari could consider himself organist of the collegiate church, but the post of *maestro di musica* had to be filled by a competitive

[1] G. Riva, *La Cappella del Duomo di Monza e il concorso di Giuseppe Verdi* (Monza, 1907). There were nine applicants (two of whom failed to appear), and not twenty-eight, as the earlier biographers say.

examination. The Verdi party had won the battle. The ecclesiastics were still able to fight a rearguard action, however, and delayed further developments for a long time. In July 1835 Verdi completed his studies with Lavigna and returned to Busseto. Feelings were still running high. The police warned the mayor that it was known that some of the town councillors had even played a part in fomenting discord. The tavern of one Fantoni was the headquarters of some of the most obstinate partisans. Giacomo Demaldè and Luigi Seletti [1] ('the 'old hypocrite') were named as promoters of strife and 'sowers of tares' in the Ferrari party and, in the Verdi party, the coffee-house keeper Guarnieri and the chemist Luigi Macchiavelli. The dragoons were ordered to stand by. Poor Ferrari, who had six children, had been informed that the Monte di Pietà's contribution of 357 lire per annum would now be put towards the salary of the music master to be elected. The municipal council, after a riotous meeting in the course of which six members walked out and an impassioned appeal was made that the youth of Busseto should not, by lack of support for the Philharmonic Society, be driven out of the temple of Apollo into that of Bacchus, voted a further 300 lire annually for the same purpose. On 29th August, in the hope of bringing an end to recurrent disgraceful scenes, a royal decree forbade the use of instrumental music in the churches of Busseto. This ban was to remain in force for seventeen years, until Verdi himself in 1852 succeeded in getting it rescinded.

Exasperated at the continuing delay, probably not uninfluenced by the ban on the Philharmonic Society's participation in the church festivals, and disgusted that the municipality of Busseto could, after all, offer him a salary of only 657 lire a year, Verdi wrote to Lavigna asking him to use his influence to help to procure him the still vacant position of *maestro di cappella* and organist to the cathedral of Monza. Lavigna's reply [2] shows that the possibility of Verdi's obtaining this post had already been discussed between them. As against the Busseto salary of 657 lire, which members of the Philharmonic Society were afterwards to raise to 1,000 lire, the post at Monza offered 2,200 lire, a house with firewood and lighting, and the possibility of earning another 700 lire by giving music lessons in a private school in the town. Lavigna and others exerted themselves on Verdi's behalf, and apparently it needed only his appearance at Monza for an interview for the whole business to be settled in his favour. But he never went there. His letter of excuse to Lavigna (15th December 1835) continues the extraordinarily tangled tale of Busseto and its music master. No sooner was his impending departure known in the

[1] These names are confusing. There were Selettis and Demaldès on *both* sides.
[2] Luzio, *Carteggi verdiani*, IV, pp. 127–8.

town than an unbelievable hubbub arose. The Ferrari party were delighted and insulted the Philharmonic members; the latter considered they had been betrayed, and hurled abuse at Verdi and at Barezzi. Not only was Verdi sharply reminded of what he owed to the Monte di Pietà and the Philharmonic Society, but he was told that if he attempted to leave Busseto he would be held back by force! He wrote to Lavigna:

If my benefactor Barezzi would not have had to suffer on my account the almost general hostility of the district, I should have left straight away; neither their reproaches about benefits nor their menaces would have been able to affect me. Even if I did receive from the Monte di Pietà a slender pension towards my support at Milan, this benefit ought not to purchase my degradation and slavery, or I should be constrained to consider the said benefit no longer a generous act, but a mean one.

So solely on Barezzi's account Verdi gave up the well-paid Monza appointment and stayed at home. Within three months he was officially nominated *maestro di musica* to the commune of Busseto after examination at Parma by Giuseppe Alinovi. Ferrari did not compete. In a letter to Barezzi dated 29th February 1836 Verdi describes his experiences at Parma:

On Saturday afternoon about three o'clock, I went to Alinovi and he examined me in the following subjects: pianoforte, singing, accompaniment from score and sight-reading. First I played my Variations, which a little later I repeated, as Alinovi liked them very much and wished to understand them better. Then he put before me various theatrical pieces which I refused to play because I knew them already; however, I played the accompaniment to a duet by Donizetti, full of mistakes (made on purpose, I believe, so that I should correct them while playing), and the thing went very well and Alinovi was very satisfied. To assure him that I was playing the new pieces at sight I asked for something of his own and he gave me a very beautiful *Laudate*, which I played without stumbling. With Alinovi I played a sonata by Herz for piano duet, and he was very pleased. . . . Yesterday I went to Alinovi at eight o'clock in the morning and a subject was given me for a fugue in four real parts, which I finished yesterday evening after six o'clock. The *maestro* examined it and said in my presence what Molossi wrote in his letter to Finola.

'Finola' was the nickname of Giuseppe Demaldè; here is what Molossi wrote to him on this occasion:

As Verdi's modesty does not permit him to say for himself how things stand, I'll tell you that yesterday about six o'clock he finished his work and Maestro Alinovi, after having examined it carefully, rose to his feet and said to Verdi: 'So far I have played the part of a rigorous examiner; now I play that of an admirer. This fugue is worthy of a consummate master; it deserves to be printed. You have enough knowledge to be *maestro* in Paris or London, rather than at Busseto. I confess that I should not have been able to do in a whole day what you have done in a few hours.[1]

This was a splendid tribute both to Verdi and to Lavigna, his teacher at Milan.

His position assured, Verdi became officially engaged to Margherita Barezzi on 16th April and on 4th May they were married. The contract with the municipality of Busseto was for nine years, but terminable by either party at the end of three or six years, provided that notice had been given six months earlier. Verdi was in fact to give notice six months before the termination of the first three years, his supposed obligation to Busseto finally absolved.

Verdi and Margherita lived, according to local tradition, in the Palazzo Tedaldi, which still exists in rather dilapidated condition, at the far end of the Via della Biblioteca, occupying the whole space between this and the end of the Via dell' Ospedale, another parallel street, at right angles to the main street of the town.[2]

This was a period of family joys and sorrows; two children were born, the elder of which died a month after the younger came into the world. Musically, they were years of frustration for Verdi, whose thoughts turned now increasingly towards Milan and La Scala. He was busy enough with the school of music and the Philharmonic Society. In the document already twice quoted he says of this period:

Back again in my home town, I began to write marches, *sinfonie*, vocal pieces, etc., a complete Mass, a complete set of Vespers, three or four settings of *Tantum ergo* and other church music that I don't recall. Among the vocal pieces there were choruses from the tragedies of Manzoni for three voices, and *Il cinque Maggio* for solo voice.

Before his appointment Verdi had played the organ in the Franciscan church of Santa Maria degli Angeli, which was not under the jurisdiction of his enemy Don Ballarini. A letter from Demaldè to Giuseppe Martini [3] describes how the Franciscan church was crowded

[1] Verdi's letter to Barezzi and Molossi's to Demaldè both quoted by Gatti, I, pp. 121–2 (second edition, pp. 106–7). But Gatti, as Luzio points out (*Carteggi verdiani*, IV, p. 76), has not understood who 'Finola' was. He includes also a few reading errors ('Minola' for 'Molossi' and 'quartetto' for 'duetto'), as may be seen from the reproduction of Verdi's letter in Lualdi's *Viaggio musicale in Italia* (Milan, 1927); Abbiati (I, p. 221) knows who 'Finola' was, but takes over Gatti's reading errors.

[2] Gatti (first edition, I, pp. 130–1; second edition, p. 112) refers to the 'Palazzo Rusca', following F. T. Garibaldi (op. cit. p. 46). No one in Busseto today can identify a 'Palazzo Rusca'. But Garibaldi, as we see from his description of Busseto (p. 3), is referring to a house in the main street just beyond the Monte di Pietà, 'then that of the Marchese Tedaldi, which formerly belonged to the Rusca family'. These old houses are known either by the names of their original owners, or by those of their present proprietors. Just beyond the Monte di Pietà is the original Palazzo Dordoni, called today 'Palazzo Orlandi', which Verdi purchased in 1845 and inhabited with Giuseppina Strepponi from 1849 to 1851. But this is not identical with the Palazzo Tedaldi. Abbiati (I, pp. 226–7 and elsewhere), also refers to 'Palazzo Rusca', without attempting to identify it.

[3] *Carteggi verdiani*, IV, p. 73.

on this occasion and the collegiate church, to the extreme annoyance of the provost, almost deserted. Probably the church music mentioned was also mostly performed at the Franciscan church, although a surviving *Tantum ergo*,[1] composed in November 1836, has an inscription on the manuscript stating that it was first sung by the Verdian partisan Macchiavelli in the collegiate church of San Bartolomeo on 1st January 1837. This would have been carrying the war into the enemy's camp with a vengeance, but the inscription, referring to Verdi as 'Cavaliere', is obviously a much later addition and may be misleading. This *Tantum ergo* reflects the conditions prevailing at the time it was written: it has orchestral accompaniment, but is provided also with a separate organ accompaniment in view of the ban on instrumental music in the churches of Busseto. The use of the organ in support of the singers was apparently assumed still to be permitted.

A letter from Demaldè to Lorenzo Molossi, dated 31st January 1837, mentions concertos or *divertimenti* written by Verdi for clarinet, for two horns, and for trumpet, performed by members of the Philharmonic Society. All the *signori dilettanti* had to be provided with opportunities to show their skill. Here is the programme of a typical *Accademia*, given in the communal theatre at Busseto on 25th February 1838:[2]

PART 1

1 Grand Overture to *Semiramide* by Signor Maestro Rossini.
2 Capriccio for horn by Signor Maestro Verdi, performed by Signor Dilettante Vincenzo Magnani.
3 Recitative and Aria by Signor Maestro Verdi, performed by Signor Rusca.
4 Introduction to *Eduardo e Cristina* (Rossini), arranged for instruments.

PART 2

Comedy by Eugene Scribe, entitled *The Artists' Garret*.

PART 3

1 Introduction, Variations and Coda for bassoon, by Signor Maestro Verdi, performed by Signor Dilettante Luigi Bottarelli.
2 Buffo duet by Signor Maestro Verdi, performed by Signori Dilettanti Macchiavelli and Guarnieri.
3 Overture by Signor Maestro Meyerbeer.

It is pleasing to find, in the second item of the third part of this concert, two of Verdi's most perfervid supporters, who had been reprimanded by the police in 1835, singing a comic duet together.

[1] In the Scala Museum, Milan.
[2] A number of these hand-written programmes are in the Museum at Busseto.

Unfortunately Verdi does not mention, among his compositions of this period, that one about which we should most like precise information—the lost opera, *Rocester*. This work, in its possible relationship to *Oberto, Conte di San Bonifacio*, the earliest surviving Verdi opera, presents a thorny problem.

In the account of his early life given by Verdi to Ricordi for use in the Italian revision of Pougin's book, the composer says that after the *Creation* performances:

> Massini, who seems to have had confidence in the young Maestro, then proposed that I should write an opera for the Teatro Filodrammatico, of which he was director, and handed me a libretto that afterwards, in part modified by Solera, became *Oberto, Conte di San Bonifacio*. I accepted the offer with pleasure, and returned to Busseto, where I was engaged as organist. I stayed at Busseto about three years; the opera finished, I undertook once more the journey to Milan, taking with me the complete score in perfect order, having gone to the trouble of copying out all the vocal parts myself. But here the difficulties began. Massini was no longer director of the Teatro Filodrammatico. So it was no longer possible to give my opera. However, either because Massini really had confidence in me, or because he wished to show his gratitude to me in some way—for after Haydn's *Creation* I had assisted him on several other occasions, rehearsing and conducting various performances (including *Cenerentola*) without ever claiming any compensation—he was not discouraged by difficulties, but told me he would do all he could to have my opera performed at La Scala, at the benefit performance for the Pio Istituto.

Massini, with the help of the cellist Vincenzo Merighi of the Scala orchestra, succeeded in persuading the impresario Bartolomeo Merelli to put on Verdi's opera for one of these charity performances, and rehearsals with the soloists were actually begun, when the illness of the tenor, Napoleone Moriani, caused the whole project to be abandoned. Then, largely through the interest shown by the soprano, Giuseppina Strepponi, *Oberto* was accepted for production at La Scala in the following season, with a different company of singers. 'I had to modify the *tessitura* of some parts of the music and to write a new piece, the quartet, the dramatic situation of which was suggested by Merelli himself, and which I had versified by Solera.'

Apart from this, most of the documentary evidence we have concerning Verdi's first opera or operas is found in his surviving letters to Massini, of which there are nine.[1] It is very difficult, or impossible, to reconcile Verdi's own account with the evidence of these letters.

As we have seen, Verdi, interrupting his studies, returned from

[1] One was published by O. Boni, (*Verdi, l'uomo, le opere, l'artista*, Parma, 1901), three more by Luzio ('*Epistolario Verdiano*', in *La Lettura*, March 1905), four previously unknown ones by Claudio Sartori ('*Rocester*, la prima opera di Verdi', in *Rivista musicale italiana*, Jan.–Feb. 1939) and another by Abbiati (I, p. 240; an extract previously in *Lo Smeraldo*, 30th Nov. 1950). Failure to consult all these letters, in chronological order, has led many biographers into confusion.

Milan to Busseto on 18th June 1834, and on 5th August of this year mentioned an opera libretto which was to have been written for him by a certain Tasca.[1] Nothing further is known about this, but it is of interest that already Massini is named as the intermediary. Verdi returned to Milan on 15th December. The performance of Rossini's *Cenerentola* by the Philharmonic Society took place early in April 1835, and all concerned were warmly commended by the critic of the theatrical paper *Il Figaro* on 8th April:

> . . . Praise to Massini, and to Maestro Verdi who conducted it; praise to the singers who performed it; to the orchestra, to the chorus, to everybody.

His studies with Lavigna completed, the composer went back again to Busseto in July 1835. On 28th July he told Massini in the earliest of the surviving letters:

> I am writing the opera (as you know) and by the time you return to Milan I hope to have sketched out all the pieces. Advise me about all the singers you have heard in the concert that by now you will have given, so that I can take into consideration the range of the voices.

The phrase 'Io scrivo l'opera' in this letter suggests that the work had actually been commenced. But it must have been intended in the sense: 'I am going to write the opera' or 'It is settled that I shall write the opera', for the next letter to Massini, six months later, shows that nothing had yet come of this project:

To Massini, 24th January 1836:

> I am sorry not to have kept my word to you. I promised you before leaving Milan to return soon to write the opera, but then I was not free, and so I have not been able to keep my promise. If I am appointed Maestro, the municipality grants me two months' holiday, September and October, and then (if you consent) I am ready to keep my word. It will be a great piece of good fortune for me if I can write an opera, and be assured that my gratitude to you will be everlasting.

Eight months later the opera was almost completed.

To Massini, 16th September 1836:

> I have long been anxious to have news from you, but the cholera has suspended our intercourse until now. I am the same as ever and am awaiting a definite reply about the opera. I foresee that there will be difficulties and for this reason wish all the more to hear from you. Meanwhile I advise you that I have finished the opera, except for those short passages that will have to be patched up by the poet.

[1] Probably the poet Ottavio Tasca. A letter from Tasca to Verdi, about the success of *Ernani* in Vienna, was published in the *Gazzetta Privilegiata di Milano* for 8th June 1844. From this letter it is clear that Tasca and Verdi had never actually met.

To Massini, 15th October 1836:

From your last letter I understand what you tell me about the opera, and although you still hold out hopes I foresee clearly that we shall not do anything about it this year.

From this group of letters we see that those who, like Toye, seeking to explain why Verdi apparently took as long as three years over the composition of his first opera, imagined that he had not yet acquired his mature fluency, were very wide of the mark. Apart from his own remarks quoted elsewhere about 'marches for brass band by the hundred' with 'perhaps as many little *sinfonie*', which he turned out at a very early age, we see that Verdi expected to be able to complete his first opera in two months, and did in fact practically complete it some time between 24th January and 16th September 1836.

The Mayor of Busseto, in a document from the same year,[1] mentions this opera completed by Verdi, 'which may possibly be heard at the Ducal Theatre', i.e. at Parma. This is an important link in the chain of evidence.

The next letter to Massini, a year later, mentions the proposal to perform the opera at Parma and gives the name of the librettist, Antonio Piazza, and the title, which is not *Oberto, Conte di San Bonifacio*, but *Rocester*.

To Massini, 21st September 1837:

It is not unlikely that I shall be able to put the opera *Rocester* on the stage at Parma this Carnival, so please go with the bearer of this letter (who is a confidential friend of mine) to the author of the libretto, Piazza, and put the matter before him. If Piazza wishes to alter the verses here and there we are still in time, and I do indeed beg him to prolong the duet for the two women, to make it a more grandiose piece. . . . Oh, I should have liked to put on *Rocester* at Milan! but I see only too well myself that I am too far away to arrange everything necessary.

To Massini, 3rd November 1837:

I spent a few days at Parma waiting for the new Impresario, a certain Granci, of Lucca. Meanwhile I secured the support of the Theatre Commission and the orchestra, all of which I was able to do easily, for to tell you the truth, not owing to my merits, I enjoy some credit at Parma. I had besides found influential people who showed themselves willing to help me. The day before yesterday the Impresario finally arrived. I presented myself to him at once in the name of the Commission and without preamble he replied that it didn't suit him to risk putting on an opera of uncertain outcome. . . . If I hadn't been the first to speak to him I should have thought that some enemy had maligned me to him, but that wasn't possible. I returned home angry and without the slightest hope. Poor young people! What a time they have of it, studying without ever a reward! Tell me, wouldn't it be possible to speak to Merelli, to see if it could be performed

[1] Gatti, first edition, I, pp. 134–5; second edition, pp. 115–16.

at some theatre at Milan? Tell him first of all that I should like the score to be submitted for examination by musicians of standing, and if their judgment were unfavourable I should not wish the opera to be performed. You would be doing me the greatest service. Perhaps you would be able to rescue me from obscurity, and I should be eternally grateful to you. Go to see Piazza and talk it over.

Here is the first reference in these letters to Merelli, impresario of La Scala. All idea of performance at the Teatro Filodrammatico would seem to have been already abandoned. We know from Verdi's own account that it *was* Massini who was chiefly responsible for arranging with Merelli that *Oberto* should be performed at La Scala in 1839. What we don't know is how far, if at all, *Rocester*, composed in 1836 and rejected at Parma in 1837, was related to *Oberto*.

At the beginning of May 1838 Verdi spent a few days at Milan alone (Margherita was expecting her second child). Then during his holidays in September and October of the same year he was there again, with Margherita. Letters to Barezzi from this period contain hints about a 'very important affair', details of which were to be conveyed by word of mouth. But a letter to an unnamed enthusiast at Busseto, enclosed in one to Barezzi on 6th October, tells us a good deal:

How the devil did you get the idea in your head that my opera is to be put on the stage by the 15th of this month? I never said or wrote that. . . . I'll tell you frankly that I came here to negotiate about the opera, but the season was too far advanced, and three operas having already been performed, with a cantata and three more operas to follow, already promised to the public (an enormous task), there is no time left to put on mine with the decorum required.

It could perhaps be performed in the next Carnival season; but it's a matter of a new opera, written by a new composer, to be staged in the first theatre in the world; I want still to think it over thoroughly. If you want the placard, wait until the spring for it. Then, if not before, you will certainly get it.[1]

Verdi had clearly met with encouragement. He had received what he took to be definite promises that his opera would be performed at La Scala in the following year, in the Carnival or spring seasons. But there was still something about which he had to think seriously. Did this merely concern changes in the libretto, considered necessary by himself, or by Piazza or Merelli? Or did perhaps *Rocester*, composed in 1836, no longer seem to Verdi fully representative of his powers in 1838? If La Scala was opening its doors to him, would it not be better to write for it an entirely new work? Whatever negotiations took place, they were probably indirect; a letter to Opprandino Arrivabene of 7th March 1874 says that, even in the spring of 1839, he had never yet spoken to Merelli.

[1] Gatti, first edition, I, pp. 150–1; second edition, p. 129.

On his return from Milan Verdi sent in his notice of resignation to the municipality of Busseto.

It is clear that the earlier biographers, including Gatti in his first edition, mistook references to *Rocester*, in the earlier letters to Massini, for references to *Oberto*. Claudio Sartori, in publishing the partially unknown letters in the *Autografoteca Pasini* at Brescia,[1] put forward the suggestion that *Oberto* was only a remodelling of *Rocester*. This suggestion was adopted without argument by Gatti, in his second edition, and by Abbiati. An American lady, Kathleen O'Donnell Hoover, taking almost the whole of her material from Sartori, has gone far beyond him in claiming to have proved that *Oberto* and *Rocester* were in fact one and the same.[2] But she is only able to do this by quite reckless manipulation of the facts. She tells us: 'Years later, in a reminiscent letter to Count Opprandino Arrivabene, the composer himself states that his first opera was *Oberto*, and that it was written in 1836.' Now if Verdi ever had made such a statement it would go a long way towards convincing us that *Rocester* and *Oberto* were indeed identical, but the only quotation Mrs Hoover furnishes from 'Verdi's own statement, in later years, to Arrivabene' turns out to be an extract from the account given to Ricordi for use in the Italian version of Pougin's biography; and neither there, nor in any letter to Arrivabene or to anyone else, does the composer state that *Oberto* was his first opera and that it was written in 1836! Further, Mrs Hoover points to the letter to Massini of 21st September 1837, with its reference to 'the duet for the two women' in *Rocester*, which Verdi wished prolonged, to make it more grandiose. She tells us: '*Oberto* contains two impressive duets, in each of which aspirations to a grandiosity not quite realized may be discerned—one (Act I, Scene i) for Oberto, Count of San Bonifacio and his daughter . . . the other (Act I, Scene ii) *for the two women*, Leonora and her rival Cuniza.' This is fantastic: there is in reality *no* duet for the two women in *Oberto*! The second duet is for Cuniza and Riccardo.

Such evidence as we have then suggests that the two operas were *not* identical in their musical contents. There was a duet for the two women in *Rocester*; there is no such duet in *Oberto*.

An important letter, which until recently has escaped everyone's notice, is preserved in the Scala Museum at Milan. It is to Emilio Seletti, the son of the man with whom Verdi stayed when he first came to live at Milan:

Sant' Agata, 14th May 1871.

DEAR SIGNOR EMILIO,

Oberto di San Bonifacio was altered and added to by Solera, on the basis of a libretto entitled *Lord Hamilton* by Antonio Piazza, a government

[1] '*Rocester*, la prima opera di Verdi' (*Rivista musicale italiana*, Jan.–Feb. 1939).
[2] 'Verdi's *Rocester*' (*Musical Quarterly*, Oct. 1942).

employee, then writer of *feuilletons* for the *Gazzetta di Milano*. Neither in *Lord Hamilton* nor in *Oberto* is there a line by Luigi Balestra.

My wife reciprocates your greetings; please give my regards to your mother.

Yours sincerely,
G. VERDI.

Seletti was probably already collecting information for his book, *La Città di Busseto* (3 vols., Milan, 1883), which contains details of the Selettis, Barezzis and Balestras, among other illustrious Bussetani. Verdi might have mentioned that Luigi Balestra did provide words for a duet which he intended to add to *Oberto* on its revival at Genoa in 1841. However, the chief interest of this letter is the reference to Piazza's libretto *Lord Hamilton*, which seems to dispose of the theory that *Oberto* was based on *Rocester*. Piazza appears to have had a predilection for fantasies about the British aristocracy; in the *Gazzetta Musicale di Milano* for 16th, 23rd and 30th June 1847 he published a story about a love affair between the composer Pergolesi and Miss Betzi Bulwer, daughter of the British Ambassador Extraordinary to the King of the Two Sicilies.

Abbiati [1] assumes that there was a double change, *Lord Hamilton* becoming *Rocester*, and *Rocester* becoming *Oberto*, but he does so on no evidence at all. Were 'Lord Hamilton' and 'Rocester' two characters in the same opera, and did Verdi in 1871 give its title wrongly? Without some such dubious assumption we must conclude that by 1879, when he gave his account to Ricordi, two early operas had become confused in his memory and condensed into one. This would be astonishing, but not more astonishing than other things in the same account, such as the confusion about the deaths of his wife and children, or the remark, 'I . . . returned to Busseto, where I was engaged as organist', which drastically over-simplifies the complicated events leading up to his appointment as music master of Busseto and makes a completely false claim to a position that was never his, but Ferrari's.

Much of the history of *Oberto* is still unclear. The following points are worth noting in case they combine with other evidence that may come to light:

(1) The *Cenni biografici* of Giuseppe Demaldè state that Verdi completed the score of *Rocester* in the spring of 1838. This is incorrect, because this opera is named already in letters of 1837, but it is interesting that Demaldè mentions the work, and differentiates between it and *Oberto*.

(2) A note in the Italian edition of Pougin's biography—one of the additions by 'Folchetto'—says that *Oberto* was written at Busseto in the winter of 1837 8. Everybody has ignored this statement, which conflicted with the long prevalent idea that Verdi spent three years

[1] I, pp. 200, 205, 222, 232–5, 326.

over his first opera; but it fits in well enough with the evidence from the letters to Massini, and suggests that Merelli may not have approved of *Rocester*, when approached by Massini as a result of Verdi's letter of 3rd November 1837, and that a fresh libretto may then have been provided. If confirmed, this would of course dispose of the tentative suggestion advanced above, that Verdi decided to replace *Rocester* with *Oberto* after his visit to Milan in the autumn of 1838.

(3) Part of the manuscript libretto of *Oberto* is in the Scala Museum. It is in Solera's hand.

(4) The manuscript full score of *Oberto* in Messrs Ricordi's archives shows signs of much alteration. Pages and groups of pages, with whole scenes and musical numbers, have been taken out and replaced. But the names of the characters have not been altered. *Oberto* was already *Oberto* before all this revision began.

(5) *Oberto*, as we have it, is not really a two-act opera, but a three-act opera of which the first act was never written. A whole page of explanation, printed in the libretto, is needed to put the spectator in a position to follow the action from the point where the opera itself begins. This page of explanation probably summarizes the action of the missing first act. In a letter to Barezzi of 3rd September 1846 Verdi's pupil Muzio writes: 'Marini wants also to sing *Oberto* but the Signor Maestro, whom they had asked to make some alterations, would not consent, because, he says, all the first act would be needed, and a month and a half to do it, and he hasn't time.' It looks very much as if Verdi and Solera had been told to keep the opera short, if they wanted it put on at La Scala.

On 6th February 1839 Verdi and his family left Busseto, to take up residence permanently at Milan. A lively picture of the city as Verdi knew it is given by Antonio Ghislanzoni in his mordant *Storia di Milano dal 1836 al 1848*.[1] What Ghislanzoni, writing from his own experience, has to say almost justifies the worst premonitions of the Bishop of Borgo San Donnino. The city, of not more than 150,000 inhabitants, was still contained within the bastions. The streets were lit by oil lamps, the pavements crossed by runnels 'which did not smell of musk'. The cathedral was admired by strangers but used as a *pisciatoio* by the local inhabitants, and on its steps the black market flourished every night. Houses of ill fame were to be found in the centre of the city, near the cathedral. Fashionable Milan woke up at about eleven o'clock, though the true 'lions' of society did not appear until 1 p.m. Top hats were worn by the elegant at Porta Renzo and in the public gardens, but it was dangerous to be seen in them in the poorer districts. There were fierce regional antagonisms within the bastions, as between village and village; and at Porta Ticinese, towards dusk, a decently dressed person risked being stoned. (Verdi lived near Porta Ticinese.) Performing fleas in a shop in the Corsia del Duomo attracted all Milan. Among the milling crowds in the streets were seen

[1] Published with *In Chiave di Baritono* (Milan, 1882).

the Austrian soldiers, Austrian officials in civilian dress, portly *monsignori* from the cathedral, police continually on patrol and students from the Conservatorio, in a uniform not unlike that of the police; above the customary shouting, the cracking of whips, the noisy games of *mora* in the *osterie*, were heard from numerous slaughter-houses the dying groans and squeals of calves and pigs. Loose women invited custom from doors and windows. Thieves were everywhere. Everyone raised his hat when the Austrian viceroy, the Archduke Ranieri or the Austrian archbishop, Count Gaisruck, passed in their six-horse carriages. Only the viceroy and the archbishop were permitted to use six horses.

Drunkenness was rife. The Teatro della Canobbiana and Teatro Carcano were the scenes of unspeakable orgies when the public balls took place. Young men about town got drunk on port or Madeira, and ended by poisoning themselves with absinthe, introduced into Milan about 1840. All serious men shaved from nose to throat. Students who grew beards or moustaches risked compromising their whole future by expulsion from the examination room. Smoking in public was not permitted. A few idlers who appeared with cigars in their mouths on the bastions, or in the public gardens while the band was playing, were considered extremely daring. 'Ladies, at the approach of a cigar, pretended to faint; at the sight of a pipe both the gentle and the sterner sex stood aghast.' The eight-mile railway between Milan and Monza was considered a wonder of the world. 'The old cried: "Now that I have seen this marvel I am content to die!" And several did, in fact, die.' The opening of the first coffee houses caused an immense sensation. At the hotels, the Falcone, the Corona, the Agnello, lodging could be had for one Austrian lira a day; at the Osteria della Foppa a three-course lunch could be got for the same price. Both hotels and *osterie* were lit by wax candles: 'Soot rained into the soup' and a boy was employed to flick away the smuts at every change of dishes.

The *literati* gathered at the Caffè del Duomo, where the *Journal des Débats* and other foreign papers were available. Elsewhere only the official *Gazzetta Privilegiata di Milano* and the various theatrical papers were read. The theatre was the greatest preoccupation of cultured society. It was dangerous to talk politics, and those who did so too openly were generally supposed to be spies and *agents provocateurs*. Nobody bothered very much. 'Men who thought of Italy, who chafed at the foreign yoke, who abhorred Austria, were very few in number. Most people did not know that Italy existed.'

Verdi's first published compositions had been a set of six *Romanze*—songs with piano accompaniment—issued in 1838 by Giovanni Canti, at Milan. They included settings of two Goethe translations by Luigi Balestra, of Busseto. Two more songs, one of them also with words by Balestra, and a *Notturno* for soprano, tenor and bass with flute *obbligato*, were printed by the same publisher in 1839. A paragraph about the *Notturno* appeared in the *Gazzetta Privilegiata di Milano* for 13th April 1839: 'Maestro Giuseppe Verdi has added to his other admired musical compositions a new work that is an inspiration, an enchantment of delicate sound. . . .' This is remarkable, for the *Gazzetta* did not normally occupy itself with such things.

On 22nd April Verdi wrote to Giuseppe Demaldè ('Finola') of Busseto: [1]

> The advice you give me concerning my opera is very just, and as soon as I got to Milan, having heard what the singers were like, I disengaged myself at once, although with great displeasure. In my place, Maestro Speranza of Parma is going to write. Poor young fellow! I wish him luck, but I'm very dubious about it.
>
> My score is still wrapped up, but is, however, not asleep. I tell you this in secret: *perhaps it will be performed at La Scala, with Moriani, Ronconi, la Strepponi and la Kemble.* I can't be sure of it yet, but I hope so. . . . Enough—soon, perhaps within a week, I shall write to you on the subject.

This shows again how complicated and confused the story of the production of *Oberto* is, and how over-simplified are all the accounts of it by Verdi himself and his biographers. The letter to a friend at Busseto of 6th October 1838, already quoted, speaks of performance at La Scala in the Carnival or spring seasons. Yet the first paragraph of this letter to Demaldè shows that Verdi had returned to Milan with the prospect of his opera being performed at *another* theatre—*not* La Scala—and withdrew from this because he disapproved of the singers available. Was this the Teatro Filodrammatico again? It is impossible to say. Even 'Maestro Speranza of Parma', who was to replace Verdi at this theatre, is not certainly identifiable.[2]

As told already, hopes of production at La Scala again faded with Moriani's illness, and then again revived. Further alterations were made to the text, the voice parts were revised to suit other singers and the quartet was added at Merelli's suggestion. *Oberto* was finally produced at La Scala on 17th November 1839, with fair success. It was performed fourteen times. Eight days before the first performance the publisher Giovanni Ricordi wrote to Giovanni Morandi: 'There is to be heard shortly another opera which *a certain Maestro Verdi* is writing.'[3] That must be the first reference to the composer in the annals of the house of Ricordi. Shortly afterwards the firm purchased the rights in *Oberto* for 2,000 Austrian lire and so established a connection which must have brought them the equivalent of several kings'

[1] *Carteggi verdiani*, IV, p. 77.

[2] Luzio identifies him as Giovanni Antonio Speranza, but this composer was born at Mantua, not at Parma, and had already produced two operas. His best work, *I due Figaro*, was heard in the autumn of this year at Turin.

[3] Giuseppe Radiciotti, *Lettere inedite di celebri musicisti* (Milan, n.d.).

ransoms. Merelli offered Verdi a contract for three more operas at eight months' intervals, the first of which was to have been *Il Proscritto*, on a libretto commissioned from Gaetano Rossi; but then, plans being changed, Verdi produced to order the *opera buffa*, *Un giorno di regno*, which had one performance on 5th September 1840 and was a complete failure.

There is not much that is new to be said about the extraordinary fact that Verdi, at the time he told Ricordi the story of his early life, had come to believe that both of his children and his wife had died within a period of about two months while he was composing *Un giorno di regno*. Gatti first established the facts: the girl Virginia was born at Busseto on 26th March 1837, and died there in August 1838; the boy Icilio was born at Busseto on 11th July 1838, and died at Milan on 22nd October 1839; both the children were thus already dead before *Oberto* was produced. Poor Margherita followed them into the grave in June of the following year. In her father's *Libro di Casa* occurs the heartbroken entry:

> Through a terrible disease, perhaps unknown to the doctors, there died in my arms at Milan, at noon on the day of Corpus Domini, my beloved daughter Margherita in the flower of her years and at the culmination of her good fortune, because married to the excellent youth Giuseppe Verdi, Maestro di Musica. I implore for her pure soul eternal peace, while weeping bitterly over this painful loss.

It has been suggested that perhaps Ricordi was responsible for the errors in the Pougin-'Folchetto' account; but the correspondence between composer and publisher shows that Verdi was sent a proof. Furthermore, although no one seems to have noticed it, the same confusion is shown in an earlier account which also has Verdi's authority behind it, that included in Michele Lessona's *Volere è potere*—the Italian equivalent of Samuel Smiles's *Self-Help*—published at Florence in 1869, twelve years before the Pougin-'Folchetto'. Here is the passage in question:

> There awaited him unutterable sorrows. He became ill, and while still convalescent while he was writing the promised opera, both his children, one three years old and the other two, fell ill and died. Shortly afterwards his wife, as a result of these afflictions, was attacked by inflammation of the brain and—the young mother following her children—she too died. All that happened between the beginning of April and 22nd June of that same year 1840, by the autumn of which he had to write an *opera buffa*.

He seems to have envisaged this section of his own life, in recollection, as if it were a page from one of the violent romantic melodramas which occupied his imagination. But the facts were cruel enough.

The story of Verdi's recovery from these disasters, and of the events leading up to the composition and performance of *Nabucco*, is best told in his own words:

Un giorno di regno failed to please: certainly the music was partly to blame, but partly, too, the performance. With mind tormented by my domestic misfortunes, embittered by the failure of my work, I was convinced that I could find no consolation in my art and decided never to compose again. I even wrote to the engineer Pasetti, asking him to obtain from Merelli my release from the contract.

Merelli sent for me and treated me like a capricious schoolboy—he would not allow me to be discouraged by the unhappy failure of my opera, etc., etc. But I stood my ground, so that handing me back the contract Merelli said: 'Listen, Verdi! I can't force you to write. My faith in you is undiminished: who knows whether, one of these days, you won't decide to take up your pen again? In that case, as long as you give me two months' notice before the beginning of the season, I promise that your opera shall be performed.' I thanked him, but these words did not suffice to alter my decision and I went away.

I took rooms at Milan in the Corsia de' Servi. I had lost heart and given up thinking about music, when one winter evening on leaving the Galleria De Cristoforis I encountered Merelli, who was on his way to the theatre. It was snowing heavily and, taking me by the arm, he invited me to accompany him to his office at La Scala. On the way we talked and he told me he was in difficulties over the new opera he had to present: he had entrusted it to Nicolai but the latter was not satisfied with the libretto.

'Imagine!' said Merelli. 'A libretto by Solera! Stupendous! Magnificent! Extraordinary! Effective, grandiose dramatic situations and beautiful verses! But that pig-headed composer won't hear of it and says it's a hopeless libretto. I'm at my wits' end to know where to find another one quickly.'

'I'll help you out myself,' I replied. 'Didn't you have prepared for me *Il proscritto*? I haven't written a note of the music: I put it at your disposal.'

'Oh! that's fine—a real stroke of luck!'

Talking like this, we had reached the theatre. Merelli called Bassi, the poet, stage-manager, call-boy, librarian, etc., etc., and told him to look at once in the archives for a copy of *Il proscritto*. The copy was there. At the same time Merelli picked up another manuscript and, showing it to me, exclaimed:

'Look! Here is Solera's libretto. Such a beautiful subject—and he turned it down! Take it—read it through!'

'What the deuce should I do with it? No, no, I have no wish to read librettos.'

'Go on with you! It won't do you any harm. Read it and then bring it back to me again.' And he gave me the manuscript. It was on large sheets in big letters, as was then customary. I rolled it up, said goodbye to Merelli and went home.

On the way I felt a kind of indefinable malaise, a very deep sadness, a distress that filled my heart. I got home and with an almost violent gesture threw the manuscript on the table, standing upright in front of it. The book had opened in falling on the table; without knowing how, I gazed at the page that lay before me, and read this line:

Va, pensiero, sull' ali dorate.

I ran through the verses that followed and was much moved, all the more because they were almost a paraphrase from the Bible, the reading of which had always delighted me.

I read one passage, then another. Then, resolute in my determination to write no more, I forced myself to close the booklet and went to bed. But it was no use—I couldn't get *Nabucco* out of my head. Unable to sleep, I got up and read the libretto, not once, but two or three times, so that by the morning I knew Solera's libretto almost by heart.

Still I was not prepared to relax my determination and that day I returned to the theatre and handed the manuscript back to Merelli.

'Isn't it beautiful?' he said to me.

'Very beautiful!'

'Well then—set it to music!'

'I wouldn't dream of it. I won't hear of it.'

'Set it to music! Set it to music!'

And so saying he took the libretto, thrust it into my overcoat pocket, took me by the shoulders and not only pushed me out of the room but locked the door in my face.

What was I to do?

I returned home with *Nabucco* in my pocket. One day one verse, another day another, here a note and there a phrase, little by little the opera was composed.

It was the autumn of 1841, and recalling Merelli's promise, I went to see him and announced that *Nabucco* was written and could therefore be performed in the next Carnival season.

Merelli declared himself ready to keep his word, but at the same time pointed out that it would be impossible to give the opera in the coming season, because the repertory was already settled and because three new operas by renowned composers were due for performance. To give a fourth opera by a composer who was almost a beginner was dangerous for everybody concerned, and above all dangerous for me. It would thus be better to wait for the spring season, for which he had no prior engagements. He assured me that good artists would be engaged. But I refused: either in the Carnival season or not at all. And I had good reasons for that, knowing it would be impossible to find two other artists so well suited to my opera as la Strepponi and Ronconi, whom I knew to be engaged and on whom I was much relying.

Merelli, although disposed to give me my way, was, as impresario, not altogether in the wrong—to give four new operas in a single season was very risky! But I had good artistic grounds for opposing him. In short, after assertions and denials, obstacles and half-promises, the bills of La Scala were posted—but *Nabucco* was not announced!

I was young and hot-blooded. I wrote a rude letter to Merelli, giving vent to all my resentment. I confess that as soon as I had sent it I felt a kind of remorse, and I feared that as a result I had ruined everything.

Merelli sent for me, and on seeing me angrily exclaimed: 'Is this the way to write to a friend? . . . But still, you're quite right. We'll give this *Nabucco*. You must remember, however, that I shall have heavy expenses on account of the other new operas. I shall not be able to have special scenery and costumes made for *Nabucco*, but shall have to patch up as best I can whatever we find best adapted for the purpose in the storerooms.'

I agreed to everything because I was anxious for the opera to be given. New bills were issued, on which I finally read: NABUCCO! . . .

Towards the end of February the rehearsals began, and twelve days after the first rehearsal with pianoforte the first public performance took place, on 9th March, with Signore Strepponi and Bellinzaghi and Signori Ronconi, Miraglia and Derivis in the cast.

With the successful production of *Nabucco* at La Scala on 9th March 1842, Verdi's glory begins and his youth comes to a close. Margherita Barezzi is scarcely heard of again.

This chapter of reconsidered legends and documents of Verdi's youth may close with a passage from the *Autobiografia dalle Lettere* (Milan, 1941), compiled from the composer's letters by Aldo Oberdorfer ('Carlo Graziani'). This book, it has been said, 'broke through the crust of biographic conformity' and certainly Oberdorfer shows courage and insight in considering in his commentary all the dubious problems, historical and psychological, of Verdian biography. Here is what he has to say about Margherita Barezzi-Verdi:

Accustomed to the comfortable way of life of the Barezzi family, whose easy circumstances, too, were reflected in her own married home at Busseto, she must have felt lost, poor, alone, in the great city. The little girl in the cemetery, out there; the little boy dead in her arms in this squalid Milanese house; Verdi, in the fever of preparing for the performance of *Oberto*, already caught up a little in the wheels of the theatre. And money was lacking for everything except essentials, and sometimes perhaps for those too—as on the day when she had to pawn her jewels to help Verdi pay the rent; at Busseto they had asked enough already of her father and mother; perhaps she did not dare to ask any more, or he wish to risk a rebuke, however affectionate, from his father-in-law. It is the only 'heroic' action that we know of in her life, poor Ghita; a good and kind gesture. We know that in the interval between the two acts of *Oberto*, on the great night of the first performance, Verdi ran home to tell her that everything was going, or seemed to be going, as they had hoped—the companion, then, of his anxieties, lovingly attentive. And we know that when she died the young man seemed shattered, let himself be led back to Busseto by his father-in-law Barezzi like a boy, with no will-power left for anything but weeping—incapable of living, incapable of working. When he tried, under compulsion, there was the fiasco of *Un giorno di regno*, when the crisis was most acute, his desperation most profound. But less than two years afterwards came *Nabucco*, glory, new life. Formally and sentimentally it was a clean break with the past. That great sorrow was not forgotten, but buried. The ladies of the *beau monde* and the *divas* of the footlights staked their claims on the heart of the fashionable Maestro. There was no more room, in that bright light, for the pallid figure that, even when she was alive, seemed born for the shadows. She disappeared—completely. And it was a kind thought to wish her remembered in the crypt of the *Casa di Reposo* beside the Maestro and Giuseppina Strepponi, but historically it was a mistake.

That is very moving—a remarkable evocation, out of almost nothing, of that pathetic wraith, Verdi's first wife. And yet, is it not only the deplorable lack of documents concerning her that allows it to be made? If we had some of the many letters that must have passed between Verdi and his 'Ghita' during the years of separation before their marriage, we should perhaps come to a different conclusion. Those few sentences preserved in the letter quoted earlier, from Galluzzi to Barezzi, though they are little enough to build on, do not suggest a shrinking, retiring nature. But Galluzzi's letter was unknown to the compiler of the *Autobiografia*. And it should be noted that Oberdorfer, with all his fine writing, his psychological acumen, has failed to read aright another of the few documents we do possess. Verdi explains in the account given to Ricordi that, after being confined to bed with an attack of quinsy, he suddenly remembered that the rent was almost due; there was *no time*, he says, to write to Busseto, to his father-in-law, for the money, as the post went only twice a week. Oberdorfer's suppositions, that Margherita did not dare to ask for more money, that Verdi did not wish to risk a rebuke from Barezzi, are entirely gratuitous.

Enough has been said to show that there is an element of fiction in Oberdorfer's commentaries on Verdi's life and letters. In another book, the posthumously published *Giuseppe Verdi* (Milan, 1949), this tendency to confuse fact and fiction was to reach alarming proportions.

Verdi may have been dazzled for a while by his lionization after the success of *Nabucco*, but not for long, and if Margherita had been still alive perhaps he would not have been dazzled at all. Hard as it is to imagine Verdi apart from Giuseppina Strepponi, is it so certain that Antonio Barezzi's daughter would not have proved equally worthy to share his throne?

CHAPTER

2

Bartolomeo Merelli, Giuseppina Strepponi and Napoleone Moriani

WHAT HAS hitherto been known, or conjectured, about the relationship between the impresario who put on Verdi's first operas and the singer who subsequently became the composer's second wife, is conveniently summarized in the following short extract from Carlo Gatti's biography:

> Merelli persuades Lanari to cede her to him for a short sequence of performances; he takes her to Vienna and protects her; Giuseppina Strepponi's fortune is thus assured.
>
> There is no better support for a singer than the protection of a powerful impresario, who dispenses fame and money, and creates the glory and wealth of his dependents.
>
> Merelli's friendship, however, costs Giuseppina anguished and unrelievable suffering in her life as a woman, of which a few people become aware.
>
> Here and there it is whispered that she is Merelli's mistress; Verdi himself, pointing her out one evening in the theatre to his sister-in-law Marianna, Margherita's younger sister, speaks about it, mentioning the son she is said to have.[1]

F. T. Garibaldi, in *Giuseppe Verdi nella vita e nell'arte* (Florence, 1904), had first disclosed in print that Giuseppina Strepponi had an illegitimate son. Garibaldi's source of information, a letter from Giuseppina to Giovannina Lucca, was published by Alessandro Luzio in his famous article '*La Traviata* e il dramma intimo personale

[1] First edition, I, pp. 158–9. In the second edition, p. 134, the passage ends: 'mentioning the son she is said to have had by him.'

di Verdi' in *Nuova Antologia* for 1st April 1937 (reprinted in *Carteggi verdiani*, vol. iv, Rome, 1947). Luzio cautiously, but certainly correctly, identified this son as the 'Camillino' mentioned by Giuseppina in a letter to Verdi of 3rd September 1849.

A few short passages, some of them expressive of profound discouragement, from Giuseppina Strepponi's correspondence with the Florentine impresario Alessandro Lanari, were published in her lifetime by 'Jarro' in his *Memorie d'un impresario fiorentino* (Florence, 1892). After her death one of her letters to Lanari, dated 23rd June 1839, was sent to Verdi by the antiquarian bookseller Giuseppe Coen, of Milan. This letter was also published by Luzio in his article in *Nuova Antologia*.

The 'Anno Verdiano' of 1951 was not remarkable for the literature it produced. Quite the most exciting and original contribution was made by Eugenio Gara, who in an article 'La misteriosa giovinezza di Giuseppina Strepponi', in the *Corriere della Sera* of 27th January, revealed, or recalled, the existence of other letters from the singer to the Florentine impresario. These letters—twenty-two from 1828 to 1842 and one from 1849—had been for more than sixty years among Lanari's papers in the Biblioteca Nazionale, Florence, but had not been utilized by any of Verdi's biographers. The additional fragments quoted by Gara were most welcome, but the study of the whole collection is necessary, together with much hard work on the operatic background, if we are to understand and interpret aright these fascinating documents. All the letters quoted by 'Jarro' are here, together with others even more revealing. This correspondence permits more than a glimpse behind the scenes where Giuseppina Strepponi, the *prima donna*, won fame and applause; here we see her in her private life, gay sometimes, courageous always, but for long periods in the toils, overburdened with cares and responsibilities—a suffering, almost desperate, human being.

Bartolomeo Merelli, impresario at Milan and Vienna, is an interesting figure who deserves more attention than he has yet received. Long before he brought out Verdi's earliest operas at Milan he had been Donizetti's close friend and first librettist.

Donizetti was the pupil of Simone Mayr at the Charity School of Music at Bergamo from the autumn of 1806, when he was nearly nine, until the autumn of 1815, when he was nearly eighteen. Among Mayr's private pupils was Bartolomeo Merelli, the son of Count Moroni's man of affairs. Merelli was born at Bergamo on 19th May 1794,[1] and was thus three and a half years older than the future composer of *Lucia di Lammermoor* and *Don Pasquale*. He was intended for the law, but showed more interest in music and literature.

[1] Precise date of birth first given by Ciro Caversazzi in *Bergomum*, April 1928.

Mayr called upon him to supervise the literary education of his brilliant pupil, the young Donizetti, and to provide verses for him to set to music. A few years later Merelli seemed to have embarked on a career as professional librettist. Four new operas with librettos by him were produced in 1818, *Alfredo il grande* by Mayr in Rome in February, *Il lupo di Ostenda* by Vaccai at Venice in the spring, and then, towards the end of the year, also at Venice, the earliest works by Donizetti to be performed in a public theatre. The impresario Zancla of the Teatro San Luca (the former Teatro Vendramin) commissioned the *opera semi-seria, Enrico di Borgogna,* from Merelli and Donizetti. The librettist, as was customary, went with the composer to Venice to produce the opera. *Enrico di Borgogna,* first performed on 14th November, was not strikingly successful. The *Gazzetta Privilegiata di Venezia* on 19th November had a few words about the authors: 'Newish, if not quite new, the so-called poet; altogether new the talented composer, who now for the first time ventures upon these arduous tasks.' The anonymous *Cenni biografici di Donizetti e Mayr* (Bergamo, 1875), based on Merelli's reminiscences, refer to an *opera buffa, Il ritratto parlante,* which he and Donizetti produced in less than a month for Zancla's second company; this seems to be identical with *Una follia,* a one-act farce recorded as having been performed at the Teatro San Luca on 15th December, although the libretto of this is sometimes attributed to A. L. Tottola. There is no comment at all on this work in contemporary newspapers.

In 1819 Merelli and Donizetti collaborated in two further one-act *opere buffe: Piccioli virtuosi ambulanti,* performed by Mayr's pupils at Bergamo in September, and *Le nozze in villa,* which was a bad failure when produced later at Mantua. In 1821 Merelli provided librettos for an oratorio, *Samuele,* by Mayr, and an *opera seria, Zoraide di Granata,* by Donizetti, which brought the composer his first considerable success when it was produced at the Teatro Argentina, Rome, on 28th January 1822. After that Donizetti's career led him for long periods away from Bergamo and the partnership broke up. Merelli subsequently wrote three more librettos for Vaccai—*Pietro il grande* (Parma, Carnival 1824), *La pastorella feudataria* (Turin, 18th September 1824) and *Il precipizio* (Milan, 16th August 1826).

For details of the next stages of Merelli's career we are dependent on the gossipy and generally unreliable Gino Monaldi, who devotes a chapter to him in his *Impresari celebri del secolo XIX* (Rocca S. Casciano, 1918). According, then, to Monaldi, after accompanying Donizetti to Rome for the production of *Zoraide di Granata* in 1822, Merelli returned to Bergamo, where he stayed for a short time, until a misadventure changed the whole course of his life.

The father of our Bartolomeo was the agent of the noble family of the Counts Moroni, and that allowed the younger Merelli to frequent their *palazzo*. Now it came about that the youth, who was of vivacious and thoughtless disposition, impelled perhaps by some considerable loss at play, or by some other motive, pocketed in a moment of mental aberration some silver cutlery, part of a splendid table service belonging to the Counts Moroni. The crime was very soon found out, to the great sorrow of Merelli's father, who, thanks to his long and honourable service with the Moroni family, was able to arrange that his son should not be punished—on the understanding, however, that he should leave Bergamo at once and never again set foot within the *palazzo*. The father then sent him to Milan. Arrived there, poor Bartolomeo, short of money, had to accept a job in one of the so numerous theatrical agencies of that time, resigning himself to the vulgar occupation of sweeping and dusting the office.

If we are to believe Monaldi, Merelli's rise from this point was meteoric indeed:

In little more than a year he had become the favourite of the house and in particular of its proprietor, who said to him one day: 'Listen, my dear Merelli, I'm not going to give you money, but I'll leave to you whatever the engagement of the theatrical company—the chorus singers, orchestral players, dancers, etc.—may bring in.' Merelli, however, was not the sort of man to be content with so little; he had quite different ideas. And one fine autumn morning our Bartolomeo suddenly leaves Milan, accompanied by a numerous company of *virtuosi* singers and dancers, and betakes himself to Vienna.

A love affair with a famous ballerina was next turned to profit. She and Merelli between them fleeced the old minister Montecucoli, who gave many presents to the ballerina before he attained his desires:

Finally the *virtuosa* capitulated, but that did not happen before Merelli had in his pocket a decree which nominated him Inspector General of the Imperial and Royal Theatres, with a salary of 12,000 florins. That office represented a real sinecure, leaving Merelli full freedom of movement. And in fact he profited by it to spread his wings and fly to other foreign shores and continue his brilliant and adventurous career. Very soon he had charge of the principal theatres of Europe—Paris, St Petersburg, Berlin, London and Vienna all had him in turn as their ambitious and fortunate impresario. In the autumn of 1836 he assumed the direction of La Scala which, with short interruptions, he retained until November 1864.

Several things call for comment here. Even Gatti, the soberest of Verdi's biographers, although he omits the picturesque details, still relies on Monaldi for the 'facts' of Merelli's life. He refers to 'a youthful error', in consequence of which legal studies were abandoned for theatrical affairs, although Merelli must have been at least twenty-eight when he stole the cutlery—if he did steal it. Gatti accepts also without question Monaldi's statement that Merelli became Inspector General of the Austrian Imperial and Royal Theatres. But of this appointment there is no trace in the Austrian State Archives. Nor is 'the minister Montecucoli' easily identified. Further, Gatti repeats uncritically what Monaldi writes about Merelli having charge of the principal theatres in Paris, St Petersburg, Berlin and London. Not a scrap of evidence for this has ever been produced. Merelli was certainly, after his establishment at Milan, the *agent* through whom singers were engaged for Italian opera seasons in other countries; the theatrical papers of the period include announcements of the engagement of singers for Mexico City, Lisbon, St Petersburg, etc., through his agency; but that is not to say he was impresario of the theatres concerned. The date given by Monaldi for the beginning of Merelli's reign at La Scala is correct; that given for its end is wrong.

More reliable information about Merelli's career is to be found in the letters of the composers for whom he worked and who worked for him, and in his own letters to Lanari, which are preserved among the latter's papers at Florence. The years following the production of Donizetti's *Zoraide di Granata* are obscure, apart from the three librettos for Vaccai. The earliest letter to Lanari is dated from Milan, 9th October 1826, and shows that Merelli was then running a theatrical agency under his own name; as the reference number of this letter is 2,095 the agency had clearly been in existence for some time. The second letter to Lanari, of March 1827, gives the address: Piazza dei Filodrammatici, Milan. In 1828 we find references to Merelli in Bellini's letters. He was not yet well known—Bellini refers to 'a certain theatrical correspondent named Merelli'—and he was not much trusted: 'between ourselves, he passes for a swindler'. He was acting as operatic middleman between the impresarios of Genoa and Parma and the composers. He had brought the composer Pacini, without having proper authority to do so, an offer from Genoa; Bellini, however, although suspicious of Merelli's credentials, did secure through him the agreement to write *Zaira* for Parma.

On 24th June 1830 Donizetti wrote to Mayr at the request of the tenor Alessandro Busti, who wished for a recommendation to Merelli. Relations between the former friends had deteriorated and Donizetti believed that a recommendation on his own part would be useless. Nevertheless, in the years that followed, the two were thrown together again fairly often by theatrical affairs. According to Alberto Cametti,[1] Merelli in 1834 was the agent of Duke Carlo Visconti di Modrone, impresario of La Scala from the autumn of 1832 until the autumn of 1836.

In June 1834 Bellini blamed Merelli for the preparation and distribution of pirated scores of his operas by Milanese publishers.

[1] *Jacopo Ferretti e i musicisti del suo tempo* (Milan, n.d.), p. 206.

A modest beginning as impresario was made at Varese, where Merelli was in charge of the short autumn season of opera from 1830 onwards.[1] He was impresario at Cremona for the Carnival season of 1835,[2] and at Como in the following August.[3] His great period began in 1836. From 1st April of that year he became joint lessee with a much older man, Carlo Balochino (1770–1851), of the Kärntnertor theatre in Vienna, and in the autumn of the same year he succeeded Visconti as impresario of La Scala, Milan. Merelli and Balochino retained their Viennese appointment uninterruptedly until the revolution of 1848; La Scala remained in Merelli's hands until 30th November 1850.

According to Raffaello Barbiera [4] the death of Malibran on 23rd September 1836 relieved Merelli of the necessity of paying 100,000 lire which he owed her under the terms of their contract.

The comments made by composers in private about the new impresario continued to be unflattering. Donizetti wrote to Count Gaetano Melzi on 26th June 1838: 'As for Milan, in the matter of Art, I sing the Requiem, for Merelli will not and (very nearly) cannot pay.' Nicolai on 20th September of the same year described the impresario in his diary as 'a scoundrel, and already known as such in the whole of Italy'.

The years during which Merelli put on the early operas of Verdi, from *Oberto, Conte di San Bonifacio* (17th November 1839) to *Nabucco* (9th March 1842) and *I Lombardi* (11th February 1843) seem to have been prosperous ones. It must be said that he treated the young and unknown Verdi very well, showing generosity and forbearance; he had his reward in the successes of *Nabucco* and *I Lombardi*, which certainly contributed largely to his prosperity. This must have been the period of Merelli's magnificent country villa at Lentate, with sixteen English horses in the stables, his luxurious apartments at Milan and his collections of pictures and *objets d'art*. The comments of the composers are now friendly in tone.

On 31st October 1843, however, Donizetti complained to Melzi about Merelli's practice of making unauthorized alterations to his operas. Having announced that the composer had revised *Fausta* for performances at Bergamo, Merelli made it appear that the work *had* been revised by adding a finale from another opera and an aria by another composer. In June 1844 *Roberto Devereux* was a failure in Vienna. Donizetti made scathing comments on the singers in this Italian season, 'which could have been one of the most brilliant, but was the most disastrous'. He added: 'And Merelli, who calls himself director of the Italian season, stays at Milan—and does well to do so,

[1] P. Cambiasi, *Teatro di Varese* (Milan, 1891).
[2] *L'Eco* (Milan), 14th Jan. 1835.
[3] *Il Figaro* (Milan), 5th Sept. 1835.
[4] *Passioni del Risorgimento* (Milan, 1903), p. 19.

for otherwise he would hear a thing or two.' The Italian season in Vienna in 1845 was even worse:

> Merelli led His Excellency the Minister of Home Security to believe that Mme Moltini was a Malibran; he bet a thousand florins that Mme Tedesco and Calzolari were two divinities, and was ready to sign a note of hand for any sum of money, to wager on a colossal success. I read his letter myself. They had to take him at his word.

The 'divinities' turned out to be two beginners, one only seventeen years old, who had never set foot on the stage before.

> It was a poor revenge for Sig. Merelli's mockery of the Viennese to see the theatre constantly empty. Only a few performances were moderately well attended. Who was responsible? *Merelli.* I was sent for. I read the letter in which the artists were listed. I couldn't say whether this was approved or not. But certainly one shouldn't write: 'I give you this singer who is a second Rubini' and 'I bet that this one will create a furore' and 'A woman of whom Mme Fedor or Pasta herself would be afraid'. . . . He made Laboccetta, a tenor of infinite grace (and therefore a weak one) make his *début* in a part that did not suit him. He ends by making him play the violoncello. . . . He has victimized all these good friends, who arrived here relying on the goodwill of the public. And why? He has three orchestral conductors capable of turning out fine operas: Nicolai, Proch and Reuling. And yet *he* decides on the opera and distributes the parts, and gives the bass the baritone part, and the contralto the soprano part. And if the artists protest he says: 'Have it altered.' He ruins operas; he ruins voices; the public hears mutilated versions of every part. He should give the scores to the conductors, who would choose the casts so as to bring honour to themselves and attract the public. Instead of which these conductors accept the scores when the management, as ignorant of music as I am of Greek, tells them: 'I have given out the parts myself.' . . . If I requested of His Majesty the complete fulfilment of my Imperial and Royal Decree [as Court Composer to the Emperor] *I* should be obliged to superintend, during my stay here, the better working of the theatre. Instead, I try to put things right without ceremony. In recompense for that he writes: 'There is in Vienna an Italian musical celebrity who wages war on me.' War? When I *ought* to wage it and *don't*?
>
> . . . .
>
> The Italian season here was Hell let loose. There were four singers who had never been on the stage before. What howls! What cat-calls! What a lesson for the good Merelli!

Things were no better at Milan. In this same year Verdi rejected a proposal that he should engage himself five years ahead to write for La Scala—for the last year of Merelli's contract as impresario. Verdi's pupil Emanuele Muzio told Antonio Barezzi: 'He doesn't want to write any more for La Scala, nor produce nor conduct any of his operas, and he says he doesn't want to set foot on that stage again.' It was hoped that the Milanese production of *I due Foscari*, with which Verdi himself would have nothing to do, would nevertheless make up for the failure of other operas:

> Let's hope that *I due Foscari* will not be so maltreated as was *William Tell*! . . . Singers, chorus and orchestra vied with one another in doing their worst. The opera was only allowed to finish out of respect for Rossini. Signora Sonta (who paid Merelli 3,500 Austrian lire to be allowed to sing) got horribly hissed and will not appear again—at least it is hoped not. Everything as bad as possible! What scoundrels!

Muzio reported fiasco after fiasco. He was perhaps a little biased.

Already in April 1845 Donizetti had heard that Merelli was in financial difficulties. In October 1846 Muzio declared that it was feared at Milan that he might go bankrupt. 'He has sold his house and still has large debts. He told one of his friends that the Carnival season will be for him a matter of life and death.' The situation was apparently temporarily saved by the successes of Fanny Elssler, a troupe of American acrobatic dancers and Verdi's *Attila*. But Verdi himself was so disgusted with the way *Attila* was produced that he wrote to Ricordi, refusing to allow any of his future operas to be performed at La Scala.

The revolution of 1848 caused the cancellation of the projected Italian season in Vienna. Richard Wallaschek, in *Das k. k. Hofoperntheater* (Vienna, 1909), provides some interesting information, not available elsewhere, on Merelli's activities at this period. Wallaschek contrasts the characters of the Italian co-lessees of the Kärntnertor theatre. He says that the elderly Balochino, after paying off the artists, ran away at the first sign of trouble, but that Merelli 'allowed himself to be employed as a spy of Radetzky's at the beginning of the Italian unrest, which brought him in such bad odour among his fellow countrymen that for a long time after 1849 he did not dare leave the confines of Austrian Italy'. Unfortunately, Wallaschek does not give us his sources for this information. It is worth noting, however, that the vice-president of the Austrian Government in Lombardy from 1844 to 1847 was Count Albert Montecucoli and that after the suppression of the Milanese rising this man became in 1849 head of civilian affairs under Field Marshal Radetzky. Montecucoli was born on 1st July 1802, so he was eight years *younger* than Merelli; he was in Salzburg when Merelli first took over the Italian opera in Vienna; and it was only during his last few years, before his death on 19th August 1852, that, as first *Sektionschef* in the Ministry for Internal Affairs, he could have called himself a minister of state. So it is difficult to identify him as 'the old minister Montecucoli' of Monaldi's anecdote. Nevertheless, the connection of the names of Montecucoli and Merelli may have some significance. It is possible that the impresario, maintaining his position with difficulty in Vienna and at

Milan, may have been driven into spying for the Austrians. Such a move would have been, from all accounts, entirely in character. Letters from the bass singer Carlo Cambiaggio to Lanari, published by 'Jarro', give a picture of Milan after the return of the Austrians and mention Merelli:

The end of August 1848:

> Milan has become a monastery, or rather, I seem to be in the country, for one sees no one except the soldiers, who make a devilish noise, dragging their sabres along the ground. The day before yesterday they shot a young man of twenty-five because they found he was wearing a dagger; today, it is said, they are going to shoot another. In order to avoid being shot, I don't even carry a cane, and I go home at eight o'clock.

16th September 1848:

> Milan is crowded only with soldiery. All the houses and *palazzi* are full of them. Soldiers cook their rations in magnificent apartments and gilded *salons*. The famous Casino de' Nobili, all the Archbishop's Palace and many churches are full of Croats and other insects. . . . At Monza they shot a man and his son because they found buried in his garden a wretched, useless fowling-piece that didn't even belong to him. New taxes are announced every day. . . . If you were here in the evening you wouldn't believe you were at Milan; in less than a quarter of an hour you would encounter twenty patrols, in war-formation, with their sentries, vanguards and rearguards. There is much talk; what is certain is that the mayor has protested that he hasn't the means to go on. Meanwhile the theatre does well, Merelli laughs and the military carouse.

Decidedly, the impresario was not a good Italian patriot.

Merelli's reign at La Scala ended on 30th November 1850. From 1853 to 1855, and probably also before that, he was again in charge of the Italian seasons in Vienna. Little is known of his later life except that he reappeared as impresario of La Scala from the autumn of 1861 until Lent 1863. When Giovannina Lucca, in 1861, proposed to Nicola De Giosa that he should write a new opera for Merelli, the composer replied: 'I hope never to have anything to do with that impresario. I know what a fine baby he is, and prefer to rot in misery rather than fall into his clutches.'[1] Someone named Merelli took an Italian operatic company, including Desirée Artôt, to St Petersburg in 1868; this may have been Bartolomeo, then aged seventy-four, but is more likely to have been his son Eugenio, who was in charge of the Italian season at the Kärntnertor theatre, Vienna, in 1864, and who is mentioned sometimes in the theatrical papers of this period.[2] The old age of the 'Napoleon of the Impresarios' was spent in retirement

[1] Franco Schlitzer, *Mondo teatrale dell'ottocento* (Naples, 1954), p. 187.

[2] The *Gazzetta Musicale di Milano* of 31st March 1867 reported that the younger Merelli had engaged Desirée Artôt, among other singers, for Warsaw.

at Bergamo, where in 1871 he was a member of the Consultative Commission of the School of Music.[1] In writing or dictating his reminiscences for the anonymous *Cenni biografici di Donizetti e Mayr*, 'raccolti dalle memorie di un vecchio ottuagenario dilettante di musica', he drew attention to Charles de Boigne's *Petits Mémoires de l'Opéra* (Paris, 1857) and Michele Lessona's *Volere è potere* (Florence, 1869). The only references to Merelli in these books concern his early recognition of Verdi and his part in the creation of *Nabucco*, of which he would seem to have been legitimately proud. He returned later to Milan, where he died of apoplexy on 3rd or 4th April 1879.[2]

Monaldi ends his history of the Fall of the House of Merelli on a macabre note:

> His only son, the advocate Luigi Merelli, who also had his period as theatrical impresario, could not or perhaps did not wish to continue to bear his famous name on the stage of the world. A few days after his father's death Luigi Merelli, at the age of fifty-four, committed suicide, together with his daughter Cristina, aged thirty-one, asphyxiating himself by means of charcoal fumes. The bodies were found in a closet, in the house they rented on the Corso di Porta Genova, clasped in each other's arms, and in a state of advanced putrefaction.

A detailed account of this 'Dramma orrendo' is to be found in the newspaper *La Perseveranza* for 11th April 1879, with additional 'tristi particolari' on 13th, 14th and 15th April. Various letters and notes were found near the corpses. On the wash-basin was a board and on this a piece of paper with an inscription in enormous letters: 'We are killing ourselves because we are tired of life. Let no one be blamed for our deaths.' Then a note in Cristina's hand: 'Please leave me dressed as I am and bury me like this, because my underclothes are clean; I changed them last Saturday.' Again:

> I ask to be buried in the clothes I am wearing, without even my underclothes being changed. I wish to be buried beside my father. Both he and I would like the expenses of our funerals to be paid out of the enclosed 250 lire.
>
> CRISTINA MERELLI.

La Perseveranza of 13th April states that the news had been too much for Luigi Merelli's sister, who had collapsed and was then in grave danger. The issue of 14th–15th April refers to another brother, Eugenio, who had a few days earlier supplied the 250 lire. So Monaldi was not right in calling Luigi the 'only son' of Bartolomeo Merelli. Monaldi gets *everything* wrong. It was Eugenio, and not Luigi, who

[1] G. Donati-Petteni, *L'Arte della musica in Bergamo* (Bergamo, 1930), p. 69.

[2] In *La Perseveranza* for 5th April he is listed among those who died at Milan on 4th April; but the obituary notice in the same number (5th April) says he died 'the day before yesterday'.

was for a time an impresario. And Luigi was fifty-one, and not fifty-four, at the time of his suicide.[1] Eugenio died on 2nd November 1882, aged fifty-seven; [2] he was therefore born in 1825. Bartolomeo Merelli must have married within a year or two of his arrival at Milan in 1822, or thereabouts. Barbiera [3] says he was twice married, the second time to a Signora Magni, his deceased wife's sister, and had seven children in all.

We turn now to the subject of Giuseppina Strepponi's origins and early career. Until her history, as well as Merelli's, has been clarified, it is impossible to decide how much, or how little, truth there is in the account of their relationship presented by Gatti and generally accepted since. Giuseppina was the daughter of Feliciano Strepponi, a musician from Lodi, who began his career under a severe handicap. While still a student at the Milan Conservatorio he had married—presumably because he *had* to—Rosa Cornalba, also a native of Lodi, and he was no more than eighteen years of age when, on 8th September 1815, his first child, Clelia Maria Josepha, afterwards known as Giuseppina, was born. A score of Mozart's *La Clemenza di Tito*, presented to Feliciano Strepponi after a concert by the Conservatorio pupils on 7th October 1819, is preserved at Sant' Agata. He completed his studies in 1820 and then secured a position as *maestro di cappella* of the cathedral at Monza, where he wrote much church music; but he soon sought fame in the theatres. His first opera, *Il marito nubile*, produced at Turin in 1822, was followed in 1823 by two others, *Chi fa così fa bene* and *Francesca da Rimini*, produced respectively at Milan and Vicenza. Preoccupation with the stage led to neglect of his duties as organist and choirmaster, and in 1828 he was dismissed from Monza. In that year he settled, with his family, at Trieste, where he was engaged as assistant to Giuseppe Farinelli, musical director of the Teatro Grande. Two new operas, *L'Allievo dell'amore* and *Gli Illinesi*, were heard there in the following year. Then *Amore e mistero* was produced at Turin in 1830 and *L'Ullà di Bassora*, with considerable success, at La Scala, Milan, in 1831. Strepponi, after an unfortunate venture into theatrical management, ending in disaster, died at Trieste on 13th January 1832, aged only thirty-four, leaving his widow in poor circumstances, with four children to support. The eldest child, Giuseppina, had entered the Milan Conservatorio as a paying pupil on 9th December 1830, exemption from the regulation concerning the age limit, refused to Verdi, having been granted in her case. She was a good pianist and showed exceptional promise as a singer. Her mother managed to pay the Conservatorio fees for 1832,

[1] *La Perseveranza*, 11th April 1879, where, however, he and Cristina are listed among 'Morti a Milano il 10 Aprile'—the date, rather, of the discovery of their bodies.
[2] *La Perseveranza*, 6th Nov. 1882.
[3] Op. cit., p. 18.

out of the receipts of a concert given for her benefit at Trieste, but was too poor to continue. Giuseppina was then granted a free scholarship, which enabled her to complete her training, and in the autumn of 1834 she carried off the first prize for *bel canto* and left the Conservatorio. A memento of this survives at Sant' Agata, in the form of a volume of manuscript music, bound in leather, with the inscription in gilt letters: 'Premio ed incoraggiamento all' alunna Strepponi per l'accademia 29 Settembre 1834.' The *Gazzetta Privilegiata di Milano* next day gave what was probably Giuseppina's first mention in print. She was praised for her performances at the students' concert of the cavatina from Bellini's *Beatrice di Tenda*, and, with other pupils, of a duet from Donizetti's *Anna Bolena* and of a quintet by Basily: 'This young singer, all heart and temperament, gifted particularly in the upper register with a neat and agile voice, will be a fine acquisition, when the time comes, for the Italian stage.' A month later she appeared in concerts at Lodi, her birthplace, where she had relatives, and towards the end of 1834 she made her *début* on the stage at Adria. A success in Rossini's *Matilde di Shabran* at the Teatro Grande, Trieste, during the Carnival season of 1835 established her as a rising star. From this time forward Giuseppina became the mainstay of the family.

The nineteenth-century Italian operatic world was controlled by the all-powerful impresarios. These competed for the singers, who often placed themselves for long periods entirely in the hands of a single impresario. A singer was said to be 'in the possession' of Alessandro Lanari or Bartolomeo Merelli, and the possessor, after making the best use of an artist in the theatres under his direction, could hire him or her, without consultation, to a colleague or rival. The young Giuseppina Strepponi is generally stated to have been secured by Lanari, who had his headquarters at Florence, but also controlled a number of theatres in other parts of Italy. Giuseppina is said to have appeared in twenty-seven theatres in the first five years of her career. Not all of these can be easily traced. According to Fétis she sang at Venice, Brescia and Mantua in 1836, at Trieste and Bologna in 1837, and in Rome, Leghorn and Florence in 1838. The Italian writers who might have been expected to clarify this dark period of Giuseppina's life, between the commencement of her professional career and the advent in 1839 of Verdi, have been content to copy from Fétis, or from each other, this string of dates and place names.

In the archives at Sant' Agata nothing remains that could serve for the reconstruction of this theatrical career—no librettos, playbills or programmes. She seems herself to have destroyed almost everything that could remind her of her former triumphs: other memories, too painful to contemplate, were bound up with them.

Books exist on the operatic history of various towns or individual theatres, from which some details of Giuseppina's stage appearances can be recovered, but the information is scanty enough, and for many towns, and very many theatres, there are no such records. The contemporary newspapers must be consulted. The *Gazzetta Privilegiata di Milano* for this period includes, not only reviews of performances in Milanese theatres, but a weekly column of operatic notes and news, with brief reports of successes and failures all over the peninsula. This is very helpful, although there are disconcerting gaps—there is almost nothing in the *Gazzetta Privilegiata*, for instance, about operatic events during the second half of 1836. The richest and most reliable sources of all are the specifically theatrical papers, of which the two most important were *Il Pirata* and *Il Figaro*, published twice a week at Milan. The files of these papers provide all the materials needed for the reconstruction from beginning to end of Giuseppina's artistic career, and against this background one can begin to understand her correspondence with Lanari. In addition, the contemporary letters of other singers and impresarios to Lanari, preserved together with Giuseppina's in the Biblioteca Nazionale at Florence, can be drawn upon for further details. They include more than two hundred letters from Bartolomeo Merelli himself.

As soon as one digs a little deeper into the records of Giuseppina's early life, one finds reason to doubt whether the accepted story is based on anything more than supposition. The Italian authorities never seem to bother to check anything. In the passage quoted at the beginning of this chapter, Gatti declares that she was taken to Vienna by Merelli, who had persuaded Lanari to cede her to him for a short sequence of performances. Now Giuseppina Strepponi's only appearances in Vienna took place in April, May and June 1835, the year *before* Merelli became impresario of the Kärntnertor theatre. The actual lessee at this time was Louis Antoine Duport, who had been Barbaja's manager in Vienna from 1826 to 1828 and was himself lessee from 1st September 1830 until 31st March 1836. This in itself does not disprove the story, as a note in the *Gazzetta Privilegiata* of 14th June 1835 shows that Merelli, although not impresario, *was* responsible, probably in his capacity as theatrical agent, for the success of the Italian season of this year.[1] So he may well have taken, or sent, Giuseppina to Vienna. But he did not obtain her from Lanari. She is not mentioned in Merelli's correspondence with Lanari of 1835. She was in fact not at this time bound to any one particular impresario, and from contemporary letters and newspapers

[1] A rival, Ercole Tinti, had announced at Bologna that he was taking over the Vienna theatre in 1836. This was denied in the *Gazzetta Privilegiata*, which stated that Merelli was then engaged, as a result of a commission received, in assuring for the Viennese public the continuation in the future of the pleasures he had secured for them in the present season.

it appears that she first sang in a theatre under Lanari's management in 1837, and first signed a long-term contract with him in 1838.

Mercede Mundula, in her delightfully written biography of Giuseppina, *La Moglie di Verdi* (Milan, 1938), follows Gatti in believing that Lanari ceded her to Merelli in 1835,[1] and adds:

> In the burning circle in which la Strepponi turns there unfolds, a little later, the almost habitual course of events of the theatrical *milieu*: the *prima donna* becomes the mistress of the conquering impresario. . . . The rash girl will never forgive herself for her lapse, which has, however, every extenuating circumstance. . . . A child is born of that union, a child that the father, legally married, cannot legitimize: Giuseppina's existence will be bound to that child of sin, as to a cross, for many years. . . . A bewildered moth has miserably burned her wings, attracted by a light that seemed brilliant, but was in reality harsh and smoky.

This is very fine, very moving—almost as good as Oberdorfer. But it is not true: it is fiction. Signora Mundula commits herself to saying that Giuseppina's illegitimate child 'saw the light in 1836 or 37—certainly before 1838', but if she had undertaken, as she should have done, the task of reconstructing the singer's career in detail, she would have found that there is simply no room, amid the crowded programme of operatic engagements in 1836 and 1837, for the birth of a baby. And how was it that, after Vienna in 1835, Giuseppina never appeared at *any* theatre under Merelli's direction until 1839? If he wished to 'dispense fame and money, and create the glory and wealth of his dependents' the obvious thing for Merelli to do for his supposed new mistress, a bright young star, would have been to engage her for La Scala at Milan and re-engage her for the Karntnertor theatre in Vienna. From 1836 onwards both these theatres were under his control. Yet Giuseppina never returned to Vienna and made her first appearance at La Scala only in 1839. As for the illegitimate child, it is possible to show fairly conclusively, from the gaps in stage appearances, that Camillino must have been born early in 1838. The newly rediscovered letters from Giuseppina to Lanari disclose that she had in actual fact, not one, but *two* illegitimate children, the second born quite certainly towards the end of 1841. And the letters show that someone else, and not Merelli, was the father of these children.

Signora Mundula is concerned to present the young Giuseppina Strepponi as a dove-like creature, the innocent victim of circumstances and the villainy of men. It is for this reason, presumably, that she places Camillino's birth very early in her heroine's career. The picture that emerges after study of the correspondence with Lanari is rather different. *One* illegitimate child may be explained away as a

[1] She is followed in her turn by Giuseppe Stefani, whose *Verdi e Trieste* (Trieste, 1951) includes, however, some new information about the Strepponi family from the local archives.

slip, the sort of thing that might happen to anyone entering, alone and unprotected, the dubious backstage world. But *two* children? When the second was born Giuseppina was twenty-six, no longer in her first youth, and, one would have thought, sufficiently experienced, after six years on the stage, to avoid the obvious pitfalls for a beginner.

The following table, compiled from the contemporary theatrical papers and other sources, gives the dates of Giuseppina Strepponi's appearances at different towns and theatres, in concerts and opera performances, from the beginning of her career until the production of Verdi's *Nabucco* in 1842. It must be understood that in most cases a long series of repeat performances followed the first performance of operas here recorded, until the end of the season in question. Precise dates of the ends of the seasons are not easy to establish; where they are known they are here given. Composers' names follow the first appearance in any particular opera. In the course of this period of her life Giuseppina sang in twelve operas by Donizetti, seven by Bellini, five by Rossini, five by Mercadante, three or four by the Ricci brothers, two by F. Campana and one each by ten other composers, including Verdi. In the last few years of her career, which constitute a quite separate period, she was to add to her repertoire only two more operas by Donizetti, one by Verdi and one by Meyerbeer.

1834

29th Sept.	Milan	Conservatorio	Concert
31st Oct.	Lodi		Concert
17th Nov.	Lodi		Concert
26th Dec.(?)	Adria	Teatro Orfeo	*Chiara di Rosemberg* (L. Ricci) (?)

1835

19th Jan.	Trieste	Teatro Grande	*Matilde di Shabran* (Rossini)
7th Feb.	Trieste	Teatro Grande	*Anna Bolena* (Donizetti)
4th Apr.	Vienna	Kärntnertor Theatre	*Anna Bolena*
29th Apr.	Vienna	Kärntnertor Theatre	*Norma* (as Adalgisa) (Bellini)
15th May	Vienna	Kärntnertor Theatre	*La Sonnambula* (Bellini)
9th June	Vienna	Kärntnertor Theatre	*Il Furioso all' isola di S. Domingo* (Donizetti)
		(Season ended 16th June)	
18th July	Udine	Teatro della Nobile Società	*La Sonnambula*
Aug.	Udine	Teatro della Nobile Società	*Anna Bolena*
Sept.	Gorizia	Teatro di Società	*Anna Bolena*

26th Sept.	Verona	Teatro Filarmonico	*L'Esule di Roma* (Donizetti)
2nd Oct.	Verona	Teatro Filarmonico	*La Sonnambula*
7th Nov.	Venice	Teatro S. Benedetto	*Nina pazza per amore* (P. A. Coppola)
1st Dec.	Venice	Teatro S. Benedetto	*Elena e Malvina* (E. Vignozzi)
12th Dec.	Venice	Teatro S. Benedetto	*La Sonnambula*
26th Dec.	Brescia	Teatro Grande	*Nina pazza per amore*

1836

Jan.	Brescia	Teatro Grande	*L'Orfanella di Ginevra* (L. Ricci)
29th Jan.	Brescia	Teatro Grande	*La Sonnambula*
		(Season ended 21st Feb.)	
9th Apr.	Venice	Teatro Fenice	*La Gazza ladra* (Rossini)
23rd Apr.	Venice	Teatro Fenice	*I Puritani* (Bellini)
4th May	Venice	Teatro Fenice	*Cenerentola* (Rossini)
7th May	Venice	Teatro Fenice	*Nina pazza per amore*
8th May	Venice	Teatro Apollo	*I Puritani*
17th May	Venice	Teatro Apollo	*Nina pazza per amore*
22nd May	Venice	Teatro Apollo	Concert
29th May	Venice	Teatro Apollo	*Il Pirata* (Bellini)
11th June	Mantua	Teatro Sociale	*I Puritani*
June	Mantua	Teatro Sociale	*Nina pazza per amore*
20th July	Piacenza	Teatro Municipale	*Un'avventura di Scaramuccia* (L. Ricci)
Aug.	Piacenza	Teatro Municipale	*L'Elisir d'amore* (Donizetti)
30th Aug.	Cremona	Teatro della Concordia	*Belisario* (Donizetti)
17th Sept.	Cremona	Teatro della Concordia	*I Normanni a Parigi* (Mercadante)
22nd Oct.	Venice	Teatro Apollo	*Norma* (as Norma)
16th Nov.	Venice	Teatro Apollo	*La Sonnambula*
3rd Dec.	Venice	Teatro Apollo	*La Straniera* (Bellini)
26th Dec.	Trieste	Teatro Grande	*I Puritani*

1837

Jan.	Trieste	Teatro Grande	*L'Elisir d' amore*
28th Jan.	Trieste	Teatro Grande	*Ferramondo* (A. Buzzola)
11th Feb.	Trieste	Teatro Grande	*La Sonnambula*
23rd Feb.	Trieste	Teatro Grande	*I Capuleti e i Montecchi* (Bellini)
		(Season ended 29th Mar.)	
15th Apr.	Bologna	Teatro Comunale	*Marino Faliero* (Donizetti)
9th May	Bologna	Teatro Comunale	*Lucia di Lammermoor* (Donizetti)
May	Bologna	Teatro Comunale	*I Puritani*

10th June	Faenza	Teatro Comunale	*Marino Faliero*
23rd June	Faenza	Teatro Comunale	*I Puritani*
28th July	Lodi		Concert
Aug.	Turin	Teatro Carignano	*La Muette de Portici* (Auber)
Sept.	Turin	Teatro Carignano	*Il Furioso all' isola di S. Domingo*
25th Sept.	Turin	Teatro Carignano	*La prova d'un'opera seria* (F. Gnecco)
14th Oct.	Turin	Teatro Carignano	*Il Pirata*
		(Season ended 2nd Dec.)	
3rd Dec.	Turin		Concert

1838

11th Mar.	Turin		Concert
25th Mar.	Turin		Concert
21st Apr.	Rome	Teatro Argentina	*Lucia di Lammermoor*
3rd May	Rome	Teatro Argentina	*I Puritani*
12th May	Rome	Teatro Apollo	*Lucia di Lammermoor*
19th May	Rome	Teatro Argentina	*Pia de' Tolomei* (Donizetti)
13th June	Rome	Teatro Argentina	*Alisia di Rieux* (G. Lillo)
		(Season ended 19th June)	
25th June	Florence		Concert
1st July	Florence	Teatro Pergola	*Lucia di Lammermoor*
14th July	Leghorn		*Maria di Rudenz* (Donizetti)
27th July	Leghorn		Concert
28th July	Leghorn		*Beatrice di Tenda* (Bellini)
14th Aug.	Leghorn		*Caterina di Guisa* (F. Campana)
Aug.	Cremona	Teatro della Concordia	*Lucia di Lammermoor*
Sept.	Cremona	Teatro della Concordia	*Norma*
14th Oct.	Florence	Teatro Alfieri	*Norma*
30th Oct.	Florence	Teatro Alfieri	*La Straniera*
2nd Dec.	Florence	Teatro Cocomero	*Lucia di Lammermoor*
8th Dec.	Florence		Concert
10th Dec.	Florence	Teatro Cocomero	*Betly* (Donizetti)
11th Dec.	Florence		Concert
16th Dec.	Florence		Concert
26th Dec.	Florence	Teatro Alfieri	*La Sonnambula*

1839

6th Jan.	Florence		Concert
29th Jan.	Florence	Teatro Alfieri	*Il Giuramento* (Mercadante)
12th Mar.	Venice	Teatro Fenice	*Le due illustri rivali* (Mercadante)

20th Aug.	Milan	Teatro Scala	*I Puritani*
18th May	Milan	Teatro Scala	*L'Elisir d'amore*
11th June	Milan	Teatro Scala	*Pia de' Tolomei*
22nd June	Milan	Teatro Scala	*Lucia di Lammermoor*
		(Season ended 30th June)	
17th July	Sinigaglia	Teatro Fenice	*Lucia di Lammermoor*
July	Sinigaglia	Teatro Fenice	*L'Elisir d'amore*
3rd Aug.	Sinigaglia	Teatro Fenice	*Il Giuramento*
15th Aug.	Lucca	Teatro Giglio	*Lucia di Lammermoor*
10th Sept.	Lucca	Teatro Giglio	*Il Giuramento*
25th Sept.	Lucca	Teatro Giglio	*Beatrice di Tenda*
11th Oct.	Florence	Teatro Pergola	*Il Giuramento*
25th Oct.	Florence	Teatro Pergola	*Maria di Rudenz*
14th Nov.	Florence	Teatro Pergola	*Beatrice di Tenda*
26th Nov.	Florence	Teatro Pergola	*L'Elisir d'amore*
26th Dec.	Verona	Teatro Filarmonico	*Parisina* (Donizetti)

1840

18th Jan.	Verona	Teatro Filarmonico	*I Puritani*
10th Feb.	Verona	Teatro Filarmonico	*Maria di Rudenz*
22nd Feb.	Verona	Teatro Filarmonico	*L'Elisir d'amore*
		(Season ended 1st Mar.)	
10th June	Florence	Teatro Pergola	*Rosmunda* (G. Alary)
July	Sinigaglia	Teatro Fenice	*Il Giuramento*
July	Sinigaglia	Teatro Fenice	*Le due illustri rivali*
16th Aug.	Lucca	Teatro Giglio	*Le due illustri rivali*
8th Sept.	Lucca	Teatro Giglio	*Giovanni da Procida* (J. Poniatowski)
Sept.	Lucca	Teatro Giglio	*Belisario*
Oct.	Florence	Teatro Pergola	*Beatrice di Tenda*
1st Nov.	Venice	Teatro Apollo	*Il Bravo* (Mercadante)
21st Nov.	Venice	Teatro Apollo	*Otello* (Rossini)
		(Season ended 3rd Dec.)	
31st Dec.	Rome	Teatro Apollo	*Marino Faliero*

1841

19th Jan.	Rome	Teatro Apollo	*Mosè* (Rossini)
11th Feb.	Rome	Teatro Apollo	*Adelia* (Donizetti)
		(Season ended 23rd Feb.)	
14th Mar.	Florence	Teatro Pergola	*I Puritani*
31st Mar.	Florence	Teatro Pergola	*Michelangelo e Rolla* (F. Ricci)
17th Apr.	Ancona	Teatro delle Muse	*Maria di Rudenz*
Apr.	Ancona	Teatro delle Muse	*Belisario*

11th May	Ancona	Teatro delle Muse	*Elena da Feltre* (Mercadante)
		(Season ended 26th May)	
1st June	Faenza	Teatro Comunale	*Maria di Rudenz*
13th June	Faenza	Teatro Comunale	*Elena da Feltre*
19th June	Faenza	Teatro Comunale	*Beatrice di Tenda*
14th Aug.	Bergamo	Teatro Riccardi	*I Puritani*
2nd Sept.	Bergamo	Teatro Riccardi	*Marino Faliero*
		(Season ended 15th Sept.)	
6th Oct.	Trieste	Teatro Grande	*Giulio d'Este* (F. Campana)

1842

18th Jan.	Genoa	Teatro Carlo Felice	*Saffo* (Pacini)
2nd Feb.	Genoa	Teatro Carlo Felice	*Il Giuramento*
13th Feb.	Genoa		Concert
		(Season ended 13th Feb.)	
22nd Feb.	Milan	Teatro Scala	*Belisario*
9th Mar.	Milan	Teatro Scala	*Nabucco* (Verdi)
		(Season ended 19th Mar.)	

Bice Paoli Catelani, in *Il Teatro Comunale del 'Giglio' di Lucca* (Pescia, 1941), p. 27, states that Giuseppina Strepponi sang in *Lucia di Lammermoor* at Lucca in 1836. This is a misprint for 1839.

Mercede Mundula (op. cit. p. 37) says that Giuseppina sang during the Carnival season 1839–40 at Venice, Verona and Vicenza. In fact, she sang only at Verona during this season. No appearances at Vicenza are recorded in the theatrical papers, and her name does not appear among the lists of artists given in Francesco Formenton's *Storia del Teatro Eretenio di Vicenza* (Vicenza, 1868).

Precise information about Giuseppina's stage *début* at Adria is lacking. It is mentioned by G. Oldrini in his *Storia musicale di Lodi* (Lodi, 1883) and by G. Baroni in *La sagra del bel canto italiano*, a *numero unico* published at Lodi in 1930, but there are no reports of operatic performances at Adria in the theatrical papers. However, single operas were often put on at small towns for a few performances during the Carnival season commencing 26th December, and as Giuseppina did not appear at Trieste until 19th January 1835 there is thus time for her to have sung first elsewhere, for a short season. A libretto of Luigi Ricci's *Chiara di Rosemberg* was published at Adria in 1835 and this may have been the opera produced there for the Carnival season 1834–5.

It was by her success at Trieste, however, in Rossini's *Matilde di Shabran*, that Giuseppina really made a name for herself. *Il Figaro* reported on 31st January 1835:

No one would have imagined that the young *débutante* Signora Strepponi would be able to open her career under such happy auspices. The management and the public expected much of her, but not as much as she achieved. And truly Madamigella Strepponi performed her part, of no slight importance, with skill such as few possess, and revealed a voice of the greatest clarity, very limpid and beautiful, in perfect intonation. Agility is another of her good qualities, so that she performed and performs things of the most notable difficulty. As regards the stage, too, we are informed that one would not have taken her for a beginner. Self-possessed, alert and always animated, she depicted the character of Matilde with the necessary variety and with more than ordinary intelligence.

In Donizetti's *Anna Bolena*, in the role of Jane Seymour, she shared the honours with the famous Eugenia Tadolini, and it was in this opera that she first sang in Vienna in the following April, with Amalia Schütz-Oldosi. Again she won golden opinions. The *Allgemeine Theaterzeitung* on 2nd May had this comment on her appearance as Adalgisa in *Norma*:

Her performance was so animated by deep inner feeling, she displayed, together with delightful vigour, virtuosity and a very considerable voice, so much charm and grace in her singing, that the effect could not be other than excellent, and the highly talented artist emphatically took today a place of honour immediately beside Signora Schütz-Oldosi. Especially admirable and pleasurable was the masterly co-operation of the two artists in the finale of the first act and in the duet in the second act, which can be called the high light of the performance, and aroused such storms of applause that it had to be repeated and the two singers were recalled four times.

There was a full house for *La Sonnambula*, chosen for her benefit performance on 15th May.

An outbreak of cholera closed many theatres in Italy during the summer and early autumn of this year, but Giuseppina's career was not interrupted. Under a minor impresario, Valentino Trevisan, she appeared successively at Udine, Gorizia and Verona, already a *prima donna assoluta* among a company of lesser fame. Everywhere she aroused the greatest enthusiasm. Citizens of Udine wrote to the editor of *Il Pirata* complaining that he had insufficiently praised her performance in *La Sonnambula*. After Verona Trevisan's company went on to Rovigo, but without Giuseppina, who had been engaged by another impresario, Camillo Cirelli, for the Teatro San Benedetto at Venice. There Coppola's *Nina pazza per amore* was not much liked, but a writer in *Il Gondoliere* for 11th November went into ecstasies about the new *prima donna*:

A real treasure, a dear young singer, la Strepponi, who at the dawn of her career treads the stage in masterly fashion and who from the first performance, or rather from the first instant in which, from the wings, we saw her open her angelic lips to intone that melancholy romance, awakened in us the keenest delight and obtained universal tributes of applause. A limpid, penetrating, smooth voice, seemly action, a lovely figure; and to Nature's liberal endowments she adds an excellent technique, which will soon cause her to shine among the brightest stars of the Italian theatre.

The same writer, a little later, criticized her excessive trills and *fioriture* in *La Sonnambula*. Bellini's opera was again chosen for Giuseppina's benefit performance and on this occasion sonnets were composed in her honour and portraits published. Within a year of her *début* she was firmly established on the stage and already in much demand.

Cirelli took his company from Venice to Brescia, where Giuseppina had a personal success in an otherwise disastrous Carnival season. The opening opera, Coppola's *Nina pazza per amore*, was coldly received and a new ballet laughed off the stage. Ricci's *L'Orfanella di Ginevra* was also a failure. Then Giuseppina, with her favourite work, saved the situation. *Il Figaro* announced on 13th February: 'At last an opera found grace and indeed favour in this theatre—*La Sonnambula*. The protagonist Strepponi was praised to the skies and accompanied in all her pieces by clamorous *evvivas*.'

Back at Venice in the spring, this time at the Teatro La Fenice under the impresario Natale Fabrici, Giuseppina appeared first in *La gazza ladra*, which was a complete failure. Apparently a ballet was performed between the acts of the opera, and, according to *Il Gondoliere*, 'it was observed that as soon as the ballet was over the theatre, which was not very crowded, was abandoned by half the spectators, and that when the concluding aria of the second act was finally reached it was not easy to decide whether the people on the stage and in the orchestra were more numerous than those that had stayed in their places in the audience'. *Il Gondoliere* did not name the singers at all, but *Il Pirata* mentioned that Giuseppina's part was much too low for her. Perhaps for the same reason *Cenerentola* too was only moderately successful, but *I Puritani* and *Nina pazza per amore* were well received, especially after the company moved from the Teatro La Fenice to the Teatro Apollo. *Il Figaro* praised Giuseppina, but issued a warning as well:

The role of *Nina*, especially, is performed by her in an enchanting way. What a pity that this fine young artist sings in so many consecutive seasons, with grave danger that she will weaken and spoil her bright and attractive voice!

Fabrici transferred his company in June to Mantua, where performances of the most successful operas of the Venetian season brought Giuseppina further applause and glowing press notices. Her benefit night on 23rd June produced 'showers of verses and flowers'. A month later she was singing at Piacenza, again under Cirelli's management. *Il Figaro* on 15th July repeated its warning:

> La Strepponi, who we believed would wish at length to rest from her continued glorious labours in various theatres, has now gone to Piacenza, where she will certainly earn as much applause as she did at Venice and Mantua. We hope, however, that excessive activity may not prove harmful, and prevent her from gathering those greater laurels to which she may before very long aspire.

The reason for this incessant activity was probably the need to provide for her mother, younger sister and two little brothers.

At Piacenza she surprised everybody by her versatility. Hitherto her greatest successes had been in serious roles, but now in Luigi Ricci's *Un'avventura di Scaramuccia* she revealed remarkable talent for comedy. 'No one could believe that this was the first time she had appeared in true *opera buffa*.' *L'Elisir d'amore* was also successful but aroused less enthusiasm than Ricci's opera.

Still she gave herself no rest. At the end of August and in September she was singing at Cremona, in October, November and December again at Venice, at the Teatro Apollo. All too often, appearing in indifferent company, she had to bear responsibility for the success or failure of the whole season. At Cremona she was 'tormented by a heavy cold' and after the first performance there of Mercadante's *I Normanni a Parigi*, Donizetti's *Belisario*, in which her role was less arduous, was restored. The Cremona correspondent of *Il Figaro* accused her at this time of a *tremolo*, of exaggeration in her acting, and of forcing her voice. At Venice, in the title-role of *Norma*, but with inferior companions, she again had to carry the whole weight of the performance on her shoulders; *Il Pirata* declared on 4th November:

> But with that Adalgisa (Signora Saglio) and that Pollione (Signor Mazzoni) there were bound to be disasters, and there were. Almost everything was received in silence, and many pieces were unrecognizable, and if those gentry ever imagined they were sometimes earning applause, in choruses, duets and trios, it is well to advise them that that applause was addressed only to la Strepponi, with whom they were singing. She is always admirable, always capable and full of spirit.

The tenor Giovanni Basadonna, who arrived back from Vienna just then, was recruited, and thanks to him and to Giuseppina *La Sonnambula* was well received. But Bellini's *La Straniera* was also put on with an inadequate cast: 'If there had been a decent bass the opera would have been praised to the skies—when Strepponi sings one expects nothing else.'

At Trieste in the Carnival season 1836–7, in Buzzola's *Ferramondo*,

Giuseppina was 'interrupted at every moment by the most flattering signs of appreciation'. On 23rd February 1837 she sang the role of Juliet in *I Capuleti e i Montecchi*, with the great Giuditta Grisi as Romeo, and did not fail to rise to the occasion. *Il Pirata*'s critic wrote:

> In the face of such a powerful rival Madamigella Strepponi surpassed herself and with surprising emulation disputed the palm with her otherwise dearest Romeo; and if she did not equal her [Grisi] in emotional expression, she certainly surpassed her in musical worth, so that, in general, judgment is suspended.

After this Alessandro Lanari engaged her for Bologna and Faenza, in which towns she appeared with the famous tenor Napoleone Moriani (1808–78) and the baritone Domenico Cosselli. Proof that this was the first time she sang for Lanari is found in the impresario's correspondence at Florence, which includes copies of many of his own letters:

Lanari to Giuseppina Strepponi, 6th February 1837:

> I am pleased beyond measure that, earlier than I expected, I am able to give you unequivocal proof of my esteem, in entrusting to you parts of exceptional importance, with famous companions like Moriani and Cosselli. I am confident that this first affair concluded between us will lead to others, to our mutual satisfaction.

Giuseppina was warmly congratulated in the theatrical papers on her successes in this distinguished company, in *Marino Faliero*, *Lucia di Lammermoor* and *I Puritani*, though it was Moriani who aroused the most fanatical enthusiasm in the audiences. There were extraordinary scenes on his benefit night at Bologna. At Faenza *Marino Faliero* was applauded from beginning to end.

It is pleasing to note that Giuseppina was not too proud to reappear at Lodi, at a concert given by the Istituto Filarmonico d'Incorragiamento, on 28th July.

A long autumn season at the Teatro Carignano, Turin, under the impresario Vincenzo Giaccone, began rather badly. Auber's *Muette de Portici*, with Giuseppina and the tenor Domenico Donzelli, was not liked and was replaced by a too hurriedly prepared production of Donizetti's *Il Furioso all' isola di San Domingo*. Later performances of *La Muette de Portici* had a better reception, but Gnecco's *La prova d'un'opera seria*, though antiquated and over familiar ('rancidissima' according to the Turin correspondent of *Il Pirata*) was the first great success of the season. Music by other composers was incorporated in the old opera, as *Il Messaggiere Torinese* reported: 'La Strepponi sang excellently and was very much applauded, principally in her cavatina and in the rondo, which pieces, however, form no part of the original score but were grafted on to it, in accordance with present custom.' According to *Il Figaro*, the 'suave notes' of Bellini's *Pirata*, on 14th October, were balm to the ears of the 'cultured public of Turin', who by this time had had more than enough of the 'most learned, deafening music of Auber'.

So far it has been possible, from the files of contemporary papers, to follow Giuseppina's uninterrupted progress from one theatre to another. But after the end-of-season concert at Turin on 3rd December 1837 she disappears from sight for over three months, until she is reported as having sung at Turin at another concert on 11th March 1838. She is nowhere listed among the artists engaged for the important Carnival season of 1837–8. Why was this? The most likely explanation is that this was the time of the birth of Camillino, her first illegitimate child. Three months' absence from the stage is about the minimum time that would have been required if a public scandal was to be avoided, for the last stages of pregnancy, the confinement, convalescence and preparation for the resumption of her career. There are only two other such gaps in the record of Giuseppina's appearances, and of these the first, from 1st March to 10th June 1840, is covered by a medical certificate which declares that at that time she was 'noticeably losing weight'—hardly a symptom of pregnancy—while the second, from towards the end of October 1841 to 18th January 1842, is quite definitely the time of the birth of her second child, as is shown by her own letters. So it seems almost certain that Camillino was born somewhere about February 1838. It is uncertain where Giuseppina lived during this period—she did not stay at Turin.

This is also the time of Giuseppina's closer connection with Alessandro Lanari. *Il Figaro*, on 7th February 1838, had this announcement:

> The distinguished *prima donna assoluta* Signora Giuseppina Strepponi has been engaged for a year by the theatrical contractor Signor Alessandro Lanari.

On 3rd March the same paper announced that Napoleone Moriani had signed on for another year with Lanari and that the impresario would be putting on a season of opera at the Teatro Argentina in Rome in the spring, with Giuseppina Strepponi, Moriani and Giorgio Ronconi.

If she had not signed a long-term contract with Lanari, Giuseppina might have appeared either in Lisbon or in London. Bartolomeo Merelli wrote to Lanari on 13th March: 'The Lisbon impresario, against all my expectations, has refused to accept your recommendation, saying that you have taken la Strepponi away from him, whom he wished to engage.' *Il Figaro* had noted on 7th March:

> The day before yesterday Signora Strepponi left for Turin, selected and engaged to sing in the concerts to be given at that Royal Court during Lent. She will then, as we have already reported, betake herself to the Teatro Argentina, Rome, with Lanari, owing to which engagement she was unable to accept the generous offers of Signor Laporte, impresario of the King's Theatre of Italian Grand Opera in London.

In Rome, in *Lucia di Lammermoor*, Giuseppina, Moriani and Ronconi won some of the greatest triumphs of their careers. Moriani, above all, drove the crowds wild with delight. At 'Tu che al ciel spiegasti l'ali', in the last act, the audience were so moved that they could not contain themselves and, according to *Il Figaro*, 'believed it must be an angelic spirit who ravished their ears, aroused their enthusiasm and permitted them to taste celestial delights'. All three singers appeared on 3rd May at a concert at Prince Massimi's sumptuous country villa, in honour of the Grand Duke of Tuscany and another royal visitor from Saxony. *Lucia di Lammermoor* was also performed once at the Teatro Apollo with immense success, and as extra items 'La Strepponi sang the cavatina from *Belisario*, to infinite applause; Moriani and Ronconi sang the duet *I Marinai* [from Rossini's *Soirées Musicales*], accompanied at the piano by la Strepponi'. *Pia de' Tolomei* opened before a restless audience, who probably wished to go on hearing repetitions of these stupendous performances of *Lucia di Lammermoor*. But after a few days *Pia de' Tolomei* also won great favour. Giuseppina was 'sublime in the poison scene in the third act', while Moriani made the spectators weep in the pathetic aria in the second act 'Mi tragge a te benefica celeste man'.

Lanari could be well content with his new acquisition and with his company generally. Before the singers separated for their various summer engagements he brought them all to Florence, as was noted in *Il Pirata* on 6th July:

> The season at the Teatro Argentina in Rome having closed on 18th June amid the most clamorous acclamations, the three champions who had gathered such laurels on the Tiber, la Strepponi, Moriani and Ronconi, moved to Florence. As soon as they arrived they were invited to appear at a brilliant concert given by Prince Poniatowski on 25th June at his *palazzo*, in honour of the Duke of Lucca, the brother of the King of Naples, the Princess of Syracuse and many other personages of high rank.

Prince Poniatowski and the Princess of Syracuse both sang at this concert; Giuseppina contributed the cavatina from *Norma*, a duet from *Roberto Devereux* with Moriani and a duet from *I Normanni a Parigi* with Ronconi. On the first three days of July three special performances of *Lucia di Lammermoor* were given at Florence. Immense and fanatical crowds filled the Teatro della Pergola and at the last performance the artists were recalled quite twenty times. After this Moriani left for his summer engagement at Sinigaglia, while Ronconi and Giuseppina went to Leghorn, to continue their triumphs.

Towards the end of August and in September Giuseppina was at Cremona, appearing with lesser singers in *Lucia di Lammermoor* and *Norma*, and leaving the audiences 'transported and ravished'. A letter to Lanari has survived from this period:

Cremona, 29th September 1838.

DEAR LANARI,

In reply to your most kind letters of the 22nd and 27th, I could not wish for more applause, through the success of *Norma*. You will have learned from all the papers about the favourable reception of that score. To tell you the truth, I should not be pleased to appear in it at Florence, as it does not seem to me the most suitable score for Balestracci, with whom I should have to sing.

On 9th October at the latest I shall be at Florence, where I hope to find your letters. I hear with much satisfaction about the brilliant success of *Lucrezia Borgia*; with the artists you have at present it seems to me impossible that it should be otherwise. I wish you continued good luck. Tell me if there is anything I can do for you, and believe me

Your affectionate friend,

GIUSEPPINA STREPPONI.

She had been singing with the tenor Balestracci at Cremona. The success of *Lucrezia Borgia*, referred to in this letter, took place at Lucca, with Moriani in the cast.

A stay of some months at Florence followed, with appearances at two different theatres under Lanari's management. Letters from Pietro Romani,[1] director of the orchestra at the Teatro Alfieri, to Lanari, who was with another company of singers at Venice, throw much light on conditions in the operatic world of that time. Engagements to sing in five performances a week were by no means exceptional. Once, towards the end of October, when Giuseppina was ill and unable to appear, she had to promise to sing *six* times in the following week. Her illness is mentioned several times:

Romani to Lanari, end of October 1838:

La Strepponi is still unwell, being assailed on the stage by bouts of coughing—it's pitiable.

Early November:

Last night the opera went very well, but in her aria in the first act la Strepponi was overcome by such a cough that she had to retire behind the scenes without finishing.

[1] Chiefly remembered today as author of the aria 'Manca un foglio', which for a long time replaced Rossini's own 'A un dottor della mia sorte', in *The Barber of Seville*.

Romani was a great admirer of Giuseppina and his letters include some fine tributes to her artistry. He wrote that she and the celebrated Caroline Unger (Carolina Ungher, in Italy) were the only *prime donne* worth anything in the whole country, and the only singers capable of executing a proper trill. Further: 'I say that among the young singers la Strepponi is Number One.'

Moriani was at Venice in the early autumn, with Caroline Unger and Domenico Cosselli, until Lanari brought these artists also to Florence and they sang at the Teatro Alfieri while Giuseppina was appearing at the Teatro Cocomero. But on 2nd December Moriani joined Giuseppina and the baritone Superchi in *Lucia di Lammermoor* at the Teatro Cocomero. Some interesting concerts were given at Florence in that winter. Giuseppina appeared twice, with Caroline Unger and Moriani, at the Grand Ducal Court, on 8th and 11th December, and at the second of these concerts no less a person than Liszt also performed. Then on 26th December a concert for Liszt's own benefit was given at the Teatro Cocomero and at this concert Giuseppina was acclaimed above all the other singers in the vocal part of the programme; Liszt himself played a Fantasia on Pacini's cavatina 'I tuoi frequenti palpiti' (from *Niobe*) and improvised on a theme from *La Sonnambula*—probably a theme from an aria sung by Giuseppina. The last item on the programme was 'a magnificent symphony by Mozart, performed with admirable accord, in an arrangement for twelve hands on three pianos, by Signori Liszt, Pixis, Leidesdorf, Doglia, Garello and Manetti'. At a concert of the Florentine Philharmonic Society on 6th January 1839 Giuseppina sang, among other things, the cavatina from Pacini's *Niobe* used by Liszt for his Fantasia in the earlier concert.

Bartolomeo Merelli had opened negotiations with Lanari for the cession of Giuseppina and Ronconi in 1838, but no mutually satisfactory agreement had been reached for that year. At length, in December, Merelli had persuaded Lanari to cede these artists, together with Moriani, for the following spring.

Merelli to Lanari, 3rd December 1838:

I shall take then Moriani, la Strepponi and Giorgio Ronconi for the spring of 1839 at La Scala, to commence on Easter Monday and end about 1st July, giving five performances a week, and three or four operas. . . . As for the price, I offer you 32,000 Austrian lire, at the current rate of exchange.

After some dispute about the price, and who should pay the travelling expenses, full agreement was reached on 19th December. But on 16th January 1839 Merelli put a rather startling query to Lanari:

Reply at once and tell me if the rumour is true that la Strepponi is five months gone with child, for how should I get on in that case?

Lanari replied from Venice on 18th January: 'As for la Strepponi, I believe all that has reached your ears is groundless tittle-tattle.' But if he was not lying he was mistaken, and was to find out his mistake within a few days. Further letters from Romani to Lanari and Lanari to Giuseppina show that this was *not* a false alarm. On 23rd January Lanari thanked Giuseppina for confiding in him and encouraged her to hope that all would go well. Romani was to coach another soprano, Amalia Mattioli, in the part Giuseppina was due to sing shortly at Venice; Cirelli was to write to Milan, arranging for this singer to be praised particularly in the papers, so as to impress the Venetian authorities: 'As for the result, it will be what it will be; I am sure that with my Peppina the triumph would have been complete, but we must be patient, and what we can't do now, we'll do another time.'

Romani rarely dated his letters, so that they are difficult to arrange in their exact order. Lanari on receipt generally noted down the month and the year. About a dozen letters from January and February 1839 refer to Giuseppina's pregnancy and its consequences. Some of these may be quoted:

> Cirelli has arrived and this morning he told me in confidence about Peppina's condition. He said you had suggested that he should confide in me and that I should find some way of having a legally valid certificate made out. I shall try to arrange everything, but would like to have the order from you, and to know what you want me to do and have done

> I wanted to put on *Gemma di Vergy* but, as I told you, Ercole is unable to learn a part in a few days, and then, as I've already mentioned, la Strepponi arouses such a furore that any opera whatsoever, given without her, would be rejected by the public. . . . In Florence one cannot say that la Strepponi is unwell; the public knows that she is pregnant, sees it, but applauds her; and I assure you that without her there would be a grand fiasco.

However unhappy the circumstances, this was a magnificent tribute to Giuseppina. The dramatic intensity of her singing in Mercadante's *Il Giuramento* was remarked on in *Il Figaro* on 6th February 1839:

> The greatest triumph of la Strepponi was in the third act, where she delivered the prayer with such deep feeling, and declaimed and sang the duet with Viscardo with such abandon, as to transport the audience, who burst into the loudest acclamation, astonished at such dramatic truth.

All the evidence we have points to the probability that the abandonment with which Giuseppina threw herself into her role in this opera brought on a miscarriage. On 9th February Romani wrote to Lanari:

> You will have heard from Gazzuoli about la Strepponi's illness. To tell the truth, among so many misfortunes I did not anticipate, in addition, this of not being able to finish the season. . . . A consultation of three Florentine

doctors has been ordered. . . . Besides the very considerable loss that this illness causes you at Florence, there is also that at Venice.

The impresario was committed to giving a certain number of performances at each of the theatres under his control, and the illness of an important singer could upset his calculations very badly. It had been his intention to call Giuseppina to Venice. Now this was out of the question for the moment, and the young soprano Amalia Mattioli was dispatched in her place. Romani's letters discuss how the situation could best be met, what use could be made, for the impresario's benefit, of the doctor's certificate, and whether it was possible to give it a false date. Lanari wrote to Giuseppina, urging her to come to Venice as soon as she could, and to Romani, asking him, it would seem, to bring all possible pressure to bear, to make her do so. Fortunately for Giuseppina, the impresario and theatrical agent Camillo Cirelli was still at Florence, and he vigorously stood up for her, insisting that she was in no fit state to resume her career. Romani's language shows his annoyance:

As soon as I had read your letter I made preparations to receive the doctors who must come to verify la Strepponi's illness. I also went to see her, and she told me the content of the letter you wrote her. Not only did I back you up, but I begged, I argued and finally I persuaded her to come to Venice. That f—— Cirelli made a bloody nuisance of himself, and finally he told me he was going to call Contrucci and would decide according to what he had to say. I have perambulated not merely half Florence, but the whole of it, and everywhere I left messages for him [Contrucci]; I wanted to speak to him, to put into his mouth the words he was to say, but I did not succeed. But with la Strepponi as I left her, I believe she will certainly come to sing for you for at least half a dozen performances. If Cirelli had not been there I should have made her leave at once, I had so thoroughly convinced her. Cirelli will also write to you about this.

Cirelli, for whom Giuseppina had sung in 1835 and 1836, proved a very good friend. He was consistently helpful, at this time and later, and it is possible that he had been Camillino's godfather, and had given him his Christian name. The responsibilities of such a relationship are not undertaken lightly in Italy.[1]

Romani was able to arrange everything according to Lanari's wishes, and even it seems to square the doctors: 'You can be sure

[1] There is evidence in Lanari's correspondence that Cirelli kept an eye on Guiseppina's finances, and on her family.

G. B. Villa, Milan, to Lanari, 11th July 1840: 'Yesterday Cirelli asked me if I had orders to pay Signora Strepponi's mother the 540 lire. I said I had not.'

G. B. Villa to Lanari, 22nd July 1840: 'I sent the 540 lire to Signora Strepponi's mother at once.'

Lanari to Cirelli, Florence, 5th April 1841: 'I am leaving tonight for Ancona. . . . Peppina leaves with me and I advise you that on Tuesday the 6th I am sending to you at Milan a package by post containing 186 gold napoleons, by order and on account of Peppina Strepponi.'

that dog does not eat dog; these grave-diggers will come to agreement among themselves.' In connection with another singer whom he had decided not to engage, he wrote: 'Carlotta told me she is pregnant, and I don't want anything more to do with pregnant women.'

A brief note from Giuseppina to Lanari at Venice survives from this time:

Florence, 23rd February 1839.

DEAR LANARI,

I am waiting for the Tuesday post, and if it brings me my orders to leave this will be the last letter you will receive from Florence. I am sorry about all your ups and downs, but for Acts of God there's no remedy. You see, however, that as far as I myself am concerned I am most willing to help you, although I cannot say that I have completely recovered. My part is almost in my head; my good will is the same as ever, and so is the friendship of your affectionate

PEPPINA.

Lanari's troubles, referred to in this note, included, besides Giuseppina's own illness, the indisposition of Caroline Unger and Ronconi at Venice. The part that Giuseppina had almost by heart was a role in another of Mercadante's operas, *Le due illustri rivali*, which, when all the principal singers had recovered, was successfully produced at the Teatro La Fenice, Venice, on 12th March, with Caroline Unger, Giuseppina Strepponi, Moriani and the bass Ignacio Marini. *Il Figaro* on 16th March had this comment:

The *prima donna* Signora Giuseppina Strepponi, having recovered, after a brief rest at Florence, from a slight indisposition, hastened to Venice, where she appeared, as already reported, in *Le due illustri rivali*. Thus were answered the prayers of the Venetians, and annihilated the rumours of those who declared she was still ill and in no fit state at the moment to take on her new and important engagements.

Together with several of her companions at Venice, she was now due to appear for Merelli at La Scala, Milan.

The Milanese season opened on 1st April with *Lucia di Lammermoor*, with Moriani, Ronconi and Adelaide Kemble, whose English accent did not please. Giuseppina made her *début* at La Scala in *I Puritani* on 20th April. This opera and *L'Elisir d'amore* were the successes of the season; *Pia de' Tolomei*, produced first on 11th June, had only three performances. Merelli was unlucky. It was now Moriani's turn to be ill.

Merelli to Lanari, 24th April 1839:

I Puritani pleased immensely for the first two acts (with the triumph of la Strepponi and also of Ronconi and Moriani) but by the third act Moriani had no voice left, so that he was unable to arouse the customary fanatical enthusiasm. At the second performance he got no further than the first act; afterwards I closed the theatre; this evening and tomorrow I am putting on *Lucia* with the substitute singer and thus (to my incalculable loss) I am letting him rest until Saturday, when he will appear in possession of all his means.

The same, 1st May:

I Puritani returned to the stage last Saturday with much better success on the part of Moriani who, however, did not sing the last number or the end of the duet with la Strepponi; on the following Sunday we had Ronconi ill and put on the opera with the substitute Berini—imagine the loss! Yesterday evening la Strepponi was indisposed but did what she could, so that today she is resting and I'm afraid I shall have to put on *Lucia* tomorrow.

This was the time when Verdi's *Oberto, Conte di San Bonifacio* was under consideration for one of the annual charity performances. The singers were given their parts to study, Giuseppina and Ronconi being much impressed by the music, before Moriani's illness put an end to Verdi's hopes of immediate production.

Merelli to Lanari, 20th May:

L'Elisir d'amore aroused fanatical enthusiasm. La Strepponi and Ronconi *non plus ultra*. Lonati and Moriani did well. After so many troubles and pains I am comforted at last, but it's little use, because now it's too late; the gentry are beginning to leave for the country.

25th May:

The furore aroused by la Strepponi in *L'Elisir d'amore* is such, and so well merited, that she is being bombarded with offers. She expressed her displeasure that among them all I stood silent, without offering her a contract. In view of that, as the other people's offers haven't got very far, so as not to lose her I decided to offer her a contract for two years, at 40,000 lire a year, for Italy alone, including Vienna, and in addition the expenses of travelling and lodgings, according to your usual style. I have told her also of my intention of doing nothing without you and she replied that she would write to you. So I advise you in advance that I shall not go beyond that sum, and that I shall await your instructions.

Lanari to Merelli, 28th May:

La Strepponi has repeatedly promised to give me the preference, other things being equal, in signing contracts for the future, after the expiration of that at present in force. After the proofs of esteem, friendship and deference that I have always given her, I am sure she will keep her word.

Before the season ended Moriani again fell ill and went away to Genoa for a week, returning however in time to appear with Giuseppina and Ronconi in *Lucia di Lammermoor* from 22nd June onwards. This work was now perfectly performed, and the season ended in a blaze of glory.

Giuseppina's appearances in the last few performances of *Lucia di Lammermoor*, in place of Miss Kemble, and comments thereon in the correspondence of the impresarios, are the subject of a letter she wrote to Lanari on 23rd June:

Milan, 23rd June 1839.

DEAR LANARI,

Cirelli has shown me a paragraph of your letter No. 1019 which concerns me, where I am amazed to find myself badly treated and unjustly accused of failing in my duty, and that according to a letter sent to you by Merelli on the 15th of this month.

I at once asked him about this and he denies the whole thing, and defies you to show me, on my arrival at Sinigaglia, any such letters of his. *They always spoke to me about doing a favour*, so I must suppose that I was not obliged to take Mlle Kemble's place; however I made no objection to the first proposal, made to me by Signor Villa in my dressing-room at the theatre on the 13th of this month, that I should take over the part of *Lucia*; I agreed after a little persuasion and the part was given to me on the arrival from Vienna of Merelli, who would have grossly lied if he had written in the terms you indicate.

What has displeased me most in this matter is that, abusing my complaisance in giving you preference over other impresarios for long contracts, you thought fit to prescribe to Merelli that he should not go beyond a salary of 40,000 Austrian lire a year, so as to be able to get me back when you need me in your theatres, having regard to the fact that, these theatres being of lesser importance, you would be able to buy me back from him at a lower fee.

As a result of that, accepting the advice of my friends, including Signor Villa, I shall never again hire myself out by the year, but shall wait and see how things turn out, since even if I should earn less money, I shall at any rate have less work to do, and shall not hear myself constantly reproved like a refractory schoolgirl.

Keep well, give my regards to your family, and believe me

Your most affectionate friend,

GIUSEPPINA STREPPONI.

The letter is interesting in that it shows Giuseppina vigorously defending herself and her interests against these old theatrical wolves and foxes. We do not know what Lanari replied, but he must have been able to convince her that Merelli, who obviously wished to secure Giuseppina for his own theatres, was playing a double game. It is true that Lanari, writing to Merelli on 28th May, had remarked that if they came to an agreement to share her services she would naturally have to be paid more for singing in Vienna or at Milan than for appearances in Tuscany or other smaller theatres. But Merelli, on 25th May, in a letter already quoted, had declared in advance that he would not go beyond 40,000 lire a year—the figure which he accused Lanari of prescribing to *him*. Giuseppina kept her word and remained under Lanari's control for the next three years. As appears from subsequent correspondence between the impresarios, she soon decided she did not wish to return to Milan.

Lanari to Merelli, 11th January 1840:

I assure you that where I make use of la Strepponi myself for some other theatre, I will let you have her on the same terms. If we come to such an arrangement, however, it would be necessary to keep the whole affair secret and allow no one to hear of it, so that la Strepponi doesn't get to know about it, she having told me that I should greatly displease her if I sent her to Milan. To this antiphony I replied neither yes nor no.

Temistocle Solera, the future librettist of *Nabucco*, contributed to the *Strenna teatrale europea* for 1840 a sketch of Giuseppina, based on recollections of the spring season at La Scala in 1839. Milan had admired in her

the most beautiful natural gifts rendered great by continual study, so that in both the serious style and the comic she caused the many celebrated singers who had preceded her to be forgotten. Gifted with extreme sensitivity, she knows how to win the hearts of the spectators by her voice and her expression. Cultured and amiable in society, an excellent daughter and sister, she has generously accepted responsibility for her whole family, and her little brothers are being educated at her expense in the best schools. Milan wishes to hear her again. It is rumoured that she is to reappear among us in 1841, when she will be free from contracts undertaken with her present manager, Signor Alessandro Lanari. And Milan is right to want her back. Most praiseworthy in *I Puritani* and *Pia de' Tolomei* (an opera that did not please very much, although she, Moriani and Giorgio Ronconi were applauded in it), great in *Lucia* and, what is more surprising, very great indeed in *L'Elisir d'amore*, it is just and natural that she should have made a profound and lasting impression on us and left here the desire to hear her again. Who is there that did not weep at her tears, in the first three of the scores mentioned above, and especially in *Lucia*, in which opera, on the first evening (not to mention those that followed), she was called back on to the stage twenty-three times? And who is there that was not made happy by her laugh in that delightful jest by Romani and Donizetti, *L'Elisir d'amore*? Find me if you can an Adina more brisk, more freakish, more lovable, and deny if you can that singers are rare indeed whom both serious and comic roles suit so well.

From Milan, Giuseppina, Moriani and Ronconi moved on to Sinigaglia, where they appeared at the Teatro Fenice, newly risen again from the ashes to which a fire had reduced it during Lanari's previous summer season there. *Lucia di Lammermoor* and *L'Elisir d'amore* aroused the usual enthusiasm; *Il Giuramento* was less successful. At Lucca in August and early September the same artists repeated their now celebrated performances of *Lucia*, before Moriani left to fulfil an engagement at Trieste. Giuseppina and Ronconi appeared together in other operas at Lucca in September and at the Teatro della Pergola, Florence, in October and November, to the unfailing delight of the audiences. For the Carnival season 1839–40 they were both engaged for Verona.

In general, Lanari must have been pleased with his season at Verona: *Parisina, I Puritani, Maria di Rudenz* and *L'Elisir d'amore* were all rapturously received, according to reports in the papers. But there was also some trouble. Giuseppina had her share of the honours, but she was not well. While the newspapers referred only to passing indispositions, Lanari was sufficiently concerned about her throat and gastro-enteric troubles, causing loss of weight, to write to Milan and engage another soprano, Giuseppina Ronzi. This singer, in a letter of 22nd January 1840, at first refused to come, saying that it would not be worth her while for six or eight performances and that she had no desire to cause displeasure to his other *prima donna*. But Lanari, two days later, assured her that the doctors had ordered Giuseppina to rest, and so Madame Ronzi appeared at Verona, with great success, in *Roberto Devereux*. Giuseppina was furious!

Moriani was at this time at Milan again and some of the rumours that had reached him about events at Verona are reported in his letters to Lanari.

Moriani to Lanari, 24th January:

A thousand stories, displeasing to me, are told here. It is said that la Strepponi can't sing any more and has commissioned you to sign up another *prima donna*, that your costumes are horrible and that you are doing hateful and niggardly things that even Trevisan and the other wretched impresarios have never done; finally that you can't even leave the house.

When you have to pay money to Regli don't make use of that chatterbox Villa any more. All Milan is saying that you have paid Regli 100 *svanziche* to praise your theatrical productions; this gossip is displeasing also to Regli himself.

Regli was the editor of *Il Pirata*.

The quarrel between Giuseppina and Lanari is referred to in one of Romani's letters: 'I am astonished at what you tell me about la Strepponi, but be careful not to release her, and if she doesn't want to sing, at least prevent her from singing in other theatres, and let her lose her pay.' Soon after this the quarrel was made up and after the end of the season at Verona Lanari gave Giuseppina two months' leave. She went to Milan and placed herself in the hands of Dr Moro, the physician officially attached to La Scala, who had treated her already in the previous year. Moriani, who was himself still at Milan, wrote to Lanari on 6th March:

I'm glad that the war between you and Peppina is over, and with much honour to both. I wish she had not been caused annoyance over that old barrel, la Ronzi.[1] I am sure she has talent and knows how to make her way in the world, and, moreover, she would be acclaimed and adored if that nasty Lame Devil didn't upset her career with his bad advice, and render her so abject in the eyes of society.

The identity of this 'nasty Lame Devil' (*schifoso Diavolo Zoppo*) is not easy to establish. A marginal note, however, on a letter from Giuseppina to Lanari of 4th April, a month later, almost certainly also refers to him: 'I have written to M . . . of Verona in such terms as to free myself entirely even from the disturbance of his letters. Rage led me to conceive the idea of marriage, but without love it was impossible to go that far.' From this it would seem that in a moment of despair at her position as an unmarried mother she had entered into relations, which she afterwards regretted, with a lame [2] admirer at Verona, some time between December and the beginning of March. Lanari, who had himself been at Verona, obviously knew all about this. He seems to have passed the news on to Moriani, who may have had special reason to be interested, as we shall see. Bad feeling between Giuseppina and Lanari, consequent on the engagement of Giuseppina Ronzi, would seem to have been aggravated by the bad advice of her new protector.

Merelli was not now particularly interested in securing Giuseppina's services:

Merelli to Lanari, 23rd March 1840:

Dispose of la Strepponi how you like! I am grateful to you, all the same, for making me pay more for her for a season than she costs you for a whole year! Accept also the offers from Rome, for I for my part give up the whole idea, it being proved conclusively that I was wrong to have come to an honest arrangement with you! . . . Please note for your future guidance that her engagement wouldn't even be approved, in view of her deterioration, noted by all those who heard her at Verona; and my management, which had anticipated these negotiations, has warned me to calculate only on permission to take her on as an extra. . . .

7th April:

About la Strepponi then we'll say no more, unless you could add Ronconi: if it would be agreeable to you to make an exchange I would give you Marini. . . .

Giuseppina's letter to Lanari of 4th April, bearing the marginal note quoted above, is full of interest. She could make witty and pungent comments on her fellow artists, but she was also always ready to recognize the good qualities, even of her rivals.

[1] According to Francesco Formenton's *Storia del Teatro Eretenio di Vicenza* (Vicenza, 1868), Giuseppina Ronzi was of 'matronale configurazione'. The word actually used by Moriani is 'Cassone'—meaning a large box, or chest.

[2] Unless 'Diavolo Zoppo' is only a figure of speech.

DEAR LANARI,

Many thanks for your news about the success of *Le due illustri rivali*. It couldn't be otherwise, as far as la Ungher was concerned. It remained to be seen how Ivanoff and la Mattioli would turn out and I am extremely glad that they both came up to expectation. La Mattioli's success will be immensely useful to you for the spring, too, for now she has acquired a reputation you will be able to employ her with confidence and more profit at the Pergola theatre. I hope you always have similar good luck in all your undertakings. As for myself, it seems that my native air, rest and medical treatment are having a good effect on my enfeebled health. God grant that I may completely recover! I have seen Alary's wife, but she did not bring me my part in *Rosmunda*, as I had begged and prayed her to do. She said that some things had been altered and that this was the cause of the delay. I should be sorry if that went on for long, and I could not study the part in my usual way. You know that I have always disdained to pay court to people, either to gain more money at my benefit performances or to facilitate a *great success*. Hence at Florence and elsewhere I am deprived of the recommendations and protection of the *Great Ones*, the *Maecenases*, who decide in part the success of a performance. So I need to seek out all the resources that art and my own small talent can suggest, adapt them as far as possible to my means, and act so that (in particular in this *Rosmunda*) the Great Ones are not hostile, and the mass of the public can appreciate at least my goodwill, as they have done in the past.

Now I'll give you an account of the opera *Marino Faliero*—a bit late, but perhaps more truthful than the others. Galli is a piece of *rococo* that one respects for its antiquity! The woman has two fine arms and is very plump. For the rest she has a few good low notes; the high ones, sometimes sharp and sometimes flat, are always unpleasant. I shall be better able to judge her manner of singing and acting in another opera. Fraschini has a fine voice. The other bass is so-so. You can deduce from that what sort of success there was. I heard the last performance of the other company, in Solera's opera and one act of Coccia's, and I admired in la Tadolini one of the greatest talents we possess, and I applauded her with conviction, along with the public. Moriani (the only time I saw him) is the same as ever. I'll tell you about the bass some other time.

If, as I hope, you reply to this, be prudent, and if you have something to tell me that must not be read by anyone else (as, having only one daily maid, I have asked Cirelli's clerk to fetch my letters from the post) write to me under another name, for instance, Signora Erminia Spillottini. I will go myself to fetch it, as I am alone until four in the afternoon, and alone all night, so can read and write freely. But in any case that's just an idea of mine, for at the moment I shouldn't know where to find any secret matters.

I will write to you about la Schütz's reception. Regards to your family; love me and believe me

Your affectionate friend,

G. STREPPONI.

Milan, 4th April 1840.

The latter part of this letter, with its suggestion of secrets and the use of a false name, is very curious. It seems that Lanari would not, without Giuseppina's assurance, necessarily have expected her to be 'alone all night'. Solera's opera, in which Eugenia Tadolini and Moriani had been singing, was *Ildegonda*, performed three times on 20th–22nd March. It is uncertain whether Moriani was still at Milan at the time of Giuseppina's letter. In the following month he wrote to Lanari from Vienna, suggesting a production of Mercadante's *Elena da Feltre*: 'In truth this would be an opera certain of effect for la Strepponi and Ronconi, and although the tenor part is not so attractive I should not disdain to sing it, there being a superb aria, which ought to suit me excellently.'

Rosmunda was a new opera by Giulio Alary (1815–91) and not by Nicolai, as Gatti believed,[1] nor by Donizetti, as stated by Rodolfo Paoli in an article to be discussed later.[2] *Rosmunda* was to be produced at Florence and is mentioned again in Giuseppina's next letter:

DEAR LANARI,

Your kind letter of the 25th received. I am grateful for your offer to allow me to rest and await better weather, but I am sorry to say I cannot profit by it, as a few hours before, to save money, I had arranged for the horses to take my carriage to Florence, and I cannot break the contract without paying a fine. So on the 10th or 12th of next month you will see me at Florence. My health seems to be improving daily, and as I hear that the production of *Rosmunda* has been postponed I shall be able to study it more easily and with less trouble with the composer. This is all the more desirable as some of the pieces must be greatly altered, or transposed down, for like all young composers, wishing to profit excessively by the top of the voice, he has written me a part that would throttle any soprano and bore the hearers with continual high notes. I certainly don't intend to sing it as it is. Thank you for the offer of the rooms; I will tell you by word of mouth why I don't accept. But please find me some others, very airy; I don't mind whether they are in a frequented locality, as long as they are, I repeat, airy, and don't cost more than about 15 scudi. I have read in *Il Pirata* my name announced for Rome. I don't believe it, as it seems impossible that Lanari would have abandoned his customary kindness, and not said a word about that to me in two consecutive letters. . . . I suppose you have prepared a pleasant surprise for me in Rome, if it's true—that is, little work to do, etc., etc., for, you know, six performances a week! . . .

Farewell, until we meet. My regards to your family.

Your friend,

G. STREPPONI.

Milan, 29th April 1840.

Rosmunda was a success at the Teatro della Pergola on 10th June, and Giuseppina certainly won over the mass of the audience. A

[1] First edition, I, p. 181; second edition, p. 153.
[2] 'La prima maniera della Peppina' (*La Scala*, Feb.–March 1944).

contributor to *Il Pirata* declared: 'For the rest, la Strepponi was received by the Florentine public as one receives a dear person, a precious friend, removed for a thousand reasons from the common sphere, and exalted through sublime powers and extraordinary worth.'

Summer seasons followed at Sinigaglia and Lucca with renewed triumphs for Giuseppina and Ronconi in *Il Giuramento*, and for Giuseppina and Caroline Unger in *Le due illustri rivali*. At Sinigaglia, while the prayer in the third act of *Il Giuramento* was 'interrupted at every phrase' by shouts of enthusiasm, the death scene was received 'in a religious silence'—the rarest of tributes from an Italian audience—until the fall of the curtain released a pent-up storm of applause. At Lucca the public was unable to decide between the two illustrious rival singers. Giuseppina had fully recovered from her setback at Verona.

A short return visit to Florence in October was succeeded in the following month by appearances at the Teatro Apollo, Venice, under Cirelli's management, in Mercadante's *Il Bravo* and Rossini's *Otello*. Revival of the latter opera was considered a hazardous undertaking, in view of the famous singers associated with the work in the past. 'Never before', reported *Il Pirata*, 'were artists of such renown as Donzelli, la Strepponi and Pio Botticelli seen to tremble as they did yesterday evening at the first performance of *Otello*.' Giuseppina had had to learn the role of Desdemona in a few days. After a shaky beginning she surpassed all expectation. During the scene in the second act where Desdemona lies prostrate at her father's feet, begging forgiveness, both Giuseppina on the stage and women in the audience were seen to be weeping. At the end of the opera she took eleven curtain calls.

For the Carnival season of 1840–1 Lanari had ceded Giuseppina to Vincenzo Jacovacci, impresario of the Teatro Apollo in Rome. She arrived there early in December, in time to be godmother at the christening of Jacovacci's daughter on the 12th. Then she caught German measles, which prevented her from appearing at the Teatro Apollo until 31st December, in *Marino Faliero*. On 11th February 1841 she took part in the first performance of *Adelia*, a new opera by Donizetti. This was not a very happy occasion. Jacovacci had sold more tickets than there were seats in the house, and the opera began amid uproar which still continued when Giuseppina made her entry. The performance was interrupted several times, two noblemen exchanged blows from neighbouring boxes, Jacovacci was arrested and the box-office receipts confiscated. *Adelia*, although repeated in calmer conditions a number of times, never became a very great success, in Rome or elsewhere.

The sculptor Tenerani made a bust of Giuseppina in Rome at this time.[1] After the end of the season she returned to Florence, where she appeared with Moriani at the Teatro della Pergola in *I Puritani* and *Michelangelo e Rolla*, a new opera by Federico Ricci. Moriani aroused the usual enthusiasm; on his benefit night he was 'unanimously acclaimed and called an infinite number of times on to the stage, which was converted for him into a lovely garden, so numerous were the flowers scattered there by the audience'. These performances at Florence in March and early April 1841 were the last at which Giuseppina shared the applause with this great tenor. He left for Vienna and Dresden; she for Ancona and Faenza. In both the latter towns she appeared again with Giorgio Ronconi and delighted the audiences.

Giuseppina's engagements after this were for Bergamo in August, under Merelli, Trieste in the autumn, under the impresario Vincenzo Giaccone, and Genoa in the Carnival season 1841–2, under the impresario Sanguineti. But she knew quite well that she would not be able to carry out the whole of this programme, for she was again pregnant.

We have now reached the crux of our inquiry. The secret history of Giuseppina's affairs has largely to be read in, and between the lines of, the letters she wrote to Lanari during the latter half of 1841 and the beginning of 1842. These letters provide much concrete information, but as Lanari already knew most of the facts, Giuseppina could make use of hints and more or less veiled allusions which can be baffling. Some less interesting matter, such as elaborate financial calculations, involving the various currencies and varying rates of exchange in different parts of Italy, is here omitted. Partial quotation can be very misleading, but in the following pages an honest attempt is made to present everything of significance.

Several of the letters were written from Bergamo. The earliest, dated 8th August, soon after her arrival there, has this passage: 'I have found Merelli particularly kind, and this very day he has written to his agent, Signor Poggiali, that I am not to be obliged to attend any rehearsals if I don't want to. The rest of my private affairs are going less badly than they could do.' There follows a discussion of the advance she was to receive from Giaccone, on account of the season at Trieste to follow. Then some proposals for contracts in the future. Lanari is asked to give his decision on suggestions for a renewal of their contract which Giuseppina had left with him: 'They have asked for me in Lisbon for that year, i.e. 1844–5, and I am not disinclined to negotiate, seeing that the work is light.' Another remark concerns the coming year, 1842: 'As I told you, if my cession

[1] The bust, now at Sant' Agata, is reproduced in Gatti's *Verdi nelle immagini*, but wrongly dated 1845. It is mentioned in the *Gazzetta Privilegiata di Milano* for 13th March 1841.

to Merelli for the Lent season is proposed, please advise me early about that, and allow me to plead for a small number of appearances.' The most interesting passage is this:

> If you have occasion to see the despicable [1] M . . . . . . kindly remind him of the *important* sum of money that through your offices he agreed to pay. You who are my friend and know all about my troubles, and my actual and future situation, will see that I cannot disregard even a small claim, having so many expenses to meet. In truth it's enough to drive one crazy, thinking of my misfortunes—but God is just and no one is beyond His reach! You who, I repeat, have shown a certain interest in my troubles—it would cost you nothing to be more careful and strict about article seven of the cession agreement. Woe when one must allow oneself to be seized by the throat, as in the present contract made at Verona, which makes me shudder every time I read it! Enough about that—a year at this pace and perhaps I shall be no more, and all claims upon one, all conflicts, end beyond the tomb. My poor children! My poor family!

'Children' here, in the plural, includes Camillino and the unborn baby. The 'family' was her mother, brothers and sister.

A letter of 16th August tells of the success of *I Puritani* on the previous Saturday—the opening night of the Bergamo summer season. It also keeps alive the subject of the renewal of the contract, about which Lanari had not yet replied, and adds: 'I should like to be able to tell you that I am well, but if I did that today I should be telling a lie. The too keen air of these hills affects my nerves and causes an indisposition which one cannot call an illness, but which affects my voice and my humour. But one must arm oneself with patience and avoid sad thoughts.' Four days later she thanks Lanari for a letter in which he seems to have suggested she should give up the idea of going to Lisbon, and stay in Italy:

> With regard to the contract, you will by now have received a letter of mine, written on the 16th, and whether we reach agreement or not I hope we shall always remain good friends. You are right to talk of beautiful Italy, but for me good pay and not much hard work is a great attraction, you know. And then I need, if possible, to go far away, for some time at least, from places that have for me too many unhappy memories. I have been too cruelly treated under the mantle of love, and thoughts of the suffering caused me and the harm done in the past, would be painful. But enough about that! I don't wish him ill, for he's father of a family, and I am not so infamous as to desire his ruin, as he has caused mine. Let's not talk of melancholy things. A year at this pace and I shall be calmer, because perhaps I shall be no more. We will wait and see the result of the steps taken by the impresarios of Genoa and Trieste, and that which I shall

[1] The first meaning of the Italian adjective *vile* would be 'cowardly'. But something more than 'cowardly' is required here, and something less than the English 'vile'. M. had been cowardly in not accepting responsibility for his actions, and thus rendered himself despicable, contemptible.

perhaps be forced to repay them will serve to remind me always of this infamy. The friend who comes forward with more than words is always that good man Cirelli. Count C. writes assiduously very amiable letters, but, in spite of my condition and my bad state of health, leaves me to go on singing to the very last moment, when by arranging in some way for assistance he could have relieved me of at least part of my work at Trieste. Or if not that, he could have written a line giving me hope of a real proof of friendship in my hour of need. Enough about that! We'll wait and see. So far his attentions have not been such as could carry any consequences for him.

I note what la Ronzi writes you. That woman is not content with her fiascos at Venice, for the second time, at Udine and now at Brescia; she wishes to continue to present herself as a target, when she could have conserved her fine reputation, with only one daughter to think about, and a good patrimony. She could have accepted an engagement at Palermo, with good pay, and chooses to come to Genoa, at other people's discretion? This woman reminds me of those birds which feed greedily on dead bodies. She went to Vicenza when poor Boccabadati had two of her children at the point of death, and on arrival there played an infamous trick on her. She came to Verona when my health required that I should not work so hard. And now I find it infamous that she should try to raise the alarm, in a certain way, and harm a poor mother of a family, such as I am. Uninvited, and depending on simple gossip, to offer herself at any price whatever? This is an action worthy only of a foolish or a bad woman! I hope that everything will be arranged (even if I can't appear on the stage on St Stephen's Day), thanks to Cirelli's kind heart, and Merelli too is very much disposed to assist me. Since I last wrote I have always been in good voice—i.e. for three days on end, for today, Friday, there is no performance. I suppose this improvement results from some powders that a doctor here prescribed for me. God help me!

The title of 'C.', the cautious admirer, is not quite certain. Giuseppina writes 'il Con—— C.'. St Stephen's Day was 26th December, the date of the beginning of the Carnival season, when she was due to appear at Genoa. The baby was clearly expected in November or early December.

The next letter, begun on 24th August, is pathetic, showing Giuseppina clutching at the hope of a lottery prize, to solve her problems:

I keep forgetting to ask you to tell Nicola that, when the results come out of the Great Lottery of Villa Mattei, drawn in Rome, to which he is also a subscriber, I should be glad if he would kindly let me know about it, and, for his guidance, I have number 11,188 (eleven thousand, one hundred and eighty-eight). You see that is very important, for if I win the first prize I shall give up this antipathetic singing profession.

The letter is continued on 27th August. It seems that the impresario Vincenzo Giaccone of Turin managed the theatre at Trieste through his son Vittorio. Giaccone the younger had passed through Bergamo recently and Giuseppina had arranged with him to be released, some time before her baby was due, from part of her engagement at Trieste. It was necessary to make a similar arrangement for the beginning of the season at Genoa. Besides Sanguineti, someone named Canzio was involved at Genoa; with him Giuseppina did not wish to engage in correspondence on such a delicate subject. In any case Lanari's interests would be safeguarded and the financial sacrifices involved in these necessary changes of plan would be borne by Giuseppina:

In that way, released entirely at my own expense, I should at least live in peace, and have time to recover both my health and calmness of mind, which fatal circumstances have caused me to lose. With that in mind I have asked the good Cirelli, who has come here to see me, to betake himself at once to Turin, and if necessary also to Genoa, and have decided, considering the uncertainty and dangers of my situation, to sacrifice to the needs of the moment that little money I should have saved this year, so as to be able to devote myself again, in good health, to my art and the interests of my family, which I have so much at heart. Write to me meanwhile if my resolution seems reasonable to you, and tell me frankly what you think. . . . My health is less than passable; nevertheless I am not failing to do my duty, and the public shows itself always benevolent towards me; I cannot but be satisfied, too, with Merelli.

Lanari was not entirely pleased with these developments. Cirelli certainly showed himself a good friend to Giuseppina in time of need, but Lanari may have objected to another impresario taking it upon himself to negotiate for her in his place. We do not know what he wrote to Giuseppina about this, but he got a stinging reply:

DEAR LANARI,

Your brusque letter received, which doesn't surprise me, most men being like that if they conceive the slightest suspicion that they are going to lose money! Now I have learned to know the world, at my own expense! Don't get upset, for as I told you the profits (considerable, indeed) you would have made out of me at Trieste and Genoa shall be repaid by me to the last farthing! In troubles, great or small, one should never reckon on the honeyed words and friendship of anyone whatsoever. In immense misfortunes, such as my own at present, there are only two courses to take—to end one's life as Nourrit did, or with a bullet in the brain, or to refuse to stoop to vileness on any account. Even if the postal expenses were also charged to you, friendship (as you say) has nothing to do with business, and so when the time comes you will only have to indicate where I must betake myself for Lent. Once again I exhort you to keep quite calm about your purse. I want nothing from you! Farewell.

Your friend,

G. STREPPONI.

Bergamo, 4th September 1841.

Adolphe Nourrit, the tenor, had committed suicide by throwing himself over a balcony at Naples on 8th March 1839. This passage is eloquent but, like others in Giuseppina's early correspondence, not entirely logical or impeccably written. The effect of the letter is softened by a postscript:

Marino Faliero was highly successful on Tuesday the 2nd: even more so than *I Puritani*, principally owing to Salvi (who at Bergamo seems a different person) and, if you will believe it, to me. Coletti and Valli sing very well, but the former doesn't seem to me to be particularly well suited to the part of Faliero. By that I don't think I do wrong to his notable talent. On Cirelli's return from Genoa and Turin I shall learn what agreements he has signed.

Lanari then did something very generous, sending, or offering to send, a large sum of money. Giuseppina's reply still has a bitter note:

Bergamo, 15th September 1841.

DEAR LANARI,

Omitting for now all mention of the contents of your last letter, of 9th September, I shall omit also any discussion about the gift of 20,000 Austrian lire, not wishing to decide if it is really meant as a gift or not. I have read and pondered over our contract and the result does not permit me to believe in this gift. No more on that subject.

The performances at Bergamo come to an end this evening. I shall leave tomorrow for Trieste, to arrive on the 20th. From there I'll write to you at greater length. Now I'm busy packing, and only have time to say farewell.

Your friend,

G. STREPPONI.

Judging from the amounts of bills of exchange mentioned in later letters, Giuseppina received the 20,000 Austrian lire, and it was regarded as a loan. The next letter is of great interest:

Trieste, 25th September 1841.

DEAR LANARI,

I reply to yours of 20th September. I forgot to tell you that I directed your letter to Giaccone and that he was most prompt in making payment. I arrived at Trieste by steamer on the 21st and I suffered greatly, as did everybody, for we had a very bad night. I know that you have leased me to La Scala for Lent, for five performances a week. I did ask you, if Merelli applied for such a lease, to let me know about it before closing the deal, but you too swim with the current, like many others. Patience! Before closing this letter I shall perhaps be able to announce the settlement of the business with Giaccone for the autumn. I believe la Derancourt has definitely been engaged to take my place, at the time when the crisis will be upon me. If the agreements, both with Canzio and with Giaccone, are definitely settled, you will be forced to exclaim: 'What a tiger's heart!' when I tell you the terms. Poor Peppina!

I have not said a word about your offer, in the last letter you wrote to me at Bergamo, to speak to the person a copy of a paragraph of whose letter you sent me. Dear Lanari, do you wish me to degrade myself still further with a man who has treated me worse than a beast? In spite of all the sacrifices, the burden of which he leaves me to bear alone, I shall certainly not take any further foolish step, as in the past, in the vain hope of moving him to compassion and justice, if not towards me, towards the child for which he is responsible [*verso chi da lui ripete la vita*]. When the business with Giaccone is settled I shall go to Venice, because there I shall have better attention, and furthermore I shall be able to procure a better nurse for my child, as here they all take them into their houses, so as to be more sure of them, and that is something that would be impossible for me to do. I am being as economical as I can, because with the disbursements I shall have to make, I shall have a not inconsiderable deficit. I repeat: God is just and will have pity on me and on my family. In spite of so much suffering I don't wish the cause of it any evil. May God touch his heart, not for me, but for his son's sake. You say that when I am calm you will tell me of something that would suit me? I'm afraid that in that case you will have to wait a long time, for calmness seems a thousand miles distant from me.

Give my regards to the Donzelli family, and to your own. Believe me,

Your friend,

GIUSEPPINA STREPPONI.

I have written a letter breaking off all relations with the person you know about at Ancona. It was a step taken in the hope of support, but he did nothing except send good wishes in his letters, not putting himself out at all, even by way of compliment. But I am quite happy about that, because I couldn't ever have loved him truly, and even if he had been what we hoped he would be, I should have refused, for I should not have been happy with him. That between ourselves. Indeed, please burn this letter at once. I have come to an amicable agreement with Giaccone; today everything will be settled, with the sacrifice on my part of not less than 3,500 Austrian lire, leaving me free from 10th November, the time when Signora Derancourt will commence her services. That's the sacrifice for Trieste alone!!!! Imagine what it will be for Genoa!!

The postscript refers, clearly, to Count C., mentioned in the letter of 20th August above. This admirer had evidently been picked up at Ancona in the previous April or May.

The season at the Teatro Grande, Trieste, opened on 22nd September, with *Zampa*, in which Giuseppina had no part.[1] She appeared only in Campana's *Giulio d'Este*, first performed on 6th October, with moderate success. Desiderata Derancourt made her *début* in *Roberto Devereux* on 20th October—earlier than Giuseppina had anticipated. A miscellaneous programme consisting of the first act of *Zampa*, the first act, or prologue, of *Lucrezia Borgia*, a duet from

[1] Giuseppe Stefani, in *Verdi e Trieste*, p. 83, says she had 'a part of no great importance' in *Zampa*. This seems to be based on a misunderstanding of a passage in G. C. Bottura's *Storia aneddotica documentata del Teatro Comunale di Trieste* (Trieste, 1885).

I Normanni a Parigi and the third act of *Roberto Devereux* was put on for Giuseppina's benefit on 23rd October. This was designed to cause her as little strain as possible; apparently she sang only in the prologue of *Lucrezia Borgia* and in the duet.

It is possible that the 'crisis' occurred earlier than she expected. The confinement may have taken place at Trieste and the following letter may have been written during convalescence, though this is not certain:

Venice, 27th November 1841.

DEAR LANARI,

I have been at Venice for some days, in a passable state of health. Cirelli has shown me your letter of the 17th addressed to him; then yesterday I received your two letters, through Signor Coin. Thank you for your offers, but I need nothing at the moment. To the person who approaches me at Genoa, to collect the money due to you, over and above the three months' salary due to me (let me know who it is), I will disburse the full sum of my debt. As I shall not be going there until towards the end of next month you can wait for the repayment of the first quarter's salary until that time. As for your answer to my request to be free, including the month I remain with you, to lend my services after Vienna, my friend Berti will write to you, and I flatter myself that you will feel like being obliging. Camillino is beginning to get on his feet—he seems quite recovered. Cirelli sends his regards and I remain,

Your friend,
G. STREPPONI.

We do not know where Giuseppina's family lived during these years —whether they had stayed at Trieste after Feliciano Strepponi's death, or returned to Lodi, or gone elsewhere. Camillino would seem to have been at Venice when the above letter was written; perhaps Giuseppina's mother had come to look after her during her confinement, and had brought Camillino with her.

Just before Christmas, the mother now of two children, Giuseppina was for a few days at Milan, where arrangements were concluded for her appearance in *Belisario* and *Nabucco* during the Lent season at La Scala. After that she was engaged for Vienna in the spring. Her contract with Lanari expired at the end of August; he wished to employ her during that month at Lucca; she hoped to be released from this obligation, and intended to be more her own mistress in the future.

She arrived at Genoa on 2nd January, and appeared first at the Teatro Carlo Felice on 18th January, in Pacini's *Saffo*. During the earlier part of the season her place had been taken by Clara Novello, who had a benefit performance on 23rd January. *Il Figaro* reported:

To honour the artist there was no lack of verses and flowers, and outstanding among the latter a wreath laid at the feet of her celebrated companion by the excellent Giuseppina Strepponi, this poet of Lesbos returned to life, who in the three first performances of *Saffo* has already aroused the audience to delirious enthusiasm. We wished to draw attention to this as an uncommon example of a generous spirit which redounds to the special glory of both singers and shows how a base thought has no place in minds truly sublime like those of la Strepponi and la Novello.

Giuseppina's letters show her again in high spirits, ready with pungent remarks about friends and colleagues. She says nothing about Clara Novello, but has this about Verdi's future Lady Macbeth, who was notoriously ill-favoured: 'I have heard la Barbieri's name announced, with the addition of Nini [Barbieri-Nini]. If *she* has found a husband no one need despair of finding one.' She mocks at the big nose and unfortunate love affairs of Pietro Romani, director of the orchestra at the Teatro della Pergola at Florence, but wishes she had him with her at Genoa, in *Saffo*: 'When he's dozing he is better than the others awake.' The next opera of the season was to be Mercadante's *Giuramento*, and to please the tenor Ivanoff it was proposed to add an extra duet from the same composer's *Le due illustri rivali*. The score of this duet was lent to Giuseppina by Lanari. But, after all, it was not made use of: 'The rehearsals began and the above-mentioned Ivanoff began: "I cut this", "I omit this other piece", "Such and such I don't sing", so that the first act became a monstrosity, without feet, hands or head—only a miserable trunk being left to us. The management, impresario and orchestral director opposed this butchery, and he was forced to sing *Il Giuramento* as Mercadante wrote it.' The opera was not a great success and had only three performances. *Saffo* continued to please: 'We are all called and recalled: my favourite pieces are the finale of the second act and the aria in the third act, after which I am called for five or six times. You know me, and know that I tell the truth, and nothing but the truth—something not too common, perhaps, among us women.' At the last performance of the season even the man who, in the last scene, represented Sappho leaping over the cliff, had to give an encore. Ivanoff got his way at a concert; he and Giuseppina sang a duet from Donizetti's *Roberto Devereux* and tacked on to it the cabaletta of the duet from *Le due illustri rivali*.

Financial matters are discussed in these letters. When she had arrived at Genoa, Giuseppina had found a bill of exchange for 13,160 francs awaiting her. She asked Lanari not to draw further bills beyond 8,500 francs, the amount of her salary at Genoa, during the Carnival season, but promised to repay the balance of her debt at Milan. The exact arrangements made are not clear. A letter of 28th January includes this passage:

Regarding the bill of exchange for 5,340 francs that you have to draw at Genoa, if you want it all together please wait a few days longer; if you'll take it in two instalments you can send a bill at once for 4,000 francs. I assure you that if you can release me from the engagement at Lucca you will please me very much, for then I should be able to put my finances in order a bit. Now (between ourselves) they are in *disorder*. Haven't you any news from Turin? Even the most just arrangement you made last year at Verona miscarried, and those 1,500 Austrian lire that are still outstanding would not cause me any annoyance just now! Enough—if you can send him a sharp reminder you would be doing me a service. They tell me that at Turin he doesn't arouse fanatical enthusiasm. I am angry with you because you haven't written me a single line. You will be busy, to be sure, with God knows how many love affairs!!! Lucky you, since now I am properly on the shelf[1]—but I'm better off so than with people like Mo . . . . near me. Goodbye, dear Lanari. My benefit night is the Saturday before Lent! I could do with a good money present from someone, as it's my benefit only in name! The Devil! The Devil!

The next letter, written a few days later, tells among other things what had happened in the previous September, after C. of Ancona received his dismissal by post. This leads to some of the most revealing passages in the whole of this correspondence:

Genoa, 3rd February 1842.

DEAR LANARI,

I have received yours of the 31st, which gave me infinite pleasure. I await your orders concerning the bill of exchange. Now I would like, in all secrecy, to ask you something, and I'll tell you later on whom it's for. Don't be afraid for yourself, on my account, because even if it were for me, from the moment when you do me the favour of releasing me from Lucca, my contract with you ends in Vienna. That premised, tell me, as a man of outstanding experience in theatrical affairs and actions at law, whether the law grants release from a contract in circumstances such as these I lay before you: A singer, or ballerina, is asked in marriage by somebody who does not wish her to appear any more on the stage. When she's married, is she indisputably released from engagements contracted as a single person? It seems to me that she is, because the Church is concerned, and the law which gives the husband rights over his wife. Please give me an early reply, as I have promised somebody to consult you on this point.

Il Giuramento, produced last night, was received neither coldly nor warmly, for the first two acts, apart from Costantini's aria; the third act pleased very much. . . . You ask what happened about C——? He came to Trieste in a fury, because they had written him an anonymous letter saying I was making love with Salvi (and, in parenthesis, I'll tell you that Salvi has always had, on me, the effect of mallow water[2]). So then I undeceived him, but I was inflexible in the matter of . . . you understand! I received him several times, always in someone's presence and with the doors

[1] This is the best equivalent I have been able to find for Giuseppina's 'poichè ora sono proprio all'asciutto'. She was 'stony broke' or 'positively cleaned out' in the matter of lovers.

[2] An emetic!

open, so as not to increase the unpleasantness that such visits could cause me in the theatre. He was, to tell the truth, reasonable, and behaved with extreme delicacy—something for which I shall always be grateful and which has persuaded me still to keep up correspondence with him. I don't even know myself what will happen now. He has imputed that M . . . . . . is despicable and infamous, but in spite of all the misfortunes and money losses to which he has seen me subjected, he has pretended not to understand a thing—in this way he will certainly remit his patrimony in the most flourishing condition. I have never been in the habit of counting the costs, for which reason I have always been deceived and made a fool of, and for an inch of evil I have always had to do an ell of penitence. Let's hope that it will soon be all over, since after Vienna there will never again come before my eyes that cadaverous face which turned my head. Listen—I feel myself strong, or, to put it better, indifferent, but if I suspected my constancy in that matter for one moment I would shut myself up among the nuns, guarded from sight, so as not to give him the satisfaction even of a glance. Farewell, dear Lanari. I have written badly because from my bed—you understand. Write to me soon about everything I have asked in this letter, and about Lucca.

Love me and believe me,
Your affectionate friend,
GIUSEPPINA STREPPONI.

There is one other letter dated by Giuseppina from Genoa, but the content shows that it was actually written at Milan.

And now—what conclusions are to be drawn from the documentary evidence here presented? The first surely is that Merelli is entirely innocent of the charges brought against him by Gatti, Mercede Mundula and their followers. We have seen that he was probably responsible for engaging Giuseppina for Vienna in 1835, although he was not yet himself officially appointed impresario there. But certainly, in view of the long, unbroken series of engagements reported in the contemporary theatrical papers, she cannot have borne him a child as the result of anything that happened between them in Vienna. There is no real reason to suppose that anything did happen. After June 1835 she did not again come within his orbit until the spring of 1839. He would have liked to have included her in his company in 1838, but did not succeed in reaching agreement with Lanari in that year. Merelli's correspondence with Lanari, in so far as it concerns Giuseppina, is strictly confined to business matters, except for the one devastating remark in the letter of 16th January about a rumour, which proved to be not unfounded, that she was then five months gone with child. Merelli, the supposed lover of Giuseppina and supposed father of Camillino, has to ask Lanari for information on this point! Subsequent correspondence shows that Merelli was eager to secure her further services in 1839, but not very interested in 1840, when her voice was reported to have deteriorated.

But it is Giuseppina's own letters of 1841 which effectively dispose of any remaining possibility that Merelli may have been responsible for her troubles. In August 1841 she was at Bergamo under Merelli's direction. It is surely utterly impossible that after writing, in the letter of 8th August, 'I have found Merelli particularly kind', she could have been referring to him, *later in the same letter*, as 'the despicable M . . . . . . '. And Merelli was present at Bergamo, while this other person was not. Again, in the letter of 20th August, she talks about her deception, under the mantle of love, by someone who abandoned her, and then, later in the same letter, says: 'Merelli too is very much disposed to assist me.' And on 27th August she writes, 'I cannot but be satisfied, too, with Merelli', at a time when she was anything but satisfied with the mysterious M.

But if Bartolomeo Merelli leaves the court without a stain on his character, who *was* the guilty party?

From Giuseppina's letters we can postulate the following:

1 His name began with 'M', and probably had six other letters. It is doubtful whether, in emotional, hastily written private correspondence such as this, the number of dots following the initial can be expected always to represent the precise number of letters omitted. But it will probably bear *some relation* to the number of letters in the full name. 'M. of Verona' is given three dots; 'the despicable M.' is given six dots, twice. Giuseppina would certainly have simplified things for her biographers if she had chosen to associate with people whose names did not all begin with the same letter.
2 He was well known to Lanari, who had occasion to write to him and to see him, and through whom some arrangement to pay compensation had been made.
3 He was a married man, the father of a family.
4 He had a 'cadaverous' face.
5 He was to have been together with Giuseppina in Vienna in the spring of 1842.

The first point leaves out of consideration a passage from the letter of 28th January 1842, which if it refers to the same person gives us the first *two* letters of the name. These two letters are followed by what look like *four* dots; but carelessness, haste or a bad pen could be responsible for there being one dot less here than we might expect. Close examination of this passage leaves little doubt that it does refer to the same person:

> Haven't you any news from Turin? Even the most just arrangement you made last year at Verona miscarried, and those 1,500 Austrian lire that are still outstanding would not cause me any annoyance just now! Enough—if you can send him a sharp reminder you would be doing me a service.

They tell me that at Turin he doesn't arouse fanatical enthusiasm. I am angry with you because you haven't written me a single line. You will be busy, to be sure, with God knows how many love-affairs!!! Lucky you, since now I am properly on the shelf—but I'm better off so than with people like Mo . . . . near me.

The mention of Verona in connection with the outstanding debt brings 'M. of Verona' again to mind. But *he* can be cleared of suspicion at once, for he was a *single* man, whom Giuseppina at one time hoped to marry, and she had herself broken off relations with him early in 1840. No, this letter of 28th January 1841, refers to the same person as the letter of 8th August 1841: 'If you have occasion to see the despicable M . . . . . . kindly remind him of the important sum of money that through your offices he agreed to pay.' It tells us that this agreement between Lanari and M . . . . . . about compensation to be paid to Giuseppina had been made at Verona, and in 1841 ('last year'). Lanari had been in charge of the Carnival season at Verona from 26th December to 22nd February 1841, while Giuseppina was singing for Jacovacci in Rome. From the sentences preceding and following those concerned with the Verona agreement it is clear that the person concerned was at Turin when this letter was written, and was almost certainly a singer. The whole passage reads logically and unfolds a consecutive train of thought, if we conclude that Mo . . . ., whose company for Giuseppina was dangerous and undesirable, was identical with M . . . . . ., who had wronged her earlier. If these arguments are acceptable, we now have the following additional pointers towards the identity of this man:

6 The second letter of his name was 'o'.
7 He was a singer, accustomed to arouse fanatical enthusiasm.
8 He was at Verona, with Lanari during the Carnival season of 1841.
9 He was singing at Turin in January 1842, reputedly with less than his usual success.

One other very important point arises from examination of this passage. If the agreement to pay damages was made at Verona in the Carnival season of 1841, this was before Giuseppina's second child was conceived, and thus the agreement concerned the *first* child. Both children, therefore, had the same father.

It is impossible to pin-point the dates of birth of the children, or to say what slight variations from the normal gestation period may have occurred. If our calculations are approximately correct, however, we have two further clues to the identity of the father of Giuseppina's children:

10 He must necessarily have been together with her at Bologna or Faenza, in May or June 1837—nine months or so before the first child was born.

11 He must have been together with her either in Rome in late February, or at Florence in March or early April 1841—nine months or so before the second child was born. As Giuseppina anticipated being able to go on singing up to 10th November, it is highly probable that this second child was conceived at Florence rather than in Rome.

We are in search, then, of a famous singer, with a name of six or seven letters, the first two of which were 'Mo', a married man, the father of a family, with a cadaverous face, who had business relations with Lanari and who was at Bologna or Faenza in May or June 1837, at Verona during the Carnival season of 1841, at Florence in March or April of that year, at Turin in January 1842—where he had less success than usual—and in Vienna in the spring of 1842.

Who was it? There can be only one answer—NAPOLEONE MORIANI.

The whole jig-saw puzzle fits together perfectly. Moriani's theatrical career, like Giuseppina's own, can be reconstructed from the contemporary papers: he was at all those places, on those dates. The *Gazzetta Privilegiata di Milano* on 5th February 1842, eight days after Giuseppina wrote, 'They tell me that at Turin he doesn't arouse fanatical enthusiasm', reprinted from the *Messaggiere Torinese* a report on the reception of *Marino Faliero*: 'Moriani . . . generally speaking, was well received, and la Tadolini also, but the duet they sang together was like Israele's aria: it didn't warm, it didn't freeze; the atmosphere was tepid, good for invalids.' That Moriani was married and had a family is shown by existing correspondence with his wife and by one of his letters to Lanari, dated 1st February 1837, in which he asks for the payment of some money owing to him because he was expecting to become a father again in that month. As for the cadaverous face, it can be seen today, in an oil painting in the Scala Museum at Milan. A white light shines on the forehead, the complexion is pallid, the shaven parts of the chin very blue and the cheeks markedly hollow. This is certainly a face that could be thought of as cadaverous even in broad daylight. How much more so, then, on the stage, as Giuseppina playing opposite him had so often seen it, in one of those dying roles for which he was famous, the corpse-like aspects of his features deliberately accentuated and underlined by make-up and theatrical lighting! They called him 'Il tenore della bella morte'. Numerous contemporary notices remark on this mortuary speciality of Moriani's. A flowery-penned critic in *La Fama* in 1844, for instance, declared: 'The extinction of life is expressed by singing that has the tints, the shuddering, of death itself; it is like a trampled narcissus that bows its head, and in whose bosom the transient echo weeps and laments'.

Counsel for the defence might bring forward Moriani's own letter to Lanari of 6th March 1840, with its references to the 'war', recently concluded, between Giuseppina and Lanari, and to the 'nasty Lame Devil' who was upsetting her career with his bad advice and rendering her 'so abject in the eyes of society'. Considered in isolation, this would seem to support the accepted story and indicate that someone else, and not Moriani himself, was responsible for Giuseppina's troubles. Less superficially examined, however, it can be seen to do nothing of the sort. It was written shortly after Giuseppina had quarrelled with Lanari and entered into a relationship which was to be short-lived, but which, at the time, she hoped would lead to matrimony with 'M. of Verona'. It is highly probable that Moriani was referring to this person, about whom he had heard from Lanari, because (1) Giuseppina could hardly have been continuing *another* relationship, at the time when she was consorting, with a view to matrimony, with 'M. of Verona', and (2) she was certainly not receiving advice, bad or good, at this time from the father of her child. It was just because she had been abandoned that she clutched at the idea of marriage. Whatever the nature of Giuseppina's brief liaison with 'M. of Verona', Moriani, it must be said, showed himself a pretty cool customer in referring to this relationship in the terms he did. In his view, apparently, it was less socially degrading to bear illegitimate children to a famous tenor than to associate, with a view to matrimony, with an obscure and probably lame admirer.

Some comment is necessary on Rodolfo Paoli's article 'La prima maniera della Peppina' in *La Scala* for February and March 1954, in which extracts from Giuseppina's letters to Lanari, more extensive than those published by Eugenio Gara in the *Corriere della Sera* for 27th January 1951, were made available to Italian readers. Both Gara and Paoli read these letters without realizing that they destroy the whole basis of the story of the relations between Giuseppina and Bartolomeo Merelli. Paoli quotes most of the interesting passages, but still identifies 'the despicable M.' with Merelli. This he is able to do only by omitting, or passing over without comment, the favourable references to Merelli in the same letters, which make this identification impossible. And when he comes to the passage in which Giuseppina gives the first *two* letters of the name, he simply omits the second letter! The text throughout is often inaccurately transcribed, and several names are misread ('Monzi' for Ronzi, 'Gianone' for Giaccone). But quite the most astonishing thing about Paoli's article is his failure to see that Giuseppina's second child was born towards the end of 1841. When she refers to her approaching confinement—'the time when the crisis will be upon me'—Paoli comments: 'There draws near what la Strepponi in these letters often calls the "crisis", i.e. that oscillation and decline of her health and her voice. . . .' The word 'crisis' actually occurs only once in all these letters. Paoli refers to Luzio's article in *Nuova Antologia*, but he cannot have read it very carefully or he would have known that Camillino's name is not a new discovery. He tries to settle the date of Camillino's birth by working back from the remarks, in the letter to Lanari of 27th November 1841, that 'Camillino is beginning to get on his feet—he seems quite recovered', taking this to mean that the child was just then beginning to walk, and was thus between ten and fourteen months old. But the phrase in question (*Camillino comincia a reggersi in piedi*) could be used, equally fittingly, in the case of an old man of ninety 'beginning to get on his feet' after an illness. Here it is definitely connected with recovery from an illness. Paoli also thinks the wet-nurse was required for Camillino, and that he may have been born at Bergamo (probably on the basis of a wrong date, the letter of 8th August 1841 from Bergamo being misdated 8th *April*). The article is highly misleading and would be better forgotten, along with the whole untrue story of Giuseppina's relationship with Merelli. Unfortunately this story has recently been given a new lease of life by Abbiati, in a monstrously inflated version, including passages from Giuseppina's letters to Lanari in Paoli's transcriptions. Moriani's name crops up here and there, with the suggestion that he was Giuseppina's lover, but there is no argument about this. The main theme is still her seduction by Merelli. Abbiati, like Gara and Paoli before him, fails to interpret correctly the letters to Lanari.[1]

In the State Archives at Milan is a letter from Giuseppina to Merelli, dated 28th March 1839, which supports the conclusions of this chapter. It concerns her engagement at Milan and the terms on which she would agree to appear in *Lucia*. It is polite and rather formal (she uses 'voi' in addressing him, as against the 'tu' of the letters to Lanari)—not at all in the style of a mistress or ex-mistress.

If, as reported by Gatti, Verdi pointed Giuseppina out in the theatre to his sister-in-law, and mentioned her supposed relations with Merelli and the child she was said to have had by him, he was passing on a rumour that was without foundation.[2] There has never been any lack of rumours, true and false, about the love affairs of

[1] I am sorry not to be able to approve of Dr Paoli's article, since it was he who, at my request and in exchange for a microfilm of music by Galuppi, procured for me a microfilm of Giuseppina's letters at Florence. In sending it Dr Paoli asked if I would mind if he wrote himself about the letters. I could have no possible objection. Hence Paoli's article in *La Scala*, Abbiati's periodical, and hence Paoli's transcriptions in Abbiati's biography. . . . Moriani's name occurs in Abbiati's version of the story as a result of correspondence with me in 1955. I have since presented the microfilm to the archives of Sant' Agata, together with accurate transcriptions of all the letters.

[2] Verdi's reported remark to Marianna Barezzi does not seem to have appeared in print before Gatti's biography. It was probably given him by Signora Carolina Prayer-Galletti, daughter of Barezzi's younger son Demetrio. In the preface to the first edition of his biography, Gatti says: 'Signora Carolina Barezzi related to me other episodes of the Maestro's life, which I faithfully transcribed.' A family tradition, re-emerging after nearly a hundred years, is to be accepted only with the utmost reserve. Elsewhere we find wholly unacceptable stories, disproved by the documents, related on the authority of the son of Giovannino Barezzi ('Ricordi Verdiani', by 'Alfio', in *Il Presente*, 30th Aug.–1st Sept. 1913).

great singers. Gatti's story has also been made the basis of a film, in which Barezzi seeks an interview with Giuseppina, discloses his knowledge of her past and the child of which Merelli is the father and forces her to renounce Verdi, which she does by pretending to have been merely playing with his affections. Verdi and Giuseppina are brought together again after some years by the dying Donizetti. It makes a good story, sympathetically presented, and the *characters* in this film are not falsified. Great liberties are taken, however, with chronology and with the facts, and now the basis of this older story has been destroyed.

The new story is different, but not less interesting. Giuseppina, whose youthful charm and gaiety shine still, after more than a century, from the files of the theatrical periodicals and the correspondence of the impresarios who employed her, rises rapidly to fame, although overworking herself in the interests of the family she supports, and, after a little more than two years on the stage, encounters the celebrated tenor at Bologna in April 1837. She is fascinated, and there develops between them, at Bologna and Faenza, one of those free associations, common in the history of the stage of this and other times, as a result of which Camillino is conceived and, about February 1838, born. Lanari brings both artists together again in Rome in April 1838. Their triumphs, together with Ronconi, particularly in *Lucia di Lammermoor*, are repeated at Florence. Before they separate in July another child is conceived, this pregnancy being terminated, however, by a miscarriage in February 1839. They appear together again at Venice, Milan, Sinigaglia and Lucca. After their next separation Giuseppina, realizing now the futility of this relationship, tries to break away from it, hoping for a short time for marriage with 'M. of Verona'. Soon she herself dismisses this admirer. Already there are signs that her voice is deteriorating. During the Carnival season of 1841 at Verona Lanari persuades Moriani to do something to make amends to Giuseppina; a sum in compensation is agreed upon; part is paid, part left outstanding. After this Lanari is able to bring them together again on the stage at Florence in March. Relations are renewed, and Giuseppina conceives another child born, in November or December, at Trieste or Venice. Lanari tries in vain to get Moriani to pay the remainder of the money owing, and probably something more for the second child. Giuseppina is finally disillusioned. 'I feel myself strong, or, to put it better, indifferent, but if I suspected my constancy in that matter for one moment I would shut myself up among the nuns, guarded from sight, so as not to give him the satisfaction even of a glance.' She had clearly loved him desperately in the past.

A catastrophic breakdown at Milan early in 1842 was at any rate to save her from the possibility of a renewal of relations with Moriani in Vienna in the spring. And here we can resume the documented narrative of her theatrical career.

The season at Genoa ended with a concert on 13th February 1842, and three days later Giuseppina arrived at Milan for the rehearsals of *Belisario*. Here is what Gatti says about her appearance in this opera:[1]

> La Strepponi presents herself again to the audience of La Scala on 22nd February in *Belisario* by Donizetti, who, everybody says, is particularly fond of her, and she is warmly applauded, praised, adulated, envied.

How very far removed from the truth this is, is shown by what Donizetti himself wrote about her at the time. In a letter of 4th March—five days before the first performance of *Nabucco*—he sends his brother-in-law a message for a Roman impresario:

> Tell him that this singer created such a furore here in *Belisario* that she was the only one who *never* received any applause, that her Verdi did not want her in his own opera and the management imposed her on him.

This is startlingly at variance with the accepted story. The truth is that the strain of years of continuous overwork, interrupted only by pregnancies, had now begun to tell and was to lead, during the production of Verdi's opera, to loss of voice and almost complete collapse. Everything that the biographers, from Monaldi in 1899 onwards, have to say about Giuseppina's enormous success in *Nabucco* is false. *Nabucco* triumphed indeed, but almost in spite of the original Abigaille, who at Milan was by no means 'stupendous', 'splendid' or 'fascinating'. The 'contemporary criticism' cunningly inserted by Monaldi in his description of the success of *Nabucco*, and copied from him by many later writers, has nothing to do with that opera; it is actually taken from the Venetian newspaper *Il Gondoliere* of 11th November 1835—more than six years earlier. The real contemporary criticisms barely mention Giuseppina. G. Romani,[2] writing in *Il Figaro*, said 'The duet between Nabucco and Abigaille would doubtless have been more effective if the principal motive had been repeated less often, and if Ronconi had not been the only person to sing it.' Summing up at the end of the season, the same writer congratulated Verdi and the singers who had appeared in his work—'Ronconi, Derivis, la Bellinzaghi, Miraglia, la Ruggeri, Rossi, Marconi and the chorus, male and female', that is, every single person in the cast *except* Giuseppina Strepponi!

Mercede Mundula, the only writer until recently to comment at all on this situation, tries feebly to prove malice on the part of the critic

[1] Second edition, p. 155; more briefly in the first edition, I, p. 183.

[2] *Not* Felice Romani, as Abbiati (I, pp. 415–17) believes. Abbiati builds a fantasy about Verdi's relations with Romani on this false foundation.

and 'indisposition on the first night' on Giuseppina's. But there is no arguing against the evidence of Giuseppina's own letters and the medical certificates:

Milan, 14th March 1842.

DEAR LANARI,

Merelli and Villa will have warned you about my present state of health. The very newspapers have written extensively about it. Merelli, surprised by my situation, came to ask me what I intended to do about the spring season in Vienna. My condition answered for me. He declared without preamble that it was necessary for him to cover himself against complaints from the powers that be in Vienna, and that he therefore intended, with the approval of the director general, to summon a medical commission, composed of the head doctor and surgeon of the province and the doctor in charge of the case who, on due consideration and after suitable investigations, would pronounce judgment on my condition.

Such a consultation took place a few days ago and, when the examination was over, they declared unanimously that I shall die of consumption if I don't immediately abandon my profession. This you can verify when you like from the authentic certificates, furnished with official signatures, which were formally delivered to me yesterday.

Now I am bound to obey this order, which deprives me and my unfortunate family of support, but God willing I shall at least preserve my life.

So much I thought well to tell you, imparting such unpleasant news, which I am sure will distress you, as it fills with bitterness

Your friend,

GIUSEPPINA STREPPONI.

A copy of the report of the medical commission is among Lanari's papers:

The undersigned went today to Cirelli's studio, Piazzale del Teatro Filodrammatico, with the object of visiting in consultation Signora Giuseppina Strepponi, leading singer of the Imperial and Royal Teatro alla Scala.

Signor Dr Moro, among the undersigned, doctor in charge of the case, discoursing for better information on the antecedent circumstances, pointed out that as far back as the spring of 1839, when she was singing at the said theatre, Signora Strepponi was subject to derangements of the respiratory passages and the gastro-enteric canal such as to render necessary several bleedings and the application of leeches to the trachea. Owing to this she was granted several days' rest by the management of the Imperial and Royal Theatres, after a report from Signor Moro himself. Some time after she left Milan the said disturbances, owing to the strain of singing, became more serious and she was noticeably losing weight, so that she obtained from the impresario to whom she was bound two months' leave, during which time she returned to Milan and put herself in the hands of the same doctor. Rest, abstinence from singing, an easy life and suitable treatment improved her health, so that she was able to appear again with honour on the stage. On her return to the Royal Teatro alla Scala in the current Lent season, her once beautiful and sonorous voice was found—also by the public—to be weak, veiled and insufficient, even when emitted with extraordinary effort. Called therefore today in regular consultation the undersigned established what follows:

The said Signora Strepponi has a very delicate constitution, and her loss of weight has become very considerable. Furthermore she is tormented by frequent coughing, with an unpleasant feeling of irritation all along the trachea and the larynx, which, she says, often becomes a burning sensation, especially after the effort of singing. Her pulse is weak and rapid; in brief, she shows symptoms of light feverish reaction, with loss of appetite and appreciable prostration. In view of all that was established the undersigned doctors unanimously declared Signora Strepponi to be affected with such laryngo-tracheal inflammation as will lead to consumption unless she at once ceases to exercise her profession and submits herself to similar careful treatment and an uninterruptedly tranquil way of life.

DR STEFANO MORO,
Principal Doctor to the Imperial and Royal Theatres.
DR ALESSANDRO VANDONI,
Imperial and Royal Provincial Doctor.
DR GAETANO CICERI,
Imperial and Royal Provincial Surgeon.

Milan, 3rd March 1842.

This document refers, of course, in the second paragraph, to the trouble during the Carnival season of 1840 at Verona, as well as to the earlier indisposition at Milan, mentioned by Merelli in a letter to Lanari, already quoted.

On the strength of the report of the medical commission Merelli wished to bring in a substitute singer immediately, but Giuseppina, whose financial situation was becoming desperate, insisted on completing the season. 'I therefore sang, or rather dragged myself, to the end of the performances,' she told Lanari. She appeared in all in eight performances of *Nabucco*. The opera was to be revived in the following autumn, with Teresa De Giuli as Abigaille, when it had fifty-seven more performances, breaking all records for La Scala.

Lanari also stood to lose money through Giuseppina's involuntary defection and seems to have reproached her. She explained in a letter of 23rd March that she had done all she could, fulfilling the Milanese part of the contract with Merelli, but to go on to Vienna was impossible:

The doctors' certificate speaks clearly enough, and I am losing much more than you. I have lost my health. I am earning nothing. Doctors, medicines and food for myself and my family are using up the little money I had. So you see you are wrong to complain and upset me. I am very displeased not to be able to go to Vienna, where besides my salary I was to have had a benefit performance with half the receipts, and not much hard work. I shouldn't be so crazy as to stay here at Milan eating up my capital if I had not been forced to do so on account of my health. We must resign ourselves to fate—with the difference that you are a fine gentleman, and I only a poor devil.

She had another engagement to sing for Lanari at Lucca, after Vienna, and the terms of her agreement compelled her to make good any time lost by illness. She appealed to Lanari to release her from this contract, and probably he did so. She was also playing again, not very hopefully, with the idea of marriage. Yet another person, it seems, was willing to consider this. On 26th March she told Lanari:

There is, too, a distant prospect of matrimony with someone not very rich, who would have to take on himself the burden of my family, large and small, a complete stranger to theatrical affairs, who wouldn't want to marry me (if at all) unless I had first brought to an end my obligations to you. The probability, or rather almost certainty, is that this marriage won't come off. But in any case I must set my mind at rest, and speak quite openly to you. You know my circumstances—more than anyone else you know what a family I have, entirely dependent upon me. The sacrifices I have had to make, through unpleasant vicissitudes that are known to you, especially in the past two seasons at Trieste and Genoa, have forced me to exhaust almost entirely the small savings I had. Add the expenses I have now, when I'm not earning a farthing, and you will have some idea of my actual situation. So without preamble, and as Villa suggests, come to a friendly settlement with me. Have in mind the mother of two children and all the rest of the family—put yourself in my position and decide as your heart dictates. If I am able to resume my career and revive the fine days of the past, there will be no lack of opportunity, later on, to show you my gratitude.

This was the lowest ebb of her fortunes. The moment that brought Verdi his first great triumph saw Giuseppina reduced almost to despair.

CHAPTER 3

Donizetti, Verdi and Giuseppina Appiani

On 18th December 1941 there appeared in the Venetian newspaper *Il Gazzettino* an article by R. L. Caro with the interrogative title: 'Verdi rivale di Donizetti?' The rivalry suggested was only to a lesser degree that of the two as musicians; they were portrayed principally as the successive admirers, and objects of admiration, of a Milanese lady, Giuseppina Appiani, *née* Strigelli.

The material of Caro's article was all taken from Gatti's biography. No one could describe that work as sensation-seeking, but it did happen that here, as in dealing with the much-discussed later question of Verdi's relations with Teresa Stolz, Gatti took a strong line. In the reasonable conviction that the composer *must* have had love affairs, he was determined to reveal them, although the surviving evidence is scanty indeed. And so, in the midst of an admirably assembled eleven hundred pages of facts, we come across occasional unwarrantable assumptions and fanciful interpretations of enigmatic documents, all the more deplorable because they are almost indistinguishable from the surrounding factual matter. We have seen in the last chapter that Gatti sometimes took over, from earlier writers or from hearsay, stories that can be shown to be untrue.

Where the existing documents present no clear case, psychology and imagination must be called in to supplement them by any biographer. The operation, however, is dangerous. The psychological probe needs delicate handling. The scalpel of the imagination, unless employed with something akin to genius, is capable of inflicting fearsome mutilations. However skilfully the biographer goes to work, such conclusions as are arrived at by deduction and manipulation of unsatisfactory and incomplete evidence are apt to survive only for a time. New documents generally turn up, sooner or later, which destroy the foundations of the older speculations and make a fresh beginning necessary. The publication of Guido Zavadini's *Donizetti: Vita, Musiche, Epistolario* (Bergamo, 1948) has enormously simplified research concerning this composer and invites re-examination of Verdi's and Donizetti's relations with Giuseppina Appiani.[1]

In 1837 the death of Donizetti's adored wife Virginia, aged only twenty-eight, turned the flowery world for him into a desert. Henceforth, although fêted and honoured almost everywhere, he was at heart a homeless wanderer, an intensely lonely man, seeking distraction from despair. The principal recipient of his confidences was his brother-in-law Antonio Vasselli, his beloved 'Toto'. To him he wrote, six days after the tragedy:

> O Toto, my Toto, let my sorrow find an echo in yours, for I have need of someone who understands me. I shall be eternally unhappy. Don't repulse me, remember that we are alone on the earth. O Toto, Toto, write to me for pity's sake, for the love of your
>
> GAETANO.

A week later:

> Forgive me, my Toto, but I am not yet able to tell you how and when I lost so much. I still believe I am dreaming, still the fatal door is shut and still I dare not remain alone. The distress I feel on your account is equal to my own; but believe it, my Toto, I spared nothing—masses, vows, three doctors, the midwife . . .
>
> This morning I gave away the new cradle that should have served. . . . Everything, I have lost everything! Without father, without mother, without wife, without children . . . for whom do I go on working? And why? Oh, my Toto, come to me . . . I beg you on my knees—come in October.
>
> Perhaps you will be of comfort to me—and I to you. . . . The house was for her, the carriage was for her—she did not even try it—Oh God, God! My Toto, write to me and forgive me if I am more importunate now than usual. You alone remain to me. I shall be unhappy until she intercedes with God for my death and our eternal reunion.

21st September 1837:

> Must I tell you? I seem to be waiting for her—it seems that she must return . . . that she is in Rome. I weep for her still as on the first day.

17th March 1838:

> I cannot write or speak of her without shedding tears—always, always, always. Yesterday I had masses said for her.

[1] Additional material is still coming to light, even after Zavadini's fifteen years of patient research. A supplementary volume of letters is in preparation.

3rd August 1842:

> I am still feeling the effects of a day most desolate for me, and your last letter increases my sadness. It doesn't matter. I shall try to distract myself, if I can.

And:

> Why do you talk of other women? Oh, laugh away, and believe me that I weep still as on the first day. . . .

Against this background the rest of Donizetti's life and activities must be judged.

There can be few more searching tests of character than the publication of a collected edition of any man's letters. Donizetti, subjected to this ordeal by Guido Zavadini—who deserves the highest praise for his scrupulous editing—emerges from it creditably. Weaknesses are apparent, but so are outstanding virtues, such as his lifelong devotion to Mayr, his first teacher, his loyalty to family and friends, his true and extraordinary modesty about his own works and, most striking of all, his wonderful generosity of mind towards rival composers—who were never treated by him as rivals. In particular, his attitude to Bellini compares very favourably with that of Bellini towards him. Whatever their comparative merits as composers, there can be no doubt that Donizetti was the more attractive character. In reading this correspondence, however, one cannot fail to remark as time goes on the increasing coarseness of language, particularly in the letters to Antonio Vasselli. Half a dozen indecencies are monotonously repeated. It is the automatic, humourless swearing of the weary conscript soldier. Must the campaign go on for ever? Will peace never come? With these meaningless oaths Donizetti helps himself along the road that leads to the asylum at Ivry.

For six months, from some time in September 1841 until early March 1842, the forty-four-year-old composer was at Milan. He was occupied first with the composition and then with the rehearsing of *Maria Padilla*, successfully produced at La Scala on 26th December. Then in the new year he was busy with the composition of *Linda di Chamounix* for Vienna. This opera was written while he was staying at Giuseppina Appiani's house, as several letters show. The fact that he never mentions *Maria Padilla* as having been written under her roof suggests that only during the latter part of his stay at Milan was he this lady's guest. During the early months of 1842 he became very friendly with her—according to Gatti and his followers, more than friendly. Although called to Bologna by Rossini, who wished him to conduct a performance of his *Stabat Mater*, Donizetti stayed on at Milan for the first performance of Verdi's *Nabucco*, on 9th March. His interest had been aroused at the rehearsals, and on the 6th he had written urging friends at Bergamo to attend at least one performance of the new opera. In the carriage that took him to Bologna, on the 10th, he sat lost in thought, taking no part in his companions' conversation, while they heard him exclaim: 'Oh, that *Nabucco*! Beautiful! Beautiful! Beautiful!'

From Bologna Donizetti went to Vicenza and on to Vienna, where he arrived on 27th March.

Meanwhile, the triumph of *Nabucco* had opened all doors to Verdi at Milan. 'He found himself suddenly beset by a crowd of friends who had need to tell him how much they had always loved him, what attention they had always given him, how they had anxiously followed his first steps. They had all known him, all protected him, all encouraged him; all had done something for him, all had divined his genius, all had foretold his brilliant success. They all wanted to press his hand, to walk arm in arm with him, to address him as "Tu".' [1] He began to frequent the drawing-rooms of the Milanese aristocracy. In the autograph album of Sofia de' Medici, Marquess of Marignano, we find on pages 18–19 an entry in Donizetti's hand, the vocal part of a song, 'Io amo la mestizia', with the remark: 'Vous êtes priée d'y faire l'accompagnement, ainsi nous serons deux auteurs.' The very next entry, after two blank pages, is by Verdi. On pages 22–4 is an otherwise unknown setting of an Italian translation of Goethe's *Erster Verlust*, dated 'Milan, 6th May 1842'.[2] From about the same period date the beginnings of Verdi's friendships with the Countess Clara Maffei, Emilia Morosini and Giuseppina Appiani.

According to Gatti, Giuseppina Appiani, *née* Strigelli, was the widow of a son of the painter Andrea Appiani. Her husband, who killed himself 'as a result of his disordered way of life', had left her with three gracious daughters. In the Borgo Monforte she held her salon, attended by the artistic bohemians of Milan. Donizetti, again according to Gatti,[3]

> sends Mme Appiani letters from Vienna, in which his longing for his distant friend and nostalgia for his abandoned cosy corner are obvious, although he protests to his relatives that his friendship with Mme Appiani is an innocent one [*sebbene protesti coi parenti che egli e l'Appiani si conoscono* '*candidamente*']. One of these letters bears five consecutive dates, as if the composer did not wish to part with the sheet of paper to which he had confided his whole heart, that it might pass into loved hands. . . . Another letter, with the dates of the two following days (the correspondence is continued for precisely a week), ends thus: 'Remember your most affectionate Gaetano and love him as he loves you.' Mme Appiani sends him a pair of slippers she has herself embroidered, and asks him for news of the opera born in her house; and Donizetti replies narrating the success of *Linda*, just performed, and the mediocre state of his

[1] Michele Lessona, *Volere è potere*.
[2] See 'Goethe's *Erster Verlust* set to music by Verdi' (*Music Review*, Feb. 1948).
[3] First edition, I, pp. 209–10; second edition, pp. 164–5.

health, invoking her, in closest confidence: 'Help me, my Peppina!' But absence lays traps for the liveliest affections. Donizetti is not a model of constancy in his loves . . . the lady, for her part, is changeable by nature. Verdi redoubles his visits to Mme Appiani, and the more he makes, the more she would like him to make.

Before we follow this romance further it must be pointed out that Gatti has confused two different women with the same surname.

On 3rd July 1843 Donizetti wrote to his brother-in-law:

Signora Cristina Appiani is coming to Rome as governess to the children of the Prince of Compagnano. I knew her when she had a carriage and horses. Her husband's suicide, as a result of his disordered way of life, left her in a bad position, with two children to maintain and endless debts to pay. She is a woman adorable on every account, highly educated, most good-natured, unhappy but always amiable. I suggest you introduce her to your wife and family and treat her with all your customary kindness. Having known her in times of prosperity, it is extremely painful for me to see her reduced to earning bread for herself and her children. If you see her make a nice face at my portrait, do not suspect things; ours is an innocent relationship [*ci conosciamo candidamente*], and she will do it because I have just lent her 300 Austrian lire for the journey. But don't mention that to her. In the good old days she was the friend of my friend Pedroni.

The incomplete text of this letter appeared in *Lettere inedite di G. Donizetti* (Rome, 1892). G. Donati-Petteni reprinted it in his *L'Istituto musicale Gaetano Donizetti* (Bergamo, 1928), and he was responsible for altering the christian name of the lady concerned, thus leading Gatti astray. Donizetti's subsequent correspondence makes it clear that Cristina Appiani in Rome and Giuseppina Appiani at Milan were two distinct persons. We are concerned with the latter. There exist nine letters to her from Donizetti, and fifteen letters and a few undated notes to her from Verdi are known.[1] Clearly we no longer have to believe that her husband killed himself 'as a result of his disordered way of life' and we no longer have to take into account a statement by Donizetti that their relationship was 'innocent'. Further information about her is given by Raffaello Barbiera [2] in discussing, in his romantic and picturesque way, the poet Giovanni Prati:

His most fervent admirer is perhaps Giuseppina Appiani, *née* Strigelli, of Milan, daughter-in-law of the celebrated painter Appiani and daughter of the State Councillor Antonio Strigelli, on whose death Prati wrote an epitaph in *ottava rima*. This lady, friend of the composers Donizetti and Bellini (who, while her guest in Via Monforte, composed suave melodies at a reading-desk that is still preserved), is distinguished for her beauty;

[1] Most of the originals were in the Museo del Risorgimento at Milan, and were destroyed in 1943.

[2] *Il salotto della Contessa Maffei* (fourth edition, 1895), pp. 101–2.

she passes for one of the loveliest women of Italy; and her charms [*le sue forme*], for which Hayez sighed, will be perfectly conserved, like those of Ninon de l'Enclos, up to her old age.

Barbiera does not connect her name with Verdi's.

It should be possible for the local historians of Milan to discover more about this lady. The sources of information, however, are by no means obvious, as is shown by the fact that even Gatti has confused her with someone else and in the past quarter of a century no one has ever noticed this. We should like to know how old she was at the time of the supposed rivalry of Donizetti and Verdi for her favours; what really happened to her husband; how many children she had and how old they were; what was her relationship to Prati and to Hayez; whether there was anyone else in the case; and how far Barbiera's comparison between her and Ninon de l'Enclos is to be pressed. If we knew all this we should be in a better position to interpret Donizetti's and Verdi's surviving letters. As it is, clues provided by these letters give grounds for supposing that Gatti has drawn wrong conclusions.

Donizetti's letter concerning Cristina Appiani, mistakenly believed by Donati-Petteni and Gatti to refer to our Giuseppina Appiani, says that she was left with two children to maintain. Gatti, doubtless on the evidence of Donizetti's letters, says that Giuseppina was left with 'three gracious daughters'. But this by no means exhausts the tale of her offspring. Donizetti always sends greetings to her 'dear and lovely daughters' and to her sons as well. A letter of 4th June 1842 names three daughters—Adele, Eugenia and Angiolina ('Angioleu'). Eugenia is mentioned in one of Verdi's letters, of 25th February 1854, from which it appears that she was a writer or composer; she was interested in a piece called *Graziella*, on which Verdi's opinion had been asked. A fourth daughter is referred to in a letter of Donizetti's of 9th March 1844: 'To the other daughter-mother whom I seldom had the pleasure of meeting, my homage.' This is perhaps the 'mamina' to whom greetings are sent in a letter of 9th May 1842. The fourth daughter was evidently already married and a mother, so that Giuseppina by 1844, and possibly by 1842, was a grandmother. There seem to have been two sons, mentioned in nearly all the letters; in 1844 one of them is referred to three times as 'the painter' and the other once as 'the wages devourer' and once as 'the architect'. The painter son was almost certainly Andrea Appiani the younger (1817–65), grandson,[1] according to the *Enciclopedia Italiana*, of Giuseppina's father-in-law, the more famous Andrea Appiani the elder (1754–1817). The *Enciclopedia* tells us that the younger Appiani

[1] 'Nipote', which, of course, could also mean nephew. The dates make this improbable. Thieme and Becker (*Allgemeines Lexikon der bildenden Künstler*) make him the 'Gross-neffe' of the elder Appiani. But the Italian for this would be 'pronipote'.

'studied at Milan under Hayez and in Rome under Minardi; painted historical and *genre* pictures and, in the church of Bolbeno in Trentino, frescoes on religious subjects'. A letter from Hayez to Giuseppina Appiani,[1] of April 1843, has a postscript: 'Kind regards to Andrea; I hope he will have done a lot of work—the days are long.' This seems almost conclusive. But one of Donizetti's letters to Antonio Vasselli, written at Milan on 4th March 1842, towards the end of his stay in Giuseppina Appiani's house, raises a problem:

> I received the box with the portraits, the stones and the prints, and have already gained good marks from the lady of the house and her daughters by the portraits. To the son of the above-mentioned lady I have given the prints (he is son of the painter Appiani and paints himself and was in Rome.)

In the passage in brackets, is the word 'son' ('figlio') a slip for 'grandson' ('nipote')? Was Donizetti himself mistaken about the relationship between these people? Or had Giuseppina's husband, of whom we know nothing, also been a painter? Without some such supposition, we should have to conclude, from this letter, that she was not the daughter-in-law but the widow of the elder Andrea Appiani. And in that case, since he died in 1817 and had been paralysed for four years before, she would have to have given birth to all her six or more children by 1813 or thereabouts. This seems highly improbable. As it is, if we accept the statements of Barbiera and Gatti that Giuseppina was the daughter-in-law of the elder Appiani, it seems that one of her children was born as far back as 1817. The second son is perhaps identifiable as the Carlo Appiani mentioned in a letter [2] from Giovanni Prati, the poet fervently admired by Giuseppina, to the Abate Bernardi, prefect of the *ginnasio* at Padua, in 1843:

> The young Dr Carlo Appiani is coming to Padua as assistant engineer at the railway station.

Donizetti, however, in the following year calls him 'the architect'. In any case, the second son cannot have been much less than twenty years of age at this time.

Such information as is available, then, about Giuseppina Appiani suggests that she was born about 1797—supposing her to have been about twenty when her elder son was born. If it should be discovered that the younger Andrea Appiani was not her son, then the existence of the 'daughter-mother' in 1844, and possibly already in 1842, would still point to a date not very much later than 1797 for Giuseppina's birth. In fact the evidence suggests that at the time of the beginning

[1] In the Masini collection, Biblioteca Communale, Forlì.
[2] Published by Carlo Giordano in *Giovanni Prati: Studio biografico* (Turin, 1907).

of the supposed rivalry between Donizetti and Verdi she was a woman of about forty-five. She certainly had six children, some of them already adult, and was a grandmother by 1844, if not by 1842. All this does not of course make it impossible that she should have flirted first with Donizetti and then with Verdi, but it does make it seem rather more unlikely, even if her 'forme' were as well preserved as those of Ninon de l'Enclos. Even the three children Gatti grants her would be a handicap in adventures of this nature, let alone the six she had in reality. And then there was the grandchild; and Prati, a notoriously unfaithful husband, who was at Milan from 1841 to 1843—precisely at this time; and Hayez, sighing in the background (he must surely have painted her portrait at some time or other),[1] and Mr Sandrini.

Verdi, in a letter dated 26th December 1843, sends greetings to 'Sandrini and all your fine family'. Donizetti in all his letters to Giuseppina Appiani sends greetings to this 'Signor', 'Monsieur' or 'Mr' Sandrini, immediately after those to her daughters and sons. Hayez, in the letter mentioned above, does the same. Who was this Sandrini? A relative? An old friend of the family? He evidently lived with the Appianis. It seems at least possible that he was a more intimate friend of Giuseppina's than any of the others, that he occupied in her life the position, say, that Carlo Tenca occupied in that of the Countess Maffei. If this could be proved it would go a long way towards showing up what has been written about the relations of Donizetti and Verdi with Giuseppina Appiani for the nonsense it assuredly is. I put forward this suggestion about Sandrini with diffidence, as a possible line of further research. But I have seldom been more surprised in the course of my own delvings than when I looked up the epitaph that Prati is supposed to have written for Giuseppina Appiani's father. It is published by Barbiera, in an appendix to his *Grandi e piccole memorie* (Florence, 1910):

There is an unpublished poem in *ottava rima* by Giovanni Prati, written for the tomb of the nobleman Antonio Strigelli,[2] magistrate at Milan, and relative of the painter Andrea Appiani.

Savio consiglio d'incorrotta mente,
Alma gentile in securtà temprata,
Nobil costume, che alla varia gente
Dona del cor testimonianza ornata;

[1] A list of Hayez's works, published with the posthumous *Le mie memorie* (Milan, 1890), includes a 'Portrait of a Lady' of 1835, commissioned or acquired by Giuseppina Appiani. But the 'Lady with the Veil' reproduced in *La Scala* for June 1953 is *not* a portrait of her.

[2] Giuseppina Appiani's father, Count Antonio Strigelli, died on 17th February 1835. He was born at Milan in 1755. (Obituary notice in the *Gazzetta Privilegiata di Milano*, 10th March 1835.)

Rigido scudo d'onestà lucente,
Iracondo de' vili alle peccata.
Nol conoscete ancor? . . . V'ò detto assai:
Il nome in questi carmi io ne segnai.

Barbiera has failed to notice that this poem is an acrostic on the name SANDRINI. And with that I hand over this problem to the historians of Milan.[1]

We have seen something now of the background of Donizetti's life at this period, and something of Mme Appiani's circumstances. What about Verdi? The biographers have little to tell us about the post-*Nabucco* period; in fact, they generally content themselves with retailing two stale anecdotes about *I Lombardi* and one about *Ernani*. Letters are not plentiful from 1843 onwards, apart from the business correspondence with the management of the Teatro Fenice at Venice. From 1844 we have the invaluable correspondence of Verdi's pupil Muzio with their mutual benefactor Antonio Barezzi. But what is written about Verdi's private life in the years immediately following the triumph of *Nabucco* is based on surmise, deriving from a handful of surviving letters to ladies in Milanese society and a few passages of later reminiscence. The tone of some of these early letters is curiously un-Verdian. 'The Bear of Busseto' they called him, and he often used the phrase of himself; but the bear revealed here is very tame, standing on his hind legs and entertaining the ladies—or trying to. The letters are written on Bath paper, the fashionable stationery of the day, and employ, rather clumsily, the language of gallantry. They offer infinite possibilities of misinterpretation.

In two letters from 1842, addressed to Emilia Morosini,[2] we find phrases like these: 'Remember that I am all tenderness; I die of tenderness,' and 'I am always tender, impassioned, ardent, half dead for you.' It would be foolish to conclude that Verdi was in love with this lady. She was, like Mme Appiani, his senior by a whole generation and mother of a bevy of daughters, four of whom are named in these letters: 'What is Peppina doing? And my dear Bigettina? A kiss to the latter and nothing to the former. With Peppina I have large accounts to settle. She won't escape me.'—'A thousand good wishes to that most kind, most amiable, most adorable Annetta; also to that naughty little Carolina; nothing to Peppina—I won't hear of it.' Peppina, one suspects, was Verdi's favourite. She was a charming, dark-ringletted girl of eighteen at this time.[3] While the family was in

[1] Carlo Tivaroni, on p. 478 of the first volume of his *L'Italia durante il dominio austriaco* (Turin–Rome, 1892), names, among those condemned to exile in 1849 after the return of the Austrians to Milan, one Giuseppe Sandrini. Was this, perhaps, Giuseppina Appiani's friend?

[2] Published by Oberdorfer ('Carlo Graziani') in *Giuseppe Verdi: Autobiografia dalle lettere*.

[3] Oberdorfer reproduces her portrait ('about 1842'), together with one of her mother by Hayez. She lived until 1909 and Verdi corresponded with her up to the last month of his life.

the country he wrote to her mother: 'The cruel one! While she wanders about on horseback, or donkeyback, with her thoughts in the third heaven, she perhaps never thinks of the wretched mortals who are in a state of desperation for her.' Annetta was rather older than Peppina and there was another daughter, not named in Verdi's correspondence, who was the eldest of all.

Donizetti's letters from Vienna to Giuseppina Appiani also offer plentiful opportunities for misunderstandings, as he himself realized when he wrote at the end of one of them: 'Don't show anyone my letters, for people might take our jokes in earnest.' They are also very imprecisely dated—often with only the day of the month—and by taking them in the wrong order it is possible, as Gatti has shown, to make them suggest all sorts of things. Every one of them has now been precisely dated by Zavadini, by study of the postmarks and collation with the rest of Donizetti's correspondence. The first, written on 3rd April 1842, is a good-humoured, garrulous account of his journey and the performance of Mercadante's *La Vestale* on the previous evening. It employs the 'voi' and the French 'vous', as do all these letters, and contains no warmer expressions than these: 'As for wanting me back at Milan, I believe you are the only one who does, and you know that one nut in a bag doesn't make any noise. Even your lovely daughters don't want me. But I'll punish them. Greet them for me. The sons as well.' And: 'Greetings to Mr Sandrini, and a thousand thanks! To you? Choose, or rather, guess!' He signs himself: 'The Lodger'.

The next letter, dated '9 or 10' and postmarked 10th May, acknowledges receipt of the embroidered slippers: 'Oh, my gigantic feet! You were never so luxuriously wrapped up!' He sends thanks first of all to Giuseppina herself, for buying the material, then to the 'dear and lovely girls, who spent so many hours working for me, after I had annoyed them for months by repeating chords upon chords for hours on end', and finally to Mr Sandrini, who seems to have been responsible for posting the slippers, or finding some other way of having them conveyed to Vienna. Gatti is thus wrong when he says that Giuseppina embroidered these slippers for Donizetti herself. Here is the conclusion of this letter:

I have just finished the rehearsal of the first act. . . . Dear Lord, how many mistakes! Horrible! And to be compelled to be silent, and not be able to make myself understood! I, who could have settled everything in four minutes, to stand there four hours for a little first act! What will happen to the rest? Oh! Pity me, *Madame et Mesdemoiselles*—and the children too. . . . Pity the poor harlequin. . . . I am very tired.

Farewell my lovely ones, my lovely one, my dear, dear ones, dear one. . . . Farewell *Biondina*; farewell lady, you who remind me of one who is no more. Farewell Crosspatch, even at the piano; farewell Angioleu—farewell male offspring. Farewell little mother, farewell *sor Sandrin.* I have heard now from General Vaccari that His Highness [1] will be at court this evening so we shall come to some agreement.

Infamous weather—rain, wet and cold. Yesterday evening Donzelli in *Otello* reminded of better days. . . . Kisses to you all. Remember your affectionate Gaetano and love him as he loves you.

Have we really to conclude that Donizetti was in love with Giuseppina Appiani? It is clear that he had been happy in her household at Milan, and that there were ties of deep affection between him and his hostess and her sons and daughters. There was evidently some physical resemblance between Giuseppina and his lost Virginia, and he had remarked on this. She was of his own generation; he felt drawn to her. It is possible that an intimate relationship might have developed if circumstances had permitted. But the fact that he does not use the intimate forms of address suggests that this had not come about yet. And he was to see very little more of her. On 26th May he tells of the success of *Linda* and of his sore throat:

I am drinking milk and hot water and sugar. It troubles me the more coming at such a time, as precisely this morning I have to begin rehearsals with the choir for the *Stabat*, to be performed on Tuesday evening without fail. How shall I get on this morning, without speaking, without shouting? Help me, my Peppina!

This is the context of Gatti's invocation 'in closest confidence'.

On 4th June Donizetti has to announce that he has been approached about the possibility of his becoming court composer to the emperor. He will be leaving Vienna shortly but is still uncertain where to go. Business affairs call him to Paris and to Naples, but his heart calls him to Milan more than anywhere else: 'If I come to Milan will you put me up? Have you the room free for the poor coffee addict?' This letter is dated: 'Vienna, 4, 5, 6, 7, 8—Saturday, in short, 1842.' It bears the postmarks 'Vienna, 5th June' and 'Milan, 10th June'. Clearly Donizetti himself was not sure of the date and, equally clearly, the letter was actually written on Saturday, 4th June. Gatti's misunderstanding is patent:

One of these letters bears five consecutive dates, as if the composer did not wish to part with the sheet of paper to which he had confided his whole heart.

The other letter 'with the dates of the two following days' (actually '9 or 10') is the second of the series, already quoted, and Gatti's 'week' stretches from 4th June backwards to 10th May.

For just over a fortnight in July Donizetti was again Mme Appiani's

[1] Probably Metternich, who had to inquire whether the empress would accept the dedication of *Linda*.

guest at Milan; a letter to a friend, dated 29th July, is written from her house, just prior to his departure for Naples. Only a few days later he was writing to his brother-in-law: 'Why do you talk of other women? Oh, laugh away, and believe me that I weep still as on the first day.' In September he asked Giovanni Ricordi to convey his regards and thanks to 'Sandrini and Signora Peppina Appiani and family'.

Verdi has not yet appeared on the scene, so far as can be judged from the available documents. The earliest surviving dated or datable letters from him to Giuseppina Appiani are from December 1843. Some of the undated notes could also be from 1843.

In all the dated letters there are only a few phrases that could be picked out as possibly implying more than they actually say. These have, needless to say, been picked out and made to imply a great deal. Without knowledge of the circumstances in which they were written and of the letters to which they reply it is not possible to decide what these few phrases really mean. But they can at least be put back into their contexts and seen in perspective. The whole correspondence is carried on in a tone of cordial but always respectful friendliness, and the lady is always addressed in the polite third person. This is so even in the series of undated notes that are supposed to represent their most intimate exchanges.

Around these notes Gatti weaves an imaginative story. He begins by ante-dating one of Donizetti's letters by more than two years. He quotes an enigmatic passage about Troy having been destroyed by love, and the dust of that city having spread itself over Vienna, and asks: 'What does he mean to say? Does Donizetti begin to suspect the relations current between Mme Appiani and Verdi?' Zavadini dates the letter in question 18th June 1845—certainly rightly, as comparison with letters on either side makes clear.[1] But Gatti is writing about 1843:

> That those relations are becoming continually closer does not escape Mme Appiani's friends, and one of them may have advised Donizetti who, disinclined to jealousy and rancour, passes shortly from scorn to joke. But Verdi is offended. Even in joke he won't endure interference in his affairs—especially in intimate ones. He likes to visit Mme Appiani's house; the courtesy and spirit of the hostess attract him. A few notes, scraps of Bath paper (the finest and most elegant of the day), sent by hand in a hurry, one after the other, some in the small hours of the morning, reveal his desire, his eagerness, for appointments far from indiscreet eyes. One of these notes says: 'Very well: I will go at three; but it is necessary for me to know where I must go. Meanwhile, a thousand thanks. Write.'

[1] Reference to the bad effect of the Viennese climate on his nerves, as in the previous letter (7th June, to Antonio Dolci); reference to the failure of Merelli's Italian season, as in the following letter (29th June, to Gaetano Melzi); reference to his impending visit to Paris.

Certainly Mme Appiani knows of the friendship between Verdi and Giuseppina Strepponi and is not ignorant of the sympathy felt by the Maestro for Erminia Frezzolini: two women (*honi soit qui mal y pense*) are already too many and not even a third favourite can be happy about it. Some pointed remark, some pretension to get the upper hand of the others, provokes Verdi's rebellion: 'I am furious, desolated, but you must renounce the position of Sultana. I thank you none the less and press your hands.'

Peace is soon restored: Mme Appiani seeks news of him, asking if he is ill. And Verdi replies: 'I am extremely well, and very soon indeed I am coming to hear the interrupted anecdotes of our common friends.[1] Good morning.' Then it is he who seeks out his lady friend and the cordial atmosphere of her house: 'Are these maccheroni to be eaten or not? I want to Neapolitanize myself at Milan.'

Honi soit qui mal y pense, indeed! How does Gatti know that some of these poor little scraps of paper were penned 'in the small hours of the morning'? How does he know in what order they were written? Or that Verdi was eager for appointments 'far from indiscreet eyes'? Or how the curious remark about 'the position of Sultana' is to be interpreted? The reference to Giuseppina Strepponi is justified, since it is likely enough that she and Verdi had already become, at any rate, good friends. The idea that there was anything between Erminia Frezzolini and Verdi is based entirely on a passage in one of Muzio's letters to Antonio Barezzi, Verdi's father-in-law, from which we learn that Mme Frezzolini's husband Poggi had opened two of the composer's letters and kept them (November 1845). But the formal and reserved terms (quoted by Muzio) in which the lady complains that she has had no reply, and the fact that Verdi told her she should ask her husband for the missing letters, make it fairly clear that Poggi's suspicions were unjustified.

By searching only a little further a fourth, a fifth, even a sixth beauty could have been added to the hypothetical harem. Was he not 'dying of tenderness' for Emilia Morosini in 1842, and at the same time 'in a state of desperation' about her daughter Peppina? And does not Barbiera, the incurable romantic, tell us in his *Passioni del Risorgimento* that 'Giuseppe Verdi, in his youth, palpitated for Gina della Somaglia, and she returned, gratefully, the sweet affection of the great man, singing with passion the popular cavatinas of the hirsute, leonine Maestro'?

At the beginning of December 1843 Verdi sent Mme Appiani the following note:

> Today I am more harassed than yesterday or the day before: tomorrow I leave for Venice. Ours is a troubled life, God knows. I'm in such good health that I'm indignant about it. Before lunch I'll come to salute you. Good morning. Good morning. This fine sunshine annoys me.

[1] Sandrini?

It would seem to have been written in tearing high spirits. But no! It reveals, we are told, 'how sorry he was to leave Milan'. And then he writes to her next time *at one o'clock in the morning*:

Venice, 26th December 1843.
One hour after midnight.[1]

You are impatient to hear news of *I Lombardi* and I send you the very latest: it's not a quarter of an hour since the curtain fell. *I Lombardi* was a grand fiasco: one of those fiascos that are truly classical. Everything was either disapproved or just tolerated, except the cabaletta of the vision. This is the simple truth; I tell it to you without either pleasure or sorrow. I am in a hurry and must leave off, begging you to greet for me Sandrini and all your fine family. Always your most affectionate friend,

G. VERDI.

Verdi often sent such brief reports to his friends immediately after a performance had ended. In this case he wrote at the same time, in almost the same terms, to Luigi Toccagni, sending greetings to the Morosini family.[2] It is therefore absurd to attach significance to the fact that he wrote to Giuseppina Appiani at one o'clock in the morning. I confess I am unable to read as much into these letters as Gatti does.

There is an interesting letter from Donizetti, at Vienna, dated 22nd January 1844. The whole of the first part (written in French) takes the form of an imaginary dialogue:

Here we are. What do you mean: 'Here we are'? Yes, here we are. After such a long silence? It's owing to the long silence that I said: 'Here we are.' Brigand! Very well! Lazy man! Quite true! Ah! But tell me, don't these names annoy you? Not at all, madame, I am disposed to hear them all and to put up with everything from a friend. Not at all, I am your mortal enemy. I don't believe it. Someone told me that, but more politely, that is to say, that you breathe, palpitate only for Verdi, and your own letter betrays you. But I approve your passion; the more you love artists of high talent, the more I shall esteem you. I cannot be offended about it. My turn for sympathy is over; another must take my place. The world wants something fresh; people have given place to us; we must give place to others. I am all the happier to have given place to a man of talent like *Verdi*. Friendship fears the worst, but you can rest assured of the success of this young man. The Venetians will esteem him as the Milanese do, for the heart is the same everywhere. In any case, if his success does not answer the expectations of his friends, that will not prevent the good Verdi from occupying before very long one of the most honourable places in the ranks of composers.

The rest of the letter contains nothing significant. It ends with the usual greeting to the dear girls, 'the painter' and Mr Sandrini. It is

[1] i.e. Actually written on the 27th.
[2] *Carteggi verdiani*, II, pp. 355–6.

evident that Giuseppina had been gravely concerned at Verdi's report on his *Lombardi* fiasco at Venice and had expressed her concern in a letter to Donizetti. She wrote to him again after the production of *Linda* at Milan on 2nd March, and Donizetti replied on 9th March:

> Your mysterious letter gave me the greatest pleasure. You speak of *happiness*, of the *future*, of *philosophical reflections*, etc., and I destroy all that with a word, which if I mistake not will certainly solve the riddle—it's all *false*.
>
> Keep therefore for others your reflections and advice, and you will do something very useful. In proof of this truth, I hope in the summer to confute these things myself and to repeat to you 'It's all false' at the top of my voice, indoors and in the garden.
>
> Thank you for the news you send of *Linda*, and for your remembrance of how and where it came into existence.

To Gatti this is 'biting irony'.[1] Considered, however, in connection with the previous letter, which Gatti does not refer to or quote, it is surely to be read as nothing more than a piece of persiflage. Giuseppina could evidently take a joke, and give as good as she got in return. It seems almost certain that she had hinted that he probably had a love affair on his hands in Vienna. 'It's all false' then makes sense, as it does not in Gatti's interpretation. This passage has nothing to do with Verdi.

March 9th was also the date of the first performance of *Ernani*, and Donizetti assured his friend in the same letter that he hoped and believed that it would have the greatest success. 'You know me,' he wrote, 'and I believe it is not necessary to tell you that my good wishes are sincere.' He praised Verdi everywhere he went and after *Ernani* had triumphed at Venice, he passed from words to deeds, making known through Giacomo Pedroni, a mutual friend, that he was prepared to assist in any way possible to secure the success of the new opera in Vienna as well. Was this perhaps at the suggestion of Giuseppina Appiani? The one surviving letter from Verdi to Donizetti concerns this pleasing incident and rare example of a composer's going out of his way to help a rival.

> Milan, 18th May 1844.
>
> HONOURED MAESTRO,
>
> It was a pleasant surprise for me to read your letter to Pedroni, in which you so kindly offer to help at the rehearsals of my *Ernani*.
>
> I have no hesitation at all in accepting, with the deepest gratitude, your courteous offer, certain that my music can only greatly gain if *Donizetti*

[1] First edition, I, p. 230; second edition, p. 182. Gatti's idea that the mode of address, 'Pregiatissima Amica', employed in this letter, indicates a more ceremonious attitude than the 'Cara Amica',' Cara Donna Peppina' and 'Chère Madame' of earlier ones is hard to maintain in view of its use in the very first letter of all, written just after he had been staying in her house.

deigns to give it his attention. Thus I can hope that the spirit of that work will be fully appreciated.

I beg you to occupy yourself both with the general direction and with such minor adjustments as may be necessary, especially in Ferretti's part.

To you, Sig. Cavaliere, I pay no compliments. You are one of those few men who have sovereign gifts and no need of individual praise. The favour you bestow on me is too great for you to doubt my gratitude.

With profoundest esteem,
Your humble servant,
G. VERDI.

Donizetti never ceased to admire Verdi and to wish him well. His chief object in watching over the production of *Ernani* in Vienna was, undoubtedly, to save the opera from the attentions of Nicolai, then first Kapellmeister at the Kärntnertor theatre. Donizetti distrusted Nicolai, and knew that he hated Verdi. The situation was curious. Verdi had achieved success with a libretto that Nicolai had rejected, and Nicolai had suffered fiasco with an opera, *Il proscritto*, on a libretto originally written for Verdi.[1] It was certainly to Nicolai and not to Donizetti, as Oberdorfer outrageously suggests,[2] that Verdi had referred in the previous year, in a letter to Emilia Morosini of 12th April 1843, on his return from the first production of *Nabucco* in Vienna: 'It was a success, a greater success than I expected after having seen the intrigues of a certain person there.' Donizetti's generous intervention in 1844 was therefore most welcome.

Verdi expected Donizetti to take over the entire direction of *Ernani*, but this was not possible. The following hitherto unknown letter of 24th May 1844,[3] from Donizetti to Giuseppina Appiani, almost wholly concerned with Verdi's opera, makes this clear and shows how he indirectly controlled everything:

DEAR AND AMIABLE LADY,

Rest assured, between M. Pedroni and me there is no single secret that may not be revealed. So no more of that. And I'll begin at once by telling you that there is no news here that would be worth the trouble of narrating in secret or in public!

The theatre languishes owing to the bad arrangements. They lost nineteen days recently in rehearsing *La gazza ladra*, which nevertheless had

[1] Here, from Nicolai's diaries, are his opinions of the *Nabucco* libretto and of Verdi: '*Nabucco*, the new libretto by Temistocle Solera intended for Milan, was utterly impossible to set to music. I had to refuse it, convinced that an unending raging, blood-shedding, reviling, striking and murdering was no subject for me.'

'The Italian opera-composer of today is Verdi. He has set to music the libretto *Nabuccodonosor* which I rejected, and made his fortune with it. But his operas are truly dreadful and utterly degrading for Italy. He scores like a lunatic, is no master from the technical standpoint, must have the heart of a donkey and is truly in my eyes a pitiable, contemptible composer.'

[2] *Giuseppe Verdi* (Milan, 1949), p. 70, where parts of this letter were published for the first time.

[3] In the Masini collection, Biblioteca Communale, Forlì.

only a very moderate success. They are now wholly given over to *Ernani*; within a few days it should be performed (so they say, for you know I don't set foot in the theatre).

The singers are very pleased with it; there has only been (they tell me) one little cut made, of a kind of waltz in the third act, owing to the inadequacy of the brass band here—which Verdi, for the rest, knows very well. As far as singing is concerned, except for a note here and there altered to suit the means of the artists, everything will be performed in the best possible way.

For the rest, Verdi has just written to me; he had already sent a letter to a stage manager. This morning I sent for the musical director, and as he couldn't come, I sent him Verdi's own letter, and I gave orders for it to be shown to the singers, and if they have need of me, they have only to tell me so. But I know from the singers themselves that everything is going very well. I shall keep you informed. Meanwhile tell Verdi that I thank him for the confidence he has in me, and *although invisible in the theatre*, I have means of watching over everything.

Who was it told you I have given up my trip to Italy? I very much hope it will take place. My father arrives on 5th June; then there will be a grand conference.

A thousand greetings to the painter, the architect, the very dear daughters, to yourself, to Mr X.[1] I am well, so I hope—I hope to embrace you soon. Meanwhile, think of him who truly loves you, and don't imagine mysteries where they don't exist.

YOUR LODGER.

Rubini is here. He sings this evening at Metternich's. Perhaps also one or two performances in the theatre! What do you say to that? La Elssler's benefit last night—called out *twenty-three* times; three dances encored; flowers, wreaths and 2,800 florins receipts, besides the season tickets. Last appearance tonight. Afterwards at Pesth. La Taglioni at Paris next month for the last time. Seven appearances.

24th May.

Donizetti was at Milan for a few days at the beginning of August 1844, and for two days in the following November. He probably saw Mme Appiani then for the last time. In December he was back in Vienna; in July 1845 he went to Paris. Shortly after his arrival he fell ill and symptoms of mental alienation before long became apparent. He grew worse, and in February 1846 had to be put into an asylum.

Meanwhile Verdi wrote occasionally to Giuseppina Appiani from Busseto, Bergamo, Naples and Venice.

Gatti tells us: 'Mme Appiani writes to him, calling him "dearest" and employing affectionate expressions, though reproving him for leaving her without news, and she sends him, as she had already done for Donizetti (now incurably ill), a little intimate gift—a pair of

[1] Illegible. It looks like a capital letter from an unknown alphabet. Undoubtedly Mr. Sandrini is meant.

braces.' This is deduced from Verdi's letter from Venice of 22nd December 1845, which includes a reference to Donizetti:

No, I'm not 'dearest' at all. I don't pretend to it. I pretend to many things, but not to amiability or beauty. No, no, certainly not: I am nothing more or less than a blundering sort of person, and yet at bottom I'm not so bad, and I think much of you and yours, although you, without really believing it, wish to reprove me for the contrary. I am extremely busy finishing *Attila*, because I should like to put it on about 28th January; I have also had to write a cavatina for la Loewe, which is her own property and which she will use for her entry in *Giovanna d'Arco*. I have not taken, nor am I taking, the rehearsals of this opera, which I yet love very much, but I should not have been able to stand up to the work and it would have been so many hours lost to *Attila*. I am very pleased with the latter and unless the devil brings us bad luck it should turn out very well. I have not received the braces. I hope I shall receive a long letter after Boxing Day, and I will write you one telling of the outcome of *Giovanna*, although I'm not going to hear it. Tell me about Pedroni and Madame Perey. If you can give me news of the *sick man* you will give me the best of presents: others would not believe me sincere, but you will. If I don't love Art for myself I am interested in it for *his* sake and for the sake of the prestige it brings our country. . . . Believe me the most affectionate of your most affectionate dear ones.

The last sentence rather more than counterbalances the first. In the second edition of his Verdi biography Gatti adds the following commentary [1] on the latter part of this letter:

The 'sick man' is Donizetti, irreparably broken in health, and the reference to Donizetti's art, the subject of this part of the letter, an art that he 'does not love', although this affirmation is in marked contrast to the praise that follows, may seem a not very persuasive justification of the tenacious spite manifested by Verdi for his predecessor in the favours of Mme Appiani.

This is positively perverse. Nothing can justify the interpretation of the general expression 'l'arte' (meaning, probably, the whole world of the theatre which had already become abhorrent to him) as a particular reference to *Donizetti*'s art. There is not the slightest trace of envy or spite in Verdi's relations with Donizetti.

Other letters followed from London and Paris in 1847 and 1848. One written on 22nd August 1847, gives an account of Donizetti's condition. Verdi had not been to see him in the asylum, having been advised not to do so, but he intended, if the opportunity presented itself, to pay a secret visit. He had been told that the sick man appeared well physically, except that his head was constantly bent forward on his chest and his eyes closed. He was eating and sleeping well, but hardly ever spoke a word. If he were more animated, even

[1] Second edition, p. 208.

raging, the doctors said, there would be more hope. As things were, only a miracle could save him. 'It's desolating; it's too desolating.'

Within a year Donizetti was dead.

After an interval of six years we have two letters from Verdi to Giuseppina Appiani from 1854. He was then in Paris. The first of these letters is that, mentioned above, in which he gives, for the benefit of Giuseppina's daughter Eugenia, his opinion of a play apparently based on Lamartine's *Graziella*; the second, dated 21st October, represents in all probability the end of this correspondence and of a friendship of some eleven or twelve years' standing:

Your letter reached Peppina by chance, by pure chance. As the address you chose to affix is unknown to the door of this house, that gracious letter ran the risk of getting lost if, I repeat, pure chance had not led me to meet the postman who, seeing a name ending in 'i', asked me about it. I took it and carried it to its destination. Peppina told me that, having renounced arts and letters, and not keeping up any correspondence except with her family and a few very intimate friends, she would be grateful if I would make her excuses and reply to a letter so *spirituelle*. And here I am, I who cannot write like you or like Peppina, in the greatest embarrassment about how to reply to a letter so well written, so fine and, I myself repeat, so *spirituelle*. But I, with my rough style, can make no parade of wit or spirit, so I will just say briefly that we are in a great hurry to pack our bags, that la Cruvelli's flight from the Opéra has obliged me to ask to be released from the contract and that I shall go straight to Busseto but shall only stay there a few days. Where shall I go then? I couldn't say! Now that you have all my news I press your hands.

One of the results of Verdi's cohabitation with Giuseppina Strepponi, for eleven years before they were actually married, was that he was cut off almost completely from the circle of his former friends at Milan. For twenty years after the rising of 1848 he never set foot in that city. With some of his Milanese friends he continued to correspond, and we find him on 9th May 1852 writing to the Countess Maffei, asking her to convey his good wishes to that Gina della Somaglia about whom, in a passage already quoted, Barbiera suspects the worst. I say 'suspects the worst' because she, too, was a married woman with a family at the time, as is seen from the fact that one of her daughters married in 1852.[1] 'In other days', Verdi told the Countess Maffei, 'she would herself have given me the news, but now this friendly relationship too, is over, and it is not her fault. It is all my fault, or rather, the fault of destiny, which strangely contrives to deprive me, one by one, of all the things that give me pleasure.'

How are we to interpret Verdi's last letter to Giuseppina Appiani?

[1] See also Abbiati, vol. i, p. 606, a passage in flagrant contradiction to another in his vol. ii, p. 284.

It seems that she had written to Giuseppina Strepponi, using her maiden name which, after all, was the only one to which she was so far entitled. It is difficult to know what to do in such cases; a letter addressed to 'Giuseppina Verdi' might have been equally offensive in her eyes, or his. It is clear that Verdi's companion had no desire to enter into correspondence under any name whatsoever; he himself, with obvious embarrassment, conveys this to his old friend. Gatti finds the letter 'mordent'. Clinging still to his romantic hypothesis, he believes that Mme Appiani 'sought to insinuate herself' between Giuseppina Strepponi and Verdi, and addressed her letters 'with offensive ostentation', until Verdi cut her short. It is hard to credit this. Verdi's life had been linked with Giuseppina Strepponi's for six years already at this time. He cannot possibly have seen Mme Appiani for six and a half years and probably not for longer. She herself was now getting on for sixty years of age. Gatti's conclusion is that with the end of this friendship

> the shade of Donizetti, dear both to Mme Appiani and to Giuseppina Strepponi, rose again beyond the tomb, deriding not the latter, but the former, who had been so complaisant of her beauty, and whose fascination had been so powerful.[1]

Donizetti's shade may still be laughing—but not, I suggest, at his good friend Giuseppina Appiani, nor at the noble woman who became the second wife of the composer whose genius he had so early recognized and unselfishly praised, but at the biographers who have made so much of a handful of letters, some embroidered slippers and a pair of braces that apparently got lost in the post.

The whole story is repeated by Abbiati, with his customary fictional embellishments.

The toils of the researcher have their compensations. One such came to me when I found, at Forlì, Donizetti's letter of 24th May 1844, about Verdi and *Ernani* in Vienna; being signed 'Your Lodger' it had not even been recognized as a Donizetti autograph. Another rewarding moment came when, in the same year, I was copying Giuseppina Strepponi's letters to Florimo, in the Naples Conservatorio. Bound up with them was a letter signed 'Peppina Appiani'. On 18th May 1837 she was in Rome, on her way to Naples to hand over to Florimo some souvenirs of Bellini. There was cholera at Naples and she wrote asking for advice and enclosing a letter of introduction that she had brought with her from Milan. This letter is also preserved in this volume of autograph letters; it is from

[1] First edition, II, p. 150; second edition, p. 492. A groundless rumour that Giuseppina Strepponi was once Donizetti's mistress is recorded by Donati-Petteni.

The careless inaccuracy of reputable Italian writers is almost incredible. Antonio Monti, in his *Milano Romantica, 1814–1848* (Milan 1946), p. 283, declares that Donizetti was in love with *Clara Maffei*, and jealous of Verdi on that account!

Giuditta Turina, Bellini's famous mistress, and with it are twenty-one other letters from Giuditta to Florimo.[1] But we are here concerned with Giuseppina Appiani. She asked about the cholera, quarantine regulations and hotels, and went on:

> Be frank and sincere: what sort of opinion have you formed of me, who without knowing you personally am writing to you with such familiarity and abandon? Don't be severe; I know you and feel affection for you. Are you not the bosom friend of the unfortunate Bellini, over whose loss we are shedding warm tears still?
>
> I had the good fortune to have that illustrious man in my house for well over a year; I had the good fortune to look after him with the utmost affection, and at a time when he was ill it was in my house that the divine music of *La Sonnambula* was born. Ah! my dear Florimo, how could we not be friends, we who share such dear and painful memories? I have here two walking-sticks and a cushion that belonged to that beloved friend; I guard them jealously; I will not consign them to anyone else; from my hands they must pass into yours. Oh, how many things we shall have to tell each other when we meet!

Here at last we hear Giuseppina Appiani's own voice. And we find that Barbiera was right when he said that Bellini had 'composed suave melodies' while her guest in Via Monforte. *La Sonnambula* was written there, eleven years before Donizetti's *Linda di Chamounix*. The nature of her relations with Bellini, when a good deal younger than she was at the time of her friendship with Donizetti and Verdi, supports the view put forward in this chapter that she was not at all the flirtatious 'Merry Widow' of the Italian biographers and journalists. The fact that Giuditta Turina herself provided her with a letter of introduction to Florimo shows conclusively that she had had no reason to be jealous. The composers who lived in Giuseppina's house were not necessarily her lovers. A truer picture is beginning to emerge. She seems to have been a music-loving lady of society, kind-hearted, hospitable and generous, with a little weakness, perhaps, for entertaining in her house the most famous composers of the day.

[1] See 'Giuditta Turina and Bellini' (*Music & Letters*, Jan. 1959).

CHAPTER

4

Muzio's Verdi: Milan before the Revolution

TWELVE YEARS after Antonio Barezzi had sent the young Verdi to Milan to complete his studies he assisted in the same way another local musical prodigy. Emanuele Muzio,[1] the red-headed son of a poor cobbler, was born at Zibello, in the Duchy of Parma, on 24th August 1821. The family moved to Busseto in 1826 and at ten years of age Emanuele entered the municipal school of music, during the period when Verdi was acting as Provesi's assistant. But Muzio at first intended to become a priest and after Provesi's death he studied music, not under Verdi, but under Verdi's rival, Giovanni Ferrari, the organist of the collegiate church of San Bartolomeo. When Ferrari left Busseto, apparently in 1840, Muzio succeeded him as provisional organist, though with only half Ferrari's salary. In 1842 the Monte di Pietà e d'Abbondanza refused Muzio a monetary grant to enable him to study at the ecclesiastical seminary of Borgo San Donnino and he abandoned all idea of becoming a priest. He seems, like Verdi himself, to have come into collision with the Provost, Don Ballarini.

The ever helpful Barezzi then took up Muzio's case and in December 1843 the Monte di Pietà decided to give him a pension for four years so that he could study music at Milan. The conditions were that he should, within fourteen days of leaving Busseto, inform the administrators of the Monte di Pietà whether he had been accepted as a pupil of the Milan Conservatorio, and, if not accepted, under which

[1] He signs himself 'Mussio' in his early letters and is so named in documents in the archives of the Monte di Pietà. This is a phonetic rendering of the local dialect pronunciation, with its soft *z* sound.

teacher he was studying privately; every two months his teacher was to report on his progress, and if he failed to make progress he would lose his pension.

So Muzio, like Verdi, came to Milan with the help of the Monte di Pietà and of Antonio Barezzi, and like Verdi he failed to obtain admission to the Conservatorio. Shortly afterwards, to his own amazement and delight, he found himself Verdi's pupil. Barezzi noted down in his *Libro di Casa* on 10th April 1844, 'a most beautiful sunny day', that he had handed Emanuele Muzio a loan in cash of 180 Milanese lire and 80 centesimi, and on 13th April, 'a day of light rain, followed by sunshine', that Verdi and Muzio left together for Piacenza, on their way to Milan. On a loose leaf he recorded:

> Emanuele Muzio commenced his musical studies at Milan under the direction of Maestro Giuseppe Verdi on 15th April 1844, according to a certificate of the aforesaid Maestro consigned to the administrators of the Monte di Pietà at Busseto.

In a long series of letters which Muzio, while studying with Verdi in the years 1844–7, wrote to their common benefactor at Busseto he reveals himself as a backward, ill-educated, naïve, but lovable and loyal youth. His teacher became and remained almost his god. In these letters [1] we have, against the background of Milanese life before 1848, a superb portrait of Verdi in his shirt-sleeves.

22nd April:

For some days now Signor Maestro Verdi has been giving me lessons in counterpoint, for no one can go to the Conservatorio, either from the Milanese province or from abroad, and if in time I shall be able to go there, it will be a special concession that the Viceroy and the Governor of Milan will make for Signor Maestro Verdi; furthermore he is going to be so kind as to write me the certificate, which I shall send to you at once as soon as I get it; many music students would pay two or three thalers a lesson if Signor Maestro Verdi would give them, but he gives them to nobody, save a poor devil to whom he has shown a thousand favours, and finally that of giving him lessons, not just two or three times a week, but every morning. I am stunned; and, what is more, sometimes when he has me do something for him he gives me my lunch as well. He, my Signor Maestro, has a grandeur of mind, a generosity, a knowledge, a heart, such that to find a good parallel one would have to set beside it your own, and say that they are the most generous hearts in all the world.

20th May:

Signor Seletti is beginning to get over his illness, and he asked me to send you his regards; when I came to Milan he was rather unwell and asked me to go to see Carrara. I told that to the Signor Maestro, and he said:

[1] *Giuseppe Verdi nelle lettere di Emanuele Muzio ad Antonio Barezzi*, edited by Luigi Agostino Garibaldi (Milan, 1931).

'No.' We went then together with the Signor Maestro to find a room, a piano, etc., for me. What kindness!

I hope that you are in the best of health; I myself sometimes get the headache. The Signor Maestro says it's the study of counterpoint, for sometimes one has to rack one's brains for an hour over a single bar; today I have a most difficult bass—the Signor Maestro said so himself and when *he* says that, you may be sure that it really *is* difficult. I only have four more to do, then I shall start on Corelli.

29th May:

I have finished Fenaroli's books on harmony. Now I am revising. The Signor Maestro says to me when I begin the lesson: 'Remember that I am *inexorable*.' Imagine how frightened I am; but little by little this disappears when he says: 'Well done'; but believe me, he doesn't pass a note—he wants everything perfect. He won't have two hidden consecutive fifths or octaves (open ones are, of course, excommunicated); he wants all the parts like a scale, without ever a jump; they must never rise all together in similar motion; and all the parts, in whatever clef they are written, must never go above this note:

The conditions are few, but the difficulty is in putting them into execution. . . . Now I am on another subject, having finished also with melodies based on the scale; and instead I am adding eight parts, all consonant, under a single note of the scale; then one note against one, two against one, etc.; this is real counterpoint; the notes being so many points put one against the other; and from this has come the word 'Counterpoint', that is, one point against the other, or note against note. (This was yesterday's explanation.) Up to now I have studied harmony and I assure you that if I had been under another teacher, apart from the fact that he would not have taught me so well, so perfectly, I should have needed almost a year, certainly, for Corbellini (I tell you this in confidence), in the six months that he has been studying, has not got half as far as I have got in the same subject in such a short time. Something depends, too, on the pupil's will to study, but it is also certain that the teacher has great influence, for those mercenary teachers never teach with the love and zeal of Signor Maestro Verdi; for when I wrote even more basses than he had told me to do, he was glad, and said I should write as many as I liked, as long as they were well done; and then the other teachers don't give such fine, minute explanations as the Signor Maestro Verdi; and in this way a pupil also comes to take a passionate interest.

I can say truly that I was born lucky: first to have found an incomparable Maecenas who supports me, secondly to have a teacher so celebrated and of European fame like Signor Maestro Verdi, who is the idol of the Milanese. . . . But when I think that in the coming summer he will go away to write the opera, very great melancholy overcomes me. . . . He's so kind to me that sometimes I can't keep back my tears; for sometimes, to finish the lesson, he lets people, no matter who it is, wait half an hour in the antechamber.

Now I go to school at eleven o'clock, because now he gets up early to write *I due Foscari*. The introductory chorus, which is the congress of the Council of Ten, is magnificent and terrible, and in the music one feels the mystery that reigned in those terrible gatherings which decided life and death; and then imagine whether the *Father of the Chorus*, as the Milanese call him, has set it to music well!!

At Milan they talk only of the Signor Maestro's *Ernani* and everybody longs for August, to hear it. The Grand Duchess of Tuscany has arrived at Milan, and the gentleman who accompanied her has expressed the desire to meet the Signor Maestro in person, as he only knew him by reputation, and I believe that he has been presented to the Grand Duchess. He says that for him such things are silly trifles.

11th June (after the production of *Ernani* in Vienna):

If you, Signore, had been in the Signor Maestro Verdi's house when the news of the great success arrived, to see coming there, for quite an hour, first one to whom Donizetti had written, then another who had received the news from a count—I don't remember his name—then another who had a letter from Merelli, and so many others that they went on for ever, and to hear the fine things that they wrote about the Signor Maestro and his *Ernani*, you would have wept certainly, for you are very sensitive; and then to see them all sitting there, first one reading his letter and then another, and with these papers in their hands they looked like so many boys at school reciting their lessons, and the Signor Maestro there in the middle, at his table, looked like the teacher, and I in a corner, staring my eyes out, was like the school beadle. It was delightful.

Ernani is in preparation at Florence and Genoa; but the Signor Maestro is not satisfied with Derivis, who will sing it at Genoa, because he lacks grace; yesterday the Signor Maestro said: 'How can he sing the delicate "Vieni meco sol di rose" with that great ugly voice of his?' Everyone says he is right. You too will be of this opinion, for you have heard Derivis. But that doesn't matter to the impresarios; as long as they can attract the public, they don't bother about anything else.

Two days ago I began the Corelli kindly given me by Signor Ricordi; I am transcribing it and studying it at the same time; it's stuff that is hard to digest, this Corelli, but already I almost understand his system, very different from the other contrapuntists, but beautiful and highly scientific.

24th June:

Often, with the Signor Maestro, we talk about you and with a certain enthusiasm we recall your good deeds; I said that you deserve to live as long as the Patriarchs; 'Longer', added the Signor Maestro, 'but with faculties preserved as in youthful years.' A most beautiful reflection! And the Signor Maestro is right, and you deserve it, for in the kindness of your heart, and with courage and vigour, you defended and gave new life to a poor devil they wanted to oppress and bring to naught. . . .

On Saturday there came a singer who wanted the Signor Maestro to write a contralto part for her in the opera he is composing for Rome. He said the libretto was already finished and he couldn't. 'That doesn't matter,' said this lady. 'Just one scene, an entry, a cabaletta . . . ' It was funny, he could not dissuade her from her purpose; afterwards she wanted him to promise at least to write a part for her in the opera for Carnival. The Signor Maestro lost patience and said: 'No, no,' and so she went away.

He is tormented by everybody; he says he won't receive anybody else, but he is so good he will never carry this out.

A composer, I don't remember his name, has written a letter to the Signor Maestro, in which he begs and prays him not to set to music *I due Foscari*, because he too has set it to music, and he fears that there will happen to his opera what happened to Mazzucato's *Ernani*; the Signor Maestro has replied that he is already engaged on the work and cannot comply with this ardent request. . . .[1]

I have got as far as the famous Opera Quinta of Corelli, the most beautiful, lengthy and difficult. This morning I began the imitations. The Signor Maestro uses the same exercises that he did under Lavigna's direction, only improved by himself. He guides me with his lamp, and illuminates the path I have undertaken. The lesson doesn't last more than a quarter of an hour—I leave you to imagine the reason. But my purse is light, and I have reckoned up and I have enough money to last until the middle of July, but on the 15th of that month I have to pay the rent for the room and the piano, and I shall have no money. Please come to my assistance; the Signor Maestro says to me: 'When you need money you must tell me quite openly,' but I haven't the courage, because he does too much already in teaching me so well, and so willingly. This morning he asked me. 'How do you think you are getting on, since you've been studying with me?' I told him: 'I have been born again.'

30th June:

Guess to how many theatres Ricordi has already sent the score of *Ernani*—to more than twenty! You will have received that article from Rome; at the bottom of that cutting I told you that the Signor Maestro is sending the music publishers mad. It *is* so. The publisher Lucca is at the moment the maddest of the lot, because he can't have an opera by the Signor Maestro, while he sees Ricordi making enormous profits from them, for just by the copies of the score of *Ernani* (not counting the innumerable arrangements) he has already made more than 30,000 Austrian lire; and if the Signor Maestro will promise Lucca one of his scores he will recover; for the rest I don't believe he will. The wife of the said publisher came to the Signor Maestro's house and wept and entreated him to give her the rights in one of his operas, and as for the price she will give him whatever he asks. He doesn't want to give her any of them. This lady said that even when they are in bed they only sigh; the Signor Maestro

[1] The composer was Francesco Cannetti. Verdi's reply was published in *La Vedetta Fascista* (Padua) for 30th March 1930, and in *Rivista musicale italiana* for April–June 1930, p. 323.

> asked her if they did nothing else but sigh when they're in bed, and in this way he makes a joke of the whole thing and gets rid of her.
>
> The reason why the lessons are so short is that the Signor Maestro sees at a glance if there are mistakes in my exercise; if it's not right he indicates where I must correct it; I correct it and he gives another glance, and that suffices. Then a few words on tomorrow's lesson, five minutes playing—that's the lesson. Does that seem little to you? Nevertheless, with these quarters of an hour I have reached a stage I should certainly not have reached with anybody else. Everything has turned out for the best.

These letters, 'a monument of ingenuousness, of mediocrity and devotion', as they have been called, are immensely valuable, in particular as a corrective to the idea of Verdi given by his business correspondence, which happens to have survived in greater measure than his private correspondence from these years. Much has been written about Verdi's peasant shrewdness, his business sense, that enabled him to hold his own in the shady world of operatic impresarios and music publishers, where so many earlier composers had been victimized. He was more than a match for the toughest of them. He needed that relentless, adamantine quality, if he was to make his way in this environment. But the picture of Verdi that presents itself to the mind's eye after perusal of his business correspondence has a hard outline. Muzio's letters soften the portrait, and give it light and shade. Here too we see him—severe and implacable in his dealings with singers, impresarios and publishers; and then—kindly in his gruff way, large-hearted, generous and charitable. These are what he used to call his 'anni di galera'—his years in the galleys—but we find that he sometimes relaxed and smiled, and even laughed aloud on more than one occasion.

The firm of Lucca, mentioned in the last-quoted letter, was particularly unfortunate in its dealings with Verdi. Francesco Lucca, born at Cremona in 1802, worked for some years as a music-engraver in Ricordi's workshops before in 1825 he founded his own publishing house. He was short, fattish and, under his brown wig, bald. His wife Giovannina, *née* Strazza, who, as Muzio reported, came to the Signor Maestro's house and wept, was an enormous and most formidable woman. She was the real head of the firm, who carried out all the most important and difficult business for her husband. Born at Fontanella, near Cernobbio, in 1814, possessed of a commercial intelligence of the first order, she brought the house of Lucca into rivalry with that of Ricordi, until, long after her husband's death, at the age of seventy-four she sold out to her rivals for the sum of a million and a half lire. But at this time she was far from thinking of dying or selling out. The two firms came into conflict almost at the very beginning of Verdi's career. The rights in *Nabucco* were held in equal parts by Verdi and by Merelli, under the terms of their agreement. On 13th March 1842 Verdi sold *his* half to Lucca. But the other half, and the rights in Solera's libretto, were bought from Merelli by Ricordi. Lucca brought an unsuccessful action against Ricordi, claiming half rights in the libretto. His petition was filed on 5th October, and came before the Mercantile Tribunal at Milan on 17th November 1842.[1] The fact that this action was pending probably explains the extremely acrimonious tone of two little-known notes from Verdi to Lucca, from September and October of this year, which are referred to and quoted by Giuseppe Lisio in *Su l'epistolario di Casa Lucca*, in the *Rendiconti* of the Reale Istituto Lombardo di Scienze e Lettere, Serie II, vol. xli (Milan, 1907):

> In the first he *invites* Signor Lucca to send him *immediately* the sum of 1,500 Austrian lire, which he was promised in the presence of *a certain person*, and adds: 'If you are hoping I shall pass this over in silence, let me warn you that it is more likely that Milan will fall in ruins.' In the second note, which is on the same subject, the form is less rude but the content no different: 'Let Signor Lucca reflect that he must make the payment *in my house*; so without further vexation kindly send me' . . . etc.

The *Strenna teatrale europea* for 1843 refers to the unfortunate litigation between Lucca and Ricordi, which was hampering and delaying the reproduction of *Nabucco* from end to end of the Italian peninsula, and this restriction of the circulation of his first big success, through the action of a grasping publisher, was something Verdi did not find it easy to forget. So Giovannina, in June 1844, got no change, in spite of her tears and entreaties. By a change of tactics, the Luccas were later to acquire three of Verdi's operas—*Attila*, which they bought, a year before it was written, from the Florentine impresario Lanari who had commissioned it, and *Alzira* and *Il Corsaro*, two poor works on which they assuredly lost money. They published also a volume of six *Romanze* in 1845 and another isolated song, 'Il Poveretto', in 1847.

It seems that not all Muzio's letters to Antonio Barezzi have been preserved: after the end of June 1844 there is a gap of several months in the published correspondence, only partially explained by the fact that Muzio and Verdi did not spend the summer months together at Milan. The letters from the following autumn and winter are perhaps a little less naïve, but it is still hard to realize that Muzio was now twenty-four, and Verdi less than seven years his senior.

In October and early November Verdi was in Rome for the first performance of *I due Foscari* at the Argentina theatre. He and the librettist, Francesco Maria Piave, sent a joint report to a Milanese friend, Luigi Toccagni:[2]

[1] Enrico Rosmini, *Legislazione e Giurisprudenza sui Diritti d'Autore* (Milan, 1890).
[2] Original in the Memorial Library, Stanford University, U.S.A.

*E

Rome, 4th November 1844.

Dear Toccagni,

If *I due Foscari* was not a complete failure, it *almost* was—whether because the singers were very much out of tune, or because expectations were raised too high, etc., the fact is that the opera was a *mezzo-fiasco.* I had a great liking for this opera: perhaps I deceived myself, but before changing my mind I want another opinion. I shall leave for Milan on Thursday the 7th and shall be there on the 12th.

Farewell,

Yours,

G. Verdi.

(Postscript by Piave):

The very expectations of the audience caused them to be rather cool, and this was then increased by the out-of-tune singing, etc., etc. Verdi, however, was called quite twelve times to the stage, but that which would be for others a triumph is nothing to him. The music of *I due Foscari* is divine and I do not doubt that this evening, tomorrow and subsequently it will be appreciated more and more. If you happen to speak of my book, remember your old promise. Farewell, dear Toccagni; it seems to be destined that I should make you aware of my existence, as when I first met you, at the moment when I am about to separate from our dearest Verdi. Retain your friendship for me and believe me

Yours sincerely,

F. M. Piave.

Muzio described on 16th November how he had travelled from Busseto to Milan by bad roads and arrived an hour before Verdi, who was himself tired out after the long journey from Rome by diligence:

The Signor Maestro is well; but when he first arrived he had all his bones broken—he was helpless with fatigue. His friends were there waiting for him at the coaching station—Maffei, Toccagni, Pasetti, Ricordi, Pedroni, etc. The day after they all came to lunch with the Signor Maestro and drank his health in Bordeaux and champagne.

Muzio was left at home when Verdi went to pay his social calls; he can tell us nothing of the composer's relations with Giuseppina Appiani, Emilia Morosini and her family, with Gina della Somaglia or with Giuseppina Strepponi. But he came to know Verdi's male friends of this period, the chief of whom are mentioned in the letter quoted above. The publisher Giovanni Ricordi (1785–1853) needs no introduction: it may have been either he or his eldest son Tito who awaited the arrival of the diligence bringing Verdi back from Rome. Luigi Toccagni (1788–1853) was another friend of an earlier generation. He had compiled an Italian dictionary, written a libretto, *Marco Visconti*, for Vaccai, translated a book on Pope Innocent III from the

German, and Chateaubriand's *Atala* and *Génie du christianisme* from the French, and was an influential journalist, a contributor to the *Gazzetta Privilegiata di Milano*. Particularly intimate with the Morosini family, he had introduced Verdi to them and to other members of the Milanese aristocracy. Giacomo Pedroni was the friend through whom Donizetti, earlier in this year, had offered to watch over the performances of *Ernani* in Vienna. Pasetti was an engineer, who had helped Verdi, to some extent, in his relations with Merelli. He is referred to, as 'Pascetti', in a later letter to Arrivabene, as 'a good man, of timid, weak character. His foible was to give out promises and protection to right and left, under the illusion of having done great things, when he had, at best, only the merit of good intentions.' [1] The poet and translator Andrea Maffei (1798–1885) was a little later to write for Verdi the libretto of *I Masnadieri*, after Schiller's *Die Räuber*. When he and the Countess Clara [2] decided on a legal separation in 1846, Verdi was asked to be a witness to the deed. He remained on very friendly terms with both parties after the separation. The countess received many of the best letters Verdi ever wrote in the course of their long acquaintance; there are fewer letters to Andrea, though probably many more were written than have survived. A letter from Maffei to his wife, though it comes from a later period, is worth quoting here:

> To increase my ill humour, there arrived Verdi's reply. He refuses, saying that he is incapable of setting to music poems of anacreontic type. He forgets that he has already set to music stupendously the drinking-songs in *Macbeth* and *I Masnadieri*, and that which I wrote at his request: 'Mescetemi il vino!' Happy he, who has an adamantine temper and can reject everything that doesn't just suit him, even at the request of an old friend! My own nature, on the other hand, is so compliant that if he had asked me to write on his old boots I should not have refused.

That is more revealing, of both men, than any of their own surviving correspondence. We see again the hard side of Verdi's nature, but at the same time the adoring devotion he inspired in those who knew him.

Other friends of this Milanese period were Giulio Carcano (1812–1884), the translator of Shakespeare, and Francesco Regli, editor of the theatrical paper *Il Pirata*. When Regli, for *Il Pirata*, or Toccagni, for the *Gazzetta Privilegiata di Milano*, needed information about Verdi's affairs they would often come to Muzio for it. They knew him for the composer's pupil and amanuensis, errand-boy and disciple; sitting together in Verdi's rooms, they would notice how, if anything needed to be done, he would just go to the window and give

[1] Letter of 31st March 1863.

[2] Clara Maffei was born Countess Spinelli-Carrara and, unlike Giuseppina Appiani, who was similarly situated, retained the use of her title after her marriage to a commoner.

a whistle, and the red-headed, uncouth but lovable youth, who often changed his lodgings but was never far distant from the Signor Maestro, would come running to see what was wanted. To help Muzio, to give him an opportunity to earn a little money, was to keep on the right side of Verdi.

Muzio's musical tastes were formed by the town band of Busseto. He went into ecstasies over the worst features of Verdi's most mediocre operas. *Giovanna d'Arco* followed hard on the heels of *I due Foscari*, and in December Muzio was declaring that if Joan of Arc had not immortalized herself by her deeds, Verdi's music would have done so for her:

9th December:

No Giovanna has ever had music more philosophical and beautiful. The terrible introduction (an inspiration that came to him, as you know, amidst the rocky precipices [1]) and the magnificent piece 'Maledetti cui spinse rea voglia' are two things to amaze every poor mortal. The demons' choruses are original, popular, truly Italian; the first ('Tu sei bella') is a most graceful waltz, full of seductive motives, that after two hearings can be sung straight away; the second ('Vittoria, vittoria, s'applauda a Satana') is music of diabolical exaltation, music that makes one shudder and tremble; in short they are divine things; in that opera there will be all kinds of music: dramatic, religious, martial, etc. Everything I have heard pleases me enormously.

22nd December:

This morning the Signor Maestro wrote the march for *Giovanna*. How beautiful it is!

29th December:

Yesterday I heard the great duet between Giovanna and Carlo, when they fall in love; this is the grandest and most magnificent piece in the opera; I have heard the finale of the third act, where there is one of the most beautiful melodies that have ever been heard.

6th January:

What marvels! You should hear how the duet between Giovanna and Carlo, when they fall in love, is conceived; the Angels' terrible words 'Guai se terreno affetto accoglierai nel petto' make one tremble, and poor Giovanna, who alone hears them, breaks into song that is all desperation for her lost virtue. Then in the cabaletta from time to time one hears the demons singing 'Vittoria, vittoria', and here Giovanna's song becomes continually louder and more agitated; then at the great final cadenza there burst out the infernal choirs, with brass band and orchestra, singing 'Vittoria, vittoria', etc.; the whole chorus can be compared with the sublime ones of Meyerbeer's *Robert le Diable*. There are so many beautiful

[1] In the passes of the Apennines, on the way back from Rome.

things that one would need a whole day to describe them. Carlo's romance; the coronation Te Deum; then when Tebaldo accuses his daughter; etc.—they are all gems.

Giovanna d'Arco was preceded at La Scala by a revival of *I Lombardi*, and Muzio provides a vivid sketch of Verdi at the rehearsals of the latter opera:

I go to the rehearsals with the Signor Maestro and it makes me sorry to see him tiring himself out; he shouts as if in desperation; he stamps his feet so much that he seems to be playing an organ with pedals; he sweats so much that drops fall on the score. . . . At his glance, at a sign from him, the singers, chorus and orchestra seem to be touched by an electric spark.

In his own studies Muzio was now passing from works of Corelli and Tartini to those of Vallotti, 'the most metaphysical and transcendental harmonist known', and copying scores by Mattei and Padre Martini. He was also trying his hand at composition, producing marches which were sent to Barezzi at Busseto, with full instructions for their performance. From one of Verdi's later remarks it appears that he had no faith in Muzio's future as a composer; but he held that he was good enough for Busseto. There the situation of ten years earlier was strangely renewing itself. When Muzio had left for Milan the provost had chosen one Enrico Landi to succeed him as organist of the collegiate church. Once installed as organist Landi, naturally enough, tried to secure also the post of municipal music master, but the Monte di Pietà insisted that this position should be held open until such time as their own candidate, Muzio, should have completed his studies with Verdi at Milan. The *maestro di musica* would then be chosen by competitive examination. Landi had also managed to win over part of the Philharmonic Society, and when renewed appeals for the lifting of the ban on instrumental music in the churches of Busseto reached the Presidente dell'Interno at Parma, he assured the Bishop of Borgo San Donnino that the old hostilities were over and that 'the greater part of the Philharmonic members' followed the lead of the organist Landi, 'under whose able direction they are already practising, and appear often in perfect accord at the municipal theatre.[1] But the then bishop, Monsignore Pier Grisologo Basetti, feared further disorders and the ban remained in force. Where Busseto had formerly been divided between the supporters of the organist Ferrari and of the absent Verdi, it was now divided between the supporters of the organist Landi and of the absent Muzio, with the further complication that the Philharmonic members were divided among themselves. When Barezzi tried to get Muzio's early compositions performed by the Philharmonic Society he met with opposition from the 'Landisti'. But the marches had Verdi's approval:

[1] Giovanni Drei, 'Notizie e documenti verdiani'.

He says that if he had not considered them good he would not have allowed me to send them. . . . The Signor Maestro has now himself played them and replayed them, and says they are good; for the rest, when they have understood the *tempi* you will see that they will please. These lines are being written under the eye of the Signor Maestro, who after reading them approves what I have said.

A little later:

If the *Landisti* don't like my marches it doesn't matter. It suffices that the Signor Maestro liked them and said they are beautiful. . . . The Signor Maestro, on reading the paragraph in your letter about the marches, laughed a lot and said: 'These Landisti think they know better than I do! *Bravi! Bravissimi!* What asses! What asses!'

These occasional quotations of Verdi's actual words, in Muzio's letters, are extraordinarily revealing. He does not say much, but the voice is unmistakable. Thus, when an expected letter from Busseto had not arrived: 'What the devil are they doing, that they don't write? Are they all dead?'

Giovanna d'Arco at La Scala on 15th February 1845 was the last opera Verdi was to write for that theatre for more than twenty-five years. He was thoroughly disgusted with the way Merelli was producing his works there, and decided to have no more to do with him. The protagonists in *Giovanna d'Arco* included Erminia Frezzolini and her husband Antonio Poggi, the tenor; Muzio depicts la Frezzolini weeping because her voice was not what it once was, and Poggi being hissed. When the Countess Samoyloff told Poggi that the Milanese did not like him, he wished to break his agreement with Merelli, but Verdi managed to persuade him to stay. *Giovanna d'Arco* was a popular success and soon the barrel-organs were playing the waltz chorus of the demons: 'Tu sei bella.' A sensation was caused later by the appearance of a monstrous barrel-organ, the largest ever seen at Milan, which played, not just a few of the more obvious tunes, but, so Muzio reported, almost the whole opera. It drew such crowds that all traffic was dislocated and the police had to ban its appearance in the streets in the evening.

The names of Emilia Frezzolini, Poggi and the Countess Samoyloff recur in these letters. These figures, too, move across the background of Verdi's life at Milan before the revolution. Erminia Frezzolini, born at Orvieto in 1818, made her *début* in 1838 and soon became known as one of the most brilliant rising stars of that time. Her father, the *buffo* bass Giuseppe Frezzolini, did his utmost to exploit her success for his own benefit; after she came of age in 1839 he made her sign away the whole of her earnings until February 1841 and agree to pay him 3,000 francs a year for the rest of his life.[1] He managed to

[1] A. de Angelis, 'Cantanti italiani del secolo XIX: Erminia e Giuseppe Frezzolini' (*Rivista musicale italiana*, Sept. 1925).

break off an engagement to the baritone Felice Varesi in 1839 and was naturally furious when, after an acquaintance of a few weeks, she accepted a proposal of marriage from the composer Nicolai at Brescia on 30th August 1840. The course of this affair can be followed in Nicolai's diaries.[1] Erminia seems to have made use of Nicolai to escape from her father's custody, and her father then to have protected his own interests by persuading her, in Nicolai's absence, to accept the attentions of Antonio Poggi. According to Nicolai's diary, Poggi more or less bought her from her father for 40,000 francs; the marriage took place at Milan on 14th March 1841. Erminia distinguished herself very much at the first performance of Verdi's *I Lombardi* at La Scala in 1843. One letter from Verdi to Poggi, friendly in tone, survives from this year,[2] and the suggestion was made that he should spend a fortnight with Poggi and Erminia at their country house in the autumn of 1844 and then they should come to Busseto to sing in a charity concert. Nothing came of these proposals, but they show that a friendly relationship existed at this time. It is doubtful whether Verdi knew the Countess Giulia Samoyloff [3] personally, since she moved largely in pro-Austrian circles, but he certainly knew her by repute: no one living at Milan and interested in scandal and opera could fail to do that. She was born in Russia on 6th April 1803, the daughter of Count Paul von der Pahlen, afterwards commander-in-chief of the Russian Army. She was thus the grand-daughter (not the daughter, as sometimes stated) of Count Peter von der Pahlen, chief of the conspirators responsible for the strangulation of the Tsar Paul I in 1801. The Countess Giulia is said to have been the mistress of the Tsar Nicholas I before he came to the throne, and then to have married Count Samoyloff. After her husband's early death, or, according to other sources, after her separation from him, she came to Milan, where she had relatives, members of the ducal family of Litta. The beautiful and immensely rich countess first appeared in Milanese society at a ball in 1828, dressed in Russian peasant costume. Tall, with opulent figure, black hair and greenish eyes, she was a passionate collector of cats, dogs, parrots, monkeys and opera singers, entertaining a succession of each in her richly furnished apartments in Via Borgonuovo. She had an affair with Giovanni Pacini (1796–1867), composer of about ninety operas. Pacini, some years earlier, had been chased everywhere by Napoleon's second sister, Princess Paolina Borghese, fifteen years his senior, and to get rid of the princess had married the daughter of an

[1] *Otto Nicolais Tagebücher* (Leipzig, 1892; more complete edition by Wilhelm Altmann, Regensburg, 1937).

[2] G. Radiciotti, 'Giuseppe Verdi a Sinigaglia' (*Rassegna Marchigiana*, Jan. 1923).

[3] Half a dozen different transliterations of the name are found; 'Samoyloff' is the form found in contemporary newspapers and used also in printed dedications of works by Malibran, Donizetti and Verdi.

old friend of his father's. After the death of this first wife he was to have married the Countess Samoyloff; a misunderstanding caused the engagement to be broken off, but they remained close friends and the countess afterwards adopted one of Pacini's daughters. Austrian officials crowded to receptions given in Via Borgonuovo and expressed their admiration in extravagant gestures. Every morning the Countess Giulia bathed in asses' milk, for which, after her ablutions, her idolators contended, in the way that Liszt's lady friends, at about the same period, collected, bottled and stored away the water in which he had washed his hands. The countess's admirers, however, are stated to have made ice-cream with the milk from her bath.

When Liszt and the Countess d'Agoult came to Milan in 1837 they made the acquaintance of the Countess Samoyloff, who is referred to, by her initial, several times in the journal of the Countess d'Agoult.[1] From this journal we learn that Poggi was then the reigning favourite:

> Moral freedom seems to be much greater here than in France. Free liaisons cause no scandal at all. The word 'lover' is used without hesitation. The Countess S., who plays the principal role at Milan, goes openly to Trieste because Poggi, her lover, is engaged at the theatre there.

Another entry credits or debits her with 'an uninterrupted succession of mediocre lovers, almost all musicians'. The populace talked about her, her carriages, her parrots and monkeys, and in all the shops one was first offered such things as the Countess Samoyloff had bought there—her favourite writing-paper, the perfumes that she used, the jewels she had chosen. A thousand stories were to be heard of her truly royal generosity and her pleasing extravagances.[2] But she drew the line at Rossini's friend, Olympe Pélissier, and when he tried to impose her on Milanese society, the Countess Samoyloff turned her back. A letter from Liszt to the Countess d'Agoult, of 29th October 1839,[3] tells how Poggi had by then been superseded, although he did not know it. But six years later he was again, or still, in favour.

The Austrian sympathies of the Countess Samoyloff were not concealed. As a result of this Pacini's operas were hissed at Milan because he was known to be her intimate friend, and the fact that she was showing renewed interest in Antonio Poggi in 1845 may have been the cause of hostility shown to him. But the countess and her friends were nevertheless keen admirers of Mme Frezzolini-Poggi.

[1] Comtesse d'Agoult, *Mémoires 1833–1854, avec une introduction de M. Daniel Ollivier* (Paris, 1927).

[2] The Neapolitan paper *L'Omnibus* for 21st August 1845 recalls how the Countess Samoyloff used to spend the summer on the island of Ischia, where she made herself much loved by paying off debts, marrying off poor peasant girls and giving pensions to the old and the crippled. On 28th July each year she gave a feast to her dependents and admirers, served with her own hands.

[3] *Correspondance de Liszt et de la Comtesse d'Agoult, publiée par M. Daniel Ollivier* (Paris, 1933), I, p. 275.

On 17th March Muzio reported:

On Saturday evening the season ended with the last two acts of *Ernani* and the last two acts of *Giovanna d'Arco*. . . . I have never in my life seen so many flowers and wreaths; it is said that la Samoyloff has spent 3,000 francs on flowers, and I assure you that she and her friends went on throwing flowers and garlands for a good half-hour. . . . They threw many to la Elssler, but more to la Frezzolini, to whom there appeared, after her death scene in the finale of *Giovanna d'Arco*, about twenty girls, all dressed in white, with bouquets of various kinds in their hands; one of these I call a Monster Bouquet; it was so enormous that it took two theatre attendants to carry it. The final terzetto of *Ernani* was repeated, and then came sonnets dedicated to la Gabussi and De Bassini. Poggi was received with hisses, and after his *romanza* various pieces of paper were seen flying through the air; everyone believed they were sonnets in his praise, and he even thanked the audience for its courtesy, with a smile on his lips and a number of bows; but there was surprise and a burst of laughter on seeing that instead of sonnets they were what the Milanese call *guzzinate*, i.e. songs the populace sings about a husband who beats his wife, a miser, a drunkard, a guzzler, etc., and I can tell you that all the Milanese are still laughing about it.

The vocal score of *Giovanna d'Arco* is actually dedicated to the Countess Samoyloff, but by Ricordi, the publisher, and not by Verdi himself.[1]

The first five of Verdi's operas had been produced at intervals, roughly, of a year; owing to special circumstances eighteen months elapsed between *Un giorno di regno* and *Nabucco*. After *Ernani* at Venice on 9th March 1844 the tempo had quickened. *I due Foscari* had followed seven months later in the same year, and then *Giovanna d'Arco* after an interval of only three and a half months. In less than another six months the next opera, *Alzira*, was due at Naples. Verdi's health in these early years was never very robust and the strain of the composition and rehearsal of these operas, one after another, soon began to tell. In addition to these tasks, there was the careful control of his interests with opera houses, impresarios and publishers, with the resultant increasing business correspondence and, from time to time, when sufficiently high fees were offered and singers were to his satisfaction, the supervision and conducting of his earlier works in various Italian towns. Verdi's troubles, probably nervous in origin, took the form of throat and stomach complaints, recurring whenever he was working at high pressure. The first manifestations had occurred in 1844, during the composition of *I due Foscari*, and now in the following year the trouble returned. On 10th April Muzio told Barezzi that Verdi had a bad stomach-ache and in subsequent letters gave further details of the malady and its treatment:

[1] Reproduction of the title page in Gatti, *Verdi nelle immagini*, p. 56.

14th April:

Yesterday the Signor Maestro expected your letters, and hoped to receive them this morning, but there was nothing at all. He can't write because they have bled him, but today he is better, and let's hope he will continue to get better. There was danger of inflammation if he delayed any longer to have himself bled; yesterday however he went out, and just for today he will stay in bed, to rest and keep out of the cold air. On Thursday I will write again and give you better news of the Signor Maestro's health, and he tells me that he, too, will write. For the opera at Naples there are only two months left; he will have a doctor's certificate made out and send it, and then go there a month later.

17th April:

The Signor Maestro received your letter this morning, but he's not writing because he is tired. His health is much improved, but his stomach pains continue and now they make him take pills. The doctors will make out the certificates to send to Naples, and thus he will write the opera when he can. . . . They had written to him from Rome, to go to stage *Giovanna*, but he's not going owing to his stomach trouble. I act as his secretary and reply to letters; however, in spite of his illness I have always had my lesson, except on the day they bled him, which was Sunday.

21st April:

The Signor Maestro has almost completely recovered his health, and after a little more rest will be quite free from his stomach trouble. All his acquaintances and friends have been most sorry about it and you, Signore, more than the others, certainly. Signor Pasetti has sent him some bottles of wine, twenty years old, and thus, taking a little glass of it every morning, he will be able more and more to tone up his stomach. I assure you it's very good, it's exquisite. . . . The opera for Naples will not be produced until July, or perhaps August, and so la Tadolini will sing in it and not la Bishop (unless, however, the former loses her voice in childbirth, of which there is some question, as she's over forty). All the Neapolitans wish the Signor Maestro to write for la Tadolini, and Cammarano, not knowing that the Signor Maestro was ill, even wrote him to seek some excuse to retard the production until the time I told you. Now the Signor Maestro has had me reply that he has no need of excuses and pretexts because he is really ill (then, not now) and will send the certificates, and thus he will get what he wants and will have a good protagonist. The opera will be composed only of thirteen or fourteen numbers. The poem is very beautiful. This is a chorus of American Indians (in the prologue) who have tied Gusmano (the Portuguese Governor) to a tree and intend to kill him:

'Muoia, muoia coverto d'insulti,
I martiri sien crudi, ma lenti,
Strappi ad esso codardi singulti
Il tormento di mille tormenti.

O fratelli caduti pugnando
Dalle tombe sorgete ululando;
L'inno insiem del trionfo s'intuoni
Mentre ei sparge l'estremo respir.'

25th April:[1]

I'm going round getting the Signor Maestro's certificates stamped and all the signatures authenticated; the only one still missing is that of the Governor, Count Spaur. If the Neapolitans accept and believe him he will write the opera later; if they don't believe him he won't do the opera at all, for the very good reason that he doesn't wish to kill himself for other people. La Tadolini has already had her baby and as soon as she has got over her confinement she will resume her place at the San Carlo theatre at Naples. . . . The Signor Maestro's illness is called *Anorexia and Dyspnoea.* He's very well, but still taking the pills. Let's hope that he will soon dispense with these too.

28th April:

The Signor Maestro continues well; he's not doing anything yet about the opera for Naples. At present he is occupied only with me, giving me lessons from ten in the morning until nearly two in the afternoon. He makes me read all the classical music of Beethoven, Mozart, Leindesdorf,[2] Schubert, Haydn, etc., then we shall come to the moderns. . . . They haven't replied yet from Naples; the certificates will already have reached their destination; so that they should arrive safely and quickly at Naples he made me frank them and then have a receipt for the letter made out by the Post Office Director, so that they can't say they haven't received them and so that they don't get lost, and thus reach the hands of Signor Flauto, who is obliged to give a receipt to the Post Office Director at Naples, and then the latter sends the receipt to the Director at Milan, and he gives it to the Signor Maestro.

14th May:

The Signor Maestro is not doing anything yet. . . . I'm in the midst of tribulations with canons and fugues. I transcribe for you the letter from the management at Naples that has infuriated the Signor Maestro, who has replied as you will see:

Naples, May 1845.

TO SIGNOR GIUSEPPE VERDI,
celebrated composer,

I am immensely sorry to learn from your favours of the 23rd and 26th of last month that you are indisposed.

The illness, however, from which you are suffering is a trifling affair and the only remedies necessary are tincture of wormwood and a prompt

[1] Not included in the published volume of Muzio's letters to Barezzi. Reproduced in Gatti's *Verdi nelle immagini*, p. 188.

[2] Carl Engel once suggested in the *Musical Quarterly* that this was a mistake for Dittersdorf, but Leindesdorf is also possible. Muzio's handwriting is generally easily legible.

departure for Naples; I assure you that the air here and the excitability of our Vesuvius will get all your functions working again and above all restore your appetite.

Make up your mind then to come at once, and abandon the company of doctors, who can only increase the indisposition from which you are suffering. Your recovery will derive from the air of Naples and from advice which I shall give you when you are here, for I too have been a doctor, and now have abandoned such imposture.

Advise me of the day of your departure so that I can prepare suitable accommodation and believe me,

Your sincere friend,

V. FLAUTO.

Reply:

Milan, 14th May 1845.

SIGNOR VINCENZO FLAUTO,

I am immensely sorry to have to advise you that my illness is not a trifling affair, as you believe; tincture of wormwood is useless in my case.

As for the excitability of Vesuvius, I assure you that that is not what I need to get all my functions working again; I have need of quiet and rest.

I cannot leave at once for Naples, as you invite me to do; if I could do so I should not have sent a medical certificate.

I advise you of all that so that you can take whatever steps you think opportune, while I think seriously about recovering my health.

Believe me,

Yours affectionately,

G. VERDI.

It will be seen that Verdi's illness occurred at a convenient moment, enabling him to defer the production of *Alzira* until Eugenia Tadolini had recovered from her confinement. This is not to say that he used the illness merely as an excuse, even though he was well on the way to recovery by the time the certificates were sent, as is clear from Muzio's letters. If the doctors had advised a month's rest, he was within his rights, and wise, to take a full month's rest. Resumption of work as soon as he began to feel a little better might well have brought on a relapse. Flauto was hard to convince that Verdi's illness was genuine, and certainly believed that if he could get the composer to Naples he would be able, in one way or another, to force the production of the opera at the time originally planned, and with Madame Bishop instead of Eugenia Tadolini. But the wily Verdi refused to leave Milan until he had everything settled in writing:

Signor Flauto has promised Cammarano and Fraschini that he will concede the month's delay requested and la Tadolini. But the Signor Maestro doesn't want words, he wants it in writing; and when Cammarano went to get that from the said Signor Flauto he didn't want to give it. What scoundrels!

Finally the opera was completed in about twenty days, except for the finale of the second act, for which Cammarano had not yet supplied the verses, and on 20th June Verdi left for Naples. As usual, he left the scoring to be done at the last moment at the place of production; for this task he allowed himself six days.

The Neapolitan correspondent of the *Rivista di Roma* described the warm reception given to the composer:

> When the news spread through the city, not only that he had arrived, but that on the same evening he would certainly be present at the San Carlo theatre for the performance of *I due Foscari*, the public, moved by legitimate curiosity, gathered in crowds at the theatre to see the famous composer in person. The galleries and the vast hall of San Carlo, packed with spectators, presented a brilliant scene. The performers, inspired by Verdi's presence as if by a charge of electricity, surpassed themselves, so that the opera, although heard an infinite number of times in the past two seasons, seemed, judging by the effect produced in the auditorium on that evening, quite new. All the singers were warmly applauded, but the enthusiastic audience wished to demonstrate its admiration for the composer of *I due Foscari*. Being called for repeatedly and vociferously, he appeared twice on the stage amid the most cordial, loud and unanimous applause.

Muzio heard about this directly from Verdi, and was delighted. 'Mercadante, Pacini and Battista will gnaw their fingers in jealous rage,' he told Barezzi. 'He says also that the journalists are all hostile to him, as in other places.' Among the singers who shared Verdi's triumph with *I due Foscari* was Anna Bishop, the runaway wife of the composer of 'Home, sweet Home', already referred to in Muzio's letter of 21st April. But because he did not want her in *Alzira*, Madame Bishop became Verdi's bitter enemy.

Anna Rivière had been born in London on 9th January 1810, the eldest daughter among the twelve children of a drawing master, Daniel Valentine Rivière. She had piano lessons from Moscheles and singing lessons from Henry Bishop, and on 12th July 1824 was elected a foundation student at the Royal Academy of Music, where in the summer of the following year she won a pencil case as a prize for composition. She sang at a students' concert in St James's Palace on 11th June 1828, in the presence of the king, and made her public *début* at a Concert of Ancient Music in the 'New Rooms', Hanover Square, on 20th April 1831. She married Henry Bishop on 9th July of the same year, less than three months after her *début* and less than one month after the death of Bishop's first wife. In the years that followed she became a well-known singer, principally of classical music, in London and the provinces, until she was induced to turn her attention to the Italian school by Nicholas Bochsa, the composer and harp player. This extraordinary character had been professor of the harp and general secretary of the Royal Academy of Music from 1822 until he was suspended in February 1826, on the discovery that he was wanted for forgeries on a grand scale, committed in France some ten years earlier. At the end of March 1817 he had decamped with the box-office receipts and all the valuable furs deposited in the cloakroom, while a concert audience was waiting for his appearance on the platform. Investigations showed that he had obtained money and goods to the value of 760,000 francs by forging the signatures of Méhul, Boieldieu, Berton, the Duke of Wellington and others, and on 17th February 1818 the Court of Assize in Paris condemned him in contumacy to twelve years' hard labour, to be branded with the letters T. F. and to be fined 4,000 francs. Meanwhile he had begun a new life in London, committing bigamy by marrying Amy Wilson, sister of the famous prostitute Harriette Wilson, whose memoirs are well known. Bochsa was bankrupt by 1824, and eventually settled with his creditors by paying them sevenpence in the pound. He and Anna Bishop went on a provincial tour in the spring of 1839 and on their return she won a great success at a benefit concert in operatic costume, arranged by Bochsa, at Her Majesty's Theatre, in competition with artists of the calibre of Grisi, Viardot-Garcia, Persiani, Rubini, Tamburini and Lablache. A month later Bochsa and Madame Bishop eloped to the Continent and, as Richard Northcott puts it, 'from that time to his death, she took no further interest in Bishop beyond occasionally singing his "Home, sweet Home"'.[1] The deplorable couple made themselves known in half Europe by concerts at which Anna sang Italian operatic arias in costume and Bochsa provided interludes on the harp. The list of his compositions makes fearsome reading, including: *Band March, in imitation of a military band at a distance*; *Caledonian Fantasie for the harp, with variations on 'Scots wha hae wi Wallace bled'*; *Grand Military Concerto for the harp, with accompaniments for an orchestra*; *Grand Polish Cavalry March*; *Tartar Divertimento*; *Mexican March*; and *Souvenir de Shakespeare, a Dramatic Fantasia for the Harp, in which is introduced some of the music in Macbeth and Hamlet, and the favourite Airs, 'My Mother had a Maid called Barbara', 'Where the Bee sucks', 'Blow, blow, thou wintry wind', etc.* Carefully avoiding France, Bochsa and Madame Bishop made their way to Hamburg, where two concerts were given. Then on to Copenhagen in October. The *Biography of Madame Anna Bishop, containing the details of her Professional Tour in England, Denmark, Sweden, Germany, Russia, Tartary, Moldavia, Italy, Switzerland, Belgium, Havana, Mexico, America, and California*, published at Sydney in 1855, is obviously 'inspired' and designed to attract attention on her first arrival in Australia in that year; it is probably highly unreliable. Only a

[1] *The Life of Sir Henry R. Bishop* (1920).

practised confidence trickster like Bochsa would have dared lay on the colour so thickly. At Copenhagen in 1839:

> The Queen of Denmark was so fond of Anna that she not only invited her to dine at the Royal Palace every Sunday, but two or three times a week visited our cantatrice at her own house, and listened to her singing for hours together. Before Anna left Copenhagen, the king presented her with a magnificent diamond brooch, as a token of the pleasure her singing had afforded him.

From Copenhagen she passed on to Gothenburg and Örebro, and arrived at Stockholm in January 1840, where she eclipsed Jenny Lind and packed the theatre every evening at tripled prices. At every performance Queen Caroline sent her chamberlain several times with her compliments, and the Prince Royal, Oscar, never missed one of her concerts. On the morning she left Stockholm all the ministers and ambassadors assembled at her house to pay their respects, the Count de Rosen, sent by the king, conducted her to her carriage, and the Countess Tobey threw over her shoulders a mantle of superb ermine. At the University of Uppsala she was serenaded by 600 students. At St Petersburg in May 1840 she lived in the palace of Baron Chabot, with nine reception rooms, where she gave a private party every Wednesday, at which the imperial family, the Russian ministers, the foreign ambassadors and the whole court assembled. Then on again to Dorpat, Riga, Mitau and Moscow. In June 1841 she was at Nijny-Novgorod, singing to audiences of Chinese, Turks, Circassians, Cossacks and Arabs, gathered for the annual fair. Here she met the last king of the Georgians, 'who, in rapture with her beautiful singing, sent to her, by several of his dwarfs, presents of sweetmeats and a rich bracelet of turquoises'. Thence to Kazan, the capital of Tartary. Anna was always ready to surprise the natives by bursting into song in their own language; the Scandinavian tongues, Russian, Hungarian, all came alike to her; at Kazan she sang in the Tartar language. On she went, to Odessa, Yassy, Lemberg, Cracow, where Countess Potoski built a small theatre in her palace for the sole purpose of hearing Anna sing, to Brünn and Vienna in March 1842, with private concerts for the emperor and Metternich, to Pressburg, with superb illuminations and a serenade arranged by Prince Esterházy and with the hospitality of the Bishop of Raab, then on to Budapest and Ofen, then Vienna again and Munich, where the King of Bavaria wrote the programme of her first concert with his own hand, and finally Italy, which hailed her at Verona in January 1843 as 'La Restoratrice del Vero Canto'. Appearances at Padua, Venice, Florence and Rome led her to Naples, where at the express desire of the King of the Two Sicilies she was engaged as *prima donna assoluta* of the San Carlo and Fondo theatres. Anna Bishop sang at Naples for twenty-seven consecutive months, appearing 327 times in twenty operas, including thirty-six appearances in Verdi's *I due Foscari*.

Composers, it seems, were less enthusiastic than kings, queens and ambassadors; Verdi refused to have her in his new opera, and Donizetti, two years earlier, had rejected her equally emphatically: 'No, for Christ's sake, not la Bishop! Are you pulling my leg?'

In a letter to Antonio Tosi, editor of the *Rivista di Roma*, written on 15th July, a few days after the rehearsals for *Alzira* began, Verdi expressed confidence that he had won the favour of the Neapolitan public, but charged Madame Bishop with bribery of the press: 'I believe the newspapers will say every possible bad thing about it, all the more as la Bishop has now increased her monthly payments to those gentlemen, because I don't want her in my opera.' [1] It seems certain that we can insert her name in a blank space left when another letter, to Giuseppina Appiani, was published.[2] This was written on 13th August, the day after the deferred first performance of the opera:

> Thank Heaven this too is over: *Alzira* is staged. These Neapolitans are ferocious, but they applauded. [La Bishop] had prepared for me a party which would have liked to force the downfall of this poor creature. But, in spite of that, the opera will stay in the repertory and, what is more important, go on tour like its sister operas.

Verdi had not yet learned that a fairly cordial reception on the first night, with all the interest aroused by the composer's presence in the theatre, was no guarantee that the opera would have enduring success. *Alzira* was not to stay in the repertory, nor did it go on tour like its sister operas. In the course of a long article Vincenzo Torelli, in his Neapolitan paper *L'Omnibus*, described how the indifferent *sinfonia* was exaggeratedly applauded by Verdi's supporters and thus from the beginning hostility was aroused in other sections of the audience. Only the cabalettas of the principal arias, magnificently sung by Eugenia Tadolini, by Fraschini and Coletti, seem to have aroused enthusiasm. The rest was comparatively coolly received. There was laboured applause, and forced calls for the singers and composer. 'We hear that some learned person had told Verdi to avoid choruses, elaborate scoring and concerted numbers, because they are not liked at Naples. Poor Verdi! How deceived he was!' Four other performances of the opera were given, during which hisses and other signs of disapproval increased in frequency and intensity, and Torelli expressed the hope that the 'bitter lesson' given to the composer by the Neapolitans would have some effect. He suggested that Verdi was writing too much and too quickly: 'No human talent is capable of producing two or three grand operas a year.' This was not bad advice.

[1] Franco Schlitzer, *Mondo teatrale dell'ottocento*, p. 135.
[2] A. M. Cornelio, *Per la storia* (Pistoia, 1904), p. 29.

It cannot be proved that Torelli was in the pay of Madame Bishop, though it must be said that other, non-Neapolitan, writers gave more favourable accounts of *Alzira* and its reception. And Torelli was certainly not much liked, or trusted. Muzio, in one of his letters from Milan, during Verdi's absence at Naples, describes how he met Maffei, who was furious with Torelli for having printed one of his private letters in the *Omnibus*. According to Maffei, Torelli was 'worse than Regli', 'a trashy writer', a journalist who had always run down Verdi without knowing anything about his works, 'one of those whom the Signor Maestro should look down upon from on high, grovelling in the dust'. Muzio also refers to an article attacking Torelli by the Neapolitan composer Vinzenzo Capecelatro, a passionate admirer of Verdi and his music, though unfortunately afflicted with the Evil Eye.

It seems from a later letter to Flauto [1] that Verdi was disgusted with the running commentary on his actions supplied by the Neapolitan journalists. When he appeared in a café, or was seen on the balcony of Mme Tadolini's apartments, or wore brown shoes rather than black, it was reported in the papers, along with 'a thousand other trifles unworthy, certainly, of a serious public or a great city'. He left Naples before the last performance of *Alzira* on 21st August, at which Mme Tadolini's cavatina was applauded and almost nothing else, according to the *Omnibus*. At this time the following doggerel verses [2] were making the rounds of the Neapolitan cafés:

Tu in prima scrivesti il *Nabucco*
E gli astanti rimaser di stucco,
I Lombardi scrivesti in appresso
Si restò press'a poco lo stesso;
Tu per terzo scrivesti gli *Ernani*
E cessò quello batter di mani,
I due Foscari in Roma scrivesti,
Ti ricordi che fiasco facesti?
A Milano *Giovanna* fu data,
E ben due volte fu spenta e bruciata;
A San Carlo scrivesti l'*Alzira*
E il Sebeto, sbuffando dall'ira,
Così disse: Chi è mai lo sfrontato
Che a San Carlo l'*Alzira* ha portato?
Forse è ignota all'ardito mortale
Che a San Carlo si fa *La Vestale*,
Che a San Carlo vi scrive Pacini,
Che rapì coi suoi canti Bellini?
Che credea con barba e mustacci

[1] *Copialettere*, p. 58.
[2] Schlitzer, op. cit., pp. 137–8. Manuscript copy in the Biblioteca di Storia moderna e contemporanea, Rome.

Ritirarsi così dagli impacci?
A San Carlo si vuol melodia,
Regolata con grande armonia.
Ci vuol canto che sia declamato,
Non cantaccio da perdervi il fiato
E costringer fin anche a stonare,
Ma Fraschini che mai potè fare?
Qui si tacque il Sebeto, ed accenna
Che si rechi all'istante una penna.
A punir l'enorme delitto
Ipso facto emanò quest'editto:
'Quel colore cotanto gradito
Da' nostr'occhi sia tosto bandito,
Trovi il verde se alcuno lo brama
Sotto il gel del *Vascello di Gama*.'

It is interesting that, of the three composers of the Neapolitan school whom Muzio had expected to 'gnaw their fingers in jealous rage', Pacini is actually mentioned in these verses, while Mercadante was the author of the two operas named, *La Vestale* and *Il Vascello di Gama*, in the face of which Verdi had dared to appear at the San Carlo theatre with *Alzira*. *Il Vascello di Gama* had been written for Anna Bishop and produced, without much success, in the previous March. It seems not improbable that Verdi knew these verses, and was referring to them when he replied to Flauto in 1846: 'Why should I be annoyed with the Neapolitans, and the Neapolitans with me? Do they lack colours in the spectrum, that they have need of *Verdi*?' The pun (*verde* = green) used here and in the penultimate line of the poem had appeared already in Torelli's *Omnibus* in 1841, in his account of the failure of *Oberto* at the San Carlo.

The subsequent career of Anna Bishop is worth an additional paragraph. Her biographer of 1855 tells us that she so charmed the Pope by 'a sacred air of Palestrina' that he conferred on her, by the hands of Cardinal Zacchia, the Ancient and Noble Order of Santa Cecilia, with a cross of precious stones. After singing in *La Sonnambula* at Palermo, in the presence of the sovereigns of Russia and Naples, she returned to England, by way of Switzerland and Belgium, giving concerts everywhere. She appeared at Drury Lane in Balfe's *Maid of Artois* on 8th October, and in Louis Lavenu's *Loretta* on 9th November 1846. She delighted the provinces with 'her favourite last scene from *L'Elisir d'amore*, composed for her by Donizetti at Naples'—a thumping lie! Then across the Atlantic, with concerts at New York, Philadelphia, Baltimore, Washington, Richmond, Charleston, Savannah, Mobile, New Orleans:

Magnificent bouquets, *corbeilles* of the richest flowers, and verses were nightly thrown at her feet, and even hats, gloves, and caps found their way on the stage as tokens of the boisterous admiration of the pit and galleries. It is said that Anna Bishop has a curious collection of such oddities, which she intends taking with her to Europe, as tokens *from the people*, not to be slighted.

In 1849 she found Mexico a true El Dorado and in the following years the 'fair cantatrice' or 'wandering nightingale' seems to have sung at almost every city in North America. On 1st October 1855 she sailed from San Francisco for Australia. Bochsa died of dropsy in Sydney on 6th January 1856, and Anna recrossed the Pacific for a tour of Chile, the Argentine and Brazil, before returning to New York where she married Martin Schultz, a diamond merchant. She spent a year in England and then returned to North America. From California she sailed to the Sandwich Islands. On 18th February 1866 she left Honolulu for Hong Kong in the barque *Libelle* (Captain Tobias) and was wrecked on a coral reef near Wake Island, losing all her clothes, jewellery and music. After being marooned for three weeks on an uninhabited, waterless island, living on provisions salvaged from the wreck, the survivors made their way in an open boat to the Ladrone Islands, 1,400 miles away. Anna and Schultz landed on Guam on 8th April and thence made their way to Manila, where the interrupted routine of concert-giving was resumed. Then to Amoy, Hong Kong, Singapore and Calcutta, where she gave sixteen concerts before undertaking a tremendous tour of India (Jamalpur, Dinapore, Benares, Allahabad, Cawnpore, Lucknow, Agra, Delhi, Lahore, Simla, Mussoorie, Bombay, Madras, Ceylon). She returned to New York, via Australia and England. She appeared in the Tabernacle at Salt Lake City, at the special invitation of Brigham Young, on 4th July 1873. After another tour of Australia she spent a year in South Africa, travelling to places like Kimberley by rough roads and across or through unbridged rivers. At the end of 1876 she was in England again, where she stayed for three years, avoiding publicity and musical engagements, before returning to New York. She made her last public appearance there on 20th April 1883 and died of apoplexy at 1443 Fourth Avenue on 19th March 1884. To quote Northcott again: 'Schultz soon afterwards degenerated into a lodging-house tramp, and died of typhus in Riverside Hospital, New York.'

After *Alzira* at Naples Verdi's next engagement was the composition of *Attila*, for Venice, early in 1846. For the libretto of this opera he reverted to Temistocle Solera, author of the words of *Nabucco*, *I Lombardi* and *Giovanna d'Arco*. This was another interesting character. Born at Ferrara in 1817, he had been sent to school in Vienna, by order of the emperor, after his father had been condemned to imprisonment in the Spielberg for revolutionary activities. One day the young Solera climbed over the wall of his Viennese boarding-school, sold his school uniform and got himself a job as riding master, poet and general factotum in a travelling circus. After a time he was tracked down in Hungary by the police and returned to Vienna. He was then sent to complete his education in the Collegio Longone at Milan. Soon he made a name for himself as poet and composer. A volume of Manzonian verses, *I miei primi canti*, appeared in 1837. Two years later a cantata, *La melodia*, words and music by Solera, was performed at La Scala, and he was always ready to make himself useful to Merelli, the impresario, as when the libretto of Verdi's *Oberto, Conte di San Bonifacio* needed revision. An opera of his own, *Ildegonda*, was produced at La Scala in March 1840, and was followed by *Il Contadino d'Agliate* in October 1841. Solera, a bull-necked, Herculean figure, incongruously flourishing a monocle, was a thorough Bohemian, lazy and not too honest. He published music by Antonio Bazzini as his own. When Verdi's *Nabucco* was performed in Paris it was found that Solera had made unauthorized use of a French drama, and in the Venetian paper *Il Gondoliere* for 15th March 1843 charges of plagiarism, citing chapter and verse, were brought by Giulio Pullè against the author of *I Lombardi*. But Solera was a fluent versifier. The *Gazzetta Privilegiata di Milano* for 20th June 1844 includes an account of his appearance at Fiume in the previous month, in a programme of improvised poems on themes drawn from an urn, with musical intermezzos by the garrison band. Solera, 'kindled wholly by the sacred Apollonian flame', improvised to a piano accompaniment on subjects like 'The Nineteenth Century', 'The Defeat of the Tartars on the Field of Grobnico', 'Count Niklós Zrinyi at the Castle of Sziget' and 'The Eclipse of 1842', to the universal acclamations of the audience. Probably he was never quite sure whether the spate of words and ideas that came into his head were his own or other people's.

Muzio to Barezzi, 13th August 1845:

The Signor Maestro has written to Solera that he is coming to Milan expressly to collect the libretto of *Attila*, out of which he wants to make his most beautiful opera; but that lazy hound of a poet hasn't done a thing. I have told Cav. Maffei and Toccagni, and they will make him do some work, and he has promised that he will keep at it day and night and that he will finish it before the Signor Maestro arrives. This morning at eleven o'clock he was still in bed, so it seems that he is not working.

18th August: [1]

Solera has almost finished the libretto and by Thursday morning will have prepared a fair copy; he is very pleased and has told me that it is beautiful, and that those who have heard it like it very much indeed. And that's good news.

[1] Misdated 'September' in Garibaldi's book, p. 217. The letter that follows it on p. 220 is also misdated, by Muzio or by Garibaldi, 'September' instead of 'August'.

26th August: [1]

The Signor Maestro is with us after an excellent journey. . . . He is getting up now, after having rested for a while, for there was no lack of the usual annoyances. He was at Milan at half past eight.

We shall come soon to Busseto, but he doesn't wish to fix the day, because when he does so he is never able to keep his promise. So we shall arrive out of the blue, just when we are least expected. Have the bed got ready, and writing materials, etc.

The Signor Maestro advises me to ask you to find a piano for me, because he wants to write *Attila* and if I waste the morning the rest of the day goes by with nothing done: the wife of the police magistrate, for instance, might help me, and a word of yours would certainly settle this for me; do it if you can and rest assured of my gratitude.

Tomorrow *I due Foscari*. Merelli sent to ask the Signor Maestro to attend the dress rehearsal but he replied with a flat 'No'. For it doesn't matter to him whether it's a fiasco or not, since the opera has been successful and is successful in all the other theatres.

Not much work was done by Verdi during six weeks of boredom at Busseto. 'This blessed, blessed Busseto!' he wrote to Giuseppina Appiani on 9th September. 'What beauty! What elegance! What a place! What society! I am enchanted and I don't know how I shall be able to tear myself away!!!!!! I found my father and mother in excellent health and happier than I am, certainly. But what am I saying? Today is a holiday and I don't want to talk of melancholy things. So let's be cheerful. As soon as I can I shall come to Milan.' Three days later, in a letter to Andrea Maffei,[2] he was comparing Busseto and Naples: 'Where one is better off, or worse off, I don't know. I know that Naples is very beautiful, that it has an enchanting sky, salubrious air, surroundings like Paradise—and that's all I know. . . . Here nothing happens—nothing, nothing; one eats, one drinks, and one sleeps twenty-five hours a day: I do so too.' At Busseto, too, there were gossiping tongues, as elsewhere, but he paid them no attention. In a postscript he added: 'Yesterday I began writing *Attila* and from now on I shall sleep only twenty-four hours a day, instead of twenty-five.' But little progress was made. In the second week of October Verdi and Muzio were back at Milan.

In Muzio's letters we have accounts of everything that went on at Milan in these years, from the introduction of gas lighting in the streets to the downfall of Louis Tour, who advertised himself as the champion wrestler of Europe and was hurled to the ground by a brawny Milanese porter and narrowly escaped being lynched by the crowd: 'If you'd only seen it! Hardly was he on the ground before benches, chairs, tables and stones flew through the air after him.'

[1] Misdated 'July' in Garibaldi's book, p. 211.
[2] G. B. Emert, 'Due autografi inediti di Giuseppe Verdi' (*Trentino*, June 1941).

Then there was the surprising flight of the aeronaut Arbon: 'The peasants to whom he had given the balloon to hold, feeling some resistance, let it go freely up into the air and, who knows, perhaps they won't find it again, because it was without any ballast and who knows where the Devil will have carried it.' The reputed former protector of the Countess Samoyloff, the tyrannical Czar Nicholas I, was at Milan in October 1845 and attended performances of *I due Foscari*; there were illuminations, bands constantly playing, processions and a magnificent mock battle lasting five hours. At one performance of *I due Foscari* attended by the Czar, the third act was performed before the second. Muzio reports other instances of Merelli's misdeeds:

La Sonnambula was performed badly at La Scala as usual. I don't believe there has ever been an occasion before when such an eminently Italian opera as *La Sonnambula* has been performed by an Englishwoman (la Birche), a German (la Stradiot) and a Frenchman (Boquet); to sing Italian operas properly fine singers are needed who are Italian either by birth or by long musical education.

Recent events at Naples were not forgotten, and no opportunity was lost for a dig at Verdi's adversaries:

At Naples *I due Foscari* has been put on again, with la Gabussi. The part of Lucrezia, which was first sung by la Bishop, has, they write, been given unexpected prominence. That's according to the *Figaro*.

At the end of October Muzio transcribed with immense satisfaction an article by Enrico Montazio in the *Rivista di Firenze*, ridiculing Pacini and his *Lorenzino de' Medici*, and apostrophizing the Signor Maestro as 'that young composer whom you affect to despise, and whom you profoundly envy for his glory and your own malice, that young composer who in *Ernani*, *Nabucco*, *I Lombardi*, *I due Foscari*, *Giovanna d'Arco*, etc., has shown more genius and inspiration than all the rest of you put together, you arid distorters of counterpoint! Verdi, in short, whom, fuming and snorting, you strive unsuccessfully to imitate, Verdi, who, sheltering under his youthful pinions the abandoned Muse of Bellini, asked her the secret of her power and was told in reply "The heart"'.

There was some surprising news on 19th November:

The Countess Samoyloff is getting married; her future husband is a singer, a certain Peri, who took the part of Carlo in *Ernani* at Lecco. They have left for Paris, where they will settle down. However, she can't marry without the authorization of the Emperor of All the Russias, and as soon as she has got it they will marry. They are selling by auction at Milan all the furniture of her house; she is selling everything and doesn't wish to see Milan again. She has made a present of 500,000 francs to Signor Peri, and in case they are unable to reach an understanding, she is obliged to pay over to him 100,000 francs a year.

La Frezzolini has finally separated from the antipathetic Poggi. It is said that he left her in the hope of being united once and for all with the Countess Samoyloff, and instead of that it is *his* turn to be given the cold shoulder. The Signor Maestro is very angry with Poggi, because when he was at Naples he wrote twice to la Frezzolini and Poggi opened the letters and kept them. This morning la Frezzolini wrote this to him: 'With fear I prepare myself to write to you for the third time, not having had a reply to the other two letters I wrote to you at Naples.' The Maestro told me he has replied that she should reclaim the two letters from her husband.

Only in Italy could the last few sentences of this passage have been made the basis of a supposed love affair between Verdi and Erminia Frezzolini.

When Verdi, in a letter already quoted,[1] wrote from Venice on 22nd December 1845 asking Giuseppina Appiani for news of Pedroni and of 'Madame Perey', he was referring, of course, to the Countess Samoyloff. A further comment on her marriage is found in a letter of the Marquess d'Azeglio, from Turin, 1st January 1846: [2]

The Countess Samoyloff is here, now Mme Perrin, seeing that she has married M. Perrin, a bass singer at Como, or Lugo, or somewhere, who, having first assured himself of an income of 30,000 francs, has thrown all the dogs out of the window, twisted the necks of all the birds and made her sell everything she had at Milan. She has lost all her property in Russia by this marriage.

Nobody seems certain of even the name of the countess's second husband, Peri, Pery, Perey or Perrin, where he came from, or where he went. He did not last long, and within a year or so she was back at Milan.

The letters to Antonio Barezzi from this winter depict two touching scenes: the first shows Verdi in bed with rheumatism, and Muzio 'continually' massaging him, so that he had almost no time for writing letters; the second shows Verdi providing Muzio, who had been shivering in his summer clothes, with a complete new outfit: 'So now I shan't feel the rigours of the cold. You can't imagine how much he loves me, and how concerned he is about me.' After that there is a gap of four months in the published volume of Muzio's letters, during most of which time Verdi was at Venice. When he went there hardly anything of *Attila* had been composed. Alterations in the fourth act of the libretto had to be entrusted to Piave, as Solera had transferred himself and his wife, the singer Teresa Rosmini, to Spain, whence he lamented the 'bitter pill' of Piave's revisions, which he had been condemned to swallow. Solera was then hoping

[1] See p. 113.
[2] *Souvenirs Historiques de la Marquise Constance d'Azeglio née Alfieri* (Turin, 1884).

for an advantageous contract for himself and his wife in Madrid. Stories of attempted assassinations, duels and romantic adventures involving Queen Isabella are probably later inventions. To Verdi he wrote of 'daily rebellions, shootings and, what is worse, an impresario who doesn't pay up. And, to increase my annoyances, letters from Milanese creditors, the most dogged of which I have directed to you'. Solera henceforth was replaced by the pliant and docile Piave, a turn of events to which the former could never reconcile himself. In later years he used to explain what a treasure Verdi had lost in the librettist of *Nabucco*, *I Lombardi*, *Giovanna d'Arco* and *Attila*. Eugenio Checchi heard from Solera verbal torrents in praise of Verdi's genius and in complaint about the difficulties of collaboration with him, and the quarrels arising therefrom: 'And it was always Verdi's fault, for, modesty apart, he will never find a librettist like me as long as he lives. He's a great composer, I don't deny it, but as weak as a woman; so weak as to accept librettos from that ass of a Piave—yes, gentlemen, that *ass*, I won't retract the word—and from that muddler, Salvatore Cammarano, who for having written the libretto of *Il Trovatore* deserves a life sentence to the galleys, at least preceded by a taste of the rope's end.'[1] Solera wrote other librettos, and is supposed to have become a secret service agent for Napoleon III and for Cavour, to have been entrusted with the suppression of brigandage in the Basilicata and to have reorganized the Egyptian police, but the only role he played henceforth in Verdi's life was as a writer of begging letters. At one time he was reduced to travelling on foot from Bologna to Florence in the middle of winter, in his thin summer clothes; later still he was seen, still sporting his monocle, earning a pittance as water-carrier at Leghorn. The Countess Maffei organized a fund to rescue him from destitution and he set up as an antique dealer at Florence. But in 1876 he was down and out in London; on 15th July of that year he wrote from 9 Glasshouse Street to a friend: 'The fatal words that Dante saw written on the gates of Hell stand now before my eyes on all the walls of London.'[2] He returned to Milan only to die, on Easter Sunday 1878.

The composition of *Attila* at Venice brought about, or coincided with, the recurrence, in much more serious form, of Verdi's illness. At first he complained of rheumatism, and then early in January 1846 he was prostrated by gastric fever. He is generally stated to have been ill for three weeks, on the evidence of a letter to the Countess Maffei on 21st January, saying that he had then just got up, in a very weak state, after twenty days in bed, which had seemed to him like twenty centuries. But he had a relapse in the following month. A

[1] Eugenio Checchi, 'Librettisti e Libretti di Giuseppe Verdi' (*Nuova Antologia*, 16th Oct. 1913).

[2] Autograph letter in the Piancastelli Collection, Biblioteca Comunale, Forlì.

letter to Francesco Lucca of 24th February says: 'I have been in bed for five days, and they have bled me.' [1] He afterwards wrote that he had completed *Attila* 'in bed, in an almost dying condition'. The opera was produced, with great success, on 17th March. Through Lucca, Verdi had arranged to go to London, to write a new opera for Benjamin Lumley, director of Her Majesty's Theatre. Two days after the first performance of *Attila* the composer wrote to a friend, Count Opprandino Arrivabene, that an obstinate gastric fever had kept him in bed for almost two months: 'Now I am better, but convalescence is slow and I don't know whether I shall be able to write the opera for London. The doctors absolutely forbid it, but I haven't decided anything yet.' [2] In the end he had to give up the idea for this year, and provided Lumley, through Lucca, with medical certificates from doctors at Venice and Milan, both of whom declared on oath that Verdi's very life would be endangered by the journey to England and the exertions involved in the composition and production of another opera. In the face of all this evidence, suggestions that Verdi was not honestly justified in his action seem impertinent.

Of course Lumley did not entirely believe him, and the Neapolitan comedy of the previous year was resumed. Lumley could not offer, as Flauto had been able to do, 'the excitability of Vesuvius' as an aid to recovery; on the contrary, he suggested that the 'less exciting' air of London would be beneficial, and followed this up with the announcement of the great success of *I Lombardi* at his theatre, in the presence of the queen-dowager and the princes and princesses of the blood royal—news he hoped would be a powerful antidote, available in larger doses in London, to the composer's indisposition. Verdi replied that natural curiosity, his self-esteem and his own interests all impelled him to fulfil this contract, but the state of his health forbade it. He had need of a complete rest.

Muzio to Barezzi, 23rd March 1846:

The Signor Maestro arrived from Venice at six o'clock yesterday evening. He suffered no harm from the journey. He has lost much weight through the illness, but his eyes are very bright and his complexion rather good. Rest will finally set him to rights.

He will write on Wednesday, because today there's a continual coming and going of people, and he will send you the newspapers too. *Attila* has aroused real fanaticism; the Signor Maestro had every imaginable honour: wreaths, and a brass band with torches that accompanied him to his lodging, amid cheering crowds.

Rossi's opera at La Scala was not liked. That's the twelfth fiasco.

I can't write more because it's time to go to the post office. The *Pirata* tomorrow will announce that the doctors have ordered Maestro Verdi six months' rest, for which reason he will not go to London.

[1] Reproduced in facsimile in *Musica d'Oggi*, Jan. 1926, p. 17.
[2] Annibale Alberti, *Verdi Intimo* (Verona, 1931), in the introductory note, p. xxvii.

22nd April:

Some private letters from London say that Prince Albert, husband of the Queen of England, wants to knight him as soon as he gets there, with the title of 'Master of the Royal Music', the said prince being a musician; a large pension goes with this knighthood.

Undated:

The *Omnibus* of Naples said: 'A Leipzig newspaper states that Verdi is dead; it is not true; he is well; perhaps they meant that his *Attila* is dead.' Regli told me he will reply to that; we shall see if he does.

For precisely six months, obeying his doctors' orders as scrupulously as he was accustomed to fulfil the terms of his business engagements, Verdi did absolutely nothing. It is a strange interlude in these 'years in the galleys'. His friends rallied round him and five or six carriages were placed at his disposal. Often he went out for drives in the country, or took the new railway—the second constructed in Italy—from Milan to Monza, or went farther afield, to Cassano d'Adda, or Treviglio, for the day, returning for an evening meal and then going early to bed. He began to put on weight again. But he was not always in a good humour. The police magistrate of Busseto had commissioned Muzio to buy him a new flute, but had not sent the money to pay for it. Muzio was unable to find the money himself and afraid to ask Verdi, who had declared he did not wish to hear anything at all about music. Furthermore: 'I don't want to importune the Signor Maestro because, to tell you the truth, he is in a rage because he lent forty gold napoleons to one gentleman, twenty to another and five to a third, and they have all left Milan without saying a word to him about it.'

In the *Copialettere* we find a prescription:

Graz water. To be taken all through the spring.

Dosage: Mix three-quarters of a glass of water with a quarter of a glass of boiling milk. For the first five days two glasses; then for the next four days three glasses; then four or five, according to taste.

Exercise and perspiration.

Muzio's letters show what a good patient Verdi was, and how much he benefited from this homely medicine, and the exercise and general relaxation.

6th May:

The Signor Maestro is well, and is now taking Graz water, and we go for long excursions outside the gates in the early morning, and we play at bowls to digest that water, and at five o'clock we go out to Poggio to dine with a select company.

14th May:

The Graz water is doing the Signor Maestro a lot of good, and most of all those early morning walks and the fine games we play. After that, you know, he has a keen appetite and eats his lunch with enchanting gusto. If you saw him now you would be surprised; he is fat, flourishing, has acquired a fine rosy complexion, and thus is in better health than he was before. The waters at Recoaro will put the finishing touch to his recovery. And now, if he undertook the journey to London, it could not harm him. But I am out of luck! Guess the proposal made by Lucca to the Signor Maestro! If he will go to London, Lucca will send me together with him, and give me 2,000 francs, so that I may help him, and be beside him, and so that he may have with him someone he can trust to do everything necessary for him. If he decided to do that it would be grand! But I have no hope at all of that. He says that he cannot go, and that it would be harmful; and rather than that he should suffer, I send to the devil all the money in the world, for he is dearer to me than the whole universe!

Verdi had been ordered by his Venetian doctor to take the waters at Recoaro later in the year, and he spent some weeks there with Andrea Maffei in July, rather bored, but undertaking long walks and donkey rides in the mountains, faithfully following medical advice. This was just after Maffei had separated from his wife.

Apart from an occasional remark, such as that about the appointment of an unpopular new official at the Milan Conservatorio: 'Vienna's choice! A present from the Germans!' politics hardly enter into Muzio's earlier correspondence. But the tremendous new impulse given to Italian patriotic hopes by the election in 1846 of the Liberal pope, Pius IX, is immediately apparent. After that scarcely a letter is without its rumours, reports and items of news taken from uncensored newspapers from Piedmont and elsewhere. In the official *Gazzetta Privilegiata di Milano* nothing was allowed to appear that could be considered an encouragement to Italian national aspirations. Muzio, however, seems to have been quite unconcerned about the possibility of censorship of letters between Milan and Busseto. He quotes freely from all kinds of sources, tells of the effect of the amnesty for political prisoners in the Papal States, the reform and partial suppression of monasteries, reductions of taxes and food prices, partial secularization of schools and some government departments, economies in the Vatican, proposals for the construction of railways and the institution of homes for poor children and the aged in some of the former monastery buildings. He reports the excited acclamations of the Roman crowds and their openly expressed fears that the new Pope would be poisoned by his enemies, the hangers-on of his predecessor, the Jesuits and the dispossessed friars. Verdi was no follower of Gioberti, who in his famous book, *Il primato morale e civile degli italiani*, published in exile in Brussels in 1842, had preached the unification of Italy in the form of a federation of states under the presidency of the Pope; nevertheless, he saw that things seemed to be moving in the right direction and shared the general enthusiasm—afterwards to be followed by bitter disillusionment—for Pio Nono and his reforms. Verdi was invited from Rome to contribute a choral work to the celebrations planned for November 1846: 'He is very sorry not to be able to accept', Muzio told Barezzi, 'for he would very much like to join with his music in honouring a man who has deserved so well of society.'

Muzio also reported the misgivings and hostility with which Pio Nono's measures of reform were viewed by the Austrians. Reinforcements were sent to Milan and there were daily military exercises as a show of strength; the Austrian ambassador was recalled from Rome: 'This is equivalent to throwing the Pope into the arms of France.' Some disaffected cardinals and officials of the Papal States got in touch with Field Marshal Radetzky and Baron Torresani, the chief of police at Milan; but they were arrested and taken back to Rome.

In *I miei ricordi* Massimo d'Azeglio recalls how the Austrians, before 1848, cleverly and successfully ruled Lombardy, as it were, through La Scala. If good entertainments were put on, if they could applaud the singing of Erminia Frezzolini, the dancing of Fanny Elssler or the feats of a troupe of American acrobats, the bulk of the Milanese public would not bother their heads with plots and revolutions. Thus the artistic decline of La Scala under Merelli's management was something that had to be taken seriously. Muzio heard from what he thought a dependable source that Baron Torresani himself was going to call on Verdi, to ask him to supervise personally the production of *Attila* at La Scala. It is not known whether Torresani did in fact approach the composer, but certainly other people did. Verdi went so far as to rehearse, unofficially, the principal singers at Eugenia Tadolini's house, and to write a new *romanza* for Moriani; but that was all: 'He says that as long as Merelli is there he will not set foot on the stage of La Scala.'

The tendency of contemporary audiences to see patriotic allusions in certain features of Verdi's operas is well known. The great nostalgic chorus in *Nabucco*, 'Va, pensiero, sull'ali dorate', sung by the Jewish exiles by the waters of Babylon, was felt as an expression of Italian yearning for liberty and independence. *I Lombardi* inevitably reminded the inhabitants of occupied Lombardy of their own warlike past. In *Attila*, which for a time had very great success throughout the peninsula, the line 'Avrai tu l'universo, resti l'Italia a me!' is said to have aroused a frenzy of enthusiasm in Italian audiences of that period. Verdi and his librettist, the firebrand Solera, cannot have been unaware of these possibilities. Nevertheless, one wonders whether the effect of these things has not been exaggerated by the biographers, whether the portrait of Verdi as Bard of the Risorgimento, composer of 'agitator's music', has not been overpainted. Accounts in contemporary newspapers do not mention, in these early years, patriotic outbursts such as Monaldi and his followers describe. It is at any rate curious that the experienced Torresani and his colleagues should, as a well-known anecdote tells, have smoothed the way for the production of *I Lombardi* at Milan, and then have tried to persuade Verdi to collaborate to secure a big success for *Attila* at La Scala. A letter from Muzio to Barezzi of 13th August 1846 provides what seems to be the earliest documentary evidence of the use of Verdi's music for political demonstrations: 'At Bologna, at the announcement of the amnesty, the finale of *Ernani*, "O sommo Carlo!" was performed at the theatre; the name "Carlo" was changed to "Pio" and such was the enthusiasm that it was repeated three times; then when the words "Perdono a tutti" occurred, cheering burst out on all sides.' In this case, of course, it was only by chance that words were found in *Ernani* suitable for the celebration of the amnesty; Piave and Verdi could not have foreseen this. But in the following spring the young Angelo Mariani, after conducting *Nabucco* at the Teatro Carcano, Milan, was to be rebuked and threatened with arrest by Count Bolza, commissioner of police, 'for having given to Verdi's music an expression too evidently rebellious and hostile to the Imperial Government'.

On 16th September 1846 a terrible fire broke out at Milan. Beginning in the court haylofts, it quickly spread to the houses and destroyed almost the whole suburb of Porta Orientale. The flames were visible as far away as Bergamo, and it was a week before they were finally extinguished. Muzio's description of this fire is quite priceless. The Signor Maestro and his disciple set out together to watch the operations of the fire brigade, but unfortunately they arrived on the scene just as the police were drawing a cordon round the onlookers, intending to compel them to work the pumps. Muzio and Verdi escaped on to the bastion of Porta Orientale, but then ran into a second cordon, coming from the opposite direction to catch the fugitives:

> The Signor Maestro acted in time and jumped down from the wall into the public gardens; I, however, was caught, while covering the Signor Maestro's retreat, and it was my lot to work at the pumps until six in the morning, when I was able to escape. I returned home covered in dirt and wet through, looking like an assassin. The Signor Maestro on seeing me began to laugh, which enraged me; he is still laughing. But then, when he told me that he had had to remain in concealment in the public gardens for an hour and a half, I began to laugh a bit myself too. Now listen to this, which is even better. When the Signor Maestro jumped down from the wall of the public gardens, the gates were all shut and he couldn't get out.

As I told you, he stayed hidden for an hour and a half; when he saw that the people on the bastions had dispersed, he tried to climb over the wall, but he wasn't able to do so as the wall was higher than he, so that he had to wander round for more than an hour gathering stones and building them up to make a sort of ladder. He told me that he scrambled up and then fell down again, and his hands, which look as if they had been scratched by a cat, vouch for the truth of this story.

This adventure has put him in the best humour imaginable.

Muzio by this time had passed beyond the pupil stage. He was busy copying parts, transcribing scores and making piano reductions for both Lucca and Ricordi, helping to score ballet music for Fanny Elssler's performances at La Scala, and giving lessons in counterpoint to pupils of his own. The question now arose as to whether he was to compete for the position of municipal music-master at Busseto. Discussion of this gave rise to one of the most moving passages in all the letters to Barezzi:

To tell you the truth I should be extremely sorry to have to abandon the Signor Maestro after he has given me a second life, and is always seeking to have me cut a good figure in society, among all the gentlemen, and is now contemplating something regarding me which, before he leaves Italy, will set the seal on all his benefactions and bring me to the attention of the whole musical world in launching me on my career. If only you could see us! I don't seem to be his pupil, but rather one of his friends. Always together at lunch, at the coffee house, playing together (for one hour only, from twelve to one); in short he goes nowhere without me accompanying him. At home he has procured a large table and we both write at the same table, and thus I always have the benefit of his advice. It is absolutely impossible for me to abandon him. Remember that he has done so much for me that I am afraid of being thought ungrateful. If it hadn't been for the Signor Maestro what should I be? A poor devil not knowing how to do anything. And now that he has taught me, and thanks to his teaching I can earn my living, honourably for now, and in time shall be able to do more—must I leave him? No, that I shall never, never do. Let them say what they like, I don't care; it's enough for me to be with my Maestro, and for him never to have to say to me: 'Now that I have taught you, you are abandoning me, you ingrate!' I should die of remorse if I gave him cause to say that to me. I have not yet spoken at length about this with the Signor Maestro; I shall avoid speaking of it, but if he brings the matter up I shall tell him what I have written to you, and something more that the Signor Maestro's modesty does not permit me to say and to write. Please reflect well on all this, and you will see that I am right. Some will say: 'Your family's need is great'; I know that myself; but if they have had patience now for two years, I hope that they won't die of privation in the course of, at most, another year. Please tell these things to my mother, because I haven't the heart to write them to her. She is good, and they are all good people, and they will understand my reasons, and I hope they will find them sound, and won't blame me; I then, for my part, will do all in my power to help my family, and be a credit to you, to my Maestro and my country.

When the Mayor of Busseto invited Muzio to compete for the post, he declined, saying that he had no wish to be the cause of further dissension among his compatriots.

It was time now for Verdi to return to the world of the theatre. His engagements had been complicated by his illness and the long period of inactivity prescribed by his doctors. The next opera was due to be written for Florence, but the choice of subject was dependent on the singers available. Maffei's *I Masnadieri* libretto was ready, and so Verdi first set to work on this, and nearly half the opera was composed before it was known that the tenor Fraschini would not be singing at Florence. Verdi then changed his plans and decided to write *Macbeth*, on a libretto by Piave, for the baritone Varesi at Florence, *I Masnadieri* being set aside for completion later, for production in London.

Muzio's letters reveal the highly strained relations between Verdi and Merelli at this time, and the parts played by Lucca and Torresani in the production of *Attila* at Milan.

> Merelli was called before the directors of the theatre, who wished to force him to give *Attila*, and this shameless creature said in public session that *Attila* is a bad opera, not in the least beautiful; however, in spite of his words, the directors compelled him to put it on as first opera of the season. Now, in hope of gain, he is doing all he can to get the Signor Maestro to conduct the rehearsals; but the latter does well not to accept and to make them pay through the nose for it; after the Signor Maestro learned what Merelli said to the directors, he sent for Lucca, the proprietor of the score, and asked him as a favour to make Merelli pay 3,000 francs for *Attila*.

Lucca went further. When Merelli approached him Lucca asked, not 3,000, but 5,000 Austrian lire for the score—an unheard-of fee for a single season at one theatre. 'When Merelli heard this Jew's demand he went straight to the chief of police, who seems to have settled for a payment of 3,000 francs. . . . Merelli then tried to get the Signor Maestro to put it on the stage, but he replied with a very decisive "No" [*un bel no grande grande*].'

Resumption of work brought a recurrence of Verdi's illness; but the new opera made rapid progress.

14th December 1846:

> Today I shall take almost a whole act of *Macbeth* to the copyist. You can't imagine the originality and beauty of this music; when the Signor Maestro lets me hear it I can't write for two or three hours, such is the enthusiasm it arouses in me. The Florentines are very fortunate to be the first to enjoy it!
>
> The Signor Maestro has been a bit out of sorts lately. He has had

intestinal pains which caused diarrhoea which gave him no peace; he did not look at all well. Then he got melancholy ideas in his head, saying that he was going to have an illness worse than last year, and many other things that nearly made me cry.

In God's good time the trouble ended, thanks to Dr Belcredi's treatment, and for three days now he has been well, and working.

Don't distress yourself, dear Signor Antonio, and remember that the Signor Maestro has near him one who loves him very much, and who does for him all those services which mercenary people would not do. For the last two days we have been working from nine in the morning until midnight, except for lunch time, and perhaps it's a bit too much, but it'll only be for a few more days, and then we shall renew our walks and our little amusements. I am writing in his house at the same table and thus I have always the benefit of his advice and we get on together so well.

19th December:

Macbeth gets better and better: what sublime music! I can tell you there are things that make one's hair stand on end! It costs him enormous effort to write this music, but he succeeds marvellously!! The first two acts are almost finished. . . . Varesi, when he left for Rome, took with him the scene of the Banquet and the Apparition and he attracted wide attention in all Milan, saying that that was the most beautiful and most dramatic of all Verdi's music. At Piacenza he said even more. In all the towns he passed through—Parma, Bologna, Florence—he shouted like a madman to everyone that he had with him Verdi's most sublime music.

27th December:

Furore! Furore! Furore! *Attila* raised the roof, as the journalists say. Clamorous applause after every number and endless recalls, even without the encores they wanted, but which the management wouldn't allow. The theatre packed, so that it was impossible to move; they opened the doors at four o'clock and we had to wait until half past seven. La Tadolini and Moriani sang as no one else can sing. . . . Marini was unsurpassable, both as actor and singer. De Bassini sustained his role well. In short, all the singers and the opera aroused fanatical enthusiasm and uproar enough to make the Old and the New Testaments tremble.

The *mise en scène* was wretched. The sun rose before the music indicated the sunrise. The sea, instead of being stormy and tempestuous, was calm and without a ripple. There were hermits without any huts; there were priests but no altar; in the banquet scene Attila gave a banquet without any lights . . . and when the storm came the sky remained serene and limpid as on the most beautiful spring day. Everyone (aloud and in their hearts) cursed Merelli for having treated *Attila* so badly. After the performance those going home past the Maestro's windows shouted: 'Evviva il Maestro!' If you had come here you would have been overjoyed.

It was after Merelli's maltreatment of *Attila* that Verdi wrote the well-known letter to Ricordi, approving the contract drawn up for

Macbeth at Florence, but insisting that the opera should never be allowed to be performed at La Scala.

> I have examples enough to persuade me that here they don't know how, or don't want, to put on operas, and especially my operas, as they should be put on. I cannot forget the execrable manner in which *I Lombardi*, *Ernani*, *I due Foscari*, etc., were produced. Another example I have before my eyes with *Attila*. I ask you yourself whether, in spite of a good company of singers, this opera could be staged worse than it is?

Field Marshal Radetzky himself enjoyed a visit to La Scala, and heard Verdi's *Attila*. The old warrior, now over eighty, was well aware of the gathering revolutionary storm, though his warnings were not taken very seriously in Vienna. Remarkably vigorous for his years, he had some difficulty in getting on his horse, but once mounted he could stay in the saddle eight hours or so. The last of his four illegitimate children by Giuditta Meregalli, a Milanese laundry-woman, had been born in the previous year. Radetzky's correspondence with Giuditta, written in execrable Italian, has been published by the Italians, but his letters to his daughter Friederike are more interesting.[1] Even better than hearing an opera he liked watching a ballet: 'I lead my usual life; I stay at the Scala theatre until half past ten when Mme Elssler dances; when she doesn't I go to bed at half past eight.' In a letter of 24th January 1847 he gives news of the former Countess Samoyloff:

> Mme Elssler caused a furore and earns well-deserved applause; Mme Tadolini does the same in *Attila*. That's all the news I can give you from here. Mme Samoyloff, who lives with her brother-in-law, is leaving on the 29th for Paris. During her stay at Milan she only gave one single dinner party; she is becoming extremely corpulent and ageing very much.

It is sad that even daily baths in asses' milk could not stay the passage of the years.

In this January there was some talk of Antonio Barezzi himself coming to Milan. He was expected on the 27th and Muzio went to meet him at Porta Romana; but the weather turned bad and Barezzi stayed at home. This caused quite an outburst from Verdi, faithfully recorded in one of Muzio's letters:

> When I came home alone the Signor Maestro became furious because you hadn't come. Then this morning, when he received your letter and that from Giovannino, he said: 'They are people afraid of a bit of snow and ice. They are well, robust, strong, with stomachs of iron, and they are afraid of a bit of snow, while I'—the Signor Maestro said—'must go to Florence in a fortnight's time even if it rains thunderbolts, and cross the Apennines covered with snow, in danger of being buried in a landslide, as on my return from Rome. They enjoy themselves; I work from eight in

[1] *Briefe des Feldmarschalls Radetzky an seine Tochter Friederike* (Vienna, 1892).

the morning until twelve at night, and I consume my life in working. What a perfidious destiny is mine!' These and other things the Signor Maestro said—I can't remember them all. But I believe that what you haven't done you will do, and that you will come to see him at Florence.

There was some further discussion of the possibility of Muzio's becoming municipal music master at Busseto, but, in the mood in which he was then, all that Verdi would say when consulted was: 'Do what you like. I won't have anything to do with it.'

Barezzi *did* go to Florence, with his son Giovannino, risking thunderbolts and landslides, and there he had a wonderful time.

Before the Barezzis arrived, Muzio and Verdi were busy at Florence with the rehearsals, Muzio being entrusted with the preparation of *Attila*, which was to precede the new opera, while Verdi took endless pains to convey to the artists his ideas of the way *Macbeth* should be sung and acted. Outside the theatre the composer made many new friends. The Countess Maffei had procured for him from Manzoni a letter of introduction to the poet Giuseppe Giusti, and through Giusti he made the acquaintance of a group of Florentine intellectuals, including the Marquis Gino Capponi, Baron Bettino Ricasoli, the poet G. B. Niccolini, and the sculptors Lorenzo Bartolini and Giovanni Dupré. Verdi also, rather reluctantly, accepted an invitation to meet the easy-going Grand Duke, whom he found well acquainted with the whole story of his life, including the battle of Busseto. Early biographies,such as the text accompanying a lithograph published in 1845,[1] and B. Bermani's *Schizzi sulla vita e sulle opere del Maestro Giuseppe Verdi*, reprinted in 1846 from Ricordi's *Gazzetta Musicale di Milano*, had made Antonio Barezzi's services generally known, and on his arrival at Florence he was made much of by Verdi's admirers. Baron Ricasoli sent his carriage, and Barezzi was shown the sights of the city, the galleries and the museums. He was able to write home, describing how, after *Macbeth*, he left the Pergola theatre with Verdi, and they were accompanied back to their hotel, a mile away, by an enormous cheering crowd. Verdi himself chose the occasion of the publication of the vocal score of *Macbeth* to express publicly his gratitude to Antonio Barezzi:

For a long time it has been in my mind to dedicate an opera to you, who have been to me a father, a benefactor and a friend. It is an obligation I ought to have fulfilled before now, and I should have done so if compelling circumstances had not prevented it. Here now is this *Macbeth*, which is dearer to me than all my other operas, and which I therefore deem more worthy of being presented to you. I offer it from my heart; accept it in the

[1] Reproduced in Gatti's *Verdi nelle immagini*, p. 185. Luzio (*Carteggi*, IV, p. 81) publishes a letter from Muzio to Giuseppe Demaldè concerning this brief biography. Demaldè supplied the materials for it; Luzio mistakenly believed that the letter referred to Demaldè's own later *Cenni biografici*. See also Muzio's letter to Barezzi of 9th June 1845.

same way, and let it bear witness to my eternal remembrance, and the gratitude and love of your most affectionate

G. VERDI.

In Baron Ricasoli and Gino Capponi, in Giusti and Niccolini, Verdi had come into touch with some of the principal political and literary leaders and agitators of the liberal and nationalistic movement in Tuscany. Giusti in *Sant' Ambrogio*, his poem about Milan under the Austrians, referred to a famous chorus from *I Lombardi*:

> Era un coro del Verdi; il coro a Dio
> Là de' Lombardi miseri assetati;
> Quello, *O Signore, dal tetto natio*,
> Che tanti petti ha scossi e inebriati.

Macbeth, even though it did, like *I Lombardi*, include a chorus of exiles, which could be turned to patriotic use, was, in Giusti's opinion, a deviation from Verdi's true path. He wrote to the composer, advising the abandonment of such foreign and fantastic subjects:

You know that the chord of sorrow is that which finds the readiest echo in our breasts; but sorrow assumes different characters, according to the time and the nature and condition of this or that nation. The kind of sorrow that fills now the minds of us Italians is the sorrow of a people that feels the need of a better destiny, the sorrow of one who has fallen and desires to rise, the sorrow of one who repents and awaits and longs for regeneration. Accompany, my Verdi, this high and solemn sorrow with your noble harmonies; do what you can to nourish it, to strengthen it and direct it to its objective.

Giusti's letter is well known;[1] Verdi's reply, of 27th March 1847, though it has been published,[2] is hardly known at all:

MY DEAR GIUSTI,

Thanks, a thousand thanks, for your most welcome letter. You have compensated me in part for the displeasure of not having been able to embrace you before leaving Florence.

Yes, you put it very well: 'The chord of sorrow is that which finds the readiest echo in our breasts.' You speak of art like the great man you are, and I shall certainly follow your advice, for I understand what you mean to say! Oh, if we had a poet who knew how to design a drama of the kind you mean! But unfortunately—you will yourself admit it—if we want anything at all effective we are forced, to our shame, to have recourse to foreign things. How many subjects there are in our own history!

Ricasoli will have told you that I wanted you to write a line of yours on a piece of paper, with your signature. If you can do so I shall be most grateful.

[1] *Copialettere*, pp. 449–50, and elsewhere.

[2] 'Una lettera inedita di Verdi' (*Corriere della Sera*, 12th May 1933, reprinted from a French periodical *Dante*). The letter has been reprinted recently by Abbiati (I, pp. 691–2) from the autograph in the Gallini Collection.

Farewell, my dear Giusti; love me, for I love you much and esteem you infinitely. Farewell!

Your

VERDI.

Verdi seems to accept the poet's rebuke. Nothing could be done about his next opera, *I Masnadieri*, after Schiller, which was already half written, but it is probable that Giusti's words weighed with Verdi in the following year in the choice of the subject of *La Battaglia di Legnano*, a piece of unconcealed patriotic propaganda.

Muzio accompanied Barezzi to Busseto and stayed there for a few days before returning to Milan, where he found Verdi and Ricordi in a rage because he had not got back in time to correct the proofs of the vocal score of *Macbeth*. Soon he was working 'night and day' on the preparation of a reduction of the opera for piano duet and on other commissions from Ricordi, but then, suddenly, all this had to be abandoned to other people, while Muzio set out on the great adventure of his life, his journey to Paris and London in the company of the Signor Maestro.

It took about a week for them to reach Paris, travelling by the St Gotthard route, through Switzerland to Strasbourg, then down the Rhine, with halts at Karlsruhe, Mainz and Cologne, and on to Brussels and thence to Paris. Muzio noted down the distances and the times taken, by diligence, lake or river steamer, and train; he counted the tunnels they passed through, and described the journey and all the sights they saw in a long letter to Barezzi. They reached Paris at seven o'clock in the morning on 1st June. Two days later Muzio was in London, alone, Verdi having heard a rumour that Jenny Lind did not wish to sing in *I Masnadieri*. Until he was assured that she would do so, as stipulated in the contract with Lumley, he would not set foot in England.

Muzio's impressions of London, its inhabitants, the climate and the English Sunday, are most entertaining:

4th June 1847:

What a chaos is London! What confusion! Paris is nothing in comparison. People shouting, poor people weeping, steamers flying, men on horseback, in carriages, on foot, and all howling like the damned. My dear Signor Antonio, you can't imagine what it's like.

Milan is nothing. Paris is *something* in comparison with London; but London is a city unique in all the world; it suffices to consider that there are almost two million inhabitants—then one can imagine what an immense city it is. . . .

I have taken apartments for the Maestro and myself, on condition that they please him, because if he can't work in peace, then we shall go into the country, for Lumley has had an apartment specially prepared in his country retreat, foreseeing that Verdi will not be able to work in the midst of all this noise. . . .

Here one doesn't do business in francs, but in sterling; the money I have spent here in one day would suffice for ten days at Milan, and that's no exaggeration. As soon as Verdi is here we shall get down to hard work and quickly flee from this Babylon. One needs patience to put up with the noise, but it's the money that counts. For three rooms I wanted to take they asked £5 a week, and ten shillings for the maid. Instead I have taken only two rooms, and I have had a bed for myself put in the parlour, which during the daytime serves as a most beautiful divan and at night becomes a bed; if Verdi likes this, very well; if not, we will take the three rooms and pay £5.

Verdi arrived a few days later.

16th June:

It's a mistake to say that all Englishmen speak French; there is nobody, one can say, in the shops and stores, who speaks French. The Englishman hates the Frenchman and his language. The high society of the Lords speak Italian well, having almost all been for years in Italy for amusement and diversion, and when one goes into society at least one can make oneself understood; otherwise it would be sheer desperation. You will have guessed, without my telling you, that we are working from morning to night. We get up at five in the morning and we work until six in the evening (supper time); then we go for a while to the theatre and return at eleven and go to bed, so as to be up early next morning. The opera progresses, and two acts are already at the copyist's, and by next Monday, perhaps, everything will be finished; then there's the scoring to be done. I am of the opinion—mark my words!—that, after *Ernani*, it's the most popular opera that Verdi has written, and the one that will have the widest circulation. . . .

We in Italy imagine that the English don't love music; this is a mistake. It is said that the English know nothing but how to pay for the pleasure of hearing great artists, but that they don't understand anything; this is a mistake that the French have spread about and that the Italians have adopted because it's a French idea. I say that no man pays for things he doesn't like and which don't give him pleasure. The English have never hissed a masterpiece. They have never received with indifference a *Barber of Seville*, as Rome has, or a *William Tell*, as Paris has, and they have never hissed an *Otello*, as Naples did on its first appearance.

Muzio found the English rather *too* fond of music, when they sat through a concert programme of fifty items, lasting six hours. Jenny Lind he thought a great artist, but disliked the way she showed off her *bravura* by arbitrary trills and *fioriture*, 'things which pleased in the last century, but not in 1847. We Italians are not accustomed to things of this sort and if la Lind came to Italy she would abandon her mania for embellishments and sing simply, having a voice uniform and flexible enough to sustain a phrase in la Frezzolini's manner'. Lumley had placed a box at Verdi's disposal. When the queen and royal family attended a performance of *Norma* Muzio 'stared his eyes out' at the rich dresses and diamonds and jewellery worn by the 'Dames and Ladies and Misses'. The latter, for their part, were equally interested in the composer and, as one paper recorded, 'devoured poor Verdi with their opera-glasses'. 'This is quite true,' Muzio told Barezzi. 'Every evening they look at nobody but Verdi. He is already popular in London, as he is in all Italy.'

It's cold in London; it does nothing but rain, with wind all the time, and the Maestro doubts whether there is any sun, for he has never seen it shining owing to the mist, which is continual. It's weather that gets on one's nerves in an incredible manner. Blessed Italy, where we have at least got the sun!

I want to make you laugh. . . . Last night the Maestro happened to see a newspaper printed in London in French, the *Revue et Gazette des Théâtres*, and there he read these words: 'Verdi, dont l'aide-de-camp, Emmanuel, un jeune maestro, est arrivé avant-hier, est attendu aujourd' hui.' 'There you are,' said the Maestro. 'They have created you my aide-de-camp,' and he made me read the paper and we had a good laugh; but I can't find out how they learned my name, seeing that the paper was printed the morning after my arrival.

Considering the time of year, Verdi and Muzio were certainly unfortunate in the weather they encountered in England. On 28th June it rained eight times, and eight times a pallid sun was seen through the mists; it was still cold and windy. Then there was 'this continual smoke, which poisons the air, blackens the face and burns the eyes'.

29th June:

Byron says: 'In England there are nine months of winter and three months without sun'; and it is Byron, England's greatest poet, who says that. . . . On Sunday not a soul is seen in the streets; they are all in church, where they make their sermons. Many, however, stay in bed almost all day, from what one hears, and others go into the country and the environs of London, for amusement and debauchery. The English say that on Sundays only dogs and Frenchmen are seen in the streets of London, and it is true that those one sees are all travellers and foreigners.

The completion of *I Masnadieri* was delayed by the depressing effect of the climate, which made Verdi 'more lunatic and melancholy than usual'. However, rehearsals with the soloists began at the end of June. Jenny Lind, on closer acquaintance, was found to be good and kind, and a profound musician. Muzio remarks on her ugly face, serious expression, big nose, Nordic colouring and very large hands and feet. But he liked her: 'She leads a very retired life; she receives nobody, but lives to herself; she told me she hates the theatre and the stage, and says she is unhappy and will not be content until she has no more to do with theatrical people and the theatre itself. In this matter she is very much in agreement with the Maestro's opinions; he too hates the theatre, and looks forward to retirement.' Verdi himself went out very little; he received many invitations but refused most of them: 'First of all because it's such a waste of time, and then because he can't eat those foods full of drugs and pepper, and all those cold dishes, and wine so strong that it's like rhum.' He even rejected an invitation, sent through Lablache, to meet the queen.

While *I Masnadieri* was in preparation a rival company of singers was appearing at Covent Garden. Muzio reported also on events at this theatre:

29th June:

It seems they're not going to put on *Macbeth*, as Ronconi says the part doesn't suit him; but that's mere punctilio and because he knows he was responsible for the failure of *Ernani* in Paris last year. Well, as soon as Verdi arrived in London, Ronconi sent Marini to say that he would be glad to go over *I due Foscari* with him, and come to an understanding about certain things that did not suit him; but Verdi sent word in reply that he would gladly have taught him *Ernani*, since he had had a fiasco with that in Paris, but wouldn't teach him *I due Foscari* because, if he wished, he has talent enough to sing that part and make a success of it. On this account Ronconi doesn't want to sing *Macbeth* any more.

18th July:

The management of the other theatre—Covent Garden—has *gone bankrupt*. Maestro Persiani, who was the impresario, has fled with his wife, leaving debts of £30,000. Salvi, the tenor, who had signed bills of exchange for 30,000 francs, has also fled—no one knows where. . . . It is possible that the theatre will close, unless they find someone willing to take over the company. Who knows whether some mad Englishman won't come forward to play the impresario? The debts amount to more than three million francs. It's true that an artist is paid well in London, but then they know *well* how to get their money back, by skinning him. You may believe me: a pound a day in one's pocket is nothing.

Those Covent Garden singers, the old ones that is, are all hostile to Verdi's music, and didn't want to put on either *Nabucco* or *I Lombardi*; they wanted to attract the public with old operas, but everyone now has his eyes open and novelties are wanted.

They put on *I due Foscari* with great success, but only for two performances, and seeing that lots of people came to hear it, they were furious and haven't performed it since, out of jealousy, saying that they didn't want to be beholden to a composer who was the rival of their theatre, and they wanted to do without his operas. And thus by punctilio they have ruined the management and ruined themselves.

Maestro Costa, who was so much in favour at court, having deliberately played la Lind's accompaniments badly, has fallen into disgrace with the queen, and recently a concert was given and he was not called for, and it is said that the queen has had him rebuked. From a *Neapolitan* la Lind could certainly not have expected anything good, for they are all envious, proud, and, not being able to do anything well or sing well themselves, they don't want anyone else to do well either.

I Masnadieri was heard for the first time on 22nd July:

The opera aroused a furore. From the prelude to the last finale there was nothing but applause, *evvivas*, recalls and encores. The Maestro himself conducted, seated on a chair higher than all the others, baton in hand. As soon as he appeared in the orchestra-pit there was continuous applause, which lasted a quarter of an hour. They hadn't finished applauding when there arrived the queen and Prince Albert, her consort, the queen mother and the Duke of Cambridge, son of the queen, and all the royal family, and an infinite number of lords and dukes. It suffices to say that the boxes were full of ladies in *grande toilette*, and the pit crowded so that no one could remember ever having seen so many people. At half past four the doors were opened and the people burst into the theatre with fury such as had never been seen before. It was something new for London, and Lumley has made them pay well for it.

The takings amounted to £6,000 and surpassed even the amount taken on the evening when the queen attended a gala performance. The Maestro was cheered, called on the stage, alone and with the singers, flowers were thrown to him, and nothing was heard but 'Viva Verdi, *bietifol*'. . . .

Tomorrow, Saturday, second performance. If the Maestro conducts on Tuesday as well, we shall leave on Wednesday for Paris; if he doesn't conduct on Tuesday, we shall leave on Monday.

Muzio's last word on the English is given in a later letter:

Verdi aroused a decided furore in London, but the English are a formal and thoughtful people, and never give way to enthusiasm like the Italians, partly because they don't understand too well, and partly because they say educated people shouldn't make a row. The English go to the theatre to show off their riches and luxury; when an opera already printed is performed they have the score in hand and follow with their eyes what the singer does and if, according to their ideas, the singer does well, they applaud and sometimes call for an encore; but they never insist, as our people do. I often went to hear the famous *Rachel*, the leading tragic actress. I saw some Englishmen with the printed tragedy in their hands, not looking at the actress, but watching to see if she said all the words.

Verdi and Muzio reached Paris on 27th July. On 8th August Muzio told Barezzi: 'Today I am leaving for Milan; Verdi is staying in Paris.' The separation was expected to be only temporary; neither Verdi nor Muzio realized that a stage in both their lives had come to an end.

Muzio, back in Milan, witnessed the ever increasing tension between the Austrians and the local populace. He invited Barezzi to come to Milan in September for the solemn entry of the new archbishop, Cardinal Romilli, the successor of Gaisruck. This was made the occasion of a patriotic demonstration by the Italians, with cheers and the singing of hymns to Pio Nono, who they hoped would lead them to freedom. A few days later there was rioting in the streets: 'A few poor devils lost their lives,' Muzio told Barezzi, 'and others will lose theirs as a result of their wounds. You will hear from the Selettis the whole sad story. All seems to be quiet at present, but only a spark is needed to set everything in flames. If I see that things are taking a turn for the worse I shall go to Paris or come to Busseto.' Muzio, clearly, was not exactly a leader of the Resistance Movement.[1]

Opposition to the Austrians was organized by a secret committee, which ordered boycotts of the lotteries, of tobacco and other state monopolies. Satires were printed and inscriptions appeared on the walls. 'House to let' was written on the governor's palace, and collaborators threatened with death. Radetzky told his daughter on 11th January 1848; 'The Countess Samoyloff was asked by two gentlemen not to receive Germans any more in her house. In the presence of those persons she sent for the porter and told him: "I am at home to every German and not at home to any Italian". However, two days later she left for Paris. Mme Carpani's life was threatened and she, too, has taken flight to Vienna.'

Great hostility was aroused by Fanny Elssler, who returned to Milan during this winter, when she objected to members of the *corps de ballet* wearing medallions of Pio Nono. Hitherto she had enjoyed enormous popularity, and not long before this her chamber-pot had been purchased by a fanatical admirer for 600 lire. But on 12th February she was hissed in the ballet *Faust*, fainted on the stage, broke her contract and returned to Vienna.

The scene was set for the revolution.

Nothing of all this was witnessed by Verdi, who stayed on and on in Paris. There he and Giuseppina Strepponi had found one another again.

[1] When the revolution occurred he is said to have thrown out of the window at the retreating Austrian troops everything he possessed except his piano, and to have fought at the barricades. Perhaps he did. But there is no justification at all for Gatti's misuse of passages from Muzio's letters to Barezzi. He passes over expressions of timidity in letters of 13th (above) and 20th September, and transplants another: 'I have had no further trouble, but I fear for the future; I shan't stay at Milan if I have serious unpleasantness', from *before* the revolution (17th February 1848) to *after* it (first edition, I, p. 314; second edition, p. 251).

CHAPTER

5

Verdi and Giuseppina Strepponi

FROM THE very beginning of his operatic career, Verdi's life had been strangely linked with that of Giuseppina Strepponi. In a sense Giuseppina discovered Verdi. Long before she had even heard of him, of course, other people had recognized his outstanding qualities. Barezzi, Provesi and Massini could all have claimed to have 'discovered' Verdi, at different stages of his development. They all did their best to encourage him and help him towards his goal, which, it soon became evident, was the conquest of La Scala at Milan. Giuseppina, however, was the first person *inside* the magic circle to sense his greatness, to recognize the right of entry that belonged to this pale, black-bearded young man knocking at the door. She was a *prima donna*, whose opinion counted for something in that world. As we have seen, in spite of what Gatti and his innumerable Italian followers have written, it is not true that Giuseppina was Merelli's mistress. Extra-musical considerations played no part in the impresario's decision to put *Oberto* on the stage after hearing the work praised by Giuseppina.

According to Gatti,[1] Verdi called to see Giuseppina in the spring of 1839, with the score of *Oberto* under his arm, and played the opera through to her:

> Before the season ends, Verdi presents himself to la Strepponi; if she, who has such influence over Merelli, thinks well of her part in the opera he has composed, there can be no doubt that it will be performed.
>
> La Strepponi, after hearing it, expresses her full approbation of the music and praises it openly.

[1] First edition, I, p. 160; second edition, p. 135.

Although this story has been taken over from Gatti's biography, where it apparently originated, by almost all subsequent writers on Verdi, it is not supported by any documentary or other evidence. It is directly contradicted by a passage in a letter from Giuseppina to Verdi of 3rd January 1853, in which she declares that the year then just beginning was the eleventh year of their acquaintance. She thus dated their personal relationship from the time of the production of *Nabucco* and not from the time of the first consideration of *Oberto* by Merelli.

Verdi himself describes the events leading up to the acceptance of *Oberto* in a letter to Opprandino Arrivabene of 7th March 1874:

> My opera *Oberto* was to have been given in the spring of 1839 for the benefit of the Pio Istituto Filarmonico. Peppina, Ronconi and Moriani were to have sung in it. The parts were already distributed, when Moriani became seriously ill and could not sing any more. One fine morning, after the end of the season, a messenger from the theatre came to say that Merelli wanted to speak to me. I had never yet spoken to Merelli and believed the invitation was a mistake. Nevertheless I went. Merelli said these very words: 'I have heard la Strepponi and Ronconi speak well of your opera. If you like to adapt it for la Marini, Salvi, etc., I will have it performed without any expense to you. If the opera is successful, we will sell it and share the receipts; if it fails, so much the worse for you and for me!'

In the account given to Ricordi for the Italian edition of Pougin's biography Verdi says that Merelli 'had overheard on the stage, one evening, a conversation between Signora Strepponi and Giorgio Ronconi, in which the former had spoken very favourably of the music of *Oberto*, and the impression she had formed was shared by Ronconi'. We know that Verdi's memory was subject to strange lapses, but, in the absence of evidence to the contrary, there is no reason to suppose that he was wrong in believing that he owed the final acceptance of *Oberto* simply to the happy chance of this conversation on the stage being overheard by the impresario.

Earlier negotiations had been taken out of Verdi's hands by Massini and Merighi. He tells us himself that he had never met Merelli. There is no reason why he should have met the singers. Giuseppina, playing over the part that had been given to her to study, or rehearsing it with the *maestro concertatore* of La Scala, divined in a marvellous way the latent talents of the unknown composer.

Nearly three years went by before their paths crossed again. During that time Verdi lost his wife, saw his second opera fail disastrously, and then, from the depths of despair, arose to create *Nabucco*. Giuseppina, for her part, experienced public triumphs and private disasters, felt passion, anguish and regret. A month or more after bearing the second of Moriani's two children, she stayed for a few days at Milan, on her way from Venice to Genoa, and during this stay at Milan she met Verdi for the first time. The date can be fixed with certainty—22nd December 1841.

In the case of *Nabucco*, when it seemed doubtful whether the opera would, after all, be produced, Verdi really *did* call to see Giuseppina and enlist her support.

Gatti states [1] that this visit took place on 23rd October—a quite impossible date, when Giuseppina was still at Trieste, and in the last stages of pregnancy. He was misled by a mistake in an article in the periodical *Verdi: Rivista per l'anno giubilare* (Bologna, 1926; only one issue appeared). This article, 'Modeste Origini', which is unsigned, includes extracts from a document of remarkable interest, a letter written by Giovannino Barezzi, who was on a visit to Milan, to his father, Verdi's benefactor, at Busseto. The true date of the letter is given in the catalogue of an exhibition: '*La Stampa*' *nel quarantesimo della morte di Giuseppe Verdi. Mostra dei cimeli verdiani* (Turin, 1941). Item 85 of this catalogue includes the letter in question, lent by Luigi Agostino Garibaldi, of Genoa:

> Two letters of Giovanni Barezzi, one dated 11th January 1841, in which he speaks of *Oberto*, the other dated 26th December 1841, in which he speaks of *Nabucco* and la Strepponi.

This precious document is given below in the unsatisfactory form in which it appears in the article 'Modeste Origini', except that the date is corrected. One suspects that parts of the editorial commentary have strayed into the text of the letter itself; the tenses may even have been altered throughout, for the sake of the narration. The original text ought certainly to be published.

After the 'Cartelone', the placard with the announcement of the operas to be performed during the Carnival season, appeared without mention of *Nabucco*, Verdi returned to his rooms in a temper and discussed the situation with his friends. What is apparently a quotation from Giovannino Barezzi's letter begins here:

> . . . and then he decides to write to Merelli in rather harsh terms. Merelli resents that and shows the letter to Pasetti and says: 'See how Verdi has misunderstood this! That is not my intention, but I did it so that I should gain credit with the subscribers when, towards the end of Carnival, I put out a new placard, with the announcement of his opera. Tell Verdi, however, to show la Strepponi her part, and if she wants to sing it I'll gladly put it on.'
>
> Pasetti sends for Verdi and they go to see la Strepponi; they explain the situation and she very willingly agrees to sing in the opera and adds: 'Come here tomorrow at half past one and I'll look through my part.'
>
> Next day—23rd [December] 1841, that is—Verdi and Pasetti go to see

[1] First edition, I, p. 182; second edition, p. 153.

la Strepponi at the agreed time; she tries over her part at the pianoforte with Verdi and then says to him: 'I like this music very much, and I want to sing it when I make my *début*,' and at once adds: 'Let's go and see Ronconi.' They get in Pasetti's cab, which had been waiting at the door, and go to see Ronconi. La Strepponi *points out to him the beauties of the opera* and Verdi tells him the plot. Ronconi, after hearing all about it, says: 'Very well, this evening I'll speak to the impresario, and tell him that I don't want to sing in Nini's opera, but that I want to sing in yours.'

It is strange that there is not a word about this episode in the account given by Verdi to Ricordi. However, as the author of the article says, the truth of the story is incontestable, for Verdi himself added his signature to that of Giovannino Barezzi, at the foot of the letter. The dates of these events are clear: the placard came out on 21st December and Verdi probably wrote to Merelli on the same day, Pasetti and Verdi visited Giuseppina on 22nd and 23rd December. Gatti, misled by the wrong date in the article, gets his chronology all wrong. He quotes the conversation of Giuseppina and Ronconi, but makes this *precede* the publication of the placard on 21st December and Verdi's angry letter to Merelli. Abbiati takes over all Gatti's mistakes and develops from them eleven pages of almost pure fiction.[1]

Pasetti's part in this episode may have given rise to stories which Verdi himself, in later years, explicitly denied. On 28th January 1876, he wrote to Giulio Ricordi: [2]

I read in *Il Pungolo* various assertions about *Nabucco.* Without wishing to underline the inaccuracies about the contract between Merelli and me, or those about the composer (it was not Nini) who refused to set the *Nabucco* libretto, I am anxious it should be known that neither Pasetti nor anybody else put down money as security, so that my opera could be performed, for the simple reason that Merelli never even thought of asking for it. In any case, I still had the greater part of the 4,000 Austrian lire paid me, in accordance with the contract, by Merelli himself (who was neither 'desolate' nor 'desperate') the day after the fiasco of *Un giorno di regno.* And may I add that if there had been need of security, and the money I possessed insufficient, I should have turned to the man who first helped me, to my second father, ANTONIO BAREZZI. To *him* I owe everything, and *only* to him! No one else ever sacrificed a *centesimo* for me. If it were worth while I should have to correct innumerable inaccurate assertions, especially about the early years of my career, but, I repeat, it is not worth while. Speak about that either to the author of the article or to the editor of *Il Pungolo*, just as you think best. I don't want to start any polemics about it.

[1] I, pp. 385–95.
[2] This letter was published in the *Gazzetta Musicale di Milano* on 30th January 1876. A very inaccurate and incomplete transcription appears in Gino Monaldi's *Verdi nella vita e nell'arte* (Milan, n.d.), pp. 105–6.

From remarks by the Countess Maffei it appears that Pasetti was in the habit of boasting about what he had done for Verdi. The vocal score of *Oberto* had been dedicated to him by Ricordi, the publisher.

Unhappily, when Giuseppina returned to Milan from Genoa, on 16th February 1842, to appear at La Scala in Donizetti's *Belisario* and Verdi's *Nabucco*, her voice was badly affected by the general deterioration of her health, as described in an earlier chapter. Donizetti's message for a Roman impresario, in a letter to Antonio Vasselli of 4th March, shortly before the first performance of *Nabucco*, is worth further consideration:

> Tell him that this singer created such a furore here in *Belisario* that she was the only one who *never* got any applause, that her Verdi did not want her in his own opera, and the management imposed her on him.

Although he had been counting on her appearance in his opera, and although he actually owed to her its final acceptance by Merelli, it is understandable that Verdi, in the circumstances, would have preferred another singer for the part of Abigaille. We have seen that what is generally written about Giuseppina Strepponi's share in the success of *Nabucco* is quite untrue. The really interesting thing about this remark of Donizetti's is the fact that he refers familiarly to Giuseppina and '*her* Verdi'. At this early date, that is astonishing. There can be no question, yet, of a love affair between them. Donizetti's remark can only be interpreted as meaning that, in her enthusiasm for Verdi's work, she had talked about him so much and so warmly that she got *herself* talked about among her fellow artists. It is a wonderful thing that the woman who was to become Verdi's second wife, and spend half a century by his side, should have been among his very earliest admirers in the operatic world, and should have played a vital role in the launching of both *Oberto* and *Nabucco*. It can be truly said that Giuseppina Strepponi, in a sense, *discovered* Verdi.

How much light a single word in a contemporary letter can throw upon the past! We can do with a *lot* more light upon this early period of Verdi's life, about which we have all too little documentary evidence and all too many romantic legends. A legend, created by Gatti, makes him, in the post-*Nabucco* period, the rival of Donizetti for the favours of Giuseppina Appiani. On examination, this legend falls to pieces, revealing itself as the product of confusion between two different ladies of the same surname, neither of whom, in all probability, ever had a love affair with either composer. Another legend, invented by Barbiera, represents Verdi at the feet of a diaphanous aristocratic maiden, Gina della Somaglia, who turns out on closer investigation to have been a sturdy matron at this time, with a family. And then there were the singers, of course, including Giuseppina Strepponi.

It is very difficult to decide just when Giuseppina and Verdi became something more than friends. Everything that has been written on this subject is based, more or less, on guesswork. We can emphatically reject, however, the outrageous statement, in Aldo Oberdorfer's posthumous volume, that the beginning of their love affair was 'in all probability *anterior to the death of Margherita*.' [1] That is the most gratuitous and odious insult that even the Italians have ever offered to the memory of their great man.

During and after the performances of *Nabucco* a warm friendship began to develop between Verdi and Giuseppina. As is well known, he came to her for advice about the figure he should ask for his next opera, and was told that he ought not to claim more than Bellini had been paid for *Norma*. The incident took place in her dressing-room at La Scala, on 10th March, the night of the second performance of *Nabucco*. In later life she used to recall sometimes, with laughter, Verdi's embarrassed demeanour, his taciturnity, his odd gloves, and hands that did not know where to rest, during these early visits to her dressing-room at the theatre or her apartments. She had little enough to laugh about at the time. She had lost her voice, ruined her health, exhausted almost all her savings; her career seemed at an end, and yet she had to support her mother, two brothers and sister and two illegitimate children of her own. On 26th March she was still contemplating the possibility of marriage with someone 'not very rich' and 'a complete stranger to theatrical affairs'. These facts need to be borne in mind in considering the development of her relations with Verdi.

The year 1842 is the least well documented of the whole of Verdi's life. It is the year, we know, of his entry into society. When Barbiera in 1892 was gathering material for his well-known book on the Countess Maffei and her *salon*, Verdi told him: 'I was introduced to her in the first months of 1842. From that time onward our friendly relations were constant as long as she lived.' No letters to the Countess Maffei survive from the earliest years of their friendship. Instead, from 1842, we have only the entry in the autograph album of Sofia de' Medici (see p. 99), the two letters to Emilia Morosini (see p. 104), written in that curious and rather embarrassingly gallant style, and the two curt notes to Lucca (see p. 123). The album entry is dated from Milan, 6th May, the first letter from Milan, 21st July; the second letter was written at Busseto, apparently in July; the two notes are again from Milan, some time in September and 13th October.

It is obviously important to discover where Giuseppina was living,

[1] *Giuseppe Verdi* (Milan, 1949), p. 66.

and if possible what she was doing in 1842, after the last performance of *Nabucco* on 19th March. It was over a year before she returned to the stage. The perpetually wandering existence of a singer had not permitted her to form a home of her own; we do not know where her family was living, nor who was looking after her children. No biographer of Verdi or Giuseppina has hitherto been able to tell us anything at all about her life at this time. The last letter to Lanari from this year is that of 26th March, from Milan. It can safely be assumed that the prospects of matrimony, mentioned in this letter, soon evaporated: she had herself, at the time, little enough belief in them. And twice before, on reflection, she had refused to purchase security without love.

A most interesting letter, written three months after the last letter to Lanari, has recently come to light and been published by Enrico Benassi in the admirable periodical *Aurea Parma*.[1] It is addressed to Giacomo Tommasini of Parma, who had been, in his day, the most celebrated doctor in Italy. Now aged seventy-seven, he had seen his theories superseded and his followers turn aside, but he was still a famous man. Giuseppina had consulted him. The tone of this letter is very different from that of the racy correspondence with Lanari. Here we find her respectful, movingly sincere, though still with a touch of light humour; the later Giuseppina, most charming of letter-writers, is foreshadowed:

After your kind reception and the concern you have shown for the improvement of my health, I ought to have written to you several times already. I wanted to do so. I set myself at the writing table, but that blessed renown of yours is so great, and I so small, that it seemed excessive boldness on my part to direct a *scrawl* of mine into your hands and cause you to lose some minutes in reading it.

I venerate all great talents, but I idolize those few who have names I can easily pronounce, names at once sweet and solemn, names that are completely Italian, like Tommasini! And yet, in the presence of such people, my intellectual faculties stand paralysed; there remains to me only the ability to thank God, who still loves Italy, since He infuses such an emanation of his Divine Power in a few chosen sons of this great and unfortunate country!

I almost feel thankful for my illness, since it turned your partial attention towards me! Dr Marardetti, whom you charged with inquiries about my well-being, will have informed you, in *technical* terms, of the effect of the medicine which you prescribed for me. My weakness, or *morbid fatigue* through overwork, as I think it better called, being centred in the bronchial tubes, the *gargling* had a tonic effect on the upper part of the throat, on the tonsils, the uvula, etc., but did not bring about any improvement

[1] Giacomo Tommasini medico di Giuseppina Strepponi' (*Aurea Parma*, Jan.–Mar. 1951).

where I feel persistent weakness and the seat of the hoarseness. I am thinking of taking the waters of Recoaro. What do you advise? I don't dare to hope for a reply, but if you did send one it would be dear to me, like a first illusion.

Honour with your friendship,

GIUSEPPINA STREPPONI.

Milan, 24th June 1842.

Tommasini did reply, very pleasantly. Giuseppina, who destroyed so much that reminded her of things in her youth she wished to forget, kept his letter. It is found in her autograph album, preserved at Sant' Agata:

Parma, 2nd July 1842.

MY KIND FRIEND,

I don't hold my renown, such as it is, in such great account as you do. But even if it were very great it would be wearisome to me, and I would gladly renounce it, if it should cause me to be thought less courteous, less accessible and urbane than any man of feeling ought to be.

In view of my *renown*, you thought it excessive boldness to write to me, and were undecided whether to do so! Yet it did not occur to me to act the *famous man* with you, either at Parma when I visited you at the [Albergo della] Posta, or at Milan when I had the pleasure of seeing you again. You oblige me, therefore, to suppose one or other of these two things: either my manners and my language are not what I would like them to be, or you in interpreting them badly have been excessively unjust to me. I don't know which of these suppositions to prefer. But if the second is the more admissible (and the words at the end of your letter, 'I don't dare to hope for a reply', oblige me to believe that), then recant at once, understand me better, set aside my *renown*, and, without cold and inopportune considerations, grant me your friendship.

The waters at Recoaro may do you good. Be careful, however, of the highly variable temperatures of that district. If you are unable to go to Recoaro, and your stomach won't bear a liberal use of those waters, minute doses of iron, continued for a long time, would also benefit you. And, better than any medicines, *rest* will benefit you, since the *fatigue* which you mention was evidently the result of overwork.

Let me know if I can help you, meanwhile, quite freely, and notice how much more just I am than you are, and how much better I know you than you know me. I am sure you will write to me before leaving Milan and I expect to receive from you, before very long, a kind and friendly retraction.

Give my regards to Dr Morardét, and believe me always

Your affectionate friend,

G. TOMMASINI.

Tommasini addressed his letters: 'All'ornatissima Signora Giuseppina Strepponi a Milano.' In this and in Giuseppina's own letter we now have documentary proof that she stayed on at Milan after the end of the season at La Scala, and therefore that the possibility existed of the further development of her friendly relationship with Verdi. The fact that she went all the way to Parma to consult Tommasini suggests very strongly that Verdi had taken a hand in the direction of her affairs. Parma, the capital of the small state in which he was born, called up in him always a vein of fierce local patriotism. This applied both to music and to medicine. He once sent to Parma for a double-bass player, to show the musicians of the Scala orchestra how a certain passage should be performed, and in 1846 he sent word to Antonio Barezzi, through Muzio, that he should not come to Milan, which was 'no place for doctors', but should rather go for treatment to Parma, where he would be cured. It is very likely that he gave the same advice to Giuseppina. And when she had recovered it was at the Teatro Ducale, at Parma, that she reappeared on the stage,[1] on 17th April 1843, as Abigaille in *Nabucco*, in Verdi's presence. The agent responsible for the engagement of the singers at Parma was her old friend Cirelli.

Mercede Mundula has pointed out that not only did Verdi go himself to Parma for this occasion, but, contrary to his usual practice of supervising only the first few performances of his operas, he stayed there for almost the whole of the remainder of the season. On 11th February he had won his second big success at La Scala, with *I Lombardi*; on 25th February he told Demaldè that he did not know yet whether he would be going to Vienna or Parma to put on *Nabucco*, this being dependent on the offers made him by the impresarios, 'for, to tell the truth, the success or failure of *Nabucco* matters little to me'. On 20th March he left Milan for Vienna, where *Nabucco* was produced on 4th April; within a week he was back at Busseto. It is illuminating to see how his plans for the visit to Parma changed, and how he constantly deferred his return to Milan:

To Count Mocenigo, 9th April:

By the 14th I shall be at Parma, where I shall stay until the end of the month.

To Isidoro Cambiasi, from Parma, 29th April:

I shall be at Milan soon.

To Count Mocenigo, 3rd May:

I shall stay another eight or ten days.

To the same, 17th May:

I shall stay here until the evening of the 22nd.

[1] It is not true, as Gatti states (first edition, I, p. 221; second edition, p. 172), that Giuseppina had already appeared in *Nabucco* at Trieste.

To the same, 25th May:

If you reply by return of post you can address the letter to Parma; otherwise to Milan.

To Antonio Poggi, Parma, 30th May:

I am leaving today for Milan.

Clearly something more than an impresario's offer attracted him to Parma and held him there, almost to the end of the season. It is not quite true to say, as Signora Mundula does, that Verdi *did not move* from Parma during all this time. Actually, he went to Bologna for a few days after the second performance on 18th April. The opera was a great success at Parma, and was given twenty-two times. The Duchess Marie Louise attended two performances and gave the composer a gold pin, with her monogram in diamonds. Giuseppina's benefit night was on 31st May, with the miscellaneous sort of programme that was usual on such occasions—parts of *Nabucco*, the third act of *Beatrice di Tenda* and a special arrangement of the *William Tell* overture, played by the brass band of the army of the Duchy of Parma. The duchess herself again attended, and presented Giuseppina with a gold ornament, decorated with enamel and pearls. The public contributed flowers and three poems in her honour. On 1st June, the last night of the season, she was again acclaimed, with wreaths and 'a bunch of flowers of enormous dimensions'. Parma had treated her well. And Giuseppina showed her gratitude by remaining there until 5th June, in order to sing without fee at a concert in aid of the local orphanage.

The letters quoted show that Verdi was detained at Parma much longer than he had anticipated, but it is not certain that he stayed there only to be in Giuseppina's company. He had dedicated *I Lombardi* to Marie Louise, by gracious permission; parts of the music had been sent to her, with a promise of a complete vocal score when it was published. Between the first performance of *Nabucco*, which she attended, and 27th May, when she again heard the opera, she had been away at Piacenza. Possibly Verdi had to wait for her return from Piacenza for an interview that had already been arranged. A few days after his return to Milan he wrote to Count Di Bombelles, Marie Louise's second morganatic husband:

YOUR EXCELLENCY,

Flattered by the kind reception which Her Majesty deigned to accord me, and by the magnificent gift with which she honoured me, I beg Your Excellency to present to her my humble and sincere thanks.

As Her Majesty, deigning to speak about the music of *I Lombardi*, asked about the reduction for pianoforte, I advise Your Excellency that a copy will be prepared as soon as possible and I shall make it my duty to send it to you.

I thank also Your Excellency for the kindness with which you received me, which I shall always remember, and which will be an encouragement to persevere in my thorny career.

With the deepest respect,

Your Excellency's most humble servant,

GIUSEPPE VERDI.

Milan, 4th June 1843.[1]

We still do not know what sort of relationship existed between Giuseppina Strepponi and the composer at this time.

The summary of Giuseppina's not very numerous stage appearances after her breakdown in 1842 show how well she served 'her Verdi', in this respect at least. In 1843, after *Nabucco* at Parma, she sang in the same opera at Bologna; in 1844 she sang in it at Verona; later in the same year she sang in *Ernani* at Bergamo, again in Verdi's presence; after a long and disastrous season at Palermo, which included performances of *Ernani*, the first Verdi opera to be heard in that city, she concluded her stage career with further performances of *Nabucco* at Alessandria and Modena in 1845 and 1846.

The following table gives details of this last phase of her career:

		1843	
17th Apr.	Parma	Teatro Ducale	*Nabucco* (Verdi)
		(Season ended 1st June)	
5th June	Parma		Concert
8th Oct.	Bologna	Teatro Comunale	*Nabucco*
		1844	
10th Jan.	Verona	Teatro Filarmonico	*Nabucco*
13th Feb.	Verona	Teatro Filarmonico	*Robert le Diable* (Meyerbeer)
28th May	Turin		Concert
11th Aug.	Bergamo	Teatro Riccardi	*Ernani* (Verdi)
		(Season ended 12th September)	
Oct.	Palermo	Teatro Carolino	*Linda di Chamounix* (Donizetti)
4th Dec.	Palermo	Teatro Carolino	*Lucrezia Borgia* (Donizetti)
26th Dec.	Palermo	Teatro Carolino	*Ernani*
		1845	
9th Mar.	Palermo	Teatro Carolino	*Belisario* (1st act) (Donizetti)
25th Oct.	Alessandria		*Nabucco*
		(Season ended 29th November)	
		1846	
11th Jan.	Modena	Teatro Comunale	*Nabucco*

[1] 'Inediti verdiani', by Ascanio Alessandri, in a special Verdi number (Numero unico) of *La Regione Emilia-Romagna* (1951).

Giuseppina's name was not at first included in the list of singers engaged for the autumn season at Bologna in 1843; she replaced Sophie Loewe, who fell ill. The impresario Camillo Cirelli wrote to Lanari from Milan on 2nd October: 'Peppina is at Bologna. I hope, if her health stands it, she will be able to do well for herself there.' On 11th October he wrote again: 'You will have heard about Peppina's success at Bologna. God grant that it may continue and that, giving up the crazy love affairs that compromise her, she may begin to think of her future.' It is to be hoped that when Cirelli referred to Giuseppina's 'crazy love affairs' (*lunatiche amorose*) he was thinking of her past history. Resuming her career in the theatres, she would be exposed to the same dangers and temptations that had earlier brought about her downfall.

The Bologna correspondent of *Il Figaro*, while confirming Giuseppina's success in *Nabucco*, remarked that the part was not really well suited to her vocal powers at that time. He recalled her previous appearances in the city (in 1837), when she had been in much better voice. She could no longer stand the strain of a whole season and henceforth appeared generally in single operas. After *Roberto Devereux*, in which she had no part, had failed, the management engaged another soprano, Fanny Maray, for *Lucia*, 'to give a very necessary rest to the Abigaille in *Nabucco*'. Performances of Verdi's opera, however, continued up to 26th November, if not later.

Comments on *Nabucco* at Verona in January 1844 were similar to those at Bologna. The opera was a splendid success and the role of Abigaille a fine one, but not suited to Giuseppina's voice.

Il Figaro mentions that 'Maestro Verdi arrived at Verona a few days before the first performance of *Nabucco*'. He had been invited to attend the last rehearsals and in asking permission to make this very short visit to Verona he told Count Mocenigo, director of the Teatro La Fenice, that it would be a good opportunity to hear a singer named Vitali, who was under consideration for a part in *Ernani* at Venice in March.

Robert le Diable, at Verona on 13th February, was applauded, but was not fully understood at first; on 17th February, however, it aroused a furore, largely owing to Giuseppina's performance, as *Il Figaro* recorded. She seems to have recovered something like her best form, and was given a very cordial reception on her benefit night, with flowers, wreaths, poems and a lithographed portrait.

There are large gaps between her engagements at this period and we have no evidence as to what she was doing when she was not singing. She may already have begun to take pupils. Probably Milan, from 1842 onwards, remained her centre of operations; a later letter to the Countess Maffei mentions a home she had at one time furnished there.

Il Figaro of 29th May mentions Giuseppina as one of four singers who appeared at a concert at the Teatro Regio, Turin. On 11th August she sang at Bergamo in *Ernani*, under Verdi's own direction, with great success. Verdi's visit to Bergamo, unknown to Gatti, but mentioned by Mercede Mundula, is recorded in *Il Figaro* for 14th August. This time, however, he did not stay for the whole season. By 28th August he was at Busseto, preoccupied with his health and the composition of *I due Foscari*. On that day he wrote to Giuseppina Appiani:

> Just a line to let you know that very soon I shall be at Milan. As soon as I am well I shall leave for the Lombard capital. My native air is not good for me. Oh, to be sure, this is an excommunicated place, right off the map! What more do you want? Be patient for once, and rest assured that no one rules over my intentions and I am not becoming the slave of anything!
>
> All your children are working desperately? I'm in a rage because I'm not doing anything, and if you knew how much I still have to do to *I due Foscari*! Poor me!

He had asked Giuseppina Strepponi, at Bergamo, to reply for him to a letter from Lucca. This is an early example of his use of her as a sort of private secretary; she wrote on his behalf to Giovannina Lucca, who was a good friend of hers.[1]

For six months, from October 1844 to March 1845, Giuseppina was at Palermo, the farthest afield that she ever went. It was a very unhappy six months. The Teatro Carolino, in this season, seemed under a curse. Nicolai's *Templario*, in which Giuseppina did not appear, was a complete failure. Donizetti's *Linda di Chamounix*, in the middle of October, fared little better. The Palermitan paper *La Fata Galante* on 30th October spoke in these terms of Giuseppina:

> In the past she was very famous and encircled by an aureole of glory. But the brilliant star that presided over her theatrical destiny seems now near to setting, and thus emits no more than a glimmer, to the feebleness of which must be ascribed her less than mediocre success. Let her rest now on her laurels; it shall never be forgotten that she was a famous singer, and one of the glories of Italy.

The same paper on 30th December commented on performances of *Lucrezia Borgia* and *Ernani* (given under the title *Elvira d'Aragona*):

On *Lucrezia Borgia*:

> The principal singers were la Strepponi, Balzar and Milesi. The first and third of these were inadequate to sustain roles which demand so much action, vigour, voice, intelligence and dramatic art if they are to stir the emotions. . . . Lucrezia was received with coldness and indifference.

[1] The letter, concerning a future contract, is published by Abbiati (I, p. 519).

On *Ernani*:

La Strepponi, although accustomed to the demands of Maestro Verdi, *L'Occhio* says, did not earn a single encomium in the part of Elvira. She gave further proof of no longer knowing how to put on the buskin, and thus of having forgotten all the exigencies of the stage. And we permit ourselves to ask her a question: Why that continual distraction, from which it seems that she is thinking of anything but the fact that she is on the stage and appearing before a cultured and intelligent audience? Why that monotony of gesture, even at moments calling for the display of strong emotion, and eloquent, rational, solemn declamation and action? We no longer recognize in la Strepponi the celebrated singer whom we heard elsewhere, not many years ago, received invariably with storms of applause and jubilation.

L'Occhio reported on 2nd January 1845 that the management of the theatre had taken energetic measures to secure another *prima donna*, Augusta Boccabadati. This artist, in *Maria di Rohan* and *La Sonnambula*, saved the situation. According to *Il Figaro* of 5th February, later performances of *Ernani* were more successful, but *L'Occhio* on 16th February referred to Giuseppina's singing in *Lucrezia Borgia* as 'the useless efforts of an expiring voice'. On 9th March Mercadante's *La Vestale* was given, together with the first act of Donizetti's *Belisario*, in which she again appeared. *L'Occhio* reported:

Signora Strepponi did not sing, but served only to represent in mime the character of Antonina, with the result that the very beautiful finale of the act fell as flat as the conqueror of Vitiges.

With this appearance as a non-singing mime Giuseppina reached the nadir of her career. If we had letters from this period [1] we should probably find that she was passing through an emotional crisis as severe as that of three years before at Milan. What was to become of her, and her family and children? It is no wonder that, as the critic in *La Fata Galante* noted, her lassitude and continual distraction were apparent even when she was on the stage.

It was more than seven months before she sang again, in *Nabucco*, at Alessandria.

Two other operas were given, Donizetti's *Maria di Rohan* and Verdi's *I due Foscari*, but Giuseppina appeared only in *Nabucco*. She must have known that her career was nearing its end; it was necessary for it to end well. And for a limited number of performances, spread over rather more than a month, she renewed her former triumphs. On the last night of the season, 29th November, she was recalled quite twenty times and presented with the usual flowers and poems and in addition a golden wreath, inscribed with her praises in magniloquent language.

[1] A brief note to Andrea Peruzzi at Bologna, from Palermo, 6th March 1845, is in the library of the Conservatorio G.B. Martini, Bologna.

The *Strenna teatrale europea* for 1846, published towards the end of 1845, included an article on Giuseppina Strepponi, with an account of her success at Alessandria. The article ended with this announcement:

> When la Strepponi has fulfilled the engagements which bind her still to the theatres of Italy (in the Carnival season she will be at Modena) she intends to betake herself to Paris, to continue her career wherever she may be required, and to propagate, as teacher of the true Italian *bel canto*, the art that made her so celebrated in the musical world.

The engagement at Modena was actually to be Giuseppina's last. She was not involved in the grand fiasco with which the season there began, on 26th December 1845. *I Lombardi*, very badly performed and produced, was hissed off the stage, the hostility aroused in the audience being such that the police did not dare to intervene. The impresario, Pietro Rovaglia, made his escape before the end of the performance and far into the night the crowds in the streets were howling for his blood. The theatre was closed. On 29th December a bill was posted to say that the second opera of the season, *Nabucco*, was being prepared and that in it the part of Abigaille would be sung by Giuseppina Strepponi. In these circumstances the success of *Nabucco* on 11th January 1846 represented a personal triumph. *Il Pirata* declared that no words could express the enthusiasm aroused by Abigaille's aria in the second act: 'The applause seemed as though it would never stop: she was continually interrupted by acclamations and *evvivas* in the adagio and the cabaletta; at the end she was called back five times on to the stage.' *I Lombardi* was then revived, with other singers; Giuseppina did not appear in this opera, although Mercede Mundula says she did. The theatre was closed in the latter part of January owing to the death of the Duke of Modena and reopened on 11th February with *Nabucco*, in which, between that date and the end of the season, Giuseppina was seen and heard for the last time on the operatic stage.

The removal to Paris, announced in the *Strenna teatrale europea*, was delayed until the autumn. An article in *La France musicale* for 18th October 1846 announces her arrival in the city 'a few days ago'. It was a bold move, considering that she was unknown in Paris and had, indeed, except for her visit to Vienna in 1835, never been out of Italy before. But Paris was a great musical centre, exercising an almost irresistible attraction upon all composers and singers of that day. There was more money to be made there than anywhere else. Giuseppina seems to have settled down comfortably in Paris, secured pupils and won friends. Verdi had given her a letter of introduction to the Escudier brothers. The article in *La France musicale*, their periodical, describes her artistic career and mentions also the esteem in which she was held personally: 'La Strepponi is known in Italy not only as a great singer, but still more as a woman of much wit and spirit. She has always been greatly sought after by the world of the nobility, who, after having applauded her on the stage, loved to applaud and admire her in their most brilliant gatherings.' She would be heard in two concerts shortly, when she would sing Verdi's song *Lo Spazzacamino* and the cavatina from *Ernani*. These concerts were announced in *La France musicale* for 25th October, to take place in the Salle Henri Herz, on 3rd and 5th November. On 15th November the following announcement appeared:

Singing Lessons
by
MADAME G. STREPPONI

The celebrated Strepponi, who made such a good impression at *La France musicale*'s last two concerts, has decided to open a course of singing lessons for ladies, designed for the finishing of amateurs or artists who wish to acquire complete knowledge of the art. Since la Ungher and Duprez, who have perpetuated in Italy the school of lyric declamation, there has been no more intelligent interpreter of that school than la Strepponi. It is to this kind of music, above all, that she owes her great successes on the Italian stage, which has not prevented her from attacking the old repertoire which demands suppleness and great agility. Mme Strepponi comes to propagate in Paris, in the world and by tuition, a style, a method, which are in harmony with our tastes and constitution. We are convinced that, this winter, this eminent artist will enjoy a vogue in the fashionable world of Paris.

Her lessons will take place at her house, twice a week, on Tuesdays and Fridays, from three to five o'clock. There will be eight lessons a month, at the price of 40 francs. For three months, 100 francs.

Two long letters from Paris early in 1847, to Giovannina Lucca at Milan, show Giuseppina again taking an active interest in Verdi's affairs. The first, dated 5th January,[1] is principally concerned with *Robert Bruce*, the *pasticcio* with music by Rossini, recently performed at the Opéra. But it includes also an inquiry after Verdi's health and a suggestion that the French rights in those of his operas published by Lucca should be sold to the Escudier brothers. The second letter,[2] dated 23rd February, tells how she had gone to the Escudier brothers' shop for some music and found them disconcerted by the peremptory tone of Lucca's letters and the unreasonably high figure he was demanding for the French rights in *I Masnadieri*. None of the operas they had bought from Ricordi, 'not excepting *Macbeth* which has every chance of a great success in Italy and is one of the

[1] In the Piancastelli Collection, Biblioteca Comunale, Forlì.

[2] *Carteggi verdiani*, IV, pp. 252–3. The original is in the Pasini Collection, Biblioteca Queriniana, Brescia.

subjects best adapted to the French stage', had cost them more than 3,000 francs. Lucca wanted 10,000 francs for *I Masnadieri*:

I don't see how it advances your interest to dismember Verdi's operas, which, except *Nabucco*, have so far all passed into the hands of these publishers, by giving them to someone else, who perhaps up till now has been a most bitter opponent of this composer, and is only ready to buy one of these scores at a high price owing to personal spite. You must consider, not the momentary advantage of a few thousand francs, but the consequences. The Escudiers have always vigorously fought all Verdi's enemies (who are not few), and it is not fair to make them pay its weight in gold for an opera which, for Paris, has two great disadvantages—*its subject and the fact of its being composed for London.* But in spite of such disadvantages they want to have it, because they have all the other operas, and because they would like to be the sole publishers in France of Verdi's music, as Troupenas was of Rossini's, and as every great composer has his own particular publisher.

In addition, if the score belongs to them, they are prepared to go to London to do everything possible to facilitate a brilliant success. However beautiful Verdi's music, it will certainly not be useless on such an occasion (in view of Meyerbeer, etc.) if someone takes a keen interest in him, and especially someone who knows the country.

If the score does not belong to them it will not be surprising if they take the matter with the utmost calmness and stay quietly in Paris.

I repeat: I am of the opinion that you should do everything possible in your own interests, but without extortion. I advise you, then, to come to terms with the Escudier brothers for many reasons, and I am convinced that Verdi would prefer these publishers to any other in Paris.

At the end of both these letters Giuseppina thanks Giovannina Lucca for attentions paid to her son, or solicitude shown for his welfare. This suggests that Camillino was living at or near Milan: he was perhaps at school there.

Meanwhile Verdi was serving his term of 'years in the galleys', when it seemed that, although he hated his career in the opera houses, he still could not bear to reject a contract that offered possibilities of gain; when he turned out opera after opera in an almost frenzied search for the wealth that alone could bring him independence. He managed his financial affairs with immense skill, turning the tables on the publishers in a way that few composers have ever been able to equal. But quite early in his life and career the idea of retirement recurs in his letters. On 21st April 1845 he told Demaldè: 'I look forward to the passing of these next three years. I have six operas to write, and then farewell to everything.' On 5th November 1845, only three and a half years after the triumph of *Nabucco*, he was writing to a friend named Masi in Rome:

Thanks for the news of *Alzira*, but more for remembering your poor friend, condemned continually to scribble notes. God save the ears of every good Christian from having to listen to them! Accursed notes! How am I, physically and spiritually? Physically I am well, but my mind is black, always black, and will be so until I have finished with this career that I abhor. And afterwards? It's useless to delude oneself. It will always be black. Happiness does not exist for me.[1]

It seems that he had some idea of a withdrawal from the scene, *à la* Rossini, as soon as he had made enough money. Already in May 1844 he had bought some farm land at Le Roncole. And in October 1845 he had acquired a large house, the former Palazzo Dordoni, at Busseto.

The idea of retirement, of a quiet life, alternated and conflicted, however, with the idea of making ever increasing sums of money. 'Who knows whether I shan't wake up one morning a *millionaire*!' he wrote to Emilia Morosini. 'What a lovely word, with a full, lovely meaning! And how empty, in comparison, are words like "fame", "glory", "talent", etc.!' Impresarios in Paris, Madrid, St Petersburg and London were beginning to compete for his new operas, and their offers were tempting.

The suggestion that Verdi should go to Paris had first arisen in 1845. Muzio told Barezzi in secret on 26th May of that year: 'Signor Escudier, editor of the French *Gazzetta Musicale*,[2] has visited the Signor Maestro, and wanted a statuette to put in his office in Paris beside Rossini and Bellini. The Signor Maestro, after he has given the opera at Naples, is going straight to Paris with the aforesaid Signor Escudier, who will come from Paris to fetch him from Naples.' Nothing came of this at the time, owing to the delay in the production of *Alzira* at Naples and the pressure of other engagements. Invitations to compose an opera for Paris, received from Léon Pillet in November 1845 and February 1846, had to be regretfully declined. A letter from Verdi to Demaldè, of 6th June 1846, expresses the wish to go to Paris, and suggests the intention of doing so, as soon as that should be possible. Demaldè had reported some of the gossip of Verdi's enemies and rivals, and received this reply:

If only it were true that one is coming who will *finally annihilate Verdi*! All the better for him, all the better for Art, and all the better for me, too, for then I should be disembarrassed of the thousand annoyances I have now. Oh, if I could cede him all my contracts I would make him a present of 20,000 francs besides! Then I should go at once to Paris, and instead of earning 20,000 or 24,000 francs an opera here, I should earn 80,000 or 100,000 francs.

[1] Reproduced in facsimile in a German autograph dealer's catalogue, of which I have unfortunately lost the reference. The letter is also listed in V. A. Heck's catalogue No. 54, but without a reproduction. The autograph was in the possession of Leonardo Lapiccirella at Florence in 1958.

[2] Actually *La France musicale*, the rival of Schlesinger's *Gazette musicale*.

A month later he had to tell a Parisian correspondent [1] that he would not be free to write for the Opéra for another two years.

It does not seem that there can have existed any very close personal relationship between Giuseppina Strepponi and Verdi at this time. After he had helped her to recover herself and resume her career their ways divided, and such connections as there were between them permitted Giuseppina not only to accept an engagement at Palermo for six months, but, in the following year, to leave Italy altogether, to go to stay for an indefinite period in Paris, at a time when Verdi's circumstances made it unlikely that he would be able to join her there, if he ever did think of Paris in connection with her, for a long time. Giuseppina needed desperately to earn money. Verdi was intent on doing the same thing. Paris offered the best field of exploitation for them both. But any suggestion that they may have accepted the necessity of a temporary separation while they each accumulated money is not supported by the evidence of their letters. Verdi's declaration to Masi, quoted above, that even after the longed-for withdrawal from the operatic scene he had no hope of happiness, is not that of a man who has solved his emotional problems, and found a life companion to replace his first wife and his dead children. He had not been able to forget so soon. The only solution of such problems, while time goes by, is to throw oneself headlong into one's work to prevent oneself thinking. And work, even writing operas, and accumulating money, can become a habit-forming drug. A passage in a later letter from Giuseppina to Verdi, beginning 'Sometimes I fear that the love of money will re-awaken in you and condemn you to many further years of drudgery', shows that she actually disapproved of his excessive preoccupation with financial gain during the 'years of the galleys'.

This seems the best point at which to mention Abbiati's extraordinary statement that 'from a revealing document, still buried on the book shelves of Sant' Agata, we know that the first passionate lover's invocation, the first confession written and signed by Verdi kneeling at the feet of his beloved, dates from October 1846'.[2] Information given me at Sant' Agata, before and after the publication of Abbiati's book, is that there was an envelope which Giuseppina wished to be laid on her heart, after her death, and buried with her. Abbiati seems to think that the letter it contained is still in existence, though it cannot be found. He does not explain how he is able actually to quote from a letter that no living person has ever seen: 'One for the other . . . we were born, we will live one for the other . . . united.' In a work full of imaginary conversations and all

[1] Probably Marie Escudier. The letter, dated 3rd July 1846, in possession of the Historical Society of Pennsylvania, Philadelphia, is published in an article 'Scoperte in America' by Renzo Bonvicini (*La Scala*, Oct. 1953).

[2] I, pp. 560–1.

the dubious devices of fictional biography it is impossible to decide even whether Abbiati intends us to take this as a literal quotation. But out of it he develops an elaborate fantasy, according to which Verdi proposed that she should secretly join him at Florence in the following year, for *Macbeth*. A miniature painting in the Gallini collection, according to Abbiati, represents Giuseppina at Florence, with the Tuscan hills seen through the window. He assumes that Camillino had already been settled at Florence, which is against all probability, and that Verdi and Giuseppina there decided upon their subsequent union in Paris.

One can only hope that Verdi's declaration of love does still exist, and that it will one day be rediscovered. Meanwhile we must rely on the documents we have. They do not support Abbiati's imaginings.

Giuseppina's letter to Giovannina Lucca of 5th January 1847, asks:

> Is Verdi at Milan? Tell me if his health has suffered any setback this year, and if he is in a good humour, for good humour, in him, is a sign of health.

If she had been corresponding with him she would have known where he was, and how he was. And Verdi's indications of his intentions when, later in that year, he finally was able to visit Paris, dispose fairly conclusively of any idea that his re-encounter there with Giuseppina was pre-arranged.

On the outward journey to London, for the production of *I Masnadieri*, Muzio and Verdi arrived in Paris on 1st June, at 7 a.m. Muzio left for London on the next day and Verdi on 4th June. Busy with the preparation of the new opera, Verdi wrote to Giuseppina Appiani from London on 27th June:

> I look forward to going to Paris, which has no particular seduction for me, but which I am sure to like because there I shall be able to live as I please. It's a great pleasure to be able to do as one likes!! When I think that I shall be in Paris for several weeks, without being involved in musical affairs, without hearing a word about music (because I shall show the door to all publishers and impresarios), I almost swoon with relief.

He arrived in Paris on 27th July. On the 29th he told the Countess Maffei: 'I shall not stay long in Paris, because I am beginning to get bored already, although I have been here only forty-eight hours,' and on the 30th he told Emilia Morosini: 'I have been here two days, and if my present boredom continues I shall very soon be back in Milan.' These are not the expressions of a lover keeping a tryst.

In spite of his talk of 'showing the door' to all publishers and impresarios, and wishing to hear nothing about music, *within a week* of his arrival Verdi had agreed to adapt *I Lombardi* to a new French libretto (*Jérusalem*) for the Opéra. This was mentioned on 8th August in a letter from Muzio to Barezzi, which also announced that Muzio himself was leaving that day for Milan, and Verdi staying in Paris. Muzio was sent back to Milan to supervise the publication of *I Masnadieri*; the necessity for this had been foreseen and already mentioned in a letter from Verdi to the Countess Maffei on 29th July. Muzio expected to return to Paris in November, or earlier if he was needed. Verdi himself, by his agreement with the Opéra, was committed to remaining in Paris until the production of *Jérusalem* in November, but he still thought he would be returning to Milan directly afterwards; on 22nd August he told Giuseppina Appiani: 'I shall be staying here until about 20th November: at the end of that month I shall see again the cupola of the *duomo*.' By 1st November he was less certain and wrote to Barezzi: 'I don't know whether I shall be returning to Italy this winter. For a year I have been working day and night: I am tired of it and have need of a little relief! I haven't yet decided what I shall do.' [1] *Jérusalem* was produced on 26th November. On 3rd December Verdi wrote to the Countess Maffei: 'I shall stay here for some time yet, to arrange various matters and also to be a long way from Signor Lucca, this tiresome and ungrateful man, who has prevented me from signing a contract for *60,000 francs*, and another that would have made my fortune, without any disadvantage to Signor Lucca.' He was snared in a tangle of contracts, actual and prospective, and Lucca had refused to release him from an engagement to compose a new opera for the Carnival season of 1848. As a result he had to start work almost at once on *Il Corsaro*, in which he took little interest. The creation of *Jérusalem* by the mutilation of *I Lombardi*, and the hasty and unwilling composition of *Il Corsaro* to rid himself of an inconvenient contract, were the least conscientious actions of Verdi's career. He was paid for *Jérusalem* as for a new opera, and was even able to sell the score to Ricordi over again, under the new title; *Il Corsaro* was sold outright to Lucca for 24,000 francs. On 14th January 1848 Verdi told Piave that he had a contract on hand for another new opera, to be written for the Opéra on a libretto by Scribe; he was only waiting to hear whether a certain singer would be available before signing the contract. 'I am well', the letter ends, 'but I look forward to returning to Italy. I hope that my affairs will be settled here in a month's time.' Listlessness and uncertainty about the future are apparent in a letter to Luigi Toccagni of 24th January: [2]

What do you want me to say about myself? That I am always the same,

[1] From a letter published by Alberto Lisoni in an article 'Verdi e Barezzi', in *Per l'Arte* (Parma) for 27th February 1901.

[2] O. Tiby, 'Una lettera inedita di Verdi' (*Giornale di Sicilia*, 5th Jan. 1952).

always discontented with everything? When fortune favours me I want it against me; when it is against me I want it to favour me; when I am at Milan I would like to be in Paris; now that I am in Paris I would like to be—where?—I don't know—on the moon. For the rest I enjoy here complete personal freedom, such as I have always desired without ever being able to obtain it. I don't visit anybody, I don't receive anybody, nobody knows me and I don't have the annoyance of seeing myself pointed at, as in Italian cities. I enjoy good health; I write a lot; my affairs go well; everything goes well except my head, which I always hope will change, and which never does change. Farewell.

The contract with the Opéra was finally signed early in February, and *Il Corsaro* completed at about the same time. Arrangements were actually made for Verdi to return to Italy, and Muzio was expecting his arrival at Milan on 17th February. But instead there arrived a letter, dated from Paris on the 12th, to say that Verdi had caught a feverish cold on the eve of his intended departure. These matters are also mentioned in a letter to Vincenzo Luccardi, the sculptor, of 17th February: [1]

I have written an opera for the publisher Lucca of Milan, and I was counting on taking it to Italy myself, but I decided to send it because I didn't feel fit to undertake the long and tiring journey at this time of year. Now I shall rest for some few days or some few weeks and then begin work on the opera for Naples.

It has been necessary to quote these passages from Verdi's correspondence in order to show that he was continually planning to return to Italy. Nothing could be further from the truth than Gatti's statement: 'He does not speak of returning to his country.' [2] The return, however, was again and again deferred, owing first to the contract with the Opéra for *Jérusalem*, and then to negotiations for a further contract, to a desire to avoid Lucca and finally to illness. During this time he was certainly seeing something of Giuseppina Strepponi and, unconsciously, his growing affection for her may have influenced his repeated decisions to defer the moment of his return to Italy. But Verdi was not a liar. He *was* bored when he first went to Paris, if he said so; he *did* look forward to returning to Italy; he *was* prevented by illness from undertaking the journey in February. The evidence is all against the conclusions of recent Italian writers who, building on the shaky foundations of some of Gatti's more incautious passages, have decided that the reunion with Giuseppina in Paris was pre-arranged, and that Muzio was sent back to Milan because of this reunion and deceived as to Verdi's real intentions. This point of view

[1] E. Faustini-Fasini, 'Una lettera inedita di Giuseppe Verdi' (*Le cronache musicali*, 1st Feb. 1901).

[2] First edition, I, p. 305; second edition, p. 242.

is presented in extreme form by Emilio Radius in his *Verdi Vivo* (Milan, 1951), described as 'the nonconformist book of the quinquagenary', and of course by Abbiati.

How do we know that Verdi was seeing something of Giuseppina in Paris? Hitherto it has been assumed that he was, without proof, but a document of remarkable interest has recently come to light at Sant' Agata which puts the matter beyond all doubt. Verdi's little known letter to Antonio Barezzi of 1st November 1847, already quoted, includes the following passage:

> I have never believed, do not believe, nor shall I ever believe, that you are capable of moving yourself out of that nutshell of yours. There are so many beautiful and ugly things worth seeing, and you, who have the means, stay shut up there all the time! If you travelled a bit you wouldn't have that trouble with your feet, and would have many other advantages which it is useless to describe. When I've finished my career, if I have a few thousand francs to spare, I shall go to see the most interesting countries outside Europe. And you—don't you want to see the principal European ones?

Barezzi had thoroughly enjoyed himself during his visit to Florence for the performance of *Macbeth* earlier in this year. So he decided to follow his son-in-law's advice and take a trip to Paris. The new document is a letter from Giuseppe Demaldè ('Finola') to Verdi, dated 31st January 1848, to which Barezzi on 3rd February added a page showing that he had recently returned to Busseto from Paris, where he had been introduced to Giuseppina Strepponi, from whom he was expecting a letter:

> Since my arrival at Busseto from Paris never a day has passed without my relating the wonderful things I saw on my journey and the kind reception I had there from you, from Signora Peppina and from your other friends, and I assure you that such memories will remain engraved in my heart for ever. . . . You give me hopes of a letter from Signora Peppina and I must tell you that I am anxiously awaiting it. Meanwhile give her my regards, together with her ladies, whom I found so kind.

Barezzi, clearly, had been charmed. He had also brought back greetings from Giuseppina to Demaldè, who had evidently met her earlier, at Milan or Parma. Demaldè wrote:

> How is Signora Peppina? I reciprocate her greetings with all my heart. Tell her that I remember her because I have reason to appreciate her gifts, her fine mind and her virtues. How I should like to see her!

In February Verdi witnessed the overthrow of Louis Philippe and the proclamation of the French Republic, with little bloodshed. He wrote about this, in a good humour, to Giuseppina Appiani on 9th March:

You will know all about events in Paris: since 24th February nothing has happened. The procession accompanying the dead to the funerary column of the Bastille was imposing, magnificent, and although there were neither troops nor police to maintain order there was not the slightest disturbance. The grand National Assembly, to decide on the government, will be on 20th April. . . . I can't hide from you the fact that I am enjoying myself very much, and so far nothing has happened to disturb my sleep. I'm not doing anything; I go out for walks; I hear so much rot that I couldn't hear more; I buy about twenty newspapers a day (without reading them, of course) to avoid persecution by the vendors: when they see a bundle of papers in my hand no one offers me others, and I laugh and laugh and laugh. Unless something important calls me to Italy I shall stay here until the end of April to see the National Assembly.

He still talks of returning to Italy. 'Something important' was to call him there before the end of April. On 18th March the Milanese rose against their Austrian masters and forced their withdrawal from the city in the heroic 'Five Days' of fighting in the streets. On 22nd March the Venetians also threw off the yoke and proclaimed a republic.

There has been until recently some doubt about Verdi's actions when he heard of the revolution at Milan. It is an extraordinary thing that in the Italian edition of Pougin's biography, issued by Verdi's own publisher in his lifetime, a special footnote was added by 'Folchetto' to the effect that the composer was feverishly impatient to return to Milan as soon as he heard the news, but that he stopped at Lyons on the way, uncertain whether he would be in time to see the city free of the Austrians, and then heard there of the sad reversal of all his hopes. This story, repeated by other early biographers, ignores the fact that four and a half months passed between the outbreak of the revolution and the return of the Austrians. In reality Verdi went straight back to Milan. All doubts about his actions were swept away by the publication in 1948 of the following magnificent letter, addressed to 'Citizen Francesco Maria Piave, Venice':[1]

Milan, 21st April 1848.

DEAR FRIEND,

Imagine whether I wished to remain in Paris, hearing of a revolution at Milan! I left immediately I heard the news, but was only able to see these stupendous barricades. Honour to these brave men! Honour to all Italy, which at this moment is truly great!

The hour has sounded—be convinced of it—of her liberation. It is the people that wills it, and when the people wills there is no absolute power that can resist.

They can do what they like, they can intrigue how they like, those that want to impose themselves by main force, but they will not succeed in

[1] *Una lettera di Giuseppe Verdi finora non pubblicata*, ed. A. Bonaventura (Florence, 1948).

defrauding the people of their rights. Yes, yes, a few more years, perhaps only a few more months, and Italy will be free, united and a republic. What else should she be?

You talk of music to me!! What are you thinking of? Do you imagine I want to occupy myself now with notes, with sounds? There is, and should be, only one kind of music pleasing to the ears of the Italians of 1848—the music of the guns! I would not write a note for all the gold in the world: I should feel immense remorse for using up music paper, which is so good to make cartridges with. My brave Piave, and all brave Venetians, banish every petty municipal idea! Let us all reach out a fraternal hand, and Italy will yet become the first nation of the world.

You are in the National Guard? I am glad that you are just a simple soldier. What a fine soldier! Poor Piave! How do you sleep? How do you eat? I, too, if I could have enrolled, would have wished to be just a simple soldier, but now I can only be a tribune, and a wretched tribune at that, because I am only spasmodically eloquent.

I must return to France on account of engagements and business affairs. Besides the annoyance of having to write two operas, I have various sums of money to collect there and many others in bank-notes to cash. I left everything behind me there, but I cannot disregard what is for me a large sum of money, and my presence there will be necessary to salve, in the present crisis, at least a part of it. For the rest, come what may, I'm not worrying. If you saw me now you would not recognize me. My appearance would no longer alarm you, as it used to do! I am drunk with joy! Only think, there are no more Germans here!! You know what sort of sympathy I had for them. Farewell. Farewell. My regards to everyone. A thousand greetings to Venturi and Fontana.

Write to me soon, because if I go away it won't be so soon—my return, I mean. Farewell, my friend. Write to me.

GIUSEPPE.

Verdi had reached Milan early in April. A comparatively short section of the journey could be made by rail at this date, and the rest by stagecoach. It took Mazzini, who had every reason to hurry, six days to get from Paris to Milan, travelling day and night, *via* Switzerland. What Verdi says about his becoming a tribune is of the greatest interest and suggests that if the republicans had won the struggle for power he would have held political office. Mazzini, whom he had met in London in the previous year, and with whom he was undoubtedly in close touch at this time, intended to make use of the prestige and glamour of the composer's name.

At the beginning of May Verdi was at Busseto, where he arranged to purchase the house and farm lands of Sant' Agata, surrendering in part exchange his much smaller possessions, acquired in 1844, at Le Roncole. One other short letter from Italy is known, written to Cammarano from Como on 31st May on the way back to Paris.

Without further letters between 21st April and 31st May we can yet be sure of the thoughts that were in Verdi's mind. The radiant hopes and the bitter disillusionment of all republicans can be read in Mazzini's own letters from Milan. The Provisional Government, at first divided in its allegiance, tended more and more to move to the Right, to support the ambitions of Carlo Alberto, without whose intervention with the Piedmontese army the revolution would probably have been crushed by Radetzky in a very short time. Mazzini wished political decisions on the future of Italy to be deferred until the war was won. 'My name, influential among the young', he wrote on 28th April, 'is suspect among men who subordinate the necessities of the war to diplomatic intrigue, to which I am naturally averse. My advice prevails sometimes, but, the day after, the energetic decisions taken evaporate as if by enchantment. . . . It seems that the Italians don't know how to be great and free, except behind the barricades.' On 18th May he wrote: 'I am nauseated by the intrigues here for the triumph of Carlo Alberto; nauseated by the Provisional Government; nauseated by everything, almost.' And in the following month: 'Fear, intrigue, materialism and ignorance govern the Italians today.' When Verdi left Italy to return to Paris the war was not yet lost, but the republican cause was doomed.

On 2nd June, while Verdi was still *en route*, Giuseppina Strepponi sat down in Paris to write to her old friend and former colleague at Florence, Pietro Romani. Some time before this she had provided a French singer with an introduction to Romani, at the request of the mother of one of her pupils. Romani had replied in affectionate terms, and asked her to write at greater length, which she now did, explaining that the occasion and her own diffidence and distrust had been responsible for the formal nature of her earlier letter:[1] 'So many things I thought impossible have happened, that I tend to doubt everything and everybody.' This time she wrote without constraint:

I know very well that quavers and semiquavers are ineffective against rifle and cannon-shot, by the ancient law of 'Might is right'. But all the notes in the world might go to the devil if there were room for hope that Italy could become great, united, strong and free! But too many crowned heads still oppress her! I had a moment of great hope, when the Milanese drove the Germans from their city; but now things have taken a turn for the worse. The Italians cannot renounce party spirit; they are always arguing—too much talk and too little action! Blood flows in impetuous, generous revolutions, but they have insufficient firmness to hold fast to the fruits of their sacrifices! They forget how much it cost to cast down a throne, and they raise another one, as if one couldn't live without a king! It is true that we shall be ruled by an Italian king, but Carlo Alberto's antecedents are not very favourable to the hope of a free constitution,

[1] Both letters are in the Piancastelli Collection at Forlì. The second letter was published in incomplete form in *Le cronache musicali* for 10th February 1901.

scrupulously observed. God grant he may not renew the betrayals of 1821 and imitate the Tartuffe who reigns at Naples! . . .

Here, as in Italy, people think only of politics. Some theatres are, or have been, closed. The artists under annual contract, those of the Grand Opera not excepted, have been put on half-pay, or their salaries greatly reduced. I say nothing of the teachers of singing, of the pianoforte, etc.! They have time to take as many walks as they please. I had begun the winter quite well, but the revolution in February came and cut short every musical resource. I haven't left Paris because, having set up house here, I should have lost much in selling my furniture at a time when money is short, and I should have incurred useless expenses in travelling. And then, where should I have gone, to do good business? To Italy? I am sure that Lanari must be losing a lot of money, and I am amazed that he doesn't put his artists on half-pay, as it's a case of extraordinary circumstances, but provided for in the contracts—war, guerilla war, etc. You envy me because I am out of Italy? You are wrong, for here the artists are as badly off as in Italy, and what with political agitations one is never sure of a quiet night's rest. So much for your guidance! You ask about my voice? How I am amusing myself? My voice has suffered and is as it was at the end of my time with Lanari. I am not amusing myself at all, because what is amusement to so many others is boredom to me. Winter is the brilliant season in Paris—society, balls, festivities, dinners, etc. Well, when I am obliged to sing at some house or other, I stay just as long as is necessary, and then run home. I don't like dancing, I don't like dinners, and if I had enough to live on without working I should perhaps stay in Paris for the freedom one enjoys here, but they would not see me any more, anywhere.

We find views expressed here that are absolutely identical with those of Verdi. More than that: not only were they both passionate republicans, not only do they say the same things about the respective claims of music and patriotism, they do so in the very same voice. The first paragraph quoted is probably a direct reflection of the lost letters Verdi wrote Giuseppina from Milan.

The evidence of the addresses used by Verdi supports the belief that it was at this time that he and Guiseppina declared their love for each other and began to live together. The stay in Paris, that was to have lasted only a few weeks and, repeatedly extended, actually lasted more than two years, was twice interrupted—first by the return to Milan when news arrived of the revolution, and then by a visit to Rome for the production of *La Battaglia di Legnano*. Before the return to Milan he wrote letters from 6 Rue neuve St Georges (1st November 1847, to Barezzi, and 17th February 1848, to Luccardi). He was back in Paris early in June, after which he gave a *poste restante* address (22nd July, to Piave). Pougin's original French biography here provides some important information, obviously based on inquiries in Paris. Pougin states that when Verdi returned from Milan he 'established himself at Passy, under the shady avenues of Ranelagh, a sojourn which was delicious during the heat of summer'.[1] It was of Passy, undoubtedly, that Giuseppina was thinking when, in a letter to the Countess Maffei in 1867, she recalled how she had persuaded Verdi to leave Paris and take a little house in the country, not far from the capital. Passy was then still an isolated village. A letter from Verdi to the Neapolitan impresario Guillaume, of 24th August 1848, refers to an absence from Paris of about a month, as a result of which he had only just seen Guillaume's letter of 29th July.

It seems fairly established, then, that in the summer of 1848 Verdi and Giuseppina were living together at Passy. It is quite certain that in the following winter they were living together, or in adjoining rooms, at 13 Rue de la Victoire. Pougin gives this as Verdi's address after his return from Rome; Verdi himself gives it (13 *bis*, however) as Giuseppina's address in a letter written in Rome.[2]

It has been rightly said that this was not a case of love's young dream. He was nearly thirty-five and she nearly thirty-three. They both had behind them bitter experiences; Verdi's mind had been stamped with pessimism for ever by the annihilation of his family, and a natural strain of melancholy in Giuseppina had been accentuated by her passion for Moriani and its consequences. They had both come to loathe the false glamour of the theatrical world. But already they had many memories in common, and Giuseppina's immediate, intuitive understanding, and Verdi's moral integrity, his kindness and reliability, shone out from the past and promised, more and more, to illuminate the future. They were born for each other, and their union, with or without the blessing of the Church, was of inestimable benefit to them both. For fifty years, now, their lives were to be joined.

It really seems that the revolutions of 1848, in Paris and Milan, played a decisive part in bringing them together. They were two Italians, old friends now, in a foreign city, when the hopes they both cherished suddenly seemed on the point of being realized. Compatriotic feeling, common ideals, excitement and dangers shared, the release from restraint that a moment of crisis brings—these must have helped to throw them into each other's arms.

The vocal score of *Gerusalemme*, the Italian version of the adaptation of *I Lombardi* produced in Paris, is dedicated to Giuseppina Strepponi. But the dedication is by Ricordi, not by Verdi, who, one

[1] Pougin, in a biography written at a time when hardly any of Verdi's letters were available, inevitably made many mistakes. He assumed, for instance, that *Il Corsaro*, performed at Trieste on 25th October 1848, was written shortly before that date, and therefore at Passy, and that Verdi went to Trieste for the first performance, as was his usual custom. It is easy to correct such mistakes now. But Pougin, many of whose books are still valuable for their documentation, knew what he was talking about when he gave Verdi's Parisian addresses after the return from Milan and after the return from Rome.

[2] To Duponchel and Roqueplan, 15th January 1849, *Copialettere*, p. 66.

cannot help thinking, would have wished to set her name, if at all, on a better work.

The political disillusionment already apparent in Giuseppina's letter to Romani, and certainly shared by Verdi himself, was to go much further. A few more weeks were to see the catastrophic reversal of all their hopes, in Italy as in France. Mazzini, from Milan, wrote to George Sand in Paris on 12th June: 'Reaction prevails here, as it does in your country. They calumniate us; they threaten us; they write on the walls: "Death to the Republicans!" They send me anonymous letters to say I must prepare for death by the dagger.' In Paris, from 23rd to 26th June, a desperate insurrection by an armed mob was bloodily quelled by General Cavaignac. This was witnessed by Verdi and Giuseppina, and may have contributed to their decision to move out to Passy. Verdi wrote to Piave on 22nd July:

> I don't know how long I shall stay in this chaos. Have you heard about this last revolution? What horrors, my dear Piave! Heaven grant they may be the last! And Italy? Poor country!!! I read and re-read the newspapers, hoping always for good news, but . . . And you, why don't you ever write to me? It seems to me that at just such moments as these friends should remember friends! . . . Let's hope for happier times. But I am frightened when I glance at France, and then at Italy.

Three days later the Italian armies were defeated at Custoza and driven back through Lombardy. Milan surrendered to the Austrians on 5th August. Verdi's name, together with that of his friend Giulio Carcano and eight others, appeared on the desperate and vain appeal for French intervention laid before Cavaignac by Guerrieri Gonzaga, of the Provisional Government of Lombardy, on 8th August. The armistice of Salasco was signed on 10th August.

In well-grounded fear of Austrian reprisals, a mass emigration from Milan had taken place. More than 120,000 persons, or three-quarters of the inhabitants of the city, fled to Piedmont or Switzerland. There are heart-rending accounts, by eye-witnesses, of the columns of exiles on the roads, in the burning sun and dust, or, physically exhausted, assembled in silent wretchedness just across the Ticino, the frontier of Piedmont. The Countess Maffei, whose *salon* at Milan had been a centre of Italian national feeling, took refuge in Switzerland, as did Carcano and Muzio. Mazzini himself withdrew to Lugano early in August.

Verdi wrote to the Countess Maffei, who had asked him what was the French reaction to events in Italy: 'Those who are not hostile are indifferent. The idea of *Italian unity* frightens these little men, these nullities, that are in power. France will certainly not intervene with her armed forces, unless some event impossible to foresee drags her in, in spite of herself. Franco-British diplomatic intervention cannot be anything but iniquitous, shameful for France and ruinous for us.' If Austria could be induced to give up Lombardy, retaining only Venetia, the republican and national cause would not be advanced: 'The result for us would be an additional insult, the devastation of Lombardy, and an additional prince in Italy.' He thought it possible that disturbances in Austria might yet bring another opportunity: 'If we know how to seize the right moment, and wage the war that must be waged, the war of insurrection, Italy can yet be free. But God save us from putting trust in our kings and in foreign nations.' In France there was little cause for optimism: 'I believe another revolution is imminent: it is in the air. Another revolution will bring about the collapse of this poor republic. Let's hope it doesn't happen, but there is grave reason to fear it.' Six weeks later he wrote again: 'I can find no consoling words to say to you about our poor Italy. Happy you, who have still some hope! I have none.' Cavaignac, in the Assembly, had refused to reply to questions about Italy and negotiations on her behalf. 'What a fine republic!' Verdi concluded bitterly.

Nevertheless, on 18th October he sent Mazzini a battle hymn 'Suona la tromba', a setting of words by the patriot poet Goffredo Mameli, and expressed the hope that it might 'soon be sung, amid the music of the guns, on the plains of Lombardy'. A fine phrase from an earlier, lost letter is preserved in Mazzini's appeal to Mameli for the poem: 'Send me a hymn that may become the Italian 'Marseillaise', and of which the people, to use Verdi's phrase, may forget both composer and poet.' But 'Suona la tromba' was not destined to become the Italian 'Marseillaise'.

Verdi's patriotic feelings found more convincing expression in the opera *La Battaglia di Legnano*, written at Passy and Paris in this autumn and early winter. Originally intended for Naples, it was offered to the Teatro Argentina in Rome when the Neapolitan contract fell through. Republican hopes were now centred on developments in the Papal States and Tuscany. Garibaldi was recruiting in Romagna. Pio Nono was no longer in control of events. It would be unseemly, perhaps, to compare a Pope to the Sorcerer's Apprentice. But he had certainly, by his well-meant liberal measures, set in motion forces that could no longer be checked. Soon he was to reap the whirlwind. He had found his name used in connection with every sort of revolutionary ferment throughout the peninsula, until, with the Allocution published on 29th April 1848, he had made clear that the Risorgimento did not, after all, enjoy the papal blessing. And with the Allocution his popularity had disappeared overnight: revolution in Rome almost came at this time. Then the failure of Carlo Alberto in north Italy had swung opinion away from Piedmont and strengthened the hands of the Mazzinian republicans. Pellegrino Rossi, called to power on 16th September, a strong man who might have been able to restore order in the Papal States, was murdered by the extremists on 15th November, and on 24th November the Pope fled, disguised as a simple priest, to Gaeta, in the Kingdom of Naples.

Verdi left Paris for Rome on 20th December. *La Battaglia di Legnano* was performed on 12th January 1849 amid scenes of hectic excitement, within a fortnight of the proclamation of the Roman republic, during the 'Dictatorship of Sterbini', who is generally considered to have planned the murder of Rossi. The last act of *La Battaglia di Legnano* was encored at every performance. Back in Paris with Giuseppina, Verdi wrote on 1st February to Piave in besieged Venice:

> I left Rome with sorrow, but I hope to return there very soon. I am trying somehow to put in order the tangled affairs I have here, then I shall fly to Italy. God bless you, my good Venetians! Whatever the outcome, you will certainly have the benediction and the gratitude of every good Italian. I am happy about Rome and Romagna, and in Tuscany, too, things are not going wholly badly. We have cause for great hopes. Two things, however, frighten me: *Gioberti* and the *Congress of Brussels*. God save us! . . . There is nothing to hope from France, and now less than ever.

We see that it was his intention to return soon to Rome, where the republic was proclaimed on 8th February. But events in northern Italy in the next month again destroyed his hopes. Carlo Alberto denounced the armistice and on 20th March his troops advanced into Lombardy again. It took Radetzky exactly four days to crush this move, by a feint retreat from Milan and a strong forward thrust from Pavia into Piedmont itself, where the battle of Novara on 23rd March brought the capitulation and the abdication of Carlo Alberto. After this the collapse of the Roman republic was only a matter of time, with the intervention, at the Pope's request, of France, Austria, Spain and Naples. The Austrians entered Florence, to restore the Grand Duke, on 25th May; the heroic defence of Rome ended early in July; Garibaldi began his epic retreat across the peninsula on the 3rd, and on the next day the French troops entered Rome. Verdi wrote to Luccardi on 14th July: 'Don't let's talk of Rome! What good would it do? Force still rules the world. And justice? What use is it against bayonets? All we can do is to weep over our wrongs, and curse the authors of so many misfortunes.' Twelve days later he announced in another letter that he would be leaving Paris in three days' time. It is generally stated, following Pougin, that the return of Verdi and Giuseppina to Italy was occasioned by the cholera epidemic in Paris, which aroused the anxiety of his parents. It seems also likely that disgust at the part played by the French in the murder of a sister republic made further residence among them intolerable.

All hope was over now, for a long time. The millenium had not arrived.

Verdi returned to Busseto, where he established himself in his house, the Palazzo Dordoni, now Palazzo Orlandi, in the main street.[1] He was busy completing *Luisa Miller*, for production at Naples later in the year. Giuseppina, at the end of August, was at Florence, putting her own affairs in order. We have two letters from Florence, written within a few days of each other, the first to Lanari, the second to Verdi himself:

Florence, 31st August 1849.

DEAR LANARI,

I am at Florence for a few days and staying at the Albergo della Luna, Via Condotti. If it's not too inconvenient come and see me, and tell Tonino that I am here and want to salute him. Do me the favour also of asking Stefano for Livia's address, which I have lost, or better still arrange to send her to me at once.

Your affectionate friend,

G. STREPPONI.

Florence, 3rd September 1849.

I shall have finished my business by Wednesday and shall perhaps leave for Parma on the same evening. Don't come to fetch me, however, until Friday evening or Saturday morning, because I should be sorry if you had to wait for me in vain at Parma. When I tell you who has charged himself with Camillino's artistic education, you will be astonished! It must suffice for now that I kissed the hands of the famous man who said to me: 'Will you confide him to me?' I have seen only a few people at Florence, but they have worked with zeal and, be it noted, mere acquaintances. No aristocrats, of course. In truth, sometimes one finds a heart where one expects only indifference, and *vice versa*.

Farewell, my joy! Now that I have almost finished my business, business too important to be neglected, I should like to be able to fly to your side. You speak of the unattractive country, the bad service, and furthermore you tell me: 'If you don't like it, I'll have you accompanied (N.B. I'll *have you* accompanied!) wherever you like.' But what the devil! Does one

[1] Researches by Signorina Gabriella Carrara-Verdi in the notarial archives at Parma show that this fine house was sold by Count Annibale Dordoni, early in the nineteenth century, to a certain Antonio Cavalli, who resold it to his son Contardo on 24th December 1825. Verdi, by deed of Ercolano Balestra, notary of Busseto, bought it from Contardo Cavalli on 6th October 1845 for 22,000 Parmesan lire.

Verdi refers to it as 'Casa Cavalli' and 'Casa ex-Cavalli' in some notes at the end of the first volume of his autograph *Copialettere*. Payment was by instalments:

For Casa Cavalli:

6th October 1845,	first instalment	10,000
	legal expenses	834.35
	present	66.30
29th December	paid as second instalment . . .	4,000
May 1846	paid	6,000

Under the heading 'My property':

'Casa ex-Cavalli, which now belongs to me, entirely paid for, lire 22,900.65.'

forget to love people at Busseto, and to write with a little bit of affection?

I'm not there yet, so can still write what I feel, which is that the country, the service and everything else will suit me very well, as long as you are there, you ugly, unworthy monster!

Farewell. Farewell. I have scarcely time to tell you that I detest you and embrace you.

PEPPINA.

N.B. Don't send anybody else, but come yourself to fetch me from Parma, for I should be very embarrassed to be presented at your house by anyone other than yourself.

It seems clear that one of the purposes of Giuseppina's trip to Florence was to settle Camillino there, in the care probably of that 'Livia' mentioned in the first of these letters. She is mentioned once before in the earlier letters to Lanari; on 19th February 1842 Giuseppina had written: 'I hear that Livia's mother is dangerously ill, so that she's terribly upset. Please send her 20 Florentine lire, and put it down to my account.' This person can be identified as Livia Zanobini, whose address at Florence is given in a letter to Mauro Corticelli of 17th February 1864,[1] and to whom Giuseppina was sending money, as many entries in her letter-books [2] show, up to as late as 1884. The 'famous man' who had charged himself with Camillino's artistic education was, as is seen from a later letter to Verdi, the sculptor Lorenzo Bartolini.

One cannot help wondering why the now eleven-year-old Camillino was established at Florence, and why a man like Bartolini should have taken any interest in him. Had the boy's father, perhaps, been persuaded to do something for him? Moriani, his singing career now practically over, was living at Florence. He had retired, in effect, about two and a half years after Giuseppina had done so. *Il Pirata* of 8th July 1848 reported what were almost his last public appearances, at Florence, in Mercadante's *Il Bravo*.[3] The poet Giusti, whose acquaintance Verdi had made in 1847, and by whom he had also been introduced to Bartolini, had been the great friend of Moriani's youth.[4] Did he know about Verdi's friendship with Giuseppina, and on this account persuade Moriani and Bartolini to do something to help her? Was he among those Florentine acquaintances in whom she had found a heart where she expected only indifference?

[1] In the Scala Museum.

[2] At Sant' Agata.

[3] He reappeared at the Pergola theatre, Florence, during the Carnival and Lent seasons of 1857, in Donizetti's *Maria Padilla*.

[4] Giusti's caustic poem, *Per un reuma d'un cantante*, of 1840, is undoubtedly addressed to Moriani. The poet recalls the days when they were both law students at the University of Pisa:

'V'è tal che, mentre canti e in bella guisa
Lodi e monete accatastando vai,
Rammenta i dolci che non tornan mai
Tempi di Pisa.'

Moriani's papers are today in the possession of the Scala Museum. They include a number of letters to his wife Elvira, from the years 1838–44, which reveal him as an affectionate husband and father. Four children are mentioned. According to Luigi Neretti,[1] these papers originally included a letter from Giuseppina herself to Mauro Corticelli, dated 10th October 1864, which is unfortunately no longer among them. How did this letter come into Moriani's hands? And what has happened to it?

It is impossible, at present, to answer these questions.

Her business at Florence concluded, Giuseppina, early in September 1849, arrived at Busseto. It was an historic moment when Verdi's carriage drew up at the Palazzo Dordoni and the amazed and scandalized bystanders and idlers under the arcades saw him dismount and enter the house in company with a strange woman. The door closed, and Busseto was provided with a subject for gossip for the next ten years.

In Paris it had been possible to live alone among the crowds, but here in this small town, where everybody knew everybody else's business, or wanted to do so, the situation was very different. Perhaps Verdi had insufficiently considered this when he brought Giuseppina to Busseto. It is true, as we have seen from her letter to him, that he had offered to go elsewhere with her if she wished.

At Busseto Verdi had enthusiastic followers and well wishers, but also enemies. The clerical party had not forgotten their discomfiture in the past. Verdi's action in living openly with Giuseppina now gave them new grounds for umbrage, and genuinely shocked and distressed many pious and narrow-minded people. Even among the well-wishers there were those who considered Verdi insufficiently recognizant towards Busseto and the Bussetani who had 'made' him, as they liked to think. Giuseppina's identity could not long be concealed. A

Then he contrasts their subsequent careers:

'Pazzo, che almanaccò per farsi nome
Con un libraccio polveroso e vieto,
Lasciando per il suon dell'alfabeto
Crome e biscrome!

'Or tu Mida doventi in una notte;
E via portato da veloce ruota,
Sorridi a lui che lascia nella mota
Le scarpe rotte.'

A cook fills the stomach and a tenor fills the ears; why bother with the intellect? The irony reaches a tremendous pitch in the lines:

'Torni Dante, tre paoli; a te, la paga
Di sei ministri.'

The vocal cords are all that matter; a plague take the useless brain!

'S'usa educar, lo so; ma è pur corbello,
Bimbi, chi spende per tenervi a scuola!
Gola e orecchi ci vuole, orecchi e gola:
Pèste al cervello!'

[1] 'Dalle carte di un celebre tenore' (*Musica d'Oggi*, Jan. 1935).

woman of the theatre, about whom rumour had been rife, come to live among them—it was too much. Giuseppina was made aware of their hostility when she went out. In the church she was left alone on her bench, shunned as though she had the plague. Verdi could treat the Bussetani with contempt, but Giuseppina, in the next few years, suffered greatly.

It seems likely that Giuseppina went to visit her mother, who was now living at Pavia,[1] while Verdi went to Naples for the production of *Luisa Miller*. He travelled in the company of Antonio Barezzi, who made notes of all the wonders they saw. Leaving Busseto on 3rd October, they were held up for a fortnight in Rome, on the way, owing to anti-cholera quarantine regulations. A fine and little known letter [2] from Verdi to Marie Escudier, from Naples on 3rd November, describes Rome under French occupation:

The affairs of our country are desolating! Italy is no longer anything but a vast and beautiful prison! If only you could see this sky, so pure, this climate, so mild, this sea, these mountains, this city, so beautiful!! To the eyes—a paradise: to the heart—an inferno!! The rule of your countrymen in Rome is no better than that of the rest of Italy. The French do their best to win the favour of the Romans, but so far the latter are most dignified and firm. One sees Frenchmen everywhere—parades, reviews, military bands that torment the ears in every corner of the city, all the time, but one never sees a Roman taking part. Whatever your newspapers may say, the demeanour of the Romans is most praiseworthy, but . . . the French are in the right . . . they are the strongest!!!

Theatrical affairs are desolating: the management is about to go bankrupt! For my part I'm not at all unhappy about that, for I desire nothing more than to retire to some corner of the earth, to blaspheme and to curse!

The delay in Rome meant that Barezzi had to return from Naples before *Luisa Miller* was staged, but he certainly made good use of his time, and enjoyed himself, as he had at Florence in 1847 and Paris in 1848:

On the 29th, with Tesorone, saw the Royal Palace, Capo di Monte, the Park, the Hermitage, San Gennaro, the Gesù Nuovo, Santa Chiara, the Campo di Marte, two large obelisks, San Severo, with a surprising marble Christ, veiled and taken down from the Cross, and in the evening with Verdi at Chiaia to watch the sunset.

On the 30th, with Arati, toured the port in a boat and visited one of the largest steamers, the *Ercolano*, and in the evening with Verdi and Signora Gazzaniga at the Teatro Fiorentini. . . .

On the 3rd went with Verdi to Herculaneum and saw the excavations

[1] Accounts at the end of the second volume of Verdi's autograph *Copialettere* record a payment by Ricordi of 3,000 lire to 'Rosa Strepponi of Pavia'. A letter to Ricordi of 19th April 1849 refers to this payment.

[2] Published in the Roman newspaper *La Tribuna* for 27th January 1907.

of the grandiose theatre, and the palace of Portici, provisionally inhabited by the Pope. . . .[1]

On the 6th with Verdi and Arati to Camaldoli on donkeys.
On the 7th with Verdi by railway to Pompeii.
On the 8th by railway to Caserta, alone. . . .

On the 10th again at Pozzuoli with Verdi and saw the Grotto of the Cumaean Sibyl, with Nero's stoves, the Temple of Serapis, the amphitheatre of Pozzuoli, and the remains of Caligula's famous bridge.

On the 11th with Verdi by steamer to Procida, Ischia, Casamicciola, Cumae and the Grotto of Fusaro.

On the 12th various other parts of Naples seen, and in the evening the sunset again.[2]

Barezzi left Naples on 14th November and was back at Busseto five days later. *Luisa Miller* was produced on 8th December; Verdi left Naples on the 13th. On 28th December he wrote from Busseto to Cesare De Sanctis, a new friend he had made at Naples, asking for the newspapers to be sent on, with accounts of the new opera 'which are awaited with the greatest anxiety by my father-in-law'.

All of which shows that as yet no shadow had fallen over the relationship of Verdi and Antonio Barezzi.

We have little information about Verdi's life at Busseto during the next two years. In February 1850 he was discussing with Cammarano the possibility of an opera on *King Lear*; in April he proposed Dumas's *Kean* as a subject to the management of the Teatro La Fenice at Venice; by August he was deeply engaged in study of *Le Roi s'amuse*; in the succeeding months he wrote part of the music of *Rigoletto* and the whole of the unfortunate *Stiffelio*, produced at Trieste on 16th November. After a struggle with the censorship *Rigoletto* was finished and produced with triumphant success at Venice on 11th March 1851.

Hostility at Busseto was met by a more and more complete withdrawal from society. In 1851, in the spring,[3] Verdi and Giuseppina left the Palazzo Dordoni and went to live in the farmhouse at Sant' Agata, two miles away, Verdi having some time earlier moved his parents to a house at Vidalenzo. Relations with Carlo Verdi, too,

[1] Pio Nono had moved from Gaeta to Portici on 4th September of this year.

[2] Barezzi's notes are published by Garibaldi in an appendix to his edition of Muzio's letters. The details of Verdi's return from Naples given by Abbiati (II, pp. 45–6) are actually those of Barezzi's return.

[3] On 28th April Verdi told Piave: 'I hope to go into the country in seven or eight days' time.' This letter is published by Abbiati (II, p. 130) who, however, regards this as a temporary move, misled, probably, by earlier writers and by the fact that Verdi continued to head his letters 'Busseto' for some time after the removal to Sant' Agata. The earliest letters actually headed 'Sant' Agata' seem to be those to Lanari of 26th April 1852 (Abbiati, II, p. 164) and to Piave of 17th August 1852 (Morazzoni, *Lettere inedite*, p. 34). But the content of letters of 1851 shows they were written there, even though headed 'Busseto'.

had almost reached breaking point; the composition of *Rigoletto* had been contemporaneous with negotiations through the notary Balestra for the payment of Carlo's debts and the firm rejection of his claim to the products of the hen-house.

At Sant' Agata Verdi and Giuseppina lived in solitude, ignoring the outside world, and Busseto in particular, occupied with country pursuits, planning the garden, planting trees and shrubs. Verdi supervised the work of the three peasant sub-tenants of the Sant' Agata farms, keeping scrupulous accounts of his wine, corn, hay, manure, flour and salt, and the profits accruing from traffic in cattle. A surviving document [1] shows that, eighteen months after the removal to Sant' Agata, he possessed four oxen, seventeen cows, ten bullocks, eleven calves and six rams, which brought in a profit of 1,714 lire over a year.

A letter of Giuseppina's, on the occasion of another visit to Florence, tells us more about her affairs, without by any means entirely clarifying them:

Florence, 18th May 1851.

DEAREST,

I delayed writing to you in vain, because so far I have not succeeded in my intent, and so cannot tell you the day of my arrival at Parma. In any case you can count on having me home by the end of the month.

If Livia's people, and she above all, had consulted Gigino (he of whom I have often spoken to you, and mentioned also in my last letter), things would have gone differently and I should not have needed to hurry to Florence. But in business affairs there is nothing worse than people of low intelligence, above all when malign influence directs them or intimidates them. From now on I am confident that things will go better. It was a great calamity for me to have met Bartolini, or, to put it better, to have set foot in poor Bartolini's studio. All these troubles arose from that—troubles not only for me, but for others besides. Fortunately I have freed myself, but there is someone else who will not escape without serious loss. Livia has become frightfully thin. Poor women, what imbeciles we are!!!

Tomorrow I should have a reply from Dini, dealer in groceries, who undertook to speak to Smith, dealer in woollen cloth. The customs union that is about to function has very sensibly diminished the business of the big firms, and this, as you will understand, is a loss for me at this moment.

I hear that Piave has written to me, flaunting his latinity, grace and wit. It's an easy triumph, because in writing to him I had no thought of such pretensions, but scribbled hurriedly a modest, intimate letter, far removed from those texts in language with long words that he receives from various *prime donne*, who write *by the pale light of the moon*, or under a *weeping willow*!!! For the rest, I shan't be able to get my own back by flaunting a like knowledge and intelligence, but I shall display a like friendship, because, to tell the truth, Piave is an excellent fellow, of whom I am fond both for his kindness and because you love him.

[1] Grazzi, loc. cit.

If you are looking forward to my arrival I am all anxiety to return. I repeat that I count on being home by Ascension Day at the latest.

I recommend you, I pray you, not to become too intimate with *your heirs*, and that not through unkind feelings, I swear to you, but because I could not endure further displeasures of the sort I have endured now for almost two years. Human nature has shown itself in such a disgusting aspect in the past vicissitudes, that it is better for us if every precaution is taken that the veil with which you covered it is never raised again.

Farewell, my Mage. I won't attempt to express my affection in words, reserving the right to do so with kisses on my return. Farewell. Farewell.

PEPPINA.

P.S. Lanari is not here, as you know. It seems that this man has done all he possibly could to render himself ridiculous, and make himself generally hated.

We see now that Giuseppina had invested the money she had saved during her last years as a singer and singing teacher in a business at Florence. To the end of her life she kept separate accounts from Verdi, buying her own clothes and contributing, as freely as her means allowed, to various charities from her own purse. She was naturally generous, not given to counting costs and keeping bills, but she made herself what Verdi wished her to be, and became a model housekeeper and wife. Livia Zanobini seems also to have been involved in business. The connection between Giuseppina's and Livia's troubles and the encounter with Bartolini remains obscure. Bartolini had died in the previous year, less than five months after he had undertaken to supervise Camillino's artistic education.

Piave, who had visited Busseto more than once in the course of the preparation of the *Rigoletto* libretto, was thus one of the first, in the outside world, to know the truth about Verdi's relations with Giuseppina. The passage in the above letter about the 'heirs' must, regrettably, be held to refer to Giovannino and Demetrio Barezzi, Verdi's brothers-in-law.

One of the few of Giuseppina's own old friends with whom she kept up correspondence was Mauro Corticelli, a theatrical agent at Bologna. About fifty letters to him are in the Scala Museum, the earliest in date being this one, which tells what happened when she arrived back at Sant' Agata from Florence:

DEAR CORTICELLI,

I got quite happily as far as one mile from Busseto. There I found a man who announced a misfortune. I hasten to add that Verdi was with me, having come to Parma to meet me. The misfortune was a burglary in the night, our country house being scaled and broken into. The thieves profited by the momentary absence of Verdi, and the consequently empty apartment, to enter by the window of my room and go straight to the drawer where the money is kept, in Verdi's room. But in forcing the secretaire, where the money was, the wood broke with a tremendous crack and the servant woke up and began to call the woman and a peasant who by chance had stayed to sleep in the house. The latter got up in a fright and their terror increased when they saw through the keyhole the lamp lit in the apartment. The woman, braver than the men, tried to open the door, but fright and some internal obstacle prevented the key from turning. They then went down to the kitchen and, having armed themselves, one with a knife, one with an axe, one with another tool, they went up again, to try at all events to get in the apartment. Indeed, they succeeded, but the thieves (who perhaps were afraid of being recognized) had seized their chance and run away, so when the peasant-servantry entered they saw nothing but the window of my room wide open, a lamp lit in Verdi's room and the secretaire open and empty! The pecuniary loss is not serious, but the fright of those poor people was very great. When we arrived they were still pale and distracted. A doctor was at once sent for to bleed them. Then there began the visits of the magistrate, the dragoons, the police, the experts, and a full report was drawn up. Now all possible inquiries are being made to discover the malefactors, but that won't be easy. . . . Verdi sends his best wishes and, as he has taken the advent of the thieves with a certain indifference, he continues to busy himself with agriculture, and at this moment is occupied in particular with the paving of the room on the ground floor, which he has had renewed. I haven't seen it yet, as it's still covered over. . . . When the tiles are uncovered and the rooms in, at any rate, decent condition, I hope you will come and join us in a good stew *alla polenta*.

Farewell, dear Mauro. Remember your sincere friend Peppina. Farewell.

G. STREPPONI.

Busseto, 1st June 1851.

Here is the earliest evidence we have that the move to Sant' Agata ('our country house') had taken place. The old farmhouse, to which the first alterations were being made, was to be constantly improved and enlarged, as the years passed, until it was almost unrecognizable. As yet, it provided a very modest, rustic home. Verdi himself tells the same story in an undated letter to Piave: [1]

One night last week, when I was away from home and Maria and Giacomo were alone in the house, sundry God-fearing persons, towards midnight, climbed up and broke a window and, having got into the upper apartment, broke open my writing-desk and stole a few gold napoleons and some rolls of Austrian lire which I kept there for daily use. Besides the loss by the theft there is the annoyance of visits by police-magistrates, police officers, gendarmes, etc., etc., and you can imagine what sort of humour I'm in. Am I never to have a moment's peace?!! I expect you at Busseto, but would like you to put off your visit for a while. For about a month now bricklayers, carpenters and the like have been working in my house, to my misfortune. They haven't finished yet and you wouldn't

[1] *Carteggi verdiani*, II, pp. 352–3. The postmark of arrival 'Venice, 4th June', can be read on a photograph of this letter in the archives of Sant' Agata.

find room anywhere. So wait a bit, and bring with you your good humour, for in this frightful solitude you will certainly need it. In another letter I'll describe the life one leads here, so that you'll be prepared for the worst. Farewell.

'Busseto', here, is Sant' Agata ('this frightful solitude'). According to a letter from Muzio to Ricordi,[1] the thieves were Verdi's own servants. Abbiati, not knowing Giuseppina's letter to Corticelli, thinks the burglary was at Palazzo Dordoni.

One 28th June Verdi's mother died, to his great sorrow, at Vidalenzo. 'I can't tell you of his grief,' Muzio wrote to Ricordi, 'it's immense. Peppina suffers in seeing him weep and it's my sad office to see to the funeral arrangements, the priests, etc.' Verdi, inviting Corticelli to pay them a visit, said: 'Certainly the place is not beautiful, and our humour is not cheerful.' Negotiations were opened for a new opera, to be produced in Madrid during the next Carnival or Lent season; Verdi's terms included the provision of accommodation and travelling expenses 'for two people'—Giuseppina would have accompanied him. But nothing came of this proposal. In December Verdi and Giuseppina left for Paris.

During this time there had been very little contact between Verdi at Sant' Agata and his friends and enemies at Busseto. There was one person who suffered greatly as a result of this. We have seen that Antonio Barezzi had met Giuseppina in Paris in January 1848, and had liked and admired her. We have seen that her arrival at Busseto had not at first interrupted the deeply affectionate relationship between him and Verdi. But then incident had followed incident until Verdi had finally turned his back on Busseto and the Bussetani and retired into solitude. There was no breach with Barezzi, but inevitably a change was felt—things were not as they were. Barezzi was hurt by this withdrawal. And now Verdi and Giuseppina had gone off to Paris without any arrangement being made, as on previous occasions, for the Barezzi family to look after Verdi's property during his absence. After an interval, Barezzi wrote, apparently complaining that he was being neglected. Verdi's reply is celebrated:

Paris, 21st January 1852.

DEAREST FATHER-IN-LAW,

After waiting so long I did not expect to receive from you so cold a letter, containing, unless I misread them, some very pointed remarks. If this letter were not signed 'Antonio Barezzi', that is to say, by my benefactor, I should have replied either very sharply or not at all. But since it bears a name that it will always be my duty to respect, I shall try, as far as possible, to persuade you that I don't deserve any sort of reproach. To do this I shall have to return to things of the past, to speak of others and of our

[1] Abbiati, II, p. 137.

home town, and the letter will become a bit long-winded and tiresome, but I shall try to be as brief as I can.

I don't believe that of your own accord you would have written me a letter which you know was bound to distress me. But you live in a town where people have the bad habit of prying into other people's affairs and of disapproving of everything that does not conform to their own ideas. It is my custom never to interfere, unless I am asked, in other people's business and I expect others not to interfere in mine. All this gossip, grumbling and disapprobation arises from that. I have the right to expect in my own country the liberty of action that is respected even in less civilized places. Judge for yourself, severely if you will, but coolly and dispassionately: What harm is there if I live in isolation? If I choose not to pay calls on titled people? If I take no part in the festivities and rejoicings of others? If I administer my farmlands because I like to do so and because it amuses me? I ask again: What harm is there in this? In any case, no one is any the worse for it.

That premised, I come to the sentence in your letter: 'I know very well that I am not the man for serious charges, because my time is over, but for little things I should be capable still?' If by that you mean to say that once I gave you heavy tasks to perform and now make use of you for little things, alluding to the letter I enclosed in yours, I can find no excuse for this, and, although I should do as much for you in similar cases, I can only say that the lesson will serve me for the future. If, however, your sentence is to be interpreted as a reproach because I have not entrusted you with my affairs during my absence, I permit myself to ask: How could I possibly be so inconsiderate as to lay such a heavy burden on you, who never set foot in your own fields, because the demands of your business are themselves too heavy? Ought I to have entrusted them to Giovannino? But isn't it true that last year, while I was at Venice, I gave him ample powers, in writing, and he didn't once set foot in Sant' Agata? I'm not blaming him for that. He was perfectly right. He had his own things, important enough, to attend to, and so he couldn't look after mine.

There, I've laid bare to you my opinions, my actions, my wishes, my public life, I would almost say, and since we are by way of making revelations, I have no objection to raising the curtain that veils the mysteries contained within four walls, and telling you about my private life. I have nothing to hide. In my house there lives a lady, free, independent, a lover like myself of solitude, possessing a fortune that shelters her from all need. Neither I nor she owes to anyone at all an account of our actions. On the other hand, who knows what relationship exists between us? What affairs? What ties? What claims I have on her, and she on me? Who knows whether she is or is not my wife? And if she is, who knows what the particular reasons are for not making the fact public? Who knows whether that is a good thing or a bad one? Why should it not be a good thing? And even if it is a bad thing, who has the right to ostracize us? I will say this, however: in my house she is entitled to as much respect as myself—more even; and no one is allowed to forget that on any account. And finally she has every right, both on account of her conduct and her character, to the consideration she never fails to show to others.

With this long rigmarole I mean to say no more than that I demand liberty of action for myself, because all men have a right to it, and because I am by nature averse to acting according to other people's ideas, and that you, who at heart are so good, so just and so generous, should not let yourself be influenced, and not absorb the ideas of a town which—it must be said!—in time past did not consider me worthy to be its organist, and now complains, wrongly and perversely, about my actions and affairs. That cannot go on; if it does, I shall choose my own course of action. The world is wide, and the loss of twenty or thirty thousand francs will not prevent my finding a home elsewhere. Nothing in this letter should offend you, but if by chance there is anything that displeases you, overlook it, for on my honour I swear I have no intention of causing you displeasure of any sort. I have always thought of you, and still think of you, as my benefactor, and feel honoured and proud of that. Farewell. Farewell.

The letter from Barezzi that provoked this reply has not survived. Probably, however, those writers who have supposed that Barezzi had written a letter 'rebuking him for causing a scandal', or 'protesting' against Verdi's relations with Giuseppina, have gone too far. It is very doubtful whether Barezzi would have dared to open a discussion on such matters as these. But he was clearly unhappy, and hurt, at Verdi's seeming neglect, with the transference to Sant' Agata and general avoidance of Busseto. The only part of Barezzi's letter quoted: 'I know very well that I am not the man for serious charges, because my time is over, but for little things I should be capable still?' might be interpreted as a reminder of past benefits—but a kindly reminder, and one, surely, revealing a sincere wish to continue to be of use. How could Verdi think for a moment that he was being rebuked for enclosing a letter to someone else in one to Barezzi, for the latter to deliver? This touchiness, this hypersensitivity, in a man who often appeared to have the hide of a rhinoceros, is seen again in the reference, after so many years, to Ferrari's appointment as organist.

It has often been remarked that although he talks about 'raising the curtain' Verdi in this letter does not actually tell Barezzi anything he did not know before. He reveals nothing at all. But perhaps he has been wrongly blamed for this. He could not tell the whole story without discussing Giuseppina's past life. It was she, and not Verdi, who for the present rejected the idea of marriage. The evidence of the letters published by Luzio is clear: Giuseppina felt herself unworthy of Verdi. Tied as she was still to Camillino and, unless it had died before this, to the second child, about which we know nothing, she hesitated to accept yet the great name that Verdi had almost certainly offered her. Remarks about Verdi 'placing Giuseppina in a position that must have been cruelly unhappy to a devout Catholic' are out of place, especially since it is more than doubtful whether she *was*, at this time, a particularly devout Catholic.

Barezzi's reply has not come down to us; it was surely conciliatory. We know that he soon took Giuseppina to his heart, and she loved him, as her later letters show. She called him her 'Nonnon' and signed herself 'your most affectionate quasi-daughter'. Visits from 'Signor Antonio' are reported in her letters from Sant' Agata during Verdi's occasional absences from home.

Giuseppina and Verdi returned from Paris to Sant' Agata in March. The reconciliation with Barezzi, and the beginning of a closer relationship between him and Giuseppina, probably followed at once. Proof that all was well by the summer is found in the reminiscences of Léon Escudier,[1] who came to Italy to convey the news that Verdi had been created Chevalier of the Legion of Honour. Escudier found Barezzi dining at Sant' Agata:

> For Father Antonio, Verdi is a demi-god. . . . He never speaks of him or of his works without tears coming into his eyes. He lives at Busseto. . . . He shows you, with a pride that makes the composer smile and shrug his shoulders, the room in which Verdi wrote *I due Foscari*. Then, if you have won his confidence, if you show sufficiently great admiration for Verdi, he allows you to see a pile of manuscripts, which he guards as the apple of his eye. These are the earliest compositions. . . . Many a time Verdi would have liked to put these old papers on the fire; a heart-rending glance from Father Antonio alone prevented this *auto-da-fé*. . . . We sat down at table. Needless to say, it was Father Antonio who led the conversation and Verdi who was the subject of it—to the great despair of the Maestro, who, tired of the struggle, gave up trying to make him be quiet.

When, at the dessert stage, the cross of the Legion of Honour was produced, Verdi frowned, trying to hide his emotion, and then shook Escudier warmly by the hand. 'Father Antonio was dumbfounded. He tried to speak, but it was impossible for him to articulate a single word; he waved his hands, stood up, threw his arms round Verdi's neck, embraced him and wept like a child.' Afterwards he borrowed the decoration, promising to bring it back the next day, and hurried off to show it round Busseto.

In the following winter *Il Trovatore* was composed, for production in Rome, and, almost contemporaneously, work was begun on *La Traviata*, for the Teatro La Fenice, at Venice. Piave was called to Sant' Agata, to work on another, unidentified libretto. This was actually finished, and Piave on the point of returning to Venice, when Verdi suddenly became intensely interested in *La Dame aux Camélias*, and made his friend stay on and draft a scenario based on this. 'You know Sant' Agata, topographically,' Piave wrote to Guglielmo Brenna, 'and you can imagine whether I am here for my amusement. . . . When it rains, I assure you, it's a case of looking at oneself in

[1] *Mes Souvenirs*, second edition (Paris, 1863).

the mirror to see if one is still in human form or whether one hasn't been transmuted into that of a toad or frog.' [1] But the result of poor Piave's tribulations was *La Traviata*. Luzio has suggested a possible reflection, or sublimation, in this opera, of the intimate drama of Verdi's personal relationship with Giuseppina Strepponi and Antonio Barezzi. Violetta's redemption through love, and the elder Germont's final recognition of her worth had had, indeed, their parallels in real life, not long before the opera was written. Giuseppina escaped Violetta's tragic end, it is true, but her health was anything but good and some of her letters exhale a melancholy, sick-room atmosphere not unlike that of the last act of *La Traviata*.

We have a wonderfully revealing group of letters from Giuseppina to Verdi, written while he was in Rome for the production of *Il Trovatore*. As yet he would not allow her to accompany him when he went to put on new operas in Italy. So Giuseppina had gone with him only as far as Leghorn, whence she could easily visit Florence while awaiting Verdi's return.

Leghorn, 2nd January 1853.

I expect to hear from you tomorrow; God grant it may be so, for I have so much need of it! I hope you spent New Year's Day a little better than I did. . . . I'm afraid I shall have lost the use of my tongue by the time of your return, having observed an almost Trappist silence since last Tuesday! I go out very little, because wandering through the streets bores me, and, for the rest, Leghorn is too small a place for one to be able to go out freely without exciting excessive attention. . . . I can't tell you with what impatience I await your return! I have taken to reading, and I read and read and read, until my eyes are inflamed, but I'm afraid that sadness and boredom will attack me, during these days when you have condemned me to the *cellular* system. You will say: 'Spend some money and amuse yourself.' First of all, I don't like you to say: 'Amuse yourself,' and then, I don't know how to set about it! If I could see you for a quarter of an hour in every twenty-four, my spirit would be glad, I should work, I should read, and time would pass too quickly, even. As things are . . . but let's not talk on that subject any more, because it makes me feel like crying.

3rd January.

MY DEAR PASTICCIO,

I have just received your letter—I can't tell you with what joy! . . . I am very glad you find yourself lost without me, and I wish you so much boredom that you'll have to renounce the barbarous idea of leaving me in isolation, like a saint of the Thebaid! My dear Mage, you have the *heart* of an angel, but your *head*, for languages and for certain ideas, is so thick that if Gall were still alive he would be able to add some curious observations to his treatise on craniology. I ask you, by way of conversation:

[1] Giovanni Cenzato, *Itinerari verdiani* (Parma, n.d.), p. 98.

Is it true or not that all those who intrigue, or interest themselves in other people's business, believe as an article of faith that I am with you in Rome? You will reply: 'Certainly it is true; let them believe it!' I retort (always by way of conversation): What would it matter to you then, if next to your bedroom there were that of your poor *Pasticcio*? An't I here in this friar's cell, with only a little mouse for company? (I forgot to tell you that I have got over my aversion for mice, since I made the acquaintance of this nocturnal companion, who comes to eat the crumbs I let fall when I dine.) Now, being able to stay all alone in my room, without any sort of distraction, instead of staying there unhappily I should stay there most gladly if I knew that at night, when you return from the theatre, or an evening gathering, before lying down you would come, as at home, to say: 'Goodnight, *Pasticcio*,' and in the morning, before opening your room to visitors: 'Good morning, *Pasticcio*.' I think no orator ever found arguments more persuasive than mine. From the moment they believe that I am with you and that you say: 'Let them believe it!' and I don't show myself either to confirm or deny that I'm there or not there, it seems to me you could be more kind and renounce the role of Dionysius, tyrant of Syracuse, because you are too generous to sign repeated sentences of exile!

The day after tomorrow I shall go to Florence, and if possible I shall go also to Pisa, to hear la Piccolomini. Were there no letters for me in Rome? I say nothing about the silence of my relatives! When I inherit 500,000 francs they will come back and write me most amiable letters! That's the way of the world! . . . Farewell. Write me a nice letter and make haste and give *our Trovatore*. A kiss on your heart.

PEPPINA.

Leghorn, 3rd January 1853.

DEAREST,

I have received your second letter, and I thank you for having thought of me on the first day of the New Year, the eleventh of our acquaintance! If I did not write to you, it was because I know your indifference about such things. But you can imagine my good wishes on the first day, and all the other days, of this and all the other years of your life to come! (God grant you may close my eyes.)

So your arm hurts? I hope it's better now, but in any case expose yourself as little as possible to the night air, and use camphorated oil. I am not very well, either, and my appetite is failing. My dear Verdi, I confess my weakness, but this separation has been, for me, more painful than all the others. Without you I am a body without a soul. I am different (and I think you are, too) from those people who have need of frequent separations to revive their affection. I would stay with you for years and years, without boredom or satiety. On the contrary, now, after we've been together for a long time, without leaving each other for a moment, I feel our separation more keenly, although you give me reason to hope it will be brief.

I'm going to Florence tomorrow, and pray heaven I may have no vexations. I shall stay there for a few days and, if I have no troubles, I shall be less sad than here at Leghorn. I have been thinking over the trip to Pisa. . . . It seems very unfitting for me to stay a night there, to go *alone* to the theatre. You will understand that when I too was a professional singer it was another matter: my name served as a sort of companion, or I could ask for letters of recommendation, etc., etc. Now, thank God, I have disappeared from *society*, and after so many years spent living with you in solitude, almost in the wilderness, I feel quite helpless when I have to go *alone* to this or that part of the inhabited and civilized world. Like me, you can say that you long for your little room at Sant' Agata! If it weren't for the contract for the opera we could enjoy, at Sant' Agata or in some other desert place, our tranquil existence, and the pleasures that are so simple and for us so delightful. Sometimes I fear that the love of money will re-awaken in you and condemn you to many further years of drudgery. My dear Mage, you would be very wrong. Don't you see? A great part of our lives has gone by, and you would be quite mad if, instead of enjoying the rewards of your glorious and honoured labours in peace, you were to sweat to accumulate money and make glad those who in the sad word 'Death' see only their infamous desires realized in the iniquitous word 'Inheritance'. We shall have no children (since God, perhaps, wishes to punish me for my sins, in depriving me of any legitimate joy before I die). Well then, not having children by me, I hope you won't cause me sorrow by having any by another woman; without children you have a fortune more than sufficient to provide for your needs, and a little bit of luxury besides. We adore the country, and in the country one lives cheaply —and enjoys oneself so much. When I think that there are, at Sant' Agata, those dear *culatelli*, Solfarin and Menaffiss,[1] who pull your modest carriage with such gusto and cost so little . . . when I think that I have my Poli-Poli, Pretin, Matt, Prevost, etc., etc.,[2] which look at me with eyes full of affection and *greediness*, which cost so little and amuse me so much . . . when I think of our flowers and few feet of garden, which gives us as much pleasure as if it were the Eden of the Earthly Paradise—I ask whether city life has ever given us such pleasures and whether, in consequence, two or three months a year of this cursed *city* are not more than enough to put us in a fever of desire to return to the country?

Don't you agree? Then I'll put a stop to my chatter, which I perceive has gone on rather too long. But you will be indulgent. If only you knew what a sad life I lead these days! . . . And you haven't written anything yet? You see! You haven't got your poor Nuisance[3] in a corner of the room, curled up in an armchair, to say: 'That's beautiful'—'That's *not*' —'Stop'—'Repeat that'—'That's original.' Now, without this poor Nuisance, God is punishing you, making you wait and rack your brains, before opening all the little pigeon-holes and allowing your magnificent musical ideas to emerge.

[1] Two horses, clearly. 'Culatelli' needs a word of explanation, even to Italians. The *culatello* is a local delicacy, a ham made from the buttock of a pig. Seen from behind, from the carriage, Solfarin and Menaffiss presented to the view two tails and four *culatelli*.

[2] All cage birds, probably.

[3] 'Livello', as she calls herself, in the dialect of Lodi means 'nuisance', according to Gatti.

Florence, 12th January 1853.

DEAREST,

Here at Florence I have received your few lines, which—be it said without intention of wronging your (calligraphic) talents—I had the greatest difficulty in the world to read. I understand, however, that you wrote to me in a moment of ill humour, and so I don't complain of the not very nice remark you make. What? Not write to you through carelessness? Because of etiquette? Listen, my dear Mage. I have nothing in the world to console me—*you* alone excepted. I love you (perhaps it's a fault) beyond everything and everybody! However great, numerous and constant my sorrows, your love is for me such a benison that it suffices to give me courage to support all my afflictions. If, therefore, an action, a word, a failing in me sometimes displeases you, forgive it, thinking of all the sadness and misfortune of my existence!

I have stayed at Florence longer than I expected; but the days are so short and walking tires me so much that it has taken me several days to pay the *necessary* calls. You will say: 'You should have taken a carriage.' I did consider it, but decided it was better not to take one, and that not *only* from the point of view of economy—though economy while travelling is very difficult. . . . Signor Ronzi, believing he was doing me (doing *you*, that is) a favour, brought me the key of a box at the theatre and I had, to my great annoyance, to go to *Le Prophète*, as la Frezzolini will perhaps not sing during the Carnival season, and spend a further 12 *paoli*!! Don't ask me anything about *Le Prophète*, or about the singers. I reserve all my critico-philosophic chatter until your return. I have also been to another place, which you are a thousand miles from guessing, but, I repeat, you will hear the story (however melancholy and boring) of these days of exile when you arrive at Leghorn.

Jouhaud is being extremely kind, and speaks of you with incredible enthusiasm!

I shall be at Leghorn on Friday evening and shall rest from all the commotion of these days. I hope that *Il Trovatore* will be staged not later than the 15th, in which case you will be at Leghorn on the 19th, if there is a steamer. I hope I shall find letters from you on Friday, having left instructions that no more letters are to be forwarded to Florence after Sunday the 9th.

Lose no time, but hurry to me as soon as your business in Rome is over. Love me, as I love you.

Your

PEPPINA.

Leghorn, 17th January 1853.

DEAREST,

I am very sorry about what you tell me concerning the opera for Venice. I hope, however, that the situation is not quite so black as you paint it, and that on your arrival at Leghorn you will have several finished pieces in your trunk. By that I don't mean to refuse to do what you wish: for a long time now I have had no will of my own. Only (and I tell you this frankly) I should be displeased if you thought up some pretext for taking me back to Sant' Agata and leaving again without me. If this is your intention it would suffice to say: 'Peppina, this is a sacrifice I ask of your affection.' I have made so many sacrifices for one who has repaid, and repays, me with immense ingratitude, that I am most happy to consent to do what pleases you, for you, who alone in the world have never caused me sorrow! So be it as you wish; let's go back to Sant' Agata, and your will be done, as long as I have my eyes open and the strength to tell you that I love you with all my being! . . .

I flattered myself you would have finished with *Il Trovatore* much earlier, but I see you throw doubt on your arrival even by the 24th. If, however, you do arrive on the 24th, we can be at Genoa on the 25th, leave again on the 26th (if you want to hear la Biscottini) and be sleeping in our own bed on the evening of the 27th. So hurry up and leave Rome.

If I were an egoist, what you tell me about Naples would induce me to advise you to accept the contract, but your health and peace of mind are worth more than all the delights of Naples, Capri and Sorrento! So, in your position, I wouldn't tie myself in any way for the present. I should look for a libretto I liked and set it to music *without any engagement and in my own time*! . . .

I shan't speak of myself! . . . I'm unbelievably sad, and woe betide me if I go on like this! At Florence I've had things to do and annoyances, not amusements, but the smoke of the steamer on the 24th will announce my Mage, and with him will return my moments of good humour and gaiety. Oh, if Sant' Agata were in France, in England, in America, who, except yourself, would ever see me again on this earth? Believe me, the aversion I show for society in general is much less than that I feel for myself.

If we could find in the south of France, in England, in Greece, in Turkey or somewhere, a patch of ground to buy, to turn upside down at our fancy, what a delight it would be for me! And for you?

I love Sant' Agata, because it's my nature to become fond of places where I've lived for a long time; nevertheless there are so many things, so many passions (good and bad) that, for another eight or ten years at least, prevent us from enjoying there that complete peace which, it seems to me, would make us young again and doubly alive.

My dear *Pasticcio*, I have spent a lot of money—and without having bought myself anything beautiful, or of any consequence. It's true that the journey to Florence (all the more as I almost never dined alone) upset my calculations; but, all things considered, as you will see from the bills, I have been very moderate. But the money just flies. It never enters my mind to sample the Bordeaux, or champagne, as when I am with you: I don't even know how a black coffee tastes at Leghorn! If you delay coming until the 24th there won't be the treasures of Croesus left over, certainly; I'm sorry about that.

I shan't write to you any more, then, and will expect you on the 24th. For the love of God, do your utmost not to fail to come. A kiss on your heart. Farewell. Farewell.

PEPPINA.

Verdi had intended working on *La Traviata* during the rehearsals of *Il Trovatore* in Rome; he had ordered a piano to be put in his rooms there for this purpose. According to Benjamin Lumley,[1] the first act of *La Traviata* was actually written at Genoa in four days, while he was detained there by bad weather. This must have been while he was still in Giuseppina's company, on the way to Rome by sea, via Genoa and Civitavecchia. We have seen that little progress was made with the new opera in Rome. The passage in which Giuseppina recalls Verdi in the act of composition at Sant' Agata, with herself curled up in an armchair near by, interpolating comments and criticism, is of extraordinary interest. She must have sung many of these world-famous melodies for the first time from the manuscript sketches. He took her advice in many things. Thus, just five days after Giuseppina wrote the above letter, we find Verdi telling Corticelli[2] that he did not wish to tie himself down by a contract to producing a new opera by a certain date; first he would compose the opera, at his own convenience, and then look round for a suitable theatre, with suitable singers. This was exactly what Giuseppina had suggested.

But if she was hoping to be allowed to accompany him to Venice for the production of *La Traviata* she was to be disappointed. Verdi willed otherwise, and Giuseppina's declining health, in any case, made it advisable for her to stay at home.

Dr Frignani, of Busseto, did not enjoy her confidence. She thought him both ignorant and malicious, recalled the mistakes he had made in treating the wife of Signor Antonio, Verdi's agent, and others, and only sent for him herself when she could not avoid it. *La Traviata* was finished at Sant' Agata in an atmosphere of gloom and foreboding like that of its own last act. Verdi himself was unwell, and already convinced that his opera would fail, as it did. Piave, from Sant' Agata, was forced to write, at Verdi's dictation, a letter[3] conveying to the management the composer's belief that the entire company of singers engaged was unworthy of the Teatro La Fenice, and that the result would be a complete fiasco. He added a postscript:

All that I wrote in Verdi's name, but now I must add on my own account that he is in a truly infernal temper, partly perhaps because of his indisposition, but more owing to his lack of confidence in the singers. I have myself read letters sent him from Rome which analyse and pulverize not only la Salvini, but *Varesi's weakness* and the *marmoreal, monotonous* singing of Graziani (those are the epithets I read!). I, also, came in for my own share of reproof, for not having told him about this *chronic condition* (as he says) of the company.

[1] *Reminiscences of the Opera* (London, 1864), pp. 395–6, footnote. Lumley says Verdi told him this.
[2] G. Morazzoni, *Verdi: Lettere inedite* (Milan, 1929), p. 36.
[3] *Verdi e la Fenice* (Venice, 1951), pp. 48–9.

A little later an anonymous letter from Venice announced that unless the soprano and the bass were changed *La Traviata* would be a fiasco. 'I know, I know,' said Verdi.

After he left for Venice Giuseppina wrote him a wonderfully beautiful letter:

Sant' Agata, 23rd February 1853.

DEAR MAGE,

I write, as I promised, to tell you I am neither better nor worse than on Sunday: however, Frignani assures me that with today's powders I shall have sensible and speedy relief. . . . He has forbidden me both meat and green vegetables, prescribing a diet of soup and eggs, to be eaten tepid; as long as it's tepid he also allows me black coffee—and you know that's my only little weakness—at table. All that I ask and hope is to be perfectly well again by your return. You can't imagine all I suffered in the last few days, seeing you, my poor Mage, working like a nigger and, on top of that, having my indisposition before your eyes! But I shall get well again and shall try, by my good humour, to make you forget past annoyances. You are so good to your Nuisance . . . and I am desolate at not being able to compensate at all for what you do for me! . . . I dare not even speak of your generous and delicate [offer?] . . . but look, not because I'm ungrateful, you know that, you feel that, you understand! More than once I have swallowed, cleared my throat, etc., to begin my discourse . . . but emotion strangles the words in my throat, I feel like crying, the blood rushes to my head, etc., and I have to renounce those sincere expressions which I would like to use and which you have the right to expect. On the other hand, knowing your fineness of feeling, I am sure you would be as embarrassed and as moved as I myself! Poor Mage! And to think that that lofty soul of yours came spontaneously to lodge in the body of a Bussetano! One needs the faith of St Thomas to believe it. I am still of the opinion that an exchange took place in your childhood, and that you came into existence as the result of some sweet lapse of two unhappy and superior beings! Write to me when you can; hurry on the rehearsals and return to your hut. Our youth is over; nevertheless we are still the whole world to each other and watch with high compassion all the human puppets rushing about, climbing up, slipping down, fighting, hiding, reappearing—all to try to put themselves at the head, or among the first few places, of the social masquerade. In this perpetual convulsion they reach the last extremity, surprised at not having enjoyed anything, at not having anything sincere and disinterested to console them in their last hours, and longing too late for that peace, which seems to me the best thing on earth, and which they have despised all their lives in order to embrace the chimeras of vanity. As long as God leaves us good health, our simple and modest pleasures and desires will cheer and comfort us even in old age; our affection and our characters, so well matched, will leave no room for those frequent and bitter altercations which diminish love and end by destroying every illusion. It's true, is it not, my *Pasticcio*, that I see life in a way that, unfortunately, people in general do not see it? If you too see it like that, the future can still be beautiful for you and for me. Farewell. I leave off because I am tired, but I hope soon to be well. Greetings to Piave. Farewell. Farewell.

Your PEPPINA.

P.S. Yesterday morning, at about nine o'clock, Demetrio came to Sant' Agata, as cool as a cucumber, to see me, but I did not receive him, both because I was ill in bed and because I thought the hour very unfitting for paying calls on a lady. I sent my excuses, and I don't know whether he took offence. . . . He said in the kitchen that he is getting married, that he has bought a new carriage, and that he had been at la Cavalli's house up till four in the morning. He really is a bad lot.

Further reports on Giuseppina's health followed.

26th February 1853.

DEAR MAGE,

Today I sent Bernardo to Borgo and he came back with a most welcome letter from you, which has consoled me. I am better, I don't know whether owing to what Frignani prescribed or owing to taking great care and to what I thought it well to do myself. After having taken the six doses ordered me, and not found the hoped-for improvement, I took, or rather I gulped down, two ounces of tamarind pulp at once, and then had Tognetta apply [compresses?] of rice water. After that I began to feel better and today for the first time since your departure I ate a little meat. Frignani came on Wednesday morning and said, after having examined me: 'The pulse is good, the tongue is fine, there is no wind in the body, etc. It's nothing! It's nothing!' After this assurance I began to get frightened, all the more as I felt very poorly late on Wednesday and the following Thursday. I didn't, however, send for Frignani again, but did as I told you above. . . . God willed that in the night from Thursday to Friday I felt considerable relief and today, Saturday, I am better and have strummed through the overture to *La Battaglia di Legnano*. I hope to be perfectly well by your return.

2nd March 1853.

DEAREST,

If, as you were hoping, the opera is staged on Saturday the 5th, it will be no use my addressing other letters to Venice after this. However, I shall know what to do from the letter that I expect to receive tomorrow. I hope that in spite of your tremendous exertions you are well. . . . I can't say as much about myself, because I've had a relapse, but perhaps, God willing, I shall have recovered my strength a little by the time of your return. If it's the cold weather that is the cause of this long indisposition, it has treated me cruelly this time! But you, who are so good to me, will arrange things so that next winter (if I'm alive) I shan't feel the rigours of the most antipathetic season of the year. If, then, we have to stay in Paris, I shall set up my winter quarters in a room with a stove at the first winds from the north, and I shall emerge when I see people dressed in their summer clothes again.

Signor Antonio came to see me on Sunday. He tells me he is not going to write to you, but begs me to give you a thousand greetings.

As you can imagine, I have had to recall Frignani: he repeats that it's nothing, and I only hope he's right. We shall see.

Forgive me, my dear Verdi, if I don't write much, but I am again on a strict diet, and you will understand that I am not very strong. I firmly believe that your return will give me back health and strength. Farewell. Look after yourself. Even if I improve to the extent of feeling well next week, I shall deprive myself of the pleasure of coming to embrace you at Cremona, from prudence, and for other reasons that I'll tell you by word of mouth—not important ones, however. Farewell once again.

Your poor Nuisance.

I have had a fairly good night, but am very weak today; I should perhaps be feeling better if I hadn't received some letters that have exceedingly distressed me. . . . I was hoping to hear from you today, but one sees, poor *Pasticcio*, you haven't had time. As long as it's not owing to illness. . . . Ricordi has written to me, and Mauro Corticelli, too, and Agostino Marchesi. I have replied to them all, in spite of not being well and my immense ill humour on account of the letters from Florence.

Come quickly. I long for you, as for God.

There are further passages in these letters revelatory of Guiseppina's attitude towards Verdi's friends and relations. Muzio she saw quite clearly:

I fear that the head of that young man will be an eternal obstacle to his fortune. He is absolutely honest, but in character exaggeratedly hotheaded and restless; all too ready to proffer remarks, spit out his opinions and give unasked advice; with so little tact in the affairs of life, which are sometimes most delicate, that few will put themselves out to help him, unless they know him well enough to appreciate what goodness, honesty and loyalty there are in his heart. I am sorry, for I am sincerely fond of him.

She also liked Piave (known as the 'Gran Diavolo') very much, though with certain reservations:

Thank the Big Devil for the few lines he wrote me and tell him not to show his friendship by *leading you astray*. I know that he has great talent and inclination for that occupation (*he has proved it to you*), but exhort him from me to show his erotic zeal with friends who resemble himself.[1] Joking apart, give him my kind regards and tell him that if poor Peppina is here among the snow (newly fallen since your departure) it is because that was the wish of him who alone in all the world commands my obedience.

[1] During his visit to Venice for *Rigoletto* Verdi had undoubtedly been flirting with a certain 'Angel', a friend of Piave's. After his return she addressed letters to him *poste restante* at Cremona and even proposed to pay him a visit. *See* the letters to Piave published by Abbiati (II, pp. 128–30).

Verdi, when he returned, brought a present from Piave, acknowledged by Giuseppina in a charming note:[1]

DEAREST BIG DEVIL,

Forgive me if I haven't written to you before now, to thank you for all the affectionate expressions in your letter and for the delightful purse sent me by means of the Big Bear. (It's true it was empty, but I count on filling it with the shekels of Sig. Capitan Piave, playing at *Sette e mezzo.*)

I repeat, please forgive my long silence, because, as Verdi has already told you, I am a poor Nuisance, who for a long time now has enjoyed very little good health. I set my hopes on the fine weather, which can't be far away.

Unappeased resentment against the Bussetani is still apparent. Even Signor Antonio got a slight scratch from Giuseppina:

Signor Antonio has been to see me once. The other day the Duke of Busseto passed and Signor Antonio went to meet him with the band; then the duke spoke to him most graciously and Signor Antonio, it seems, was on the point of fainting at such an honour, at such a joy! Amen.

This little weakness of Barezzi's had been referred to by Verdi himself in the letter of 21st January 1852, when he wrote: 'What harm is there if I live in isolation? If I choose not to pay calls on titled people?' Barezzi himself, however, was before long to outrage conventional opinion at Busseto. On 29th August 1853 his wife Maria died, in spite or because of the attentions of Dr Frignani; within a year, on 18th May 1854, Barezzi, aged sixty-seven, married Maddalena Fagnoni, aged about thirty, his former domestic servant.[2] This cannot have been much to the liking of Giovannino and Demetrio, considered by Giuseppina to be avidly awaiting their inheritance.

Giuseppina's own children, after this, are lost in obscurity. Of the younger child absolutely nothing is known. A vague tradition at Sant' Agata holds that Camillino died in an institution at Florence at about fourteen or fifteen years of age. According to our calculations, he would have been just about fifteen when Giuseppina wrote of receiving distressing news from Florence, but she may, of course, have meant news about her business affairs. Was it Camillino of whom she wrote that he had repaid her for her many sacrifices with immense ingratitude? It is possible.

After *La Traviata* Verdi *did* renounce the role of Dionysius, tyrant of Syracuse, and signed no more 'sentences of exile' for Giuseppina. As a result of this, and perhaps also of the death of Camillino,[3] we have very few more letters from her to him, for they were seldom

[1] *Carteggi verdiani*, II, p. 351.

[2] From the registers at Busseto, by courtesy of the Parroco and Signorina Gabriella Carrara Verdi.

[3] I was once told that Camillino did *not* die at fourteen or fifteen, but lived as a carpenter in the neighbourhood of Busseto. My informant said he could document this.

separated. On 9th September 1853, in accordance with Giuseppina's expressed wish to be spared another winter at Sant' Agata, Verdi asked Cesare De Sanctis if he could find an apartment at Naples for two persons, and if a lady, coming with him with passport in order, would suffer annoyance from the police. De Sanctis replied that the lady would have nothing to fear; to bring a letter of introduction to a banker would be the *non plus ultra* of prudence. However, Verdi and Giuseppina did not go to Naples, but to Paris again. The departure was preceded by a further explosion of wrath against Busseto. This concerned the proposed appointment of Muzio as *maestro di musica*, which, after Verdi had persuaded him to apply, came to nothing owing to the vexatious and humiliating conditions attached to the appointment. Verdi told the Philharmonic Society that he would never again have anything to do with the musical affairs of Busseto: 'In any other town, in a musical matter, I should have succeeded in obtaining what you and I want; in any other town I should have had the support of the civil and ecclesiastic authorities. . . . Elsewhere I should have succeeded; at Busseto (it is ludicrous!) I have failed. The proverb is old: *Nemo propheta in Patria*!!!'[1]

Verdi and Giuseppina returned to Paris in the middle of October, to the Second Empire of Napoleon III, which had succeeded the Second Republic. They were now to stay in France for more than two years. The long promised libretto by Scribe and Duveyrier, *Les Vêpres Siciliennes*, was delivered at the end of December. Most of the music of this opera was written in 1854, very slowly, and without enthusiasm. Verdi's thoughts were often elsewhere. He told the Countess Maffei he had no idea of settling permanently in Paris: 'I love too much my desert and my sky.' He had 'a fierce desire to return home'. To Cesare Vigna, who had reported the successful revival of *La Traviata* at Venice, he wrote: 'A time will come, and it's not very far off, when I shall say: "Farewell, my public; have a good time; my career is over: I'm going to plant cabbages."' The summer months were spent in the country, at Mandres, and from there in September Verdi reported that he had finished four acts of the new opera. Rehearsals were begun in October, but interrupted by the disappearance of the principal soprano, the eccentric German singer who called herself Cruvelli. Verdi made use of this to ask for release from his contract. In a letter to Giuseppina Appiani, already discussed,[2] he said that if he obtained his release from the contract he would at once return to Busseto, but only for a few days. 'Where shall I go? I couldn't say!' Probably he would have taken Giuseppina Strepponi to Naples, to avoid another winter amid the mist, rain and snow at Sant' Agata. But la Cruvelli reappeared, and it was necessary

[1] Giovanni Drei, 'Notizie e documenti verdiani' (*Aurea Parma*, 1941), *fasc.* I–II.
[2] See p. 114.

to stay in Paris. Seemingly endless and exhausting rehearsals followed; *Les Vêpres Siciliennes* was not produced until 13th June 1855.

On 28th June Verdi told the Countess Maffei that he hoped to be in Italy in a fortnight; but he was kept in Paris for another six months, struggling to prevent his operas being given in an unworthy manner, and without payment of royalties, by Calzado, a Spaniard who had taken over the management of the Théâtre Italien. During this time he was also engaged in lengthy and often acrimonious correspondence with Tito Ricordi about translation rights, performing rights, contracts, printing errors, piracy, royalties and publishers' trickeries. Ricordi's agent had not done his duty: 'So I have to stay in Paris, wasting my money! As usual, the expenses and annoyances are for me, the profits for other people!' He reminded Ricordi that the latter's 'colossal fortune' derived largely from *his* operas. 'I have never been considered as anything but an object, a tool, to be made use of as long as it works. Sad words, but true!'

Towards the end of December Verdi and Giuseppina were back at Sant' Agata. On 7th February 1856 Verdi described his life there to De Sanctis: 'Total abandonment of music; a little reading; some light occupation with agriculture and horses; that's all.' Piave was sent for, to discuss the transformation of *Stiffelio* into *Aroldo*; this was not regarded as a difficult task. On 1st April Verdi told the Countess Maffei: 'I can't help admiring your goodness and constant friendship for this poor Bear of Busseto. I'm not doing anything. I don't read, I don't write. I walk in the fields from morning to evening, trying to recover, so far without success, from the stomach trouble caused me by *I Vespri Siciliani*. Cursed operas!'

Nevertheless, on 15th May he signed a contract for a new opera, to be given at the Teatro La Fenice, Venice, during the next Carnival season. This was to be *Simon Boccanegra*. And he was still considering writing an opera based on *King Lear* for Naples. In June, on medical advice, he went with Giuseppina to Venice for the sea bathing; at the end of July they returned once more to Paris. This was intended to be a visit of about a fortnight, to dispose of his house and furniture. 'Verdi is coming to Paris', Escudier was told, 'but the Maestro remains in Italy.' But as usual he became involved in musical affairs, in spite of himself. He brought, and lost, a lawsuit against Calzado, an attempt to prevent him giving *La Traviata* and *Rigoletto* at the Théâtre Italien, and then agreed to supervise the production of *Il Trovatore* in French at the Opéra. These things kept him in France until January 1857.

Back at Sant' Agata, with his stomach 'torn to pieces', he had to work on *Simon Boccanegra*. The opera was eventually produced, not very successfully, at Venice on 12th March.

More and more the theme of country life, farming, 'the fields', recurs in his letters. 'My dearest Vigna,' he wrote on 11th April 1857, 'I too shall be frank with you (as for the rest I am always, with you and with everyone) and shall tell you that I haven't written before now because from morning to evening I am always in the fields, in the woods, among the peasants and animals—the quadrupeds being the best. Arriving home tired, I haven't until now been able to find time and courage to take my pen in hand.' Vigna was asked: When will you find the courage to come to spend a fortnight or so in these sandy wastes? Peppina and I would receive you with open arms, for you know how much we love and esteem you.' Giuseppina herself wrote to Léon Escudier on 4th July of the same year: 'His love for the country has become a mania, madness, rage, fury—anything you like that is exaggerated. He gets up almost with the dawn, to go and examine the wheat, the maize, the vines, etc. . . . Fortunately our tastes for this sort of life coincide, except in the matter of sunrise, which he likes to see up and dressed, and I from my bed.'

Giuseppina had accompanied Verdi to Venice for the production of *Simon Boccanegra*. She accompanied him also to Rimini, where *Aroldo* was produced on 16th August. The days of her 'exile' were over; she now passed everywhere as his wife. Her letters from these years are rather scarce, so that it is not possible to decide precisely when she began to use Verdi's surname. We have nothing between the note to Piave of 27th March 1853, which, five years after they had set up house together, is still signed 'G. Strepponi', and a letter in French to Léon Escudier of 15th February 1857, which is signed 'Josephine Verdi'. It will be recalled that she seems to have objected to the use of her maiden name by Mme Appiani in 1854. Abbiati [1] makes the neat point that in July 1856 her handkerchiefs bore the initials 'G.V.' All the other letters we have from 1857 and later are signed 'Giuseppina (or Josephine) Verdi', where a surname is used at all. On 24th December 1857 Verdi himself told De Sanctis: 'I shall come to Naples with my wife.'

The visit to Naples, early in 1858, lasted nearly four months. It was embittered for Verdi by the fierce struggle with the Neapolitan censorship over the opera eventually known as *Un ballo in maschera*; in the end, the opera was not given at Naples at all; claims for damages for breach of contract were dropped when Verdi agreed to return later in the year to put on *Simon Boccanegra*. However disagreeable the litigation over *Un ballo in maschera*, Giuseppina enjoyed her long-planned winter at Naples and made a host of new friends. These included Cesare De Sanctis and his family, the cartoonist Melchiorre Delfico ('the Great Neapolitan Nadar'), the librarian of the Conservatorio, Francesco Florimo ('Lord Palmerston'), Baron Giovanni Genovese, the poet Nicola Sole, the painters

[1] II, p. 365.

Domenico Morelli and Filippo Palizzi, Vincenzo Torelli and many others. They are all immortalized in the cartoons of Delfico, together with Verdi, Giuseppina and the tiny Maltese spaniel Loulou, presented by Piave.

Neapolitan resistance to Verdi's supremacy in the Italian operatic world had now almost wholly collapsed. Torelli had surrendered long ago. Mercadante, who in 1853 had still been fighting bitterly,[1] had also laid down his arms. This is shown by a letter preserved in Giuseppina's autograph album:

To the celebrated
Signor Cav. Giuseppe Verdi,
from Mercadante.

24th March 1858.

DEAREST FRIEND,

Yesterday my wife dropped in to see you, to ask you, together with your good lady, to spend the evening of the 26th at my house, where some pieces of music are to be performed.

Not having had the pleasure of encountering you, the present letter serves to renew the invitation and declare myself

Your affectionate

SAVERIO MERCADANTE.

By the end of April Verdi and Giuseppina were back at Sant' Agata. 'After the turmoil of Naples', Clarina Maffei was told, 'this profound silence is more welcome than ever. It would be impossible to find an uglier place than this, but on the other hand it would be

[1] Reminiscences of Mrs Squires, an American soprano who, under her maiden name, Lucy Escott, sang in Mercadante's *Violetta* at Naples in 1853, are published in Blanche Roosevelt's *Verdi: Milan and Othello* (London, 1887):

'Verdi had conquered northern Italy, but in Naples Mercadante reigned supreme. He would not listen to the sound of the former's name. He declared even *Rigoletto* was bosh—you know I was then singing Gilda at the Teatro Nuovo; he had the court and highest society for his patrons, and managed to set everybody against poor Verdi. Things went so far that he organized a cabal against him at court, and when *Trovatore*—which, by the way, after Rome, the people would have—was brought out at San Carlo, Mercadante had so ingratiated himself with the censor, Lord Chamberlain, and I don't know who else, that they only allowed two acts of *Trovatore* to be sung, and there was a perfect revolution in the town until the third and fourth acts were accorded the management. . . . It is impossible to conceive the tricks and cabals against Verdi put up by old Mercadante. One would have thought that, as he was old and nearing his grave, and his last opera at San Carlo had been a failure, he would have had some consideration for the young and struggling artist; but on the contrary *he kept Verdi out of Naples as long as he could*: the people finally wouldn't stand it any longer; they weren't going to put up even with Mercadante at his best when there was a fresh new composer taking Italy by storm, when every Italian capital was singing his operas, and Naples, according to all, the very *seat* of fine arts, the only city deprived of hearing Verdi and acclaiming his works. . . . The worst of all was to see that poor Mercadante. . . . I had been singing a year every night in Mercadante's *Violetta*, but even that success was feeble compared with the enthusiasm over the new work; as we say in America, Mercadante went about growling like a bear with a sore head. . . .'

A crazy campaign on Mercadante's behalf, against Verdi, has been fought in recent years, single-handed, by Biagio Notarnicola. I have dealt with his writings, with as much seriousness as they deserve, in 'Mercadante and Verdi' (*Music & Letters*, Oct. 1952).

impossible for me to find a place where I could live in greater freedom.' He asked for news of Milan: 'It is ten years since I last saw that town, which I loved so much, and in which I spent my youth and began my career. How many dear and sad memories I have of it! Who knows when I shall see it again?' To Torelli at the end of May he wrote: 'You have retired to the country, and I am in a real desert. I have not seen anybody now for a month: I run all day from the house to the fields, from the fields to the house, until, when evening comes, dead tired, I throw myself into bed, in order to begin all over again next day. Peppina reads, writes, works: I do nothing at all. A real brute.' In August he was supervising the construction of a bridge over the stream in front of the house.

Signor Antonio had a slight stroke, causing everybody great concern. 'But he has been so well looked after', Giuseppina told Léon Escudier on 19th August, 'that no trace of it is now to be seen. Indeed, yesterday he insisted on going down to his shop to count the money! We scolded him thoroughly, but as our voices haven't a silvery sound he turned, and will always turn, a deaf ear to our remonstrances.' Giovannino Barezzi in the same month asked for a loan of 6,000 francs. He got it, together with a lecture about the way people at Busseto, commencing with Giovannino himself and almost all of his associates, continued their ill-natured gossip about Verdi's affairs.

Giuseppina was spared another winter at Sant' Agata by the return to Naples for *Simon Boccanegra* and then by a stay of two months in Rome for the production of *Un ballo in maschera*. The Roman impresario concerned was Jacovacci, whose daughter, Giuseppina's godchild, was now eighteen years old.

In 1859 politics burst again into Verdi's life.

Between 1849, when the last Republican hopes had been destroyed, and 1859 we have no evidence whatsoever as to the composer's political views. Comments on politics disappear from his letters as completely as does the patriotic, warlike vein from his operas. The withdrawal into domesticity and the silence of the fields was of immense benefit to his art, the increasing humanity, warmth and grace of which can be counted not the least of the achievements of Giuseppina. But Verdi's heart bled for Italy all the time, and the mere success of his operas meant less and less to him. He told Piave that if it were known how incredibly indifferent he was to the warm reception given to *Un ballo in maschera* people would be roused to hostility, would tax him with ingratitude and with caring nothing for the art he professed. 'But no!' he exclaimed, in a rarely confidential outburst, 'I have adored, and I adore, this art, and when I am alone, and occupied with my notes, then my heart throbs, tears rain from my eyes, and my emotion and pleasure are indescribable. But when

I think how these poor notes of mine must be cast before beings without intelligence, before a publisher who sells them to serve for the entertainment and the sport of the mob, oh, then I love nothing any more! Let's not talk about it.' [1] The theme of retirement, of 'farewell to the muses', recurs ever more frequently, every additional work being forced from him, by unforeseen circumstances, by the plotting of friends, by the sudden ignition, almost against his will, of the creative matter buried beneath the ashes. To tend his farm lands, to become a peasant, as he kept saying, was all he cared to do.

From this spiritual inertia, despondency and disillusion, he was rallied by the bugle call of Cavour and Vittorio Emanuele.

Cavour had been prime minister of Piedmont since 1852, except for a very brief interval. By skilful diplomacy, by playing off one power or party against another, by forcing through unpopular measures which paid dividends later, he had created the possibility of a successful renewal of the war with Austria and a move towards the unification of Italy under Vittorio Emanuele. By sending Piedmontese troops to the Crimea, to fight beside the French and English, he had raised the prestige of his country and assured it of benevolent support in the future. On 10th January 1859 Vittorio Emanuele had declared before Parliament that he was not insensible to the cries of sorrow reaching him from many parts of Italy. In the same month a defensive alliance between Piedmont and France was signed and Princess Clotilde of Savoy married Prince Jerome, cousin of Louis Napoleon. All this was just before the production of *Un ballo in maschera* in Rome, and it seems that it was at this time that the cry 'Viva Verdi!' came first to imply: 'Viva Vittorio Emanuele Re D'Italia.' [2]

Austria was provoked into delivering an ultimatum on 23rd April and, three days after the ultimatum was rejected on 26th April, the Austrian army crossed the Ticino and invaded Piedmont. This was precisely what Cavour wanted them to do. Napoleon III honoured his agreement and came to Piedmont's assistance, and in a series of battles the Austrians, under General Gyulai, who was far from being a second Radetzky, were defeated and driven back, out of Piedmont and Lombardy. Soon the Dukes of Parma and Modena fled from their territories and the provisional governments set up sought the protection of Vittorio Emanuele.

Sant' Agata was not actually in the front line, but it was near enough to it at one time. Giuseppina wrote to De Sanctis on 21st May:

We are well, and unafraid, but preoccupied with the grave things that are happening. At eight o'clock this morning the gates of Piacenza, about

[1] *Carteggi verdiani*, II, pp. 353–4.
[2] It is highly unlikely that it bore this meaning already at Naples in 1858, as stated by some writers.

eighteen miles distant from us, were closed and the drawbridges raised. Part of the Franco-Piedmontese army is moving to the assault of that fortress and we shall hear tomorrow, or perhaps this evening, the thunder of the guns. Verdi is serious, grave, but calm and confident in the future. I am certainly more disquieted, more anxious, but then I am a woman and of more lively temperament than he. For the rest, you will understand that the thought of such things is not calculated to excite a senseless merriment.

Before long gunfire was heard almost daily, but farther away, the Austrians having blown up the forts of Piacenza and retired. Things were going well. On 20th June Verdi drew up a subscription list for the benefit of the wounded and the families of the fallen. He headed the list himself with a contribution of 25 gold napoleons; Giuseppina followed with an independent contribution of 4 gold napoleons, and the next names were those of Verdi's father, Verdi's bailiff, his friend Dr Angiolo Carrara, notary of Busseto, and Antonio Barezzi. 'What miracles have happened in these few days!' Verdi wrote to Clarina Maffei on 23rd June. 'It doesn't seem possible. Who would have expected such generosity from our allies? For myself, let me confess and say, *mea grandissima culpa*, that I did not believe the French would come to Italy or, in any case, shed their blood for us, without any idea of conquest.' There followed the victories of Solferino and San Martino. But then, on 12th July, Napoleon signed the Treaty of Villafranca, which brought peace, but left Venetia still in Austrian hands. Verdi was shocked and disgusted. 'Where then is the longed-for and promised independence of Italy?' he asked Clarina. 'What is the meaning of the Proclamation of Milan? Isn't Venice a part of Italy? After such victories what a result! How much blood shed in vain! How many poor young people deluded! And Garibaldi, who has sacrificed his old and constant beliefs for the sake of a king, without obtaining the desired result! It is maddening!'

According to Gatti, Toye and many other writers, Verdi and Giuseppina were married at Collonges-sous-Salève in Savoy on 29th April 1859—the very day of the Austrian invasion of Piedmont. This is a mistake, deriving from an inaccurate copy at Villanova d'Arda of the entry in the registers at Collonges. The marriage took place on 29th *August* of that year.[1] The officiating priest was the Abbé Mermillod, then rector of the church of Notre Dame at Geneva, who had made all the arrangements. According to Verdi himself the parish priest of Collonges was 'sent out for a walk' and the only witnesses were the bell-ringer and the cabman who had brought them

[1] A true copy of the entry is given by Luzio, *Carteggi verdiani*, II, p. 29, from the *Journal de Genève* of 8th October 1913. Don Ferruccio Botti procured, independently, a copy of the entry from Collonges and pointed out the mistake in the *Gazzetta di Parma* for 5th November 1951. Verdi himself mentions that the date is wrong in the copy now at Villanova d'Arda, in a letter to Giuseppe Piroli of 17th April 1869 (*Carteggi verdiani*, III, p. 63).

from Geneva. The marriage is not mentioned in any of the composer's letters from this time.

If the war of 1859 had not brought fulfilment of all the Italian hopes, much had yet been gained. Lombardy was free, and Parma, Modena and Tuscany opted by plebiscite for union with Piedmont. Verdi, representing Busseto, was among those chosen to convey the result of the plebiscite to Vittorio Emanuele at Turin. The delegates saw the king on 15th September and two days later Verdi, by arrangement with Sir James Hudson, British minister to the court of Piedmont, paid a visit to Cavour, who had resigned at the news of the Treaty of Villafranca and retired to his estates at Leri. What Herzen called Cavour's prose translation of the poetry of Mazzini won Verdi's whole-hearted support. The passionate republican of 1848–9 became in 1859 a loyal subject of Vittorio Emanuele.

Cavour returned to office on 21st January 1860. By the Treaty of Turin on 24th March Napoleon recognized the annexation of the central Italian states, following the plebiscites, in exchange for the secretly pre-arranged cession of Savoy and Nice to France. This was the price that had to be paid for the supposedly generous French intervention, to the indignation of many, including Garibaldi, a native of Nice.

The year 1860 saw immense progress in the unification of Italy. Garibaldi, taking matters into his own hands, landed with his thousand volunteers at Marsala on 11th May, outwitted the Neapolitans and entered Palermo on 27th May. On that day Verdi wrote to his friend Mariani, the conductor: 'Hurrah, then, for Garibaldi! By God, he is truly a man before whom one should kneel!' Soon all Sicily, except the forts of Messina, was in Garibaldi's hands. On 20th August he crossed to the mainland and on 7th September entered Naples in triumph. Cavour, alarmed at the possible effects of Garibaldi's impetuosity, sent the Piedmontese army, under General Cialdini, into the Papal States. We have a comment on this in another of Verdi's letters to Mariani: 'Tell me of other music. . . . What of the quavers and semiquavers of Cialdini, Garibaldi, etc.? . . . Those are composers! And what operas! What finales! To the sound of the guns!' After the annexation of the Papal States had been completed, and Garibaldi had placed the Kingdom of the Two Sicilies in the hands of his king and retired to Caprera, his island home, Giuseppina wrote to Antonio Capecelatro at Naples: 'Do you love Giuseppe of Caprera? I hope so. It is impossible that you should not be an enthusiastic admirer of the purest and greatest hero since the world was created.'

The last of what may be called the love letters of Giuseppina to Verdi dates from towards the close of this year.

Many years had passed since they had first set up house together, but the burden of Giuseppina's letters had not changed. Still she felt lost without him. Still the shadow of her past hung about her. And the news from Busseto was still of bad weather, ill health and the shameful calculations of the Barezzi brothers:

Tuesday evening, 4th December 1860.

DEAREST,

This accursed place! You perhaps won't receive the letter I wrote this morning until Thursday. Cristoforetti did not make his usual second round today. I am sorry, but it's not my fault.

Here it is raining in torrents, uninterruptedly, and I'm afraid that at Genoa it will be doing the same. Poor Verdi, what fine entertainment for you!

I sent Giovannino to Busseto and he has consulted the oracle Sancho Panza. It seems that instead of being in debt to his father, he is his creditor to the extent of 29 gold napoleons. What do you say to that? For the rest, the affair is progressing and I believe they will bring it to an end without your further assistance. Good luck to them, and long life to him whom they wish dead!

My stomach has left me a little in peace today, but in order to try my patience my tooth has been very troublesome; add to that the dreary weather and you will understand what sort of mood I'm in! Today I dined in the hall, taking about ten minutes over it; this evening I had supper in my room. The big hall without you is too deserted and that empty place at table makes me sad. In going to sleep think of me—think of the com panion who has lived with you for so many years and would like to go on living with you for as many centuries. Don't pull an ugly face! I would seek and perhaps find in my heart a way of never being tiresome or a hindrance to you, and so as not to be so now, either, I'll say farewell and go to bed. I wish you a quiet night and a blue sky tomorrow.

5th December.

It's idle to contemn the climate of Paris so much, when here there are fortnights of leaden skies, like those that oppress us now. Doors, windows, etc., are swollen by the recent torrents of rain, and it seems as if the marrow of one's bones were swimming in this unhealthy fluid—unhealthy, at any rate, when absorbed in that way. And what are you doing? How are you? Are you enjoying yourself? I hope you are enjoying yourself, but I'm not *very* hopeful about it, unless the sun is shining at Genoa. Have you seen Marcellino? Has the corrupting city air begun to seduce him? I don't know what to do about Gigia. There are so many pros and cons that I hover irresolute between yes and no, like the tomb of Mohammed between heaven and earth. You, who are now far away and free, therefore, from all influences, give me your opinion, instinctively, without reflection.

Giuseppina had this constant need to communicate with Verdi. One letter had been finished on Tuesday morning, another begun on Tuesday evening and continued on Wednesday. And on Wednesday evening she added this:

Perhaps when this letter arrives you will be at Turin, if, as you intended, you decide definitely to see Cavour and Sir James. What a thing it is to have genius! One goes to pay calls on ministers of state and ambassadors, just as I go to see Giovanna. And yet that which obliges the world to take off its hat to you is the quality about which I never think, or hardly ever. I swear to you, and you won't have difficulty in believing it, that many times I am quite surprised that you know anything about music! However divine that art, and however worthy your genius of the art you profess, yet the talisman that fascinates me and that I adore in you is your character, your heart, your indulgence for the mistakes of others while you are so severe with yourself, your charity, full of modesty and mystery, your proud independence and your boyish simplicity—qualities proper to that nature of yours, which has been able to conserve a primal virginity of ideas and sentiments in the midst of the human *cloaca*! O my Verdi, I am not worthy of you, and the love that you bear me is charity, balsam, to a heart sometimes very sad, beneath the appearance of cheerfulness. Continue to love me; love me also after death, so that I may present myself to Divine Providence rich with your love and your prayers, O my Redeemer!

One would like to close this chapter with this sublime passage, this great hymn, in which a noble woman lays her heart bare. But the letter goes on, and we cannot afford to neglect any part of these uniquely revealing documents. Giuseppina continued:

I re-read this shapeless letter, that perhaps I ought not to send you, but I haven't the courage to copy it out again. Although it's the pure expression of my feelings, I ought to have written to you in a different style and with ideas much more serene. Forgive this *spleen*, which for some time has persecuted me, and which is not the predominating defect of my character, but rather of yours. Oh, at last I've found a defect in you, a fault! I'm delighted that you've got at least one. I shall keep it in mind, and remind you of it on the first occasion that arises.

I am not very well. I have had no further attacks of cramp, but continual threats of them, of short duration. Tomorrow I shall be better. I hope so, for your sake. These disturbances prevent me from smiling, and I have need of quiet and good humour to get rid of them, and not to present you, as I did, with the spectacle of dolorous crises, which I wanted to hide, but I had not the strength.

It seems to me that everything is going on in the house as usual. I must, however, tell you that I only went down once, and you will hold me excused on account of my health. In any case, the iregularities will concern only a bit of bread or meat given away without my permission. When we are dead there will be oxen, corn and money left over, of which we shall not have been able to make use. So let's close our eyes to these compassionate insubordinations, and agree that they are small troubles among the grave miseries of humanity. You will say: 'What a St Augustine you are!' It's true, but I'm not always like this. Good night, my *Pasticcio*. Enjoy yourself, but remember that I am at Sant' Agata.

Your PEPPINA.

There is something rather mysterious about the circumstances in which this letter was written. During the summer Verdi had embarked on repairs, additions and improvements to the house at Sant' Agata. Workmen were still busy during the following winter. The expenses of the building operations were a drain on the ready money available, and it had been decided that this winter must be spent at Sant' Agata. Yet Verdi, as Giuseppina told De Sanctis, felt a strange desire to explore the world, just at the time when it was necessary to economize by staying at home. On 1st December he had told Giuseppe Piroli: 'I am leaving tomorrow morning for Genoa, where I shall stay for about two months.' And he had gone, leaving Giuseppina, who was unwell and had, indeed, passed recently through more than one 'dolorous crisis', in charge at Sant' Agata. One does not know what arrangement there was between them, and certainly there is no sign of a quarrel or shade of reproach in Giuseppina's letter. There is only the phrase: 'Enjoy yourself, but remember that I am at Sant' Agata.'

Verdi, however, before he could have received Giuseppina's letter, had already made up his mind to return. He told De Sanctis on 6th December: 'I came to Genoa because I felt the need of moving, but tomorrow I shall return to Sant' Agata, where I hope to find Peppina better.' So, instead of two months, he was away only five days.

CHAPTER 6

Giuseppina at her Writing-desk

GIUSEPPINA's surviving letters to Lanari and to Verdi have enabled us, in earlier chapters, to explore the mysterious world of her youth on and off the stage, and to catch more than a glimpse of her subsequent life with Verdi, in retirement at Sant' Agata and elsewhere. Apart from these two series, we have only a handful of other letters from early years. But from the time when she became everywhere recognized as Verdi's inseparable life-companion, and of course from the time when she was actually married to him, we have a mass of correspondence from her, a source of invaluable information and unending delight. As soon as she was allowed to accompany him to Venice, Naples, Rome and other places, and thus to make the personal acquaintance of many of his friends and admirers who could not visit Sant' Agata, she was able to relieve Verdi of much of the burden of his private correspondence. Giuseppina wrote fluently and charmingly in Italian and French; she could also write, less fluently but no less charmingly, in English. Next to a letter from the Maestro himself, the friends could wish for nothing better than one from Peppina. She possessed outstanding narrative powers; she could be witty, wise and sympathetic; she had great understanding and much common sense; an occasional sparkle of malice adds savour to her writing. When occasion demanded she could take off her elegant gloves and administer a sharp and salutary verbal box on the ear. Her charity, sometimes in abeyance where Busseto was concerned, deepened as she grew older. Her goodness, her kindness and her devotion to Verdi's welfare stream out from her letters and compel one to love her. The most revealing things are often tiny vignettes of domestic life at Sant' Agata, as when she tells how she is able to relax if she knows that the house is clean, that the dinner won't turn out too badly and that none of Verdi's buttons is missing, or explains that the periodical deterioration in her handwriting is due to Verdi banging his fist down on the other side of the table, where he is playing cards with a friend.

A letter to Vincenzo Torelli,[1] editor of the Neapolitan *Omnibus*, opens appropriately for the purposes of this chapter with a description of the postal service in the backwoods of the Duchy of Parma:

Busseto, 12th September 1858.

DEAR TORELLI,

If I paid attention to Verdi I shouldn't be writing to you even now, because today as always he goes on repeating: 'This evening I'll write to Torelli myself and I'll give the letter to the carrier tomorrow.' Let it be told in secret, so that Verdi doesn't take offence: here at Busseto there is no post office yet. A man arrives twice a week, modestly mounted (on Shanks's pony), to distribute and collect the very few letters of these illustrious citizens, who perhaps think a lot, but hardly ever write at all, and what little they do write reduces itself to an occasional business letter offering to buy or sell fat pigs. You know the *salami* are exquisite in this progressive town! But let's go back to where we started: I am writing to you in spite of what Verdi says. He once, after promising me to write to a certain person, whom you don't know, let almost two years go by! In the end I wrote myself and asked forgiveness for his long silence, without however promising that he wouldn't repeat the offence. Verdi in this respect will die impenitent. The person concerned had the goodness to reply at once, and to forgive, even though it was two years!

You, Vincenzo Torelli, as it's not yet one year since Verdi last wrote to you, do you feel sufficiently generous to forgive, without comment? I believe you do, because although there are some people who consider you a Big Devil (mind, it's better to be a Big Devil than a big . . . something else!), I am not altogether of their opinion. I think (not to make a comparison, but to express my idea) you're a bitter-sweet sauce. Well then, unfortunate is he who bumps into you and sets in motion the bitter substances; fortunate, however, he that happens on the sweet ones: you are capable of much good. I hope that this letter arrives in one of these honeyed moments and thus that you will pronounce the *ego te absolvo*, the absolute pardon for Verdi's silence.

You are well; Mariannina, Maddalena and all the Torellis are well; I am glad and I pray God (will He follow my advice?) to give you good health, plenty of money, peace and fine pictures, without the dangerous proximity of Verdi, who would end up by stealing some of them from you. I am fairly well now, but I have been poorly for a long time. 'But the past is past; think of the future' (Piave's words—I don't want to take credit for what is not mine).

As for Verdi, he is fantastically well (keep your fingers crossed!) and, judging by his complexion, is worthy to go to the colonies to plant sugar-cane. I can swear to you that in all these months he hasn't written a note!

[1] *San Carlo. Numero unico* (Naples, 1913–14).

As for letters, he has perhaps written a thousand—minus the last two noughts! But he has given close attention to the construction of a bridge in front of the house, and not a tree has been planted or uprooted without him being present in body and in spirit. Now he's beginning to give an occasional glance at the cover of the new score, which will almost certainly be given in Rome. I put my trust in the bad weather and the impossibility of going out, so that he may find it necessary to take up his pen again.

This letter illustrates Giuseppina's insight into human nature. Torelli, a difficult, rather unscrupulous man, was not popular with some of Verdi's other Neapolitan friends. De Sanctis thought him a heartless and vindictive egotist, and reported various things to his discredit in letters to Sant' Agata. But Giuseppina respected his independent character. Torelli himself referred in a letter to Verdi to 'that amiable and acute Signora Peppina, who understood us before we spoke, and distributed rewards and punishment so graciously, making peace between us all'. Another instance of her judgment is seen in a letter to her old friend Mauro Corticelli,[1] called 'Don Cappellari' from his aptness to take offence (*prendere cappello*), who had announced that he was giving up a career as theatrical agent and impresario at Bologna to become secretary to the actress Adelaide Ristori:

Rome, 15th January 1859.

Giraldoni has given me your letter, which I read with greater pleasure than the other ones. God be praised! You are leaving that vicious atmosphere, in which your honest nature could not help but suffer. I told you from the first moment when you plunged into that stinking swamp: 'Corticelli, that's no place for you, no occupation for you!' You could have got out of it sooner, but at any rate you have got out in time. Well done, my dear Cappellari! I am exceedingly glad that you have accepted la Ristori's proposals and are putting your intelligence and probity at her service. I don't know la Ristori personally, but I follow with interest her artistic triumphs, and still more her actions, which are noble, in truth, and worthy to be put on a level with her talents. So I repeat again: I am sincerely glad. May God always bless her, you and all honest hearts that resemble yours.

Verdi is so tired, sated, disgusted with the stage that there is every probability that he will say regarding the theatre what Rabelais in his last moments said regarding life: 'Bring down the curtain; the farce is over!' His will be done. No man, certainly, can boast of being more honest than he is, or of having earned with more dignity the means and the right of leading an independent existence.

The beginning of 1860 saw an important development, when Giuseppina began to keep letter-books, on the lines of Verdi's own

[1] The originals of most of the letters to Corticelli quoted here are in the Scala Museum. They were used in part by Gatti.

Copialettere. She was to continue to do so up to 1892. Five large foolscap volumes, preserved at Sant' Agata, record the bulk of her correspondence over more than thirty years. And here, in addition to her own letters, we find, in her hand, drafts of many letters which, with little or no modification, were subsequently copied and sent off by Verdi as his own. Giuseppina, in fact, had become a sort of ideal private secretary. Now and then Verdi would alter a too flowery phrase, erase or condense a passage, or substitute a more energetic expression for that used by Giuseppina. Sometimes he had to soften a too outspoken remark of hers. But in general she was astonishingly successful in drafting letters for Verdi in his way of writing, practically indistinguishable from those he wrote himself. A few of the entries are copies of his letters, others *may* be copies, or may have been dictated by him, but the vast majority of the letters in Verdi's name in these books are certainly Giuseppina's work, as the appearance of the pages, with erasures, fresh starts, corrections and alternative passages shows. The dates of the drafts in Giuseppina's hand in the letter-books are often one day, and sometimes several days, earlier than the dates on the letters themselves.

A fairly close description of the first group of letters in the first volume will give some idea of the nature of the contents and of Giuseppina's activities as Verdi's private secretary.

The volume opens with the draft of a rather stiff letter from Verdi to Tito Ricordi, in Verdi's own hand, but with slight revisions by Giuseppina. Tito Ricordi, owing to his indifferent health, tended to leave too much in the hands of subordinates. Complaints received from Rome indicated that the parts of *Un ballo in maschera* had arrived late and were still full of mistakes, although these had been pointed out in the previous year:

> I indicated all these mistakes to you, but I have reason to believe that nobody in your business has deigned to glance at this poor opera. As a new work is concerned, it would be worth the trouble to do something about it, if not for its musical value, or for the good name of the composer, at least for the honour of your establishment. Similar complaints have been made to me many times, and I have never written to you; but now, feeling that things are going too far, I think well to tell you frankly that if you cannot or do not wish to occupy yourself with your and my affairs, you should find people either more able or more willing to do so.

In order to by-pass the secretary through whose hands it was supposed Ricordi's correspondence would pass, this letter was sent by Giuseppina to Tito's wife, with a covering note from herself. The copy of this covering note, dated 15th January 1860, is on the next page of the letter-book, and is Giuseppina's own first contribution.

The following entry, dated from Busseto, 15th March, is a draft or copy, in Giuseppina's hand, of a letter of recommendation addressed by Verdi to the governor of Milan, Massimo D'Azeglio, on behalf of Piave, who had transferred himself after the Treaty of Villafranca from Venice to Milan. Piave's formal application for the post of producer at La Scala [1] is dated two days after this entry in the letter-book. On 15th March Giuseppina also drafted for Verdi a letter to the mayor and municipality of Milan, who had invited him to compose a national anthem. She tried to sweeten the inevitable refusal by a paragraph in which Verdi was made to promise to do his best in this matter when Italy should be wholly free from the foreign yoke. But all this passage was then crossed out by Verdi himself. On the following day Giuseppina drafted for him another refusal, this time of the post of provincial councillor.

It fell to her lot to prepare a large part of Verdi's French correspondence. In this same month of March he had been invited to join Auber, Berlioz, Halévy, Thomas and others in a printed denunciation of the musical notation and teaching of Émile Chevé. His reply is found in Giuseppina's letter-book.

> I have read very carefully the brochure about the *Chevé* question. That is another of the numerous follies of those with a mania for innovation at all costs! I believe myself to be as progressive as anybody else, and I declare myself ready always to approve everything that I recognize as good and useful. But what is the use of changing the names and the signs universally known and adopted in music? I do not think there is any serious musician who could conscientiously approve of the chaos in which music would find itself if M. Chevé's bizarre fancy were, so to speak, sanctioned and officially adopted. That is why, gentlemen, I unrestrictedly approve the ideas and observations expressed in your brochure, and, since you are pleased to consider me worthy, I beg you to add my humble name to your own.

This is wholly in Giuseppina's hand, with the spelling of some words heavily corrected, perhaps after consultation of a dictionary (*consciencieusement*, *chaos*, *bizarrerie*).

There follows, also in March, the earliest known letter to Giovanni Minghelli-Vaini, who was to be defeated by Verdi in the following year in the election for the deputyship of Borgo San Donnino in the Italian Parliament. But in 1860 Verdi had no thought of such a development. He had promised Minghelli-Vaini his support in the coming elections; then Minghelli-Vaini had decided not to contest the seat and asked Verdi to support another candidate whom he hardly knew. In this letter drafted by Giuseppina, with various alterations also in her hand, Verdi refuses: 'I know too little about the person you propose I should support, and I should like to give my push (however feeble) to one I know very well. You could draw

[1] Reproduced by Gatti, first edition, vol. ii, p. 21.

my attention to the fact that we ourselves haven't known each other very long. That is true. But I am perfectly well acquainted with your genealogy and know very well that you are a *vieux de la vieille*, and not a Liberal of yesterday!'

Patriotic feeling could occasionally bring Verdi again into superficially amicable relations with Busseto. Even Giuseppina, when a demonstration of loyalty was called for, was prepared to emerge from her retreat. The next entry in the letter-book is her own, a copy of a circular address to the women of Busseto:

> The ladies of Parma forming part of the committee constituted at Bologna have deputed me to collect subscriptions among my fellow townswomen towards a gift to be offered to the king in the name of the women of Emilia.
>
> Busseto has hitherto shown itself on every occasion to be sincerely Italian, and thus I have reason to hope that the women of Busseto of every class will not fail to associate themselves with the rest of the women of Emilia, to give this brave and most Italian king a demonstration of affection and gratitude.
>
> The poor and the rich can contribute according to their means, since to give testimony of love for the king is not the privilege of the wealthy, but the right of every good Italian.
>
> GIUSEPPINA VERDI.

The response seems to have been lukewarm. A cancelled draft of a letter to the committee members at Parma begins: 'Living always in the country and having very little to do with Busseto, I haven't been able to collect a larger sum than that which will be handed over to you by Signor . . .' The final reply, dated 9th April, says she had hoped to raise a larger sum, but it was not possible, there having been too many subscription lists in recent months.

Between the cancelled draft and this final reply is a copy of a private letter, dated 1st April, from Giuseppina to the composer and impresario Achille Montuoro, then in Paris, ending with a cordial invitation to Sant' Agata, in spite of the alterations then in progress, and promising food to his taste with plenty of *maccheroni* and no cold meat. Another of Giuseppina's private letters follows, the draft of that to Cesare De Sanctis of 14th April, published in the *Carteggi verdiani*, with the delightful confession: 'We have been for a month now in our solitude, which merits that name more and more, because, except for Signor Antonio, we see literally no one. I assure you I am almost losing the use of my tongue, a rather strange thing in a woman. . . .'

She made up with her pen for the loss of the use of her tongue.

The first eleven entries, then, include one letter in Verdi's hand, five drafts or copies of letters written by Giuseppina for Verdi and three official and two private letters of her own. The importance of these letter-books is all the greater since the period of Giuseppina's most active secretarial collaboration largely fills the enormous gap from 7th October 1858 to 20th September 1867 in Verdi's own *Copialettere*. Luzio devotes about fifty pages of the second volume of the *Carteggi verdiani* to Giuseppina's letter-books. The material, however, is of vast extent and would fill several volumes the size of the Verdian *Copialettere*, as published.[1] Giuseppina included much of her private correspondence, whereas Verdi did not, and as a result her letter-books present a far fuller picture, and are altogether more personal and intimate in character than his. Besides the letters, there are also occasional entries in the form of diary notes, never kept up for long, but of the highest interest. Here secrets are recorded that would otherwise have been lost for ever. To read the letter-books from beginning to end is to live over again in imagination Giuseppina's life during thirty years—an enthralling experience, at times exalting, at times profoundly saddening and disturbing. One emerges with enormously enhanced sympathy and respect for this wonderful woman in her difficult role of wife to a man of genius.

A letter to Léon Escudier of 30th April 1860 describes Verdi's intervention at Busseto, inspired by patriotism and common sense:

> He has persuaded the municipal authorities to present the king with a gun, on which will be inscribed: 'Offered by Busseto.'
>
> He told them, in a brusque but feeling manner: 'Illuminations and celebrations are useless and do nothing to drive away the enemy, who is still at our gates. They don't even prove our love for our king. We shall do that better by providing him with the means of fighting the Austrians and rendering our country strong and respected. He has need of soldiers and of arms. We have given all we could of our youth. We have subscribed towards rifles for Garibaldi. Now, instead of celebrating his expedition with illuminations and other frivolities, let us present the king with a gun.' And the poor Bussetani voted unanimously to give the king a gun, with full equipment. . . . You will perhaps smile at these small matters, but if you were in Italy you would be moved, witnessing the exertions of a people *rising from death to recompose itself as a nation.*
>
> And to think that you have allowed Lamoricière to come and associate himself with the Croats, to extinguish this divine spark of national feeling!

We know very little about the later history of Giuseppina's family. Some information can be drawn from her letters and letter-books. On 14th July 1860 (9th July in the draft) she told De Sanctis: 'You didn't read very carefully what I wrote about Locate. . . . That is not my home town, but my mother lives there. I went to see her because she was seriously ill. I was born in the glorious city of Lodi, which has the best milk and the best cheese in the world.' Locate Triulzi is

[1] Including the huge appendix, that is, with supplementary material added by the editors.

about ten miles south of Milan. Giuseppina's mother lived there after she left Pavia until November 1868, when she moved, or was moved, to Cremona with her younger daughter Barberina. Both Giuseppina's brothers had died at an early age. A letter to De Sanctis of 14th December 1860 refers to a black shawl, left over from mourning worn for the death of one of the brothers, which could then be put to other uses by the addition of a coloured border. The letter-books record no correspondence with Giuseppina's mother, who was perhaps illiterate like Verdi's parents, but there are many letters to Barberina Strepponi, who in later years was a frequent visitor to Sant' Agata. Barberina was a lifelong invalid, a nervous wreck with supposedly consumptive tendencies, who nevertheless proved surprisingly tenacious of life, long surviving both Giuseppina and Verdi, and dying at a great age during the First World War. Many later entries in the letter-books show Giuseppina continuing to contribute towards her sister's support:

4th April 1867:

[in English] Written to my sister, and send a quarter of pension, 17 gold francs.

27th June 1867:

Written to Barberina, [in English]. Hundred francs to pay looking-glasses and remaining for her.

17th December 1867:

[in English] Written to Barberina and send, instead of 340 francs, 400 francs. The 60 francs for Christmas day and pays for her windows.

Mercede Mundula has charmingly said that almost the only trait of the nineteenth-century *prima donna* which Giuseppina retained in later life was the love of an *entourage* of animals—dogs, cats, peacocks, pheasants, parrots and other cage birds. Among all the pets the favourite was the little Maltese spaniel Loulou,[1] on which was lavished all the maternal affection of a childless woman's heart. Verdi, too, loved this dog:

December 1860, Giuseppina to Léon Escudier:

I shall only speak *en passant* of my nightingales, so as not to make you jealous. They are in my room and sing as if it were May. As for my peacocks (I have eight of them!!) they are very unhappy! They like to sleep in the open air and this inexorable continual rain soaks them to the marrow. My white Loulou whom you saw when he was quite small is the most beautiful dog in the world and all the world has to obey him. Verdi has the patience to walk around with his dog under his cloak, in such a

[1] Giuseppina writes 'Loulou', always; Verdi writes 'Lulu'. It was a dog, and not a bitch.

way that just his nose is outside, so that he can breathe. Our country house will be given a name, and the name will be that of Loulou.

It had been proposed that Verdi should contest the deputyship of Borgo San Donnino in the coming general elections. He was himself resolutely opposed to this idea. But in January 1861 he received a personal appeal from Cavour, urging him to lend the prestige of his name to the first Italian national parliament. He left at once for Turin, intent on securing release from what to him would be an onerous and unwelcome distinction. During his absence a letter arrived from Minghelli-Vaini, seeking confirmation or denial of the rumour that Verdi was to stand for election. Giuseppina wrote to Minghelli-Vaini on 16th January:

> Verdi is away from home at the moment, and as I am authorized to open his letters, I am replying briefly, so that you won't accuse him of negligence. I know for certain that he is disinclined to play the role of deputy, so you can go ahead without fear that he will oppose you. Moreover, I can add that it is just to obtain exemption from such an honour that he is at Turin, and I hope he will succeed.

As it happened, this was the wrong reply, and it would have been better if she had waited. For Verdi was persuaded by Cavour and Sir James Hudson, the enthusiastic British minister at Turin, to accept, after all, the candidature of Borgo San Donnino. The rather comical ensuing correspondence with Minghelli-Vaini is printed in the appendix to the *Copialettere*. Both the letter of 23rd January, in which Verdi refuses to accept the suggestion that he should offer himself as a candidate for election elsewhere, leaving Borgo San Donnino to Minghelli-Vaini, and that of 29th January, in which, with unnecessary emphasis, he insists on his integrity and his horror of intrigue, are found in Giuseppina's letter-book, in her hand. The former was certainly written by her; there are two drafts; the first, after many alterations, was then erased; the second has small alterations in Verdi's hand. The letter of 29th January is dated one day later in the letter-book: someone made a mistake in the date, but Giuseppina's version appears to be the first draft.

Verdi defeated Minghelli-Vaini in the election on 27th January, but by an insufficient majority; a second ballot on 3rd February resulted in his definitive victory. His last letter to his opponent had ended: 'I have said and I repeat for the hundredth time: I shall accept, against my will, if I am nominated, but I shall never do anything, nor ever say a word, to secure nomination. Let that serve to close a correspondence between us that should never have been opened.' But Minghelli-Vaini still could not let well alone. He addressed himself to Giuseppina, who would seem to have known him before Verdi. She replied on 13th February:

First of all, let's correct a mistake: our friendship is not of twenty years' duration, but of fourteen or fifteen. I know that wine and friendship acquire excellence by age, but women lose it. Now although I am near to acquiring what is called a venerable appearance, I am nevertheless a woman and in consequence not at all disposed to accept, even from the best friend in the world, the unwelcome gift of half a dozen extra years. The first point being settled, let's go on to the second.

Verdi, although surprised and nauseated by the re-staging of these elections, has nothing against you *and is convinced that in spite of your desire to be deputy you have done nothing in the least shady*. For the rest, I, who have been your friend for forty years (!) and know you well, have assured him that you cannot help being what you always were—*un homme franc et loyal*. He shakes your hand and begs you to excuse him if for the present he does not reply in person, occupied, enraged and tormented as he is by preparations for his journey, and by arrangements he has to make for his house here before leaving. I, too, am going to Turin, and that will certainly make serious inroads on my savings. I am getting out and folding the tail coats.

The first Italian parliament met at Turin on 19th February. Various patriotic Bussetani went to see what could be seen and were questioned eagerly on their return by Antonio Barezzi. A letter of his to Verdi includes the passage: 'I am very glad that Signora Peppina is well, but I would so much have liked to know whether she was present in parliament on the first day. None of our people could tell me for certain.' Giuseppina reassured him in an affectionate letter on 25th February:

Verdi being very busy in the Chamber of Deputies, he charges me to reply to your most welcome letter of the 23rd. I shall skip everything connected with the recent celebrations at Turin. You will have read detailed descriptions of them in the newspapers, so 'amen' to all that.

I was present at the opening of parliament, in a very good position. Armed with my opera-glasses, I was able to study at my convenience the physiognomy of the king, the ministers, the ambassadors, the generals and as many of the others as attracted my attention by name or dignity. If the gentry from Busseto weren't able to give you exact information about that, it was either because they hadn't access to the Chamber, or because they did not know me personally.

Verdi hasn't received even a line from his bailiff. Perhaps when the latter addressed his letter he was thinking about the world of the moon, and in his distraction directed it to Peking. Any letter to 'Giuseppe Verdi, Parliamentary Deputy' will reach its destination. Tell him so, adding that the Parliament at Turin is meant, not the English one in London.

I don't know where Signor Ciro Demaldè got his information that we are lodged in a private house. Your son Giovannino came to see us on the 19th and found us at the Hotel Trombetta. . . .

Last night Verdi went to the Teatro Regio, in a reserved stall, hoping to remain incognito. But at the end of the second act of *La Favorita* he was recognized and they began to shout 'Viva Verdi!' and everyone, from the boxes to the pit, stood up to salute the Great Composer of *Le Roncole*. If they only knew how well he composes *risotto alla milanese* God knows what ovations would have showered on his shoulders!

I have related these little stories because I know that you, my excellent Signor Antonio, do not share the opinion of the Preacher, who in his Ecclesiastes says: 'Vanity of vanities, all is vanity,' etc. Ovations for Verdi have always made you weep. Get out your handkerchief, for I am convinced that at this moment you are wetting the spice-box.

Verdi's earnings were largely invested in land and property. The extensive alterations at Sant' Agata had left him short of ready money, and this fact increased the attractiveness of an offer, early in 1861, of 60,000 francs, with all expenses paid, for a new opera to be written for the Imperial Theatre at St Petersburg. The tenor Enrico Tamberlik acted as intermediary between the management of the theatre and the composer, and his proposal reached Sant' Agata enclosed in a letter from Corticelli, whose travels with Adelaide Ristori had led him at this time to St Petersburg. The course of the negotiations which eventually resulted in the composition of *La forza del destino* can be followed in Giuseppina's letters to Corticelli. The idea of a trip to Russia seems to have appealed to her from the start:

Verdi will reply direct, as soon as he is back; in what terms I don't know, but from certain words that have escaped him it seems he is no longer so averse to taking up his pen again. . . . If I were not afraid of committing forgery, I would gladly alter that imposing figure of twenty-two below zero, which will make him open his eyes wide in fright. As for myself, I took refuge almost under the stove, reading that sentence, as if the frosts of Russia had already assailed me. . . . In any case, however poor an advocate I may be, I shall gather together, on this occasion, the shreds of my eloquence, to try to persuade him to expose his nose to the danger of freezing in Russia. If I don't succeed by eloquence, I shall employ a means which, as I've been assured, succeeds even at the frontiers of Paradise with St Peter, and that is, *to insist, to make a nuisance of oneself*, until one gets what one wants. It's true that Verdi is less patient than St Peter, and if, in the end, he sends me to bed, it won't be the first time, and I shall have to be quiet.

She was not sent to bed, and Verdi proposed Hugo's *Ruy Blas* as the subject of the opera for St Petersburg. But it was thought there would be difficulties with the censorship and a telegram from Tamberlik led Verdi to believe that the management had uncompromisingly rejected the idea of *Ruy Blas*. No other suitable subject could be found and Giuseppina almost lost hope. Then, when it was seen that Verdi would not commit himself to write an opera before he had a subject to his liking, suited to the singers available and approved by the authorities, the Russians changed their tune. Tamberlik's son Achille was sent with wide powers to Turin to negotiate with Verdi, who had himself, meanwhile, had second thoughts about the possibilities of *Ruy Blas*. In a letter to Corticelli, then in Paris, Giuseppina on 17th April told of the successful outcome of Achille Tamberlik's mission:

He arrived, saw the terrain not too favourably disposed, and swore to conquer, in spite of the fact that Verdi, profiting by the veto on the subject pronounced by the famous telegram, was much more concerned with the Chamber than the theatre. Then he quietly began to discharge his mission, rectifying the mistake of the dispatch and declaring with the utmost calm that Verdi could set to music *Ruy Blas* or anything else, he having instructions to grant every possible condition that could be asked, except only that of obliging the Czar Alexander to proclaim a republic in Russia. Verdi scratched his head, pointing out that there was this difficulty about *Ruy Blas*, that difficulty about other plays he had looked through; that a certain play he had once read, and liked, could not be found. That was enough, and, the title being made known, behold us making the rounds of the bookshops and second-hand dealers of Turin, leaving no alleyway unexplored. Nothing! Not to be found! In the end it was given to Verdi (who, to be just, was as active as the rest of us, since he sees no seemly way of getting out of it) to seize by the scruff of his neck a certain person who was going to Milan, where alone it would be possible to find the play, and whence he in fact received it within twenty-four hours, to the great consolation of Tamberlik, who, although he affirmed with the greatest pleasure in the world that he liked Turin and would gladly stay there for a month, yet as soon as the Gordian knot had been untied hurried off and will have halted, I think, only in Paris. So now it is ninety per cent certain that Verdi will write for St Petersburg. This being the probability, I have already begun to have dresses, petticoats, vests and shirts lined, adapted and trimmed with fur. I think not at all about how—before we arrive in Russia—the month of July must pass; the idea of the cold we shall have to suffer next winter puts out of my head the idea of the heat we shall probably have to suffer this summer. And to think that after the disasters and the cold of 1812 there are still to be found meridional animals like ourselves who of their own free will dare to approach the polar bears! Oh men, men, mad from head to foot, including that rib from which we poor women were made! Enough! *Au revoir* then, dear Mauro. (Now I think of it, you would do well to change your name, because when I write it or pronounce it I seem always to be calling the cat—miaow, miaow, miaow.) In any case, if you wish to keep it I shall like you just the same, certain as I am that your character does not resemble that of that clawed little animal.

By the end of May they were back at Sant' Agata; within a few days the contract for *La forza del destino*, based on a Spanish play by Ángel Pérez de Saavedra, Duke of Rivas, had been signed. Then there arrived the terrible news of the death on 6th June of Cavour. The well-known letter from Verdi to Arrivabene of 14th or 15th June on the memorial service for Cavour held at Busseto is found in draft form in Giuseppina's letter-book. But Verdi made some changes in it, and for the better, deleting a reference to members of the Philharmonic Society who had refused to lend their services without payment, and generally tightening up the style. The result of this collaboration is a completely characteristic Verdian letter, in his best lapidary manner. A letter of Guiseppina's own, to Léon Escudier on 3rd July says:

You know the calamity that has befallen Italy—the death of Cavour!!! To tell you that Verdi has wept as at the death of his mother is to tell you little. He knew intimately that extraordinary, fascinating, marvellous man. That man of state who had conserved (unique privilege!) a heart in the midst of diplomacy and politics! Well, this beloved man, venerated by the Italians, has vanished for ever! A month has already passed since his death and I cannot speak of it without my eyes filling with tears.

After this Verdi, who had always voted with Cavour, was rarely seen in his seat in the Chamber of Deputies at Turin.

Adelaide Ristori was to appear again in Russia in the following winter, when the new opera was due for performance. 'So we shall all meet among the perpetual ice-creams of St Petersburg,' Giuseppina told Corticelli on 17th July.

Verdi says he has done a foolish thing in signing this contract, because it obliges him to work and therefore to sweat too much in the summer, in order to go and cool himself down too much in the winter. Quite perfect *tagliatelli* and *maccheroni* will be needed to keep him in good humour amid the ice and the furs. For my part, to avoid all storms, I intend to agree with everything he says from mid October to the end of January, foreseeing that during the hard labour of composition and rehearsal it will by no manner of means be possible to persuade him that he is wrong about any single thing! When, therefore, the atmosphere becomes too oppressive I shall go and take the air. Wait a bit, though! I was forgetting that the air of Russia freezes one's nose! I shall go to bed, the only place, I believe, where one can be comfortable in those boreal regions. By the way, while I remember, if la Ristori believes she will hold superiority in the matter of *tagliatelli*, Verdi counts on eclipsing her with *risotto*, which truly he makes in divine fashion.

Since, in spite of your peregrinations and *entourage* of actors, you remain what you always were, an excellent friend, we gladly accept your offer and beg you to provide for us too. We shall stay in Russia about three months, from 1st November to the end of January 1862, and there will be four of us to provide for—master, mistress and two servants. If an interpreter is indispensable, and if it is the custom to give him his meals, instead of four of us there will be five. You could provide for us, in proportion to our numbers, as you do for la Ristori in the matter of rice, *maccheroni*, cheese, salt provisions and those things which you know are not to be found in Russia or which are only to be found there at an exorbitant price. As for wine, here is the number of bottles and the qualities which Verdi would like:

100 bottles of light Bordeaux dinner wines,
20 bottles of fine Bordeaux,
20 bottles of champagne.

Perhaps it will cause you less inconvenience to provide more abundantly for la Ristori and then to cede to us the portion superfluous for her and necessary to us. I will then settle accounts with you on arrival in St Petersburg, having risen from the position of singer to that of housewife, a position I much prefer, as you will not find it difficult to believe, knowing as you do how little love I had for the boards of the stage. Don't tax me with being prosaic! Take note that there can be as much poetry in humble and, so to speak, solitary domestic occupations as in that kind of delirium one feels and sometimes communicates from the stage to the crowded auditorium.

Her pen would often take flight in the course of copying a letter. The beautiful conclusion here was such a sudden afterthought, and does not appear in the letter-book where, as Luzio says, 'about her own dispositions Giuseppina limits herself to saying: "You know me, and know how much I longed to leave the ugly boards of the stage."'

The solitude of Sant' Agata sometimes became oppressive, but uninvited visitors, including Giuseppina's relations, were not encouraged. There had been attempts at intrusion. On 19th July Giuseppina drafted a reply to a communication, after a long interval, from an aunt of hers, Giovannina Strepponi, at Lodi.

Your letter of yesterday was a pleasant surprise. So far from having forgotten *you*, I thought I had *myself* been forgotten—and deliberately forgotten. I am glad it is not so. . . . After it occurred to that cousin of mine, whom I'd never met, to present himself at the house of persons unknown to him, with very insistent and extravagant pretensions (to use no other term), I wrote you a long letter explaining in detail my position and circumstances, and asked you at the same time to tell the said cousin to leave me in peace, because his words, his letters and his visits were not such as could be to my taste, and much less to that of Verdi. To this very long and important letter I received no reply, not even an acknowledgement of receipt. The thought at once occurred to me that it could have been taken from the post by some culpable person anxious to see from what I had written to you what was to be expected on the part of Verdi and myself. Your letter of yesterday almost confirms me in this suspicion, which would account for my and your silence for so many years. While we are on this subject, let me in all frankness ask you never to direct here any of my relations, because it would be time and money wasted for whoever came. . . . As for Verdi, I would go to the world's end rather than abuse the kindness he has always shown me. . . . You know, dear Aunt, that I have always been fond of you; you know, in fact, that you are the only relation (apart from my own family) that I have ever loved spontaneously and through sympathy, without considering the ties of blood that bind us. And as you have had the most blessed idea of breaking the icy silence that divided us, write to me from time to time and I will make it, not my duty, but a real pleasure to reply, with all the affection I feel for you. It is not impossible even that I shall come for a moment to press your hand before the winter which I shall spend in Russia. Not a word, however—I could in that case only stay for an hour, nor should I wish during that hour to see other people who might come to profane this colloquy, perhaps the last, with the only surviving member of my father's family, with a person who amid the sad reality of life has known how to preserve the poetry of the heart!

She continued to correspond with this aunt for many years. She also sent her money from time to time, as later entries in the letter-books show:

26th December 1868:

[in English] Written to my Aunt Giovanna and sent forty francs.

1872:

To Giovannina Strepponi, with 50 francs.

A visitor whose presence at Sant' Agata was both welcome and necessary was Piave, to whom the libretto of *La forza del destino* had been entrusted. He came several times from Milan during the summer and autumn of 1861 and was given a number of household commissions:

DEAR PIAVE,

A silver cruet-stand made at Milan would cost 350 francs?!!! Full stop and begin again!

Poet most gracious, buy the plated cruet stand and bring it to Sant' Agata, not full of oil and vinegar, but provided with a little Cayenne pepper and with what can't be found in this Eden to fill the six little vessels. As for the effect it could have on the Natives, there's no need to bother about that. The Natives, as you know, don't frequent the modest and tranquil house of him who has honoured the town as artist and Italian.

An inimitable account of another of Piave's visits is given in a letter of 9th October to Tito Ricordi: [1]

Verdi and I were surprised to see friend Piave arrive looking like a commercial traveller, furnished, that is, with boxes, packages and parcels. As someone else was present, he could not at once embark on his Dulcamara-like harangue, expounding the wonderful virtues of the elixirs contained in the mysterious packages. But as soon as we were left alone and unsuspecting, behold him brandishing pincers and hammer: *piff, paff, puff,* out with a ream of paper, from which emerged a most novel pendulum clock; *tric, trac,* he opened the suitcase and lo! among men's stockings and ladies' stockings (don't ask me why Piave carries ladies' stockings

[1] Giovanni Cenzato, *Itinerari verdiani* (Parma, n.d.), pp. 127–8, and previously in the *Corriere della Sera* for 11th August 1934. The draft in the letter-book is dated 6th October.

about with him!) there appeared a pocket case containing a most elegant pin. Then, setting his glasses astride his nose, he began to speak: 'Lady and Gentleman! Excuse the liberty, and for love of your poet accept these two trifles, which . . .' 'Be quiet, Dulcamara! Poets don't give presents to anyone, and for good reasons.' Then, with all the airs and graces of an ambassador, he added: 'It is Tito who, returning from Switzerland and his one hundredth cure, offers through me, and begs you to accept, these two souvenirs.'

We are much obliged to Signor Tito, but Tito was wrong to indulge in compliments with a composer who indulges very little in them, and loves contracts with short words and big figures. If such be his will, however, thanks to him, on my own and Verdi's account, for this act of exquisite courtesy.

La forza del destino completed, they set off for St Petersburg towards the end of November, stopping only in Paris to pick up a new dress suit, ordered in advance from Verdi's tailor, Laurent Richard. What happened in St Petersburg is told in Giuseppina's first letter to Opprandino Arrivabene, whom she had apparently met for the first time at Turin:

St Petersburg, 1st February (20th January) 1862.

SIGNOR CONTE,

I should have liked to open my correspondence with you in a very different way. Certainly, the news I am going to give you will make you open at once your eyes, mouth and ears! But however you may exclaim in every tone of your deep bass voice 'Oh!' 'Ih!' and 'Ah!' the news is none the less true—Verdi will not be giving his new opera in St Petersburg this year.

Alas! The voices of singers are as fragile as . . . (I leave you to finish this phrase) and the voice of Signora La Grua is, to her and Verdi's misfortune, a desolating example of this fragility. Well then, lacking the *prima donna* for whom he had written, and there being no other singer here suitable for that part, Verdi asked for release from the contract. The reply to this request was a decided 'No', however preceded, followed and seasoned by the most beautiful phrases in the world. Then they agreed to give the opera next winter, on condition, etc., etc., etc.

Here then is Verdi, condemned to confront twenty-four, twenty-six, twenty-eight and more degrees of frost—Réaumur! Nevertheless, this frightful cold has not troubled us in the least, thanks to our apartments. *One sees the cold, but one doesn't feel it.* Let's be clear about this, however. This strange contradiction is a benefit reserved for the rich, who can indeed exclaim: 'Hurrah for the cold, the ice, the sledges and other terrestial joys!' But the poor people in general, and the coachmen in particular, are the most unhappy creatures in the universe. Imagine, Signor Conte, many of the coachmen stay sometimes all day and a part of the night immovable on their boxes, exposed to deadly cold, waiting for their masters, who are guzzling in warm and splendid apartments, while perhaps some of those unhappy beings are freezing to death! Such atrocious things happen every year! I shall never be able to accustom myself to the sight of such sufferings. But I don't want to bore you with too long a tirade. I promised to write to you and I have kept my word.

They returned to Paris, where they spent about a month. Verdi was expected in London in the spring, with his contribution to the opening ceremony of the International Exhibition of this year. In Giuseppina's autograph album is preserved a letter of intolerable prolixity from one F. R. Sandford, Secretary to Her Majesty's Commissioners organizing the exhibition:

The object in naming so early a date as the 1st of February 1862 for the transmission of the scores, was to prevent the possibility of any failure in the execution of the music in a manner that should be worthy of the eminent composers who had been requested to represent their respective countries on such an occasion as the opening of a great International Exhibition. Her Majesty's Commissioners, however, would regret to think that the naming of a particular date was in any way likely to interfere with the prospect of their being favoured with a work from your distinguished pen. They are quite willing to leave it in your own hands to fix the time at which you will be able to send the music of the march.

As is well known, Verdi decided to contribute a cantata, the *Inno delle Nazioni*, instead of a march, and his work, for reasons that are not clear, was not performed at the opening ceremony, but was put on by Mapleson at Her Majesty's Theatre a little later. Before he came to London, Verdi made a brief visit to Turin and Sant' Agata. Giuseppina crossed the Channel by herself, about three weeks before he did. She occupied herself with study of the English language. No anthology of her letters would be complete without some examples of her English correspondence. The letter-books include a series of enchanting little notes addressed to S. M. Maggioni, a sort of resident poet and translator at Covent Garden and other theatres:

In London. Mister Maggioni.

If you can and it does not derange you too much be so kind as to lend me during my abode in England a French and Italian Dictionary.

Laugh at me at your pleasure, but I will read, write and speak in English at random till I shall be able to understand this infernal language.

Do not forget what we settled today with regard to Verdi.

Good night.

DEAR MISTER MAGGIONI,

I have just now received a letter from my Husband and he can't be at London till Tuesday or Wednesday.

If you have nothing better to do tomorrow come, I beg you, dine with me. I have a Leg of Lamb, a Fish, Soup, Salade, *at your service*.

DEAR MISTER MAGGIONI,

Verdi arrived last night. He desire to grasp your hand. Then come, I beg you, as soon as you can.

Without doubt, you must to dine with us.

Good morning.

One has a suspicion that Giuseppina was sometimes poking fun at some of our national institutions, as in the following note, in Italian this time, to the baritone Leone Giraldoni:

DEAR GIRALDONI,

Verdi wants a word with you.

When you have eaten your ten pounds of meat for breakfast, come and see us for a moment.

Good morning, and *au revoir*,

Your affectionate friend,

GIUSEPPINA VERDI.

London, 29th April 1862.

Another letter in English, with the postmark 4th May, is addressed to Corticelli:

DEAR FRIEND,

Well! very well! You have some good aptitude for commercial style, and I shall employ you as a Secretary when I shall be able to open a Cheesemonger Shop. But, you must submit yourself (before I put you in possession of such a noble charge) at an experiment with closed doors.

You are right in giving all your mind and time to your important *things*. I am not so silly to pretend, that a future Cheesemonger's Secretary, ought to occupy himself with trifles: but I am very glad to know it, because things being so, I shall buy some trifle in London myself.

I beg your pardon, for every error that I am sure, you shall find in my letter. Be indulgent, and think, Mister Secretary, that I am *all alone* without hope today to see some english person able to correct it.

I send you the requested *autograph*, and beg you to remember

JOSEPHINE VERDI.

On the reverse is this in Italian:

DEAR CORTICELLI,

If I have enough time and paper I will translate my letter; and *please understand* that this scrawl in English must be kept to yourself and Signora Ristori, because while I love to joke, I don't want to become an object of ridicule. As I wrote it quickly and without the help of *anybody*, *anybody at all*, I'm still too much a blunderer in this language not to have made some mistakes, and God knows of what calibre! Tell me if you really are unable to bother about my rags, so that I may buy here myself a few things of which I have much need.

It is curious that she relied on this friend to buy some of her clothes.

Possibly, acting in Ristori's name, he was able to get discount. It is also curious that Verdi's wife, apart from occasional presents, still paid for all her own clothes, out of her own money. Corticelli was now in Paris; a letter to him from London on 6th May says:

I prefer the cloak—black, of course, plain black. For the rest, I believe you are sufficiently well acquainted with my tastes, which are for quiet colours—*violet*, *emerald green*, *black*, *grey*, etc.—for day dresses. As for evening dresses, my lord and master is going to give me one this autumn, so don't bother, unless it's a case of an excellent bargain going cheaply. I count on you, and on your affection for me, to be economical. Did you see that a most charming, brand-new dress in a first-class establishment in Regent Street can be had for £5 10*s*. 0*d*.? Let that be your *point de départ*.

Her meticulously kept inventories of the contents of her wardrobes include several dresses bought in Paris in the spring of this year.

From contemplation of the Regent Street shop windows her thoughts turned to Sant' Agata where she was soon to return: 'Perhaps if the solitude of that place were not so absolute, and at times sepulchral, I should completely forget that cities exist. And in truth I only think of them when months and months go by in the profound silence and complete solitude of the fields. A single family near us would suffice to break the monotony of that existence.'

There were visitors at Sant' Agata in the summer, but it was a melancholy time. The stay of the tenor Fraschini was clouded over by the illness of the beloved pet dog Loulou. Mariani proposed to bring Sir James Hudson with him in August, but Verdi had to ask for the visit to be deferred. The house was still full of workmen and not a single room was completely finished. Several of the servants were ill with tertian fever. Loulou died, and Giuseppina was prostrate with grief. Worst of all, Barberina Strepponi was thought to be going into a decline; she came to stay at Sant' Agata, apparently for the first time. 'She is so calm', Giuseppina told a Russian friend, Marie Lavroff, 'resigned like a saint, and happy to be with me, whom she loves beyond everything and everybody.' A letter of 14th August to Corticelli says:

The first and most serious of the things that afflict us, and afflict me in particular, is the illness of my sister, who is declared consumptive. She is here with us, and I shall take her home on Sunday, and be back on Monday evening, the 19th. She is the only one left to me, out of four brothers and sisters. . . . The second affliction (and perhaps some people will smile, but I am weeping still as I write) is the loss of my dear Loulou. Four days of atrocious sufferings carried him off to rest eternally under a willow in our garden, where you too will come to say goodbye to the memory of that faithful and charming friend. . . . Verdi is well, and is scoring the opera for Russia.

All went well on the second trip to Russia. 'The opera was successful', Giuseppina told Corticelli, 'in spite of the colicky contortions of the *Teutonic* party, for whom, on the other hand, I feel sorry, since after so many years of shouting to all the winds that German operas are the best, the public obstinately leaves the theatre empty when they give them, and runs in crowds when this ugly rubbish *Un ballo in maschera*, *La forza del destino*, etc., is announced. Imagine, eight performances of *La forza del destino* have already been given, with the theatre constantly packed. A fine sight for the impresario! The Czar, who attended only at the fourth performance, having been prevented before that by acute eye and throat trouble, called for Verdi by name, and wanted, too, to have him in his box, where he and the Czarina smothered him in compliments. On the day of his annual departure for Moscow he sent Verdi, *motu proprio*, the Order of St Stanislas (Commander's Cross, worn round the neck). As for the indemnity for having come twice to Russia, it was highly satisfactory.'

There are no outstanding letters from the year 1863. A visit to Madrid for another production of *La forza del destino*, followed by a tour of Andalusia, did not inspire Giuseppina. A stay in Paris, where Verdi had promised to superintend a revival of *Les Vêpres Siciliennes*, terminated in a breach with the Opera and return to Sant' Agata. Then the bailiff ran away; his defection is commemorated in the letter-books in a sonnet in dialect. Life at Sant' Agata was restful, after the journeyings in Russia, England, France and Spain, but rather dull and, as the winter came on, dreary. These are not very exciting years in the lives of Verdi and Giuseppina.

The letter-books were neglected altogether in the year 1864, but the correspondence with De Sanctis and Corticelli fills the gap. The Neapolitan friends were often lectured on family limitation—without much effect—and on their political attitude after the collapse of the Bourbon régime. Baron Genovese, whose bald head is so conspicuous in Delfico's cartoons of Verdi at Naples, had apparently fled from the city on the approach of Garibaldi's legions in 1860. A letter in Verdi's hand in the National Library, Vienna, of 3rd January 1861, says: 'After this permit me to say that you were wrong to be afraid, to sell out madly, and above all to leave your country at a time like that.' The letter to Genovese was drafted by Giuseppina and appears in her letter-book under the date of 29th December 1860—five days before it was actually copied by Verdi and sent. Now on 3rd January 1864, in a letter of her own, she discussed with De Sanctis the problems of Italian unity:

Your political point of view has rejoiced our hearts. So there *are* Neapolitans who understand the position, see the difficulties that exist, and are just enough and of sufficiently good faith to recognize them? God be praised! Unfortunately, however, there are among the Neapolitan and Sicilian deputies some great talkers, full of violence and anything but in favour of the unity of Italy under Vittorio Emanuele. They would like to fish in troubled waters, with the Prophet of London and his associates. As for the ingenuous Garibaldi, he has come down a great deal in the opinion of right-thinking people.

This probably represents the views also of Verdi, and shows again how far to the right he had moved since the days when he had written *Suona la tromba* for Mazzini. Garibaldi had incurred disapproval through his ill-advised misadventure on Aspromonte in 1862.

We have several letters about doctors. A recommendation to Corticelli of a young surgeon, who was going to practise at Florence, says: 'I know that virtue matters little when it's a question of amputation, of cutting off a leg or an arm; but it matters a great deal when he who is capable of doing that occupies a position where humanity and justice are the comfort, and sometimes the *only* comfort, of unhappy beings condemned to their beds, where often they suffer as much morally as physically.' But she had little belief in Dr Frignani and his colleagues. Caterina De Sanctis had recently brought another baby into the world, which had not lived long. Giuseppina on 27th March 1864 comforted her, and suggested various cures, to be taken all at once:

The first is good humour, sovereign remedy indicated by the great Rabelais, celebrated as doctor and philosopher in his day. I, a country lady-doctor, unrestrainedly approve and warmly advise it. Begin then by ceasing to weep for the little angel who has returned to God's bosom. He is better off than we are and without fear for the future. For the rest, if you had no other children I should be a bit sorry for you, but as you already have a sufficient number of them and possess, too, a factory in full activity for the multiplication of the De Sanctis, I can't feel sorry for you at all. So dry your tears quickly and read my second prescription.

Send to the Devil all doctors, great and small! One hundred and one out of every hundred don't understand a thing and are charlatans, with the appetites of musicians! I believe (I speak seriously) in the ability of a surgeon who amputates properly an arm or a leg—that is something I can see. I believe in the efficacy of certain waters, but as for the chatter, the prescriptions, the opinions of those conceited asses who pretend they know all about our insides—I don't believe in them at all! Take twenty doctors and it will be pure chance if two find themselves in agreement. Guesses, guesses—and one understands why. Medicine does not yet possess a microscope, telescope, stereoscope, or whatever you like to call it, for examining and seeing well the bowels! Therefore don't sublimate yourself with sublimate, but pack your bags and come to see us. A grand cure is a change of air and the distraction of travelling! And fifteen miles from our shanty there are two miraculous springs—and I have seen the miracles with my own eyes. It's an ugly bathing establishment where one does not dine in Lucullan fashion, but where many regain their health.

The 'shanty' was still undergoing repairs and alteration. In April it was 'an Inferno', with workmen everywhere. On a visit to Genoa Giuseppina herself fell ill, and spent nearly three weeks in bed with gastric fever. She wrote to Corticelli on 7th July:

As you know, we are back home again, after the unhappy, forced sojourn at Genoa. Enough—it is over now and convalescence is proceeding regularly, although I feel physically exhausted. And you are off to Egypt? A mere trifle to you! Do you intend, perhaps, to give performances in the interior of Africa? I hope you enjoy it! Give my respectful regards to the crocodiles, the pyramids and the mummies. Among the latter perhaps you'll find the Marchese Sampieri. If so be careful, for the Love of God, *not* to give him my regards. He would be quite capable of reviving, to come and annoy me, and annoy the musical world as he did for the space of so many centuries!

The Marchese Francesco Sampieri (1790–1863), friend of Rossini, musical dilettante and composer, would seem to have been among Giuseppina's early admirers. The letter continues:

In truth, in spite of my weakness and a certain hypochondria, the consequence of my gastric fever, I can't help laughing at the thought of you going to perform in Italian to the Egyptians. What famous gipsies you are!

I do beg of you to write to us, to stay fond of us, and to find sometimes a way of coming to spend a little time at Sant' Agata, where, I assure you, the quiet is like Paradise. Verdi is well, sends his kindest regards, and hopes to see you dressed as a Pharaoh. He has been, as always, full of affection and solicitude during my illness and, what will seem strange to you, but is nevertheless true, he has even found the way to be patient! As you can imagine, I am grateful to him for that, with all my heart!

Our greetings to the Ristori family. And you, excellent and most dear friend, accept a paw-shake from your affectionate

GIUSEPPINA VERDI.

She was feeling a bit catty when she next wrote, on 17th September: 'The Morchio family, Father, Mother, Daughter and Holy Ghost, were here at Sant' Agata. Teresa had four or five photographs of Bianca in divers poses which (the *photographs*, not the poses!) added to the forty-five left behind at Genoa, will make up the fifty!!' Again: 'Don't talk to me of Sicily, of the province of Naples, of Spain, etc., etc. They are countries, peoples, nations, full of pride, ignorance and lice!'

At the moment I'm in such a black mood that I would make a great roast of the human race. Don't be afraid, for if I had such power I should make a few exceptions and should scatter here and there some Cadmuses,

Deucalions and Pyrrhas, to repopulate, in rather better fashion, this earth, which, physically speaking, is in great part very beautiful.

Corticelli was not entirely happy in his position and talked of giving it up. Giuseppina, who knew him well and suspected that he had been quarrelling with someone, or perhaps again too easily taken offence, gave him some characteristically sensible advice:

> Listen carefully, homoeopathic *mortadella*! If you wish to separate from la Ristori because you find that kind of life too tiring for you I have nothing to say, as you must think first of all of your health. But if it is for another reason, and the travelling is not too much for you, consider also your interests and as long as a certain delicate point of honour is not involved (you know what I mean) don't pay for your punctilio out of your own pocket. Do you understand? . . . I warmly embrace you, and hope you'll become more of a gipsy than ever, if that's possible, for then you will travel with your gipsy band to California, Australia, New Zealand and the interior of Africa, and we shall thus gain precise ideas of those distant parts.

Cesare De Sanctis had lost his wife early in August, in spite of all medical and lay prescriptions. Giuseppina wrote to him on 19th September: 'I really flattered myself, until your letter came, that we should see you arrive at Sant' Agata to pass a few days in this profound quiet, which calms the blood and, if it does not heal the sorrows of the heart, sets on them, nevertheless, a seal of mystic melancholy and grave solemnity that helps one to bear them with courage and resignation.' Again and again she speaks of the profound silence and peace of their life in the country. But again and again, too, she refers to her dread of the winter at Sant' Agata, with its ennui and isolation. There is a letter of 22nd October 1864,[1] from Verdi to Tito Ricordi, the opening of which, though not found in her letter-books, was assuredly drafted by Giuseppina. It is, exceptionally, wholly in the manner of her own private letters and not a bit in Verdi's style: 'It rains and it rains and it rains! Farewell to the country, farewell to our walks, farewell to the beautiful sun, which now we shall only see pallid and sick; farewell beautiful blue sky, farewell infinite space, farewell desires and hopes of coming to Como! Four walls will now replace the infinite: the fire instead of the sun! Books and music will replace the air and the sky; boredom instead of pleasure!' Verdi was occupied in this winter with the revision of his *Macbeth*, suggested by Escudier, but Giuseppina had too much time on her hands. 'Try to persuade Verdi to come to Paris', she wrote on 2nd November, 'without leaving me at Sant' Agata, where at this time of year I am *most royally* bored.' Then a little later: 'Verdi doesn't seem disposed to undertake the journey to Paris, or any other journey, so behold us

[1] *Copialettere*, p. 617, wrongly dated 1862.

still here at Sant' Agata on 3rd January, while it is wantonly snowing!' There was a brief escape to Genoa in February and early March, but concern about his father's health brought Verdi back home again.

The revised *Macbeth* had its first performance at the Théâtre-Lyrique in Paris on 21st April 1865, but was not particularly successful. Nevertheless, the management of the Opéra soon afterwards opened negotiations for a new work. Giuseppina wrote to Escudier in June:

> It seems that Verdi has not replied with a refusal to Perrin's offer. That is already much, since for a very long time now I have heard him singing in every tone: 'I don't want to write,' and frankly I am anxious that he should write, because, although I love the country very much, three hundred and sixty-five days a year in the country are too many—far too many! We have never stayed so long in the midst of these cretins. I feel myself stick out my claws like a wild animal and a furious desire for movement and destruction overcomes me, to avenge myself for this eternal immobility! I am no longer young, it is true, but intellectual life is ageless and here it is completely lacking. It would seem that the great difficulty about writing for the Opéra would be the libretto. I put my trust in the imagination of the poets. . . . I know him; once he is engaged the scene will change. He will abandon his trees, his building, his hydraulic engines, his guns, etc. He will allow himself, as always in such cases, to be overcome by the artist's creative fever; he will devote himself wholly to his poem and his music, and I hope the whole world will benefit by it.

Before that happened, however, 'these cretins' were to occasion a tremendous outburst of wrath.

Many pages of Giuseppina's letter-books are devoted to a sort of dossier concerning Verdi's feud with Busseto, which came to a head in the summer of 1865. The municipal theatre, long projected, was nearing completion and the authorities expected that Verdi would allow the theatre to be called by his name and would use his influence to secure some of the most famous singers of the day for the opening ceremony. Possibly they hoped, too, that he would write a new opera for them. These hopes and expectations seem to have been based on remarks he had let fall in private many years before, when the idea of the new theatre at Busseto had first been mooted. But the mayor now declared that the composer had given his solemn promise of adherence to these schemes and the theatre had been built for him. Verdi reacted violently, as always when he felt that an attempt was being made to force his hand. His angry but reasoned reply, published in the appendix to the *Copialettere* (pp. 434–5), without the recipient's name, was addressed to Giovannino Barezzi, who had come forward as spokesman for Busseto, although he was not a member of the theatre commission.

*I

Meanwhile Giuseppina had begun to gather together and copy out documents and notes for the presentation of the case against Busseto.

She turned first to two letters Verdi had written twenty years before to Antonio Barezzi. Only part of the first is transcribed:

In the name of the *Father, Son and Holy Ghost*! I cross myself before replying to your most welcome letter and put myself in God's grace, so as not to talk rubbish. A theatre at Busseto? I don't believe it, I never shall believe it! . . . Poor us, if that came about! The end of the world is at hand! . . . I'll write the opera (if you like), subject always to my engagements—and everybody knows that I've six operas to write. I can't promise anything about la Frezzolini and Poggi, but there is every probability. . . . Take courage, and as you are building castles in the air, let them be beautiful ones!

The rest is condensed by Giuseppina: 'The letter continues, speaking of Paris, of Escudier and the affairs he proposes. It ends with these words: "I commend to you the theatre. Dream well!" This letter must be—is, in fact—of 1845.' Here was probably the *fons et origo* of the claims made upon him, for in that remote period he had certainly not frowned upon the idea. But the castle, at that time, had only been built in the air. It had been discussed again about ten years later and the mayor held that it was then that Verdi had committed himself. Construction of the theatre had been decided on on 28th August 1857, and work had begun two years later. At some time during his deputyship (i.e. after 3rd February 1861) Verdi had suggested that work on the theatre should be suspended and the money contributed to the national cause. But the building had been completed, except for the interior decorations, by 18th October 1864.

The first document in Giuseppina's dossier is otherwise unknown. The second ('Copy as above of a letter of Verdi's') appears without precise date in the *Copialettere* (pp. 14–15). Giuseppina, however, would seem to have retrieved the originals from Barezzi for her purposes. Her transcription of the second letter is precisely dated and differs in many details from the version in the *Copialettere*. Verdi, in this dispute of 1865, added annotations to his old letter:

Milan, 12th June 1845.

I have read the theatrical project, and I must tell you with my customary frankness that I am not happy about it. (1) In truth it was not a very delicate action to make use of my name and compromise me before the authorities on account of a word I may have said in confidence between friends; and if it was wished to make public use of this word of mine I should first have been asked. (2) In all the towns in the world they have built theatres without having anyone to write an opera for them, or to sing it for them, and if Busseto had that advantage it should have availed itself of it without calculating on it and making it its principal basis. By that I don't intend to withdraw my word, but how can one speak now of

1847? (3) Haven't I got to write in that year for Naples and for the publisher Lucca? And isn't it enough that I promise for myself? Must I promise for the singers too? That is something quite new! Here are the words I said in this connection: 'Perhaps, perhaps, we could get la Frezzolini and Poggi' (in saying that I did not promise anything). In a moment of enthusiasm (for I don't deny that I liked the idea of a theatre at Busseto) I flattered myself about that, because, besides the friendship existing between me and those artists, when I last said goodbye to la Frezzolini she said: 'We are resting this autumn; come for a fortnight to stay with us in the country, and we will come to you at Busseto and there we'll give a concert for the benefit of the poor.' I replied: 'I take you at your word but not for this year, because I haven't a house yet; however, next year I expect you without fail.' But if in the year when they want to open the theatre la Frezzolini has in her hands a contract (which means to say 40,000 or 50,000 francs), who will be so crazy as to propose she should come and sing for nothing at Busseto? . . .

(1) Those who occupied themselves with the theatre at that time at least had the grace to show me the project.
(2) Discretion is not an outstanding virtue in general. It seems that at Busseto they regard as official any word that may have escaped one by way of conversation, when this word furthers their interests and aims. Nor do they seek, as persons who act with delicacy and prudence should, to have this or that word, said *en passant*, confirmed, but they invent that word, or they take him who uttered it *by surprise*. For them the law changes its purport, and they keep their word, even the most formal and written word, only when and as it suits them.
(3) And in any case, if in 1845 it was impossible to speak of 1847, that means to say that it is more absurd to speak in 1865 of a word (even admitting there were such) spoken academically in 1854–5. One must also take into consideration the different circumstances. . . .

From the ancient history of the theatre Giuseppina turned to 'the affair of Emanuele Muzio', transcribing, probably from the same source, two documents relative to the climax, in 1853, of the long-drawn-out negotiations concerning the post of *maestro di musica*. Just as Verdi had been induced to give up a much more lucrative post at Monza for the benefit of his home town, so Muzio, who was beginning to establish himself as a conductor, had agreed to return there, stipulating however that he should be left some free time to pursue his career in the theatre. Giuseppina copied out his letter to the Mayor of Busseto about this:

I have the honour to advise you that after many difficulties I have succeeded in obtaining a promise in writing of my release from the engagement which bound me to the direction of the theatres of Padua for a period of three years. Now (and with pleasure) I am able and prepared to accept the vacant post of Maestro at Busseto. I believe it unnecessary to recall to your memory that, as in the past, so today I should refuse to submit myself to a competitive examination. Among the new conditions there are some too onerous for me to accept, so it would be necessary to modify them by common consent.

Should you decide to proceed with this matter, it would be necessary not only that I should have a reply, but that everything should be settled by 12th September, as at that time I have to leave for Bologna, and write definitely to Padua as to whether I accept or not the requested release from contract.

The result had not been all that had been hoped. To objections from Busseto as to Muzio's terms Verdi had replied, probably to Antonio Barezzi, in these words:

I am frank and always say what I think. Emanuele, this time, is not wrong. Must he wait and hold himself at the disposition of the affairs of Busseto? And even if he had written, or should write, to say he would accept, would he be sure of obtaining the post? Must he then renounce everything and, I repeat, hold himself at the perpetual disposition of the indecisions of Busseto? He has a contract with Padua (I myself arranged it) which binds him for the season of the autumn fair and carnival. He has accepted for the season at Alessandria and now Mariani (in my presence) offers him in the name of Cavour, Minister for Internal Affairs, the post at the Teatro Regio at Turin, which perhaps he won't be able to accept owing to his engagement at Padua. The mayor says he has had the salary from the Monte di Pietà increased. It's natural enough that the salaries of the employees should be increased, since the funds have grown and the cost of living gone up. But that wasn't enough; they should have given up the competitive examination (which is the most stupid thing imaginable) and they should have offered—mark well—*offered* the post to Emanuele. If the Minister of Piedmont offers the post at the Teatro Regio at Turin, Busseto could well have offered, without loss of dignity, that miserable post. But Busseto has a vanity and ridiculous pretensions not found in the great cities. It's the defect of that town!

To settle this business now is more difficult than ever. Nevertheless there is still one thing worth trying. Let the mayor offer the post to Emanuele in writing to me. I will try with this letter to induce Emanuele to accept, and to release him, or at least to come to some arrangement with those with whom he has engagements. This is the only way. And let the mayor settle about the competitive examination and settle with the priests. Let him think too about getting an increase from the ecclesiastical authorities, because the present emolument is wretched. This, you know, is the only way in which past mistakes can perhaps be remedied. If the mayor can't do that, say no more about it and content yourselves with some imbecile of a foreigner obtained by competitive examination, instead of a native who is certainly no imbecile. The old proverb is very true: *Nemo propheta in patria.*

In the event, not only had it not been found possible to modify the terms of Muzio's proposed engagement, but, not long after he had thrown up the whole idea in disgust, one Ferdinando Savazzini, of Parma, had been nominated *without* a competitive examination. This had actually been done on the orders of the minister Salati at Parma, who had had enough of these squabbles, but Verdi put it down to the account of Busseto.

These documents from 1853, preserved in Giuseppina's letter-book, are otherwise unknown.

On 20th July 1865, after further correspondence about the theatre, and what he had, or had not, promised to do about it, Verdi, or Giuseppina in his name, wrote to Angiolo Carrara, notary of Busseto:

Although tomorrow is Friday, if you could come here at six in the evening I should be very grateful. There is perhaps reserved for you a fine part in the ugly comedy being performed these days at Busseto. I won't tell you what this part is, because I want curiosity to act rather as a spur. . . .

The succeeding pages of the letter-book are filled with notes about the various ways in which Busseto and the Bussetani had offended. These notes are all in Giuseppina's hand, but it is not easy to decide exactly what they represent. They are mostly written in the first person singular, in Verdi's name, but just once there is a reference to him in the third person. It seems most likely that the notes were set down, largely from Verdi's dictation, to serve as the agenda, as it were, of the meeting with Carrara. Or possibly they were taken down by Giuseppina at Verdi's request during the actual interview with the notary, who is clearly the 'you' of the opening paragraph.

Here is the voice of Verdi in his anger:

The gravest *affront* is that, having put words and promises into my mouth, and demanded, in bad faith and by surprise, the actualization of them, which I naturally refused, they have made me out to be a man who doesn't keep his word. It is necessary to destroy, by letter or however you think fit, the effect of Sunday's commission, and relieve me of the responsibility that another has put upon me to relieve himself.

The affair of Emanuele as *maestro*—the competitive examination for him, the nomination of somebody else without examination.

The letter they want to write to America,[1] to prove that I am a man who breaks his word. Fine way of acting—delicate and honest!

Apart from my word (which I have never given) why do they want to exact so much from me? Is it perhaps on account of those 27 francs and 50 centesimi a month[2] which they gave me and which they couldn't refuse me?

Is the merit theirs, if they gave them, or the testators'?

And all this fuss for 1,200 francs?

[1] Muzio was then in America.
[2] Actually, 25 francs a month.

Haven't they given them, and aren't they obliged to give them in perpetuity, to four youths every year? Cialdi, Bottarelli, etc.—aren't they included? Do they wish to punish me, perhaps, for the name I've acquired and the honour I've done to the town?

For the rest, it's a vain and ridiculous mania of the town to wish to play the Maecenas by the merit of the dead and 30 centesimi from the living.

There follows a passage which seems to be Giuseppina's own, since it refers to Verdi in the third person:

The pensions were left by those who are no more and the merit belongs not at all to those who now cry out so much in the piazza, in the taverns, in the cafés and shops, against Verdi who, whether they like it or not, made known to the whole world that Busseto was on the map.

The living, when they go to the theatre and spend a few centesimi, think they're the benefactors of the actors, singers and instrumentalists. In their view they have benefited all those who have come to Busseto, including la Ristori, who, if it hadn't been for them, would not have laid the first stone of the edifice of her glory and her fortune.

It's time to throw off the bandage and to look round rather, and see how the world progresses.

There is another instalment, in briefer notes on the left-hand sides of some divided pages. This amounts to a really savage indictment of the unhappy town:

Do they make claims on me because I am rich? Sivioli, Lanbroni—aren't they rich too?

Fofino—breaks into my house. And this is found a matter of indifference perhaps because done to me.

Old Frignani—tries to find out, by direct question, how and by what means my wife lives, because the town is not clear about that. By what right?

The engine—for the water.

La Landriani—to whom was read, but not given, the letter of reparation for what was done and written to her by Arfini, who is still in his post.

Investigation, or rather inquisition, into everything that is done or said in my house.

How no one can frequent my house without becoming an object of hatred and persecution on the part of the Bussetani.

Giovanni B.—cries out in the piazza, and writes with a velvet paw. Two-faced, like so many of the rest. Hasn't the courage of his own opinions.

Diverse opinions.

To say at every moment this phrase, which, if ridiculous, is still offensive: '*We made him.*' It's the business of the 27 francs again. And why didn't they 'make' the others, then, since the means were the same?

If I in this connection, without departing from the truth, were to write a short letter for publication, I could make them look ridiculous before all Europe.

It's better to have done with it—both with the 27 francs 50 centesimi and with the kind of inquisition that has been practised for sixteen years.[1]

I have, so to speak, withdrawn from Busseto. If my annoyance increases I shall withdraw from Sant' Agata, and I shan't be the one that will cut the worst figure.

Confession, communion, days of abstinence, mass, novenas, etc. Can't one have then individual liberty, when one lives honestly in one's own house without offending against the laws or morality?

Observations on how much one buys at Busseto, at Cremona, etc., on how much one eats. . . .

Our opinions are at the antipodes. I am Liberal to the utmost degree, without being a Red. I respect the liberty of others and I demand respect for my own. The town is anything but Liberal. It makes a show of being so, perhaps out of fear, but is of clerical tendencies.

Not all the persons mentioned can be identified. La Landriani was the school-teacher. In the previous May, Verdi had written, probably to Carrara, about her case: 'La Landriani, whom I did not know, has been here. According to what I was told, nothing could be more unworthy and odious than the scene that occurred between her, the superintendent and the school director. I have seen the letter of this last, Arfini, and it is unbelievable that an educated man, a priest, could exaggerate in that way. It's the letter of a Jesuit and an inquisitor! It's a letter that deserves to be presented to the minister, so that he may know in what hands is public instruction!'

'Giovanni B.' was certainly Giovannino Barezzi. He mistakenly believed that as Verdi's brother-in-law he was in a position to smooth over all the difficulties about the new theatre at Busseto, and wrote suggesting that he and the mayor should call at Sant' Agata. This is the answer he got:

Why should Corbellini come to see me? And why with you? What is your position? Why the slight to the commission, with whom he was at Sant' Agata? Why the slight to Angiolo Carrara and to the municipal authorities? And if you wish the gossip to end, begin by talking less yourself. For the rest, since they dared to tell me *officially* that I had promised, so I believe it is necessary for the truth to be officially admitted —that is, *that I have never, never promised.* I know sufficiently well the system of many people, who in private, in the taverns and cafés, say one thing, and in public say another.

I don't know why you meddle in this business, not being a member of the municipal council or the commission. Is it perhaps in the capacity of a friend? In truth, you can't say you've been one on this occasion! *As for being averse to gossiping, you, who ought to be the one not to do so, were the first to shout things utterly false and unseemly at all the street corners.* Doesn't it seem to all of you that it's time to leave me in peace?

Giovannino wrote again and Verdi, instead of replying, passed his

[1] i.e. from 1849, when Verdi had brought Giuseppina to live with him at Busseto.

letter on to Angiolo Carrara, with an accompanying note ending: 'Send for Barezzi and tell him to spare me his proposed visit.' There are four drafts for this short note in Giuseppina's letter-book. On 1st August Verdi wrote again to his brother-in-law. The draft of this letter is almost illegible owing to innumerable erasures, alterations and additions in the hands of both Verdi and Giuseppina. This can be made out:

> I did not think fit to reply to your last letter, out of consideration due to Signori Angiolo and Leopoldo Carrara. Today the affair is about to end, the disputes are settled, and I take up my pen again to reply once and for all to your last letters.
>
> And first of all, where did you, who call yourself my *old friend*, find the nerve to go about the piazzas, the cafés and the taverns, crying out against this your *old friend*, cursing and speaking ill of him?
>
> How could you disapprove his actions, without knowing them, and condemn him, without defence?
>
> Do you know that even between enemies, when they are honest, accusations are made, but discussions take place before acquittal or condemnation!!? And you, my *old friend*, have behaved worse than an honest enemy! You adjudged me in the right in your letters, and you cried out against me in the piazzas.

What follows is a version of the letter published, without the recipient's name, in the appendix to the *Copialettere* (pp. 436–7).[1] He returns to the subject of the words 'We made him', which he had overheard during his last visit to Busseto, eight or ten days before; he discusses again the question of the pension he had received in his youth from the Monte di Pietà; now, through Dr Angiolo Carrara, he has put forward conciliatory suggestions: 'Whatever the result, it's a matter I never wish to speak of again. This letter is a reply to yours; it's not worth answering. But if you do decide to write to me again, since you won't be able to say anything new, or anything to which I haven't replied in anticipation, don't be surprised if I conserve the profoundest silence. I ask only one thing of you: *quiet* and, if you like, *oblivion*.'

Exit Giovannino, devoted companion of former days, veteran of the wars of the 'Coccardini' and 'Codini'.

After making the municipal authorities eat their words, Verdi, through Dr Carrara, conceded that the theatre should be called by his name. He refused to accept, as a gift, the box in the theatre offered him; instead, although he never intended to use it, he would pay them 10,000 francs for it.

The last of this miserable episode is heard in Giuseppina's private comment in her letter-book:

[1] Part of this letter has been quoted in another chapter (p. 12).

To the minor and modest composer Coppola, the people of Catania, as a token of their joy over his return to his country after fifteen years, are having a gold medal coined, valued at 1,227 francs.

To Giuseppe Verdi, who has filled the world with his glory, the Bussetani make recompense by poisoning his life by every sort of vile action, and reminding him at every word, at every step, of the wretched sum (which they could not refuse him, because it was an old endowment) of 1,200 francs!! By infinite abuse, lies, violent acts, they exacerbate him, annoy him and, so to speak, oblige him to make an end, once and for all, of these daily goadings, and throw in their faces the conspicuous sum of 10,000 francs!!!

So be it! Thus will be paid off that *so-called* benefaction, one hundred per cent, materially! And a thousandfold in the glory that shines on that filthy and unworthy town!

She ends with a touch of characteristic melancholy poetry:

Alas! at every hour the tree of illusions loses its leaves. . . . I, poor woman, have almost reached the point of desiring the repose of the majority and the shades of death, so as not to see any more the work of men. . . . My beautiful peacock, that stands watching me, tells me that the animals are the best of living beings. That's what my poor Loulou always told me, with his big eyes full of affection and fidelity. Poor Loulou!

During this summer Verdi was at his most unapproachable. The editor of *La Scena*, who had sent one of his publications and, apparently, a request for an interview for his paper, got this flung back at him on 10th September:

It would be a good thing to add to the booklet, which I herewith return, the following appendix: 'One must leave in peace persons whom one doesn't know, who live in retirement and neither ask for nor desire biographies, articles or anything else written in their praise.'

More politely, the same thing was said to Filippo Filippi, music critic of *La Perseveranza*, on 26th September:

If you honour me with your visit, your talents as biographer will find little satisfaction in narrating the marvels of Sant' Agata. Four walls in which to take refuge from the sun and inclement weather, amid the vastness of the fields; a few dozen trees planted in large part by my own hands; a dirty pool which I shall honour with the pompous title of lake when I can get the water to fill it. All that without plan, without architectural order, not because I don't love architecture, but because I detest discordances, and it would be a bad one to set up anything artistic in so unpoetical a place.

This was all drafted by Giuseppina, as the style might have led one to guess. In the definitive form of the letter, which is well known, Verdi made small alterations, adopting a variant reading already indicated by Giuseppina, and omitting the word 'pompous' and the phrase about the vast fields. The latter part of the draft in the letter-book shows Verdi and Giuseppina in active collaboration within the same sentence. The following passage begins in Verdi's hand:

> I know that you are an enthusiastic and able musician. Alas! Piave and Mariani will have told you that at Sant' Agata [*here Giuseppina takes over the pen*] no one ever plays or speaks of music [*here Verdi resumes and finishes the sentence*] and you run the risk of finding a pianoforte perhaps without any strings.

In the letter as sent the last phrase became: 'you run the risk of finding a pianoforte perhaps not only out of tune but without any strings'.

Verdi often made use of Giuseppina as intermediary, knowing that a word from her to the right person at the right moment would save him much bother and embarrassment, or bring forward the positive proposals he desired. Those who had business with him, too, would often sound Giuseppina first, to discover whether the moment was propitious. The skill and diplomacy she displayed in her position between Verdi and the outside world were beyond all praise. Acting sometimes in collusion with Verdi, sometimes on her own initiative and impulse, she dealt out friendly hints, reminders, words of warning. Above all, Verdi's publishers found her an invaluable go-between. With his marvellous insight into all the complex financial and commercial possibilities in the international sphere of his own operas, there were always some things in which he held that Ricordis had done less than they might have done in his and their interests. From time to time a storm would blow up. Then Giuseppina's help would be sought by the publishers, and freely given, in so far as she could do so without disloyalty. She is seen in her role of intermediary in two letters to Giulio Ricordi of October 1865, though it is not clear what the particular point at issue was. On the 17th she wrote:

> I have received your kind letter and in making it my duty to reply immediately *I profit by the ungrateful privilege of age to speak frankly and without preamble.*
>
> Be assured, Signor Giulio, that no one made it his deplorable office to turn white into black. If there is some cloud in the mind of Verdi, *it derives from the atmosphere prevailing for a long time, too heavily charged with heterogeneous elements*; it derives from circumstances and facts of which you cannot be ignorant *and which are not ignored at Sant' Agata, since, after all, this hovel is not outside the bounds of the known world!*
>
> From your letter I learn (*not without surprise*) that you know of the chance conversation between your father and me. I say 'chance conversation' because, passing hurriedly through Milan and believing you all on the Lake, I was very far from expecting a visit from Signor Tito. But since you know the substance of that conversation, you ought also to know

that what I said was on my own impulse and in no way by Verdi's agreement or authorization. It's not that those words of mine did not express Verdi's ideas, but he did not know (nor could it have been otherwise) that I would be seeing your father, and he still does not know of that *chance conversation*. If he did, I am sure that with that little laugh of his that I know so well he would say coldly: 'You were wrong to speak about it because you have done something useless,' and would go back to the garden to plant cabbages.

However, I can assure you, dear Signor Giulio, that if you will honour us with a visit you will be welcome. Verdi could perhaps receive a stranger coldly; he will always receive an old acquaintance in a friendly and cordial manner.

Giulio and his father came to Sant' Agata and afterwards, on the 31st, Giuseppina wrote again:

Verdi is in the garden all the time he is not sleeping or eating. He has already made the necessary arrangements for the little island in the pond to take another shape. Today the plants arrive from Bordin and if by mischance the moon shines tonight we shall have, until God knows when, to put as many of them as possible in their places, seeing that tomorrow is a holiday, when it'll be impossible to get any work done. Verdi speaks with great respect of your father's botanical and agrarian talents. Both of them will probably end up as gardeners, for the greater glory of the art of music, and so be it!

From the very few words exchanged at the last moment on the business *en question*, you will have been able (with your acumen and good sense) to perceive how much logic and justice there is in the cause producing that kind of *cloud*, which disturbed the serenity of the long-standing relations between my husband and your House.

On this occasion, clearly, little was conceded. One has the impression that it was not to discuss plants and gardening that they came to Sant' Agata. All the Ricordis were astute, and none more so than Giulio, but they needed to get up very early in the morning to get the better of Verdi.

Towards the end of November the long stay in the country came to an end; the winter months were spent again in Paris, where negotiations with the Opéra resulted in the signing of the contract for *Don Carlos*.

A good friend of Giuseppina's was Don Giovanni Avanzi, parish priest of Vidalenzo and canon of the collegiate church of Busseto, who was respected by Verdi, too, for his learning and his liberal tendencies, rare in country priests of that time. Giuseppina wrote to him:

You will say: 'Twenty-seven days in Paris, and you haven't found twenty-seven minutes to write to the poor Canon?' Ah, Signor Canon, I have spent these twenty-seven days . . . in the midst of tribulations. The house in which and from which I write is the third we have lived in: the cook who will prepare our dinner tomorrow is the fourth to enter our house in these few days. Verdi, most happy about all these difficulties, all these tribulations, that I have to surmount and conquer, strokes his whiskers, and waits for me to ask him in grace to return to an hotel.

But she was determined not to do so, and they settled at length in the Avenue des Champs-Élysées, No. 67. The contrast between life at Sant' Agata and life in Paris was extreme, and Giuseppina, perhaps to her surprise, found that the advantages were not wholly on the one side.

Here everything proceeds feverishly, at a furious pace. The mass of the population work, talk, dance, run to the theatres, to festivities, to outings —today, tomorrow, in summer, in winter, always, always!! At Busseto and similar places they hardly vegetate; in Paris they devour life. Who is right? Neither of them, I think. (I live amid the giddy whirl without taking part in it, just watching this life of convulsions.) In those towns where activity is minimal and everything reduces itself to a material, and grossly material, existence, every aspiration to higher things, to progress towards ideal perfection, is buried in the task of digestion and the need of sleep. In the great cities, like this Paris, the artery and heart of modern civilization, life is synonymous with frenetic activity, with desire to possess, to enjoy. Glory, power, luxury, pleasure . . . and, above all, money! Money!

And all too often it was transmuted into a golden key opening all the doors leading to Armida's garden.

Drafting a letter for Verdi on 11th February, however, to the baritone Filippo Coletti, born at Anagni, but living in Rome, Giuseppina found at the bottom of her inkpot a drop of gall:

Your letter, received the other day, was very welcome. It was proof that you have not forgotten an old friend. What happens to you at Anagni doesn't surprise me: all small towns are retrograde, dirty, hypocritical, impossible! You fled from Anagni and I avoid as much as possible entering Busseto, because like you I am pointed out in the streets as an atheist, a proud man, etc., etc. You and I are honest men—that is one of our offences. The other is more serious: our fault is to have made our fortunes by our talents. We are persons, therefore, a little distinct from the generality. What a crime in the eyes of the spiritless sheep! We should perhaps have found some indulgence if our backbones were more elastic, for the making of bows, but dignified politeness sets these pretentious insects of the small towns in a fury. May the light of progress purify the corrupt atmosphere of those parasitical and ill-behaved populations! Amen!

Good news had arrived that Giuseppe Piroli, a close friend of Verdi's though born at Busseto, had been elected deputy in his place. Another friend in the town was Cesare Finzi, to whom Giuseppina wrote on 23rd February: [1]

[1] *Nozze Liscia-Formiggini* (Spezia, 1901).

You will be justifiably surprised that I haven't yet replied to your kind and sensible letters, but in Paris, if *man proposes, time disposes*. That is my case and although I don't run around, like the Parisians, to balls and festivities, yet, living in this restless atmosphere, one is drawn, willy-nilly, to right and to left, with much strain on body and spirit, much waste of time, and little or no satisfaction.

I am glad to hear that Signor Antonio is well, and is keeping himself amused. I propose, on return to Sant' Agata, not only to make him repeat, twenty times over, all he has said and done at Parma, but to make him draw in chalk all he has seen in the ex-capital; I'm quite sure no previous description has ever been given with greater exactitude or at greater length.

I won't mention politics, because I cannot cry 'Hallelujah' about our affairs, as I should like to do and would be able to do if the personalities and parties concerned weren't so mean, violent, egoistic and cruel towards this mother country of ours, this ancient land of heroes, of poets, of scientists . . . and let's add, to our shame, this ancient land all too celebrated for its civil wars!

I can't tell you what pleasure Piroli's nomination has given me. First because Piroli is neither retrograde nor headstrong, but follows the straight road that every citizen and representative should follow, so that the Italians may become a strong, united and powerful nation. Then I love Piroli as a fine, courteous, sincere, well-informed man, and all that without that oppressive arrogance of the pedants, which I detest as much as and more than my own sins.

Dantan, as you will perhaps have seen from the newspapers, has done a bust of Verdi and, out of regard for the eminent sculptor and making an exception to our usual habits, we gave a kind of soirée at which Verdi, the sculptor and the bust were acclaimed with loud hurrahs by the friends assembled for the occasion.

I hear with pleasure that my father-in-law is not too much tormented by his disabilities. Greet him warmly from us, along with Filomena and all the family.

Verdi and I beg you to salute for us Pesci and the few friends we have. We both send our kindest regards and I in particular greet you as

your servant and friend

GIUSEPPINA VERDI.

Towards the end of March 1866, after a few days at Genoa, she found herself back at Sant' Agata, and quietly happy to be there, amid the first flowers, the singing birds and sunshine of an early spring. The watchdog Black had made them welcome. 'The poor thing is getting old, like his master and mistress,' she told Arrivabene. 'If you had seen him on our return from Paris, you would have been moved. I thought he would fall dead in convulsions of joy at seeing us again. I don't know whether a monkey is a degenerate man, but certainly man, where the heart is concerned, is far from being a perfected dog.' Additions to the menagerie were contemplated. Verdi dissuaded her from having another pet dog, since the loss of Loulou had nearly broken her heart. But a parrot was sent by Mariani from Genoa. 'The parrot is here in my room, in the warming sun, after having eaten some polenta, from among the various things offered. It seems really to have a gentle disposition, for it gives its claw, it comes on my shoulders, and it gave me, too, in its way, a few kisses, a proof of sympathy that I accepted with much prudence, not unaccompanied by some apprehension.' The arrival of a monkey was expected, but it died prematurely.

Just how good a friend Giuseppina could be is seen in a letter of 12th April to Corticelli, who had got into difficulties and tried, unsuccessfully, to obtain an advance or borrow money from his associates:

> I perfectly understand your position and, knowing you so well, I know how much it must weigh upon you. What you tell me about the request made to those gentry, and the reply you got from them, distresses me but doesn't surprise me. I don't know whether there is any truth in spiritualism, magnetism, somnambulism; what I do know is that, to my fortune or misfortune, I see through people as though they were made of crystal, and I've seen enough of those people of yours to anatomize them morally better than you who have been together with them for so many years. Take them as they are, and, by honesty and prudence, try to put your affairs in order, so as not to let yourself be caught unawares. You were very wrong, in your moment of need, not to send me word. I don't need very much for my *toilette* and (especially of late) the liberality of my protecting angel is sufficiently great to permit me some small savings. I should have sent you at once that little hoard of mine, no one would have known anything about it, and you would have spared yourself disillusionment over those gentry, which must have been very bitter for you. I hope you never find yourself in such a tight place again, but, in any case, as far as the modest purse of your old friend will reach, draw upon it freely.

She had learned a good deal from Corticelli about Adelaide Ristori, already past her prime, but unable to accept the idea of retirement. The actress is referred to in these letters as 'the Invalid' (*l'Ammalata*); her disease was a craving for applause:

> As for your Invalid's intention of making an end in 1867, I don't believe in it at all! Avarice, vanity and *the exigencies of her disease* will cause her to wander to all the corners of the earth, until the boredom and disgust of those who will have, so to speak, to suffer her, will force her to bring down the curtain. But then she will be, I'm afraid, and I shall regret it, unhappy —most unhappy!

There are several other passages on this subject. The prediction was accurate enough: for another twenty years la Ristori was to wander round the world.

Meanwhile Verdi was working at Sant' Agata on *Don Carlos*, plagued as usual when composing by chronic throat trouble. By early

May he had reached the beginning of the fourth act, but political developments were distracting him from his work. Italy had recently concluded an alliance with Prussia, and was preparing herself for a renewal of the struggle with Austria. Verdi's attitude before hostilities commenced was positively bellicose: 'War is inevitable. Things have reached such a stage that even if the whole world didn't want it, we should want it. The mass of the people can't be held back any more—that is no longer even in the power of the king—and, come what may, war must be waged.' As the young men of Busseto were called up, mothers and wives wept, the farmers complained of the loss of their labourers, but things went better than he had expected. 'As for the priests,' he told Piroli, 'their attitude is decent enough. They daren't show themselves hostile. It is certain, however, that if they saw the tip of the nose of a German they would go to meet him, with monstrance, censer and sacrament.' If war came, Sant' Agata would be in the front line, and it would be necessary to leave. 'It's certain that I should become a target, not so much for the Germans as for the priests.' War did come, and the windows of Sant' Agata were shaken by the gunfire. Reports in the London *Musical Standard* and elsewhere that Prince Umberto had made Verdi's house his headquarters were untrue. The Italian army advanced and met with disaster at Custoza on 24th June; the Prussian victory at Sadowa nine days later more than redressed the balance, and put Italy on the winning side, but she was humiliated. Venetia was ceded by Austria to Napoleon III, who after a plebiscite was later to pass it on to Vittorio Emanuele.

On 5th July Verdi and Giuseppina had moved to Genoa to the Albergo Croce di Malta, whence Giuseppina on 13th July wrote to Corticelli:

> Verdi is in a black mood, and I am too. . . . No Italian of any feeling could be, at this moment, tranquil and gay, especially those who are obliged to go to the Capital of the Braggarts. . . . Don't tell anyone that I've written that perhaps we shall go to Paris, because, with Verdi in this mood, I shouldn't be surprised if he sent to the devil the Opéra, Perrin, Paris and everything else, and returned to Sant' Agata.

The next day Verdi asked to be released from his contract. But his request was refused; it was necessary to go to Paris. There is a curious letter to Escudier, dated 18th July, asking him to go personally to see Madame Baratte, owner of the house in the Avenue des Champs-Élysées, Verdi's lease of which had not yet expired, and insist that the carpets should be thoroughly beaten before his arrival, dust having fatal effects on his throat. The last act of *Don Carlos* was written partly in this house in Paris and partly at Cauterets, a watering-place in the Pyrenees. From there Giuseppina wrote on 20th August to

Corticelli, who was about to leave, not altogether happily, for an eight months' tour of the United States with Adelaide Ristori and companions. She assured him that the gates of Sant' Agata would always be open for him and asked him to bring back from America 'a beautiful cockatoo or a macaw—whatever you like, as long as it's a beautiful creature', to add to her collection. On 22nd September, from Paris, she wrote to Antonio Barezzi: 'We are back from Cauterets. I am well, Verdi is well, Paris is well, and would be better still if the cholera would wholly depart; I know that you are well, Maddalena is well, my father-in-law is well, Filomena, the household servants and Signor Polly Parrot are well, and God grant that all of us may stay well at least until the year 2866! What do you say, Signor Antonio? Another thousand years or so wouldn't be bad, eh?' This letter is an example of a kind of word-spinning at which she was expert; there was nothing much to say, but she knew the dear old man was always thinking of them, and longed to hear from them; in a cloud of light banter and gossip she conveyed all her affection. Barezzi's own surviving letters to Verdi and Giuseppina are without literary value; some of them are in the hand of his second wife and ex-servant, Maddalena, who could not spell; they reveal only his goodness, his great simplicity and his boundless love.

Many letters of this year to Giuseppe De Amicis and, in particular, to Mariani, concern the choice and the furnishing of an apartment they had decided to take for the winter months at Genoa. This was in the Palazzo Sauli, on the hill of Carignano. A letter to the previous tenant, named Muller or Müller, is addressed to 100 Albany St, Regent's Park, London. Part of Muller's furniture was being taken over, together with 662 bottles of wines and liqueurs, and the letter, in September, complains that Verdi's friends had found that there were actually less than 600 bottles left. The *gran salone*, the reception-room, dining-room, and Verdi's and Giuseppina's bedrooms were to be furnished anew; also the billiard-room, Verdi refusing to have Muller's billiard-table at any price. Some of the new furniture was bought in Paris. While Verdi was scoring and rehearsing *Don Carlos* Giuseppina was almost equally busy, shopping, packing things up, dispatching them to Mariani at Genoa, and corresponding with everybody concerned. All this, and the bustle and noise of the French capital, tired her out. On 15th November she told Canon Avanzi: 'I want Verdi to finish this *Don Carlos* quickly, so that we can return to Italy. I have need to *vegetate*, or rather, to live in silence and quiet for a while. In this Paris life is just a violent, rapid, exhausting fever that bears one panting towards the grave. . . . I am tired without working, I have time neither to read nor think, in the city they say is the most intellectual in the world. I cannot stand this unbridled movement of men and things any longer. I have reached the point almost of feeling benefit and relief when I see a funeral pass. In death is calm and repose! Blessed are the dead, in the kiss of God!' To Corticelli she wrote: 'It doesn't surprise me that charlatanism and imposture are greater in America than in France, since the *Barnums* were born, or were invented, in America. Only the French are the charlatans *par excellence* of Europe, though one must agree that they have much wit and, I would dare to say, *good nature* in their charlatanism. Perhaps they will perfect themselves by the example of the Americans, but for the present they are slightly less dishonest.' Another letter of 7th December says:

Verdi, with his opera, cannot give a thought to anything that might distract him. You know that we have settled on an apartment at Genoa, and that this apartment has to be furnished and decorated . . . and all that with the least possible expense, because money doesn't rain on us from the sky as it does on you people. So I have had, and still have, to run to right and left, and, God willing, in eight or ten days everything will be packed up and I shall be able to breathe a little. Add that, through I don't know what aberration, we have begun to give a little dinner-party every week! . . . *Don Carlos*, God and the Tortoises of the Opéra willing, will perhaps be put on at the end of January. What a punishment for the sins of a composer is the staging of an opera in that theatre, with its machinery of marble and lead! Just think! I am burning with impatience to go to Genoa and put in order and enjoy the apartment, and at the Opéra they argue for twenty-four hours before deciding whether Faure or la Sasse is to raise a finger or the whole hand.

One joy at this time was to see Muzio again, who had returned after several years in the United States, where he had married a young singer, Lucy Simons. After he went to Italy in December Giuseppina wrote him an affectionate letter: 'Your departure from Paris has left a great void in the restricted circle of our friends. Seeing you every day again, after so many years' absence, had rejuvenated us and carried us back to the time when you often lived with us and were like a relation, or rather, better than the general run of relations, an intimate and most dear friend. Perhaps it would have been better if you hadn't returned to Europe. We were resigned to separation; now, when you go back to America (where you must return, if you have faith in the advice of your old friends), we shall seem to lose you a second time.' She told him he would find Signor Antonio, Giovannino, Carlo Verdi and the rest quite unchanged at Busseto. To Corticelli she remarked: 'I don't know whether Emanuele has done well to marry a woman so young. There must be at least twenty-five years' difference between them.' And, in another letter: 'I am fond of Emanuele, but I'm afraid that he is still, and will remain for a long time yet, a boy, as far as knowledge of the world is concerned.'

Bad news arrived in January of the sudden death of Carlo Verdi at

Busseto; he was buried, in accordance with his last wishes, beside his wife Luigia in the little churchyard at Vidalenzo. Verdi being absorbed in the preparation of his opera, Giuseppina took on practically the whole correspondence necessary in consequence of this bereavement. Besides letters to Angiolo Carrara about funeral and family arrangements, she wrote to almost all Verdi's friends for him, to Barezzi, Muzio, Piave, De Sanctis, Mariani, Morchio and others. To Corticelli she wrote:

> Your letters are always welcome, but at this moment of great sorrow they are a drop of dew on an afflicted heart. Verdi's father, an octogenarian and ill for four years, ceased to suffer and rendered his soul to God in the night of the 14th of this month! Although his age and illness made us foresee that his end was near, yet his decline and death were so rapid as to augment, if that is possible, the sorrow of this loss. Verdi is extremely grieved and I, in spite of the fact that I have lived very little with him, and that we were at the antipodes in our ways of thinking, feel the keenest regret—perhaps as keen as that of Verdi. Poor old man! God have mercy on him, and bless him, with us, in all eternity!

All the letters she wrote on this occasion are different, deeply felt, in no way conventional. A passage in one to Angiolo Carrara says: 'I thought little Filomena had gone back to her mother during those days of anguish, but I hear that you have kindly taken her into your house. Verdi and I sincerely thank you.' Filomena, already mentioned in letters to Barezzi and Finzi, was Verdi's second cousin, a girl of seven, who for some time had lived with Carlo Verdi at Busseto. Her parents, poor peasants with a large family, lived at Le Roncole. Verdi and Giuseppina took a great interest in her, had arranged for her to have lessons from the school-teacher, Signora Landriani, and were a little later to take her into their own home and practically to adopt her. After adoption she was called Maria. In Angiolo Carrara's house, where she found shelter after Carlo Verdi's death, she was afterwards to find a husband.

The production of *Don Carlos* was deferred from the end of January to the end of February, and then to 11th March. 'You can well imagine', Giuseppina wrote to Corticelli, 'that the next day the trunks will be ready for our return to Italy. I have never so much wanted to return to the peasants as this time! . . . Don't misunderstand me: to the peasants, not to Busseto.' And the day after the first performance they did leave. 'It was not a success,' said Verdi. On 14th March they arrived at Genoa, and took possession of their new home in the Palazzo Sauli, where a very busy time began for Giuseppina. She wrote to Giulio Ricordi on 29th March: 'It's very difficult to give a sign of life when one has been almost buried for eight days amid the dust and the rags that encumber every corner of this enormous apartment. Add—and it isn't a small thing—that there are bricklayers, paperhangers, carpenters, painters, etc., etc., and I am alone here to direct and to fight with this cohort of blunderers, since Verdi has thought well to stay out of it and plant cabbages in the Athens of Italy, which is to say, in the neighbourhood of Busseto.'

A most affecting episode took place in May 1867. Giuseppina, still occupied with furnishing problems, went from Sant' Agata to Milan, alone. There, without forewarning, she summoned up her courage and called to see Clarina Maffei, introducing herself by sending in Verdi's portrait. The visit was an enormous success; Giuseppina and Clarina, laughing and weeping, fell into each other's arms. Clarina then had the wonderful idea of taking Giuseppina to see Manzoni, her 'Saint', idolized also by Verdi, who had yet always hesitated to approach him in person.

The draft of Giuseppina's first letter to Clarina Maffei, written at Locate on 17th May, is found on a loose sheet of paper inserted in her letter-book:

How wrong I was to be so nervous about my daring venture, presenting myself before you with only my little portrait to introduce me! I ought not only to have hoped, but to have been sure that you would have thrown your arms round my neck, as you did, and confused in your angel's heart your old friendship for Verdi with the new one with which you have honoured poor Peppina. When, however, here in the quiet of this room, I think of all I did the other day, I hardly recognize myself and almost break into a cold sweat of embarrassment! But throwing a glance at the precious things spread on my table, which I owe to you, my embarrassment vanishes and—in spite of my rotundity—I jump for joy, and kiss your little note and the violet and the ivy-leaf. . . . At sight, however, of the portrait of Manzoni tears come into my eyes; I jump no more, but there is such consolation in this feeling of respectful tenderness that no festival in the world could compare with it. To have seen him, to have spoken to him and touched the hands of that Saint, is an occurrence and a memory that will remain indelible in my mind and heart all the days of my life. This honour I owe to you, excellent creature, not on my own merits, but because you love my Verdi with unalterable friendly sentiments, and because, I being his wife, doing for me something so welcome, so longed-for, you knew you were doing it still, and at the same time, for Verdi himself. . . . Verdi has always spoken to me about you as of his dearest friend, and the most worthy of being that, so although we saw each other for the first time only the other day, we have nevertheless loved each other for a long time.

Then came the joy of breaking the news to Verdi on her return home. The story is told in a second delightful letter to Clarina, the draft of which, in the letter-book, is dated 21st May:

The exertions and emotions of recent days raised my temperature to boiling point, and I arrived home with a magnificent headache, which, if it prevented me from writing yesterday, yet allowed me to give Verdi an account of all that happened at Milan. He was waiting for me at Alseno station, with little Filomena, and as soon as we were in the carriage he asked about my family and what I had done at Milan regarding the furniture. I said that I had been all over the place without finding anything I wanted, that I had seen the Ricordis and Piave and his charmers, and that, although pressed for time, I should have called on you if he had given me a letter for you, in spite of a certain reluctance owing to the *embonpoint* which for three years now has excluded me from sentimental women's gatherings. While he, laughing, bestowed on me the flattering epithet 'Capricciosa' (given only to young women, and for a long time I have not been that), I very quietly extracted your little note from my handbag, threw it on his knee, and procured for myself, as soon as he had glanced at it, the sight of a big row of teeth, including wisdom teeth!

I told him then very quickly, at breakneck speed, how you had received me, how (an extraordinary thing for you) you had gone out with me, how foolish I had been to wait so many years before making your acquaintance; and he kept on saying: 'It doesn't surprise me; it doesn't surprise me; I know Clarina.'

Wishing to push on as fast as possible, I said with affected indifference: 'If you go to Milan I'll introduce you to Manzoni. He expects you, and I was there with her the other day.'

Phew! The bombshell was so great and so unexpected that I didn't know whether I ought to open the carriage windows to give him air, or close them, fearing that in the paroxysm of surprise and joy he would jump out! He went red, he turned deadly pale, he perspired; he took off his hat and screwed it up in a way that reduced it almost to shapelessness. Furthermore (this is between ourselves) the most severe and savage Bear of Busseto had his eyes full of tears, and both of us, moved, convulsed, sat there for ten minutes in complete silence. Oh, the power of genius, of virtue and of friendship! Thank you, my good Clarina, at once in Verdi's name and my own. Since Sunday, in this solitude, your name and that of our Saint are repeated at every moment, and with what accompaniment of praises and affectionate words I leave you to imagine.

Now Verdi is thinking of writing to Manzoni, and I laugh, because if I was so overcome, confused and foolish when you procured me that great honour of finding myself in *his* presence, it pleases me that those, too, who are much more than I am, feel also a bit of embarrassment, pull their whiskers and scratch their ears to find words worthy of saying to the mighty.

The more I think of it, the more I marvel, not at my gross foolishness, but at the incredible, and yet sincere and profound modesty . . . of whom? —of him who wrote the greatest book of modern times!

Like all the best letter-writers, Giuseppina reveals to each of her different correspondents a different aspect of her personality. In writing to Clarina Maffei she employs for her sprightly narratives a more studied, literary vein, born of an immense desire to please and the consciousness of her new friend's intellectual background. This letter from Genoa, of 14th June 1867,[1] is justly celebrated:

I have been wishing that my teeth, the carpenters, the paperhangers and all my present tyrants would leave me one day's breathing-space, in order to have the pleasure of writing to my friends in peace. It is seven o'clock in the morning; Verdi left yesterday for Sant' Agata, and I am writing all alone in a large hall with a view of the sea—that sea which I adore, and which gazes at me (the deceiver!) calmly and smilingly, like a happy bride the day after her wedding.

The bride and you, my dear Clarina, are able to be happy, because you don't know the unpoetic fever of removals and of furnishing a house. As for myself, I have been so often afflicted with these calamities that I ask myself sometimes whether I really once belonged, more or less worthily, to the company of singers in or out of tune, or whether I did not rather serve a long apprenticeship in Righini's or another upholsterer's shop. For the rest, Verdi, circumstances and I myself have been the cause of the setting up of these many different homes, and thus of my present troubles.

Many years ago (I dare not say how many), since I loved the country so much, I asked Verdi, with some insistence, to leave Paris, to go and enjoy, under the canopy of the open sky, those salutary baths of fresh air and sunshine which bring strength to the body and tranquillity to the mind. Verdi, who, like Auber, had almost a horror of country life, consented after much persuasion to take a little house a short distance from Paris. The pleasures of this new way of life were a revelation to Verdi. He came to love it so much, so passionately, that I found myself surpassed, and my prayers only too well answered, in this cult of the woodland gods. He bought the estate of Sant' Agata, and I, who had already furnished a house at Milan and another in Paris, had to organize a *pied-à-terre* in the new possessions of the illustrious professor of Le Roncole. We began with infinite pleasure to plant a garden, which in the beginning was called 'Peppina's Garden'. Then it was enlarged and became *his* garden, and I can tell you that in this garden of *his* he now reigns like a czar, so that I am reduced to a few feet of ground in which, by agreement between us, he has no right to poke his nose. I could not conscientiously affirm that he always respects this agreement, but I have found a means of calling him to order by threatening to plant cabbages instead of flowers. This garden, which was progressively enlarged and made more beautiful, called for a rather less *rustic* dwelling. So Verdi turned architect, and I can't tell you how, during the rebuilding, the beds, the wardrobes and all the furniture danced from room to room. Suffice it to say that, except for the kitchen, the cellar and the stables, we have slept and eaten our meals in every corner of the house. When the fate of Italy was in the balance and Verdi, with those other gentlemen, took to King Vittorio the results of the plebiscites in the different States, Guerrieri, Fioruzzi, etc. came to Sant' Agata and had the *honour* of dining in a kind of ante-room or passage-way, in the presence of families of swallows, which flew calmly in and out through a grating, bringing food to their young. When God willed, the house was finished,

[1] Drafted in the letter-book on 13th June.

and I assure you that Verdi directed the works well, and perhaps better than a real architect. And that was the fourth home I had to furnish.

But the sun, the trees, the flowers and the vast and varied family of the birds, which make country life so lively and beautiful for a great part of the year, leave it sad, mute and bare in the winter. Then I love it no longer. When the snow covers these vast plains, and the trees with their bare branches look like desolate skeletons, I can't bear to raise my eyes and look out. I cover the windows with flowered curtains, up to eye-level, and I feel an infinite sadness, a desire to flee from the country, and to feel that I live among the living, and not among the spectres and the silence of a vast cemetery. Verdi, an iron nature, would perhaps have loved the country even in winter and known how to create for himself pleasure and occupations adapted to the season, but he had, in his goodness, compassion on my isolation and my sadness, and, after many hesitations over the choice of locality, we have pitched our winter tents facing the sea and the mountains, and now I am engaged in furnishing the fifth and certainly the last home of my life.

But this correspondence, so happily begun, takes on, too soon, a sorrowful note:

24th June, in the letter-book, copied and sent on 25th June:

The ivy leaf that you send me, and the lock from that venerable head . . . would have greatly moved me at any time, but now, in our present affliction, have really made me cry. Verdi's old father-in-law, whom I love, and by whom I am loved like a daughter, is in grave danger of his life. Ill for a long time, his condition in the last two days has got suddenly much worse, and we see, to our infinite sorrow, that honest face become more pale and cadaverous every minute. We see those eyes, almost moribund, fixed upon us with affection so profound that it rends our hearts. Thank your Saint for the good and the honour he does us, in remembering us. He, whose faith is sincere and absolute—let him pray God to have mercy on this poor old man and leave him longer with us, who love him so much.

6th July:

We thank you again, with particular warmth, for your sympathy in our sorrow. Poor Signor Antonio is in a pitiful state, and for every few hours of relief has many in which his life is in gravest danger. The other day they called us at midnight; we left in all haste for Busseto and we found him so much worse that certain *most zealous* relations thought well to have a *priest* in readiness! Towards two in the morning the fever abated and the poor old man recovered a little. Today (Saturday) has been tolerable. This morning Verdi and I went to play the upholsterer, adjusting a certain green blind so that air can circulate in the room without the light disturbing him. If only you could see the affection with which he gazes at us! . . . how he clasps our hands when we are about to leave, as if he wanted to keep us near him by main force, the tears would come into your eyes, even without knowing him! Poor old man! Oh, if God would leave him with us for a few years more, what a consolation it would be, for Verdi and for me! But at eighty, there is little hope!

22nd July:

He is dead—dead in our arms! Farewell, beloved old man; our sorrow, our benedictions, our affection, will follow you beyond the tomb. The memory of your goodness, and of all you did for Verdi, will be forgotten only when we, in our turn, close our eyes. His last word, his last glance, was for Verdi, for his poor wife and for me. I can say no more, for I haven't the strength. Weep with us and pray for the peace of the soul of this man we loved so much.

Verdi presses your hands, and I press you to my heart. Farewell. Farewell.

Corticelli was now back in Italy, tired of travelling, and without employment. He was offered the position of bailiff at Sant' Agata, and accepted gratefully. This was in October 1867. A loose draft of Giuseppina's letter to him, conveying the offer, survives. She told him that if he found the isolation and monotony of country life too much for him, he had only to say: 'My friends, I have need to return to a more lively and varied life.' He would be at liberty at once, without any sort of reproach.

This year, which had seen the deaths of Carlo Verdi and Antonio Barezzi, was not to end without a further catastrophe. In December, Piave had a severe stroke which left him paralysed, deprived of speech and reason. Clarina Maffei urged that Verdi should come to Milan; others advised that it would be pointless and terribly distressing for him. Giuseppina wrote to Ricordi on 10th December:

I have just received your letter, which expresses exactly what we thought and still think. Verdi understood that, as you so well put it, Signora Clarina let herself be carried away by an access of feeling. Let us settle things, then, with regard to this journey, which, in the present circumstances, would be of no benefit to the sufferer, and would be most painful for Verdi. If ever poor Piave, recovering awareness, should show in some way a desire to see Verdi and, in the opinion of the doctors, this visit could have no harmful consequences for the sick man, you will have the kindness, Signor Giulio, to send a telegram to Verdi, who will come for a moment to Milan. Otherwise it would mean causing painful commotion to one with no benefit to the other. Verdi has shown, and will show, to Piave and his unfortunate family, what he feels—in a way more efficacious than that of a useless visit, which could even be fatal.

Piave was to linger on, in a helpless state, for more than eight years, sometimes in hospital, sometimes in his home. Correspondence with his wife Elisa appears in Giuseppina's letter-books, concerned with his welfare and that of his young daughter. A letter of 11th April 1868 includes this passage:

I shall say nothing of our surprise at the offers of Sig. Giovanni Barezzi. Only I think it my duty to advise you that it would not be possible for us to pay our respects and thank him in your name, since for a long time now we have had nothing further to do with that gentleman. As for sending Didina for some months to Busseto, to stay with that family, you would be doing something that would certainly be very displeasing to Verdi.

Giovannino Barezzi's offer of hospitality to Piave's daughter does him much credit. He had known the librettist well, ever since he had gone to Venice in 1844 for the first performance of *Ernani*. But this letter shows how implacable was Verdi's resentment against his brother-in-law.

It is pleasant to return to the relations with Clarina Maffei. It must be remembered that Verdi had not seen her for twenty years. Giuseppina, without a word to him, arranged for Clarina to pay a surprise visit to Sant' Agata towards the end of May. 'He received me like a sister,' the countess told a friend. 'He knew me at once, but he didn't believe his eyes. He gazed at me in astonishment; then he blurted out exclamations and embraced me. . . . The house is elegant and most comfortable, the garden vast and beautiful; we shall carry back to Milan whole forests of flowers. This morning Verdi talked to me about rose-trees, of which I send you a leaf for a souvenir. Today we are going to Busseto, and then to visit the house where he was born.' [1] She stayed a week; they talked of the past, and Verdi promised to go to Milan and to meet Manzoni. After Clarina left, Giuseppina wrote:

I go from time to time, as is my custom, to visit the rooms upstairs. I go into the room that you occupied and I ask myself: 'Is it true? Was Clarina at Sant' Agata? In this bed?' Yes, that good, that excellent creature was here to visit and bless the old and new friends that her heart has joined in a single, most holy embrace. . . . Thank you, Clarina, for this appearance of yours, which has warmed my heart. You arrived amid flowers and left amid flowers, almost like a visionary being! And the sadness, the silence, that your departure has left in this house, is not without life and delight! The mind is at rest, thinking of you, who made (in *our* century!) of friendship your temple, your god and all your joys! Bless you! Verdi will write to you. It is still his firm intention to take a trip to Milan and on the Lake. So he'll come before Manzoni leaves for the country. It is fitting that that Saint should clasp the hand of my Verdi, who is worthy of his benevolence.

The visit to Manzoni took place on 30th June; Verdi was deeply moved. It was strange for him to be at Milan again, after so many years. He noticed how the city had grown, admired the new Galleria, and felt again the ties that bound him to the scene of his first successes.

The decision once taken to adopt little Filomena (Maria), there were inquiries about schools at Piacenza, Genoa and Turin. In the latter part of this year, too, Giuseppina's mother and sister were moved from Locate to Cremona, in easier reach of Sant' Agata. In

[1] Barbiera, *Il salotto della Contessa Maffei*, pp. 279–80.

the letter-books are lists of all the expenses of the furnishing of the house at Cremona, with indications of the respective contributions of Verdi and Giuseppina.

There is a flash of wit in a letter to Léon Escudier's wife, on 6th January 1869:

> I thank you most warmly for your kind and affectionate letter. I won't hide from you the fact that I needed two pairs of spectacles to decipher your English handwriting, in the form of the wavy line indicating a trill ∿∿∿∿∿∿∿∿∿∿. When you write to me again, dear Laure, kindly make use of Chinese handwriting. That will always be easier to read than this trill.

Apart from that, there is little gaiety in the letters of this period.

Giuseppina was capable of the most intense attachments—to people, to places, to pet animals—and hence suffered correspondingly intensely at partings, deaths and disillusionment. Verdi was armoured against such things, but she was not. The melancholy silence that sometimes descended on Sant' Agata had been enlivened by the presence of Maria Verdi, as we must now call her. Giuseppina's love for this child was almost more than maternal. But Verdi had decreed, with his usual strong common sense, that Maria should go away to the chosen boarding-school at Turin, the Istituto della Regia Opera della Provvidenza. After the gates of this institution closed behind Maria, Verdi went to Milan, to rehearse the revised version of *La forza del destino* at La Scala, while Giuseppina returned alone to Genoa. She told Canon Avanzi: 'I shouldn't have the courage to do it over again, and at the moment I'm not at all sure whether I shall have the courage to persist in the determination taken to separate from her for so long. I have suffered so much! I weep every time I think of her and I seem to see that open, smiling face in every corner of the house. But she's not there. The school is imposing; it seems to have the greater part of what is necessary to produce pupils *well brought up* and *seriously instructed* . . . but . . . but it seems to me that I, too, should have been able to bring her up well and have her very well taught.' She refused at first to come to Milan, until Verdi went back and fetched her. Afterwards, again at Genoa, she drafted another long letter to Clarina Maffei in a vein both sad and sweet:

> Arrived at a certain age, the most agreeable and the most sorrowful things, those that are longed for and those that are feared, pass, fly away with vertiginous rapidity. Verdi was at Milan, after so many years' absence and such great desire on the part of his friends to see him again! He returned to that box at La Scala, witness of his first successes, of his struggles, of his first artistic experiences—those that are the frontispiece of the book of life for a man of genius! He saw you again every evening, he embraced Carcano, Tenca and other old friends of the 1840's, returning for

a moment to the years of his youth, to the customs and memories of that time. . . . It has all passed, and we have come back to calm, to silence, almost to solitude. Verdi has gone, for a few days, to talk to his trees and flowers at Sant' Agata. I have stayed at Genoa; I don't go out, I am rather neglecting the house, I am reading a lot, and thinking a great deal.

In meditation there is something severe and melancholy which is yet not deprived of delight! As I get older I incline very much to this disposition of mind. I pass in review men and things: in this kind of mental phantasmagoria I see a world by turns laughing, weeping, moved, enraged, and so I go on, abandoning myself to the interminable chain of emotions that different sad or smiling thoughts arouse in me.

It seems to me that the beginning of this letter has nothing to do with what I wished to write, which is, first of all, that I want to thank you again for the affectionate friendship of which you gave me fresh proof during the few days I spent at Milan. Seeing you every day, knowing you to be so good, so indulgent and *sincere* with everybody, including myself who have so much need of that, was a real consolation! You are one of my saints, in the world of my mental apparitions. And with the thought of you in my heart I evoke, as in a dear and mysterious world, the few people in my life who have sincerely loved me, and before whom I have been able to burn, without subsequent regret, the incense of affection, esteem and veneration!

I have sent our visiting-cards to Manzoni. God grant we may be able to send them for many years yet, on that blessed day! When one knows Manzoni one would like to begin life all over again, to make oneself worthy of his esteem and friendship!

As you can see, I have nothing to tell you of my own life, passed as it is these years almost wholly within domestic walls, whence however one can see the mountains and the sea—this eternal marvel among the marvels of creation.

Excuse me, dear Clarina.

This letter of 9th March allows much of her recurrent depression to be read between the lines. There were excellent reports of Maria's progress at school. But Giuseppina had plenty of other worries. At Cremona her mother was behaving like a madwoman, and it was thought she would have to be put into an asylum. Barberina was constantly ill; in a recent letter she had expressed a wish, almost, to die: 'I thank you for the sacrifices you make for me, who never get better, nor does the Lord take me to His bosom.'

Giuseppina was sending money from time to time to Barberina and her mother at Cremona, to her aunt Giovannina at Lodi, to Livia Zanobini at Florence and probably also to Elisa Piave at Milan. A note in her letter-book on 4th April records that she wrote to one Filippo Pagliai, with the comment: 'N.B. Not sent this time any money.' Pagliai was Livia Zanobini's brother-in-law; he is mentioned several times in Verdi's letters to Piroli, who was asked to find for him a minor post in a government office. Giuseppina had noticed that he only wrote when he thought there was a possibility of getting some money from her, and complained to Livia: 'If you really wanted to know more about my health, there are 365 days in the year and you could have chosen one that wasn't always precisely Christmas or Easter. That was a kind of importunity, or demand, which has ended by offending me. What I can or wish to do, whatever the person concerned and the circumstances, I want to do spontaneously, without it being imposed on me by anybody whatsoever.' Payments continued, however, for many years after this.

Verdi had two plans for helping the Piave family. Didina being now of school age, he settled 10,000 lire on her, the interest to pay for her education, the capital to become her *dot*. He also went to great trouble to arrange for the publication of an album of songs by himself, Mercadante, Federico Ricci, Antonio Cagnoni, Auber and Ambroise Thomas, to be sold for Piave's benefit. Mercadante's contribution was brought to Sant' Agata by Cesare De Sanctis in this year; it was dedicated to Giuseppina. Her letter of acknowledgment of 5th July 1869 survives in a loose copy.

There was a misadventure at Sant' Agata to relate to Clarina on 18th July:

> God be thanked, it's over now: and that being the case it's unnecessary for me to try to give you a palpitatingly tragic description of it, but all the same you may know that the *dirty pool*, the infamous dirty pool, very nearly became our tomb. . . . Verdi was in the boat and held out his hand to help me into it. I got one foot in, but in setting down the other the boat capsized and down we both went to the bottom of the lake—really to the bottom! Verdi, thanks be to God, to chance or to his presence of mind, feeling the boat lightly touch his head, was able, raising his arm, to thrust away that sort of coffin-lid. This movement, I don't know how, helped him to get on his feet, and in that position, with incredible promptitude and vigour, helped by Corticelli, he was able to pull me out of the water, where I was unable to move, caught by my dreadfully distended silk clothing, and also almost unconscious of my situation and thus making no attempt to save myself. I'll say nothing of the alarm, the desperation, of my poor sister, who ran off crying 'Help!' or of the fright of all who saw us at that terrible moment. I myself hadn't, so to speak, time to get frightened, because losing my balance and finding myself with two fathoms of water over my head occurred in a flash. I was about to faint when, opening my eyes, I found myself supported by the arm of Verdi, who stood upright on his feet with the water up to his throat, and I thought he must have jumped in on purpose to save me. It was only later that I learned how things happened, and then I was seized with terror, thinking of Verdi and the consequences that unhappy, involuntary bathe could have had for him and for art. I don't matter, being nothing to the world . . . but let's think no more about it. . . . My sister, my mother . . . Blessed Jesus and Mary, how many misfortunes if. . . !

Tell Giulio what happened, as I don't want to have to repeat it over and over again, but for the love of God save us from the newspapers and their lying exaggerations.

Verdi took the incident much more calmly: 'It would certainly have been better if the affair of the lake had not occurred, but there could be no danger. It was impossible for me, reaching the bottom, not to get on my feet, and once on my feet, even with the water up to my throat, all was saved.'

A letter to Draneht Bey in Cairo, drafted in French by Giuseppina for Verdi on 10th August, shows that he was first approached, in the negotiations that led finally to the composition of *Aida*, for a 'hymn' and not for an opera, to be performed at the inauguration of the theatre built in celebration of the opening of the Suez Canal.

The last two volumes of Giuseppina's letter-books are essential for the study of the domestic crisis which overshadowed much of the latter part of her life. But the general interest of the volumes diminishes. Verdi had now resumed his own *Copialettere* and made fewer calls upon her in her secretarial capacity. And as she grew older a good deal of the sparkle went out of her writing.

There are complaints about the servants and advice to Corticelli on how to deal with them. There is news of Canon Avanzi and his numerous ailments, of Maddalena Barezzi, Signor Antonio's widow, with whom conversation was exhausted in ten minutes, and of poor Barberina: 'She lives to take a few steps in the garden.' There is correspondence with Lucy Muzio in Italian and in now very halting English: 'When I shall send word to you in French or in Italian you must think: "She has no time to turn over her dictionary."' There are letters to Verdi's cousin Carlo Uttini, founder of the first kindergarten in Italy, at Piacenza.

Giulio Ricordi sent some of his piano pieces, published under the pseudonym 'J. Burgmein', and Giuseppina had to confess that they were too difficult for her: 'Once upon a time I knew my *do*, *re*, *mi*, *fa*, but now it is only when everybody has gone out for a long walk that I dare, with great respect, ask the pianoforte if it will allow me to touch it!' A little earlier she had told Ricordi that owing to the persistent laziness of her left hand she had given up all idea of making her *début* in a Chopin concerto at Milan: 'Alas! one must resign oneself little by little to renouncing everything—the world, the flesh, the devil, and playing with the left hand!'

In January 1870 Giuseppina's mother died at Cremona.

The unheroic final attainment of Italian unity in 1870, by the absorption of the Patrimony of St Peter after the withdrawal of the French garrison from Rome, gave Verdi little pleasure, 'It's a great thing,' he wrote to Clarina Maffei, 'but it leaves me cold. Perhaps because I feel it could be the cause of trouble, both at home and abroad. For I cannot reconcile Parliament and the College of Cardinals, freedom of the press and inquisition, the Civil Code and the Syllabus. . . . Perhaps tomorrow there will come a shrewd and clever Pope, such as Rome has had so many times before, and he will ruin us. *Pope* and *King of Italy*—I can't see them together even on the paper of this letter.' The Franco-Prussian war and its aftermath greatly grieved and concerned him and Giuseppina. 'It is true that the *blague*, the impertinence and presumption of the French were, and are, in spite of all their miseries, insupportable. But, after all, it was France that gave liberty and civilization to the modern world. And if she falls, let us be under no illusion, all our liberties and civilization will collapse.' Verdi foresaw the wrath to come:

> Our literary men and politicians praise the knowledge, the science and even (God forgive them!) the arts of these conquerors. But if they examined them less superficially they would see that there still runs in their veins the ancient Gothic blood, that they are immeasurably proud, hard and intolerant, despisers of everything that is not German, and of limitless rapacity. Men with heads but no hearts; a strong but uncivilized race. And that king who is always talking of God and Providence, and with the help of these is destroying the best part of Europe! He thinks he is destined to reform the conduct and punish the vices of the modern world!!! A fine sort of missionary! Attila of old (another missionary of the same sort) drew back before the majesty of the capital of the ancient world; but this one is about to bombard the capital of the modern world. . . . I should have liked a more generous line of politics, and the payment of a debt of gratitude. A hundred thousand of our men could perhaps have saved France. In any case, I should have preferred to sign peace, after defeat beside the French, to this inertia that will make us despised one day. We shan't avoid a European war, and we shall be devoured. Not tomorrow—but it will come!

Giuseppina had spent, off and on, about seven years of her life in France. Her letters to her French friends, after the fall of Paris, are highly charged with emotion. She added this note to a letter from Verdi to Camille Du Locle on 14th February 1871:

> Paris, this great Paris, that you call *le Grand Cadavre*—I love it and am proud of loving it. You are, morally, more glorious than you have ever been! I have only one desire—to come and kneel down and kiss the dust of that great country, where my friends have suffered so much! You know me, and know that I tell the truth, and that my words are sincere.

Correspondence of exceptional interest took place in 1872 between Giuseppina and Cesare Vigna, the alienist, at Venice, to whom, twenty years earlier, Ricordi had dedicated *La Traviata*. Vigna, on 2nd May, sent to Sant' Agata a pamphlet he had written, with the intention of confuting Verdi's opinion that it was impossible for a doctor to be a spiritualist: 'I am one, nor am I ashamed of being one, because he will see, if God gives him the patience to read me, that science is not wholly on the side of the adversaries, as the positivists of today make out.' Giuseppina's letter in reply, of 9th May, is well known, having been published by Luzio together with his selection of the letters to Clarina Maffei:

Verdi esteems you too much not to believe your words and to number you, although you are a doctor, among the spiritualists. But, between ourselves, he presents the strangest phenomenon in the world. He is not a doctor, but an artist. Everyone agrees that there fell to his lot the divine gift of genius; he is a shining example of honesty; he understands and feels every delicate and elevated sentiment. And yet this *brigand* permits himself to be, I won't say an atheist, but certainly very little of a believer, and that with an obstinacy and calm that make one want to beat him. I exhaust myself in speaking to him of the marvels of the heavens, the earth, the sea, etc., etc. It's a waste of breath! He laughs in my face and freezes me in the midst of my oratorical periods, my divine enthusiasm, by saying: '*You're all mad*,' and unfortunately he says it in good faith.

Attempts have been made to pervert the clear meaning of this passage, by those who, at all costs and in the face of all the evidence to the contrary, wish to represent Verdi as a Christian and a Catholic. They tell us that the exclamation 'You're all mad' does not refer to the substance of Giuseppina's discourse, but to her poetical manner of talking.[1] The passage, however, which they are careful not to quote in its entirety, simply will not bear this interpretation. Furthermore, the draft in the letter-book shows a crucial variant. There it reads: 'this *brigand* permits himself to be an *atheist* with an obstinacy and calm that make one want to beat him'. She chose subsequently the less drastic form, but first she wrote 'atheist'.

It has been universally assumed that Giuseppina herself was a devout Catholic all her life. The evidence of the letter-books, surprisingly, does not support this idea.

She suggested to Vigna that, if they could meet, he would be a powerful ally in such discussions with Verdi about religion. Vigna at first took up the suggestion with enthusiasm. He replied on 12th May:

Anyone who can write a letter like your last one can be something more than a simple intermediary in the most vital question I would wish to pursue in Verdi's company.

While he, without knowing it, is much stronger than I, even in argument on such a subject, if we, reciprocally helping each other, should succeed in

[1] Lorenzo Alpino, *Verdi umorista* (Milan–Rome, 1935), p. 7; Don Ferruccio Botti, *Verdi e la religione* (Parma, 1940), p. 6.
Mercede Mundula, op. cit., p. 309, and Marcel Moré, 'La foudre de Dieu' (*Dieu vivant*, No. 26, 1954), consider that Giuseppina misunderstood Verdi here.

lessening that painful emptiness, that cruel scepticism which at times poisons the purest joys, the noblest satisfactions, the most sublime aspirations of life, might I not consider myself fortunate in being the occasion and instrument of such an achievement? Let him by all means represent the adversary's role—nothing better, it's the more difficult one. There could come about the case of the philosopher who had never been able to demonstrate God's existence, but became a fervent believer when he studied for all he was worth to disprove it. . . .

You're all mad! Verdi has said it to you more than once. But I, who must at least know more about madmen than he, could add hat often *in delirio veritas* and that sometimes even madmen are to be listened to.

Luzio, who published these extracts from Vigna's letters,[1] deduces from them that he decided in the end not to confront Verdi in open argument, but to leave the hoped-for conversion to providence and the action of time.

Subsequent entries in Giuseppina's letter-books, passed over in silence by Luzio, are of vital importance. The following is from a letter of 29th May:

I believe in God, the first, unknown, unique, omnipotent source of all creation. I feel within me that spark, that atom, emanation of the Divine Spirit, which gives life and movement to the universe and which we call the soul. Thought, conscience, the heart—mysterious powers that move me, approve of me, condemn me—are superior things and will survive my body, destined to die. Death!! The science, the sophisms, the metaphysical subtleties of the theologians and the learned of all the religions of all the ages, strike vainly against this mystery of death, as against that of life, and have nothing to say, just as they have never been able to say, believing it and proving it: *God does not exist!* Even the sceptical Rabelais in his last moments exclaimed: *Je vais quérir le Grand Peut-être.* So he had laughed all his life, to die with doubt in his heart. Other sceptics, or sophists, lie even as they die, saying, out of pride and not conviction: *There is no God!!!* Religions—my dear Vigna, don't be alarmed; I am favouring you with my ideas, my convictions about religions. If you have managed to read me up to this point I admire your patience and indulgence for my boldness.

This passage, on the right-hand side of a divided page, seems to be a collection of notes in preparation for the proposed debate, rather than the draft of a letter:

'Who knoweth whether the spirit of the beasts goeth upward or *downward*?' Admirable and respectful confession for a wise man like Solomon! At any rate he confesses his ignorance concerning the Great Mystery of death and the future.

I have a certain attachment—almost childish, I should say—for the

[1] *Carteggi verdiani*, IV, pp. 285–7.

religion in which I was born; going back, however, to the Gospel of Christ. I would not change, because I dislike apostasy in religion, in politics, in everything else. Conviction alone can justify certain changes, which too often have their origin in the passions or in material interests.

I believe that the religions are the work of cunning or superior men, who, to dominate their fellows or to do them good, have profited by their weakness, by terror, by misfortunes, etc. After all, we have need to invoke a Supreme Being, and man tends always to materialize it, to give it sensible form. And this form and the theocratic laws according to the climates, the needs and the nature of the men who receive these laws. Hence a priesthood originally convinced, exalted; then corrupt, cunning, venal.

Coming from Giuseppina, these are astonishing remarks. From Verdi they would be less surprising, but they are certainly not his. The past participle 'born', in the second paragraph, has the feminine ending (*nata*).

Another letter to Vigna, on 25th June, says:

I believe that on the subject of religions, although in perfect agreement about everything concerning the divine person of J.C., there would be a kind of bifurcation in our opinions regarding the observance of rites before the face of God.

On 3rd September, to Clarina Maffei, Giuseppina wrote:

Verdi is busy with his grotto and his garden. He is very well and in the best of spirits. Happy man! and may God keep him happy for many long years to come! There are some virtuous natures that need to believe in God; others, equally perfect, that are happy not believing in anything, and simply observing rigorously every precept of strict morality. Manzoni and Verdi! These two men give me cause for thought—are for me a true subject for meditation. But my imperfections and ignorance render me incapable of solving the obscure problem they present.

It seems utterly beyond dispute that at this time Verdi was an unrepentant atheist, and that Giuseppina herself, although deeply religious, in the sense that she believed in a God, a Supreme Being, was yet very far indeed from being an orthodox Catholic.

The letter-books have documents of the highest importance to contribute to the study of another controversial subject, to which we must now turn our attention—the relations of Verdi with Angelo Mariani and Teresa Stolz.

CHAPTER

7

The Breach with Mariani

TWO SCHOOLS of thought exist in Italy today among those who write about Verdi. On the one hand are the followers of Gatti, with whom it is axiomatic that Verdi had a love affair with the singer Teresa Stolz, and that this was the root cause of the breach between the composer and his friend Mariani; on the other hand are the followers of Luzio, to whom this idea is anathema. *Parti pris* informs the writings, and deforms the arguments, of both schools; an objective examination of all the evidence is totally lacking.

In the early 1870's, just before and just after Mariani's death, rumours were circulating about Verdi's relations with Teresa Stolz; echoes of these rumours are to be found in contemporary letters. An outrageous account of their supposed relations was actually printed in 1875, running as a serial in the *Rivista Indipendente* of Florence from 4th September to 9th November. This will concern us later.

After Verdi's death, the earliest direct reference to these matters is found in Franco Ridella's 'Giuseppe Verdi: Impressioni e ricordi', published in the periodical *Per l'Arte* of Parma for February and March 1902. Ridella's reminiscences were reprinted separately in booklet form in 1928; the fact that they were actually written much earlier and published in a periodical only a year after Verdi's death, and before biographical controversy had begun, gives them considerable importance. Here is what Ridella has to say about the breach between Verdi and Mariani, in the version published in *Per l'Arte*:

Alas! This beautiful friendship was to be dissolved, or rather broken off. Various versions of the cause of this rupture were current. Some spoke of a celebrated singer, still living, who had dazzled them both and given the palm of victory in the end to the more eminent contestant. True; but the dispute did not begin there. According to others, Mariani had promised his friend to conduct *Aida* at Cairo, and then, having leagued himself with the publishing house of Lucca, Ricordi's rivals, as is known, and in consequence hostile to Verdi, had broken his promise, for the honour of conducting Wagner's *Lohengrin* for the first time in Italy, at the Teatro Comunale at Bologna. This report is, in part, inexact, and I believe I can tell the truth about this matter. Verdi, although he had the greatest esteem for his friend's ability as conductor, could not approve of certain sides of his character, had already accused him more than once of capriciousness, and for some time had been a bit cool towards him. One day in the spring of 1871 the two friends were dining as usual at the Ristorante della Concordia, in Via Nuova (today Via Garibaldi), at Genoa. During the meal they were seen to be conversing animatedly. On leaving, Verdi was heard to say to Mariani: 'Anyone who breaks his word is not a man, but a boy.' They separated, and never saw each other again. Mariani, giving vent to his feelings afterwards with a friend of mine, complained that Verdi would not believe in his illness, which really did not permit him to undertake the hardships of a trip to Africa. Nor was the poor fellow telling anything less than the truth, for although he did go to Bologna to conduct *Lohengrin* he bore within him a cancerous growth which two years later was to bring him to the grave. He died on 13th June 1873, in the arms of a cultured and rich Genoese aristocrat who was desperately in love with him.

The 'celebrated singer, still living', was clearly Teresa Stolz, and Ridella more than implies that it was true that Verdi, like Mariani, fell in love with her. The 'cultured and rich Genoese aristocrat', in whose arms Mariani died, is generally identified as the Marchesa Teresa Sauli Pallavicino.

The altercation in the Ristorante della Concordia had already been reported in print by Ferdinando Resasco, in his *Verdi a Genova* (Genoa, 1901), without reference to any rivalry in love. Resasco only says that rumour had it that Mariani, drawn into Lucca's orbit, had broken his promise to go to Cairo for *Aida*, and then put on *Lohengrin* at Bologna.

In 1907 Giuseppe Lisio, discussing Lucca's correspondence,[1] referred again to Teresa Stolz, without actually naming her, although she was by this time dead. He wrote of 'Angelo Mariani, the famous conductor, whose mistress (they say) Verdi carried off, ruining his life, and it was on this account (they say) that he set up Wagner in Italy in opposition to Verdi'.

The next witness is Gino Monaldi (1847–1932), author of a long series of volumes of musical small talk, in which the same anecdotes recur, though often in slightly different forms. After hinting in various earlier publications that he could reveal the real cause of the quarrel between Verdi and Mariani, he stated in *Le prime rappresentazioni celebri* (Milan, 1910): 'Today, after forty years, it is useless to disturb

[1] 'Su l'epistolario di Casa Lucca', loc. cit.

the ashes of a fire that is spent, and cause the dead to speak when they do not wish to be disturbed. We will say only this: a divergence involving the passions, ending in Verdi's victory, was the pernicious seed from which germinated in Mariani's heart the desire for vengeance.' Only three years later, in *Il Maestro della Rivoluzione Italiana* (Milan, 1913), Monaldi brought himself to say much more:

More than once, treating of Verdi, his life and his works, I have wanted to strike this unknown chord, to open the mysterious gate whence issued that painful disagreement, but I was restrained from doing so by regard due to people then still living. Today, however, when the tomb has closed for ever over the protagonists of that love drama, history claims her rights, and I obey.

Resasco is correct in indicating 1870 [1] as the date of the breach between Verdi and Mariani. The beginning of the conflict, however, goes back to 1868. At that time, and precisely in the month of June, Mariani was at Pesaro, where he had been called to conduct the wonderful Rossini Commemoration, the like of which, perhaps, is not recorded in contemporary history.

I lived, or rather, I was a guest, like Mariani, in the beautiful house of the Carnevali brothers, and our rooms were adjacent. Although young, it had been my good fortune to win the benevolence of the great conductor and to be considered worthy of his confidence. Thus I was witness of his jealous outbursts and his secret torments. In those moments of abandon and discouragement, violent at times, given Mariani's genuinely Romagnolo character, two names often issued together from his lips—those of Giuseppe Verdi and Teresa Stolz. Mariani's love for the famous singer was one of those loves for which one lives and dies!

Monaldi goes on to describe an incident that occurred at one of the Rossini Commemoration concerts at Pesaro, conducted by Mariani. Many famous instrumentalists had lent their services, including the trumpeter Giacomo Brizzi, of Bologna. Tremendous enthusiasm was aroused in the *Inflammatus* section of Rossini's *Stabat Mater* by the combination of Teresa Stolz's high C and a prodigious blast on Brizzi's trumpet. Brizzi considered that he should have been invited to acknowledge the subsequent applause, along with Mariani and the singers, and showed his resentment by not reproducing, on the repetition of the piece, the expected apocalyptic trumpet call. Afterwards Mariani, absolutely beside himself with rage, rushed at Brizzi and violently abused him:

During that ugly scene la Stolz moved neither lip nor eyelid, but remained imperturbable. Mariani was dismayed by her demeanour. On returning home I found him alone, weeping in his room, exclaiming continually between the sobs that choked him: 'That woman doesn't love me any more! And it is he, my friend, my brother, who robs me of her

[1] Resasco actually says, 'after 1870'.

love, which was my whole life! Oh, but I shall avenge myself, and my vengeance will be much grander and more beautiful than that of the cowardly Brizzi! I shall die of it, but I shall avenge myself.'

And his revenge was *Lohengrin* at Bologna, that *Lohengrin* that Mariani had never wished to read or to hear, and of which, by a miracle of genius, he divined every most subtle and delicate shade and movement, surpassing, almost, the intentions and aspirations of the composer, devising and obtaining new effects, which have remained traditional ever since.

Monaldi always gets his dates wrong. He says the incident occurred in 1868 'and precisely in the month of June'—before Rossini was even dead—whereas we know from documentary sources that the Commemoration at Pesaro took place in August 1869.

After another eight years Monaldi had apparently forgotten that he had ever published this story. He decided, in *I miei ricordi musicali* (Rome, 1921), 'to raise the veil that up till now no one has ever dared to raise'. He told the story of Brizzi again and explained:

Mariani was passionately in love with Teresa Stolz, and his love for her had become the law of his life. This he confided to me, with tears in his voice, one night during which the impetus and the anguish of jealousy had driven him from his bed and brought him to my room, there to seek relief and give vent to his feelings. I would not like to say if, or how far, that jealousy was well founded; but certainly poor Mariani was cruelly tormented by his jealous anguish and he had neither doubts nor excuses. He could not understand how the infinite blessing of that love could be stolen from him by his dearest and most trusted friend. 'It's infamous!' Mariani cried, violently beating his fists on the table, at the risk of wakening all the occupants of the house, 'but I will avenge myself! I shall die of sorrow over it, but I will avenge myself.'

We may note in passing that the scene of Mariani's confession has changed. In the earlier account he is found alone, weeping in his room; in the later one he comes in the night to Monaldi's room.

In the same year as Monaldi's *I miei ricordi musicali* there appeared Tancredi Mantovani's *Angelo Mariani* (Rome, 1921), an excellent short book. Mantovani made no bones about mentioning the relationship between Verdi and Teresa Stolz: 'I think there is nothing impermissible and indiscreet in revealing completely what many people knew and know.' He dates the beginning of the affair from the performance of *Don Carlos* at Bologna in the autumn of 1867: 'The Maestro had been present at the last rehearsals of *Don Carlos*, and from then onwards a decided current of sympathy, a reciprocal admiration, perfectly understandable, was established between the great composer and his magnificent interpreter. Sympathy passed from the sphere of art to that of sentiment, and soon became love.'

Monaldi repeated in *Verdi aneddotico* (Aquila, 1926) what he had first published in *Il Maestro della Rivoluzione Italiana*.

The first small voice raised in Verdi's defence seems to have been that of Lorenzo Alpino, who in his article 'Verdi, Mariani, la Stolz e Gemito' (*Corriere del Pomeriggio Illustrato*, Bologna, 19th–20th January 1927) declared that it was absolutely false that the composer ever had a love affair with the singer. Alpino's article was based on information given by Luisa Cora Mancinelli, widow of Luigi Mancinelli, the conductor, who had lived at Genoa in apartments in Palazzo Doria on the floor above those occupied by Verdi. 'Mancinelli's widow denies, curtly and angrily, that there were ever relations between Verdi and la Stolz other than those of the purest and most disinterested friendship. Verdi was never in love with la Stolz and the relations between the celebrated singer and the Verdis were always straightforward, loyal, beyond suspicion.' A more prosaic reason for the breaking off of relations with Mariani was here given:

> Mariani lived at Genoa in the Palazzo Sauli at Carignano, where up to 1877[1] Verdi and la Strepponi also lived. With Mariani was Teresina Stolz, to whom the great conductor was engaged to be married, and the singer had entrusted him with a considerable sum of money, the proceeds of her artistic exertions. They were to have married, and so full and absolute confidence reigned. But one unhappy day la Stolz and Mariani quarrelled and all idea of marriage vanished. La Stolz, who wished to break off relations completely, asked for her money back from Mariani, who first grumbled and then refused, on various pretexts. And then la Stolz asked Verdi to intervene in the financial dispute. In money matters Verdi was very correct and he did everything possible to make Mariani do his duty towards la Stolz, but in vain. It seems that Mariani had lost the singer's capital in unfortunate speculations. From that time onwards Verdi had nothing more to do with Mariani. But love, clearly, did not enter into the matter.

Another of Verdi's friends at Genoa, Giuseppe Perosio, in his posthumously published *Ricordi verdiani* (Pinerolo, 1928), also denied that Verdi and Mariani quarrelled over Teresa Stolz. 'Here I could disclose the real cause of the breach between the two illustrious artists, about which the most erroneous and strange things have been said and written, even by publicists usually well informed. But in due regard to the memory of the illustrious dead, I don't think I ought to discuss the subject; I will only say that the cause of the breach was not a question of a lady, nor of a phrase attributed to Mariani when he conducted *Lohengrin* at Bologna.'

In *Il Lavoro* (Genoa) for 4th September 1929, Alpino, under the pseudonym 'C. Belviglieri', again discussed these matters, in an article 'Un romanzo amoroso di Giuseppe Verdi?' He referred to Perosio's reminiscences, and drew upon the memories of Luisa Cora

[1] This date is incorrect.

Mancinelli, repeating the story about Mariani having speculated with and lost money entrusted to him by Teresa Stolz when they were living together in Palazzo Sauli. This article drew an indignant letter from Maria Cortesi Schnitzer, Mariani's niece, published on 11th September. 'First of all, it is false, absolutely false, that Mariani cohabited with Signora Teresa Stolz; she lived always in the Palazzo Corallo, by the bridge of Carignano, in the Canestri family's house. Mariani never indulged in speculation; the cause of the breaking off of relations between him and Teresa Stolz was quite different. Signora Stolz left him because she was jealous of the fact that Mariani nourished a strong passion, which was reciprocated, for a lady of the Genoese nobility'.

Thus we return to the Marchesa Teresa Sauli Pallavicino.

Such were the conflicting reports, and evidence from witnesses of varying reliability, available when Carlo Gatti came to write his Verdi biography of 1931. It must be remarked that none of the many earlier Italian biographers discussed the story of the supposed love affair at all, either to confirm or deny it. In spite of what had been written by Ridella, Lisio, Monaldi and Mantovani, not a word was heard in Verdi's defence until 1927, and then it came from Mancinelli's widow, whose acquaintance with the composer dated only from later years, from the Palazzo Doria period. Giuseppina's letter-books show that she first wrote to Luisa Cora, as she was then, on 14th August 1879. Perosio first met Verdi in 1876. In the circumstances it was hardly surprising that Gatti, who knew also the article in the *Rivista Indipendente* of 1875 and the correspondence of Mariani with his friend Teodorico Landoni, threw the immense weight of his authority into the scale against Verdi. In Gatti's biography there is no argument on this subject; it is just taken for granted that Verdi *did* betray his friend and Giuseppina.

Our own Francis Toye, writing at about the same time as Gatti, approached the problem with apparent impartiality:

> Verdi would not have been the first man of fifty-seven to have an intrigue with a young and attractive woman. Peppina, a very remarkable and broad-minded person, would not have been the first wife to make friends with her husband's mistress. Moreover, in the operatic world where she had acquired her standards of conduct, the matrimonial tie cannot be said to be regarded in quite the same way as in ordinary society.

But, having seen the article by 'Belviglieri' in *Il Lavoro*, he accepted Luisa Cora Mancinelli's explanation, she having been 'in a position to know the facts' and the explanation itself being 'more consonant with subsequent events as well as with the psychology of everybody concerned'.

From 1931 onwards Alessandro Luzio courteously but persistently attacked Gatti's assumptions and conclusions in this matter of Verdi's relations with Teresa Stolz. It is a fault in Gatti that he seldom argues, but writes out of assumed omniscience. Luzio, for his part, argued readily, and supported his arguments with documents whenever possible. He had wide access, as Gatti had not, to the archives of Sant' Agata and was able to contribute material of capital importance, such as letters of Mariani and Teresa Stolz to Verdi and extracts from Giuseppina's letter-books. The results of Luzio's researches are available in the *Carteggi verdiani*, which include articles originally published in the *Corriere della Sera* and *Nuova Antologia*.

Some short extracts from Verdi's and Giuseppina's letters to Teresa Stolz were published in the *Corriere della Sera* for 30th October 1932 by Giovanni Cenzato; they included no sensational revelations.

A fierce counter-attack on Luzio's position was made by Umberto Zoppi in *Mariani, Verdi e la Stolz* (Milan, 1947), a book of nearly 400 pages, based on the correspondence of Mariani and Carlino Del Signore. Zoppi showed himself singularly ill-equipped to deal with the undoubtedly valuable material that had come into his hands; his commentary is violently prejudiced in Mariani's favour; his arguments are often fallacious and his knowledge of the Verdi literature is evidently superficial; his style verges on the ludicrous. But one can admire his courage, and the letters he publishes certainly cannot be ignored.

A new and revised edition of Gatti's biography appeared in 1951. As so often in similar cases, the result of the revision was not entirely happy. Neither time nor biography stands still. New facts and documents are constantly coming to light which make, every generation or so, a new approach necessary. But biographers grow old, and lose touch with their subjects. Unable to face the task of beginning again and revising, not only their own writings, but their own opinions of earlier years, in the light of the latest information, they generally do what Gatti did—add a little, here and there, cut a little, and ignore what is inconvenient. One can readily admit that the refutation of Gatti's presentation of the Verdi-Stolz relationship became almost an obsession with Luzio in his old age. Some of the arguments he put forward were puerile. But others demand and deserve earnest consideration. They did not get it from Gatti, who ignored them all, together with almost the whole of the *Carteggi verdiani*, Luzio's own great contribution to Verdi literature.

Franco Abbiati's enormous work of 1959 includes much new material concerning Mariani and Verdi, and Verdi and Teresa Stolz. Abbiati adheres, decidedly, to the school of Luzio, and yet the final impression left by his treatment of this subject is strangely equivocal. Some of the documents he publishes raise questions he does not attempt to answer. Faced with a difficult problem, he slips back into sentimental fiction.[1] We are left still without an impartial survey of this crisis in the relations of Verdi, Giuseppina, Mariani and Teresa Stolz.

In a manuscript autobiography,[2] copies of which are preserved in the Biblioteca Classense at Ravenna and the Archiginnasio library at Bologna, Angelo Mariani says: 'I was born at Ravenna on 11th October 1824.' A note has been added on both copies: 'He was born and baptized on 12th October 1821 (thus Dr Romani's certificate of 24th July 1873)'; the copy at Ravenna has a further correction: 'He was born, rather, on 11th October 1821, and baptized on the 12th.' Documents concerning Mariani's early musical activities at Sant' Agata Feltria and Rimini, dated respectively 24th October 1842 and 20th September 1843, bear remarks in his own hand: 'I was then barely eighteen years of age' and 'I was barely nineteen years of age'.[3] He was actually just twenty-one and almost twenty-two years old, respectively, on those dates.

Thus, in almost the first documents to which one turns in sketching the life of Mariani, one seems to find already evident two of his leading characteristics—vanity and untruthfulness.

After directing a brass band at Sant' Agata Feltria, and playing the viola and violin in orchestras at Macerata and Rimini, he was appointed teacher and orchestral conductor to the Philharmonic Society of Faenza. When just over twenty he had married Virginia Fusconi, a girl from the same district as himself, and they had a daughter, who died of consumption at an early age. Matrimonial differences came to a head at Faenza, where Mariani, as Zoppi tells us, 'ended by surrendering to the flattering smile of a local countess'.[4] After scenes of jealousy and face-slappings in the theatre, the breach became irreparable and Mariani separated from his wife, who did not long survive her daughter. When it suited him, Mariani left Faenza 'almost forgetting, or not caring about, his contractual engagements with the Philharmonic Society'. These actions, too, seem entirely typical.

Encouraged by Rossini, he studied composition for a time at Bologna, interrupting his studies to direct, as 'maestro concertatore', a season of opera at Trento in June 1844.

[1] See, for example, the end of his third volume, where a truly sensational document, Giuseppina's draft letter to Verdi, is followed by a mawkish commentary, false from beginning to end.

[2] It was written in November 1866, at the request of Giulio Ricordi, and was used by Ghislanzoni for a biography of Mariani published in the *Gazzetta Musicale di Milano* in the following year.

[3] Umberto Zoppi, 'Documenti sulla giovinezza di Angelo Mariani' (*La Scala*, Nov., 1953).

[4] *Mariani, Verdi e la Stolz*, pp. 73–4.

Mantovani, Zoppi and others state that Mariani made his *début* as operatic conductor at Messina in the Carnival season of 1844, which would normally mean the season commencing 26th December 1843. Mariani himself, in his autobiography, says he was engaged at Messina for the autumn and Carnival 1844–5. This was the long Sicilian season, customary also at Palermo, where at this same time Giuseppina Strepponi was singing, from October to the following March. Zoppi says Mariani's position was that of 'primo violino direttore', conducting with his bow, as was then the practice, from the first violin desk. Mariani himself says he was engaged as 'maestro concertatore e direttore d'orchestra'. 'But in that season', he goes on, 'it was not possible for me to give proof of what I could do because the musicians of the orchestra protested that they did not want to play under a *foreign boy*.' He conducted concerts, however, for the Philharmonic Society of Messina and wrote orchestral and vocal music for them, and marches and other pieces for the band of the Royal Orphanage. In April 1845 he left Messina, spent a month at Naples, where he was encouraged by Mercadante, and then returned to Bologna. After a short season at Bagnacavallo he was back at Messina in November 1845, again as 'maestro concertatore e direttore d'orchestra'.

> But in that year, too, I was able to do little or nothing except write a few pieces for the Philharmonic Society and the Royal Orphanage, since for the players in the theatre it was still my crime to be a *foreigner* and a *boy*. I left Messina before the season ended, because I was bored with that life, but more because I was becoming a target for the hatred of a high government official who, at the instigation of one of my enemies, did everything he could to banish me from Messina.

A later passage of the autobiography says he believes he was the first in Italy to abolish the old post of 'maestro concertatore', as distinct from the orchestral conductor, which made any unity of conception in performance impossible. Perhaps he tried to put his ideas into practice at Messina and thus aroused hostility among the players.

After another month at Naples, he went in May 1846 to Milan, where his real career as a star conductor began.

On 2nd July 1846 Muzio reported to Antonio Barezzi: 'Last night *I due Foscari* was produced at the Teatro Re. The performance was so perfect that it left nothing to be desired. The choruses were very much applauded. And from beginning to end of the opera there was continuous applause, continual cries of "Viva Verdi!"' This was Mariani's Milanese *début*, and his first appearance as conductor of an opera by Verdi. Two new operas were produced later in the month; both were failures, and the performances of *I due Foscari* were resumed. In August Mariani moved from the Teatro Re to the Teatro Carcano:

In that theatre I was able to show myself to be also a tolerable violinist, playing in Verdi's *I Lombardi* the well-known violin solo, which I had to repeat every evening. See p. 276 of the *Gazzetta Musicale*, Anno V (1846), the 'Milanese Weekly Gazette', where the Wrath of God is called down on everything except my violin solo. Please note, however, dear Giulio, that since I first went to Bologna I had entirely neglected that instrument, and if after several years without practice I could still arouse applause, playing at the Teatro Carcano, that shows that from boyhood I played the violin well. Since then, however, I have given it up entirely.

This quotation from the autobiography does not support Zoppi's views on Mariani's position at Messina and elsewhere, and still less does it support the statement of Mario Ferrarini, in a discussion of Zoppi's book,[1] that even at the Teatro Carlo Felice at Genoa Mariani was only the first violin and leader of the orchestra. However big a liar Mariani may have been, he could not have told Ricordi that he had given up the violin entirely, many years ago, if his known position demanded that he should continue to play it daily. The truth seems to be that the old titles of 'primo violino direttore d'orchestra' and 'maestro concertatore' were retained in some theatres long after the functions had changed to those of principal and assistant conductor.

The performances at the Teatro Carcano on which the *Gazzetta Musicale* called down the Wrath of God are also mentioned by Muzio. He told Barezzi that *Ernani* left much to be desired and that he had never seen a worse performance of *I Lombardi*. Apparently the singers were inadequate. But the theatre was crowded, and the season successful.

Verdi's interest had already been aroused. Mariani's name occurs for the first time in the composer's surviving correspondence in a letter to Lanari of 19th August 1846: 'I am vexed and surprised that you haven't replied to the letter in which I complained of Mariani's pretensions.'[2] This has been interpreted, probably correctly, as meaning that Verdi would have liked to have had Mariani as conductor of the new opera he was engaged to write for Florence (*Macbeth*, as was later decided), but that Mariani, already fully conscious of his worth, had asked higher fees than Lanari was prepared to pay.

After engagements at Stradella and Vicenza, Mariani was back at the Teatro Carcano, Milan, in the spring of 1847, when he conducted Verdi's *Giovanna d'Arco* and *Nabucco*, with Ricci's *Michelangelo e Rolla* and a new opera, *I Baccanti*, by Uranio Fontana. For reasons best known to themselves, the Austrian police insisted that *I Baccanti* should be produced on a certain date, before there had been time to

[1] 'Il romanzo "Mariani, Verdi, Teresina Stolz" e le inesattezze storiche di un bel libro' (*Aurea Parma*, July–Dec. 1947).

[2] *Copialettere*, p. 25.

rehearse it properly. A fiasco seemed inevitable, but Antonio Ghislanzoni, who was to sing the baritone role, deliberately absented himself from the theatre on the night of the announced first performance. *Nabucco* had to be substituted for *I Baccanti* at the last moment and the audience seized the occasion for a political demonstration. It was after this performance of *Nabucco* that Mariani was rebuked and threatened with imprisonment by Count Bolza for having given Verdi's music too evidently rebellious expression. Ghislanzoni, who himself tells this story, got off with a few days in jail.

After another season at Vicenza, Mariani left in November 1847 to direct a season of Italian opera at the Court Theatre in Copenhagen. This was interrupted by the death of King Christian VIII on 20th January 1848. Mariani composed a Requiem Mass, and was offered a permanent position in Copenhagen as director of the Royal Chapel, but he renounced this in order to return to Italy during the revolution and war of 1848.

It remains dubious whether he ever actually did any fighting against the Austrians. *Il Pirata* for 26th July 1848 announced that the Teatro Re would be reopening soon with a season of opera: 'The conductor of the orchestra will be the famous Maestro Angelo Mariani.' It looks as though he had found himself a job behind the lines with the equivalent of E.N.S.A. But the announcement in *Il Pirata* appeared on the day after the Italian defeat at Custoza, and by 5th August the Austrians were back at Milan. In the autobiography he only says: 'I came to Milan, I enrolled as a volunteer, and I have never forgotten 5th August 1848, before Porta Romana, and the re-entry of the Austrians.' Zoppi plays with the idea that Mariani may have fought under Garibaldi, after this date, in the last skirmishes around the lakes. But the autobiography says: 'I stayed at Milan until the beginning of September, and then left, having been engaged by the impresario Naum for the new Italian theatre of Pera in Constantinople.'

He travelled by the Austrian Lloyd steamer from Trieste.

Our voyage was somewhat disastrous. We had no little stormy weather, and having gone ashore at Smyrna for a few hours to get something to eat, we found there more than a thousand cases of cholera a day. After leaving Smyrna we had, too, the misfortune to see cholera manifest itself on board, and you can imagine, my dear Giulio, how that cheered us up.

When we were in the Dardanelles, near the Isles of the Princes (it was night-time), we saw Pera in flames! You can't conceive what a desolate impression this made on us; it was such that, having disembarked from the Lloyd steamer, at the sight of that heap of smoking ruins we wished above all things to return to Italy. But the brother of the impresario Naum, suspecting our intention to repatriate, had recourse to the police to prevent us embarking.

Then, by the next steamer, all the company of singers arrived, and so we began at once the rehearsals of *Macbeth*, adapting ourselves perforce to the semi-barbarous life led by foreigners at Pera.

My destiny willed, however, that I should make the acquaintance of Prince Galitsin, at that time First Secretary of the Russian Embassy to the Sublime Porte, and he, a very accomplished 'cellist and a great music-lover, introduced me to His Excellency the Russian Minister, Sig. de Titoff. The latter, in his goodness, conceived such benevolence and esteem for me that in April 1849 he offered me hospitality in the Russian Palace and I remained there until 5th December 1851, when I left Constantinople.

In the Scala Museum are some fragments of a diary kept by Mariani in Constantinople, which give some impression of his social activities there, showing him horse-riding, attending Lady Canning's ball, buying gloves for a young prince, taking tea with His Excellency, delighting the company with improvisations at the pianoforte, composing dance music and drawing-room romances, singing and playing the violin.

His compositions of this period include a new Turkish National Anthem, an album of songs, *Rimembranze del Bosforo*, and two so-called dramatic cantatas, *Matilde*, or *La fidanzata del guerriero*, and *Gli Esuli*, which are probably fragments of a never completed opera.[1] The diary fragments include these passages, of uncertain date, but from 1850 or 1851:

Sunday, 12th. I stayed home all day to study Verdi's *Luisa Miller*.

I stayed in the city in the evening to hear the opera. . . . I liked the opera (Verdi's *I Masnadieri*), but the singers were perhaps a bit weak.

The autobiography explains why he was not himself conducting in the theatre:

I remained director of the Pera Theatre until May 1850, for having been attacked by a chest complaint, which greatly afflicted me and gave reason to fear for my life, I was obliged to stay in almost complete retirement until my return to Italy, so I had to give up the theatre. Sig. de Titoff and all my friends of the Russian Embassy were greatly concerned about me and some of them accompanied me on various journeys in Asia Minor and Egypt. But the symptoms of my illness persisted and left me prey to unspeakable physical and moral depression, so that I thought my end was near when, invited to go to Messina for the opening of what is now the Teatro Vittorio Emanuele, I hoped that the climate there would be beneficial and I accepted the invitation. So on 5th December 1851, as mentioned above, I most regretfully left the Russian Palace in Constantinople and went, by way of Malta, to Messina. I stayed in that town until April of the following year (1852) and the orchestral musicians, who some

[1] They are little more than single arias for soprano, with cabalettas. The words of both are by De Dominicis. In the Piancastelli collection at Forlì is the manuscript of a chorus 'Il piè vacilla', not part of either cantata, headed 'Chorus of Exiles weeping for their distant homeland, taken from the opera *La fidanzata del guerriero*'.

years earlier had not wanted to play under my direction, received me favourably and were prodigal with their praise. However, all that was a matter of indifference to me, for my chest trouble persisted, filling my mind with the utmost sadness. I suffered in consequence from the most desolating melancholia; I was resigned to die! From Messina I went once more to Naples. The good Mercadante received me with his usual courtesy, dedicated to me one of his compositions and arranged always for my *salon* pieces to be performed at his musical evenings. Maestro Florimo too was very friendly, but as my illness still continued, all these demonstrations of affection were almost painful to me, in that they rendered yet more bitter my leave-taking from life.

A letter of introduction to Sir William Temple at Naples, from Stratford Canning, was apparently never presented, since it remained among Mariani's papers:[1] 'Although a great Liberal and having taken active part in the events at Rome [*sic*] in 1848, and bled in the defence of the Cause, he has during the last eighteen months uninterruptedly enjoyed the hospitality of the Russian Minister, M. de Titoff. Lady Canning and I have also seen enough of him to appreciate his talent and amiable disposition to be warranted in recommending him to your favourable notice and kind offices.' It is news that he had 'bled in the defence of the Cause', and certainly curious that a great Liberal should have accepted such favours from the representatives of the most despotic power in Europe. The autobiography continues:

In Naples I learned that at Genoa they were looking for an orchestral conductor, and as I had decided to go to Germany with Sig. de Titoff, who had followed me to Naples, I resolved to pass through Genoa. On arrival at the landing-stage of this city on 1st May, I found Maestri Gambini and Venzano waiting for me. At the Albergo Croce di Malta I received a visit from the Deputy Mayor, Sig. Viani, and, liking the climate, I decided to stay at Genoa for about two months, i.e. just for the spring season at the theatre, which had already begun.

The evening of 15th May 1852, then, was the first on which I appeared before the public here as orchestral conductor. See the *Gazzetta Musicale* of that year, p. 94, the letter from Genoa, where it is stated, too, that after a few hours I conducted *Robert le Diable* at this theatre without rehearsals. It went well, my dear Giulio, but it was the rash act of a careless boy.

When the spring season ended, pleased with my stay at Genoa, I received from the municipal authorities a definite appointment as conductor of the civic orchestra. In the summer I returned to Ravenna, and my native air was very beneficial, so that, by taking great care, in the course of a few years in this temperate climate I succeeded in freeing myself from the chest complaint that had made me so wretched.

Thus began an association with Genoa, its municipal orchestra and the Teatro Carlo Felice, which lasted for the rest of Mariani's

[1] In the Biblioteca Beriana, Genoa.

life. The appointment, sometimes felt as irksome, nevertheless left him free to conduct elsewhere for fairly long periods. In this first spring season the operas performed included Verdi's *Luisa Miller* and *Ernani*, but it was *Robert le Diable* that scored the outstanding success, being given twenty-eight times. Zoppi and Mantovani list the dates of the performances of Meyerbeer's operas under Mariani at Genoa, but it is quite false to suggest, as those writers do, that these works were little known in Italy before Mariani's time. Mantovani says that *Robert le Diable* was new to Italy; Zoppi seems to think it had previously been heard only at Florence. In fact, it had been performed at Florence in 1840, Padua in 1842, Parma in 1843, Verona (with Giuseppina Strepponi) in 1844, Milan (Teatro della Canobbiana) in 1844, Venice in 1845 and Milan (La Scala) in 1846. All these performances preceded those at Genoa in 1852, for which Mariani was not even initially responsible, since he took over the orchestra after the season had begun under another conductor. Then *Les Huguenots* had been heard at Florence, Padua, Turin, Venice, Milan and probably many other places before it was given at Genoa in 1857; and *Le Prophète* was heard at Florence, Turin, Parma, Milan and Venice before it reached Genoa, also in 1857. That much being said, it can be agreed that Mariani found in Meyerbeer's operas a superb vehicle for the display of his virtuosity, and the operas found in him a superlative interpreter.

It is probable that Verdi had made Mariani's acquaintance at Milan in 1846 or 1847. It seems certain that he spent some time in his company in December 1852, when held up at Genoa on his way to Rome for *Il Trovatore*. The first reference to the conductor in Giuseppina's correspondence occurs in a letter to Verdi of 2nd January 1853, from Leghorn, in a passage concerning the reported relative merits, at that time, of two singers, Erminia Frezzolini and Teresa De Giuli: 'I shall take a trip to Florence to hear and judge with my own ears, which are not ass's ears. Mariani has anything but ass's ears, and is a million times greater and better musician than I am, yet I fear that *sex*, sympathy, friendship, vanity, etc., etc., make him a judge sometimes less than wholly the servant and devotee of the laws of Themis, and that not through bad faith, but passion.'

The earliest surviving letter from Verdi to Mariani is that published by Monaldi in *Il Maestro della Rivoluzione Italiana*, p. 90, which must have been written on 7th March 1853 from Venice:

> *La Traviata* was a grand fiasco, and what is worse, they laughed. However, I'm not disturbed about it. Am I wrong, or are they wrong? I believe myself that the last word on *La Traviata* is not that of last night. They will see it again—and we shall see! Meanwhile, dear Mariani, register the fiasco.

The second person singular, the familiar form of address, is already used, as it is in the earliest surviving letter from Mariani to Verdi, in the archives at Sant' Agata, which is from the autumn of this same year, and is concerned with the possibility of a revival of *La Traviata*. Mariani wrote from a summer resort not far from Genoa:

Arenzano, 25th September 1853.

MY VERDI!

I have need of your approval and of your assistance. I am desirous of reviving on this stage your so unfortunate *Traviata*, with the honour that such a stupendous work deserves. I wrote about it to our friend Ricordi, but he replied *that since you had made known to him certain particular and special distinctions concerning that opera, it was necessary for me to approach you and come to an understanding with you alone* (those are his words), *and that, for the rest, following a favourable reply from you, everything could easily be arranged.*

I believe, O my illustrious friend, that I could have no more propitious occasion of satisfying my desire, as la Salvini-Donatelli and Graziani, for whom you wrote that opera, are already engaged for the Carnival season, with the baritone Cresci, a young man gifted with a voice and artistic feeling, and always ready to accept the advice *of those who know*. What do you say? As for the performance of the orchestra and the chorus, of the *ensemble*, in short, it will be my concern to see that everything goes precisely as it should, and as can be expected of those who make up the family of this theatre, now *one of the best in Italy*.

Of the stage-settings and the costumes, it suffices to tell you that Canzio is responsible for them, and in consequence they will be unique and as sumptuous as possible.

For first opera *Il Trovatore* will be given, and I assure you that the performance will be such as is fitting, in every part.

For second opera we shall give *Rigoletto*, desired by everybody, and for third, if you are kind to me, *La Traviata*.

Please don't forsake me!

I should cut a very poor figure, having already vociferated that *La Traviata* shall rise again on the stage of the Carlo Felice.

I am writing from the country, where I have been living happily for a month, surrounded by the most enchanting display of nature. The day after tomorrow I return to town for the rehearsals of *Scaramuccia*, with which the autumn season will open on 1st October. . . .

Forgive me for writing in such haste, but what do you expect? I'm just back from a shooting expedition and a boat is already waiting to take me out fishing!

I await a consolatory reply from you at Genoa. Remember me kindly to Signora Giuseppina. Greetings from your

ANGELO MARIANI.

Verdi's reply is lost, but it may be taken as certain that he refused to sanction the performance of *La Traviata* at Genoa, precisely *because* two of the original singers were engaged. Mariani, however, deserves credit for his proposal, preceding that of Antonio Gallo at Venice, to revive and make a success of the opera.

After this there is a gap in the correspondence of the two men, reflecting an enforced interruption of their personal relations. A month after the above letter was written Verdi left for Paris, and he stayed in France for the best part of the next three years.

Mariani, apart from his summer excursions, remained at Genoa. Another valuable source of information about him is his correspondence with the Dante scholar Teodorico Landoni, the most intimate friend of his youth at Ravenna.[1] The following uncommonly revealing and beautiful letter illustrates the passionate attachments of which Mariani was capable—of which, indeed, because of some inherent weakness in himself, he had need:

Genoa, 30th September 1855.

MY TEODORICO, DEAR FRIEND OF MY HEART,

. . . I am trying to follow your example, and although I feel tired, sometimes, of the bitter war waged on me by base malignity and envy, I end by despising them, and laughing at my enemies, who have recently been harassing me not a little. I imagine myself following you, and it seems that you say to me, holding out your hand:

> Vien dietro a me, e lascia dir le genti:
> Sta come torre ferma che non crolla
> Giammai la cima per soffiar de' venti.

Today has been a very happy day for me, for in hearing from my good mother I had from her also news of the beloved friend of my childhood, my dear Teodorico. . . .

You are far from me, and so I treasure the friendship, formed not long ago, of the most worthy Marchese Pallavicino, a man of wide literary culture, who had the honour of being secretary of the Eighth Scientific Congress at Genoa. This good creature, I assure you, O my Teodorico, is a second father to me, and through him I experience the comforts of the studious life, which I should vainly seek among the silly multitude who encumber my steps.

The happy days of our childhood are always present in my memory, when, clasped in friendship's close embrace, we went to pass whole days, almost, in our poetic Pineta, now the desire of my heart. Do you remember, beloved friend, our readings together of *Daphnis and Chloe*, of the *Decameron*, of the *divine* Plutarch, and Alighieri's sacred poem, in the coolness of those perennial shades? I assure you that when I have need of tempering a little the bitterness of this my pilgrimage, it helps if I recall to mind those blessed days, for I do not believe that sentence is true which says:

[1] There are fifty-eight letters to Landoni in the Archiginnasio library at Bologna. I have consulted, as did Gatti, the copies in the Biblioteca Classense at Ravenna.

Nessun maggior dolore
Che ricordarsi del tempo felice
Nella miseria.

In fact, what greater pleasure is there, for him who lies in darkness, than remembering the light; or for him who is in exile, than remembering his country? The soul flies on the wings of hope to times of serenity, and its confidence grows that perhaps they will come again.

For the rest, be sure that I regret unceasingly that destiny drove me out alone in this ugly world, and that if by chance I have acquired a little fame, so great were the sufferings I had to undergo in order to win it, and so great my disillusionment about this wretched combination of skin and bone that is called humanity, that I have to confess I should have been happier if I had never left my humble home and my friend.

Tomorrow the rehearsals begin, at the Teatro Carlo Felice. For nine months now I shall have to wrestle again with that singular race of the so-called *Signori Virtuosi*. La Bendazzi is once again our *prima donna assoluta* and she has chosen (very badly, in my opinion, for it's a very old opera for this public) Verdi's *Ernani* for the first opera of the season.

The Marchese Pallavicino, here mentioned for the first time, was the father of that Teresa Sauli Pallavicino (Sauli would seem to have been her mother's maiden name) with whom Mariani is said to have had a love affair, and in whose arms he is said to have died. She was a young girl at this time. Among Mariani's numerous *salon* compositions is a volume of songs, *Il Trovatore nella Liguria*, dedicated 'alla nobil donzella Teresa Pallavicino'.[1]

In July 1856 Mariani came to London to arrange for the publication of some of his compositions. He never conducted in this country but, according to the *Gazzetta Musicale di Milano*, he took part in the course of about a month in sixteen musical evenings at the houses of Lord Malmesbury and others. Mariani, as we have seen, liked always to move in high society.

The first actual musical collaboration between Mariani and Verdi was the production of *Aroldo* at Rimini in the summer of 1857. Eugenio Checchi[2] tells how during the rehearsals Mariani made the orchestra repeat over and over again the storm music in the last act, without being able to get the effect he wanted, and how Verdi at last told him to give it up and get on with the rehearsal. Afterwards he explained: 'God preserve me from doubting even for a moment your ability or that of your excellent players! But didn't you perceive that it was ineffective because the scoring is faulty? I promise it will be rescored by tomorrow evening.' Checchi regards this simply as the ingenuous confession by Verdi of his mistake, an example of 'the

[1] Precise date of publication unknown. Four songs from *Il Trovatore nella Liguria*, all with this dedication, are included in a volume of twenty-two *Melodie Italiane* published in London in 1859 by Ewer & Co.

[2] *Verdi* (Florence, 1901), pp. 142–3.

simplicity of truly great men'. But Gatti, as is his way, sees more in it than that. He says that Mariani was wounded and began, from that time, to seek means of opposing Verdi, setting up against him, above all, Meyerbeer. Nobody who had had access to Mariani's letters to Verdi could possibly believe this. It is the first of several mistaken conclusions by which the whole chronology of the history of the relations of these two men has been falsified. As for the other anecdote, according to which, when people at Rimini were talking of Verdi's music, Mariani said: 'But this is music that won't last. Talk to me about that of Meyerbeer!' we shall see later that it is drawn from a letter that has been first misdated and then misinterpreted, and that Mariani himself flatly denied he had ever used such words.

After *Aroldo*, in reality, an increasingly warm friendship developed between Verdi and Mariani. On his journeys by sea, to and from Naples and Civitavecchia, Verdi generally spent a few days at Genoa, where Mariani made himself useful and agreeable. A letter to Cesare De Sanctis of 29th April 1858, after the conclusion of the battle with the Neapolitan censorship over *Un ballo in maschera*, says: 'At Genoa I visited the theatre, but in strictest incognito. Mariani had me enter by a secret door and, without meeting a living soul, I went to a box in the fourth tier where (bchind drawn curtains) I heard the first two acts of *Mosè*.' Mariani's first visit to Sant' Agata took place later in this year. And from this year onwards his surviving correspondence becomes almost superabundant.

There are two hundred and twenty-nine of Mariani's letters at Sant' Agata, many of them of enormous length, from the years 1858–70. Only eight letters were published by Luzio in the *Carteggi verdiani*; others are included in Abbiati's volumes. Verdi's surviving autograph letters to Mariani are divided between the Biblioteca Beriana at Genoa and the Biblioteca Classense at Ravenna: the two collections together comprise fifty-three letters, dating from 1858 to 1864. After the latter date we have to rely, for the Verdian side of the correspondence, on about a dozen entries in Giuseppina's letter-books and a single letter in the composer's own *Copialettere*. Luzio's commentary in the *Carteggi verdiani* is heavily biased against Mariani. He did not know of the letters at Ravenna, although they had been published,[1] and supposed that all Verdi's letters after 1863, the date of the last at Genoa, had been destroyed by Mariani or his heirs because they presented the conductor in an unfavourable light. In contrast with this, according to Luzio, stands 'the eloquent fact that the very voluminous correspondence of Mariani is conserved at

[1] Partly by Zabery, 'Lettere inedite di Verdi e Petrella ad Angelo Mariani' (*Musica*, 16th March 1913), and partly by S. Muratori, 'Lettere del Verdi al Mariani' (in a *Numero unico, Centenario di Giuseppe Verdi*, Ravenna, 1913). The letters at Genoa are well known, at any rate in extracts, from the appendix to the *Copialettere* and from various articles.

Sant' Agata in its entirety'. This is untrue. For instance, between May and December of 1860 we have thirteen of Verdi's letters and *none* of Mariani's. Few such collections survive complete.

Mariani's letters are essential for the understanding of his relations with Verdi. The difficulty in discussing them is that they are almost endlessly long-winded, repetitive and generally badly written. And yet only by reading them in bulk can one gain a clear picture of this man, in his boundless devotion to Verdi and all his works. Mariani *worshipped* Verdi, and would have allowed himself to be cut to pieces to give him pleasure. That, above all, is what emerges from examination of this correspondence.

Such an attitude of intense respect and devotion was a prerequisite for any close friendship with Verdi. Given it, he would relax his severity and treat with a kind of laughing indulgence the weaknesses of natures less adamantine than his own. Not that Mariani was ever allowed to forget that he *had* weaknesses. His pen or his tongue could easily run away with him; his volatility, his indecision and frequent lack of judgment were deplored by Verdi. All this side of Mariani was summed up in the sobriquet 'Wrong Head' (*Testa Falsa*) given him by the composer. On the comparatively rare occasions when his conduct could be entirely approved he was called 'Right Head' (*Testa Giusta*) or 'Good Head' (*Buona Testa*). The subject of these nicknames recurs continually in Mariani's correspondence for many years; there are periods when every letter has some reference to it, when, after fulfilling one of Verdi's numerous commissions, he instances this as an example of his reliability and pleads, only half humorously, for a revision of opinion and the abandonment of the offensive nickname. A few words of praise send him into ecstasies; he is happier if Verdi only omits a few letters, calling him 'Wro . . He . .'; he is grieved when the full nickname is resumed; in the end he accepts it resignedly, in the knowledge that in Verdi's eyes he could scarcely ever do anything right.

In 1858 Verdi's temporary passion for collecting the autographs of famous men was at its height. Mariani made numerous contributions to the album at Sant' Agata, providing autographs of Guerrazzi, Massimo d'Azeglio, Ugo Foscolo and, after a second visit to England, Brougham, Bulwer and others. The Foscolo item was a bill of exchange from the English period, signed with a pseudonym preceded by the poet's true initials. Mariani explained this and added that it was all the more precious as 'an eternal witness to the privations which that noble soul had to suffer in the time of his dolorous pilgrimage *in hac lacrymarum valle*. Poor Foscolo! To think that at times he hadn't even £2 to pay his housemaid!' This was written in a despondent mood, similar to that which found expression in the letter to Landoni already quoted, but in this case Mariani's variations on an unoriginal theme take on a tone of quite grotesque exaggeration: 'It is all too true, O my sweetest Verdi (and you know it by experience)—the lives of great men must always be tormented by the wickedness of this stinking carcass that calls itself *humanity.*' Before recognition comes: 'It is necessary for your heart to be only dust, for your head, with all its immense ideas, to be nothing but a bare skull, for a tombstone to crush that boiling breast in which glowed the most noble passions, the most noble sorrows; and real happiness is impossible for you to discover among this stupid swarm of parrots!' Such ridiculous language helps to explain why Mariani was regarded sometimes at Sant' Agata as a sort of involuntary court jester. Nevertheless, his constant love and desire to serve Verdi are most touching. The letter that accompanied the Foscolo autograph ends:

Continue to love me, for even if I *had* a wrong *head,* that would not invalidate a heart wholly devoted to you and a soul able to nourish itself on your sublime musical inspirations.

Your ANGELO MARIANI,
Good Head.

'Good Head' is thrice underlined.

A projected return visit to Sant' Agata came to nothing because Mariani stayed longer in England and France than had been anticipated. 'You say nothing more about coming to Sant' Agata,' Verdi wrote. 'Were you too bored? . . . You are not wrong, for the place could hardly be more horrible.'

Shortly before Verdi returned to Naples in October 1858 he asked for information about the steamers leaving from Genoa. Mariani replied in minute detail, at great length, on the time-tables of the various shipping companies, Neapolitan and Piedmontese, every corner and all the margins of the paper being utilized. Some of Mariani's letters have to be seen to be believed. When he had reached the end of his notepaper but not the end of his thoughts he would turn the letter sideways and continue at right angles to what he had already written. The result, particularly when the ink has passed through the paper to the other side, is an inextricable tangle of words.

Giuseppina had a nickname of her own for Mariani. She called him 'Frate Lasagna', which is untranslatable, implying a combination of laziness and foolishness; 'Brother Ass' seems to be about as near as one can get in English to this term, which Mariani himself applied to Piave. A letter from Giuseppina to Florimo from Rome 15th February 1859 [1] refers to a love affair between Mariani and one Elena Massa, of Genoa, and to the former's seeming reluctance to commit himself to matrimony:

[1] In the library of the Naples Conservatorio.

I have to advise you that Brother Ass (the former Angelo Mariani) has not yet replied to my letter. *Perhaps* because he's so busy; *perhaps* he intends to write when the wedding is over . . . perhaps he has *taken the bait*. . . . What do you think? It has already been proved that the greatest men have weaknesses even greater . . . so our Mariani may also have them. For the rest, he's a good friend, a distinguished conductor and a musician of immense gifts.

In view of what has been written about Mariani's attitude after the production of *Aroldo* at Rimini, a letter of his of 25th March 1859, from Genoa, is worth quoting at some length:

ILLUSTRIOUS MAESTRO, FRIEND OF MY HEART!

Although I know it is extremely distasteful to you to hear talk of the theatre, of yourself and your works, nevertheless this time I take the liberty of boring you a bit by announcing that your *Aroldo* had here a fanatical success.

The tenor Agresti was able to raise himself to the heights of his role, and it was truly great good fortune for him to appear in this beautiful *Aroldo*, which brought him ovations for the first time in this theatre, to which he could else never have aspired, so low had he fallen in public esteem in the preceding operas. I assure you, O illustrious Maestro, that Agresti sang the part of Aroldo in accordance with your intentions, and with that I think I have said everything. Pizzicati and la Parepa, too, did well. Not a movement, not an *accelerando*, not a shade of colour that was not yours! Such stupendous music, performed according to your *sacred* intentions, could not help meeting with public approval, and it did so truly, so that the auditorium of our severe Carlo Felice resounded with applause such as had not been heard there for a long time. . . .

I would like you to read the official newspapers of this city, to see how they justly proclaim *Aroldo* a worthy opera of yours, to be ranked among the most beautiful works of modern music, which truly has no reason to envy that which was written twenty years ago! I am really happy that *Aroldo* went well. What would you have said of me, *poor Wrong Head*, if I had proved incapable of bringing out all its beauties, by a loving and zealous performance? It is true that you would have laughed, but nevertheless I should have been mortified to the point of tears, because not only was an accomplished work of yours concerned, but a score which I had the honour of conducting under your own eyes at Rimini, where it went so well and pleased enormously, and which I consider now a most sweet part of my own heart, since its melodies recall to me days I spent happily with you and your wife, for whom I feel, more than a loving affection, a veneration that shall be eternal like my soul.

It is quite impossible to believe, after reading such letters as this, that Mariani was seeking to supplant Verdi, in the operatic hierarchy, by the exaltation of Meyerbeer or anyone else. Nor can any credence whatsoever be given to rumours collected at second hand by Zoppi[1]

[1] pp. 144–5.

that at Rimini Mariani always silenced Verdi in debate, and sometimes even insisted that he should not attend the rehearsals. We know that the conductor, seeking effects of superficial brilliance, used to take liberties with the scores, and that the composer objected to this. It is evident that there had already been discussion between them on this point, and that Verdi had imposed his will on Mariani as he did on everyone else.

A batch of letters from April, May and June 1859 is wholly concerned with the course of the war against the Austrians. Verdi, in the depths of the country, was anxious for news; Mariani, at Genoa, saw all the Piedmontese newspapers and the official bulletins, and himself witnessed the disembarkation of the French troops and the arrival of the emperor. He supplied, in astonishing profusion, what Verdi wanted. The following extracts represent only a small part of Mariani's almost daily news-letter service:

26th April:

Eight frigates and two warships with French troops have just arrived in our port. Some arrived last night, too, from Corsica; it was the 33rd, 34th, 37th and 38th regiments of the line. Tomorrow evening two batteries of artillery and five thousand cavalry are arriving from Africa. . . . Volunteers continue to arrive—three or four hundred a day. Twenty-eight thousand of them are already in the regiments. . . .

I would advise you to leave instantly. Come to Genoa, a safe city, where you can live in retirement, and keep yourself informed about events which must interest you so much.

12th May:

I have been waiting with real anxiety for your letter. I thought that it would be so: you haven't received regularly the official Gazette that up to today I have always sent you. Well, we must be patient, and I'll give you the news directly. Thus I'll have the advantage of being often in touch with you, a thing most sweet to me, and you will know better what is happening here, for a decree has been issued by the government forbidding all newspapers of this state to mention the movements of our army or anything regarding politics. So we only have the official bulletins, somewhat meagre, and anyone venturing to give news that had not first been announced by the government would incur most severe penalties, and would probably be arrested. As several bulletins are issued every day, and these say very little, it wouldn't be possible for me to send you them all, first because they wouldn't reach you, and then you wouldn't learn from them what I can write you privately.

Nevertheless he copied by hand many of the bulletins, as well as passing on, in defiance of the censorship, all the information he could gather:

First of all then, I'll tell you that up to last night the French army that passed through Genoa has amounted to about a hundred thousand men, the greater part *Zouaves*, *Turcos*, of the Imperial Guard, the most formidable soldiers, as you know, that France possesses. The artillery has guns on a new system with a range of eight thousand metres, and these guns they have allowed no one to see, so jealous are they of the invention. At any moment now the Emperor Napoleon will arrive. The whole city is decorated for his arrival. In all the French troops the most lively enthusiasm reigns. I can't tell you anything about the Piedmontese troops because they're all on the field. The French, too, as soon as they arrive, go on straight to the field. Once Napolcon is there the great battle will take place on which, in large part, the success of this holy war depends.

This letter, resumed later, has an exalted outburst, written under the immediate impression of the events described:

Here he is! I hear the batteries of the port announcing by their salvoes the arrival of Napoleon! It is two o'clock in the afternoon. By God! It sounds like the end of the world! The bells are ringing in celebration and all the forts with their cannonades are saluting the Head of the great Warrior Nation that has stretched out a fraternal hand to Italy, to aid her efficaciously to win at last her longed-for independence. The cheers of the people near the port and on the walls of the city can be heard from here! What enthusiasm! What a beautiful festal day! How moved I am! Oh! my Verdi, *sommo Maestro*, why aren't you here, with your kind Signora Giuseppina, to enjoy this unique spectacle, impossible to describe! Oh! how imposing is the sight of an army and a people, throwing themselves with assurance into battle, in the war between tyranny and justice and civilization! Long live Italy, God's true blessing! Long live those who generously come to shed their blood for her!

23rd May:

I don't understand it at all. I have written to you continually, and today I receive your kind letter of the 18th, in which you say you haven't received my letters. I wrote to you on the 12th, 13th and 14th of this month; I wrote you, too, another letter which I posted the day before yesterday. . . .

I advise you to leave at once, and move to a place where you'll be safe. Come, my Verdi, don't stay in an exposed position, where you are, because if the Austrians, as seems likely, retreat, they will probably be hindered in this from the direction of Cremona, and there is every probability that the fatal action will take place on those plains. The fact is that the Austrians are behaving barbarously everywhere. Yesterday, for example, at the inn near Torrialla they shot a whole family. So put in a safe place everything you possess in the way of jewellery, silverware, linen and valuable things. You must, in short, bury everything, for the times are most perilous, and you know better than I do that that horde of barbarians respects neither celebrity nor talent, neither works of art nor men, and much less women and children. . . . If you want to leave Sant' Agata, I warn you that you won't be able to pass by Piacenza, since the bulk of the Austrian army is there.

Repeating himself a great deal, he beseeches Verdi, in various letters, to evacuate Sant' Agata; then resumes his account of the war:

27th May:

Garibaldi is at Varese, reached by crossing the mountains. Yesterday at four in the morning the Austrians, to the number of 5,000, attacked him, and by seven o'clock they had already been driven back beyond Malnate, with very heavy losses. The Alpine Brigade, led by the valiant Garibaldi, to the number of 4,000, the greater part volunteers, fought valorously, charging with the bayonet. The town of Varese contributed effectively to the defence of the barricades. To the cannon-shots of the Austrians the populace replied with cries of 'Viva l'Italia!', 'Viva Vittorio Emanuele!'.

3rd June:

Garibaldi's tactics show how expert he is in the art of war. He reappeared at Varese when they thought he was at Como. When at Como they thought he had retired into the mountains, here he is again in the town, after having soundly beaten the invader, who for a moment had thought of re-occupying those towns, which perhaps now he will no longer be in a position to attack. . . . Today I met a French soldier wounded at Montebello, who told me that the Austrians are very much afraid of the bayonet, but that they are *méchant* at the same time. On that field of battle there were found the bodies of some French officers with their eyes gouged out. The sight of such barbarity so inflamed the French soldiery that they set off in pursuit of those cannibals and all those they found had their throats cut without mercy. It is said that the Emperor Napoleon has written a letter to the Emperor of Austria, reproaching him for the infamous manner in which his hired assassins wage war. He threatens that if such barbarity occurs again he will give no quarter to the prisoners, but put them all to the sword. . . .

What will our poor Pantaloon, Piave, do at Venice? The French squadron has already announced the blockade of that city from the sea, and when it's blockaded from the land also the position there will be extremely serious.

4th June:

King Vittorio Emanuele has already given proofs of immense courage. At Palestra he was in the thick of the fight and by words and example encouraged the soldiers, and in the very forefront at the head of the Zouaves captured several guns from the enemy. The Zouaves (and it is said that about 800 of them were killed and wounded in that action) were astonished at such boldness, singular in anybody, but most singular in a king. When the guns, of which I told you in my last letter, were taken, the Zouaves shouted, in their outspoken way: 'Ah! ce bougre de Roi, c'est le Roi des Zouaves!'

On the sixth page of this very long letter, of ten pages in all, he asked: 'Tell me, my Verdi, doesn't it bore you to read my letters? Do you read them all? To tell you the truth, I write, write and write, because if you wish to have precise and genuine news you can have it, but then you can attach whatever importance you think to my letters.'

At length he got his reward. 'Dear Mariani,' Verdi wrote on 12th June, 'You have a *Good Head* and an excellent heart. I have received your letter of the 7th as well, and thank you for that and all the others. Poor Mariani! What a lot of trouble I've given you! But now you can stop, because I have the *Gazzetta di Milano* sent me, and then we have the news from near by.' Mariani's reply, of 16th June, for all its semi-humorous tone, shows clearly how much he had suffered from Verdi's attitude, and how much a word of praise rejoiced his heart:

God bless you, dear Verdi! At last you have seen the light; at last you have come to your senses; now I concede that you have every good quality to glorify your high intelligence, for you have become perfect! It was truly unworthy of a great genius, such as you are, not to concede that which is due to me. Perhaps you were severe with me in order to put my constancy to the test? Well, after all, you have had to agree! . . . You're a follower of St Thomas, aren't you? He wanted to touch the wounds of Christ, to convince himself, and you have put my *Good Head* to the test!!!! I gladly accept, then, your approval of this great virtue of mine, and from the depths of my soul I thank you for what you add about my *excellent heart*. . . . Now I am happy, and I assure you it was more painful to hear myself called 'Wrong Head' by you than it would have been if you had called me a *bad musician*, for I know I am that. No more '*Wrong Head*', then, and so be it!

The letter is signed:

ANGELO MARIANI
Good Head.
Approved.

The Treaty of Villafranca brought a convulsive re-appraisal of the actions and motives of the French emperor. In June Mariani had gone so far as to say: 'If the first Napoleon was great, the third Napoleon is certainly not inferior, and perhaps will leave a name more glorious in history.' In July, like every Italian patriot, he was angry, indignant and humiliated. Correspondence was resumed after an interval:

5th September:

Your kind letter of the 3rd, from Parma, was welcome beyond measure, because it brought me news of you, of which I had been deprived for a long time. To tell the truth, receiving no reply to my last letter, I was much troubled, and was afraid of having displeased you in some way or other. Now I am wholly content. You have shown that you haven't forgotten me, you honour me still with your favour, and I express over again my feelings of gratitude for your benevolence, which makes me so happy.

As soon as certain duties at Genoa permitted, he proposed to return to Sant' Agata, 'to express again by word of mouth my feelings of devotion, to pay my respects to kind Signora Giuseppina, to wrestle for an hour with that ugly great animal of yours, *Black*, and to talk a little about the wretched political events forced on our king, the only true man of honour among the crowned heads'.

It was Mariani who arranged, through Sir James Hudson, for Verdi to visit Cavour, in retirement at Leri, when he came to Turin with the other representatives of the states that had voted for union with Piedmont. Sir James Hudson was a particular friend of Mariani, who often stayed in his house.

After this the visit to Sant' Agata took place. The friends went shooting, and Mariani made the acquaintance of Barezzi and his wife. The signed photograph, inscribed with a phrase from *Luisa Miller*, that is reproduced in Zoppi's book,[1] was given Mariani before he left at the end of this visit, on 29th September. From Broni, near Stradella, where he stayed with the Massa family and other friends, he wrote next day:

You and your wife will have forgiven me, won't you, if I was at fault in anything? You are so good, I know, so you will be indulgent with me.

I shall write to Cavour.

Tell Signora Giuseppina, that profound student of the history of Sant' Agata, that I have already executed her commission. . . .

Give my affectionate regards to Signor Antonio Barezzi and to his good-natured consort, Signora Maddalena. My Verdi! My soul is full of gratitude for all you have so generously lavished on me.

On 7th October he sent verbose birthday congratulations from Genoa. This is one of the letters in which his adoration is expressed in a manner at once touching and absurd:

Sunday will be a delightful day for me! It's my Verdi's birthday! At twenty past four (exactly half past four by your watch), fixing my eyes on your beautiful portrait, which I have already had framed, I shall drink your health, and with this toast I shall send you a salutation of the soul as fervent as the prayers I raise to heaven always that its benedictions may aid you. And as I am firmly convinced that your house will be enlivened on that happy day by the presence of the angelic Signor Antonio Barezzi and his consort, I should like to ask you, O my best Verdi, in your gathering kindly to recall my poor name, because thus it will be most sweet to me too, to live where my heart has remained and where my wandering spirit strays. . . .

As I've told you, I had a frame made for your portrait (it was my first thought) and so that this precious gift of yours may be kept in good condition I shall also have made for it a little curtain of green silk, to

[1] Facing p. 32.

preserve it from the light, which is always harmful to photographs. . . .
I would give ten litres of my blood to be beside you with my gun.

> Nessun maggior dolore
> Che ricordarsi del tempo felice
> Nella miseria.

Oh! Happy this sheet of paper of mine that is going there!

Sir James Hudson had given Verdi a letter of introduction to one of Garibaldi's officers, Clemente Corte, at Modena, who would be able to assist him to secure one hundred and seventy-two rifles for the National Guard of Busseto. Corte agreed to help, indicated the firm of Danovaro at Genoa, but then seemed to lose all interest in the affair and did not reply to Verdi's subsequent letters. So it fell to Mariani's lot to clear up the confusion caused by Corte's defection, to inspect with an expert friend Danovaro's stock, the best part of which had been sold while a firm fresh order from Verdi was awaited, to reject some guns of inferior quality, and after about a month's activity to purchase and dispatch some brand-new ones from a consignment that had just arrived from St Étienne. By these services Mariani earned Verdi's gratitude and unqualified approval. Afterwards he paid another visit to Sant' Agata.

In December Giuseppina wrote to Florimo:

Mariani is here! . . . Open your eyes as wide as you like, but he has been here for eight days, amid the snow, without seeing a living soul except Verdi and me, me and Verdi. This is a proof of friendship to astonish the world! As you can imagine, we often speak of you, with the affection and esteem that you deserve. . . . We speak also of the Massa family and in particular of Signorina Elena, who is still Signorina Elena Massa, and for my part I have little hope of seeing her become one day Signora Elena Mariani. You know the good qualities of our friend; but one must confess that in this matter he is a great *Ass*! We shall be making a short stay at Genoa, and I shall make use of that time to vex and torment him in such a way that he decides either to marry her or to leave her alone. Perhaps he'll send me to. . . ? All the worse for him! Sincere friends are too rare to be contemned.

Mariani himself added a postscript:

I am most happy in this cave covered in snow, because, as you know, Verdi and his wife take the place of everything else and form a world in themselves. Yes, my dear Florimo, I have spent nine days here in full contentment and today I am sad because I must return to Genoa tomorrow to recommence my tiresome occupations in the theatre. I shall feel better there when the Verdis have arrived.

The first winter sojourn at Genoa, anticipated in this letter, lasted from 3rd January to 11th March 1860. For some time now Mariani had been busy inspecting houses and flats on Verdi's behalf. 'I wish

Genoa were a Paradise', he wrote, 'so as to be worthy of receiving you within its walls.' But in the end Verdi and Giuseppina stayed in a hotel, the Croce di Malta, in Via Carlo Alberto.

After the visit was over Mariani continued to look over houses, including some on the hill of Carignano. 'What happiness would be mine if I could find something to suit you!' he wrote on 13th March. 'Genoa without you is insupportable.'

In the wilds of Sant' Agata, Verdi and Giuseppina often had occasion to ask their friends in the larger towns to buy things for them. The friends were glad to do so, and no reader of the letters published here could suppose for a moment that Mariani resented the demands made on him. But certainly he was given plenty to do. A letter of Verdi's of 21st March, almost domineering in tone, is remarkable in this respect:

In the days when you were just a musician, I wouldn't have dared to write you a letter like the present one; but now that you have become a capitalist, a speculator and usurer, I am giving you various commissions, as the result of which you will be out of pocket for a few days (*only for a few days*) to the extent of a few hundred francs, which will soon be repaid, together with interest, broker's fees and similar robberies, etc., etc.

First of all, you will go to collect my portrait, and you will pay for everything, as detailed in the enclosed letter.

In the second place, you will make Maestro Gambini take you to that nurseryman, and you will buy *ten Magnolia Grandiflora* about a metre and a half high, but in any case not less than a metre high. Let them be carefully dug up and wrapped in straw, and that only the day before you leave.

In the third place, you will go to Noledi, and ask him if he wants to exchange my St Étienne gun for his Liège one that I like, calibre 13–14. You know it, and I will give him four gold napoleons in addition. You can assure him that my gun can be said to be new, for I've only used it for a part of the month of December, and the iron and the wood shine like new. For the rest, if Noledi wants to see it first, write at once, and I will send it to you by rail, in a box. I want you however to try out the Liège gun, and see that it shoots straight and doesn't kick. If that's not the case, leave it. It's necessary to try it with five and six grains of powder.

The snow has gone; however, if you wait a few days longer the ground will dry out and we shall be able to go into the woods.

You will bring everything with you, putting it all on the railway as your baggage. You will take a ticket to Piacenza; at Piacenza you will have it renewed as far as Borgo San Donnino. You will leave at ten in the morning, arrive at Piacenza about three, wait half an hour at Piacenza and be at Borgo after four. You will find a carriage for Busseto, but as this carriage waits for the connection from Parma, you will be very late in leaving Borgo. You can dine at Borgo while waiting for the said carriage or hire a gig expressly to take you to Sant' Agata; or you can write to me the day before, and I will come or send my horses to Borgo.

Do you understand?

One sees that Verdi, in his practical way, was intent on getting his trees replanted as soon as possible. But, all the same, it was a monstrous thing to expect a friend to carry ten magnolias about with him, as part of his personal baggage, to say nothing of a gun and the 'portrait', which, as an invoice at Sant' Agata shows, was not a painting but a heavy marble statuette by Luccardi. If Mariani failed to appear at Sant' Agata on this occasion, however, it was not because he objected to being made use of in this way. His letters show that he did everything possible to satisfy Verdi. The gun, he found, had already been sold. The nurseryman indicated by Gambini had some well-branched magnolias, a little over a metre high, for which he asked five francs a tree. Mariani made a note of this, promised to return later, and then made a tour of all the gardens and nurseries of Genoa. He found a shop in the Via Carlo Alberto which could supply ten magnolias, a metre and a half high, at half the price of the others. This was on Friday, 23rd March. During Holy Week, commencing 2nd April, he would have to be at Genoa for services in the cathedral. So he proposed that he should come to Sant' Agata on Thursday, 29th March, and stay until the morning of 2nd April. If Verdi would reply at once, confirming these arrangements, the trees could be ordered on Tuesday, dug up and packed on Wednesday and be ready to leave with Mariani himself on Thursday.

Verdi replied on 26th March:

> If you can only stay here for four or five days it would be better if you came immediately after Easter, so that we should have plenty of time to go into the woods with our guns. For the rest, you can come either now or after Easter, and whenever you wish, for you know you can never be at all in the way and I'm always pleased to see you. . . . Collect the portrait and pay all the charges, both for transport and customs dues, and when you come here (either now or after Easter) bring it with you as your baggage. Do the same with the magnolias; take those at two and a half francs, and if there are some more than a metre and a half high (paying more for them) better still.

Having decided to visit Sant' Agata, as he had suggested, before Easter, Mariani, armed with Verdi's letter, returned to the nurseryman and ordered the ten largest magnolias he could find, magnificent specimens costing five francs twenty centimes each. In the morning of 28th March he took the marble statuette to the station and returned in the evening with the magnolias. Then calamity overtook him. The enormous package, almost three metres high, was too big to go in the luggage van. The station-master advised him to take it to the goods station the next morning, where it could be put into an open truck, covered with a tarpaulin to prevent sparks from the engine setting fire to the straw wrappings. Poor Mariani, in great distress, explained all this the same evening in a long letter, promising to get up before seven the next morning to go to the goods station and find out the quickest and safest way to send the trees to Borgo San Donnino. That evening Verdi wrote again:

DEAR MARIANI,

Wednesday evening.

If you haven't left, and if you haven't sent the magnolias, instead of ten bring *twelve*. It would be better if they were more than a metre and a half high, even if they cost more. In haste. Farewell.

G. VERDI.

On 29th March, having sent off the ten magnolias by the only means possible, slow goods train, Mariani, 'poor Wrong Head', as he called himself, assured Verdi that they would be all right, packed as they were, for up to fifteen days. Not having been able to carry out his instructions to the letter, and having lost another day in arranging the dispatch by goods train, he decided to put off his visit. He wrote again on 1st April:

This morning there arrived from Naples a box containing the magnificent portrait of your wife, some other pictures and various books.

Yesterday I received your letter and I am awaiting the nurseryman's convenience before sending you the other two magnolias, which I hope to be able to send by express train, since a small package, not very heavy, is concerned.

I hope you will have received the other plants by now, and your portrait in marble. You will also have received my letters and thus know of my anguish over the difficulties I encountered in connection with the plants. I await with anxiety a consoling letter from you.

The ten magnolias, the statuette and the box from Naples all arrived safely. The order for the two extra magnolias was subsequently cancelled, as Verdi found he could buy them locally.

On 1st April Giuseppina wrote to Achille Montuoro: 'We are at Sant' Agata, but lively correspondence about the purchase or exchange of guns continues with our friend Mariani, who continues, too, the dispatch of bric-à-brac, and indeed we expect a box to arrive this very evening.' Bric-à-brac, she called it! Giuseppina had little faith in the marksmanship of either of them: 'Mariani is coming to Sant' Agata after Easter and then Verdi and he will start their walks in the woods near the Po, after game. However, if we eat woodcock, pheasant, etc., at home, it will be when I have been able to find some to buy in the market.'

In Giuseppina's letter-book, under the date 19th April, is found the acknowledgment of another parcel from Genoa, containing three pounds of powdered orris-root and thirty yards of black lace, the latter commissioned from Signora Paolina Massa, the mother of

Mariani's friend Elena. This letter is one of Giuseppina's narrative masterpieces:

My best thanks to you, dear Mariani, and to *the very amiable lady*[1] Signora Paolina. The orris spreads its sweet scent about my room; the lace will serve to adorn a little my ugly person. Ask Signora Paolina if I may wear the lace without scruple, because, the price being so low, I'm almost afraid it must have derived from the protégés of Mercury! Joking apart, the lace is just what I wanted and the price lower than I expected.

I am glad you are accompanying the Massa ladies as far as Borgo, and I am sure that if you warn us in time we shall come to shake them by the hand.

So Signora Paolina is also a bit hard up? A real affliction of humanity! Instead of making me sorry for her, it almost gives me pleasure—the pleasure of the damned, to be sure, but still, pleasure! I am myself so often hard up that I am glad to know that others are sometimes in like case. But please don't be anxious about your credit, Mariani. As I told you in an earlier letter, I am sufficiently in funds at the moment and, certainly, temptation to spend money can come to no woman who lives at Sant' Agata, however much of a coquette she may be.

But when one begins the year badly, one continues in the same strain, however much one tries to break the spell and be prudent to avoid loss. There are certain destructive little spirits which receive orders to torment this or that individual. This year, 1860, I have a malevolent and spiteful one which persecutes me in a thousand ways and empties my purse without any advantage to me. It began by stealing my wrap at Genoa; for, believe me, I didn't lose it—it was stolen. Spirits in the form of pickpockets and thieves are doing excellent business this year. From Fontana, the Parisian jeweller, 250,000 francs' worth of loose precious stones were stolen this month, in his shop, under his very eyes!!! How much easier to steal a black wrap, packed in yellow paper! Accursed colours, always fatal to the Italians![2] Now can you guess what form this spirit took at Sant' Agata in order to harm me? The form of an enormous grey mouse, with whiskers as long as those of our Vittorio Emanuele! This rascal (the mouse, not Vittorio!) began operations in my room a few nights ago, and as it's the way of sprites to be eccentric, the idea occurred to it of banging on certain metallic hangings until I awoke.

I light the lamp; the noise stops. I put out the lamp; the noise begins again. I began to laugh, thinking that the peasants, because they are ignorant, and the priests, because they are ——, would say it was the result of excommunication.

I said nothing and fell asleep again.

In the morning Gigia comes to me and says: 'Signora, there must be a big mouse here, because it has pulled a carpet this way, a towel that way.' I run to see . . . alas! the excommunication had vented itself on various things, and above all on a shawl of mine, reduced to a sieve, and a pair of new shoes, not even worn yet! I look for the mouse, right and left. Nothing

[1] These words in English.
[2] The colours of imperial Austria.

to be found. Serafina enters armed with a stick and with Dindin (Dindin is the cat) under her arm. We close the doors. I get up on a trunk, Gigia on a chair. Serafina, who is more of a soldier than me, begins to wave her stick and mutter between her teeth: 'Son of a ——, you've got to come out.' Dindin begins to get restless because he's half strangled under Serafina's arm. After ineffectual manœuvres, we raise our eyes and see the mouse on the curtain-rod, seeming to make fun of us! Give it him! Bang! Bong! The enemy, reduced to his last defences, falls headlong from his throne. Serafina flings Dindin on the mouse, and victory is ours—Dindin's, that is, who from now on will be called 'Zouave'.

This affair of the mouse means a loss of about a hundred francs. Let's hope that the troubles are ended with Easter. . . . We hope to have you here with us soon, and then we will pay our debts.

This brilliantly witty letter is a precious memorial of a friendship that seemed as if it would last for ever. Verdi himself, though he treated Mariani at times almost like a servant, and often assumed the role of a heavy father rebuking an irresponsible schoolboy, was quite uncommonly open and cordial with him, and untiring in his invitations: 'Come, then, to Sant' Agata, and send London and Paris to the devil! If you abstained from coming from fear of disturbing us you would be the most wrong-headed person in the world. I have always treated you *sans façons*, so as to make you understand that you can stay here for months and months without being at all in the way. So come, now or later, whenever you like, and send your scruples to the devil.'

In the autumn of 1860 Mariani conducted his first season of opera at the Teatro Comunale at Bologna. *Un ballo in maschera*, *La Favorita* and *Le Prophète* were all very successful. He was delighted with the orchestra, which compared very favourably with that available at Genoa. His contract with the municipality of Genoa was due to expire in the following spring and moves were afoot to secure him permanently for Bologna, not only as conductor at the Teatro Comunale, but as director of the Liceo Musicale. Mariani himself, however, tended to favour another offer which had reached him from Naples. But he wavered a good deal between the two. Writing from Genoa to Stefano Golinelli at Bologna on 22nd December,[1] he apologized for not having replied earlier and explained:

Besides the bother of the theatre I had the most sweet company of Verdi, who decided to come here with me, and stayed until yesterday, so, as you can easily imagine, whenever I had a moment's freedom I had to devote it to him. Florimo has written to me from Naples, inviting me to go there as *absolute* director of that great theatre. I showed Verdi the letter, but he too is of the opinion that I should stay at Bologna, where the musical resources, especially the vocal ones, are better. And then, as he

[1] In the Piancastelli Collection.

says, at Naples there is such confusion in the organization of the theatre and the Conservatorio that many years would be needed to get them in order, and there would be a risk, perhaps, of not succeeding at all, for the demoralization there extends into everything.

The postscript of this letter is touching:

Verdi was astonished when he saw the enormous cigar you gave me; I presented it to him—he was so much in love with it.

Mariani was attracted by the Neapolitan offer because it was made directly to him and did not depend, as did the appointment to the Liceo at Bologna, on the deliberations of a committee. By the end of January 1861 he was on the point of signing the contract to go to Naples. Both Verdi and Giuseppina gave him their advice in writing. It is curious that Verdi's letter, dated 31st January,[1] begins and ends in exactly the same way as Giuseppina's, dated 1st February in her letter-book. The advice given is the same; Verdi is more concise, Giuseppina more sprightly and amusing:

Thank you, thank you a thousand times for Loulou's passport—though I would have preferred the city of Turin to be indicated, where Loulou will perhaps have to go very soon. Verdi is in a bad temper, fearing to obtain that majority of votes which would make any other candidate happy. Such is life!

We come now to the question of Naples, on which, since you are kind enough to attach some value to it, I will give you my opinion in a few words.

From time, I should say, almost immemorial, Naples has had orchestral conductors born in those parts and a foreigner would wound those municipal susceptibilities, to eradicate which many many years will be needed. It's quite true that since Festa they have had only conductors who are mediocre to say no worse. . . . But they are Neapolitans, and have the advantage of possessing fecund wives, who make them fathers of dozens of children! Now at Naples to be father of a large family means to have a claim to protection, interest, sympathy. These sentiments are highly moral, these claims of father and mother are most sacred, and would be most praiseworthy always, if they weren't in most cases used as means to commit injustice and employ inept people and do every sort of bad thing.

The present conductor is a Neapolitan and father of a family. He is therefore doubly armed to wound anyone who should wish to drive him from his post. There will be many, certainly, who will have the good sense to say: 'But this conductor is a pigmy; Mariani is of the stuff of Festa, Rolla, Costa, etc., etc.' Yes, but the croaking of frogs is often more powerful than the song of the nightingales, and in this case you would have to put up with the chatter of the idle, who are numerous in all towns and in Naples more numerous than elsewhere. Now among your eminent qualities I haven't noticed that *sans-souci* needed to laugh at the swarm of

[1] Gatti, first edition, pp. 41–2; second edition, p. 399, and elsewhere.

insects which buzzes and stings all the more gleefully the more annoyance it causes. On the other hand, if at Genoa they grant you the pension, why throw into the sea so many years of hard work? Will Naples grant you, or, to put it better, will Naples take into account the years not spent in its service? You will say: 'Naples is an artistic city, and I am an artist *par excellence*!' It is true: Naples is an artistic city; Genoa is a commercial city; but at Naples, too, there are many troubles, and at Genoa good qualities are not lacking. The very activity of the population leaves it no time to bother about other people's affairs, and this freedom, this absence of inexorable daily gossip, is really God's great blessing on the earth!

If, then, you feel your spirit strong enough to despise all obstacles, sustained by the idea of making the Neapolitan orchestra what it once was, the finest in Italy, and to sacrifice your peace of mind (at least for a time) on the altar of art—Hail, then, friend Mariani! Arm yourself with shield and lance—that is, with your violin and magic bow—and *en route* for Naples!

With Angelo Catelani and Gaetano Gaspari urging him to come to Bologna, Florimo seeking to persuade him to come to Naples, and Verdi and Giuseppina leaving him in no doubt that they thought he would do better to stay at Genoa, Mariani was utterly unable to make up his mind. Another friend joined in, regretting his very apparent infirmity of purpose. On 28th February Mariani wrote to Verdi at Turin: 'I've just received a letter from Sir James Hudson, in which he tells me you called to see him yesterday and he is enchanted with the resolution of your mind and character. Indeed, he told me that if I had only a tithe of your firmness and perspicuity, I might become somebody. A fine discourse, eh? But I can't help it. God made me with a Wrong Head and I shall have to stay as I am in my littleness.' Verdi commented on 3rd March: 'Your letter made me laugh, for I can see you took great offence at Hudson's words.' Mariani replied, denying this, in a whirl of words:

I did not *take offence* at what Sir James wrote to me in relation to you. What he says is quite right; it's what I too think of you, and I've always told you myself that one has to esteem you not only as the greatest musical genius of our day, but as the most honest man, of exemplary character and extreme firmness, that it has ever been given me to know. I'll bring you that letter from Sir James; it's a just tribute to your rare excellence, and that is why I at once wrote to you about it, and not to complain of his most just reproaches *that I haven't even a minimal part of your firmness of mind, and that a boy is enough* [he alludes to the young Neapolitan Baron Cianciolo, of whom I told you in another letter] *to put me in a fury and make me threaten even my true friends.*

An example of the sort of thing Hudson meant followed almost at once. Mariani reported on 18th March:

Florimo wrote to tell me that at Naples there are big intrigues against me, that Capecelatro has fallen and there is someone now in power in the theatre who doesn't want any *foreigners* (!) and that to overcome these people I should write to Cavour and have myself officially appointed by him. I replied that it was never my intention to accept their offers, that we people of central and northern Italy do business with more honesty and frankness, and that they will greatly oblige me if they will leave me in peace.

This is a typical piece of confused thinking. It was untrue that it had never been his intention to accept the position, since less than seven weeks before this he had told Catelani that he had all but concluded a new contract with Naples, and had asked for Verdi's and Giuseppina's advice. It is dubious whether the remarks about honesty and frankness have reference to the Neapolitan intrigues or to the suggestion that he should approach Cavour; but since his opponents would obviously be very glad to leave him in peace, what he says could only hurt Florimo and his other supporters at Naples. The person now in power in the San Carlo theatre was Mercadante, as is clear from a later letter.

A word of reproach from Verdi could reduce Mariani to a state of grovelling abjection. It seems to have come to the composer's ears that *Un ballo in maschera* was being prepared for performance at Genoa with an inadequate cast. In a sudden gust of anger he had complained of this, in a letter that has not survived. Mariani wrote four times to Verdi and once to Giuseppina, in the course of nine days, before and after the production of the opera. 'You are quite right, but I am not to blame,' he said on 27th March, in the course of an enormous letter, very difficult to read because the ink has passed through the paper:

As a result of this misfortune I am in hell! You know how I adore you and how I venerate all that is yours. What am I to do? Tell me what you want, by return of post, and I will obey you. I am ready to do anything. If you think fit send Tornaghi at once; he will be able to see how the last rehearsals go.

There was no answer, but the opera when produced was a brilliant success. He advised Verdi of this in another endless letter on 1st April:

Heaven be thanked! I am really happy, and God knows what I've suffered! As I told you just now by telegram, your *Ballo in maschera* aroused fanatical enthusiasm and went very well. You will hear the news from other people besides, so, frankly and without fear of being vainglorious, I can tell you the truth, that I was so pleased that I was moved to tears. Have the kindness, my Verdi, to write me just one line, so that I know you are not angry. Poor Wrong Head! Let me know at least that you haven't abandoned me.

Still there was no reply, and he wrote again, in a pleading tone, after the second performance, two days later:

> Oh, Don Peppino! Don't be angry any more with your poor Wrong Head! Write to me, for I really have need of a letter from you, to tell me that you don't hold anything against me. What could I do? That c—— Montuoro had put me in an embarrassing position. Be indulgent with him, too. . . . Be graciously pleased to give my regards to Donna Peppina. *She* is truly an angel of goodness, but you are too cruel to me. Oh, Don Peppino! Have the kindness to write to me—I need it so much.

At length, at midnight on 4th April, he was able to write:

> Thank you, Don Peppino! So you aren't angry with me? I am so glad. Now I know that I have an angel in heaven who prays for me.

Mariani was not yet forty. According to his own reckoning, since he always insisted that he was born in 1824, he was not yet thirty-seven. It is strange that on 5th July he could write to Stefano Golinelli:[1] 'I shall go away to London, where an independent existence will bring me in enough to get along for the few years of life that remain to me.' He worried a good deal about his future, and there is this to be said for him: he was not well off; his salary at Genoa was only 3,600 lire a year, and out of this he often sent home money to his mother. Probably only Landoni, among his friends, knew how much trouble his relatives caused him; his sister Bradamante wrote him begging letters, and in the past winter he had had to refuse to pay his brother's debts at Ravenna. There was good news on 7th July, when he wrote to Verdi: 'The municipality of Genoa has decided, *by way of exception*, that my pension shall be determined on the same terms and conditions as those of the other employees. . . . So my future is assured. In short, I shall not any more have to fear a miserable old age, for I'm assured, at least, of bread.' In spite of repeated entreaties from his friends at Bologna, he had refused to compete for the post of director of the Liceo Musicale: 'I suppose I've done the wrong thing as usual.'

He agreed, however, to return to Bologna to conduct the autumn season of opera at the Teatro Comunale. On the way he stayed for a few days at Sant' Agata and marvelled that Verdi, busy composing *La forza del destino*, could work amid all the bricklayers, carpenters and blacksmiths employed in rebuilding the house.

Mariani complained often of the restricted musical resources of the Teatro Carlo Felice, which no longer satisfied him. There were certainly some serious shortcomings, as a letter to Golinelli of 20th December shows:

> Accustomed to the vigour, the *brio*, to that wave of sound that satisfies

[1] Piancastelli Collection.

one's soul, of the *truly excellent* Bolognese orchestra, the Genoese one seems enervated, feeble—so lifeless that it depresses me. Add to that the complete lack of double basses, the incompetence of some of the players of the principal instruments, the difference between the dead acoustics of this theatre and the sonority of the Teatro Comunale, and you will easily understand how disgusted I am by the ensemble I find again here. I seem to have a spinet under my fingers, and I am not exaggerating when I make the comparison between a *spinet* and an *Erard* grand piano, for such is the difference between this orchestra and that one. . . . Verdi writes to me from St Petersburg that he is happy and his new opera will be staged about the 20th.

Few of Mariani's letters to Verdi have survived from this period, but amicable correspondence certainly continued all through the composer's visits to Russia, France and England. Another letter to Golinelli of 5th June 1862 says:

Verdi writes to me from London to say that he has prepared a room for me in his lodgings. It's a great temptation, and if I hadn't got to finish some short works I have on hand I should go there at once.

Later in the month Verdi was back in Italy, and looking forward to seeing Mariani again:

I've been some days in Italy and I've never written to you! You'll excuse me, won't you? I am on the train from Turin to Piacenza. I am bringing with me two fine guns bought in London from one of the leading gunsmiths: a carbine like Sir James Hudson's but perhaps finer, and a double-barrelled rifle on the *Le Faucheux* system. When are you coming to try them?

Too much is made by Gatti of the occasions when Mariani failed to appear at Sant' Agata, after pressing invitations. There were many visits, besides those mentioned in Verdi's surviving letters. Even though Mariani had to be asked not to bring Sir James Hudson, in the summer of 1862, because the house was in disorder, the servants ill and poor Loulou dead, he was asked to come himself for a few days, and did so.

5th August 1862:

Poor Loulou! The news of his death has immensely upset me. He was your faithful companion, your friend, your affection, your pastime. In short, I considered him a part of yourself, and therefore I tenderly loved him.

19th August 1862:

How good you are! I'll pay you a visit at the beginning of September. I'll stay only one day, so as not to vex you.

In 1863 Mariani received the offer of an engagement in Peru, and at about the same time learned that Bagier, the new director of the

Théâtre Italien in Paris, was in search of a conductor. The idea of this latter position attracted him, but he hesitated and prevaricated as usual, and asked the advice of Verdi, now become a veritable father-figure in his life. The negotiations concerning this projected appointment fall in a period from which Verdi's letters survive, but not Mariani's. In this episode the actions and reactions of both men were highly characteristic.

Verdi was on the spot, in Paris, and prepared to do what he could to secure the appointment for Mariani. He warned him, however, that there would be other aspirants, also with influential friends, and that while there were financial advantages the position offered no security: at any time Bagier could dismiss all his employees, and if that happened all the years of hard work at Genoa would have gone for nothing.

It appears that, in spite of what he had written two years earlier about his pension rights at Genoa, Mariani was still uncertain of his position; probably he had received only verbal assurances, but nothing in writing. Verdi, on 12th April, told him how to deal with the municipal authorities:

DEAR MARIANI,

No more hesitation then! Write resolutely but very calmly and politely to the municipality, asking either for the pension or for your release. And if you want to achieve any useful result, keep it a secret. Consult a solicitor and write in such a way that the municipality is obliged to give you an answer. Take note that the municipality will believe that your application is only the whim of a moment or a boyish trick, and won't reply, and that is why I say that you must find a way of getting an answer of some sort. I repeat: don't hesitate any longer, and think how hesitation has caused you to lose ten of the best years of your life. If the municipality guarantees you the pension I advise you to stay where you are. If not, make up your mind, as you think best, either to go to Lima or to aspire to the post at the Théâtre Italien in Paris. The post in Paris cannot guarantee you a pension, and its only advantage is that of living in a great musical centre. The pay would be (if you take the pianoforte rehearsals as well) 9,000 or 10,000 francs (I believe). Employment for seven months: about four performances a week. I shall be staying in Paris all this month and towards the end of the month Bagier is due back from Madrid to draw up the contract and settle everything. In the meantime, order your affairs so as to be able to write to me *definitely*

either that you are staying at Genoa,
or that you are going to Lima,
or that you aspire to come to Paris.

In this last case I will then tell you what else you have to do.

Hardly was this admirably practical and most helpful letter in the post when information reached Verdi that caused him at once to stiffen and withdraw. The following note is dated 14th April, in Mariani's hand, on the back:

I know that you have approached others about the post at the Théâtre Italien in Paris (you were wrong to do so) and I know that Bagier has made proposals to you concerning this. You will do what you please, but from this moment I declare that I don't come into the affair any more and if you value my friendship a little you will not make use of my name in this connection, and much less will you speak of the present letter.

The effect of this, with its warning of a possible breach in their friendship, seems to have been to paralyse Mariani's initiative completely. Three weeks later he wrote to Verdi asking what he was to say to one Toffoli, probably Bagier's agent, with whom he had been in touch about the Parisian appointment. Verdi replied on 5th May:

You really are a *Wrong Head*! You expect me to tell you how to reply to Toffoli?!! You absolutely do not understand me, you have never understood me, and you know nothing at all about business. When I told you that from the moment you had dealings with Toffoli I did not wish to enter into this bungled affair any more, you ought, without hesitation, to have either accepted or rejected those proposals. That is all I can say, and I say it again.

Bagier's return to Paris was long delayed. By the end of the month, no doubt after lengthy explanations and protestations from Mariani, Verdi was mollified and again willing to be helpful. Some negotiations of his own concerning the Théâtre Italien had come to nothing; if Mariani really wished to secure the post of conductor at that theatre he needed to take early action: 'I can no longer be any use to you, except by a word to Bagier when he returns. It would be necessary for you to authorize me to do that, by a letter that could be shown. If that suits you I am at your service.' The storm had blown over; the atmosphere was clear again. The old cordiality returned, and the old commissions:

The sherry is still on the high seas? Escudier seems also to have sent a case of wine to Genoa, addressed to 'Chevalier Mariani, for Verdi'. If so please collect it, paying the charges, for which I will reimburse you. We'll drink these wines at Sant' Agata, where you'll come, I hope, as soon as I'm back.

The letter ends with a request for information about a small steam-engine of about four horsepower, suitable for working a pump at Sant' Agata.

When Bagier finally returned to Paris Verdi found himself, after all, unable to put in a good word for his friend, for reasons that are not clear. Mariani had not, therefore, been so very unwise in approaching Toffoli as well.

The end of this episode is reflected in Verdi's last three letters from Paris:

10th July:

In spite of myself, I cannot help you at all with Bagier, and at Sant' Agata I'll tell you why. Meanwhile, if you are set on coming to Paris, you can put your terms to Toffoli. Come to a clear understanding, and don't harbour any illusions. I'm sorry I can't help you at all, but it's against my will.

15th July:

I have received your letter and seen Toffoli. Your request is all right, and is just. Hold firm for Paris only. That is advice given *inter nos* and as a friend, for I wouldn't like to see you running like a mountebank from Paris to Madrid, and *vice versa*. Reflect, however, on the *safe position* you are leaving; here you will be insecure always, and Paris is not entirely a *bed of roses*. Finally, if Bagier agrees—*good*; if he doesn't (don't despair)—*better*. There is my opinion, frankly and clearly!

20th July:

I leave tomorrow evening (Tuesday). I shall be at the Hotel Trombetta, Turin, about midnight on Wednesday. I shall stay at Turin for two days and at 4 a.m. on Saturday I shall be at Sant' Agata. Does that inspire you, perchance? It would be a good idea to take your bag and come to Turin, and we'll leave for Sant' Agata together. You can help me unpack my trunks. . . .

Thank Providence on your bended knees that you didn't allow yourself to be taken in at Paris!

Very few letters, either of Verdi or Mariani, survive from 1864. The established pattern of their relationship, however, does not change. Part of February was spent by Verdi and Giuseppina at Genoa. In this year too Mariani entered into negotiations for the post of conductor at the Théâtre Italien in Paris, only to decide again to stay where he was. On 20th July Verdi asked Léon Escudier to advise Bagier to give up the idea of producing *Aroldo* in Paris: 'Without Mariani that opera is impossible.'

The days of the first performance of *Aroldo* at Rimini are referred to in an important letter published, probably from a loose draft or copy at Sant' Agata, in an editorial footnote to the *Copialettere*.[1] This was the reply to a lost letter of Mariani's, in which he had mentioned that a story was circulating, according to which Verdi had described him to General Cialdini as 'a fine conductor who overdoes all his *tempi*'. Taking this for a complaint, Verdi explained:

[1] pp. 256–7.

The last time I saw General Cialdini I said to him, among other things: 'How is the theatre going at Bologna?'

'So-so; but the orchestra does well.'

'I don't doubt it—under Mariani's baton.'

'However, the other evening I heard the overture to *Semiramide* and was not too pleased; I thought the *tempi* were rushed.'

'That's quite possible: Mariani has that tendency, to give more *brio* to the pieces.' And then (jokingly): 'It's better so—it's all over sooner! For the rest, I should have this tendency to speed things up myself if I were a conductor; Costa has it, who is one of the greatest conductors in Europe.'

Those, and no others, were the words about music exchanged by the general and myself. *C'est le ton qui fait la chanson*, says the proverb, and the simplest things take on another aspect when they are reported; the proof of which lies in the contradiction in the phrases referred to: '*A fine conductor, who overdoes all his tempi.*' But, by God, if you are a *fine* conductor you can't overdo your *tempi*, and if you overdo all your *tempi* you can't be a *fine* conductor. People with a bit of experience of the world take no notice of such silly stories, and to give you proof of that I'll tell you one that is told of yourself! One evening when we were together at Rimini, among a lot of people talking about music, and my music in particular, you said: 'But this is music that won't last. Talk to me rather about that of Meyerbeer, etc., etc., and then we're in agreement.' Well! I have never mentioned this to you, and this is the first time I have spoken of it, to prove to you that one should take no notice.

This is undated in the *Copialettere*. Mantovani,[1] however, after quoting it, says: 'And this letter of December 1870 was the last that Verdi wrote to Mariani.' This is a mistake that has led Gatti, Zoppi and others astray, and caused them not only to attach undue significance to this letter in relation to the quarrel with Mariani, but also to misunderstand what Verdi says. For they state as a fact that Mariani at Rimini *did* make this comparison between the music of Verdi and Meyerbeer, whereas the sense of the letter is that Verdi had heard the story but attached no importance to it, knowing the way things got twisted out of recognition in the mouths of idle or ill-natured gossips. There is no reason to believe, with Zoppi,[2] that after brooding over these words for thirteen years he 'spat them back in Mariani's face'. The letter was actually written early in December 1864, as is shown by Mariani's reply from Bologna, dated 6th December of that year:[3]

In an hour's time I leave for Genoa. Thank you for your last kind letter; please believe that I related that silly story for no other reason than to let you know of it. I know how much you love me and I know the nobility of your character.

[1] p. 44. [2] p. 144.

[3] No one is more confused in this matter than Abbiati, who corrects the date of Verdi's letter in his second volume (p. 428) and then reprints it under the wrong date in his third volume (p. 434).

For the rest, I don't remember having said that which you bring to my attention, concerning an expression of mine at Rimini, when we were there.

It doesn't seem possible that I should have pronounced such words, since they do not express what I feel. If I had said them I should have been mad, or stupid, and as I've never been that, someone has decided to attribute to me things I wouldn't even wish to hear, from anyone, and I would permit nobody to blaspheme in that way.

In this autumn, after an interval of two years, Mariani had returned to Bologna to conduct the season of opera at the Teatro Comunale. During this season Teresa Stolz had made her very successful *début* there, in *Ernani* and *William Tell*. It has been almost universally assumed that the love affair between them began at this time. Before we consider whether this could possibly have been the case, it will be necessary to explore, rather more thoroughly than has been hitherto done, Teresa Stolz's career, which can be reconstructed, like Giuseppina Strepponi's, from the theatrical papers of the day. First, however, a few words about her origins.

Teresa Stolz, born at Elbekosteletz in Bohemia on 5th June 1834, came of a very musical family. Five of her eight brothers and sisters studied at the Prague Conservatoire and became professional musicians. They included the twin sisters, Francesca (Fanny) and Ludmila (Lidia), both sopranos, who immortalized themselves by their relations with the composer Luigi Ricci. The twins, born on 8th May 1827, and thus seven years older than Teresa, left the Conservatoire in 1843 and made their way to Trieste, where Ricci had been established since 1837. Lidia made her *début* in a small part at the Teatro Grande during the Carnival season of 1844. The twins were probably identical, and Ricci seems to have fallen in love with both of them at first sight. In this most difficult situation he obtained a year's leave of absence, beginning in April 1844, from the authorities at Trieste, and took the sisters, with other singers, to Odessa. He wrote for them an opera, *La Solitaria delle Asturie*, first performed at Odessa on 20th February 1845. The story of Ricci and the Stolz twins would have been a wonderful subject for Richard Strauss and Hofmannsthal. Florimo was told by Federico Ricci, Luigi's younger brother, that at Odessa the composer and the twin sisters lived in apparently separate lodgings, which were connected, however, by a door concealed by a wardrobe from which the back had been removed. This led to most comical and embarrassing scenes, as when, while Ricci was receiving visitors, one of the girls emerged suddenly from the wardrobe. . . . The twins at this time were only seventeen, and Ricci nearly forty years of age. From Odessa they moved on to Constantinople before returning to Trieste. In the autumn season of 1845 and the Carnival season of 1846 Fanny and Lidia Stolz sang at the Teatro Grande, Trieste, and afterwards at Milan, Cremona and elsewhere. By a strange chance, they were among the singers engaged at Copenhagen in the winter of 1847–8 under Mariani, and if the death of Christian VIII had not cut short the season they would have appeared in another opera by Ricci, *Il diavolo a quattro*, which he was commissioned to write for them. After the revolution of 1848 they were all back at Trieste. In 1849 Ricci married Lidia Stolz, but continued to live with both sisters. Lidia was the mother of the first of his two children, Adelaide, born on 1st December 1850, and Fanny was the mother of the second, Luigi, born on 27th December 1852. . . . It comes as no surprise to learn that some years later the fell consequences of some earlier amorous adventures became apparent: Ricci went mad and died in Prague in 1859 of general paralysis.

Such was the background of Teresa Stolz's early life.

Teresa, destined to become the most famous member of the family, seemed at first to be the least gifted. Entering the Prague Conservatoire in 1849, she studied under an Italian, Giovanni Battista Gordigiani, until October 1851, when she was advised to give up hopes of becoming a singer. She returned discouraged to Elbekosteletz but in the next few years her voice developed strongly and she went back to Prague to study with Voitecha Cabouna. On 21st November 1855 she appeared in public at a concert at Zofine. After this she joined the irregular establishment at Trieste and had further lessons from Ricci. She sang at Trieste in a concert given by his pupils on 26th July 1856, and in the following year made her operatic *début* at Tiflis. The whole first phase of her career was spent in the most distant outposts of the far-flung Italian operatic empire. She appeared, like her sisters, at Odessa and Constantinople, and repeatedly at Tiflis. In 1863 she was hoping for an engagement at Milan: on 16th July the theatrical paper *Il Trovatore* mocked at the idea that one who had been for five seasons the *prima donna assoluta* at Tiflis should aspire to appear in Milan, but on 20th December the same paper reported her 'stupendous success' in *Il Trovatore* at Nice. In February and March 1864 she sang in *Mosè* and *Norma* at Nice, and in April in *Ernani* at Grenada. On 9th July it was announced that she had been engaged for the autumn season at Bologna:

> Teresina Stolz, the young and already accomplished soprano *prima donna*, who gave such an excellent account of herself recently at Grenada, as earlier at Nice, has been engaged for the coming season at the Teatro Comunale, Bologna, and for Carnival and Lent 1864–5 at the Teatro Bellini, Palermo.

It is already clear that Mariani did not 'discover' Teresa Stolz, at Trieste or anywhere else; nor was he responsible for her appearance at Bologna, as is so often stated or implied. She happened to be among the singers there, when he returned after two years' absence to conduct the autumn season.

The following table, based on reports in the theatrical papers, shows the whole course of her career from the time of her *début* in Italy up to the production of *Aida* at Milan in 1872. The first performances listed were generally followed by others, of course, up to the end of the season, the date of which is given where known. A capital M in the left-hand column indicates that Mariani was the conductor. A capital V indicates that the opera was staged under Verdi's supervision.

	10th Sept.	1864	Spoleto	Teatro Nuovo	*Il Trovatore* (2 perfs. only)
M	25th Oct.	1864	Bologna	Teatro Comunale	*Ernani*
M	Nov.	1864	Bologna	Teatro Comunale	*William Tell*
	Dec.	1864	Palermo	Teatro Bellini	*La Juive*
	Feb.	1865	Palermo	Teatro Bellini	*La Vendetta Slava* (Platania)
	Feb.	1865	Palermo	Teatro Bellini	*Rigoletto*
	Mar.	1865	Palermo	Teatro Bellini	*Macbeth*
	May	1865	Florence	Teatro Pagliano	*I Lombardi* (4 perfs. only)
M	Aug.	1865	Cesena	Teatro Comunale	*William Tell*
M	Aug.	1865	Cesena	Teatro Comunale	*Un Ballo in Maschera*
	23rd Sept.	1865	Milan	Teatro alla Scala	*Giovanna d'Arco*
	4th Nov.	1865	Milan	Teatro alla Scala	*Rebecca* (Pisani, 1 perf. only)
	18th Nov.	1865	Milan	Teatro alla Scala	*Lucrezia Borgia*
	Dec.	1865	Palermo	Teatro Bellini	*I Vespri Siciliani*
	Feb.	1866	Palermo	Teatro Bellini	*Parisina*
	Mar.	1866	Palermo	Teatro Bellini	*William Tell*
	2nd May	1866	Reggio Emilia		*Robert le Diable*
	Oct.	1866	Treviso	Teatro di Società	*Un Ballo in Maschera*
	Nov.	1866	Treviso	Teatro di Società	*Lucrezia Borgia*
	Nov.	1866	Treviso	Teatro di Società	*Jone* (Petrella)
	26th Dec.	1866	Parma	Teatro Regio	*La Juive*
	9th Jan.	1867	Parma	Teatro Regio	*Robert le Diable*
	Feb.	1867	Parma	Teatro Regio	*Un Ballo in Maschera*
	20th Feb.	1867	Parma	Teatro Regio	*Norma*
			(Season ended 12th March)		
M	27th Oct.	1867	Bologna	Teatro Comunale	*Don Carlos*
M	3rd Dec.	1867	Bologna	Teatro Comunale	*Un Ballo in Maschera*
	26th Dec.	1867	Rome	Teatro Apollo	*Jone*
	9th Feb.	1868	Rome	Teatro Apollo	*Don Carlos*
			(Season ended 25th February)		
	25th Mar.	1868	Milan	Teatro alla Scala	*Don Carlos*

M	May	1868	Genoa	Teatro Carlo Felice	*Un Ballo in Maschera*
	Aug.	1868	Vicenza		*La Juive*
	Aug.	1868	Vicenza		*Un Ballo in Maschera*
M	4th Oct.	1868	Bologna	Teatro Comunale	*La Juive*
	26th Dec.	1868	Milan	Teatro alla Scala	*Don Carlos*
V	27th Feb.	1869	Milan	Teatro alla Scala	*La Forza del Destino*
	20th Mar.	1869	Milan	Teatro alla Scala	*Fieschi* (Montuoro, two perfs. only)
	24th Apr.	1869	Parma	Teatro Regio	*Don Carlos*
	July	1869	Padua	Teatro Nuovo	*Don Carlos*
	Aug.	1869	Vicenza		*La Forza del Destino*
M	22nd Aug.	1869	Pesaro	Teatro Rossini	Rossini Commemoration (*Stabat Mater*, repeated 23rd Aug.)
	20th Sept.	1869	Trieste	Teatro Comunale	*Don Carlos*
	17th Nov.	1869	Trieste	Teatro Comunale	*Robert le Diable*
	26th Dec.	1869	Turin	Teatro Regio	*Giovanna di Napoli* (Petrella)
	22nd Jan.	1870	Turin	Teatro Regio	*Don Carlos*
	15th Mar.	1870	Turin	Teatro Regio	*Il Favorito* (Pedrotti)
M	17th July	1870	Sinigaglia	Teatro Fenice	*Don Carlos*
	26th Dec.	1870	Venice	Teatro Fenice	*Don Carlos*
	7th Feb.	1871	Venice	Teatro Fenice	*Ruy Blas* (Marchetti)
	1st Apr.	1871	Venice	Teatro Fenice	*Linda d'Ispahan* (Malipiero)
	Aug.	1871	Brescia		*Robert le Diable*
	26th Dec.	1871	Milan	Teatro alla Scala	*La Forza del Destino*
V	8th Feb.	1872	Milan	Teatro alla Scala	*Aida*

From this table we see that between her *début* at Bologna in the autumn of 1864 and her reappearance there in *Don Carlos* three years later, Teresa Stolz sang under Mariani's direction only at Cesena, in August 1865. This combines with other negative evidence to suggest that there was in fact no close bond between them during this time. Singer and conductor could not be always together, but if they were in love they could surely have arranged things better than this. There is nothing to show that they met between engagements, and all that has been written about their living together at Genoa is based only on assumptions.

Some initial attraction is possible enough, before Teresa Stolz went off to sing in Sicily and Mariani returned to Genoa. His letters at the turn of the year show him ill and melancholy, and Giuseppina, on 3rd January 1865, wrote this to him:

I have received your most welcome letter, written in an access, and excess, of sentimentalism—the result, perhaps, of some storm raised up by the blindfolded god. Let's hope that the pains, inflammation and ill humour will have gone by now, thanks to the opportune arrival of a perfumed *billet-doux* to play the doctor. In case there is something positively wrong, take little medicine and lead a very regular life, which is the best of all medicines.

Verdi and I are growing old, but our health is good, and our hearts and heads are sound. Thank you for your good wishes, which we very sincerely and cordially reciprocate. It seems that we shall be coming to Genoa, but not just yet. Verdi or I will write and tell you when, on condition that you keep it secret, for callers as soon as we've arrived get in my way and give me the *spleen*.

Permit me this suggestion: look after yourself, *wear flannel over your intestines*, talk little, sigh even less, and we shall find you well and lively as a cricket, ready for the joys of the Carnival.

Most of February and early March were spent at Genoa.

It is surprising to find Verdi writing in June to Escudier, confident, in spite of past experience, that he could persuade Mariani to go to Paris as conductor of the Théâtre Italien: 'Why don't you try to get Mariani again? It's something I could arrange, if Bagier wishes. But see that no one interferes. If Bagier wants that, let him make equitable conditions; I undertake to get them accepted. Then you will have a good conductor at last.' It is not clear why he now favoured an appointment he had thought undesirable for Mariani in 1863.

In a letter of 2nd July Mariani suggested that he should visit Sant' Agata for advice. If he had done so punctually he would have been there at the same time as Escudier, with whom the Parisian appointment could have been seriously discussed. But Mariani was detained at Genoa.

One of the surprises of these letters is the discovery that Teresa Sauli Pallavicino, with whom, before and after his relations with Teresa Stolz, the conductor is supposed to have had a love affair, was a married woman. It is clear from Mariani's letters that her married name was Teresa Pallavicino Negrotto. She appears to have been a highly eccentric and emotionally unstable person. A crisis in her affairs was responsible for Mariani not coming at once to Sant' Agata:

2nd July 1865:

The poor Pallavicino family has suffered a most terrible misfortune. The daughter, Signora Teresa, who already had unexpectedly decided to return with her husband, has gone mad. All the family are with her in the country, at the house of Marchese Negrotto, the son-in-law.

9th July 1865:

An affair of the utmost importance to me prevents my departure, as I had intended, this evening, and I shall have to stay here a few days longer. . . . I'll tell you all about it by word of mouth, and you know that your poor Wrong Head is most capable of *good deeds*.

Giuseppina, ever sceptical where Mariani was concerned, commented on 31st July in a letter to Giuseppe De Amicis at Genoa: 'Mariani was here and imparted to the telling of the story you mention in your letter the most sentimental and philanthropic colouring imaginable. For my part, I think that a little *confiteor* would be in place in the mouths of all the characters in that quasi-tragedy. If they do recite it, I pray God to forgive them, and set them on the right road.'

Mariani's letters from Cesena, in late July and August, include the first brief references to Teresa Stolz. In *Un ballo in maschera*: 'La Stolz, the *prima donna*, did very well indeed, and so did Pandolfini, the baritone.' The Parisian project was discussed in several letters. Bagier again wished to combine the appointment at the Théâtre Italien with the direction of a season of opera in Madrid and offered 50,000 francs for this. Mariani was tempted, but wished first to have Verdi's approval: 'I shall do nothing, settle nothing, without advising you and without your advice. You are all I have in the world, and it is certain that I owe every satisfaction and the contentment of my life to your benevolence, to the kindness you squander upon me. My Maestro! I shall always be your faithful servant.' The other subject of these letters is the epidemic of cholera that raged in the area. He describes the arrival of a train full of cholera victims from Ancona; a man vomiting out of the window while his sister lay dying on the floor of the carriage, without attention, guards being posted to keep people at a distance. Mariani had the crazy idea that water-melons were anti-choleraic: 'I continue my usual way of life, eating melons and fruit. I feel very well, and in any case, if cholera gets me, you will write my Requiem Mass. I tell you the truth: I would most gladly die so that Italy and the whole world might have such a fine present from you. A Requiem Mass by Verdi! Enough of that—we shall see what happens.'

But it was not for Mariani that Verdi was to write his Requiem Mass.

This time Mariani got as far as going to Paris to see Bagier. But again nothing was settled. It is truly a great pity that so many of Verdi's letters from these later years have been lost or destroyed. One would like to know what he wrote to produce the following reply, from Genoa, on 26th September:

> On my return from Paris I found here your *tremendous* letter, which I read with resigned devotion, since in it you tell me some home truths that I too feel in the depths of my heart, and I wish I hadn't provided occasion for them to be told me. It's true! *Mea culpa, mea culpa, mea maxima culpa!*

Batti, batti, o bel Maestro! There really was a masochistic element in Mariani's nature. Then, having admitted his fault, he begins to shuffle and excuse himself: 'But, believe me, my Maestro, from what I can gather, this year my having delayed coming to Sant' Agata is not of moment, for I have come to no agreement with Bagier.' Another conductor had already been engaged. Clearly, however, this had not happened until Bagier had despaired of getting a decisive answer from Mariani, after several months.

After some rather confused negotiations with both Perrin, director of the Opéra, and Bagier, Verdi himself had decided to go to Paris in the coming winter.

During his visit to the French capital Mariani had attended two performances of *L'Africaine* at the Opéra, and his impressions, as reported in the letter of 26th September, are of great interest, and astonishing in view of his reputation as a fanatical admirer of Meyerbeer:

Musically speaking, it's a poor thing; *staged, however, stupendously*, and that is why I say I have *seen L'Africaine*, since it's more to be seen than heard. You too will *see* it, and *in this* you will be of my opinion. Then, if I must tell you the truth, I found the orchestral playing cold, and one can hear that it was rehearsed by old Fétis, called specially from Brussels, and the French say that the *tempi* of *L'Africaine* are old-time *tempi*. . . . For the rest, those sixteen bars in unison, that they always have to repeat, in the last scene of the fifth act, are truly stupid as a composition, and that's the only thing that is moderately well played, for being a *unison* passage for the stringed instruments, which are good, especially those ten violoncellos, reinforced by clarinets and bassoons, it produced a fine effect. When you see that passage of sixteen bars, to which *all the papers* have given such importance, you will laugh. It's really a case of wishing to make famous what is in reality mediocre in the extreme. By God! It seems to me that in Paris very little is needed to make an effect.

Coming back to myself, I'll tell you, my Maestro, that I was only sorry not to have accepted the Parisian offer when I was told that you were going there next winter, and that you will be at the Opéra and the Théâtre Italien. You can't imagine the sorrow I felt for having to stay at Genoa without *you*, and knowing you to be in Paris without *me* will render me desolate. But believe me, my Maestro, this year it was impossible to come to agreement with Bagier. . . . So don't abandon your poor Wrong Head, and be sure that all you do for me I will accept with my eyes closed.

This very autumn he was to conduct *L'Africaine* at Bologna and arouse enormous enthusiasm in his audiences by those same sixteen bars in unison which he had ridiculed to Verdi. Towards the end of the year he wrote to Lucca [1] of the 'stupendous music' of Meyerbeer's opera.

Verdi in Paris signed the contract for *Don Carlos* and returned in March 1866 to Sant' Agata. In Giuseppina's letter-books we find evidence of further dissatisfaction with the way his operas were

[1] Piancastelli Collection, letter of 22nd December 1865.

performed at Genoa. There is the draft, subsequently cancelled, of a ferocious letter to Ricordi in May:

I believe that *La forza del destino* would gain by being sung and not *barked*, as it was by that pack of dogs who are howling at Genoa! What do you say? Do you think that if it had been one of Lucca's operas he would have allowed it to be given in those conditions, and so near Milan? Never! Never! Lucca is a *bourgeois* publisher, who lowers himself even to look after the merchandise he has acquired. For shame! How prosaic! An aristocratic publisher lets them be massacred, murmuring haughtily:

Non curiam di lor ma guarda e passa.

What a difference!

Then a milder rebuke for Mariani:

Permit me to ask, *en passant, sans rancune*, and so that you don't think me too much of a blockhead: If the company of singers who had to perform *La forza del destino* was so bad, why did you yourself show such interest on your impresario's account, even going so far as to ask Ricordi for moderation in the fees? Are my operas created, then, to be thrown to the dogs, just as you please, as a *pis aller*? Ah. . . . I was forgetting—my name ends in i.

Mariani took evasive action, reporting the successful performance of another work, in the course of a short visit to Bologna. Giuseppina replied, on 13th May:

Verdi, as you can imagine, is very busy with the opera for Paris, for which reason he begs you to excuse him if he does not reply directly to your letter from Bologna. . . . He says that if the *Inno delle Nazioni* was a success at Bologna he is glad, without being surprised, and that not on account of the quality of the music but because of the good *ensemble* of performers. He would have preferred, however, that such an *ensemble*, and all the elements necessary, should have been got together for *La forza del destino* at Genoa. . . . Although the orchestra can perform miracles on its own account, it can't sing, paint the scenery, make the costumes, etc. In the first production of such an opera, and others of that sort, everything must work together to form a homogeneous whole.

For years now Mariani had been in search of a suitable home for Verdi at Genoa. He found it at length in the Palazzo Sauli, the property of his friend the Marchesa Luisa Sauli Pallavicino, the mother of Teresa Pallavicino Negrotto. The whole upper floor of this, the *piano nobile*, would be vacant from the autumn. No finer choice could possibly have been made. A splendid building by Alessi, situated on the hill of Carignano, amid gardens with cypresses, cedars, palms and magnolias, with wide views over the port and the shining sea, it was isolated and peaceful, and yet within a few minutes' walk of the centre of the city. In recent years other buildings have encroached on the grounds, the view towards the sea has been cut off, but the tragic bombed palazzo, amid its wildly overgrown gardens, casts a spell even today. The address remains what it was in Verdi's time: Via San Giacomo 13.

Palazzo Sauli, between the wars, was used as offices by the Società Elettrica Terni, and the interior entirely altered, so that it is no longer possible to envisage, from the building itself, its internal aspect when Verdi, Giuseppina and Mariani were its occupants. In a letter written after the breach, quoted by Luzio, Giuseppina has a remark about Mariani having 'spontaneously, not to say arbitrarily, taken possession' of his apartment, which he had then to be asked to leave. Zoppi, who has drawn some largely erroneous conclusions from information conveyed in the inventory of Mariani's effects, is incredulous and indignant at Giuseppina's remark. 'But is it not known,' he asks, 'has it not been printed by all the biographers, that the Verdis went to live in that villa in 1866, at the suggestion and with the intermediation of Mariani, who had already been renting rooms there for years?' [1] The answer is that all this is indeed stated or implied by many biographers, including Gatti, but that none of them has taken any steps to find out where Mariani lived before this, and they have all *assumed*, quite wrongly, that he was already installed in Palazzo Sauli before Verdi decided to go there. Mariani's correspondence makes quite clear that something of the sort described by Giuseppina did take place.

Another most misleading assumption is that Teresa Stolz was also living at Genoa at this time. Opinion is divided as to precisely where she stayed. Gatti, probably on the evidence of Maria Cortesi Schnitzer's letter to the editor of *Il Lavoro* in 1929, says she lived in the nearby Palazzo Corallo, by the bridge of Carignano. Zoppi and most Italian writers follow Gatti in this. Francis Toye, following Belviglieri's article and ignoring Maria Cortesi Schnitzer's protest, says Teresa Stolz actually lived with Mariani in Palazzo Sauli. This view of things still prevails among English writers and a few minor Italian ones. All the biographers present the picture of Verdi and Giuseppina, Mariani and Teresa Stolz, living on the most intimate terms, almost like a single family, at Genoa in 1866. But this is absolutely impossible.

Our table of the career of Teresa Stolz in the Italian theatres shows her singing at Palermo during the first three months of the year and at Reggio Emilia in May. Then there is a gap of about five months before she reappears at Treviso in October. This gap is accounted for by the war with Austria. Verdi himself, during this time, was first in Paris and then at Sant' Agata, working on *Don Carlos*, until on 5th July he came to Genoa. By 3rd August, having failed to obtain release

[1] p. 376.

from his contract with the Opéra, he was back in France, where he remained for the whole of the rest of the year. He was thus at Genoa for just less than one month, at the height of the war, during which Teresa Stolz, an Austrian subject, cannot possibly have been in Italy.

There are no further references, so far, in Mariani's letters, to the woman with whom he is supposed to have been having a love affair. There is a total lack of any sort of friendly greetings to the Verdis from her, such as might have been expected if they were all already on intimate terms.

During the short stay at Genoa it was finally arranged for the new apartment in Palazzo Sauli to be got ready for the following winter.

An entry made in Giuseppina's letter-book in Paris on 27th September begins:

> Alas! That's how it is! Put yourself out on your friends' behalf, look for an apartment, find it, see that everything runs *comme sur les roulettes*, send a booklet of measurements, and silk-twist for matching colours, give orders to the servant to dust the furniture, so that it doesn't deteriorate, in short, go to endless trouble. . . . And then? And then find you've done it all only for ingrates! Thus, perhaps, a certain Mariani, unjustly called Wrong Head by Verdi, will have muttered. If so, let the lamentations of Jeremiah cease, and learn that if you have sent me a booklet of measurements, I am disposed, in an outburst of gratitude, to send you a volume of thanks.

He deserved no less. Out of twenty-one letters sent to Paris during the rehearsals of *Don Carlos*, eighteen are addressed to Giuseppina and are concerned almost entirely with Palazzo Sauli and its decoration and furnishing. This is another batch of letters that really has to be seen to be believed. In endless detail, and at astonishing length, Mariani provided every scrap of information that could conceivably be useful. The 'booklet of measurements' mentioned by Giuseppina was a letter of twenty-three pages, dated 9th–12th September, containing the description and plans, with all the measurements, of forty-nine different rooms, corridors, doors, staircases, etc.

Some extracts from the letters to Giuseppina will make clear the situation in Palazzo Sauli. Mariani uses the word 'mezzarie', derived from Genoese dialect, for that part of the building he proposed himself to inhabit; sometimes he calls it the 'mezzanine' but that, as we shall see, is misleading. A Signor Tuvo had been his predecessor in these rooms.

9th September:

> As for the *mezzarie*, I repeat that I need only four or five rooms, including the servant's room and the kitchen. You will be able to furnish the remainder for your friends, if they come, and I shall like that, because it will seem as if I have a large apartment at my disposition.

11th November:

The Signori Pallavicini are still in the country and will not be returning until towards the end of December. As Tuvo is leaving, that palazzo will be left wholly uninhabited, so if you and the Maestro permit I think it would be as well, as soon as everything is in order, if I began to have my things moved in. . . . Further, I must tell you, my Signora Peppina, that, hoping you would be returning in December, I have given up the apartment I am living in at present.

28th November:

I have agreed with the person who is taking over my little apartment to let him have it from the fifth of next month, but the *mezzarie* cannot be ready on the fifth of next month, since it has been necessary to whitewash the walls and varnish the floors, which were in a very bad state. . . . So I shall have to have all my things carried for the time being into the *gran salone* of the *appartamento nobile*, and keep them there until I can have them carried upstairs. . . . As I told you in my last letter, I shall only occupy in the mezzanine an entrance hall, another room (of which I shall make my little drawing-room) and the bedroom. These three rooms can't be separated. Then there'll be another one which will absolutely have to be joined to mine, as there's no other way of getting into it. Thus, then, my little apartment (if you and the Maestro agree) could consist of an entrance hall, a little drawing-room, the bedroom, which would serve also as my study, and another room to the left of the entrance hall, which I could keep at the disposal of my friends. I'll put my servant to sleep in a little room attached to the kitchen of the mezzanine. In this division of things one room would remain free, wholly independent. . . . But, I repeat, I shall settle nothing without your consent, which you will give me only on your return. So for now I'll put myself in two rooms, with their entrance hall, and that's enough. If then you and the Maestro think fit to let me have all the *mezzarie*, as Signor Tuvo had, I'll pay you 600 francs rent annually, as he paid, otherwise I couldn't accept it. I tell you again, my Signora Peppina, it's such an honour for me to be able to have my *nest* under your roof, to be able to live in such a pleasant situation, and to be *the guardian of Verdi's house*, that truly I don't know how to repay you, in gratitude for the favour you have wished to squander on me. So, my Signora Peppina, we're agreed.

A good many of Gatti's and, particularly, Zoppi's illusions are destroyed by these passages. We can see now how Palazzo Sauli was divided among its inhabitants. The proprietress, the Marchesa Luisa Sauli Pallavicino, retained the ground floor, where some members, at least, of her family lived. The whole of the rest of the building, consisting of the *appartamento nobile* and the *mezzarie*, was rented from her by Verdi, for 3,700 lire a year.[1] There is no sign in Palazzo Sauli of any rooms on a mezzanine level, between the two

[1] Giuseppina's letter-book, 29th November 1866: 'Wrote to Mariani, and sent 4,000 francs, 3,700 of which to pay the rent and the rest to remain at our disposition.'

main floors, and since Mariani's luggage was to be taken *upstairs* from the *appartamento nobile*, the first floor, it is clear that the *mezzarie* were the series of low rooms on the attic level, distinguishable in photographs as a row of small windows at the top of the building. Mariani's 'nest' was, in fact, a comparatively small and humble one, immediately under the roof. It is important to note that he was Verdi's sub-tenant. The final arrangement was that he should pay 400 lire a year for the rooms he had suggested in his letter of 28th November, the rest of the *mezzarie* being retained by Verdi for the use of his guests. This explains the statement in the inventory of Mariani's effects that when the seals were removed from the third door, on the left as one entered, it was found locked on the other side, since it led to rooms occupied by Verdi. It led actually to his spare bedroom in the attic storey.

On 9th December Mariani announced: 'I rise from bed, after sleeping for the first time in your future residence, the enchanting Palazzo Sauli in Carignano.' Soon he had the joy—it was no less for him—of again fetching and carrying for Verdi. In the new year the furniture began to arrive from Paris: 'Thank God, thirteen cases are already in the house. They arrived the day before yesterday. I at once got busy. I ran to the director of the customs, to the town hall; all due formalities were completed and yesterday, towards the evening, your thirteen cases came out of the customs, without paying any dues, either to the Government or the municipality.' Eight more were to follow. 'Will the other cases be long delayed? The fact is, I am enjoying myself and it's a real satisfaction to me to be able to serve my Maestro and my Signora Peppina.' He saw to everything. He installed the billiard-table; he laid in supplies of fuel for the kitchen. 'The beds are all in order,' he wrote on 23rd February, 'for which I have the new linen; only blankets are lacking, but I can get those at any time.' He supplied a list of sailing dates of ships from Nice to Genoa. Early in March he was almost ecstatic with happiness at the idea of their arrival, and on the 14th was able to welcome them to their new home.

Gino Monaldi, in half a dozen publications since 1898, tells how Mariani had accompanied Verdi to Paris for the production of *Don Carlos* and comforted him afterwards for the relative failure of the opera: 'I'll have it performed and conduct it myself at Bologna, and then we shall see.' This is seen to be simply untrue, since Mariani was not in Paris with Verdi. Variants of the story are given by many later writers, including Mantovani, Gatti and Zoppi. Gatti, in his first edition, followed as usual by Zoppi, sends not only Mariani but also Teresa Stolz to Paris, at Verdi's invitation. As our table shows, she was singing at the time at Parma. Gatti himself, in the revision of his work, became aware of this, from a letter from Verdi in Paris to Ferrarini, the conductor at Parma, asking for information about the Bohemian singer. So the passage about the trip to Paris is deleted in Gatti's second edition, although by an oversight it remains in the analytical index, under Mariani's name. It is a pity Gatti did not give us the whole text of the letter to Ferrarini, otherwise unknown. It seems obvious that Verdi had never yet met or heard Teresa Stolz.

Even while Mariani was settling himself and his belongings in Palazzo Sauli he had been discussing in correspondence with Cesare Dallolio, a member of the municipal council of Bologna, the possibility of removal to that city, as permanent director of the Liceo Musicale and the Teatro Comunale—the old project that had been revived several times since 1860. It seems that he had recently been given an increase of salary, from the 3,600 lire, less 7½ per cent for the pension fund, mentioned in earlier letters: 'My salary here is 5,000 francs a year. I am a civic employee, with corresponding pension rights, and I already have fourteen years and seven months' service. . . . Besides this, I am *maestro di cappella* of the cathedral of Sant' Ambrogio, for which I get another 600 francs a year.' Typical of his thinking, at once ingenuous and tortuous, is the argument in these letters that secrecy was necessary, because the municipality of Genoa had been very good to him, and if they got wind of the proposal that he should go to Bologna, they might so load him with favours that he would find it impossible to leave.

The spring of 1867 was spent by Verdi and Giuseppina in Palazzo Sauli, though there were frequent excursions to Sant' Agata. Mariani's letters recommence after their final removal to the country for the summer. We now have further news of the proprietors of Palazzo Sauli:

6th July:

The Pallavicino family left on the first of the month and are again in trouble. Their daughter ran away to Paris. She left one day before her mother, whom she awaited at Turin, and from there continued the journey with her to Paris. She left with only the clothes she was wearing, without money, and in despite of her husband, who is beside himself with anger. She did not manage to take even a handkerchief with her. Poor Signora Luisa! She certainly won't enjoy her trip to Paris.

17th July:

The Pallavicino family wrote to me from Paris, and as you can imagine their stay there is disturbed by the incubus of the daughter who inconsiderately played one of her tricks. God grant that everything may be settled this time too, but in any case it's a nasty business.

Now Mariani really was to go to Paris with Verdi, and to hear *Don Carlos* at the Opéra. The letter of 17th July continues: 'We shall see you there, if you are still disposed to betake yourself, with your wife of course, to Paris. It will be a real joy to your poor, faithful Wrong Head to make that journey in your company, all the more since I feel in better health, so that I shall be crazier than ever.'

In an obituary notice of Teresa Stolz in Ricordi's periodical *Musica e Musicisti* for 15th September 1902 it is stated that someone pointed her out to Verdi as a suitable interpreter of the role of Elisabeth for the first Italian performances of *Don Carlos* at Bologna, and that on being offered the part she went to Paris, heard the opera three times and then telegraphed to Ricordi: 'I accept.' The essential truth of this is confirmed by an item of news in the *Gazzetta Musicale di Milano* for 4th August 1867; 'Signora Teresina Stolz has arrived back at Milan from Paris, where she went to hear *Don Carlos*.' A fortnight later the *Gazzetta* announced: 'The illustrious Maestro Verdi has left Genoa for Paris, in company with Maestro Cav. Angelo Mariani.' This is in accordance with what Verdi wrote to Camille Du Locle on 16th August: 'On Monday morning I shall be in Paris with my wife. With us will be my friend Mariani, who wants to hear *Don Carlos*. So if there is a performance on Monday evening, please keep an orchestral stall for him, in a good position. He needs to hear well and see well, so it would be best if it were not too near the orchestra.' The fact that Teresa Stolz, before accepting the engagement to sing in *Don Carlos* at Bologna, went independently to Paris and back, only just before Verdi and Mariani did the same, very strongly supports the view that they were not all living together 'almost like a single family'. Mariani's letters to Ricordi [1] show that he was initially in favour of another singer, Antonietta Fricci, for the role, going so far as to declare that one of her legs alone was worth the whole of Teresa Stolz. This is not exactly the language of a lover.

It becomes more and more clear that the accepted chronology of the relations between Verdi, Mariani and Teresa Stolz, based as it is on pure surmise, is in need of drastic revision. There is no evidence at all, up to this time, that Mariani was in love with Teresa Stolz, or that Verdi even knew her, except by repute. We have seen, in our introductory survey of the historiography of the supposed affair, that Mantovani dates the beginning of Verdi's love for Teresa Stolz from the time of the last rehearsals of *Don Carlos* at Bologna. He is followed in this by Gatti, in his first edition, and by Zoppi, who tries to account for the continuing friendly relations between Verdi and Mariani by explaining: 'It is one thing to fall in love, and another to attain love's perfection. Nothing prevents us conjecturing that there was a period of waiting, between that falling in love and that perfection. A time of doubt, like a shuddering and germinal March day, of temptations, of delicious and tormented perplexities, perhaps too

[1] Abbiati, III, pp. 133–5.

of scruples, of anticipated remorse on one side or the other.'[1] But Verdi, in reality, did not attend either rehearsals or any performance of *Don Carlos* at Bologna. This is another thing quietly corrected by Gatti in his second edition.[2]

Abbiati, in all these matters, is quite hopelessly confused. He tries to reconcile old assumptions and new documents by fictional elaborations worse even than Zoppi's, and far longer.

All through the autumn of 1867 correspondence continued between Mariani at Bologna and Verdi and Giuseppina at Genoa and Sant' Agata. There was no lack of gossip and scandal concerning friends and neighbours:

Bologna, 7th October:

Corticelli is here and comes to wake me up every morning. He too has contracted the bad habit of maltreating me always, for he says I stay up late at night in the café. He's a proper grumbler. I have been assured that he is a woman chaser *par excellence* and that Bologna is full of his former mistresses, old and young. . . . I received a letter this morning from the Pallavicino family, with the usual greetings for you and your wife, and among other things they tell me there has died of cholera the young Count De Sonnaz, object of the jealousy of the Marchese Negrotto, the daughter's husband. That ass now delights in tormenting that poor creature, manifesting to her his infernal joy at this death, and he says that God has avenged him.

This was just before Corticelli, when his fortunes were at a low ebb, was engaged as Verdi's bailiff at Sant' Agata. Suddenly, by this very fact, he became an object almost of veneration to Mariani:

14th October:

This morning the good Corticelli told me he had received Signora Giuseppina's letter, and wept with consolation. You really are angelic creatures! You have rendered happy one who is the king of men of honour, and the admiration of all the honest. Poor Mauro! He comes to see me every morning and his company is so dear to me, because I consider him part of yourself and of that dear creature, your wife. Are you coming to Bologna? You can be sure you would not be annoyed. There is a fine exhibition of pictures. Come, my Maestro, it would be such a consolation! I would allow myself to be made fun of, too—but do come!

With the performance of *Don Carlos* at the Teatro Comunale on 27th October Mariani attained the first of the twin peaks of his career. Under his direction the great but ponderous work, in its original five-act form, took flight as it had not done in Paris and as it has never again done since. Contemporary criticism recognized his great contribution to this result. Filippi wrote in *La Perseveranza*:

[1] p. 197. [2] p. 500.

The success was immense, the performance phenomenal. The first and greatest credit for this marvellous achievement is due to the conductor, Angelo Mariani, for whom no praise, no epithets, can suffice. In him, one may say, all Verdi's opera is incarnate, for not only did he rehearse and conduct the score, but he thought of everything, down to the smallest detail of the staging. From the orchestra his genius (it really is genius) sparkles; one would say that by richness of colour, by fire, by the magic of sonority, he creates another *Don Carlos* within the *Don Carlos* of Verdi.

Perhaps the composer, if he had been present, would not have approved of all Mariani's ways of doing this, but it is certain that the revendication of his opera gave him no little satisfaction. He was enabled to write to Escudier:

It seems that *Don Carlos* has had a very great success at Bologna. Everybody says that the performance is marvellous, and that there are some most powerful effects. I can't help reflecting: here, it's not a month since the rehearsals began, and great effects are obtained; at the Opéra they rehearse for eight months and the result in the end is an anaemic and cold performance. See how right I am to say that one single hand, if secure and powerful, can work miracles. You have seen it with Costa in London; you see it in greater measure with Mariani at Bologna.

Almost before the first echoes of the triumph of *Don Carlos* at Bologna had died away, Mariani was again in trouble. We do not know what Verdi wrote to cause Mariani to reply on 2nd November, six days after the first performance: 'I thank you for the letter you have had the goodness to write me, as I thank my good Signora Peppina for the kind words it pleased her to send me. I know full well that I must always, always, always be maltreated by you, but your censures, your rigour and severity, are more dear to me than the praise of anyone else, and I shall be eternally grateful.'

His contract at Genoa required him to be available there from the beginning of November to the middle of May. Each time he conducted the autumn season of opera at Bologna he needed the permission of the municipality of Genoa, if he was to stay away until the end of the season. In this year of 1867, when Meyerbeer's *Dinorah* (*Le Pardon de Ploërmel*) was due to be performed at Genoa in November, there was a considerable body of opinion, headed understandably by the impresario of the Teatro Carlo Felice, Emanuele Gattorno, which considered that Mariani should return to his post.

Mariani's letters from Bologna in November are concerned with the later performances of *Don Carlos* and with profuse explanations of the situation at Genoa and his views on his own moral and contractual obligations to the municipality.

4th November, after the fifth performance of *Don Carlos*:

As I told you, then, when I left Genoa I agreed with the assessor of the theatre (Avv. Brosca) and the deputy mayor (Avv. Bixio) that if I arrived in time to be able to conduct the three first performances of *Don Carlos* at Bologna and then return to Genoa for the orchestral rehearsals of *Ploërmel*, I would gladly do so, but that if I knew I could not get back there in time I would warn them to find someone to take my place. In fact, in due time, I wrote to Ricordi, proprietor of the score of *Ploërmel*, and at the same time to the above-mentioned two municipal assessors, as well as the impresario, that they should agree among themselves to find me a substitute. From Genoa I had no reply to my letters. I only learned from Ricordi that Mazzucato had undertaken the task of rehearsing and conducting *Ploërmel*, and for that purpose would stay at Genoa until the 10th of this month. I did not write again to anyone, except when, a few days ago, I received a letter from Avv. Bixio in which he congratulated me on the great success of *Don Carlos* and said he hoped I would return to Genoa by the third of this month. To this letter from the assessor Bixio I replied that I was grateful for his kindness but that it was useless for me to return now to Genoa, because my sense of delicacy did not permit me to take over the direction of an opera that was rehearsed and directed by another most able conductor and that, not knowing the work at all, I could not suddenly put myself in a position where I should only have been an embarrassment and no use at all. And that therefore they should keep Mazzucato as long as he could stay there and afterwards there should succeed him Maestro De Ferrari, who took the pianoforte rehearsals, or my normal substitute Signor Preve, who has been present all the time and subject to the will of the aforesaid Mazzucato. And that if after *Ploërmel* they gave another familiar opera, this could be conducted either by the said De Ferrari, or by Preve, who is quite able.

I ended by saying that my presence was more necessary at Bologna than at Genoa, and that I hoped they would understand my position and leave me here as long as possible. I heard no more. I know that that beastly impresario Gattorno spoke ill of me, and that the members of the municipal council keep telling him that there are circumstances at times before which egotism and private interests have to give way, and that if they did not quickly grant me this permission I should leave the Teatro Carlo Felice. I know too that the said impresario did not fail to protest to the municipality about my absence. I don't know what reply was given him; I only know that all this gets on my nerves and that if Signor Gattorno (with whom I have nothing to do) doesn't stop it, I shan't go back any more and all will be over.

Whatever the cost, I shall not leave *Don Carlos* now. I like it too much, I feel satisfaction such as I have never felt in any other of the highly important performances I have had the honour of directing; and now that the poor impresario is making up for the enormous expenses he has incurred in putting on this imposing spectacle, I must not egoistically abandon him. I'll tell you, too, that here in Romagna, if they knew I had gone away, in the adoration they have for you, they would condemn me and I should be universally blamed.

Then the municipal authorities here sent for me this morning and offered me, *on the terms I should myself have wished*, the directorship of the Liceo Musicale and of the theatre, and everything I pleased, counting the years of service I have at Genoa and leaving me at liberty as many months as I wish, to go where I please.

I asked for time before replying, and this was granted. I don't know what to do. It's quite possible that Gattorno's way of going on will spur me to accept the offer of this classical city; in any case, however, I shall spend all my free time at Genoa, or wherever you and Signora Peppina are. I should like to have (*in all confidence*) your opinion of these proposals.

6th November, after the sixth performance of *Don Carlos*:

They have written again from Genoa, to induce me to go there instantly, but I am standing firm, saying that I must not and cannot take over the direction of an opera rehearsed and directed by another *renowned* conductor.

Meanwhile I'm staying here, whatever happens.

I can't help it, my Maestro. Real artistic pleasures and satisfactions are so rare that when there is one to be had, one must not disdain it and leave it suddenly in the lurch.

I am enjoying these performances; they give me satisfaction, and I feel I am an artist. I have suffered too much in the past, and since I don't believe I shall ever again have a complex of opera and performers like this, I am making up now for what I could not get in the past and what will never be given me to obtain in the future. What a divine creation is this *Don Carlos* of yours! What enchanting music! What a stupendous *ensemble*! I say that in all possible truth and with the utmost sincerity of heart.

The dispute with the municipal authorities at Genoa could not long be kept from public knowledge and on 16th November the local newspaper *Il Movimento* published a letter from Mariani to the assessor of the theatre. If in this there are not quite so many evasive twistings and turnings as in the letter to Verdi of 4th November, it still reveals a fundamental illogicality, and presents alternative and contradictory reasons for his actions. He would have liked, he untruthfully said, to have been back at his post by 10th November, but due regard to his distinguished colleague Mazzucato did not permit this; at the same time he asked the municipality and the Genoese public not to consider him a man who had failed to keep his engagements, as might appear, but an artist constrained by the *force majeure* of art to stay at Bologna to conduct, for the glory of Italy, the latest work of Verdi.

The impresario responded by pasting bills, giving his point of view, on all the walls of the city.

Towards the end of the letter published in *Il Movimento* Mariani wrote: 'I scarcely need to add that as soon as the autumn season at Bologna is over I shall infallibly return to Genoa to take up my duties again.' A few days later even this was in doubt:

21st November, after the fifteenth performance of *Don Carlos*:

Imagine! Last night and tonight we had to repeat *four times* the famous eight bars for orchestra that conclude the trio in the third act. . . . I so revel in this divine music of yours, with these soloists and chorus, this orchestra and brass band, that I feel I'm in Paradise, and during the five hours I spend in the theatre I forget the troubles caused me at Genoa. . . .

It's true I promised the municipality to return there for the Carnival, but unless I receive better news I am thinking of paying heed to the doctors here at Bologna, who assure me that, for my health's sake, I need a few months' rest and an assiduous cure.

If one excuse was not good enough, another, it seems, could always be found.

It struck him then that he had received no comments on all this from Verdi:

24th November:

I have been deprived for so long of your dear letters, and that makes me very sad. Have I perhaps been involuntarily at fault in some way? However much I examine my conscience I have nothing with which to reproach myself, yet if, through *foolishness*, I have pained you by one or other of my letters, I beg you, in the name of the devotion I bear you, to relieve me, by a line in your hand, from this most painful condition, and tell me where I have been at fault and I will offer my apologies.

Tonight is the seventeenth performance of your *Don Carlos*.

The reply came from Giuseppina:

Verdi left last night on his last trip to Sant' Agata before settling definitively in winter quarters at Genoa. He did not read the article sent him, as he knew it already, together with the letter printed in *Il Movimento*. I can't conceal from you, dear Mariani, that the impression made by that letter of yours, on all those who are fond of you, and especially on Verdi, was a very bad one. A lot could be said about the style and the content of that letter, but since it concerns exclusively your own affairs, it's not my place to speak about it. I'll only say, as indeed I must say, that you were wrong to bring into it *Don Carlos* and Verdi's glory, when you should only have spoken of your own affairs with the municipality and the management of the theatre, i.e. whether you had or had not the right, whether you had or had not formal and legal permission, to absent yourself from your post for the whole season. From that letter of yours it almost seems as if Verdi weighed in the balance of your decision to stay at Bologna, somewhat in despite of the Genoese! . . . Your publicly involving him in such delicate affairs, not his concern, doesn't please Verdi at all, in character stern, decided and very reserved, as he is.

This is taken from Giuseppina's letter-book. The rest of the draft is all crossed out and we do not know how the letter, as actually sent, continued. But the erased passage makes clear what Verdi and Giuseppina thought:

> I heard (is it true?) that you had no regular permission, but only verbal leave to stay at Bologna up to a certain fixed time. In that case, forgive me for saying so, but the Genoese are right, and I who am your friend and sincerely fond of you, to my regret am constrained to find you in the wrong. If you wished to stay at Bologna for the whole season and could not get regular permission to do so, you ought either to have handed in your resignation at once or, at all events, to have returned to your post after the first few performances of *Don Carlos*. And while we are talking of resignation: these hesitations and that threat which, like the sword of Damocles, you have hung for such a long time over the head of the municipality and the management of the theatre—'If you don't do such a thing, don't grant me that other thing, I'll go away'—for an honest man, and a great artist such as you are, they really are unbecoming. One discusses terms, one accepts or refuses an engagement, a position, but once one has accepted one doesn't return every moment to the past. You know that the Genoese are above all business men, and your contract with the municipality is a business affair like any other, concluded and settled between the two parties. The one who fails . . . is wrong.

Raffaello De Rensis, in an article 'A proposito del *Lohengrin*: I primi voli del "Cigno" in Italia' (*Giornale d'Italia*, 26th January 1927), quotes a letter in his possession, from Mariani to Franco Faccio, written from Bologna, probably on 6th December:[1] 'I have not yet entirely got over all that unpleasantness, but I am more resigned and next week I shall return to Genoa and there will be ended for me the most perfect theatrical season I have ever known, which will leave in my mind an impression at once most sweet and sorrowful. There is no rose without a thorn, but this time my thorn was exceedingly cruel.' De Rensis, misled by the imaginings and false chronology of Monaldi and Mantovani, misinterprets this passage as a reference to Verdi's supposed betrayal of his friend during the rehearsals of *Don Carlos*: 'The allusion is clear.' We see now that the allusion is actually to the dispute with the municipality of Genoa.

Mariani in January asked Dallolio for confirmation of the terms, as he had understood them, of the proposed appointment at Bologna. According to this letter he had been offered 5,000 lire a year for the directorship of the Liceo Musicale with complete liberty to go elsewhere during the Carnival season, and 3,600 lire for conducting the autumn season at the Teatro Comunale. There is no further mention of pension rights in this letter.

We must return to the problem of Mariani's love affairs.

At the beginning of 1868, at Genoa, Giuseppina made some diary notes in her letter-book. An entry on 4th January says: 'Mariani

[1] The date given, 6th October, is impossible.

burst out against Genoa and the bad moods of la Ma . . . He praised to the skies Bologna and all its inhabitants.' It seems certain that the lady concerned was Elena Massa, whom *nine years earlier* Giuseppina thought Mariani had already been courting long enough. In that case her 'bad moods' were understandable. Then there was, or had been, another friend, referred to as 'my Elisa' in a letter to Verdi of 5th July 1864, and perhaps identifiable as the Elisa Galli who sang some of Mariani's songs at a concert under his direction at Genoa on 4th June 1867.[1] As for Teresa Pallavicino Negrotto, we know that the recent death of the Count De Sonnaz had created a vacancy in the succession of her admirers, and although Mariani writes of receiving a letter about this from the Pallavicino family, his comments suggest that he had heard rather from the lady herself. Would any other member of the family have told him about the husband ('that ass') delighting in tormenting her ('that poor creature') and manifesting his infernal joy that God had avenged him? We may suspect, then, that Mariani had assumed the dangerous role of confidant and comforter to Teresa Pallavicino Negrotto, whom he had known since girlhood. They were now probably living under the same roof in Palazzo Sauli. In one of his letters, just after this winter stay at Genoa, Mariani asks Verdi to send one of his cards to this friend: 'From what I have been able to understand, Signora Teresa has got it in her head that you can't bear her.'

We have *some* evidence, then, concerning Mariani's relations with these three women. What of Teresa Stolz? There is still nothing to show definitely that they were having a love affair. He is silent about her in the surviving letters from Bologna. It is not unlikely, however, that the attraction she had for him played its part in making him reluctant to return to Genoa when he should have done, although he himself gives almost every possible reason *except* this. She was to sing under his direction at Genoa in the following spring, in *Un ballo in maschera*. During that visit to Genoa she was to meet his intimate friends, Carlo and Teresa Del Signore, and begin to correspond with them. We have proof that later in this year she and Mariani were contemplating marriage. The production of *Don Carlos* at Bologna, then, far from being, as has often been supposed, the occasion of Verdi's falling in love, seems more likely to have brought about the love affair between Teresa Stolz and Mariani.

Before she went to Genoa, however, the singer had other engagements to fulfil. These included the *première* of *Don Carlos* at La Scala in March. Gatti states, correctly, that she was not available for the rehearsals, under Mazzucato, before the end of February. But, in a passage added in his second edition,[2] he accounts for this quite wrongly:

[1] *Gazzetta Musicale di Milano*, 9th June 1867. [2] p. 504.

> Verdi was displeased that la Stolz had not presented herself at La Scala to sing in *Un ballo in maschera* [i.e. earlier in the season]: a precaution to which he usually has recourse, to dispose the public to receive favourably this or that new opera, trying the singers out first and assuring himself that the public liked them. But Mariani had kept la Stolz with him at Genoa as long as he could.

What are the facts? She had not been with Mariani at Genoa at all yet, but was singing in Petrella's *Jone* and in *Don Carlos* in Rome from 26th December to 25th February, when the season ended at the Teatro Apollo. *This* is why she could not come to Milan before the end of February.

Verdi and Giuseppina, during the three months they spent in Palazzo Sauli, must have heard a good deal about Teresa Stolz from Mariani. The composer wrote to both Escudier and Du Locle, regretting that Marie Sass in Paris had not thought better of the part of Elisabeth in *Don Carlos*: 'Do you know that la Stolz made of it the leading role?' When the opera was produced with almost equal success at Milan, Giuseppina (not Verdi) attended a performance. On 11th April she wrote to Elisa Piave: 'The ovations to Signora Stolz give me pleasure, being homage to real and very distinct merit.' This is the first reference to the singer in Giuseppina's letter-books. Verdi had written to Du Locle on 8th April: 'And what effect la Stolz creates in the part of Elisabeth! Peppina has been to Milan, and has spoken to me especially highly of the fifth act.'

It is just possible that Teresa Stolz may have been introduced to Verdi at this time, if she came at once to Genoa after the end of the season at Milan on 8th April. Verdi and Giuseppina returned to Sant' Agata on 15th April, and Mariani's letters begin again on that very day.

Just before this Emilio Broglio, Minister of Public Instruction, had written a letter to Rossini, outlining a plan for the formation of a society of music lovers, with Rossini at its head, which should take over from the Government the administration and financing of the Conservatorii. The situation was desperate, according to the minister, and demanded a desperate remedy. The music of the pre-Rossinian age was not worth discussing; Rossini's own music was immortal but there was no longer anyone who could sing it (Broglio's wife was an ex-singer); and 'since Rossini, that is, in the last forty years, what have we had? Four operas by Meyerbeer. . . . How can such grave sterility be remedied?' In May, with Rossini's half-mocking reply, Broglio's letter came to public notice and aroused general indignation. Verdi, who had just been made Commendatore of the Order of the Crown of Italy, sent the decoration back. At the beginning of June Giuseppina told Giulio Ricordi: 'I know nothing of Mariani. I believe he is engulfed up to the neck in the business of the decoration refused by Verdi—all the time, however, with the air of ridiculing it.' This was unfair to Mariani, who was in a most comical and cruel situation.

What happened is that Verdi asked Mariani to make public the fact that he intended to return the order to the minister, and Mariani chose to do so by publishing in *Il Movimento* the letter he had received from Verdi:

Sant' Agata, 15th May 1868.

DEAR MARIANI,

Our friend Corticelli gives me *Il Movimento* of the 13th, where I read that I should do well to return the Cross of the Crown of Italy. That is precisely what, some days ago, I decided to do, as soon as I should receive the diploma. But now, without waiting any longer, I authorize you to declare that, with or without diploma, I do not accept the Cross of Commendatore of the Crown of Italy. As for the project, in letter form, for musical restorations, of which Rossini has not refused the presidency, for my own part I have not, and probably never shall have, anything to say. Only I find it fine and edifying in an Italian minister that he should so severely condemn an art that still carries with honour the name of Italy to every part of the world.

In haste, farewell, farewell,
Affectionately,
GIUSEPPE VERDI.

Then followed an inimitably Marianian misadventure. On the very day on which he published Verdi's letter he received the same decoration himself from Vittorio Emanuele. Was he to keep it, or to send it back?

I find myself embarrassed, and also humiliated. I am not Verdi. I did not receive the Cross from the Minister Broglio, or at his suggestion, but from the king. I was not at the mayor's banquet, but it was sent to me at home with a letter from the first secretary of the king's private cabinet. I repeat: in art I am a nullity! It seems to me that I ought not to set myself on your level by returning the Cross. It is still there, that Cross, I have neither accepted it nor refused it, and I don't know what to do. I see the effect your letter has had and I see, too, how everyone is talking about it. How do you expect me, a poor insect, to pretend to cause a stir by an action that in me I shouldn't know how to qualify? . . . I can't tell you how embarrassed I am, how much in two minds. What must I do?

It was damnable. Probably he had done the wrong thing again, he thought, in publishing that letter, and arousing a storm of controversy such as he knew Verdi intensely disliked. But what else was he to do? And then, why did his pleasure in this honour from the king have to be spoiled like this? How much better it would have been not to be embarrassed in this way at this moment! Then he had a sudden idea—why, of course, *Corticelli* was to blame! He wrote to him on 24th May:

Like the revolutionary you have always been, like the enemy of public order you have always declared yourself, you have succeeded in creating a political disturbance and procuring such blame for the government that the wise *Opinione* of Florence has justly accused you in the face of the world. You sinned, and now you must do penance.

Like the great rogue you have always been, you succeeded in your intent, drawing the chestnuts from the fire, like the monkey, with the paws of the cat. Maestro Verdi would certainly never have published that most noble letter of his if you had not given him the *Movimento*. The Maestro never reads newspapers, so that Broglio's foolish epistle would have escaped his notice. Certainly Verdi would not deign to write to a journalist. A third party, therefore, was needed to serve as intermediary between the Maestro and the journalist. I was that person, and by that Verdi honoured me. . . .

And so on. Mariani and Corticelli seem to have considered this blustering vein appropriate in the correspondence of two hot-blooded sons of Romagna, as they liked to think themselves. It allowed them to express something of the mutual dislike that underlay the apparent cordiality imposed by their common relationship to Verdi. In the end, of course, Mariani kept the decoration: 'I am Cavaliere of the Crown of Italy! And you, *Verdi*? I am ridiculous, aren't I?'

This episode occurred while Teresa Stolz was singing in *Un ballo in maschera* at Genoa under Mariani's direction. She is mentioned, quite formally, in a letter of 28th May: 'Sivori is here and will play in the concert I am giving for the benefit of the Philharmonic Provident Fund, in which Signora Stolz will also take part.' They were now more or less engaged to be married.

After leaving Genoa, towards the middle of June, Teresa Stolz wrote from Milan in very affectionate terms to the new friends she had made, Teresa and Carlino Del Signore:

Scarcely four days have passed since we separated and it seems ages to me. I hope you arrived safely at Florence. You can't imagine the distress I felt in leaving you, luckily I was alone in the compartment and could give free vent to my barely restrained tears. without making an exhibition of myself to the curious and the indifferent. What are you doing? How are you enjoying yourselves? How I wish the happy days we spent together in your attractive Genoa could return! Now, when I think of it, it seems like a lovely dream, from which I have awakened in the sad reality of the so-called *artistic* life, which is beautiful, I won't deny it, but one would need to have no heart, to look on everything with indifference, to make no acquaintances of any sort, not to become fond of anybody—then one would be all right, and would not suffer as I am suffering at this moment. . . . I have received a long and affectionate letter from our common friend Mariani. He too seems to be suffering from our separation; he writes a lot to me about you and one sees that he loves you dearly, but that is natural enough: I think it impossible not to love you, once one has had the good fortune to meet you.

Here, for the first time, we hear the voice of Teresa Stolz herself. A number of her letters to the Del Signore family are among the valuable correspondence published by Zoppi.

Mariani, after another visit to Sant' Agata, went to take the waters at San Pellegrino, near Bergamo. A letter to Gaetano Grilli says:

I hope I shall benefit. I have been vexed for some time by an affection of the bladder, which torments me very much. I suffer in silence, since my acquaintances, seeing me looking well, deride me and say that *my trouble is all imagination*. Would to God it were!—I don't wish anyone such martyrdom. The worst of it is that this physical indisposition induces a dark and desolating melancholy. Work is very hard and I flee as much as I can the company even of those who are fond of me. Enough: it's for me to think about this, and God's will be done.

More and more often, as time goes on, he complains in his letters about his health, and describes, at ever increasing length, his symptoms and all the details of his medical examinations and cures. He must also have talked at great length on the same subjects, until people were tired of hearing about his troubles and grew unsympathetic. One of the most unpleasant features of the later relations of the Verdis with Mariani is their refusal to believe that there was anything seriously wrong with him. They knew he suffered from piles and all his symptoms were put down to this unromantic complaint. The rest, they believed, was exaggeration. But Mariani died, within a few years, after horrible torments, from cancer of the bladder or the anus.

Monaldi's suggestion that Mariani died of venereal disease is utterly false.

In the autumn of 1868 Teresa Stolz was singing again at Bologna, in *La Juive*. Mariani mentioned her in a letter to Verdi of 23rd September: 'It seems to me that la Stolz performs her part very well and I am sure (sympathy apart) that this time too she will very much distinguish herself.' The singer invited Teresa Del Signore to visit her at Bologna. She envied her friend her peaceful summer stay in the country, prolonged now into the autumn, while she herself was tied to the theatre: 'I hope that I too shall soon end this life of vagabondage, and then I too shall satiate myself with good country air, among a few good friends.' This was a reference to her anticipated marriage. We know from one of Mariani's later letters to Del Signore that at the end of this season at Bologna, he went to Ravenna to procure documents necessary for the marriage, which was to take place at the conclusion of her engagements in the following spring. According to Mariani the wedding was then deferred because she had taken on further engagements. It would seem that he wished her to give up her career on her marriage, and that she, when it came to the point, was reluctant to do this.

During the Carnival season of 1868–9 she sang again at La Scala, in a revival of *Don Carlos* and in the first performance of the revised version of *La forza del destino*. Franco Faccio was the conductor, but the whole preparation of *La forza del destino* was directed by Verdi himself. The success was very great: 'La Stolz and Tiberini were sublime,' Verdi told Escudier. He returned to Genoa immediately after the first performance. On 11th March Teresa Stolz wrote to Teresa Del Signore:

> What you have heard from the good Maestro concerning me is not all true; you must attribute a large part of it to their goodness, because truly both Maestro Verdi and his kind wife have been indulgent to me. It is certain that the Milanese will always remember that beautiful evening when they had the good fortune to be able to applaud once again the celebrated Maestro. Dear Teresina, you can be sure that if you had attended that performance you would have felt indescribable emotions. Imagine me, then, who had to sing! I felt tears in my eyes every moment. Enough! Now I am glad that it's all over, and that Maestro Verdi was fairly well satisfied with me.

Although it is just possible, in our revised chronology, that she could have been introduced to Verdi at Genoa in the previous year, their encounter at Milan for the rehearsals of the revised *Forza del destino*, in February 1869, is the earliest for which we have documentary evidence.

In Giuseppina's letter-book is a list of names of those to whom, on 22nd March, she had sent cards, in response to congratulations on her and Verdi's joint name-day, S. Giuseppe, always celebrated on 19th March. Teresa Stolz's name is included. This is the earliest evidence of any correspondence.

Early in April Giuseppina wrote to Escudier:

> We have resumed our calm and silent life—all the more so since Mariani, that great babbler and provoker of babbling, is not at Genoa at the moment. He is running after *La forza del destino*, which he is destined, it seems, not to hear. He will not be back in his apartment, that photographer's shop, until the end of the week.

She referred to the signed portraits with which his rooms were cluttered. He was in time for one of the last performances at Milan. After the season at La Scala ended Teresa Stolz, who was due to sing *Don Carlos* at Parma on 24th April, seems to have paid a short visit to Genoa. Giuseppina told Du Locle on 17th April, just after she and Verdi had returned to Sant' Agata:

We left the handsome Mariani in the midst of his victims. He attended a performance of *La forza del destino* at Milan, and truly heard it.

Verdi did not visit Parma for the performances of *Don Carlos*.

We come now to the history of the collective Requiem Mass for Rossini, projected by Verdi, written, but never performed. The episode is crucial in the relations of Mariani and Verdi. The story has been told many times, the facts seem established, but here again the study of Mariani's letters leads to a surprising new conclusion.

What is well known and not in dispute can be passed over briefly here. On 17th November, four days after Rossini's death, Verdi had put forward his proposal in a letter to Tito Ricordi: the leading Italian composers should collaborate in the composition of the Mass, which should be performed in the church of San Petronio at Bologna on the anniversary of Rossini's death and then the manuscript should be sealed up in the archives of the Liceo Musicale, never to leave them except, perhaps, on the occasion of a later anniversary tribute. The idea was favourably received by the city council and the Accademia Filarmonica of Bologna, and a committee was formed at Milan, consisting of Lauro Rossi, Alberto Mazzucato and Stefano Ronchetti-Monteviti, all of the Milan Conservatorio, with Giulio Ricordi as secretary. Eleven composers were chosen by the committee and assigned their tasks, Verdi's being the *Libera me*, at the end of the Mass. Mariani agreed to conduct.

Another commemoration was planned by the town of Pesaro, Rossini's birthplace, for August. Mariani agreed to conduct this too, and the Pesaro committee relied largely on his advice in all musical matters. Practically, he was the musical dictator of Pesaro, and he threw himself with all the energy and enthusiasm of which he was capable into the preparations. We have twenty-five of his letters, some of them very long, written to Gaetano Grilli at Pesaro, between 17th December 1868 and 11th August 1869, entirely devoted to the planned commemoration.[1] He had first to disabuse the committee of their idea that Verdi might compose a work for them: 'As I've said before, and as is universally known, Verdi initiated another proposal for Bologna and, there being no Requiem Mass among his compositions, he would not agree to write one specially for Pesaro.' He declared that he had explained to Verdi what they intended to do and had received his blessing and approval; the programmes, however, had not then been settled. One of his first actions was to secure the collaboration of Teresa Stolz, especially with a view to the performance of Rossini's *Stabat Mater*, in which she had sung at

[1] Published, together with other letters to Grilli, by Ernesto Paolone, in 'Inaugurazione della statua di G. Rossini nel 1864 e pompe funebri in onore dello stesso nel 1869, a Pesaro, attraverso spigolature epistolari' (*Rassegna Dorica*, serially, from 20th October 1935 to 20th July 1936). The originals are in the library of the Conservatorio at Pesaro.

Palermo in 1865. Grilli, in default of a Requiem Mass by Verdi, suggested that one might be found among the works of Mercadante, but Mariani overruled him, urging instead the claims of Cherubini's Requiem Mass in C, which he had already performed with splendid effect at Genoa. For this, permission for the use of women's voices would be necessary, but if there was a local church controlled by the local authorities, there would be no need to approach Rome for this concession.

Cherubini's Mass in C major is a creation so serious, so noble, that the effect of the women's voices creates no scandal, but imparts, rather, a more religious colouring to the sacred ceremony. It is absolutely necessary to perform this Mass, and with all due resources. I don't believe that Mercadante has a Requiem Mass, but even if he had (this I say to you alone, in confidence), it would be more theatrical and profane with men's voices only than that of Cherubini with all the women in the world. . . . It isn't the women's presence that creates scandal in church music, but the profane style of the compositions of these days, which are, in general, ugly copies of theatrical music in the worst taste. You will recall the ridiculous effect of the music that was performed recently at Bologna for Rossini's obsequies.

He referred again, in another letter, to the 'scandal' of these ceremonies in the church of San Giovanni in Monte. Rossini's own *Petite Messe solennelle* was given in the Teatro Comunale at Bologna at the beginning of April; the performance, conducted by Muzio, was highly praised. The same work, later in the month, was almost a fiasco at La Scala; it was in preparation at Genoa, too, but Mariani was not in favour of including it in the programmes at Pesaro. 'I am rehearsing Rossini's Mass at the Teatro Paganini,' he told Grilli on 22nd April. 'The fugue of the *Cum Sancto* is very beautiful, and the *Sanctus* is very effective, but for the rest I am still for the *Stabat*.' After the performance at Genoa he sent Verdi a long and far from enthusiastic account of this 'semi-serious score'. For a time he still hoped that permission for the use of women's voices would be granted: 'The municipal authorities of Bologna have already written to Maestro Verdi that in San Petronio there will be no difficulty in that respect.' But if at Pesaro consent was withheld, he had another work in view: 'I have examined Cherubini's other Mass, for male voices, in three parts; I find it beautiful, most convincing.' In the end it was decided to perform this Mass in D minor, for male voices, in the church of San Francesco on 21st August, and Rossini's *Stabat Mater*, with the overture to *William Tell* and the famous prayer from *Mosè*, in the local theatre on 22nd and 23rd August. A popular concert, of twelve or more items, would follow on 25th August. Singers for the chorus would be drawn from choirs in all the towns of the area; the orchestra would be formed from the best artists in the whole country. The municipal brass band of Bologna, which was famous, under its conductor Alessandro Antonelli, a friend of Mariani's, would also perform daily.

When Arrivabene asked Verdi, on 1st August: 'Have you seen the spectacular manifesto of Pesaro?' he received this answer:

I know nothing of the Pesaro manifesto, because Mariani is at Vicenza. It's an ill-arranged festival. I'm not very enthusiastic about Rossini's Mass, but if ever circumstances and place were adapted for it, it was at this Pesaro festival. I can't understand why Mariani did not insist on this idea.

I am writing my piece for the Requiem Mass.

Petrella, after having accepted, now refuses to write the piece assigned to him. Not much loss! But it's the action of a *lazzarone*!

Is there a trace of pique here? Far from being 'an ill-arranged festival', the Pesaro Rossini commemoration did the greatest credit to its organizers. None of the major cities of Italy had produced anything like it. And for his choice of Cherubini's Mass Mariani had sound artistic grounds.

He was at Vicenza for the production of *La forza del destino* with Teresa Stolz. In nine long letters he reported to Verdi on every detail of the rehearsals and performances. It was natural enough that he should concentrate on his immediate problems, and on the Pesaro festival, for which he was largely personally responsible and which was due to take place shortly—three months before the as yet unfinished collective Requiem Mass was due at Bologna. But he had kept the latter in mind. A letter to Verdi of 6th August is important:

I received your letter of the 4th yesterday, after the rehearsal, and you'll forgive me if involuntarily I forgot to tell you, in my previous letters, that I was waiting, before replying to what you ask me about the Mass, for the arrival of Signor Casarini, to learn what artists he can dispose of at Bologna next autumn. In fact, he only arrived yesterday, and told me that for the Teatro Comunale there are engaged la Galletti, la Berini and a certain Garbato, all impossible, *according to my way of thinking*, for your purposes.

I thought of another arrangement. I know that Signora Fricci has to go to St Petersburg, but I believe she has to be there only at the beginning of December. In that case, since a piece of your music is concerned, I believe she would lend her services, with the kindness that has always distinguished her. As you probably know, Signora Fricci lives at Bologna, and further, I know that last year she stayed there, before going to St Petersburg, up to about the end of October. Well then, next Monday she will be here at Vicenza: I shall ask her if she can stay at Bologna until 13th September [13th November must be meant] and if she says 'Yes' I shall not fail to ask if she would be disposed to undertake the performance *just of your piece*, which you are composing, and I'll write to you at once about that.

Signora Stolz, as you probably know, is going to Trieste in the autumn and it's not possible to have her. In any case, if la Fricci can't oblige you, it will be necessary to look elsewhere for a voice for your purpose, and to tell the truth I wouldn't know where to turn, for we're very short of beautiful voices with good intonation. It is certain that the artists of which the Teatro Comunale can dispose this year are not those of past years, and I believe, therefore, that Scalaberni's idea of giving *Lohengrin* will end in smoke, as I can't *conscientiously* guarantee the singers to the proprietor of the score, as the latter would wish.

Enough! As soon as I've spoken to la Fricci I shall be able to tell you something, and then I am always ready to do what you please and to put myself wholly at your disposition, in all my littleness.

Apart from the slip in the date, poor 'Wrong Head', as he still sometimes called himself, was making a bad mistake in proposing to ask Antonietta Fricci to consent to sing just in Verdi's contribution to the collective Mass, the *Libera me*, since the plan, drawn up by the committee at Milan, called for a soprano voice also in the *Quid sum miser* (Cagnoni), *Recordare* (Ricci), *Lacrymosa* (Coccia), *Domine Jesu* (Gaspari) and *Lux aeterna* (Mabellini). But probably he had never seen this plan. 'Next Monday', when the singer was due at Vicenza, would have been 9th August, but he does not seem to have seen her before he left for Pesaro, about the middle of the month. On 17th August he wrote from Pesaro:

This morning I heard the choir that is to perform Cherubini's Mass. It's truly stupendous, being made up of the best singers from all the choirs of the neighbouring towns. The men number 112, the women 56. They are partly from Macerata, from Fano, from towns of the Marche. They are pupils of the schools of music, have very beautiful voices, read at sight stupendously and have intelligence enough to obtain every desired effect. To give you an idea of their ability, I'll tell you that they sang me the fugue of the *Stabat* very well *without accompaniment*. Shall we have a similar choir at Bologna? What will the Milanese committee do to procure it? Do they perhaps think they can make use of the theatre chorus? I don't consider them competent for that sort of music!!!! I will keep you informed of how everything goes, and if I can be of use to you, you have only to command me.

The committee at Pesaro had invited Verdi to attend the commemoration, and Mariani urged him to accept. He wrote again on 19th August:

I have received your two letters. You can imagine how happy I should be if you really decided to come to Pesaro. Come, come, and come! The *ensemble* of the performers, in general, is excellent, and I think you will admire it. You will be indulgent about the performances, because you will understand that it is not possible, *in three days*, to rehearse as one should Cherubini's Mass, the *Stabat* and a concert including twelve or fourteen items. The choir was unable to get here on the date arranged owing to a broken bridge between Fano and Pesaro, which interrupted the regular railway service.

I am rehearsing, rehearsing and rehearsing, but the voices tire, especially the tenors, for whom Cherubini's Mass is very high. At all events I hope everything will go off—if not very well, at least passably. I am at your disposition. Here you won't find hotels, but you will have the hospitality you deserve. You will be lodged in one of the principal private houses; in any case, I am lodging with the Carnevali brothers, in a house with every convenience, most decent, cordial and, what is best, with no women of any sort, and if you like, I shall be very happy to give up to you my apartment. You have only to write to me and I shall do everything that you wish, and you will see that you will have no annoyances. If I don't do well you may beat me. As soon as I return to Vicenza I shall execute your commission with Signora Fricci. For Bologna you will have a stupendous choir; I've already found the way to procure it. Signora Stolz sends her most respectful regards and begs you to remember her to Signora Peppina, whom please greet also from me.

I kiss your hand and repeat that I am for life

YOUR ANGELO.

It seems obvious that Mariani was, up to this point, fully prepared to do everything in his power to prepare for, and ensure the success of, Verdi's own project of the collective Mass at Bologna. He was well acquainted with the ability and limitations of the chorus of the Teatro Comunale. His experience at Pesaro had suggested the possibility of forming, for Verdi's purposes, a superlative choir by calling on the best singers among the pupils of all the Conservatorii of Italy. It was an excellent idea, easily realizable by the Milanese committee, with Verdi's backing. If nothing came of it, it was because Verdi, on receipt of Mariani's first letter from Pesaro, of 17th August, sent this astonishing reply:

Genoa, 19th August 1869.

Sleep in peace, for I've already replied that I can't come to Pesaro.

I take up again your letter of yesterday, because I don't fully understand two phrases in it: '*What will the Milanese committee do?*' and further on: '*If I can be of use to you, you have only to command me.*' Do you mean to say that we've got to entreat you, in order to obtain the chorus you have at Pesaro? First of all you should have understood before now that my *ego* has vanished, and that now I am nothing but a pen, to write as well as may be a few notes, and a hand to offer my obol for the effectuation of this *National Celebration.* Next I'll tell you that nobody in this case should have to entreat, or be entreated, because a duty is involved that all the artists must and should perform.

I have never been able to discover whether the project of the Mass for Rossini has had the good fortune to be approved by you. When one does not act in one's own interest, but in that of art, and for the glory and decorum of one's country, a good deed has no need of anyone's approval. All the worse for him who does not know that! A man, a great artist, who marks an epoch, dies: one individual or another invites his contemporaries to honour that man, and in him our art; music is expressly composed and performed in the greatest church of the city that was his musical home, and so that this composition may not become the prey of miserable vanities and hateful self-interests, it is deposited, after the ceremony, in the archives of a famous institution. Musical history will necessarily have one day to record that 'at a certain time, on the death of a famous man, the whole art of Italy united to perform in San Petronio at Bologna a Requiem Mass expressly written by many composers, the original of which is conserved under seal in the Liceo at Bologna'. This becomes an historic fact, and not a piece of musical charlatanry. What does it matter, then, that the composition lacks unity, that the contribution of this or that man is more or less beautiful? What does it matter if the vanity of this composer or the arrogance of that performer is not satisfied? Here individuals are not concerned: it's enough that the day comes, the ceremony takes place, and finally the *historic fact*—mark well, the *historic fact*—exists.

This admitted, it's the obligation of us all to do what is in our power to attain the objective, without expecting entreaties beforehand, or praise and thanks afterwards.

If this solemn ceremony takes place, we shall indubitably have done something good, artistic and patriotic. If it doesn't, we shall have shown once more that we act only when our own interest and vanity are rewarded, when we are flattered and shamelessly adulated in articles and biographies, when our names are shouted in the theatres, dragged into the streets, like charlatans in the piazza; but when our personalities have to give way before an idea, and a noble and generous action, then we disappear beneath the mantle of our egoistic indifference, the scourge and the ruin of our country.

This is a fine outburst of moral indignation, but after reading Mariani's letters one asks oneself in vain what he had done to deserve such reproaches. Responsibility for the organization of the collective Mass rested with the Milanese committee; Mariani was not a member of that committee; it was no part of his duty to negotiate with Signora Fricci or offer advice on conditions at Bologna and the formation of the choir. If he did these things, it is clear that Verdi's project had his support. There seems no justification for Verdi's letter.

It will be recalled that Monaldi claimed to have heard from Mariani's lips, after the incident with the trumpeter Brizzi during the Pesaro Festival, these words: 'That woman doesn't love me any more! And it is he, my friend, my brother, who robs me of her love, which was my whole life! Oh, but I shall avenge myself, and my vengeance will be much grander and more beautiful than that of the cowardly Brizzi. I shall die of it, but I shall avenge myself.'

Biographers are necessarily dependent on the material available to them at the time of writing. Gatti in 1931 knew nothing of Mariani's letters to Verdi. He accepted Monaldi's evidence at its face value, and was led to interpret the conductor's feelings in the light of Verdi's irate letter. According to Gatti, if Verdi did not attend the Pesaro Festival it was because he knew that Mariani did not wish to have him there in the company of Teresa Stolz. But Luzio, in 1934,[1] totally demolished this idea by publishing Mariani's letter of 19th August, with its cordial invitation: 'Come, come and come!' and offer to give up his own accommodation to Verdi. Luzio also pointed out that Monaldi's narrative was anachronistic, in view of the whole tone of Mariani's subsequent correspondence with Verdi. This view is further supported by all we know of the extreme unreliability of Monaldi in other matters, and by Mariani's letters to Del Signore and others, which reveal his continuing close relations with Teresa Stolz. On the evidence of Mariani's letters, it was not until early in 1872 that he had any suspicion of an affair between Teresa Stolz and Verdi. Gatti, in 1951, in the revised version of his biography, completely ignored Luzio's objections and repeated that Mariani did not want Verdi to attend the Pesaro Festival. Luzio, however, went much too far in pretending that the letter of 19th August was just a 'good-natured' reply to Mariani's offer to give up his own rooms. Here Zoppi was quite right to point out that Luzio himself, before he was so anxiously involved in the last-ditch defence of Verdi's every thought, word and deed, had much more accurately described this letter of 'cutting reproaches, that seem to be slashed in his face'.

The one thing on which all these writers are agreed is that Mariani did not reply to this letter. But in fact he did.

The eight letters published by Luzio in the *Carteggi verdiani* are all taken from a packet enclosed in a folder on which Giuseppina has written, in English: 'Put together in 1870 some papers that have some reason to be keeped.' There is nothing in Luzio's writings to show that he had studied the other packets of Mariani's letters at Sant' Agata, which when I was working there in May 1957 were only in part arranged in chronological order. In one of the packets I found Mariani's reply to Verdi's letter of 19th August. At this date it is impossible to say whether it was ever included among those in Giuseppina's folder; she may have overlooked it, or it may have been abstracted at some time, by Luzio or another, and conveniently forgotten. Common justice to Mariani demands that it should be published:

Pesaro, 24th August 1869.

Your last letter of the 19th has very much distressed me, and you can't believe how sorry I am that I was not able to reply at once.

I did not ask: '*What will the Milanese Commission do?*' because I wanted to be asked for anything, or, *as you write*, to concede the choir that

[1] 'Un "Romanzo" degno di revisione: Verdi e Mariani' (*Corriere della Sera*, 2nd January 1934); materially reprinted, in extended form, in the *Carteggi verdiani* of 1935.

is now here at Pesaro. I didn't assemble it, it doesn't depend on me, and I have no power over it.

Since I know the chorus of the Teatro Comunale, I only asked if the committee intended to make use of this chorus, or to call upon all the schools of music in Italy.

And then, if I offered you my services, you mustn't believe, Oh my Maestro, that I think myself worthy of serving you: I think I have no need of explanations to show what veneration I feel for your person!

Since the Milanese committee wrote to me some time ago, inviting me to that solemn ceremony, and I replied that I was at their disposition, I think I have done no more than my duty in offering you my services, which I shall always offer you, not in artistic matters, for I know I am a most miserable object, but far more, in that devotion I feel for your, to me *Sacred*, person.

I shan't say it to you again, and I am sorry you have misinterpreted my words.

As for the project of the Mass for Rossini in San Petronio at Bologna, if you will have the goodness to recall to mind the letters I wrote last year to friend Corticelli, just at the time when that most noble project of yours was announced, you will see that I applauded it, and found it worthy of you and of your immense genius. By word of mouth, too, I spoke to you about it with all the admiration that I felt, and if I have not bored you further on this subject it was from fear of causing you extreme tedium.

He had sent some newspapers, with reports on the performance of *La forza del destino* at Vicenza, and there would seem to have been some comment on this in Verdi's letter of 19th August, as sent, although there is nothing about it in the version known to us from the *Copialettere*, for Mariani's letter continues:

And then, I don't know why you reproach me about the newspapers, of which I've always taken very little account; if I sent you some from Vicenza it was so that you could read the true story, written by those who were present at the first performance of *La forza del destino* at Vicenza. I also sent some of these papers to the Pallavicino family, because I know they like to have them, and because in that way I saved myself the bother of having to write long letters. I know that you despise such tittle-tattle, and to me it's a matter of indifference.

I beg you not to write me such severe letters any more, because you make me wretched. I shall not take the liberty again of writing to you for anyone whatever, and if you think fit to give me your orders, do so at will.

The letter from Verdi to the Rossini Committee at Pesaro, referred to in the following passage, is not known to have survived:

I have seen your letter in reply to the Rossini committee here: it is most beautiful and written with unique finesse. You have touched on *certain phrases*, expressed by them, with an acuteness worthy of your high intelligence. I have not seen the letter they sent you, but I understand from your reply that it must have been a stupid thing. The best of it is that Perticari took it all for shining gold, but when Filippi saw it he understood what it was all about and advised the committee not to publish it. Men of intelligence say that this letter of yours is a real masterpiece.

I'll say nothing of what has been done here, because I know it would bore you. On Thursday evening I shall be at Vicenza again and shall stay there until about 12th September.

I know from the servant at Genoa that you have returned to Sant' Agata, where I am addressing this letter.

What I don't wish to hide from you is that it's been infernally hard work here and I feel as if all my bones were broken. However, I know I have done my duty, for it is a sacred duty to honour the memory of those great men who have ennobled all humanity by their talents and the power of their art. Give my regards to Signora Peppina and to Mauro, and write me just one line, to say that I expressed myself badly in my previous letters.

If you permit me, I shall come to pay you a visit before going to Bologna. Do believe that if I do things badly it is not through ill will.

I kiss your hand and repeat that I am what I shall always be

Your faithful servant

ANGELO MARIANI.

It was quite true that he had not been responsible for assembling the choir at Pesaro from the pupils of the schools of music in the neighbouring towns. The idea was Grilli's, as is clear from the correspondence preceding the festival. Mariani's extension of this idea, the formation of a choir from the pupils of all the Conservatorii of Italy, would have lent the commemoration at Bologna a truly national character. One would have expected this to appeal to Verdi.

But the 'one line', for which Mariani begged, did not come.

The Milanese committee could think of nothing better than to ask Scalaberni, the impresario of the Teatro Comunale at Bologna, to lend his orchestra, chorus and solo singers for the performance of the collective Mass on 13th November. Scalaberni, however, refused to do this, explaining on 6th October in a lively letter to the *Monitore di Bologna* that he was a business man, with six children to support, and not a Maecenas, and that it was idle to pretend that the rehearsals and performance of the Mass would not interfere with the course of his opera season. The municipal authorities then proposed that the commemoration should be deferred until early December, when the opera season would be over. Verdi, questioned about this by Giulio Ricordi, would not budge from the terms of his original proposal. The whole thing was pointless except on the anniversary of Rossini's death. It was next suggested that the collective Mass could be performed elsewhere—at Milan perhaps? Verdi, while taking the line always that he was now nothing more than one of the contributors, subject to the rulings of the committee, left Ricordi in no doubt of his own views. The work lost all significance unless it was performed at Bologna, on 13th November.

Having said this, in a letter to Ricordi of 27th October, Verdi continued:

> If the Mass is performed, for example, at Milan, shall we find resources sufficient, in number and ability, for an imposing performance? The ordinary theatre chorus lacks musical knowledge (I say nothing of style, for this depends on the conductor). A *fugue* is not so easily performed as the *Rataplan* in *La forza del destino*. At Bologna it was easier to find the necessary resources, thanks to the choirs of the city itself and the neighbouring towns, and Mariani, in this, could have been a great help to us, but he has failed in his duty as a friend and an artist. Furthermore, who would be the conductor at Milan? It cannot and must not be Mariani.

Is this not astounding? Verdi is here putting forward the ideas expressed, in only slightly different form, by Mariani himself, in a sincere attempt to be helpful, in the letter that had brought down upon his head vials of wrath.

In a letter to Clarina Maffei, on 19th November, Verdi wrote: 'The Bologna affair is an ugly business for many people, including my distinguished friend Mariani, who has not lifted a finger in this affair which I so recommended to him. The Milanese committee, in my opinion, can do only one thing: restore the pieces to their respective composers and say no more about it.' A little later, in a letter to Arrivabene, he blamed the municipal authorities of Bologna, the impresario and Mariani: 'He has not done that which he should have done, both as artist and as my friend, perhaps a little piqued because he was not included among the composers. *Vanitas vanitatis*, etc.' As a result of these statements Mariani has gone down in history as the person principally responsible for the fiasco of the collective Requiem Mass for Rossini. Such a verdict is grossly unfair. There is no evidence whatever that Mariani aspired to a place among the representative composers of Italy in the collective Mass. His letters to Verdi, long suppressed, show that he was prepared to do all he could to make the Bologna commemoration as great a success as that of Pesaro. He had advanced the most reasonable and helpful suggestions to Verdi and in return had nearly had his head bitten off. His anguished pleas and explanations had been ignored. No replies had come to his letters. What encouragement had he been given to do more? It is very hard to stand up straight when one has been savagely kicked in the stomach.

After examination of all the evidence one is forced to the conclusion that if nothing came of Verdi's pet project of the Mass for Rossini it was principally his own fault. If anyone else deserved a rebuke it was surely the unimaginative Milanese committee.

Why did Verdi act as he did? What was it that made him, at this time, incapable of understanding the plain language of Mariani's letters? What led him, normally the embodiment of fairness and justice, to make such wildly misleading statements about Mariani in his letters to his friends? There is something mysterious about the whole of this episode. One feels that some malign spirit was abroad, poisoning all the wells of friendship.

As for Mariani, he just did not know what was happening to him. He would have been willing to crawl on his hands and knees from Pesaro to Bologna at Verdi's bidding. What had he done to be thus cut out of the life of the man he idolized? He could not understand it, and was desperately unhappy. On 28th November he wrote from Bologna to Corticelli at Sant' Agata: 'My dear Mauro, I know that the Maestro and Signora Peppina are already at Genoa; I haven't the courage to write to them, for you can't believe what displeasure I feel when I see that they don't reply to my letters. If, however, you have occasion to write to them, greet them on my behalf.' This letter is among the others in Giuseppina's folder.

Early in December Carlino Del Signore told Mariani that he had need to speak to him as soon as he arrived at Genoa. Doubtless he warned him to keep out of Verdi's way. Some weeks passed before there was an attempt at a reconciliation. Mariani, in the attic of Palazzo Sauli, wrote to Verdi, on the first floor. The letter, which unfortunately has not survived, was sent first to Del Signore, to be read by him and forwarded. Verdi replied to Del Signore:

Genoa, 11th January 1870.

The solicitude you show on your friend's account is most praiseworthy, but you will understand, my dear Carlino, that it would be very embarrassing for me to reply to Mariani's letter. What could I say to him? Could I reproach him? Accuse him? He will always reply: 'I have done nothing wrong.' I don't accuse Mariani of having acted wrongly: I accuse him of not having acted at all. No one has insinuated anything against him and, furthermore, words have no influence on me when deeds speak. He cites my Pesaro letter to justify his strange and unusual silence. But that letter was not intended to say anything other than: '*Whoever is truly an artist must work for the realization of this project*, etc.' and, it was understood: '*It will also be a proof of friendship.*' If there was anything in that project he didn't like, he should have refused the commission assigned to him by the Milanese committee. But, having accepted, he was doubly under the obligation to act. What did he do? Nothing! . . . All right: I accept that, but it is impossible for me to accept that he has acted as he should have done, as an artist and a friend.

Mariani asks if he may speak to me: so be it, but I want you to be present at that interview.

'He cites my Pesaro letter to justify his strange and unusual silence'

—this is almost incredible, when the silence had been on Verdi's own part. It is this passage, of course, that has led everyone to believe that Mariani did not reply to Verdi's letter of 19th August.

Del Signore's son, questioned by Zoppi, could not remember his father ever having spoken of the proposed meeting. Gatti, in a passage added in his second edition, says: 'The interview, so far as we know, did not take place.' It certainly did, and some sort of armistice was patched up. In the archives of Sant' Agata there are thirty-two more letters from Mariani to Verdi, after this date, besides six to Giuseppina.

But nothing could ever be the same again. An apologetic, cringing note recurs in Mariani's letters. Teresa Stolz was singing this year at Turin, in *Don Carlos* and *Il Favorito*, a new opera by Pedrotti, and Mariani went to see her. On 1st March he wrote to Verdi: 'Signora Stolz asks me to give her regards to you and your wife, to whom also kindly give my own affectionate greetings. I should enjoy myself here if I were not far away from you and from the good Signora *Pepolina*, but there's no rose without thorns. Talking of thorns, please remember me to Mauro. . . . Forgive me, my Maestro, if I annoy you with these stupid letters of mine, but how can I help it? Now that I've written to you, and lingered with you a while, I feel more happy and satisfied.' And on the next day: 'You will say I'm a nuisance but I want to write to you again to tell you that last night I went to hear *Don Carlos* and that (with my friend Carlino's permission) I was very satisfied and on the whole better pleased than at Milan. I'll give you particulars by word of mouth. . . . Forgive me if I have annoyed you so much, and believe me for life your faithful Angelo Mariani.' Several consecutive letters end in almost the same way. One of 5th April addressed to Paris, where Verdi and Giuseppina had gone for a short visit, says again: 'Forgive me, my Maestro, if I annoy you with these stupid letters of mine, but today, now that I've written to you, I feel happier.'

We have seen that the evidence is against the picture, drawn by the biographers, of Verdi, Giuseppina, Mariani and Teresa Stolz all living together on intimate terms at Genoa, like a single family. They were, however, all there for some weeks in April 1870. A season of comic opera was given at the Teatro Nazionale, under Mariani, the programmes including the first performances in Italy of Federico Ricci's *Une Folie à Rome*, which had been highly successful in Paris in the previous year. The *Gazzetta Musicale di Milano* of 1st May records that the fourth performance was attended by Verdi and his wife and by Teresa Stolz.

Giuseppina, writing to Clarina Maffei from Sant' Agata on 14th May, declared: 'Mariani has not married, and will not marry, la Stolz—*this at least is our opinion.*'

In a letter to Carlino Del Signore, whose wife was expecting a baby, she sent greetings and thanks to various friends at Genoa:

> A kiss, then, to your Teresa, together with the recommendation to take care of herself, in the condition in which, by your fault, she finds herself; a kiss to the other Teresa, who should be Mariani's, if Mariani's head were as sound as the rest of him, and if he weren't his own worst enemy—in spite of self-love. A handshake then to that friend of ours, of whom we might one day become. . . . No, God forbid! I want to keep the affection of the few friends I have, and I would like to be able to love and esteem them all. Tell him I will write to him later. . . .

The implication was ominous: a friend who might one day become an enemy.

A letter to Teresa Del Signore of 20th May says: 'Mariani replied to a letter of mine, and greeted me on our friends' behalf, without naming anyone in particular! He talks of his health, *still very much affected*, but that's a fable in which no one believes.'

Mariani's health was bad enough to cause him to spend the whole of June at Bologna, in the care of two doctors. The surgeon Pietro Loreta found no reason to operate, spoke of 'glandular irritation' and recommended a course of cold shower-baths.

On 24th June Verdi wrote to Del Signore:

> It is probable that at the end of this month or the beginning of the next I shall be coming to Genoa for twenty-four hours. Let me know at what time and on which days I shall be able to find you. Tell me also if Signora Stolz is at Genoa and, if she is, how long she will be staying there. I need to speak to her, or write to her, if you will tell me where she is. I have heard nothing of Mariani for a long time. Du Locle is here.

Although the news had not yet become public, the composition of *Aida* had now been decided on. Zoppi, in publishing the above letter, suggests that Verdi was already thinking of assigning the name-part to Teresa Stolz. However, her engagement at Venice for the Carnival season of 1870–1 had already been announced,[1] so that she would not have been free to sing either in Cairo or Milan at the time originally fixed for the first performances of *Aida*. Verdi's immediate object was to secure her services for a projected production of *La forza del destino* in Paris, under his own direction. This is mentioned in some of Mariani's letters, and in Muzio's correspondence. Zoppi does well to remark that the above letter shows that Verdi was not at this time informed of Teresa Stolz's movements. Mariani, if he had been asked, could have told him that she had gone from Genoa to Florence to see her sister. Verdi's remark on 24th June, 'I have heard nothing of Mariani for a long time', is rather misleading.

[1] *Gazzetta Musicale di Milano*, 20th March 1870.

There are letters dated 2nd, 5th and 9th June at Sant' Agata. A long one was to follow on 27th June, with endless descriptions of the state of Mariani's health, his treatment and the course of the shower-bath cure at Bologna.

In July and early August Teresa Stolz was singing in *Don Carlos* at Sinigaglia, under Mariani's direction. They were both engaged also at Baden-Baden later in the year, but the Franco-Prussian war caused the cancellation of this and also put an end to the Parisian project. Meanwhile, news of *Aida* had leaked out from Cairo. Mariani wrote to Verdi from Sinigaglia on 28th July:

MY MAESTRO!

You can't imagine the pleasure your little letter gave me. I had been deprived of your news for so long, and so my happiness was doubled at receiving your letter and I thank you for it really from the depths of my heart. It's enough for me to have just one line from you and to know that you are well. . . . I have heard nothing more from Baden. . . . I still hope that nothing will come of it, and I should be sorry indeed to find myself in the theatre of war. Signora Stolz, too, would like to have done with this uncertainty and looks forward to hearing something decisive, yes or no. Today I'll write again to the impresario and tell him I shall not leave Italy without advice from him, and Signora Stolz will do the same. She sends you her kind regards and charges me to tell you that she will reply tomorrow to your letter. . . .

Now I must tell you that Signora Galletti has written to me from Pesaro to tell me that you are writing an opera for Cairo, and she wants me to recommend you to give her the preference; indeed, she asked me for a couple of lines to you to enclose in the letter she intends to write to you about that. As you know, I don't care to get involved in such things, and I replied that she should write to you direct and I would write to you privately. Imagine! (I tell you this in confidence) she wanted me to thrust her upon you and sing the praises of her . . . *artistic* virtues! In my reply I told her that the latter was not necessary, since she was known to and admired by everyone. That is what I've done, and I believe I have acted as I should.

Isabella Galletti-Gianoli was to sing in Cairo in the following winter and would probably have been the first Aida if production of the opera had not been held up by the war. She was a most voluptuous-looking woman,[1] and at Sant' Agata Mariani was suspected of having designs upon her. He may have been known to have had an affair with her already.

The letter of 28th July includes also this passage:

[1] Portrait in Gatti, first edition, vol. ii, facing p. 65. On this lady compare also Rossini's remarks, in a letter to Domenico Liverani, known as 'Menghino', of 12th June 1867, in the Piancastelli Collection: 'Execute my commission, Sig. Menghino, with lowered eyes, for I'm told Signora Galletti is Too Seductive!!!'

Yesterday I was at Loreto (don't laugh) because, feeling no improvement, as a result of the cure, in my physical sufferings, who knows but what the Madonna won't heal me? You will laugh, but so it is!

In reply, a few days later, there came this truly odious letter—from Corticelli:

On the eve of that saint whose name you should bear (31st July),[1] you chose to spit out one of the most insolent farragos of nonsense that have ever been spoken in our time. And were you sincere? No! Your measureless vanity obliges you always to pose, even to the point of wishing to appear one of the most vulgar bigots among the adherents of the Pope! Verdi handed me, between a little laugh and a *pouah!* of disgust, this sacristan's letter of yours. That you go to Loreto to get your faith and devotion to the Madonna talked about—tell that to the formerly assisted husbands and to the women in relationship to whom it doesn't suit you to be what you asked to be, and pretended it suited you to be, some time ago. Considerations of vanity and egoism may weigh in your own balance, when turning your coat, but that you dare so ostentatiously to try to make a fool of Verdi and of your most humble servant—oh no, by God! We prefer your vanity to go on making you transcendently ridiculous, in impudently saying that Napoleon III drew up his horse to exclaim: 'Are you Mariani? What can I do for you?' 'Sire, save Italy!' *And 100,000 Frenchmen hurled themselves over the border to please you.* Such charlatan's tales, in their incommensurability, have the merit of raising a laugh. But that you are such a hypocrite as to wish it believed that you visit the Madonna so that she may heal those precious guts of yours, the eternal subject of discussion with everyone! . . .

Finally, Mariani, if it matters to you to conserve your relationship with Verdi, already so much compromised last autumn, be careful in speaking, writing and acting, and in *advising* your friends, male and *female*, not to deviate from the truth, not to exaggerate, and not to act in ways that are not perfectly open, worthy, honest and loyal. I know that you will not reply to this, or will reply with a letter in pamphlet form, but I have told you what I wanted to tell you and I shan't return to this subject. You can burn this letter, so that posterity won't find it among those you keep to flatter your memory.

This atrocious document was drafted in Corticelli's name by Giuseppina. It is found on a loose sheet in her letter-book, entirely in her hand and with alterations and erasures that leave no doubt at all that it is her work. It does no one at Sant' Agata any credit. Once again, it is difficult to understand the violence of the reaction to Mariani's letter. Corticelli, like Verdi at this time, was an atheist, but there is nothing to show that Mariani shared their views; many phrases in his letters, as Zoppi remarks, suggest that he was a believer. He had every right to go to Loreto without being subjected to this sort of

[1] i.e. St Ignatius Loyola, founder of the Order of Jesuits!

vulgar abuse. But just to have mentioned it was considered an offence against Verdi! The latter part of Giuseppina's outburst in Corticelli's name would seem to have been occasioned by Mariani's advice to Isabella Galletti, though it is hard to see what there was to object to in that. Possibly some knowledge of his relations, past or present, with this singer aroused the suspicion that the whole thing was a put-up job between them. The formerly assisted husbands (*mariti ex-ajutati*) would then include Gianoli, with, perhaps, the Marchese Negrotto or someone else at Genoa. The women it did not suit Mariani to marry, in Giuseppina's opinion, certainly included Elena Massa and Teresa Stolz.

Verdi seemed incapable of putting anything but the worst possible construction on Mariani's every word and action. Some evil force was at work, destroying their friendship and driving them apart. The revulsion of feeling, the failure to comprehend, the harshness, were all on Verdi's side. We do not know what, if anything, Mariani replied to Corticelli. But certainly, once more he swallowed his bitter medicine. Within a few days he was writing again to Verdi, reporting on the remaining performances of *Don Carlos* at Sinigaglia, and telling of his illness and, after his return to Bologna, the further course of his useless 'cure'. He was humbly, pathetically grateful when Verdi deigned to reply: 'Yesterday was a happy day for me—I received your dear letter. It's unnecessary to send me that money; you can give it me when I have the good fortune to see you again.'

On 28th September he wrote:

> You will be busy with your new opera. . . . Remember that if you think of staging it in Cairo, if you permit me, I'll come with you, desiring as I do to see the East again. Afterwards we could go to Constantinople and from there return by way of Vienna. Why not? One only lives once, and it's best to pass this poor life in the best way possible.

This was as near as he dared to go to suggesting that he should be chosen to conduct the first performance of *Aida* in Cairo. Verdi, who had already decided to send Muzio, replied evasively.

The subject came up again about two months later:

Bologna, 18th November 1870.

MY MAESTRO,

Since I have been honoured with your benevolence I don't think I have ever importuned you about my private affairs, and indeed I remember that two years ago when I was invited to go to Padua and by a combination of unforeseen developments someone else was chosen, you, in your goodness, reproached me for not advising you about that. Well then, mindful of that attention of yours and of the kindness you have always shown me, I venture to bring up a matter which I should never have brought up if I had not been impelled to do so by the enclosed letter from Gianoli, Signora

Galletti's husband, who is in Cairo, addressed to Maestro Antonelli, whose guest I am here at Bologna, as you know. Please read the said letter and tell me if there is any truth in it. Whatever your reply, you may be sure, my Maestro, that no living soul will learn of it, and that I swear to you on the soul of my poor mother.

But you know, if what Gianoli writes is true, I should owe my fortune to you and I should cease to lead a financially pinched and highly dependent life.

But let's set aside the 50,000 francs: half of that would be enough for me. And then what about the honour that would be mine in being sent *by you* to Cairo on such a solemn occasion? I'll speak frankly and tell you that I should consider myself the most fortunate of men if such a benefit came to me through you. You are all-powerful, and to your proved generosity I leave my fortune.

Truly, last night, after having read Gianoli's letter, I could not sleep for excitement: it would be fortune enough for me to reach the apex of that to which I have so long aspired, i.e. a little private income, already coming in, so as to be able to live an independent life. Better than a pension! I should have it in my own hands. As for Genoa, you can be sure that I should find no difficulty about absenting myself, even in the winter, for two months; and then, in any case, if difficulties were made, I should bid them a perpetual farewell, that is to say, I should bid farewell to the Teatro Carlo Felice, which this year must have an impossible company of singers.

I say no more, my Maestro, and I think I have bothered you enough already. My fortune depends on you, if I can be of service to you.

The ninth performance of *La forza del destino*, too, was crowned with the same success as the earlier ones, with the theatre packed. Tomorrow and Sunday, the same opera again, and it is that which has put the management on its feet again. On Wednesday of next week we shall put on *Macbeth*; on the days when *La forza* is performed I don't hold rehearsals, so as not to tire the chorus and orchestra, who perform divinely always.

Have you received the Savoy biscuits?

Hearty greetings to Signora Giuseppina and to Mauro.

I kiss your hand; believe me always

Your faithful servant

ANGELO MARIANI.

P.S. Please return Gianoli's letter, because I must give it back to Antonelli, who doesn't know I have sent it to you.

It seems clear that Gianoli's letter had told of rumours in Cairo that Mariani was to be sent by Verdi to conduct *Aida*, at a fee of 50,000 francs. This would have solved Mariani's financial, and perhaps also his matrimonial, problems. But the rumours were baseless. A copy of Verdi's withering reply is found in Giuseppina's letter-book:

Gianoli would do well to look after his own affairs and not to interfere in mine. Antonelli can tell him from me that there is no truth in that letter, which stinks of the theatre at a thousand miles distance.

You wrote to me once before that you wanted to accompany me to Cairo: I replied that I wasn't going. If I had thought fit to send you in my place I should have asked you; if I did not do so that is proof that I did not think fit and that I had entrusted the task to someone else.

This letter of Gianoli's is an ugly business for him, for you and for me.

Verdi seems to have looked on the whole affair as a second attempt to force his hand, as something privately arranged between Mariani, Antonelli, Gianoli and Isabella Galletti. Why was it 'an ugly business' for Gianoli, except on the assumption that he was conniving at his wife's supposed love affair with Mariani, and had been induced by her to write this letter? 'Gianoli would do well to look after his own affairs and not to interfere in mine. . . .'

If the production of *Aida* had not been held up by the Franco-Prussian War, it would have been conducted in Cairo by Muzio, probably with Isabella Galletti in the title-role; at Milan the part would have been taken by Antonietta Fricci. As already mentioned, Teresa Stolz was not available, being engaged for Venice. When the production of the opera was put off for another year, the casting, for Milan and for Cairo, had to begin all over again. Giulio Ricordi got busy at once. Verdi's choice of singers for Milan in the following year included Antonietta Fricci, again, as Aida, and Teresa Stolz as Amneris. The extensive range of the latter's voice permitted her to undertake either of the two chief women's roles. Antonietta Fricci was already engaged for Lisbon, but Ricordi hoped to be able to secure her release. On 31st December 1870 he wrote to Verdi:

La Fricci is agreeable to everything, *even to diminution of her fee*, as long as she succeeds in singing *Aida*. So on this side I have *carte blanche* from la Fricci and the management. . . . As for la Stolz, I have *carte blanche* concerning her as well, it being pressingly important to secure this artist too. Thank you for your advice about that, which I am following entirely. . . . I am awaiting another letter from you and then either I myself or someone else will leave at once for Venice, to blockade, *ipso facto*, la Stolz.

He went himself to Venice and secured a verbal agreement, but a few days later there arrived a letter from the singer:

I write in accordance with what was agreed between us on 3rd January, when you were at Venice, i.e. to let you know in writing all the conditions I would like set down in the contract between me and the Teatro alla Scala at Milan for the next Carnival season, 1871–2.

The first condition would be *to have my fee guaranteed either by the municipality or by a sound banking house.*

2 The fee to be 40,000 francs, free of brokerage and all taxes.
3 All the operas to be chosen by common consent and (*if possible*) I to have the right to appear in Maestro Verdi's new opera *Aida*.
4 No more than three performances a week.

5 *I* to be the *prima donna d'obbligo*.
6 To have the right to the customary eight days' sick leave.

Those are all my express conditions. Now, dear Signor Giulio, do all you can to get them accepted, *especially the first one*, and I shall be ready to sign the contract at once.

Ricordi was furious, and replied that he was unaccustomed to having his good faith doubted, that she had circumscribed their original agreement with so many conditions as to alter it entirely and that he could not propose such conditions to the management. He withdrew from the negotiations. He also told her she had been 'very badly advised'. What he meant by this is seen by what he wrote to Verdi on 7th January: 'Signora Stolz's letter is really a dirty trick. I see Mariani's hand in it, and if I had him here at this moment I would kick his backside and treat him as he deserves. He is ruining Signora Stolz's career too!' Antonietta Fricci was not released from her contract to appear in Lisbon and by the end of the month Ricordi was wondering: 'Shall we have to go back to la Stolz?' Meanwhile the authorities in Cairo were also trying to make up their company for the new opera.

Muzio was no longer free to go to Egypt as conductor, so Draneht Bey, director of the khedive's theatres, tried to secure, through the theatrical agent Lampugnani at Milan, Mariani as conductor and Teresa Stolz as *prima donna*. Here is a passage from an interesting letter, written at Venice on 13th March 1871, from Teresa Stolz to Lampugnani: [1]

As soon as I got your letter of the 9th I wrote to Mariani for his *ultimatum* (as you call it) about the Cairo business. Here it is: Mariani writes to me precisely these words: 'To go to Cairo, I would accept from 30,000 to 35,000 francs for the whole season.' As you know, I would myself accept 120,000 to 125,000 francs for the whole season. There you have the whole thing. Now I beg you, dearest friend, to keep these negotiations of ours secret, because there are people at Milan who don't look favourably on my giving preference to theatres outside Italy!!! Perhaps you will understand who could have such strange ideas and who is concerned about the presentation of new works by the great composers in Italy! Please do me the favour of telegraphing at once to Cairo to let them know my final demand and that of Mariani.

Here we see that she was demanding three times as much as she had asked from La Scala. All the artists seem to have regarded the new theatre in Cairo as a perfect gold mine. On 24th March Draneht complained to Verdi about this. The tenor Mongini wanted 125,000 francs and a benefit night; he had been offered 100,000 francs and a benefit. Draneht went on:

[1] From a copy in the possession of Franco Schlitzer.

I have also approached Madame Stolz and Mariani, her future husband, but there, too, I have had to contend with exaggerated pretensions. I have offered 125,000 francs for the two of them, and a benefit that can be reckoned at 35,000 or 40,000 francs,[1] which seem to me very reasonable terms.

During these negotiations, Verdi and Mariani were both living in Palazzo Sauli at Genoa, except that in March Verdi made a trip to Florence to preside over a commission appointed by Cesare Correnti, Minister of Education, to consider the reform of the Conservatorii. He took the opportunity to hear a performance of *La Traviata*, with Anastasi Pozzoni, whom he recommended to Draneht, and who in fact became the first Aida. There are several letters from Mariani to Verdi and Giuseppina at Florence, about the commission, about the apartment and about the joy of Lorito, the parrot, on hearing of the imminent return of his master and mistress. Verdi replied to Draneht on 30th March: 'As soon as I was back at Genoa I made haste to speak to Mariani, but I did not find him disposed to go to Cairo. Unless he changes his mind (which is easily possible) you must not count on him. . . .' Reference to Mariani's perpetual irresolution was no doubt justified, but Verdi, too, had changed his mind. Only four months earlier he had made clear, in a manner most wounding to the conductor's self-esteem, that he was not his own first choice for the task. Now, since Muzio was no longer available, he wanted Mariani to go. In another letter to Draneht on 14th April he said again: 'Mariani could easily change his mind'; in the same letter he announced: 'Madame Stolz is engaged for Milan.' This he had learned from Giulio Ricordi, who had written from Bologna station at half past two in the morning:

I have just arrived from Venice and while waiting for the train to Milan I hasten to give you news of my trip to see Signora Stolz, who has finally accepted the Scala proposal, after *a telegram from friend Mariani.*

But are they married then, or not? Enough—that's for them to worry about! For my part I am happy to have succeeded in settling the matter with both.

Nothing now remains but to come to agreement on the secondary terms of the contract, but about that I know the management is quite prepared to satisfy Signora Stolz. As for the fee, I know the way to ensure that it is *quite safe*!

Teresa Stolz was now detached from Mariani, as far as *Aida* was

[1] These figures are perfectly clearly written on the original document, which I have checked at Sant' Agata, but they seem impossibly high. *L'Art musical*, Escudier's paper, commented on 11th April 1872 on reports in the newspapers that Marie Sass had received 40,000 francs from a benefit night in Cairo: 'The highest receipts amount to about 6,000 francs. M. Naudin's benefit, which was one of the most productive last year, did not go beyond that figure.' In 1874 Teresa Stolz's benefit night, with the highest receipts of the season, brought her 5,653 francs.

concerned. It would be interesting to know whether it was at Verdi's insistence that Ricordi, swallowing his pride, and reopening negotiations from which he had earlier withdrawn, made his hasty return to Venice to secure her services for Milan.

After this, Verdi continued to urge Mariani to go to Cairo. And Mariani of course prevaricated. He did not *want* to go, in a poor state of health, as a second-best choice, at a fee less than that he had stipulated, and without his *fiancée*. There is no doubt that Verdi subjected him to considerable pressure. This is certainly the time of the dispute in the Ristorante della Concordia, recorded in print by Resasco and Ridella in 1901 and 1902, which ended with Verdi saying: 'Anyone who breaks his word is not a man, but a boy.' This indicates that at some point in the discussions Mariani had weakened and agreed to go, or at any rate that Verdi believed him to have done so. Now again he begged for more time to think it over. Verdi was to leave Genoa for Sant' Agata on 22nd April.[1] Mariani promised to bring his final decision before he left, after consulting Teresa Stolz, who was apparently staying at Sestri, south of Genoa, and his employers, represented by Bixio, the deputy-mayor. But it was by letter that Verdi received, at Sant' Agata, Mariani's unhappy final refusal, communicated, as ever, in an oddly evasive way:

Genoa, 23rd April.

MY MAESTRO,

I have been to Sestri but I did not find the person there: I shall only be able to see her this evening.

Bixio is not at Genoa.

Don't believe that I tell you that to gain time; I want only to prove to you that my asking you to wait until today for my reply was not just an excuse.

I thank you for the kindness you have shown me, on this occasion too. Be sure that I shall be eternally grateful, and I am sorry not to be able to profit by your favours.

Please give my regards to Signora Peppina and believe me, kissing your hand, always

Your servant A. M.

Verdi's version of these events is given in a letter to Carlino Del Signore:[2]

And Mariani? . . . Do you know that I left Genoa without a reply about the Cairo affair? You will know that on the very day of my departure he wrote me a short letter, begging me AGAIN to wait for his decision until the next day. The next day, he didn't come!!! *Ah! c'est vraiment trop fort! trop fort! trop fort!*

[1] Verdi to Du Locle, 21st April: 'We shall leave Genoa tomorrow.'

[2] Published by Zoppi, pp. 225–6, who states that it is well known, because included in the *Copialettere*. But it is *not* in the *Copialettere*.

From this it appears that he had delayed his departure at Mariani's request until the 23rd.

The friendship was now over. Verdi had finished with Mariani. The latter, hoping still that he had not committed the unforgivable sin, tried to excuse himself, through other people, and through a letter, the last that has survived, delivered by a common friend, the Spanish painter Serafino De Avendaño, on 18th June:

> I haven't written to you any more because I hadn't the courage. I hope, however, that Carlino's letter will have persuaded you that I have never regarded myself as having let you down. If involuntarily I happened to do so, I beg your forgiveness, and you can be sure that I am very sorry you could so much as suppose it. I know the goodness of your most noble mind, which leads me to hope you will relieve me of the anguish I am suffering at never receiving news from you or the worthy Signora Peppina. I'll say nothing of myself, or of my health, for fear you should believe I am looking for sympathy. I live in retirement and try to get well. I must confess, however, that this condition is beginning to vex me unbearably. Enough—it's my business!

There was no reply. Del Signore tried to arrange another meeting. Mariani, who had gone to Bologna to put himself again in the hands of his doctors, advised Verdi that he would be at Genoa from 29th June to 1st July. But the composer did not stir from Sant' Agata until 19th July, by which time Mariani was back at Bologna.

The unexplained remark: 'God be with the worthy Signora Stolz, and inspire her for her own good!!!' occurs in a letter from Giuseppina to Del Signore. From Mariani's own letters it appears that he and Teresa Stolz were still on terms of close intimacy.

Two years before this the possible performance of *Lohengrin* at Bologna had been discussed. It had been mentioned casually by Mariani in a letter to Verdi. Now the idea was revived. The course of events, and Mariani's involvement in them, can be followed from the correspondence with Del Signore, which here becomes of great importance.

The introduction of Wagner's music into Italy was a consequence of the bitter commercial rivalry between the firms of Ricordi and Lucca. Verdi's operas, since *Il Corsaro*, which he had been compelled to write, against his will, by a contract from which Lucca had refused to release him, had remained firmly in Ricordi's hands. Lucca and his remarkable wife had countered the Verdian domination of the Italian theatres by presenting important foreign works, such as *La Juive*, *Faust* and Meyerbeer's long-awaited *L'Africaine*.[1] Tito Ricordi, in his correspondence with Verdi, speaks of his rival with hatred and contempt, but Verdi, in spite of his own dislike of Lucca, was not

[1] Of Meyerbeer's earlier operas, *Robert le Diable* and *Les Huguenots* were shared by both publishers; *Dinorah* and *Le Prophète* were Ricordi's property.

above using him as a bargaining counter in dealings with Ricordi. In December 1866, after a bad performance of *Un ballo in maschera* at Venice, when the curtain had to be brought down half way through the first act, he wrote:

> Since we are able, as you say, to talk as one friend to another, allow me to tell you that I should not be at all unhappy if my operas were in the hands of someone who better looked after them. The affair of *Un ballo in maschera* at Venice was scandalous! Observe how Lucca has managed so that *L'Africaine* is always well performed, and when the management of the Teatro Fenice asked him for *La Juive*, his first condition was the imposition of a new conductor. The fact is that the operas of which Lucca is proprietor are always well performed, and with his three operas he now has the principal theatres of Italy in his hands.

He startled Ricordi by suggesting that he should take the first favourable opportunity and combine the two publishing houses in one. Ricordi replied: 'Your advice about forming one big establishment by merging my firm and Lucca's would be excellent if the latter were a different sort of man, and if it were possible for him and me to get on together. But, by God, when one thinks of his past, and recalls the old proverb about the wolf . . . there is reason enough for hesitation, not to say for alarm. . . .' [1]

Lohengrin was Giovannina Lucca's trump card. This indomitable woman, who used to declare that if Verdi avoided Milan it was because he was afraid of having his ears boxed by her, adopted towards her own composers, of all ages, a maternally protective attitude. Whatever her husband may have been, Giovannina was sincere, generous and loyal. Her ungrammatical letters have a genuine warmth, far removed from the tone of normal business correspondence. Her relations with Wagner would be worth a study in themselves. Her understanding of his music was limited, to say the least, judging by the fantastic proposal she made to him in person, that he should prepare for Italy a condensed version of the *Ring*, to be performed on one single evening. But she passionately believed in his cause and fought for it, tooth and nail.

Earlier views on Mariani's part in the events leading up to the production of *Lohengrin* at Bologna have had to be profoundly modified as a result of the letters to Del Signore published by Zoppi. Readers should be warned that Zoppi's commentary is often very misleading; but he has things to say, at this point of the story, that badly needed saying.

It can now be stated with certainty that the performance of *Lohengrin* was never planned by Mariani as an act of revenge, noble or otherwise, on Verdi. In a sense it *became* something of the kind,

[1] Letters quoted by Giuseppe Adami in *Giulio Ricordi* (Milan, 1945), pp. 50–4.

but by force of circumstances rather than as a result of the conductor's turpitude. The stages by which he progressively became involved can be followed in his correspondence with Del Signore.

He was at Bologna in the care of his doctors while the project matured. The leading spirit in the whole enterprise was the mayor, Camillo Casarini.

Mariani to Del Signore, 19th July:

From what I have heard, the municipality here is absolutely set on the performance of Wagner's *Lohengrin* at the Teatro Comunale in the coming autumn season. I am only concerned to get well, nor do I want to involve myself in what doesn't concern me. So let them all, beginning with the proprietor and publisher, perform what bestial actions they please!

This does not sound much like admiration for *Lohengrin*.

30th July:

Nothing has yet been settled about the coming autumn season. The mayor and the city council were considering having *Lohengrin* performed, but Lucca having put forward unacceptable terms, I believe nothing will come of it. Imagine! Among other things Lucca wanted Bülow to come as *my adviser*, and all the artists to be Germans who had already sung in *Lohengrin* with success in other theatres, in Germany, under Wagner's own direction. This demand of Lucca's aroused the indignation of the mayor, the council and the entire population, and it was treated as a question of national decorum. The municipality behaved, truly, with dignity and exemplary firmness. It gave full satisfaction to me and the Italian artists, saying that *it preferred to keep the theatre closed rather than permit this affront to the musical decorum of Bologna and all Italy*. Filippi has written a letter to the mayor saying that he approves his noble conduct and that I am *the only person* capable of conducting Wagner's operas. Lucca's wife, too, wrote to the mayor, indicating that she has never doubted my *renowned ability*, but that she had suggested the *advice* of Bülow, as the person most familiar, *as she says*, with the music of *the mighty Wagner*. Casarini (the mayor) has replied to Lucca that here there is no need of Bülow, or even of Wagner himself, and that if he wants the work performed he is to hand over the score unconditionally otherwise, good night!

Verdi, writing to Ricordi, had held up Lucca as an example of a publisher who took care that his operas were properly performed. That was what, perfectly reasonably, he was doing here. But in seeking to introduce Wagner's work into Italy in the best possible conditions he had come up against national and civic pride, and Mariani's own vanity. The conductor abased himself before Verdi, in many of his letters, in exaggerated terms. He was 'a nullity', 'a poor insect', etc. But actually he was very vain. Ghislanzoni, writing only a few years after his death, remarked on this.

Mariani's letter to Del Signore of 30th July continues for another page to express his mingled indignation and satisfaction. Then:

> Perhaps the Maestro knows nothing of this trick that Bülow and Lucca tried to play on me. If so, all the better, for, knowing how much he has at heart the honour of Italian art, I am sure it would have displeased him; so don't tell him anything about it. I would ask you to give him my regards. But what is his attitude towards me? Do what you think best.

Zoppi is absolutely right—these are not the words of a man guilty of ingratitude, of rebellion and defection to the enemy's camp. He still loved Verdi, and was still unaware of having irreparably offended:

9th August:

> Oh! how sweet it is, amid the perversities of the world, to know that one possesses a true friend! Of you I am sure, as I am sure of the affection of all your angelic family. How can I help it? I have faith, too, that the Maestro and his wife have not entirely forgotten me. I should like you to give him my regards, and make him understand that if I did not write to him any more it was because I lacked the courage. How is it possible not to love Verdi and his wife? Apart from his genius, does it seem to you a little thing to find a man of such exemplary virtue? With me he was sometimes severe; perhaps it was my fault, my involuntary fault, but I was afraid of him. Please, give him my regards, and the same to his wife, and if they disdain my salutation, don't tell me, for it would hurt me too much.

There is much in this letter, too, about what he saw as Lucca's ingratitude and villainy, and about his own satisfaction at Bologna's reaction. From subsequent correspondence it is clear that he insisted on going through with the whole business alone, because his injured vanity demanded that he do so. The score was now ceded without conditions. Lucca and his wife, with the stage designer and technicians of the Teatro Comunale, went to Munich to see how the work was staged there. Mariani stayed at Bologna, intent on demonstrating that he had no need of anybody's advice. As he studied the work he came to admire it greatly. He sent Del Signore a copy of the vocal score: 'Examine it carefully', he wrote, 'and you will find some beautiful things.'

In the war of the publishers, the fact that *Lohengrin* was to be performed at all represented a tactical victory for Lucca. If it could be exploited and a Wagnerian break-through into Italy achieved, the consequences for Ricordi would be very serious.

These events were seen at Sant' Agata in the light of what Ricordi's agent at Bologna, Luigi Monti, reported to his employer. Luzio, in the *Carteggi verdiani*,[1] briefly summarizes a letter from Monti, a copy of which, with commentary, is found in Giuseppina's letter-book. It is not made clear in the *Carteggi* that the letter is addressed

[1] II, pp. 34–5.

to Ricordi, and had been forwarded by him to Verdi. It is dated 5th August, from Bologna, and must have reached Sant' Agata at about the time Mariani was writing: 'I have faith, too, that the Maestro and his wife have not entirely forgotten me. . . . How is it possible not to love Verdi and his wife?' Here is the full text of Monti's letter:

In continuation of my letter of today: I stayed in town this evening because I wanted to hear the outcome of today's discussions in the town hall about our theatre. There were two proposals, one from that society of forging rascals, the other from Gaiby. The mayor wouldn't accept the proposal of the former, and proceeded to discussion of terms with Gaiby, giving him to understand, though without insisting, that *Lohengrin* was wanted. Gaiby drew attention to the big risk involved in giving this somewhat hazardous score, and offered him *Don Carlos*, with la Latti or another singer, with la Galletti, the tenor Capponi, Pandolfini and other artists acceptable to Mariani. The mayor had a meeting with Mariani and, in Gaiby's presence, put forward this idea to Mariani, who suddenly said that *Lohengrin* had got to be given, and that he had already chosen the singers for the impresario who had taken the Teatro Comunale, and the company consisted of la Blume, Capponi, Destinn and I don't know what others, and that he had already had wires sent to these because he knew they were acceptable to Signora Lucca, and that they must also be engaged by Bolelli's agency. You will understand how pained Gaiby was, for knowing how Mariani had spoken in the past of the opera, of Lucca and of the affront he had received because Lucca had excluded him from conducting this score, he hoped that Mariani would have supported his proposal; but this *chameleon* insisted instead in wanting this score, revealing himself wholly on Lucca's side, and the reason he adduced for not giving *Don Carlos* was that he didn't believe it would come off well, and that if *Lohengrin* were not given, he would prefer to repeat *L'Africaine*. Then Gaiby said that he would think it over and draw up estimates concerning this score which is wanted, and which upsets his whole proposal, based on other ideas.

But tell me, is it possible to be more of a rascal and deceiver than that fellow? I have been to see him twice, but he kept out of sight, ashamed perhaps of the infamous role he played in this business, which would give me the right to tell him that as an artist he is worthy of all respect, but that as a man he is the most abject creature that exists. Note that these matters had already been initiated even when he told me to let him have *Die Königin von Saba* at once, giving me to believe he would look through it immediately, for if he found it suitable he would suggest it to the mayor; instead of which I know he hasn't even opened it. I confess I am so angry that I don't know what I should say to him; I should never have thought him such a rascal; I have always said that as a man he is a buffoon and a chatterer, but such an intriguing deceiver I should never have believed him. Enough—let him do what he likes. Speaking for myself, I've finished with him; you do what you think best, it's enough for me that I've informed you of everything and you know all about it.

I think I have sufficiently explained matters and relieved my feelings a bit, and I feel better. Farewell.

One would like to know what Ricordi wrote when he sent this letter to Verdi, and what the latter replied. That the whole affair was viewed at Sant' Agata in the worst possible light is shown by Giuseppina's commentary, in which Mariani's crimes, over the years, are totted up:

Note by the Copyist.

And the *mascherade* about going to Cairo to conduct *Aida* when la Galletti was there, and it was thought the opera could be given in that season?

And the Mass at Bologna?

And the *ibis* and *redibis* (I mean in a bad sense) concerning the engagement of la Stolz at Milan, on the pretext of his rights as her future husband?

And the generally unknown but not less infamous and cowardly underhand dealings and lies concerning his old and new mistresses, and the continual deceit of la Stolz?

And the daily, hourly, lies? And his sordid avarice, when his vanity is not in question?

And the ill spoken of la Pallavicino, when, bored by his interminable lying rigmaroles, she has moments of impatience?

And the lies told to la Frugoni?

And his lack of restraint with Carlino and family, whether other people are present or not?

And la Massa?

And the affair of the Mayor of Bologna, in which he played the part of the laziest and vilest person in the world? . . .

And the position in which he placed Verdi, *after having agreed* to go to Cairo for the opera to be given there positively this year?

The words of this man are mire, like the mire of his soul, and his pretension is to pass as the most *chaste* of men.

Things had changed indeed since she had written, eleven years before, that she loved him like a brother.

Carlino Del Signore, often employed as intermediary, must have heard from Verdi and Giuseppina some of their complaints. He sometimes passed on warning words and recommendations that were not welcome to Mariani. A sudden bitter note, in a letter of 13th October, disturbs the normal warmly affectionate tone of the correspondence with Del Signore: 'I know no joys, and if I had any I should not tell of them, so as not to arouse envy and attract slander and new enemies. Let each one keep to himself his pains, sorrows, disillusionments and anguish, and await in resignation the hour when it will please God to liberate him and recall him to His bosom.' In response to an inquiry about his *fiancée*, he added: 'Signora Stolz went into the country on the 23rd of last month, to Maestro Verdi's house, and stayed there until yesterday. Now she is again at Florence. This is all I can tell you, knowing no more myself.'

Lohengrin at Bologna, on 1st November, made operatic history. It was a sensational success, and Bülow himself, after hearing more than one performance, had high praise for Mariani. He wrote an article for *Die Signale*, in dialogue form; one voice raises objections, the other replies. Reference is made to the numerous cuts; the reply is that much worse things, in this respect, happened in Germany. On the whole, Bülow's impressions were very favourable, as were those of the leading Italian critics, with the notable exception of contributions to Ricordi's *Gazzetta Musicale di Milano*. Wagner sent his portrait, with the inscription: 'Evviva Mariani!!!'

This triumph was achieved in spite of intense sufferings, physical and moral. Mariani's world was collapsing all around him. Everything he had suppressed in his letter of 13th October came out a month later, in two enormous screeds. In floods of words, he poured out his heart to his friend:

Bologna, 14th November 1871.

Yesterday morning your letter of the day before arrived, and it was welcome, because it is proof of the benevolence you still feel for me, in spite of those defects with which, according to your way of seeing things, and that of a few others I believed my friends, I have to reproach myself. But you at least, my Carlino, open your heart to me, you want clarifications of such misunderstandings as may have arisen between us, you treat me, in short, as an honest man and not as a twisting rascal, in the way that, it is all too true, I have been treated by persons I believed of very different nature and character. I cannot and must not give you now the reasons that led me to doubt even you, and you wouldn't believe how painful it was to me to hear myself unjustly reproached by you. Oh, my Carlino! Perhaps you have unwittingly contributed greatly to harm me, and above all you can't imagine how bitter it was to have to believe of you things I should never have wished to believe.

You, who have a penetrating eye and have, as you say, recognized my defects, why haven't you taken the trouble to scrutinize also those of other people? You ought to have considered carefully whether in my conduct and actions there were failings, or crimes. If sometimes I showed myself undecided, irascible, disgusted with everything and everybody, you should have considered whether that was caused by my nature or by the malice of others. I really feel that I have nothing, nothing at all, with which to reproach myself; and where, unwittingly, I may have failed in some things, my *true* friends should have corrected me kindly, and punished me too, but not treated me with harshness and scorn, as they have done. Oh my Carlino! Put your hand on your heart, and consider how I have been treated by Maestro Verdi, by his wife, and by another person who should have behaved towards me in a very different manner. What have I done to Maestro Verdi? You know, since everything passed through your hands. Is his attitude towards me a fitting one? What has happened to the benevolence and friendship that he said he had for me? What is the reason for the severity with which he treats me, as if I were the vilest creature on this earth? If he wanted me to go to Cairo he should have said so, and I would have gone to the end of the earth for him. I did not believe I should so rouse his anger, seeing that he had declared it was a matter of indifference to him whether I went or not, by not accepting an offer that came to me from some director or other and a theatrical agent. I thanked him and afterwards I wrote to him again, asking forgiveness if I had involuntarily done something he did not like; he did not reply, nor did he reply to the third letter I sent him, which was delivered to him, *open*, by Avendaño. I learned from this friend of his that in Verdi's house it was no longer possible to mention my name, and if someone dared to do so, everything possible was done to change the subject. And what is the reason for all that? Am I become a creature so vile that a conversation is considered contaminated just by the mention of my name? Must I be treated with such harshness? Don't you find here, my Carlino, excessive malice and vulgarity of heart? If Maestro Verdi or his wife had reason for complaint against me they should have pointed it out to me, if I had really failed them so as to deserve their anger; I don't therefore consider that my memory should be detested by them to the point of feeling revulsion at the mere mention of my name. From the sublime to the ridiculous is but a step and when haughtiness is pushed to that degree it becomes despotism, a thing ridiculous in our day. If all my failings were like that which has lost me the Maestro's esteem, believe me, my Carlino, they would not condemn me to hell, nor deprive me of the regard and benevolence of kind and good hearts. So about that I feel no remorse, but rather most painful disillusionment.

Now I'll tell you something about the lady from Prague, and mind, my Carlino, I tell it to you alone.

I'll tell you the facts; you will consider them dispassionately and if you feel I am at fault I will submit to your reproaches.

As you know, after having been at Genoa a few days at the beginning of August, I returned through Bologna to Florence, with the sole purpose of talking things over with the lady. I stayed there about ten days, I returned to Bologna for the first rehearsals of the chorus, for *Lohengrin* (that was about 20th September) and, as the lady had told me she had to go to Sant' Agata, I returned to Florence to accompany her on her journey as far as Bologna. I did not fail to bring to her notice (when she revealed that she was going to Verdi's house) that that trip of hers was inopportune, considering Verdi's attitude towards me, and that she was going to put herself in a position that would be embarrassing for us. I pointed out also that I should not be able to write to her, seeing that, if my letters arrived in that house, it would be unfitting for the lady from Prague not to give my regards to her host and hostess, and not to try, as a kind and truly *friendly* person should, to bring about a reconciliation. But nothing of the kind! In parting from me at the station she told me that she would stay only a week in Verdi's house, that on her return she would stop at Bologna for two or three days, and that then she would return for the production of *Lohengrin*. Instead, she stayed at Sant' Agata for twenty days; she wrote to me three times to say that Verdi and his wife were overwhelming her with kindness, that she was studying her part in the new opera, that she was very pleased with it, and that she was happy.

I replied to her reservedly about everything, not knowing what attitude to adopt. She repeated by letter her promise to stay at Bologna, but then she did not keep it. One morning there arrived a telegram to say she would be passing through the station here at three in the afternoon. I went, the train was about three-quarters of an hour late, so that the lady only stopped for fourteen minutes. . . . Two days after she reached Florence she wrote to me, treating me coldly, with despite even. I did not fail to complain of that in my replies, begging her to be kind, for in those circumstances I had more need than ever of her comfort and moral support (I was at the culmination of the rehearsals of *Lohengrin* and God alone knows in what physical and moral anguish). We staged *Lohengrin*, but the lady did not appear; I had not failed to let her know that I had reserved a box, but she replied nothing about that, limiting herself to saying that although *our present relations could not be what they had been in the past*, she was yet still an artist, and did not wish to deprive herself of the pleasure of hearing a fine performance in the theatre, and that therefore on passing through Bologna she would stay one night. I replied that I could not believe her letter, or suppose her so cruel. She repeated her letter, declaring that she did not wish to deceive me and that between her and me *there existed henceforth only simple friendship, as between fellow artists*. Such was the gratitude and the comfort I had in those circumstances from the woman to whom I had consecrated all my affection, and my whole future. . . .

Once she wrote to me that she would be staying at Genoa until she went to Milan: that is natural, she being now very intimate with Verdi [*in gran tenerezza con Verdi*], which proves what affection she had for me!! Who would ever have thought that my friends, the two persons I esteemed and loved more than myself, would have united in treating me as they have done!!!!! I hope that you will remain my friend, my Carlino, for if I lost you too I should be more desolate even than I am! Oh! how painful is disillusionment!!!

Forgive me if I have written badly, but how can I help it? I began this letter out of bed, but I have had to lie down again, suffering insupportable spasms of pain. My exertions and emotions, and above all my moral sufferings, have affected me physically, so as to cause a recrudescence of my old trouble. Oh! if God would only call me to Him! It would be the greatest, most longed-for favour He could grant me. And to think that I have to conduct *Lohengrin* four times a week, in this state, before ever fresh audiences, for the concourse of foreigners is very great, and consequently I feel each time the emotions of the first night! I hide my sufferings from everyone: to whom should I tell them? I should only give satisfaction to my enemies, to the malicious, and I should not improve my most painful condition in the least.

It is impossible to decide just how much truth lies behind these whirling words. One has the impression that he must also have talked in this breathless style, and said or wrote the first things that came into his head. Afterwards he calmed down, forgot all about it and was surprised that other people remembered and resented his words.

*N

It seems above all impossible to accept his claim that he did not know that Verdi wanted him to go to Cairo. It may well have been true that Verdi's expressed attitude was: 'I'm not asking you to go myself, but I have now to reply to Draneht. Are you going—yes or no?' But he must have known that Verdi really did wish him to go. One important fact emerges quite clearly from the above letter: Teresa Stolz broke off her engagement to Mariani immediately after her visit to Sant' Agata. It is hard not to believe that she did so in consequence of what was said to her there about him.

The next letter, of 17th November, is even longer. Parts of it must be quoted. Del Signore had not been able to accept all Mariani's protestations of innocence. By replying to the question: 'What have I done to Maestro Verdi?' he brought down upon himself another torrent of words:

This was not the moment to come and throw in my face the sins I know, by God, I have not committed, to give me to understand that I deserve the despite of persons so perfect and of exemplary virtue. If I were the nullity you think me, shouldn't you, who talk so much of friendship, recognize that even the beasts feel pain, and in consequence should you not have soothed rather than exacerbated my anguish?

But just as you like! I submit to everything with the resignation of one who knows he has nothing with which to reproach himself, or of which to be ashamed or repent.

In truth the fault you wish to ascribe to me concerning Maestro Verdi is quite new to me—that *of having spoken ill of him, whoever was present*, and you yourself have heard me. I don't remember ever having lost my head, and if I did what you say I did I should have been acting against my own self, and must have been demented. I remember, rather, disgusted as I was by the severity and rigour with which the Maestro had always treated me, having relieved my feelings with you and your wife, but I did not believe that you would have interpreted that just outburst in the sinister way you have. In any case, you, such a close friend, ought at the time to have recalled me to my senses and not allowed me to offend against myself. I have never spoken to other people about what passed between the Maestro and myself; you can be sure of that and I can swear it, if you except the lady of whom you speak with such reverence in your letter—the only person perhaps to whom I may have repeated the same outbursts. But how could I help it? I believed that she too was a friend of mine, and instead she never was. Then I declare to you here, in the face of God and men, and all those who may accuse me, that I have never spoken ill of Maestro Verdi to anyone, and that this is a rascally invention to excuse the rather severe way in which I was treated, to denigrate me with false arguments and insinuations. Oh, Carlino! if you knew how many things I have kept buried in my anguished heart!!!

Among pages and pages about the history of his relations with Teresa Stolz, this passage is important:

The providential opportunity had arrived, as you know, but the lady declared she wouldn't hear of it and would follow the impulses of her heart, which called her to Milan, and this most harsh sentence she repeated to me several times, with infernal sarcasm. You know all the rest and what happened concerning the Milanese negotiations, on the part of the lady and of the Maestro. But that was just play-acting, which ended with all looking after their own interests and I being left in the wrong, with a broken head.

This can only mean that he would have gone to Cairo if Teresa Stolz had been willing to come with him. It can only refer to the end of March or the first half of April 1871, the time of the delicate cross-negotiations with Cairo and Milan, unless indeed, as is not impossible, Mariani thought his *fiancée* should break her contract with Milan and accompany him to Cairo. What would Verdi have said then?

Towards the end of this letter occurs another bitter passage:

I thought I had in the Maestro a true friend, in the lady from Prague an affectionate and devoted heart, in you a brother. The first thinks it necessary to treat me as he does; you say he is right, and so be it. The second is too virtuous to be guilty of an unjust action, so I must be unworthy of her. As for you, the least of the three, though you can't make up your mind to cast me off, you recognize that I don't deserve anyone's esteem, owing to my dubious and dissolute life, so I must consider myself a most miserable creature. I am sorry, but if God made me like that, it's not my fault. You others stay then in your lofty stations, and accept the homage of those who have the honour and good fortune to approach you, and leave me in my mire.

Carlino Del Signore must have been a man of great sweetness of character, gentle and forgiving. Such words would have sufficed to ruin many another friendship. But not this one, and three days later Mariani was writing again:

In order to avoid further misunderstandings and irritation and any misinterpretation, the weight of which, as on so many other occasions, I should have to bear, I must tell you what has happened, because if ever the Maestro should speak to you about it, it will be well for you to know the truth.

Yesterday afternoon, between two and three, I was at the station, summoned there by an old friend in the retinue of the Russian Grand Duke Michael. I saw Signor Luigi Monti, Ricordi's agent. I asked him what he was doing there; he replied that he was waiting for someone who had not arrived.

Hardly had he said these words when, a few yards away, I saw the Maestro. I went towards him, greeted him and tried to relieve him of his travelling-bag. He would not allow me to take it. I understood that he was not pleased that I had seen his arrival. I gave him my word of honour that no living soul would learn of it from me. He went away, and I remained at the station. Half an hour later I went home in a carriage and lay down as usual on my bed. I got up for dinner, I did not speak to a living soul and at the usual time I went to the theatre. I perceived, from certain imperfections in the performance of the soloists and chorus, that there was some excitement on the stage. After the first act, when I complained of that I was told that Maestro Verdi was in the theatre, in box 23 of the second tier. I replied that it was not true. I was told to go and see him, from the peep-hole in the drop-curtain. I found la Sacconi and she too told me she had seen him and in reply I called her an imbecile. After the second act I heard Luigi Monti shout from the directors' box: '*Viva il Maestro Verdi!*' —the response to which was general applause from the audience, prolonged for about a quarter of an hour. You can imagine how it affected me! 'Now I'm in a fine mess,' I said to myself, 'the Maestro will think I spoke about it and will believe I broke my word.' The Maestro, naturally, kept out of sight and I think he did well. I know that even the mayor went to ask him to appear, but all in vain. I asked how they had known and was told 'from some Milanese who had arrived by the same train and who had seen him enter, and then in the box, where Corticelli and Monti were on show'—something that clearly indicated that the Maestro was within. He could be seen, moreover, from the directors' box, and the soloists and half the chorus had seen him too. The Maestro left the theatre at the end of the opera; I was told that he departed last night. I did not know he was staying at the Hotel Brun, nor did I go there, so as not to displease him. This is the real truth and I hope that the Maestro has not blamed me for something that was not my fault.

The Maestro's presence had terrified soloists, chorus and orchestra, for there were imperfections in the performance that had never occurred before. I was upset about it, and I tell you that to persuade you all the more that not only would I not have broken my word for all the gold in the world, but I would not have wanted such a thing known—something that naturally paralyses those who have to give of their best.

Verdi's remarks, such as 'horribly out of tune' and 'badly performed, a real mess', in the famous annotated vocal score of *Lohengrin* at Sant' Agata, take no account of the disturbing effect of his own presence. No condemnation could be too severe for the tasteless and loutish action of Monti, Ricordi's creature, in provoking a demonstration. But Mariani did not complain of this. His sole concern was that Verdi should not think he had broken his word. The little incident at the railway station, when he was refused permission even to help Verdi with his bag, is unspeakably sad. This was their last meeting.

Verdi had come all the way from Genoa to hear *Lohengrin*, and to Genoa he returned. A letter written by Del Signore to Mariani, probably after a visit to Palazzo Sauli, provoked an indignant reply: 'I am surprised at your advising me to move house. What then, am I a thief? Am I so despicable a being that I disturb others with my contaminating presence? I shall do what my dignity and my quiet way of life demand, and you can be sure I am able to despise those unworthy of esteem.' The poor man was mortally wounded, and desperately ill. By a supreme effort he conducted three performances of *Lohengrin* at Florence early in December and then returned to the care of his doctors at Bologna. He was still being treated for haemorrhoids and complications, and underwent a minor operation for the removal of necrotic tissue. He was in constant pain and, in spite of morphine, unable to sleep. Reports on the state of his health appeared in the newspapers and finally even Verdi and Giuseppina were persuaded that his troubles were not all imaginary. On 19th December Mariani wrote to Del Signore:

> Regarding the advice you give me to write to Corticelli, I don't feel I have the strength to do so. I have suffered too many humiliations already and would rather stay as I am in my misery. My Carlino, I know I'm a worthless person, but Signor Corticelli could have written to me, in the circumstances. And then, if certain high personages deigned to ask after my health, you should not deduce therefrom that they have benevolent feelings towards me.

Giuseppina's friend Nina Ravina had also tried to heal the breach:

> I don't know why that kind lady goes to the trouble of putting in a good word for me to those who have treated me with injustice. I have suffered many humiliations and don't wish to expose myself, to no purpose, to others.

But he sent two cards to Palazzo Sauli for the New Year. 'If the man was severe with me, and unjust, that cannot diminish my respect for the artist.' There came no acknowledgment.

We may recall here Luisa Cora Mancinelli's story that Mariani had speculated with, and lost, money entrusted to him by Teresa Stolz during their engagement. A belated Italian translation of the biographical part of Francis Toye's *Giuseppe Verdi* appeared in 1950. The text was unrevised, but a footnote was added to the discussion of the cause of the quarrel with Mariani. Mr Toye, as we have seen, originally accepted Luisa Cora Mancinelli's story; in his footnote of 1950 he added that he had since read Zoppi's book, but that it had not caused him to change his mind and did not invalidate 'the greater psychological probability of the financial explanation'. This is curious, because the one thing that Zoppi succeeded in demonstrating beyond all doubt was that Mariani repaid the money entrusted to him. The sum involved was 42,000 francs. Zoppi published a whole series of letters about the return of this money in December.

There are two brief references to Mariani in Verdi's letters from January 1872. On the 13th he wrote to Arrivabene: 'Mariani was, and still is, very ill. I hope he recovers and I wish him well, but . . . his conduct towards me . . . I'll say no more!!!' On the 15th he exclaimed in a letter to Corticelli, apropos, apparently, some proposed further performances of Wagner's opera: 'Poor devil! His vanity will survive on his tomb. It seems impossible . . . to talk of *Lohengrin*, in that state!' These letters were written from Milan, where the rehearsals for *Aida* were in progress.

The first performance of the opera on 8th February was a great triumph for the composer and his singers. Some of Mariani's friends at Bologna wished him to think otherwise and brought back stories to which he lent an only half unwilling ear. On 13th February he wrote to Del Signore:

> There was sent me from Milan a bundle of newspapers which speak of this opera and truly I find that they all talk a lot of nonsense. People from Bologna who heard it three times are agreed that the opera is a blunder, but as I don't know a note of it, I want—though I recognize my own nullity in the matter of music—to see it and study it for myself before I can persuade myself of the truth of that assertion, for it seems impossible that Verdi should have failed to do himself justice. What surprises me is that the *prima donna* was inadequate; it seems to be a role of a kind completely at variance with her vocal means and her manner of singing. To say she was surpassed by la Waldmann is to say everything. It seems, too, that she paints her face an impossible green colour, and thus gives herself a disagreeable appearance. I really can't understand all that. And I can't understand the numerous other rumours about her, rumours which, if true, would indicate in her a depraved soul. But, I repeat, they are probably only rumours, promoted perhaps by misleading appearances.

Towards the end of the month, feeling rather better, he returned to Genoa and on 9th March wrote to Landoni, his closest friend at Bologna:

> As for my *fellow tenant*, I can tell you nothing. He is here, but I have never seen him, nor do I seek him out, not wishing to suffer any more of those humiliations that move me to anger and poison my soul. I shall not forget what you said to me the last night we were together, and truly, my Teodorico, you hit the nail on the head. I have nothing with which to reproach myself in my relations with that gentleman, and above all I am sorry to have had to persuade myself that he is not the man I thought him. His behaviour towards me was not the most fitting. I'll leave this subject because it's painful to me: all I'll say is that if the gossip one hears, about him and another person, who also behaved very badly towards me, were true, they would both deserve contempt. You may be sure I don't speak or write to anyone about these things: I confide them only to you, and I know by experience your discretion and the friendship you bear me. You are all I have in the world! If you ever want to know anything about what is said at Milan and elsewhere about the two persons I mean, you can, without mentioning my name, sound Antonelli who, back from Milan, must have heard something. Note again, though, that I have never spoken to anyone at all of what will be for ever a secret to my own self, but which

I will confide to you alone when I have the joy of re-embracing you, and that will be soon. Oh, it's an ugly world; but I laugh at it, and you may be sure I am able to despise those unworthy of esteem. Those who don't want me don't deserve me, and you make up to me for all the others.

In another chapter we shall approach the problem of the nature of the relations between Verdi and Teresa Stolz from another direction. Here we shall only remark that these two letters from Mariani to Del Signore and Landoni, both from 1872, are the earliest documentary evidence we possess that tongues were wagging. We will note, again, the impossibility that Monaldi could have heard from Mariani what he claimed to have heard at Pesaro in 1869 (or 1868, according to his own crazy chronology). It is not only that Mariani, in 1872, writes: 'I have never spoken to anyone at all of what will be for ever a secret to my own self'; the whole idea was obviously new to him, and still he did not know whether he could believe it. Rumours about Verdi and Teresa Stolz first began to circulate during the rehearsals for *Aida*. We shall see that it was precisely at this time that Giuseppina herself began to wonder a little what was happening.

Now we find expressions of open hostility on both sides:

Mariani to Giovannina Lucca, before the production of Petrella's *Manfredi* at Naples on 24th March 1872: [1]

I am sure another triumph awaits him there, in despite of him who would like to be alone in all the world, but who has been put in his place by circumstances and the reason of men of good will.

Verdi to Ricordi, before the production of Meyerbeer's *L'Africaine*, under Mariani, at Reggio Emilia in May 1872: [2]

Avenging Jove wants to reduce us to ashes, and we must all feel ourselves honoured by the thunderbolts of the god. Only we shall have to see that the ashes are not dispersed too much by the wind. For my own part, if in the past it was my intention to do the work of ten men, now I shall do the work of twenty!

This is what Teresa Stolz was writing about Mariani in her letters to Verdi:

Parma, 19th May:

Maestro Rossi has just come to give me news of *L'Africaine* at Reggio. The performance went fairly well, but not superlatively well. The company was considered mediocre; a certain Preny distinguished herself in the role of Ines. There was much applause but also some hissing of the chorus; repetitions of the usual eight bars; wretched *mise-en-scène*!!

Padua, 22nd June:

In July Venice too will have a grand opera season, and Mariani will go

[1] Lisio, loc. cit.
[2] Monaldi, *Verdi nella vita e nell'arte* (Milan, n.d.), pp. 14–15.

to conduct it. It seems a real persecution! I was at Parma, he at Reggio; now I'm at Padua, he at Venice!!!

Padua, 15th July:

At Venice things are not going too well!!! This year Gallo is not making money; our performances are partly to blame for that! I'm not malicious but I'm just a little bit glad, for another time there won't be so much *blague* from the *illustrious personage*!!!

Brescia, 19th August:

Yesterday I had a letter from Gallo. I don't know whether you remember a conversation we had at Parma, when I told you something of my affairs, and among other things I told you I had some money in Gallo's hands; he should have paid me in April but asked me to wait until October 1872. Now he writes that he can't pay me—repay me, that is—having lost a lot of money by his theatre, and he asks me to wait till next year. . . . On the one hand I'm sorry, because thus I have to wait for the restitution of my 8,000 francs, but on the other hand I'm a little bit glad! He did not want to undertake the staging of *Aida* and believed that M. alone would fill his theatre! But something more than just the *magic baton* is needed!!

The season at Venice included performances of *Un ballo in maschera*.

In the autumn, at Bologna, Mariani put on his second Wagner opera, *Tannhäuser*. It was first performed on 7th November, amid cheers and jeers. According to what Mariani himself wrote, in his last surviving letter to Del Signore, there were hisses and whistles before the opera even began. They came from a 'camorra' sent to Bologna from elsewhere and paid to wreck the performance. The first night was stormy, the second less so and by the third the opposition had been defeated. *Tannhäuser* was not the tremendous success that *Lohengrin* had been, but it was far from a failure.

At this time Verdi and Giuseppina were at Naples, where they had gone for the production of *Don Carlos* and *Aida* at the San Carlo theatre, with Teresa Stolz and Maria Waldmann. On 16th November Giuseppina commented on the performances of *Tannhäuser* at Bologna in a letter to Giuditta Ricordi:

The Bolognese are fine people and we will suppose that the scandalous scenes were all made by outsiders. . . . As for the *Divo*, he has been deified too much by his coterie and the papers, including yours. His multiple apotheosis has caused his little brain to lose, not the right road, for he has never even glimpsed it, but that kind of semi-modest cunning by which he tried to keep himself hidden in a cloud, like Father Jove when he committed his Olympian obscenities, offending against Juno. Now the *Divo*, wounded perhaps because some mortals refused to burn incense on his altar, has uncovered himself, and alas! nudity does not exactly augment the beauty of his figure. He, in his divine fury, has thrown down a gauntlet of challenge, which no one picked up because a contest of that sort is not for a *divo* of his class.

Verdi sent Corticelli instructions to go to Genoa at the end of November, when the next year's rent was due for the apartment in Palazzo Sauli. He was to pay 3,700 lire to the Marchesa Pallavicino's agent and find out the exact terms of the lease; he was also to go to see Carlino Del Signore and arrange for Mariani to move out of the house. The affair was to be settled amicably if possible, but if no agreement could be reached in that way Mariani was to be given as short notice to leave as the law permitted. Many pages of Giuseppina's letter-books are filled with correspondence arising out of this.

The agent, acknowledging receipt of the money, announced that the rent would be raised in the future. Verdi replied, with great dignity, that the marchesa was quite right to raise the rent for such splendid apartments but that he was not inclined to pay more and would therefore vacate Palazzo Sauli by 1st December 1873. He told Del Signore on 5th December: 'In all the coming year I shall perhaps only be at Genoa for a few hours. So Mariani can come and go just as he pleases. Only tell him that in this matter he has nothing more to do with me.' Mariani, Verdi's sub-tenant, then deposited his next year's rent with Del Signore. On 24th December Giuseppina wrote to Corticelli:

> Carlino Del Signore will try to find out whether we are going to stay at Genoa or leave. Say nothing at all, and leave their curiosity unsatisfied. *En passant* you can ask Brighenti, or whoever you think best informed, if Danovaro has apartments to let in his new houses, and of what size, on which floor and at what price. All that, however, with finesse, prudence and *relative* secrecy. . . . You will know that Mariani has deposited in Carlino's hands the 400 lire for the rent, reserving the right, if he is the first to leave, to pay only in proportion to the time! He's always an Ass in all his actions! He fears, then, that Verdi might profit by some fifty francs or so, without that *Nota Bene*! And to think that Verdi has said and written in a thousand ways: 'He can pay, or not pay; he can do as he pleases, as long as he goes away and no more is heard about him!' Now he can stay there eternally if he likes, for it no longer matters to us in the least.

Earlier in the year Teresa Stolz had written: 'So the *illustrious personage* is not thinking at all of looking for an apartment? Probably he believes he is *himself* the proprietor of the house!!!! by way of the old and renewed sympathy shown him by the proprietress of the Palazzo!!! Enough, let him live in peace!! let him allow others to live, however, without disturbing them with his presence!' Another of her letters, a little later, refers to Mariani's illness and remarks that he 'is not thinking in the least of doing penance for his sins. Probably he will have some *St Luisa* to intercede for him, but I think she too will have enough to do, if she wishes to be absolved of her own sins!' Here is a final surprise concerning Mariani's relations with the Sauli Pallavicino family, for these two passages [1] seem to imply that it was the Marchesa Luisa, rather than her daughter Teresa, with whom he had had an affair.

Lengthy and tediously repetitious correspondence followed, with the agent, the Marchesa Luisa, Corticelli, Del Signore and Nina Ravina, through whom the marchesa tried to restore good relations. Verdi objected to suggestions that it was *he* who had given notice, when the deciding factor had been the unacceptable increase in the rent. No one knew the terms of the original contract, which probably never existed on paper. On 3rd January Giuseppina wrote to the marchesa: 'When by means of Signor Mariani we took the apartment in your Palazzo, he told us that the rental was for six years, which would end exactly on 1st December 1873. We asked perhaps a hundred times for the agreement, but putting us off always from one day to the next, he wore down our insistence in asking for it, while persisting in his negligence to procure it for us.' On 14th February she wrote to Nina Ravina:

> Is it six, nine or five years? Mariani always told us that it was six years. Now who has told the truth? In whose interests is it not to tell the truth? We believe that Mariani and the Marchese Cheut [?] played a large part in the ugly intrigue that has brought us to this pass. On her side the Marchesa, deceived by those two Gentlemen in the matter of the house, and in part by false or altered accounts of the causes of the breach in friendly relations between Verdi and Mariani, thought fit to give her old friend the pleasure of a little vendetta.

The most curious thing about all this is that there was an elementary mistake in Verdi's arithmetic: he took these rooms from 1st December 1866, and if the contract was for six years, as he believed, it had already expired. From 1866 to 1873 is *seven* years. The contract was due for renewal, therefore, when the increase in the rent was notified.

A letter from the marchesa to Nina Ravina a few months later said that the suggested new terms were agreed between her agent and Corticelli. She herself had been absent from Genoa at the time and very concerned about her daughter's health; the first news of Verdi's intention to leave had reached her through Mariani, who had it from Del Signore. She concluded: 'I am very sorry about what has happened and I very much hope that the two old friends will renew their former friendship and continue to live in my house. I should be very glad.' Verdi and Giuseppina saw this as a piece of hypocrisy, since

[1] Abbiati, III, pp. 576 and 635. These letters were not among those I myself examined at Sant' Agata.

they had made up their minds that the raising of the rent was an act of petty revenge. Giuseppina copied the marchesa's letter and sent it back to Nina Ravina:

Apart from tact and refinement your noble friend is completely revealed in that note of hers which you sent me and which I return. It's a true self-portrait. Her insistence in laying the blame on poor Corticelli's shoulders is pitiful. That may be very convenient, but is not equally honest. In short it's a complex of dear persons worthy of associating and understanding each other. . . . Verdi, to whom I read the note in question, limited himself to the exclamation: *Pouah!*

Those words were written the day before Mariani's death.

We have long since finished with the conductor's letters to Verdi; we have come to the end, also, of those to Del Signore; there remain only the last letters to Teodorico Landoni, contemporary with the confused and acrimonious correspondence concerning Verdi's tenure of Palazzo Sauli.

31st December 1872:

Since I have returned here I pass the greater part of my time in bed, suffering as I still do so much that I am now tired of this wretched life. I get up, with great effort, only to go in a carriage to the theatre, for, as you know, I would die rather than fail in my duty. I know that a few days ago you had a long conversation with Professor Loreta about me. Oh, if he had some drug to give me, to relieve me a little of this torment that tears me to pieces! But I know only too well that he has nothing efficacious to give me back my health again, and I must submit to my fate, which, I assure you, my Teodorico, is perverse indeed.

23rd January 1873:

I am beginning to improve a bit, and I hope before long to be wholly free from the intestinal spasms that have caused me to suffer so much. When you write to that excellent creature, Sir James Hudson, thank him for the interest he has shown in all my sufferings, and express my regret for the four months' torment that he, too, has had to put up with. Oh, you are quite right, my Teodorico, it's always the good people that have to suffer. . . . Give Assunta a thousand affectionate greetings from me, and thank her for her kind offer to come and look after me. For the moment I don't need it and if I should find myself in need of rigorous attention I should have to go to hospital, since my lodging would not accommodate anybody else, there being barely room for my own bed and that of my servant. In a few months' time this *calamity* will disappear, because I shall be able to have far more space, having obtained from the owner of the house, from that time, the addition of two more rooms to my apartment. So if you like to come and spend a month or so at Genoa next year I shall be most happy to have you with me, and to offer you a nice room with every convenience. I am taking a homoeopathic cure and I really feel great benefit from it.

25th February:

My Teodorico, I repeat, there's no need to worry on my account; it's only a matter of a rigorous cure I'm taking, to try to rid myself of that torment which for some years now has rendered life odious to me. It's true, however, that I asked the municipality to be released from service in the theatre, so as to be able to take this cure. What was I to do? I couldn't stand it any longer. Since the beginning of November (I was then at Bologna) my sufferings had become so unbearable that I thought I should go mad. I spoke about it to Professor Loreta but he did not bother himself at all. Several times I returned to the subject, but I found in him an attitude of great indifference and for fear of boring him I said no more about it.

Then the haemorrhages began and the spasms when I evacuated, and torments each time I had to pass a little water. My Teodorico, truly I suffered greatly. How many evenings when I left our favourite café to pass water, spasms of pain threw me to the ground! I said nothing to anyone, because I saw how indifferent they were. I suffered and suffered, until I returned to Genoa. Here the haemorrhages continued and it was reckoned that I was losing eight or even ten ounces of blood a day. . . . I put myself in the care of Dr Damba. An assassin! He applied twelve leeches, which brought on deadly convulsions, taking from me the little blood I had left. I remained in the care of this Dr Damba for a fortnight, but feeling that he was killing me with his leeches, purges and drugs, I thanked him and resigned myself to keeping my disease.

I don't know who it was then that procured me a visit from the homoeopath Gaiter. This doctor has achieved some marvellous cures, especially in my type of malady. . . .

11th March:

I'm still taking the cure and the doctor assures me that soon I shall be better. So I suffer and hope. That's all, and don't worry, for we shall soon see each other again.

16th April:

I haven't written before because I was hoping very soon to be able to come to Bologna. The return of the bad weather, however, has caused some recrudescence of my sufferings, so for the time I shall stay here.

4th May:

If you want to know how I really am, go to see the excellent Professor Loreta and he'll tell you, because he was here at Genoa to visit me and in his goodness stayed two days. He arrived without my knowledge and I assure you that on seeing him I thought he was an angel come down from Paradise, because for four months I had been suffering like a dog, without a shadow of hope of improvement. Enough. . . . You'll learn the rest from that good friend of ours, and truly I don't know how to express to him the gratitude I feel for such great kindness! Enough, if God will heal me I shall have time to think of everything. Loreta has prescribed for me a new cure, under the direction of a pupil of his who lives at Genoa. . . . When you see Professor Loreta thank him yourself for his kindness in coming all the way to Genoa to help me; if he had not come I should be dead. . . . Tell the Professor I shall write to him in a few days about the effect of the cure he has prescribed, and give him a kiss for me, for truly he is an angel of goodness.

28th May:

I have not replied until now to your last most affectionate letter because I did not know, nor do I now know, what I am to do. I mean, whether I shall stay at Genoa, to suffer here the fate that awaits me, or whether I shall go to Bologna. To tell you the truth Bologna attracts me, because you are there and Loreta is there, who are the best of my friends, and I am sure that his care and your affectionate attentions would give me back my lost health. And I have so much need of that. Do you know, Teodorico, my sufferings have been unbearable, to the point even of depriving me of that little intelligence that God gave me? The young doctor to whom Loreta recommended my cure has not come back since he visited me at Genoa; a relative fell ill and he had to leave Genoa; it's true, no doubt, but the fact remains that I am here without anyone looking after me, suffering more than ever, so utterly depressed that inertia has seized me, and I assure you that I would not take a step, nor any sort of decision, even if I knew that it would bring about my complete recovery. How can I help it? I have suffered too long, have lost all hope.

He would have liked to return to Bologna, where he hoped Loreta would find him a place in a hospital; anxiously he awaited a reply about this, but none came. Landoni explained with embarrassment that, not being a doctor, he was unable to invite him to stay in his own house. He must have learned from Loreta that the case was hopeless.

The last letters of all are appalling. Devoured by cancer, enfeebled by daily haemorrhages, without doctor's care or alleviating drugs, alone in the attic suite of Verdi's house at Genoa, Mariani surely expiated all his sins before he died.

4th June:

You are lost in idle talk, while I am perishing from day to day, abandoned by everybody, and no one heeds my pleas to be relieved of my sufferings. You say again that Loreta has told you he does not think me fit to undertake a long journey and that I must first receive treatment from the doctor in whose care he left me. Well then, I don't know what language I am to employ, for I have told Loreta many times already that his Dr Massini only came twice and then I saw him no more, so that for a month now I have been suffering like a dog without anyone bringing me relief. Indeed, attacked by diarrhoea which I really feel is killing me, I wrote to Loreta repeatedly, but he never replied. Perhaps I didn't make myself clear, but in my letters to you, also, I repeated that the doctor left by Professor

Loreta had not returned and truly I thought this a singular way of treating me. And Loreta, too, has never replied to me! So I must die alone, like a dog, and so I shall die. I know I'm not wanted at Bologna and I should never have decided to go there if it had not been for the fact that I have been abandoned by everyone here. Now I know what it's all about and I shan't cause you any more bother. Loreta, instead of answering me, let me know through you that he doesn't think me fit to travel, which means to say I must die here alone like a dog and alone I shall die. . . . The pain I suffer is so great that truly I no longer have the strength to bear it. You can imagine in what state I am, without any sort of comfort. It's true I am resigned, but mine is too excruciating a death. Enough, it had to be so. . . .

I dare not call in other surgeons because I am sure it would be useless and they would kill me. . . .

I am so beside myself with wrath that I don't know what I am doing. . . .

And Loreta does not answer me!

Dr Massini recalled his Hippocratic Oath in time to witness, with the Marchese Francesco Pallavicino, the drawing up of a will on 13th June. Mariani left everything he possessed to his sister Virginia, and nothing to his brother and his other sister Bradamante, who had repeatedly borrowed money from him during his lifetime. But the will remained invalid. Irresolute to the last, he failed to sign it, although he said he was able and although the notary repeatedly asked him to do so. Delirium supervened and towards midnight he died.

It is said that when Verdi was told he remarked: 'What a loss for Art!'

CHAPTER

8

Verdi, Giuseppina and Teresa Stolz

THE BIOGRAPHER seeks the truth. How shall he find it?

He is generally working long after the events he is describing. Although he may not be able to remember what he was doing himself on the Tuesday of the previous week, he has to convince his readers that he knows what happened between certain people, say, one hundred years earlier.

If the lapse of time is not too great there may be eye witnesses still living, able and willing to tell what they saw. But only the most incautious and inexperienced biographer will accept at its face value evidence so obtained. Those old people who seem to retain, with miraculous clarity, their vision of the distant past, will relate with passionate conviction things that cannot possibly be true, or that are in conflict with the accounts of other survivors, or with the available documents. Apart from deliberate lying, which can be comparatively easily detected, if the persons consulted have themselves been actively involved in the events described, their recollections will, in most cases, have been coloured, unconsciously, by the action of an automatic self-defensive mechanism in the mind. There is practically no limit to this process of self-deception. A few meetings, a flirtation, may be magnified into a fateful love affair or into an engagement to be married, frustrated by circumstances. Or a passionate affair may become, in the course of time, only a beautiful friendship, in the memory, in spite of the existence of dozens of letters to prove the contrary, as in the case of Teresa Guiccioli's recollections of Byron. Even in the cases of people not emotionally involved, self-importance, a love of tidying up or the pleasure of telling a good story may lead to misrepresentation.

Written reminiscences, in this matter, are not much different. Spontaneity may be lost and the tidying up be more thorough. Often, where there is literary ability, what Norman Douglas called 'the novelist's touch' will come into play. 'The facts may be correct so far as they go, but there are too few of them; what the author says may be true, and yet by no means the truth. That is the novelist's touch. It falsifies life.'

In 1906 Annie Vivanti (Mrs John Chartres) described [1] her first meeting with Carducci. She had come to Bologna, from Milan, to ask him to write a preface to her poems. She climbed the steep and narrow stairs of his house and knocked on the door:

> A man opened the door. 'Is Signor Carducci in?' 'Yes.' 'Will you tell him', I stammered, 'that I have come—that I have arrived—that I have travelled far to see him?'
>
> 'Si, Signora,' said the man, and vanished. He reappeared. 'Il Signor Carducci says that he is not King Solomon. Please walk in.'

She found herself in the presence of the great man:

> 'What do you want?'
>
> 'Good morning. I should like a preface to my poems.'
>
> 'Oh, you are a poet. I thought you were the Queen of Sheba.'

Now these reminiscences have been republished fairly recently, by Pietro Pancrazi,[2] together with the correspondence of Carducci and Annie Vivanti, which shows that, in actual fact, she wrote to him from an hotel at Bologna, and sent him her poems, before she ever saw him. Her first letter, of 5th December 1889, includes the sentence: 'I am a woman, twenty years of age, and have come very far to see you.' She asked if she could come to his house, or if he would come to the hotel. He seems to have replied, in a letter that has not survived, that he was too busy. She wrote again on 6th December, stating that she was prepared to wait as long as Esau, in the Bible, waited for Jacob's daughter. Carducci replied that he could not receive her in his house, which was cold and unattractive, and where there were eighty steep stairs to be climbed, and continued: 'You, certainly, are younger than the Queen of Sheba and, doubtless, less boring than she. But I am not as wise as Solomon, and am at least as boring as he.' Here we can see the very elements out of which, sixteen or seventeen years later, memory and imagination created an entirely false picture.

This example illustrates the aberrations of which the mind is

[1] In English in the *Fortnightly Review* for 1st October; in Italian in *Nuova Antologia* for 1st August.

[2] *Un amoroso incontro della fine ottocento. Lettere e ricordi di G. Carducci e A. Vivanti* (Florence, 1951).

capable, in a comparatively short period of time, in a non-controversial matter. A much more powerful impulsion towards the distortion of the truth is present in matters involving passion, self-interest, family reputation, religion or patriotism, including *campanilismo* or parochial patriotism, that lovable vice still rampant in Italy.

Some 'Ricordi verdiani' were published by one Alfio in *Il Presente* (Parma) for 30th–31st August and 1st September 1913, based on information provided by the son of Giovannino Barezzi. Here, surely, was a valuable source, in the traditions of the Barezzi family? The article includes some curious stories. One relates how Verdi and Margherita, with Margherita's sister Marianna and her husband, all slept together at one time, four in one bed. Another tells of an 'amorous adventure' of Verdi's with the Baroness Soldati, wife of a minister of the Duchy of Parma. But it is impossible to believe these stories, otherwise unknown, because on every single point where the reminiscences can be checked against established facts and documents they are seen to be false. We are also told how Verdi and Giovannino encountered the baroness again, many years later, when *Aida* was performed at Parma (1872), and how Verdi sent Giovannino a ticket for *Otello* (1887), with a very curious note to say that the opera was not worth the trouble of the journey. These are inventions, intended to conceal the fact that after 1865 Verdi had nothing at all to do with Giovannino. The tale of the Baroness Soldati may also have been related out of spite against Giuseppina, who had very little use for the younger Barezzis. We have seen that the untrue story that she had had an illegitimate child by Merelli originated in that family.

What are we to say of Gino Monaldi, another 'eye witness', except that his innumerable shallow publications have been responsible for half the apocryphal stories current about Italian composers of the last century? He had an Olympian disregard for awkward facts, habitually touched up the texts of any original documents he had occasion to quote, and almost invariably misread or misprinted their dates. His unreliability has been noted more than once in the course of this book. Here is a further and final instance. In an article in the *Rassegna contemporanea* for November 1911 Monaldi told how Boito, after the failure of *Mefistofele*, had smashed up the contents of his room and been found by his friends, exhausted, 'like Marius among the ruins of Carthage'. Piero Nardi found a copy of this article among Boito's papers, on the margin of which he had written: 'Lies, lies, lies!'

It is safer to stick to the documents. But here, too, there are traps for the unwary. In the article on Verdi in the fifth edition of Grove's *Dictionary of Music and Musicians* (1954) I quoted passages from letters said to have been written by Giuseppina to her confessor, Don Francesco Montebruno, and to the Archbishop of Genoa, Monsignor

Salvatore Magnasco.[1] These letters were published in the *Corriere della Sera* by Lorenzo Alpino,[2] who stated that he had taken them from an old exercise-book, into which they had been copied by Don Medicina, Montebruno's secretary. They include references to the relations between Verdi, Mariani and Teresa Stolz:

So much has been said about the case of Mariani—too many words with little foundation. Don't let us talk about myself, who have nothing with which to reproach Verdi in this matter, nor my dear friend Teresina, who has always behaved as a faithful friend should, without thought of abusing or betraying the friendship of those who have always wished her well. If Mariani decided to act as he did, he is his own master and responsible for his own actions. But Verdi is a perfect man of honour and gentleman and has nothing with which to reproach himself. . . . You, who at Palazzo Sauli have seen and learned many things, are in the best position to know and to judge.

Further:

For a few moments, owing to malign tittle-tattle, some doubt may have come over me, but I have always been more than persuaded that I need think no evil of my good friend Teresa. She has been at Sant' Agata again this summer and her eye was limpid and sincere, and her words were frank and pure. Verdi laughed and made fun of her (forgive him!) as usual. Oh! I am not the person (you know everything, Father, about me) to judge what Teresina did for Mariani and what their relations were. But as one woman judging another I am led to think that she was trusting and believed that all would end well. As was my own experience. Instead of which it's all over now, and I'm convinced that Verdi gave her good advice, and only for her good, and that everything will go well.

Giuseppina writing to her confessor on these hotly disputed matters—this is a biographer's dream. Unfortunately, it is no more than a dream. For these letters are *forgeries.*

Alpino gives few dates, and my attempts to date the letters from internal evidence disclosed some puzzling features. Those quoted above seemed to have been written during Mariani's lifetime ('he is his own master . . .'). The first of them begins: 'We have been in Paris for more than a fortnight now.' Yet after 1867 Verdi and Giuseppina did not visit Paris until July 1873, when Mariani was already dead. Where Alpino does give a date other problems arise. A letter to Monsignor Magnasco, said to have been written in 1872, thanks the archbishop for the honour of a recent visit, arranged through the good offices of Don Montebruno, and goes on to discuss Verdi's attitude towards religion:

[1] In the Grove article I mistakenly said that Monsignor Magnasco was her confessor. The first two passages quoted (vol. viii, p. 742) are from letters said to have been written to Don Montebruno.

[2] 'Quattro lettere inedite della moglie di Verdi' (13th October 1939) and 'Religiosità di Verdi: Quattro lettere inedite di Giuseppina Strepponi' (21st July 1942).

Verdi is not communicative and expansive, but his soul is very sensitive and grateful for every courtesy shown to him. There are those who wish to make believe that he is very different from what he really is, especially in certain matters concerning his intimate, spiritual life. Verdi's soul, since several years ago, has changed much in this respect; not changed substantially, because there was no need, but formally and apparently. Much of this change is owing to the work of the Abbé Mermillod—the most worthy priest who married us at Collanges—who knew how to find the way to reach efficaciously his soul and his heart. If externally and for reasons concerning politics, on which I cannot and must not make pronouncement, because I don't bother myself with them, Verdi does not appear that which in effect he is, one must not judge him solely by appearances. He is respectful towards religion, is a believer like me and never fails to carry out those practices necessary for a good Christian, such as he wishes to be. His conflicts with certain persons are incidents that do not touch his faith and his conscience, even if they withhold him from some practical demonstrations. Verdi is a good Christian, better than many others who wish to seem so more than he.

How is it possible for this to have been written *in the same year* as the letter to Cesare Vigna in which Verdi is described as 'very little of a believer' and, in the first draft, as 'an atheist'? Is the date misprinted, perhaps—something that could happen easily enough in a newspaper?

When I was able to study Giuseppina's manuscript letter-books, in the archives of Sant' Agata, one of the things I was most eager to do was to establish, from the drafts or copies, the precise dates of these letters. *Not one of them was there.* Other letters to Montebruno were to be found, but none of these. This in itself would have sufficed to raise doubts in the mind as to the authenticity of the letters published by Alpino, though such purely negative evidence could never have settled the matter. Fortunately, the letter-books provide also a positive contribution to the establishment of the truth.

Don Montebruno, founder of the Institute of Little Artisans, for poor and orphaned children, at Genoa, played an important role in Giuseppina's life. The letter-books show that she was brought into contact with him by her Genoese friend Nina Ravina, who lived in Via San Giacomo, No. 18, almost opposite Palazzo Sauli. Don Montebruno wrote to Giuseppina before he had actually met her. On 19th January 1872 Giuseppina wrote to Nina Ravina from Milan: 'Tell Don Montebruno that when I have the courage I will reply to his letter, which has moved me, and in which I seem to discern a distant sadness, overcome, at least apparently, by an iron will and the gift of faith. A precious gift!' She wrote to Montebruno himself for the first time on 17th February:

You are not unknown to me. If like so many others I don't know you *materially*, in person, I know of your work, and I know and I *feel* that your name brings benediction, and I feel too that it must be benediction both for those who suffer materially and for those who suffer morally. I am grateful to Nina for having given me the opportunity and the courage to enter into relations with you, and if it is true that the style is the man, the style of your letter is such as to render me still more glad of this wholly spiritual relationship of ours.

It is possible that she became personally acquainted with him on her return to Genoa a few days later, though this cannot be proved. It is certain that in later years he was her confessor. On 24th October 1887 she wrote to him: 'As soon as time and my knees permit I will come to do the washing, as usual. I wish I were able to say: '*I have no further need to do it.*' Only too well I know that's not the case, and I believe (a poor consolation) that very few people indeed have *a clean sheet.*' There is little doubt that Montebruno led her back to more orthodox beliefs. But what of Verdi? In the last of the letter-books is a loose, undated card addressed to Nina Ravina, with the postscript: 'Father Montebruno performed the miracle of appearing briefly in our house and he was an enormous success [*ha fatto un furorone*]! That handsome face, honest, open, sincere, made the best of impressions on Verdi!' The date of this is given by another entry in the letter-book, of 29th January 1888:

Father Montebruno. Verdi, happy to have made your personal acquaintance, sends his respects, thanks you for your visit (most agreeable to both of us) and begs you to accept what is enclosed, with his card, for your little artisans and your poor.

This is devastating, since it proves that Verdi did not know Montebruno before 1888. Now we look back at the first of the letters published by Alpino: 'You, who at Palazzo Sauli have seen and learned many things, are in the best position to know and to judge.' Palazzo Sauli was given up in 1874. How can Montebruno have 'seen and learned many things' there, without making Verdi's acquaintance?

Another of these letters says: 'I have never been a mother.' We know that in her youth she had had two illegitimate children. Was she lying, then, to her confessor?

Three of the letters are published with the signature 'Giuseppina Strepponi-Verdi'—a form she never used.

There can be no further doubt: the letters published by Alpino are pious forgeries.

Alpino, who had been one of Montebruno's 'little artisans' in his boyhood, also published personal reminiscences of Verdi and Giuseppina. These, too, like his other very numerous articles, are full of dubious and more than dubious stories. Under his pseudonym, 'C. Belviglieri', he was also responsible for the publication of some forged Verdi letters—those about which there has been so much discussion, hostile to Alfredo Catalani.[1]

When all the lies and the forgeries have been discounted, we still have to consider the problem of what may be called the relative truth of the authentic documents. No man gives himself away entirely in his correspondence, and certainly Verdi never did. He was most relaxed and open, perhaps, in his letters to the Countess Maffei, that old and well-tried friend. We do not know how he wrote to Giuseppina because, except for the texts of a few telegrams, nothing has survived of his correspondence with her. With others, though there were various degrees of intimacy, an ultimate barrier of reserve remained.

Giuseppina herself was much more spontaneously communicative. The wonderful letters to Verdi quoted in an earlier chapter certainly bring us very near to the truth. They are written in love, with absolute trust and confidence, and nothing is held back. Unfortunately, only two such letters survive from later years. There are drafts of a few others, of the highest interest and importance, in the letter-books. She had other friends with whom she could disburden herself, such as, at one period, Nina Ravina at Genoa. But some of the most celebrated of her letters, such as the first ones to the Countess Maffei, about her return to Sant' Agata after the visit to Manzoni, and about Verdi and country life, are at a slight remove from reality. She was here more studied than was her wont—too intent on pleasing to tell quite the whole truth. Something similar is found in later letters to another literary lady, Caterina Pigorini-Beri. There is a forced note in some of the letters to Teresa Stolz.

Studying her letter-books, we find passages written and then erased which are more revealing than anything actually sent. More than once she can be caught telling a white lie, as when she writes that she has not shown Verdi a letter sent, has not spoken to him about a certain suggestion, while phrases of the draft replies are found to be in Verdi's own hand.

The surviving letters of Bellini to his famous mistress, Giuditta Turina, reveal nothing about the real nature of their relationship. We know from what Giuditta wrote to Florimo that disaster followed on the discovery by her husband of letters from Bellini of a very different sort. Many other cases of the existence of an official correspondence,

[1] For a full investigation of Alpino's activities, see my articles 'Verdian Forgeries' in the *Music Review* for November 1958 and February 1959. Abbiati, deceived as I was when I wrote the Grove article, quotes the forged letters to Montebruno and Magnasco in support of his views of Verdi's religious beliefs and on the nature of the relations with Mariani and Teresa Stolz (I, pp. 573–4 and 596–7; III, pp. 609–10 and 702; IV, pp. 6–8). Although he had full access to Giuseppina's letter-books he failed to notice that Giuseppina first wrote to Montebruno in 1872 and Verdi first met him in 1888. Abbiati gets over the difficulty of the reference to Mariani being his own master by quietly altering 'is' to 'was'.

side by side with an intimate one, could be cited. The fact that all the surviving letters from Teresa Stolz to Verdi are perfectly formal and 'correct' does not in itself prove that their relationship was a wholly innocent one. It is one piece of evidence, an important one, to be considered together with all the rest.

A closer look at the background will perhaps help us to reach a convincing conclusion. What was Giuseppina's home life with Verdi like?

It is idle to pretend that the sun shone always at Sant' Agata, and that the hearts of its inhabitants were never for one moment estranged from one another. Late family traditions, based on memories of the composer in his serene old age, have played their part in creating a falsely idyllic picture. This is mirrored in Mercede Mundula's charming book, and elsewhere. No one had better opportunities of discovering the realities of the matter than Luzio; he preferred, however, to suppress them. In the *Carteggi* [1] he published two short passages from a sort of diary, from July 1867, found in Giuseppina's letter-book. The diary was kept for only a few days, but the entries are more extensive and reveal a much more unhappy state of affairs than Luzio allowed us to suspect. For vividness, these diary notes are unsurpassed. Suddenly the mists of time are dispersed and the past is before us, as it really was. It is like discovering a forgotten film of a few scenes of domestic life at Sant' Agata:

July 1. Note. Decidedly, there are things which are repugnant to the conscience of an honest person, but which calculation would advise one to do, and perhaps women who don't disdain certain cunning little tricks do well to employ them. Whence it is worth while to be hypocritical, coquettish and affected with all men, from the highest to the lowest. To occupy oneself exclusively with one man may be admirable in theory; in practice it's a mistake. I try to cheer Verdi up about his indisposition, which perhaps his nerves and imagination make him think more serious than it is. He says that I don't believe him, I laugh, etc., and he blames me for that. He is subject to intestinal inflammation, and the restlessness, the running about, the hard work occasioned these days by the engine, and his natural inquietude, are causing some abdominal upset. He comes into my room many times, without staying ten minutes in peace. Yesterday he came and, as usual, especially in recent days, as soon as he had sat down, got up. I said to him: 'Where are you going?' 'Upstairs.' And as it's unusual for him to go there I replied: 'What for?' 'To look for Plato.' 'Oh! don't you remember? It's in the cupboard in the dining-room.' It seems to me there was nothing at all natural about these questions and answers, and for my part I was thinking all the time of not seeing him stay quiet, as he needs to do, and of saving him unnecessary exertions. . . . If only I hadn't said

[1] II, p. 26.

it! It was a serious business, premeditated on my part and almost an abuse of power! . . .

Finally he is so worked up against the servants and against me that I don't know with what words and in what tone of voice I am to speak to him, so as not to offend him! Alas! How things will end I don't know, for his mood becomes continually more unquiet and wrathful. To possess such eminent qualities and to have a character at times so harsh and difficult! The copies of letters contained in this book prove that at times he has confidence in my character and believes me to have a bit of sense. . . . Yet sometimes, recognizing in the address of a letter the handwriting of a friend, I ask: 'How is he?' That suffices to irritate him and give him the idea that I poke my nose where I should not! Isn't this excessive susceptibility and contention?

July 2. A row this evening, too, about an open window, and because I tried to calm him down! He got into a fury, saying he will dismiss all the servants, and that I take their part, who don't do what they ought to do, rather than his part, when he makes the most just observations. But my God! In his bad mood he sees these failings of the servants through a magnifying glass, and furthermore the poor devils need someone to watch over their interests a bit, because they are poor and, in the generally corrupt mass of servants, not bad. God grant he may calm down, for I suffer very much from it, and I lose my head.

July 3. Marcellino, the last time he was at Busseto, went to see Maddalena and told her, weeping in torrents, that he's afraid he won't be staying in the house long, because his master shows how displeased he is; that he does what he can, and his failings are not through ill will, but through excessive nervousness; that if he should have to go away from the house he would be so desperate that he would leave the town, because he loves his master and mistress.

After reading these things, what can one say of Luzio's remarks [1] on the misinterpretations of the biographers who, he alleged, have created a picture of Verdi as a domestic tyrant, completely at variance with reality, and have similarly distorted the 'imperious and virile' character of Giuseppina, 'respected and feared very much more than her roughly good-natured husband'? What can one say, except that Luzio, in the service of a wrong-headed pious tradition, was himself deliberately intent on falsifying history? Consider in this connection the following passage from a letter, written six weeks after the diary entries, from Verdi at Turin to his agent Paolo Marenghi at Sant' Agata:

I leave tomorrow evening for Paris and I repeat once again the orders given, to see if for once I can't make myself understood and obeyed.

1. Besides your general inspection, you will watch over the horses and the coachman, in whom I have little confidence in the matter of

[1] *Carteggi*, II. pp. 12–13.

orders. Let him exercise the horses every two days, without going to Busseto.

2. You will tell Guerino that he was wrong to hand over the key of the engine, that now he must clean it and lock it up until further orders.
3. You will repeat to the gardener what I said to him. The garden closed: no one must enter, nor must the people in the house go out, except the coachman for the short time needed to exercise the horses. If anyone goes out, he can stay out for always.

Take note that I am not joking, for henceforth I intend to be master in my own house.

The servants, according to the third order, were not even allowed to leave the house! What was this, if not domestic tyranny of a truly monstrous order?

But it was not only the servants who suffered under this harsh regime. It comes as a shock to find that he could behave in this way towards Giuseppina. No better instance could be found of what I mean by the 'relative truth' of the various documents, for how different are the scenes depicted in the diary notes from anything that could be suggested by the contemporary letters to Clarina Maffei!

The diary notes were written during the last illness of Antonio Barezzi, when his end was already foreseen. Verdi's explosions of churlish wrath against Giuseppina, so that she hardly dared to speak to him, might be explained psychologically as a result of this. Bound up with his love for Barezzi were memories of his early happiness and early sorrow, life with his lost Margherita, the brief joy of fatherhood, followed by annihilating loss. If his thoughts were drawn back to Margherita by the approaching death of his father-in-law, a wave of revulsion from her successor would be understandable. Perhaps it was so. But psychology can prove nothing, can only put forward suggestions. And another set of diary notes, in French this time, from Genoa, at the beginning of the following year, show little change in the situation. Here is another forgotten roll of film, tantalizingly brief, miraculously surviving from the past:

January 1. Apart from the rather serious dispute yesterday about the house at Genoa, the cook, who doesn't please him, and the thousand things that vex him, while I do everything possible to see him satisfied at home, as he deserves to be, the day passed pretty well, and he wished, absolutely, to give me a new year's present, which I did not want and did not expect at all, in view of the heavy expenses of the year, for the apartment, the bricklayers, etc., expenses that seem to weigh upon him and that he blames me for his having been drawn into incurring, for the house I showed I wanted at Genoa. First of all, and as basis of the memoirs or notes I have promised to keep from the first day of 1868, there is this: that if I wanted to have a *pied-à-terre* in a district near the sea, which I admire to the point of adoration as one of the great marvels of God and of Nature, nevertheless I never wanted anything splendid, but only a little nest in view of the sea, in which to pass the rigorous winter months—months which are very gloomy in the country, and very expensive, without corresponding comforts, in hotels where one is always among other people. He has given me, then, a very beautiful present, for he is a *grand seigneur* and *generous*. I was touched by that, as by all he does for me, and has done for me always, without ostentation and without reproaches . . . exemplified three times in recent days! . . .

January 2. A serene day! The dinner was found good. I am content. He is calm.

January 3. We played billiards, as almost always recently. He is busy playing the carpenter, the locksmith and the piano. He found nothing of which to complain or to grumble! My God! it would be so easy to be happy, when one has health and a little money! Why isn't he always like that, instead of finding fault no matter what I do, *while what I do is done always with one and the same intention*—to make his life comfortable, pleasant and serene?!!

January 4. Alas! The clouds have reappeared! Last night the Marquess of . . . . . came to pay us a visit, with her husband. Mariani burst out against Genoa and the bad moods of la Ma . . . . He praised to the skies Bologna and all its inhabitants. I took part in the conversation, giving my opinion, in terms I thought fitting . . . but for a sufficiently long time now I speak, as it always seems, badly, and out of season. Verdi gets irritated by intonations of voice too soft or too shrill, so that I am brought to ask myself what can be the *juste milieu* to suit him! In the morning at breakfast he reproached me *vis-à-vis* Corticelli and Maddalena, on the subject of what he said about Mariani. I played billiards badly, and as he said something to me brusquely I replied: 'Didn't you sleep well?' Afterwards, in going to my room, I asked: 'What did I say last night to merit your observations?' He replied: 'It's the way you say it. . . .' But, in God's name! have I, at my age, to speak and contain myself like a young girl? . . . He affirms that my pretension is to think myself a perfect wife (!) and that one can't touch me, or say a word about what I say and do, above all about my housekeeping! My God! If, when something doesn't suit him, he would tell me so with a little less brusqueness! . . . And besides, is it a great crime to occupy myself so conscientiously, as I do, with matters that are, in their extreme modesty, essentially feminine concerns? How many men there are who would like to see their wives occupied in that way, above all when one retains at the same time poetic tastes for reading, for the arts, and for elegance in conformity with one's age?? But having renounced society and the world (and gladly!) in order to occupy myself exclusively with whatever can be of use or necessity to him, wouldn't it be fair to bear that in mind, with a word of satisfaction *at least* once a year?! But perhaps that's where I've gone wrong, in not having acted as most wives do, who, having succeeded in attaining an ardently desired goal, afterwards recommence a life of extravagance and amusements, etc. I wished to become *a new woman*, worthily to respond to the honour I received in becoming his wife, and to the benefits I receive continually from this man, who, to be perfect, lacks only a little more sweetness and charm in daily relations with one who has no other happiness than that of an amiable word! With his immense gifts, he should recollect that bread is necessary to material life . . . but that there is another life, besides the purely material one! . . .

Half past two. Now he is playing the piano and singing, with Mariani.

No one could form any idea of the true nature of these diary notes from the excerpts published by Luzio. Nor is his sketchy paraphrase of a letter from Giuseppina to Verdi of 3rd February 1869, with tendentious commentary,[1] much more than a smoke-cloud concealing the truth. When this letter was written Maria (Filomena) Verdi had just been taken to her boarding-school at Turin, to the great distress of Giuseppina. From Turin Verdi had gone on to Milan for the rehearsals of *La forza del destino* at La Scala, and Giuseppina had returned to Genoa. One does not know the precise form given to the letter as sent; there are passages that seem disconnected in the draft in the letter-book, and there are, as so often, cancellations and alternative phrases. But what can be made out is of absorbing interest. Here first is a passage concerning Maria:

I have heard from Turin and send you the news at once, being sure that even amid your occupations and distractions you will be thinking sometimes of that dear child who is no longer with us. She is well; she cried again on Sunday evening and on Monday morning, waking up amid so many strange faces! It seems that she is calming down (so Canon Berti writes to Lessona), but I, who read between the lines, can see that she has suffered and is still suffering greatly. But it's for her own good that she should stay at school, and so be it. Although I was sure I should feel the parting keenly, I did not expect it would prove so bitter. I have let nobody know that I am back at Genoa, because I have no wish to see anyone. At the same time, these enormous rooms seem like sad deserts to me now, populated by phantasms.

One must consider her distress on this account in judging the significance of the whole. But what are we to make of the following extraordinary passage?

I have thought it over carefully, and I shan't come to Milan. Thus I shall spare you from having to come mysteriously to the station, at night, to slip me out like a bundle of contraband goods. I have *pondered* your profound silence before leaving Genoa, your words at Turin, and your letter of last Tuesday, and my presentiments counsel me to decline the offer you make me, of coming to attend a few rehearsals of *La forza del destino*. I feel all there is that is forced in this invitation, and I think it a wise determination to leave you in peace and stay where I am. If I don't amuse myself, at any rate I don't expose myself to further and useless

[1] *Carteggi*, II. p. 30.

bitter experiences, and you, on the other hand, will be completely *à ton aise*. When, last spring, my heart gave me the courage to present myself to la Maffei and Manzoni, in order to return to you with my hands full of welcome things, when I was happy thinking of the lovely surprise Clarina's visit would give you, when we made our trip to Milan together, and the visit to Manzoni and the excursion on the lake, and the consequence of all this was your coming together again with the city that saw your earliest successes. . . . I did not think of the strange and bitter consequence with which I am faced, *of being repudiated.* [*Cancelled passage:* You will understand that when years and years and years have passed in a silent, retired, modest life, one has no craving to go to amuse oneself at Milan.] No, Verdi, I could not imagine that in spring we could present ourselves together before the august presence of Manzoni, and that in winter it would be a prudent thing to repudiate me. That's how it is. Permit my exacerbated heart therefore to find at least the dignity of refusal, and may God forgive you [*Alternative version:* and sufficient affection to forgive you] the most acute and humiliating wound you have dealt me.

For Giuditta and Clarina, who write (I don't know why and for what end) asking me to join you at Milan, you will find some pretext to justify my refusal. I will reply tomorrow or the next day. About the child I will write to you again as soon as I myself have further news.

This is the reverse side of the picture, from which one sees all the heartbreak behind the charming descriptive letters to Clarina. What bitter feelings there must have been, to cause Giuseppina to pen such a phrase as 'to slip me out like a bundle of contraband goods'!

We are now fairly launched on the main subject of inquiry in this chapter, and in a position to assess it on a realistic basis. According to our new chronology, Verdi probably first met Teresa Stolz, briefly, at Genoa in 1868, either in early April or in the second half of December. He first spent any length of time in her company during the rehearsals of *La forza del destino* at La Scala in February 1869. One thing emerges with crystal clarity from Giuseppina's letter of 3rd February—Verdi's behaviour before he left to take charge of these rehearsals was such as to lead her, rightly or wrongly, to believe that she was not wanted. It is true, as Luzio assures us, that she *did*, after further persuasion, go to Milan and afterwards wrote letters of thanks for the kindness shown her there. I do not find these letters, however, 'overflowing with inexpressible happiness, with enthusiastic praise of her Verdi, with unlimited faith in him', as Luzio did. There is this passage to Ricordi: 'It's true, isn't it, Giulio, that in Verdi the man surpasses the artist? For many years now I have had the benediction of living beside him and there are moments when I don't know which is greater, my affection or my veneration for him, for his heart and his character.' But the contemporary letters to Clarina Maffei are pervaded by a vague sense of unease and depression. It is not easy to expunge from the memory the letter to Verdi of 3rd

February: 'May God forgive you the most acute and humiliating wound you have dealt me.'

Abbiati quotes parts of this letter,[1] and then dismisses it as the product of 'a quarter of a hour's ill humour', imagining an 'instantaneous reconciliation' when they saw each other again. His version of the second of the two sets of diary notes [2] has eight omissions totalling 680 words, out of 893, by which the prevalent mood is concealed.

After this, as described in the last chapter, the friendship of Verdi and Mariani broke up, the first really serious breach occurring within a few months, in August of this year, ostensibly over the Rossini commemorations at Pesaro and the abortive preparations for those at Bologna. The relationship survived precariously for two more years, and then, as we have seen, Teresa Stolz broke off her engagement to Mariani immediately after her first visit to Sant' Agata, from 23rd September to 12th October 1871. In Giuseppina's letter-books only two cards to Teresa Stolz are recorded before this—one on 22nd March 1869, after name-day congratulations, the other at the beginning of January 1871, reciprocating good wishes for the new year. The real correspondence begins only after the visit to Sant' Agata.

Here again we shall allow the documents, as far as possible, to speak for themselves. Giuseppina's letter-books have a most valuable contribution to make at this point. This passage is from her first letter to Teresa Stolz, written on 16th October 1871, four days after the end of the visit to Sant' Agata:

I am glad you had a good journey; I want to hear that your and your sister's affairs are equitably settled, so that both of you may enjoy that peace of mind without which there is no happiness on earth. After that, what I want above all is to embrace you again and stay as long as possible in your company, because I love you, esteem you and am attracted by your frank, sincere and elevated character, in no way tainted by the air of the *coulisses*!

I blushed a little, in spite of my *venerable* age, in reading the praises you shower upon me with such indulgence. I don't deserve them all, but one part I don't disclaim, and that is, of being a firm and loyal friend, when I say I am a friend, which occurs very, very seldom. [*Deleted:* Now I feel inclined to form a sacred friendship, dear Teresa, with you, and I hope you will not disdain to return this sentiment, the most blessed and most worthy known to man.] I am a little better and tomorrow I am going to pay my annual visit to poor Barberina, to whom your greetings will certainly give great pleasure. By the middle of November, unless something out of the ordinary happens, we shall be at Genoa, where we count on seeing you.

[1] III, p. 248 [2] III, p. 157.

In November and early December Teresa Stolz, with some of the other singers, was at Genoa, studying her role in *Aida* with Verdi. She went then to Milan, where she had decided to make her home. Giuseppina wrote to her again on 13th December:

After having made your closer acquaintance, I cannot but think good of you in all things. So it is that if you have not written to me first, apart from the fact that you were under no obligation to do so, it is a sign that you could not. And then I myself, being lazy and knowing what it is to have to put a new apartment in order, am extremely indulgent in the matter of *letters*, having need myself of infinite indulgence.

My health is improving, but very slowly. Speaking is still hurtful, and to avoid frequent conversations I have not yet sent any cards to my few acquaintances at Genoa. Unfortunately I was not able, as I should have wished, to do anything for you during your stay at Genoa. So you do not owe me, even formally, any thanks. In coming to see me you performed two good actions at once: the first of charity, of visiting the sick, that is; the other was particularly welcome to me, because I love and esteem you and hope to conserve these two sentiments unchanged, where you are concerned, for the rest of my life. *Ergo:* let ceremonial phrases be banished between us, and let us adopt the cordial language of friendship.

Verdi believes he knows the apartment at 8 Via dell'Agnello. It must be that formerly occupied by Signora De Giuli. It must be a bit melancholy, but if you like it *c'est tout ce qu'il faut.*

It seems that Mariani is really and seriously ill. Stripping away all the useless embroideries, one understands that the malady that torments him is still his old trouble, haemorrhoids, brought now, thanks to his monstrous efforts over *Lohengrin*, to such a state of inflammation and irritation as perhaps to necessitate an operation. The recent Florentine caravan has been the *coup de grâce* and he has dragged himself back to Bologna and put himself to bed. We shall have *definite news, free from exaggeration*, tomorrow or the day after, and I shall send it on to you. Mariani was born the most fortunate of men, but it pleases him to be, morally and materially, his own executioner. He could be a friend, a husband, an envied artist, happy, esteemed by all. And what is he? A great orchestral conductor, now. [*Cancelled:* A man who busies himself in tortuous ways, searching for clay to raise a monument to his own glory.] And later? Alas, alas, poor humanity! [*Cancelled:* They will say: It seems he was a great conductor and a great liar.]

One of Luzio's principal arguments against what he called the 'odious legend' of a love affair between Verdi and Teresa Stolz was always that Giuseppina's letter-books show that it was she, 'exclusively',[1] who induced the singer to break off her relationship with Mariani, and opened her eyes to the latter's true character. Luzio's view was accepted with much satisfaction, by Francis Toye among others:[2]

[1] *Carteggi*, II, p. 11. Cf. also IV, p. 193 and 273 ('estraneo totalmente Verdi').
[2] 'New Verdi Correspondence' (*Music & Letters*, Oct. 1936).

> One thing of primary interest to the Verdi student emerges from [Giuseppina's] letters. It was she, not Verdi, who weaned Teresa Stolz from Mariani. Thus, the whole imaginative fabric of a Verdi-Stolz intrigue constructed by imaginative biographers in Germany and Italy on this episode falls to the ground. I am particularly delighted at the establishment of the truth because, with the facts at my disposal at the time I wrote my book on Verdi, I had already come to the conclusion (there stated) that the whole thing was almost certainly moonshine.

It is a little strange that Verdi's defenders should be so positive that he had nothing whatever to do with this manœuvre, when they had earlier accepted Luisa Cora Mancinelli's story of the financial origin of the breach, in which the composer's punctiliousness in money matters was certainly involved. But, apart from that, my own examination of Giuseppina's letter-books at Sant' Agata produced nothing that could justify such positive assertions as were made by Luzio on this subject. Probably, if asked to produce his evidence, he would have pointed to the above letter. We see now, however, since Zoppi's publication of Mariani's correspondence with Del Signore, that Giuseppina was writing two months *after* Teresa Stolz had broken off all relations with Mariani, following her visit to Sant' Agata. Who knows what was said to her during that visit? And by whom? One cannot think that all the talking on this subject was left to Giuseppina.

Continuing our examination of the letter-books, we find Giuseppina not particularly looking forward to the visit to Milan for the rehearsals and performances of *Aida*, nor particularly enjoying it when it came:

To Clarina Maffei, 24th December:

> The thought gladdens me of embracing you again and coming to spend a half-hour or two with you in intimate *causerie en tête à tête*. Thank you for your kindly offer to put yourself at my disposition, but I want you to promise me not to alter your usual habits in the least, especially at this time of year and with your delicate health. I shall come to see you (without abusing my privilege) at times when it will be least inconvenient to you and when your society will shine by its *absence*. My plan in coming to your beautiful city is to pass from my room at Genoa to another at the Albergo Milano. My long indisposition, my tastes, which are becoming more and more solitary, do not permit me anything resembling the agitated life of the generality. It's quite settled that I shall not accept any dinner or other engagements. I shall make no single new acquaintance—*none*. I shall go a few times to see Tito Ricordi and poor Piave. I shall often come to see you and if I feel like it I shall go sauntering alone (I am fond of solitary walks) with my nose in the air, or against the shop windows, and then return to my room to read, write or do nothing. Before leaving Milan, if to do so would not be too indiscreet, I shall come to kiss the hand of the High Priest of literature and good morals. There you have, from alpha to omega, what I wish and intend to do during my stay at Milan. *Sine qua*

non, I shall stay at Genoa. God bless you and all who are like you—how small the scope of this blessing!

To Nina Ravina at Genoa, from Milan, 19th January 1872:

I have been only once to La Scala and I don't think I shall go again except for *Aida*. I am not going out much and so far have held firm to my resolution to avoid all new acquaintances. We shall see whether I succeed in warding them off. There is at Milan much noise and movement. It is absolutely a big city, with the air of the capital of a great nation . . . but (I whisper it in your ear) I long for the silence and calm of my solitudes at Genoa and Sant' Agata. Nothing re-awakens in me any desire to amuse myself, in the usual sense of the word. Verdi is well, is working hard, is in a good humour, pays visits to some of his old acquaintances and continues to love Milan. *Tant mieux!*

And what are you doing? Let me hear from you, about your family, and tell me if your troubles are over. Poor Nina! You so deserve to be happy!

At this time there began, at the suggestion of this friend and near-neighbour at Genoa, the correspondence with Don Montebruno. Nina Ravina, a married woman, was engaged, as entries in the letter-books over a wide period show, in a long struggle to overcome an attraction towards the painter Avendaño. She and Giuseppina had exchanged confidences and considerable intimacy had grown up between them. Here is a passage from another letter to Nina Ravina, a little later in this year:

What you tell me in your letter, most welcome in any case, wrings my heart. There is always some part of our unhappiness of which we must accuse ourselves, but there is, too, another very large part which we owe to destiny and to the *goodness* of men. In saying, with Montebruno, '*Patience!*' I add '*Courage!*' to continue the struggle, and about this I should have a whole volume of things to say, some of them already discussed between us, during those intimate evenings spent together in my room at Genoa.

Some of the autographs of Giuseppina's letters to this friend still exist and when they become accessible we may learn a great deal more about her secret anxieties. The letter-books do not give us a complete record of her correspondence. Some pages have been cut out and copies were not kept of every letter sent.

There are fairly numerous brief records of uncopied letters to Teresa Stolz from this period, after the return to Genoa:

23rd February: 'To la Stolz.'
1st March: 'Wrote to la Stolz.'
7th March: 'To la Stolz—a word.'
? March: 'To Mme Stolz.'

Early in April Verdi was at Parma, directing the rehearsals of *Aida* at the Teatro Regio; Giuseppina stayed at Genoa, preparing for the removal to Sant' Agata. She wrote to Verdi on 7th April to say that except for putting away the carpets she was all ready, but that he was not to worry about coming to fetch her if it was not convenient while he was busy in the theatre, and if he was not able to come at all she would set the household caravan in motion herself. This is a scrappy letter '*à la Mariani*', as she herself admitted, but it includes some interesting things. 'I don't know what to do for la Stolz . . . fearing by my letter to renew her sorrow. I'll see about it later.' This refers to the death of the singer's mother, and not to her separation from Mariani. Then: 'Give my cordial regards to la Stolz. Why don't you suggests Castione to her? The position seems to me a pleasant one, for a site in the plains.' The idea seems to have been for Teresa to take a house for the summer. Nothing came of it, but the reference is to Castione dei Marchesi, between Busseto and Fidenza, about six miles from Sant' Agata, as Gatti says, and not to a place near Genoa, as Luzio and Abbiati think.[1]

She came again to Sant' Agata after the end of the season at Parma. In Giuseppina's letter-book, under the date 26th May and the heading 'Theresa Stolz' in German script, is found this:

> I am glad you found your stay at Sant' Agata both delicious and too short. It certainly seemed very short to us, because your company is dear to us. As for it being delicious, your affection for us made it seem so to you, but we cannot agree, or we should seem to be beating the big drum to draw compliments to ourselves and our possessions. This is a privilege we don't envy certain persons of our acquaintance and which we leave wholly to them. If it is true that you feel so at home with us in our modest house, prove it by staying a long time, and in the most complete freedom. And don't imagine you are too reserved. No, you are that which a serious and affectionate woman should be, without mealy-mouthedness and exaggerations. I love you as you are. I like to be sure that when I shake your hand I shake the hand of a sincere and loyal woman, who loves me a little. A friendship like that growing up between you and us has need of a sound foundation and I believe we have all contributed our corner-stone, to render it such as may be confidently relied upon all the days of our lives. So write to me when you wish; don't write to me when time or inclination is lacking. I hope, at all events, that your affection and esteem will never fail me and I likewise believe I was not deceived in judging you in every way worthy of the friendship of my Verdi and myself.

This was as far as she copied the letter in her book, the entry going on: 'I continue talking of la Melloni, of *Don Sebastiano*, of the trunks,

[1] Gatti, revised edition, 1951, pp. 586–7; Luzio, *Carteggi*, IV, p. 274; Abbiati, III, p. 577. It is amusing to note the different interpretations of this passage by the first two of these writers.

Gatti is wrong in quoting at this point from another undated letter from Giuseppina to Verdi: 'I embrace you tightly, as in the *active* period of our life'; Loulou is mentioned in the same sentence, and Loulou died in 1862. This letter is actually from December 1860.

etc., etc., and end the letter more or less in these terms: "You have no need of my advice, and in talking of that person at Milan I invited you to think it over because you had told me of your position and your isolation, and an honest man, as you say he is, is not a companion to be despised."' This introduces a new element into the mixture we are trying to analyse: Teresa Stolz had another admirer at Milan. But the person here indicated is unidentifiable, and nothing more is heard of him in the available documents. All one can say, for the moment, is that there is evidence that she was seriously considering, in this year of 1872, a close association with another man, who was not Verdi.

But Giuseppina's oppression of spirit continued. It was intensified by an unhappy letter from Clarina Maffei. On 25th June Verdi sent her a cordial invitation to Sant' Agata and Giuseppina added:

OUR DEAREST CHIARINA,

Don't write us any more such letters; that is, don't be ill again. Verdi is very upset, and I with him. For some time now I have had a tendency to sadness, to tears, I would almost say to desolation! Why? Knowing you are ill, guessing, or rather feeling, from your words all the melancholy in your heart, hurts me, hurts me, hurts me very much, and increases my sadness. I love few people in the world, and you I love most of all, after my Verdi and my unhappy sister! I love you as if you had been my friend for twenty years. My Clarina, get well, and come to stay with us for a while. We have need to weep together; to speak together of that Saint, who alas! perhaps has not long to live! I embrace you, my Clarina, tight, tight to my heart!

She was doing her best to set, as she said, the new friendship with Teresa Stolz on a firm foundation. The effort it cost her, however, can be felt. Altogether different, warmer and deeper, was this friendship with Clarina Maffei:

9th July:

I am glad to hear you are better, but I need to hear you are well. As one advances in years the number of persons one loves is continually diminishing, and one's affection seems to concentrate itself and to become increasingly intense for the friends who are left, above all when one loves with the tenderness Verdi and I have for Chiarina Maffei! I am so sorry you were not able to come to see us this year. The profound silence of these fields and the almost claustral calm here would have done you good. My disposition of spirit is so sad, my mood so depressed, that sometimes I weep and sometimes I am almost afraid of myself. We should have had long conversations and you, who are so expansive, would have cheered me up and cured me of this depression, that will be fleeting, I hope. I am a savage, who flees the banal affection of the multitude, but I avidly need my few friends to love me and tell me so; precisely because I love so few people, I love them so much and I like to tell them so repeatedly. So,

*O

hoping that God will allow me to live till then, I'll wait for the days you can spare me next year.

Giuseppina had seen Verdi taking considerable interest in Teresa Stolz's affairs from the time of her first visit to Sant' Agata. He had sought advice from Piroli about her position in Austrian law, asking whether it permitted, as did Italian law, her brothers and sisters to demand at any time a share in her fortune. He had personally undertaken to procure from the firm of Granger in Paris the stage jewellery she was to wear in *Aida* at Milan. There is some quite agitated correspondence with Du Locle about these jewels, although it could hardly have mattered much whether the Ethiopian slave girl wore a bangle or two more or less. Giuseppina had had to serve as intermediary and secretary to arrange, initially through De Sanctis and Torelli, for performances of *Aida* under Verdi's direction at Naples in the following winter. In a letter to De Sanctis on 21st January she had reported a conversation with Verdi on this subject, his conditions including the engagement of Teresa Stolz and Maria Waldmann. In the draft of this letter only one singer is mentioned: 'Mark well that the primary condition is la Stolz, *sine qua non*; all talking is useless otherwise.' When Torelli announced her engagement for Naples in his paper, and sent her a copy, he received it back 'refused by the addressee'. He was very annoyed, but Verdi told De Sanctis: 'I was present in the theatre when la Stolz received the paper and I myself advised her to send it back.' According to him, the dispatch of that issue of the *Omnibus* at that moment could only be interpreted as a form of blackmail: 'Subscribe to the paper or expect my hostility.' Another thing Verdi's wife noticed: it was his custom to see his new operas launched on their first three performances and then to leave them to make their own way; only rarely did he ever attend later performances. In the case of *Aida* he returned more than once to Milan, so that Giuseppina remarked in a letter to Clarina Maffei that if things went on in that way he would do well to take a season ticket for the railway.

There was nothing wrong in any of these things, but they did show an unusual personal interest on Verdi's part, and Giuseppina did not altogether like it. After the performances of *Aida* at Parma she noticed with dismay the frequency of the correspondence between Verdi and the singer. And one day in August she picked up the letters that had accumulated and looked through them.

Many letters from Teresa Stolz, to Giuseppina and to Verdi, are preserved at Sant' Agata. Sixteen of them were published by Luzio. Abbiati has recently given us extracts from many others, including some which Luzio apparently did not see, and which were not among those I myself examined. These additional letters, however, are exactly like the others, and reveal no particular secrets.

On the top left-hand corner of a letter of 15th August 1872 is a pencil note in Giuseppina's hand:[1] 'Sixteen letters!! in a short time!! what *activity*!' Luzio remarks that 'this shows that she had her eyes well open from the first'. It certainly does. The imagination boggles at the thought of what Verdi must have said to her when he found the annotation. Another letter, a little earlier, is signed 'Aida'; one would have thought she had a perfect right to use this signature, but there have been added in pencil a note of interrogation and two exclamation marks. If Giuseppina did this she was a very jealous woman.

In the content of the letters, as Luzio says, there is nothing to which she could well object. The tone is respectful; the polite third person singular is used throughout; there are many kindly references to Giuseppina herself; everything is open, and little or nothing can be read between the lines.

As for the 'activity': from the year 1872 there are letters from Parma on 17th, 18th, 19th and 27th May; from Florence on 10th June; from Padua on 17th, 22nd and 27th June and 2nd, 4th, 8th, 15th and 20th July; from Brescia on 30th July, 15th, 19th and 22nd August and 6th and 9th September. Why did she have to write so often? What were the letters all about?

Some are concerned with arrangements for visits to Sant' Agata and the disposal of her luggage; most, however, consist of theatrical reports and gossip. Verdi liked to know, almost from day to day, how the early performances of *Aida*, when not directed by himself, were going, artistically and financially. He received these reports from Teresa Stolz, as he had received from Mariani, earlier, similarly frequent ones on the performances of *Don Carlos*. The tone of the later correspondence, as preserved, does not change, and the subject-matter, right to the very end, is the same. The letters from Milan, after her retirement, form a fairly close chronicle of events at La Scala, with sharply critical remarks about many of the operas and the artists.

It will be best to give here a selection of passages from this first group of letters, from 1872, particularly as Luzio published nothing dating from before the end of the following year.

Parma, 17th May:

DEAREST MAESTRO,

Thank you for your kind letter of the 15th. This time I am a bit behind-hand with my theatrical chronicle and I ask your pardon. The fact is that the poor chronicler was in bed for three days, with a heavy cold. . . . I can hide nothing from you, dear Maestro. I must tell you that last Monday's

[1] It is strangely unlike her normal hand, but one does not know, of course, in just what circumstances she wrote. After initial doubts, close examination and comparison of the letter formation, and discussion at Sant' Agata, I believe these remarks are indeed Giuseppina's. This was also Angiolo Carrara-Verdi's opinion, as well as Luzio's.

performance was downright bad. Capponi sang flat in the most terrible manner and ruined the whole finale of the first act; many lapses of intonation were heard, too, in the fourth act, from the internal chorus (in the final duet) and I did not feel well and therefore made my own contribution to the bad result!!! . . .

A great sensation has been made here by Filippi's article in *La Perseveranza*, which speaks very well of our performances here, and says every imaginable bad thing about me and la Waldmann. It wouldn't have mattered so much if he had only spoken ill of me, but where does poor Waldmann come into it!!! Of all this tangle of intrigue I shall be able to speak when I have the good fortune to see you at Sant' Agata. For two more evenings I shall be Aida and then I shall become my usual self again, la Stolz, for a while. I look forward to the end of these performances and then on Tuesday I shall come to embrace dear Signora Peppina. It really seems a thousand years since I saw her!!! I should like to come in the morning, however, the more to enjoy your[1] dear company, because on Wednesday I should return again to Parma. This time I shall come alone, without Maria [Waldmann].

As for my opinion on the Padua affair, I'll say this, dear Maestro. I know that theatre, because I have sung there before. They promise everything imaginable, and then one gets nothing, owing to the extreme economy they try to practise in *everything*. If you, as Maestro Verdi, ask me if you should consent to go to Padua, I, as la Stolz, say frankly: Don't go; but if, as *composer of Aida*, you ask me, then, as *prima donna*, I reply at once: Come to Padua and your *Aida* will have the shining success it had at Milan and Parma. Your presence influences *everyone*, makes everything go well. . . .

Parma, 18th May:

In my letter of yesterday I forgot to ask you, dear Maestro, not to put yourself or anyone else out by coming to meet me at Borgo San Donnino, all the more since a sufficiently early hour is concerned, for I would like to leave Parma on Tuesday morning at 9.52.

If you think fit, however, to send the carriage, and if Signor Corticelli has no other business that morning, I should be most happy to find him at Borgo, but if by chance he is busy, do nothing about it—I'll find my own way. We are agreed then! I don't want you to go to any special trouble, nor should I ever permit dear Signora Peppina to put herself out either; I am only paying a hasty visit, in order to embrace her and to tell her many, many things (whether she will listen to me will depend on her kindness). But poor lady!! Already I hear her exclaim: 'Poor me! I must prepare myself to hear Teresa's endless chatter!' All right, I'll try to be brief.

Parma, 19th May:

DEAREST MAESTRO,

I have just received your kind letter of yesterday, and reply at once, confirming what I wrote to you yesterday: i.e. on Tuesday morning at

[1] 'Your' in the plural (*loro*).

10.36 I shall be at Borgo. Again I beg you not to go to any special trouble. I don't wish you, dear Maestro, to put yourself out, and still less do I wish Signora Peppina to do so. If you like to send Corticelli, very well. If not, do nothing at all. When I hinted to Maria that perhaps I would take her with me, she began to jump up and down as though she were crazy!!! so if it won't cause too much bother during the twenty-four hours I shall stay at Sant' Agata, I'll bring her with me. If then those twenty-four hours become forty-eight, it will be as a result of your[1] goodness, to which I shall submit with the greatest pleasure.

In insisting that he should not come to meet her, and in bringing Maria Waldmann, in spite of her stated intention not to do so, she seems to have been trying to avoid anything that might suggest she wished to be alone with Verdi. The next few letters are concerned with his invitation to Padua, for the production of *Aida* there:

Florence, 10th June:

Consult the good Signora Peppina again. She, with the discernment she shows in everything, will certainly be able to suggest the best thing to do.

Padua, 17th June:

DEAR MAESTRO,

I still await your reply to my letter from Florence. Are you going to be good, or obstinate in repetition of your solemn *No*? The theatre management told me they sent you another invitation yesterday. . . . So, dear Maestro, don't be naughty [*cattivo*] and come, and thus you will make *everyone* happy and especially, I think, poor Faccio, who is really very dissatisfied with the orchestra here, and much afraid he won't achieve a good performance! How is dear Signora Peppina? I can just see her rambling about that delicious garden, sometimes with Lorito on her shoulder, and in thought I accompany her everywhere. I wish it were reality, but one must be patient!! Please give her my very kindest regards. . . .

P.S. I reopen my letter to tell you that I have just received your kind letter of the 15th. To tell you the truth the contents of the same give me no pleasure at all! My poor hopes!! and these poor gentlemen of the management here, who hoped so much!!! I lack courage to insist further, but you are naughty!! naughty!!

A few brief references to Mariani, and the money owed her by Gallo, have been quoted in the previous chapter. Everybody seems to have borrowed, or tried to borrow, money from her:

Padua, 20th July:

Gallo owes me more or less the same sum as Carlino [Del Signore]. They will pay me when they can and, who knows, perhaps we shall end by becoming enemies, as has happened in the case of another lady, also

[1] 'Your' in the plural, again.

of your acquaintance. To you, dear Maestro, I can tell everything. I was Signora Ravina's friend before you were, and we used to call on each other. One day her husband wrote to me asking if I had any money to give him, for him to invest in business for me. I refused, and from that day our good relations ceased, and now, if we are not enemies, we are not far off that. Such is the way of the world. But it doesn't matter; I have found other friends who are much dearer to me, and God grant I may keep them always!!

So *Carlina* wanted to come and stay with you in the country? She told me all about it in a letter, indeed she added that she is coming to Sant' Agata next week, together with her husband!!! I think Signora Peppina is perfectly right: one should not take such liberties with *Maestro Verdi*. He is not like an ordinary mortal, and must therefore be treated differently. Oh, the vanity of men! One's *amour propre* is very flattered, certainly, when one can say: 'I have sent my wife to stay with Maestro Verdi in the country'!! I think Carlino would have told the whole world about it, through that same vanity of men!! I am wicked, no doubt, but I know these people a little!!!!

Towards the end of July a charity performance at Padua had to be deferred owing to her indisposition. This was misunderstood by the public and she was hissed on her next appearance in the theatre. She then told the management she would not sing in the deferred charity performance. 'On Sunday there was much talk about this in the town,' she told Verdi, 'but no one attached much importance to it. They all believed I should let myself be won over by a few bunches of flowers that they prepared for me on Sunday and would certainly sing on Tuesday. But, poor things, there they made a mistake! I am a conscientious artist, I do my duty as best I can, but I wish also to be respected, as an artist, and still more so as a woman!! I cannot allow myself to be unjustly insulted nor can I permit them to say I am capricious and unkind!!' Verdi did not think she had acted well, and told her so, as appears from a letter to Faccio of 16th August:[1]

She wrote to me at length about the affair at Padua, and I replied telling her what seemed to me the truth. It is true that she was treated unworthily by the public, but a person of integrity goes straight ahead and takes no notice of such caprices. If she had not thanked me for my frank words and sent me a telegram after the first performance of *La forza del destino* I should have thought she was a bit annoyed. But that is not so, and cannot be so.

One gains the impression from Teresa Stolz's letters that she was garrulous, sometimes rather malicious, and not particularly intelligent. She was, of course, writing in a foreign language. As for her looks, Luzio considers that the well-known pastel by Gariboldi, in the Scala Museum, gives a romantically exaggerated impression of

[1] Raffaello De Rensis, *Franco Faccio e Verdi* (Milan, 1934), p. 133.

her beauty. It may however be a good likeness from an early period. One can agree that the photographs give her a plainer, more stolid appearance. But if at this period, approaching forty, she was not exactly a 'blonde bombshell', one yet has to remember that Mariani, a noted connoisseur, had been desperately in love with her. This is something that Luzio, in his attempts to minimize her attraction for Verdi, leaves wholly out of account.

Whatever Giuseppina felt as she read these letters, she had to keep up appearances, reply herself from time to time, and agree to further visits:

Brescia, 19th August:

Yesterday I had a welcome letter from Signora Peppina—I'll say rather from dear Peppina, since she has permitted me to call her that.

Brescia, 6th September:

Please let me have two lines to say whether I may come to Sant' Agata next Thursday. If that should cause you even the slightest inconvenience, then you can yourself indicate the day, and the hour, too, when I must be at Borgo. Please forgive me if I speak with such freedom (impudence, almost) of my arrival at Sant' Agata. You have spoiled me by your kindness and as you see I am taking advantage of it—too much, perhaps!!!

For nearly five months, from the middle of November until nearly the middle of April in the following year, they were all together at Naples, for performances of *Don Carlos* and *Aida* at the San Carlo theatre. The stay was lengthened by Teresa Stolz's illness, which delayed the production of *Aida*.

Further indications of Giuseppina's uneasiness are found in correspondence from Sant' Agata immediately after this long stay at Naples. Verdi's first letter to De Sanctis, most intimate of the Neapolitan friends, has a postscript: 'Peppina is well, but very sad.' Giuseppina herself, writing at the same time, enclosed this note on a separate scrap of paper:

I am curious to know whether the gossip circulating about that matter of which you told me there is so much talk at Naples, has reached the ears of la S . . . .

If you should by chance come to mention this stupid and infamous tittle-tattle, and learn something about it, it will suffice if, when you reply, you write on a little piece of paper: 'She knows that.'

'She knows that' is in English. It is all very well for Luzio to cite, as he frequently does, the words 'stupid and infamous tittle-tattle', applied here to rumours of an affair between Verdi and Teresa Stolz, as though they settled everything; there are many other signs that Giuseppina was seriously disturbed. She put a brave face on it, however, and renewed her invitations to Sant' Agata. Her letters to the singer are in carefully chosen words, with recurrent faint notes of warning amid the cordiality and the transparent desire to think nothing but good of her.

In her letter-book, after an entry dated 20th April, is this fragment:

MY DEAR TERESA,—Your words of affection are so spontaneous that they have really done my heart good, and if in my eternal suspicion of men and things I could abandon myself . . .

She broke off, and began again, under the heading 'Stolz':

From the 13th to the 21st without replying! This must have set you wondering. Alas! It is human nature to torment oneself with suppositions, when one can't account for certain things and certain appearances. I did so myself and sometimes I still do, so that I should think it very natural if you had done so on this occasion on my account. Be indulgent with me, in view of the *chaos* of occupations I have these days, with a bumpkin for housemaid, with my health not yet fully restored, and my mood as grey as the skies we have generally had so far at Sant' Agata. If you suffered in separating from me, I too greatly suffered, and if I wept, in spite of my unfortunate difficulty in weeping, that means to say I was sincere in my spontaneous words. I really have need of your affection. But let's be clear about it—love me truly, for myself, without *arrière-pensée*, loyally, limpidly. [*Erased:* Love me with my qualities and my defects! What a rare and precious treasure is true friendship!] . . .

The garden is beautiful and flowery, in spite of the cloudy skies. You could now, if not eat grapes, gather flowers and row on the pond and there will be fruit too later, but you have, after Ancona, so many splendid projects of exhibitions, journeys, baths, cold shower-baths, etc., that you will be unwilling even to think of burying yourself for a time in this tiny corner of the earth before going to Cairo to earn that *trifling sum.* If, however, you find you can make that *sacrifice* for the composer of *Aida* and his wife, your room will be got ready at once.

The death of Manzoni on 22nd May led to Verdi's decision to compose the *Requiem*, to be performed in the following year. He and Giuseppina spent the summer months in Paris, returning to Sant' Agata in September. Teresa Stolz paid a visit, as suggested, before she left to sing in *La forza del destino*, *Aida* and *Un ballo in maschera* in Cairo. A letter to Verdi from Alexandria on 18th October describes the voyage from Brindisi on an English ship and the week's quarantine on arrival. As always, the plural forms of 'you' are employed in all passages expressive of affection:

I shall never forget your kindness, and can find no words to express my gratitude. It seems to me that every time I say goodbye to you I become more mute; grief and pain constrict my throat and there are moments when I think I shall suffocate!!! Poor me! I wonder what you said after I left? I feel quite mortified when I think of those last few moments before my departure. The good Peppina was right when she said that one should either never have any friends, or should live with them always, in the same town, so as never to have to separate from them.

Maria Waldmann had also received a letter and had wept with joy. The fact that Verdi was engaged in fairly frequent and affectionate correspondence with her, a much younger and far more beautiful woman than Teresa Stolz, does not seem to have troubled Giuseppina in the least. Maria Waldmann's career was very short; before long she was to marry Count Galeazzo Massari and retire from the stage; from various indications in the letters it appears that she was already being courted, if not yet actually engaged to be married. In her Christmas letter to Teresa Stolz, Giuseppina wished the same thing for her:

I seize the occasion of the coming festival, and the new year, to wish you the continuation of those good things that alone can procure you true happiness—good health, riches, the affection and esteem of all, and a woman's necessary complement—an honest man for husband, on whose arm you can lean in the certainty that he will be your faithful companion to the end of the road that God has marked out for you.

The most revealing of Giuseppina's letters are always those to Clarina Maffei. One of 5th March 1874 shows her in a very black mood:

I think Verdi really will take another trip to Milan in the next few days, but I shall stay at Genoa. He has many things to settle concerning his Mass, and will settle them better in person than by writing letters for two months. It's true: arrived at a certain age, one lives much on memories. We all have them, happy, sorrowful and dear, but alas! we are not all so fortunate as to conserve unchanged the affection and the friendship of the living, or at least the illusion of possessing those things, which make life dear. Happy you, who believe, who possess and deserve to possess the affection of your old and new friends! I—in profound discouragement I tell you this—I no longer believe in anything or anybody, almost. I have suffered so many and such cruel disillusionments as to become disgusted with life. You will say that everyone has to tread the spiny path of disappointment, but that only means to say that, stronger than I, others have retained some hope and some little faith in the future. Instead of which, now, when anyone tells me they love me, I laugh. . . . Even my religious enthusiasm has vanished and I scarcely even believe in God, when I look at the marvels of creation!

The original of this letter is in the Biblioteca di Brera, Milan. Gatti, suppressing the date, quotes it a little out of chronological order, and sets it against the background of the rehearsing of the soloists, including Teresa Stolz, for the approaching performance of the *Requiem*, in Verdi's house at Genoa. But there were no such rehearsals at Genoa, and when this letter was written Teresa Stolz was still in Egypt. It was another six weeks or more before she arrived at Milan, and by that time Verdi and Giuseppina were back at Sant' Agata. All rehearsals for the *Requiem* took place at Milan. These facts, however, scarcely diminish the value of the letter as an indication of Giuseppina's distress. The draft in the letter-book, dated two days earlier, has a variant: 'A grey veil has fallen over my spirit and I no longer believe in anything. This lack of faith at times makes life very wearisome to me and makes me all the more desire the completest solitude, to give me what I want, which is rest.'

It was decided that after the first performance on 22nd May, the anniversary of Manzoni's death, in the church of San Marco, and three others at La Scala, the *Requiem* should be given also in Paris, with the same soloists. Giuseppina very unwillingly agreed to go. 'Verdi does not seem disposed to leave me in Italy,' she told Corticelli. To her sister Barberina she wrote from Milan on 15th May:

> My ideas are so confused, I am so tired, physically and morally, that I hardly know how to express myself in words!
>
> I never have a day's peace and, what with the noise outside and the chattering inside, I go to bed so worn out that every day I seem to grow older by a year! It wouldn't be so bad if Milan were the end of it, but the complications I feared have arisen and it is settled that six performances will be given in Paris, with Verdi present, at least for the rehearsals. I understand that the immediate repetition of an unknown work in the capital of the modern world, simply because they have faith in the high fame and genius of the composer, is a fine thing, artistically speaking, but for myself, apart from the satisfaction of seeing Verdi so greatly and so universally honoured, I am desolate at not being able to come at once to Sant' Agata. It's not even certain that it will be possible to pay a visit between Milan and Paris, because the six performances of the Mass in Paris have to be finished by 20th June at the latest.
>
> I believe that we shall then finally be able to return home. There will be the removal at Genoa, but that will be done when it can be done, and in any case won't take long. Next year it seems to me there should not be anything to take us away from the peace of the country. But will God give me the strength to live that long?

Teresa Stolz's letters from this year are of the same character as those already quoted; they are full of theatrical gossip, rather sharply critical of her fellow artists, very respectful in tone and not really very interesting. One includes this passage: 'Excuse the length of my letter, but when I write to you or Signora Peppina I forget myself always and I chatter away as if we were in Peppina's bedroom in Paris, where we used to talk together after every performance of the Mass!!! Do you remember those days? I recall them always with the greatest pleasure.'

Fairly numerous uncopied letters were recorded by Giuseppina:

21st July: 'Wrote to la Stolz.'
27th August: 'To M.me Stolz.'
14th September: 'Wrote to la Stolz.'
19th December: 'Wrote to la Stolz.'
20th January: 'Wrote to Sig.a Stolz.'
26th January: 'Wrote to Sig.a Stolz.'

The letters themselves may have begun: 'My dear Teresa'; never once does she employ the Christian name in her own records of her correspondence.

The Carnival season of 1874–5 at the Teatro Apollo in Rome brought a serious interruption of the singer's career. On 17th January 1875 she appeared in *La forza del destino* but later in the month withdrew half way through a performance. She told Verdi on 1st February that she had bronchitis: 'Oh truly, I'm beginning to dislike this career in the theatres. All goes well when one's health is good, but hell begins when it fails one.' She was not fully recovered when she appeared in *Aida* on 17th February, and a week later she had to retire again and to cancel her contract.

She did not sing again in public until she went on a tour of the European capitals with Verdi and the *Requiem Mass*, the other soloists being Maria Waldmann, Angelo Masini and Paolo Medini. There were seven performances in Paris between 19th April and 4th May, four in London, in the Albert Hall, in May, and four in Vienna in June, with two performances of *Aida*. A projected visit to Berlin was cancelled, to Verdi's annoyance. All the performances were conducted by Verdi himself and the tour was a complete triumph. After this he considered that the *Requiem* could stand on its own feet and refused invitations to conduct it, with the same singers, at Venice and elsewhere. From Teresa Stolz at Venice on 11th July came the usual long report, ending:

The presence of the composer was all that was lacking at yesterday's festival! How many times, during the loud applause, la Waldmann and I said: 'What a shame that our good Maestro is not here!' In looking round the boxes my eye searched in vain for the dear and sympathetic figure of Signora Peppina; how lovely it would have been to see her there enjoying the triumphs of her dear Verdi!!!

In a word, your absence was much felt last night, and I in particular missed the comforting presence of two dear friends whom I sincerely love; but one cannot always be happy in this world!!

The second performance will be on Tuesday.

Now that I have bored you with my chatter nothing remains but to send my loving regards to you all, with lots of affectionate kisses to Signora Peppina and Signora Barberina.

Love me a little and remember your grateful and affectionate

TERESA STOLZ.

It is difficult not to believe that the writer of these lines was honest and sincere.

In the summer of this year a new access of vitality and energy is apparent in Giuseppina's correspondence. The veil of melancholy that had fallen over her spirit had now lifted. She wrote in exalted terms of the music of the *Requiem*, in which, she recognized, Verdi had touched a higher point than ever before. The fact that he had done so in a religious work probably contributed to her happiness and satisfaction. It sometimes seems as if Verdi's music, and the tributes paid to him, would have brought her back from the dead. We have a whole series of splendid letters from this summer of 1875: To Daniele Morchio, 12th July:

As you seem to know, the journey to the lands of *oui*, *yes* and *ja* was truly a happy one, and would have been more so without the hot weather that liquefied us in London and Vienna. I am glad that friends and Italians were so moved and proud of the results obtained by Verdi on this artistic tour. It is not my place, as his wife, to say it, but truly, truly, without shame Italy can say: This is my son!

To Clarina Maffei, 15th July:

Along with the many letters you must receive from your host of friends and acquaintances here is one from me too, since you were so kind as to say you would like one. Permit me not to repeat the description of Verdi's successes, and the endless praises, sung in good and bad style. Apart from the fact that you seem to be well informed already, I could find no words to tell of the general enthusiasm and the almost religious ecstasy of my own admiration for this man so blessed by God! There are certain geniuses who, as I feel, are to be praised and honoured in a way all their own. The orgy, the Bacchanal of applause—so it seems to me—must offend their high natures. But the fashion in our time (above all in Italy) is to manifest enthusiasm by exuberance of almost savage howls and shouts, and my Verdi, this chief and prince of modern music, has perforce to emerge from his cloud of glory to thank the public for these hosannas, which are sincere, certainly, but sometimes excessive, tiring, deafening and not always in the best of taste. Not everyone is of my opinion and perhaps I am wrong and the others right. However that may be, if no man of genius was ever praised and admired like Verdi, no man of genius has ever less sought the incense of praise, or remained more calm and dignified than he, amid the general intoxication.

To Cesare Vigna, 22nd July:

By Tuesday evening the performances of the Mass will be over. The last stroke of the *Asperges* will have returned to silence sounds, songs and enthusiasm. *Requiem* then, but not *aeternam*, to this *sublime* creation, which is truly an emanation of the Divine Spirit. We who are living will hear it and know it is being repeated in every corner of the civilized world. Posterity will place it, with wings outspread, in domination of all the music of mourning ever conceived by the human brain. I am sure you will not make use of *empty phrases* in giving your impressions of the Mass. That is why I wanted you to write about it; I can't tell you with what satisfaction I see you take up your pen. Nothing I have read on the subject has wholly satisfied me. It seems to me that in order to discuss it worthily one must raise oneself nearer to the Throne of God. You see, dear Vigna—to you I dare confess it—the feelings aroused in me by this music were so profound, raised me in spirit so far above the real world, that I found myself at certain moments painfully wounded by the public's loud applause, recalling me to earth.

To Teresa Stolz, 3rd August:

Since the mountain has not come to Mohammed, Mohammed will go to the mountain. In this case I am Mohammed, and present myself before you to remind you of your promise to come and spend some time this year, too, under the roof of our modest house. . . . I am going on Tuesday to Turin to fetch Maria and shall be returning on Thursday by the train that passes through Piacenza at . . . [*omission in the draft*] on 12th August. There is one that arrives from Milan ten minutes earlier. Would it be convenient for you to take that one, so that we should arrive together at Borgo San Donnino? I shall have the pleasure of seeing you a little sooner in this way, unless indeed you feel inspired to anticipate by a few days your arrival in the Capital of Sant' Agata. Now you have neither rehearsals nor performances, steal a little time from your amusements to write me a line, so that I can give the last touches to the grandiose apartments that you are to occupy, and that you already know! Verdi is in perfect health and in a mood very different from that in London. . . . I say no more because we shall have time to chatter at Sant' Agata.

This is the old Giuseppina again, with much of her former vivacity and charm. She had now an idea for the commemoration of Verdi's fame at Busseto too, and carried it through with characteristic vigour and independence. Luzio in the *Carteggi verdiani* [1] says that in September of this year she bought Verdi's birth-place, with the intention of having it restored as a memorial. He has totally misunderstood, perhaps wilfully, the evidence of her letter-books. Verdi's birth-place was at Le Roncole, as we know, and belonged to the Marchese Pallavicino; Verdi would have liked to buy it and have it pulled down, if the marchese had been willing to sell. But the house Giuseppina bought was the Palazzo Dordoni, the present Palazzo Orlandi, where she had lived with him when she first came to Busseto in 1849. And the person she bought it from was Verdi himself. It had remained in his possession all these years and become rather dilapidated. He had paid Contardo Cavalli 22,000 lire for it in 1845; now in 1875 he sold it to his own wife for 18,000 lire, a

[1] II, p. 45. Luzio is followed by Abbiati (III, p. 770), who is confused in this as in many other matters. Elsewhere (II, p. 29) he states correctly that Palazzo Orlandi was bought by Giuseppina in 1875.

reduction being allowable, as it says in the deed, 'in view of the huge expenses involved in the repairs and restorations indispensable for the preservation of the property'. On 7th August Giuseppina wrote to Dr Carrara:

> I discharge my material debt to you and at the same time charge friend Corticelli to convey to you my deepest appreciation of the tactful and solicitous friendship shown me in my acquisition of Verdi's house at Busseto. You know that my only intent was to secure that this house, decently restored, should remain (at least for this and the next generation) as an historic memorial to a man who, from the humblest origins, succeeded by his genius, and by every private and public virtue, in raising himself to the highest social spheres and honouring the town he inhabited for some time and Italy, our common motherland. I think that friends and enemies, men of both wide and limited intelligence, if they have feeling hearts as men and citizens, will approve my action.

There is a gap of more than two years in Verdi's *Copialettere* at this time, and Giuseppina's own letter-books show her once again busily engaged in secretarial work, with the utmost competence and decision. A tremendous storm blew up, almost wrecking relations between Verdi and his publishers. It is impossible not to admire the way it was dealt with by Giuseppina, the intermediary and Ricordi's only hope of reconciliation, by a combination of sympathy and firmness. A number of pages of her letter-book are devoted to correspondence on this subject, headed by the entry: 'First German affairs broken off owing to Tito's stingy, hesitant, niggardly spirit.' This dossier recalls that of the great dispute over Busseto and its theatre in 1865. As soon as the storm burst, Tito left hurriedly for a cure at San Pellegrino, leaving his son Giulio to try to sort things out. Giulio appealed to Giuseppina and received in reply a long lecture on the situation, how it had arisen, and what the attitude of the publishers to a man like Verdi was and should have been:

> Everything in this world has a beginning and an end, and in every properly administrated business house an account is kept of Profit and Loss. The House of Ricordi can open its ledgers for affairs with Verdi from 1841–2 to 1875—thirty-four years, that is!!!—and put in the balance the Profit and the Loss. It's a matter of weight and calculation. You must know that very well and you will have to agree that the Verdian *goods* have been a rich mine of wealth for the firm of Ricordi. So much for the material fact. Then, especially for a publisher, there is a higher question. There is a sort of self-esteem, of glory, I would almost say, in keeping a banner flying that decorates the House, and in retaining the friendship of one whom all the world honours, both as man and artist. Well, my dear Giulio, for a long time now that man and that artist has had no reason to be very satisfied with the whole procedure of your firm in affairs that concern him.

She reminded him that some years earlier Verdi had wished to undertake a tour of Germany with *Aida*, which had come to nothing owing to the tight-fisted, mercenary spirit of the firm:

> It did not see, or did not wish to see, that in Verdi's artistic aim, which was to have his music performed in Germany according to its true spirit, lay hope of planting it on sound roots in that musical territory, and once planted the publisher would have been largely compensated by the redoubled sale of his publications. But the firm lacked the courage to risk a few thousand francs. It wasted time, hesitated, and ended by writing Verdi, at the last moment, a letter reading like a certificate of destitution, to excuse the wretchedness of the compensation offered. Verdi took great offence, and refused it!

The success of the *Requiem* in Paris had led to the recent tour of European capitals. A small deficit over the first of the performances in London, however, had scared Ricordi and led to the cancellation of the visit to Berlin. Then the question of financial compensation had again arisen. When first asked what they were to give him Verdi had replied: 'What you like.' For some reason that is not clear he was extremely annoyed at being asked about it again in Vienna. Probably he felt that an unfair appeal to his generosity was being made, after the publishers had shown concern over the expenses of the tour.

These things, however, were not the most serious causes of the dispute. These lay, as Giuseppina wrote, in what they were all pleased to call 'irregularities' in their accounts. 'I don't know what they would be called in legal terms.' Verdi considered that he had received less than his due from some recent contracts. His reaction was immediate and tremendous. He sent Corticelli to Milan to fetch all the contracts between his publishers and the various theatres from *Rigoletto* (1851) onwards! These contracts he settled down to study. He spent days and days going carefully through them, arriving more and more firmly at the conclusion that he had been cheated. The publishers sought to lay the blame on Tornaghi, who had charge of the contracts department. They got little encouragement to pursue this line: 'But who is the proprietor, please? Signor Tito, I think. Who has been corresponding with Verdi in recent times? You. How then could you and your father not know about Tornaghi's actions? And, knowing of them, how could you pass them over?' They tried a new approach, with a tearful letter from Tito's wife. Giuseppina's reply was sympathetic but unyielding:

> If Verdi did not think it opportune to see Tito, one could call that an apparent lack of consideration, but on the other hand I ask you yourself, who have such talent and knowledge of the world, how could he come for an interview, having before his eyes those contracts, which I have seen myself, and would rather not have seen, because . . . because they won't

do! The thought of your moral sufferings and those of your family really rends my heart. I wish all this were just a bad dream. But think yourself for a moment of Verdi. How could this man, who for so many years has brought riches and honour to your firm, how could this man, I say, imagine that in the House of Ricordi *irregularities* were being committed, to his detriment, wounding him thus materially and morally? No (I say it again), no one, no one, you understand, here or elsewhere, has wished in malice to influence Verdi against you. Nor is he a man to allow himself to be influenced. In this painful business he has had to surrender to the evidence! . . . I am suffering greatly these days and try every possible way of bringing a little calm to the hearts of us all, but I must tell you that if, by God's will, this great wound is to heal, it will not be by a simple *fiat*, or with a stroke of the pen. I told Giulio and I repeat to you that only after the complete examination of the contracts will Verdi take such measures as he thinks just and reasonable. For the moment I am absolutely unable to say more.

On 7th August she wrote again to Giulio:

I should have replied before this to your letter of the 3rd if I had been able to tell you what I should have liked to be able to tell you. Unfortunately the state of affairs is still the same as it was at the beginning. I have done everything possible to mitigate Verdi's attitude of mind. I have not succeeded and I now despair of succeeding. To every attempt at defence on my part he opposes reasons all too . . . mathematical!! Seeing that my attempts at conciliation are ineffective, I don't wish to seize on, as it were, your thanks in anticipation and your expressions of gratitude, when I am conscious of not having succeeded in doing anything worth while. I promised, loyally and sincerely, to act for you, and I did so. With my heart full of anguish, but with the same loyalty and sincerity, I believe it my duty to warn you that I cannot, at least for the moment, allow myself to touch on this unhappy subject further.

After some months Ricordi agreed to pay Verdi 50,000 lire in compensation. When, much later, Tornaghi wrote to Giuseppina pleading that he should not be excluded from the general amnesty, she had to convey to him Verdi's inexorable reply: 'Matters were settled with the House of Ricordi, as far as business interests were concerned, by means of an indemnity. There has been no reconciliation, in the moral sense of the word, and no one has been excluded. I repeat, a financial settlement was reached. Nothing more.' Tornaghi's relations with Ricordi were not his business.

The great dispute with the publishers in the summer of 1875 shows Giuseppina in her very best form, active in Verdi's affairs as she had not been for years. Her contemporary private correspondence, with its expressions of something like reverence for Verdi's character and genius, its almost ecstatic happiness over his triumphs with the *Requiem*, gives the impression that a great load had been lifted from her heart.

Just at this time there appeared in the *Rivista Indipendente*, of Florence, a scurrilous article on Teresa Stolz and her relations with Verdi. The *Gazzetta d'Italia* had announced, correctly, that the *Requiem*, with the soloists who had taken part in the European tour, would be performed at Florence. The *Rivista Indipendente* at first denied this. Then on 22nd August it stated that the impresario Ducci had attempted to hire the Teatro Pagliano for four concerts, without disclosing his true intention, which was to perform the *Requiem*. Readers were promised shortly a discussion of 'certain intimacies of Signora Stolz, both with Maestro Mariani and now with Verdi, intimacies that have some connection with the present case, and other similar cases'. Scalaberni was impresario of the Teatro Pagliano and it seems that, in view of the part he had played in the fiasco of the collective Requiem for Rossini at Bologna, care had been taken to prevent his putting obstacles in the way of the Requiem for Manzoni at Florence. Verdi had refused him permission to perform the *Requiem* at Florence in the previous year. Now Scalaberni found it was to be performed in his theatre, which he had sublet to Ducci for 'four concerts'. Teresa Stolz describes in a letter to Verdi his affected indifference, amid the excitement of the Florentine public, and calls him 'a truly poisonous insect, hated and avoided by everyone'. Possibly the article in the *Rivista Indipendente* was Scalaberni's revenge. The editors of the paper were Leopoldo Pasquali and Giuseppe Pasini, neither otherwise known to Verdi literature. In the course of the article the *Requiem* is compared, very unfavourably, with the masses of Teodulo Mabellini and Luigi Vecchiotti, but it seems improbable that these composers were responsible for such a virulent personal attack.

The campaign began on 4th September, with the editorial declaration: 'Determined always to conserve the complete independence of our paper, we shall not draw back from the task we have undertaken, but shall tell the truth always, without passion or prejudice, even when the truth is not to everyone's liking.' This is just like one of our less reputable Sunday newspapers of today, introducing its salacious 'exposures' with hypocritical show of concern for the public good. After further protestations of impartiality, the article launches into a malicious and highly inaccurate account of the singer's career:

Teresa Stolz, of German origin, now aged about forty-eight, of proud appearance and bearing, and very homely manners, made her *début* abroad, where she stayed for ten years; the annals of her career are unknown, but they must be inglorious, if she and the press have buried them in absolute oblivion. About 1866 this soprano arrived in Italy and tried to begin a career in our theatres, after having, perhaps, failed abroad. Boasting herself celebrated in interpreting the role of Elvira in *Ernani*, which she called her battle horse, she managed to get herself engaged for the Teatro Comunale at Bologna and, amid expectation worthy of a better result, made her *début* in *Ernani*. But alas! the battle horse turned out a sorry jade, and the celebrated soprano fell headlong from the saddle, in a manner so indecorous that the management of the Teatro Comunale at Ferrara, where la Stolz was to have sung in the following spring, warned by the failure at Bologna, and fearing that the battle horse would this time go lame, protested against her engagement. And behold the proud soprano sheepishly packing her bags to return to Austria, when a propitious star lit up her path, and this star . . . was the never to be sufficiently lamented Maestro Mariani.

He persuaded her to stay, and coached her for the role of Matilde in *William Tell*, with the result that she seemed a different singer and had a great success. They found themselves together again at Bologna for the first performances in Italy of *Don Carlos*:

A vague, indistinct but true rumour announced that it was one of Verdi's minor works and that in Paris it had left few pleasant memories and perhaps been a bit of a fiasco. Fortune willed that the orchestra was directed as usual by the tireless and insuperable Mariani, who, overcoming every difficulty, gave the opera the colour that it lacked and that they had not been able to discover in Paris, and Verdi as composer and la Stolz as singer had a splendid success. And Verdi and la Stolz saw in that conductor a saving Angel, and protested their eternal devotion and undying gratitude. But la Stolz, this tempting Eve, turned too desirous glances towards the composer of *Ernani*, who in a moment of weakness fell at the feet of Cupid of the golden wings and . . . la Stolz and Verdi became ungrateful. As a result of this painful incident a coldness developed in the relations of Mariani and la Stolz, and the latter, a practised courtesan, burned incense before the more splendid star, Maestro Verdi.

The composer allowed himself to be led by the nose by Teresina. 'He has to ask her permission about everything and sometimes cannot fulfil his promises because his *alter ego* intrigues, imposes her will and commands. And Verdi obeys. Poor fame, poor name, how low you have been brought!' She had forbidden Verdi to come to Florence; perhaps she had another lover in the city?

Mariani, deeply affected, complained to his friends, who wrote to la Stolz asking her to write Mariani an affectionate, consoling letter, at least, but she replied that Mariani (her benefactor) mattered little to her, and Verdi (because his purse was full) mattered a lot.

And Mariani sickened and died. Then comes the story of Verdi's wallet, lost and found in Teresa Stolz's room in an hotel at Milan:

Staying there, by accident or design, was Verdi, composer of the *Messa da Requiem*, written for Manzoni, or for whomsoever instructs his heirs to pay for it, and the celebrated (according to him and to her) Teresa Stolz. They were not (see how up to date) staying in the same hotel but that did not prevent Maestro Verdi from going soon to honour with his visit (platonic, we believe) the rotund and appetizing soprano. Signor Verdi was received with all the honours and the duties incumbent in such visits, and a little later the amorous couple stretched themselves out, that is to say, did not stretch themselves out, but accommodated themselves, made themselves comfortable, sat themselves, on a soft sofa. What strange things they did on that sofa, what contests took place, what disputes, why they became so agitated, we don't know, to tell the truth, because we were not in the room and the door was shut. But the fact is that without la Stolz or Verdi, in the heat of the struggle, noticing, a wallet containing 50,000 lire slipped out of Verdi's pocket. . . .

After he returned to his own hotel he became aware of his loss and began to blame the servants. One of the waiters, however, who knew where he had been, went to Teresa Stolz's hotel and asked in Verdi's name for his wallet. It was found, amid general hilarity and to the singer's embarrassment, on the sofa.

Teresa wished to be introduced to Giuseppina, who received her kindly:

But when the good lady became aware that la Stolz, besides showing off Verdi's operas, was showing off her *chignon*, she thought well to leave her in the dust of the boards of the stage. *Inde irae*. And Verdi thus miserably lost his domestic peace, without la Stolz being guilty of anything but of loving too platonically the maestro who had raised her so high. Blindness of la Strepponi, to believe that a soprano would permit herself other than platonic loves!

At Vienna, on the tour of the *Requiem*, Verdi's wife was able to see with her own eyes that his intimacy with the singer had not lessened, and this led to a cooling of relations between the two women.

The *Rivista Indipendente* on 9th November promised further instalments but in fact nothing more appeared. It is remarkable that such things should have been published in the composer's lifetime. Probably most of the popular ideas on his relations with Mariani and Teresa Stolz ultimately derive from this article. A version of the story of the wallet found on the sofa occurs also in a letter from Luigi Illica to Mascagni's wife, the scene being transferred, however, to a hotel at Cremona. Something of the sort probably occurred, though no one can possibly know in what circumstances the wallet fell from Verdi's pocket.

One cannot be sure that Giuseppina knew, at the time, of the appearance of the article. Teresa Stolz certainly did, and she seems to have written to suggest that her visits to Sant' Agata might not be entirely welcome or opportune. On 15th September, eleven days after the publication of the first instalment, Giuseppina replied:

Calm down again if you are angry. Assume that I replied to you at once, as I wished to do, and would have done if opposing currents had not drawn me to right and to left, not permitting me to sit down in peace at my writing-desk. By this time you will be at Florence, where I think it best to address this letter. That you love us I know, or rather we know, we believe it, and are glad to believe it, and we are confident that over you we shall never suffer disillusionment. That we love you you know, you believe it, you are glad to believe it, and you are just as sure as we are. For you, we shall be the same as long as we live. So, my dear Teresa, the fear of *being in the way*, because you saw in me a tinge of sadness, is a fear to set beside that which made you, in dread of disturbing us, go to your room at an early hour with the famous phrase: 'If you'll excuse me I'll retire.' With us you will never be in the way, as long as you and we remain the honest and loyal persons we are. And with that and a kiss I close the paragraph.

This is one of the most convincing of Giuseppina's letters. She is obviously sincere; one does not detect a forced note; what she says takes into account the whole background of rumour and suspicion and magnanimously dismisses it.

From Florence Teresa Stolz's career took her to Trieste in October and then for the whole of the winter to Russia, where she sang in *Aida* and the *Requiem* in Moscow and St Petersburg. Verdi rejected an offer of 6,000 roubles, conveyed in a letter from her, to go himself to conduct four performances of the *Requiem*.

There was an interval of about six months before they all met again, when they went to Paris for the first performances of *Aida* in France and repetitions, for the third year in succession, of the *Requiem*.

Verdi was now sixty-two years old, Giuseppina was sixty and Teresa Stolz was nearly forty-two. Nearly everybody seems to be agreed that, if there ever was a love affair between the composer and the singer, it had by this time faded and given place to a calm and affectionate friendship. In spite of the late date of publication of the scandalous article in the *Rivista Indipendente*, this is certainly the impression given by our own study of Giuseppina's correspondence so far. However, there is a severe shock in store: we turn one more page of her letter-book and find ourselves, in 1876, at the very heart of a tremendous crisis. Before we turn that page, let us read part of some 'Observations by a Philosopher on the heart of Woman, set down by him for the guidance of Men'. These are found, in Giuseppina's hand, among her surviving letters to Verdi:

1 From the age of twenty to thirty, a woman takes courtship and everything else as a joke—no danger, or almost none.
2 From thirty to forty, the affair is more serious: at that critical age a woman is in a dangerous state of mind! She dreams of transgression and is intent on debating the question of the remorse she . . . desires!!

When a woman of that age shows you kindness, she *parades* remorse for what she feels and says she fears transgression. Oh! she is very much disposed to commit it! She has need of a bit of scandal, to draw attention to herself! Let the man keep well clear!

3 There remains the woman of forty to fifty. Oh! Oh! . . . one must act here with extreme prudence! Whether she's beautiful or ugly, and especially if she's ugly, her heart is like an Aeolian harp that throbs and sighs in every wind. A man is lost if he lets become apparent the very faintest amorous aspiration! With women of this age one must limit oneself to speaking of love in general terms—don't risk a glance or a sigh. . . .

Did she copy these things from a book? Or did she invent them herself? It hardly matters; it seems certain that she sent them to Verdi by way of warning, in a moment of jealous anxiety. But there came a time when she spoke out more clearly.

Turning the pages of the last of her letter-books, which is much larger and, generally speaking, less interesting than the others, after an entry of 21st April 1876, followed by a blank page, one finds oneself staring dumbfoundedly, almost unbelievingly, at this:

'It didn't seem to me a fitting day for you to pay a call on a lady who is neither your daughter, nor your sister, nor your wife!' The observation escaped me and I perceived at once that V. was annoyed.

It seems to be the beginning of a diary note, such as those already quoted, but is changed then into the draft of a letter, undoubtedly addressed to Verdi. 'V.' becomes 'you'. Owing to alterations, cancellations and alternative passages, it is very difficult indeed to present a definitive text of the draft, and no one will ever know the precise form of the letter as sent, or as left for Verdi to read. This is as close a reproduction as is possible in print of this vital page from the letter-book:

'It didn't seem to me a fitting day for you to pay a call on a lady who is neither your daughter, nor your sister, nor your wife!' The observation escaped me and I perceived at once that you were annoyed. It's quite natural, this ill humour of yours hurt me, for, as she's not ill and there's no performance, it seemed to me you could spend twenty-four hours without seeing the said lady, all the more since I had taken the trouble, so as not to fail in attention towards her, of asking her personally how she was; I told you as soon as I reached home again.

I don't know if there's anything in it, or not . . . I do know that since 1872 there have been [*added and erased:* febrile] periods of assiduity and attentions on your part that no woman could interpret in a more favourable sense. [*Erased:* I know that I have never failed to show cordiality and courtesy to this person.] I know that I have always been disposed to love her frankly and sincerely.

You know how you have repaid me! [*Erased:* There is no biting word . . .]

With harsh, violent, biting words! You can't control yourself. [*Partly erased:* But then I open my heart to the hope that you will see this person and things as they are.]

If there's anything in it . . . Let's get this over. [*Erased:* If you find this person so seductive] Be frank and say so, without making me suffer the humiliation of this excessive deference of yours.

If there's nothing in it . . . Be more calm in your attentions, [*added and erased:* don't display such agitation], be natural and less exclusive. Think sometimes that I, your wife, despising past rumours, am living at this very moment *à trois*, and that I have the right to ask, if not for your caresses, at least for your consideration. Is that too much?

How calm and gay I was the first twenty days! And that was because you were cordial. . . .

Luzio saw this entry when he was working on the letter-books and, in his old-maidish way, hastily covered it over with a thick blanket. In the *Carteggi verdiani* [1] he says: 'From some few indications in the letter-books it is evident that her frank and virile character was not such as to resign itself to indecorous transactions. Having ascertained by a frank *aut aut* that she could continue tranquilly to "despise past rumours", she set aside all suspicion and in the spring of 1876 travelled happily to Paris with la Stolz and la Waldmann to restore the fortunes of the Théâtre Italien with *Aida*.' This can only be described as another deliberate falsification of history. The episode actually took place in an hotel in Paris, some time in the second half of April, and the letter quoted is only the first of several that survive to document this great domestic crisis of 1876. For Giuseppina it was a year of the most bitter unhappiness.

The letter to Verdi explains a great deal. It sets in proper perspective the expressions of affection in her letters to Teresa Stolz and the brave invitations to Sant' Agata on which so much of the case for the defence has been built up. It provides a date, 1872, for the beginning of Verdi's attentions to the singer, which is perfectly consistent with everything we have learned from other sources, and especially from Mariani's letters to Del Signore and Landoni. The visit paid to her hotel in Paris, which led to Giuseppina's protest, shows the sort of thing that had given rise at Milan (or Cremona, according to Illica) to the malicious gossip retailed in the *Rivista Independente*.

I was once discussing this subject with some Italian friends and described this entry in Giuseppina's letter-book. I was asked with a smile: 'And are you still doubtful?' My reply was that, though tormented with anxiety, *after four years*, Verdi's own wife was still doubtful. This is a point that deserves the most serious consideration. She could accuse him of nothing but 'febrile periods of assiduity and attentions'.

[1] II, p. 46.

Now she wished to know the truth. What did Verdi reply? Nobody knows. My own guess would be that he admitted nothing, but blustered and overwhelmed Giuseppina, once more, with 'harsh, violent, biting words'. It seems to me now beyond all doubt that he was in love with Teresa Stolz. But to fall in love is no crime; everything depends on how one behaves in that predicament. How did Verdi behave? Brutally to his wife, certainly, but did he actually have a love affair with the singer? Was she his mistress? We do not know. If she was, then in view of what she wrote in her letters to Verdi and Giuseppina both before and after this year of crisis, Teresa Stolz must have been about the biggest hypocrite that ever lived. Reading these letters over again, it is extraordinarily difficult to believe it.

The only writer who has actually seen Verdi's surviving letters to Teresa Stolz is Giovanni Cenzato;[1] no one knows where they are now. In 1932, when Cenzato examined them, there were sixty letters, but this total includes many from Giuseppina. All the most interesting things he quotes are Giuseppina's, known to us also from her letter-books. What remain of Verdi's letters seem to be mostly unimportant, sometimes rather enigmatic notes:

> Content! Happy, most happy! I'll write on Monday and tell you many, many things. Farewell, farewell, and always farewell!
>
> O joy! What joy! I receive the letter which drives away the black mood that for forty-eight hours has oppressed me.

He uses the second person plural ('voi') except in one very late note, after Giuseppina's death, which employs the second person singular ('tu'); but two days later he reverts to the less intimate form. Teresa Stolz consistently uses, right up to the end, the more formal third person singular ('Lei'). It has been remarked that Verdi's notes resemble those, equally enigmatic, that he wrote to society ladies at Milan, in very early years.

If one seeks in the rest of his correspondence for echoes of the domestic drama revealed to us by Giuseppina's letter-books one finds nothing at all. He continues to instruct Corticelli on every detail of his duties; he comments pessimistically on political developments; he invites people to visit Sant' Agata; he sends calm, affectionate letters to his old friends. Was there ever another man who so carefully covered his tracks?

[1] Zoppi remarks (p. 12) that Luzio seems to have known Verdi's and Giuseppina's letters to Teresa Stolz only from a résumé given by Cenzato in the *Corriere della Sera* of 30th October 1932. He adds: 'Fortunately we have more than a 'résumé'. Cenzato was reviewing in that paper an *opuscolo* published at Milan, edited by Prof. Melchiorre Rinino, in which, by permission of Prof. Rienzi Ricci Stolz, great-nephew of the incomparable interpretress of *Aida*, were gathered about sixty most interesting, most significant epistolary documents.' This is just bluff, and based on a misreading of the article. Zoppi himself quotes nothing that is not quoted by Cenzato, who has personally informed me that he was *not* reviewing a published *opuscolo*, but working from the originals. Zoppi misled Gatti (*Revisioni e rivalutazioni verdiane*, Turin, 1952, p. 95) into a false statement about this non-existent *opuscolo*.

It is only from Giuseppina's correspondence that one can discover, or divine, what was happening. Back at Sant' Agata, she wrote on 15th July to Giuditta Ricordi, Giulio's wife: 'In Paris I had nothing much to do, but though apparently in a bed of roses, I was pricked by many thorns and disturbed in the quiet that is so dear to me. But we won't talk of that either.' She was alone at the time. 'Nor do I know when Verdi will come to Milan. He is quick to make up his mind and to catch the train. But as for myself, I think it will be a long time before I see again the *Patria Meneghina*.' One week before this Clarina Maffei had written to Verdi:[1] 'I have seen la Stolz several times and she seems absolutely determined to leave the theatre and, I'm glad to say, settle at Milan.' Clarina was one friend who thought no evil, but one must remark that it was absolutely contrary to Verdi's normal habits to make flying visits to Milan, on the spur of the moment, as he evidently had been doing.

Next, a letter from Giuseppina to Teresa Stolz herself, addressed to Tabiano, the watering place in the hills on the other side of Parma, on 8th August:

I am sorry, but it's impossible for me to come to Tabiano this year. Without seeking other reasons, there are the two following ones, which you will easily understand: *It's too early—It's too late.* Too early because, since the baths are still crowded, besides being ill lodged, one would have to bother about one's *toilette*, and I really don't feel disposed to put up with that frivolous tyranny. Too late because Maria, who is not at Sant' Agata, has to take her final examinations about the 20th or 25th of August and I shall have to stay some days at Turin, both to attend some of the examinations and to complete the formalities imposed by such an occasion. For the rest, even if I did burden myself with the antipathetic task of packing and making my *toilette*, there would be only a few days left to take the cure, so that I renounce Tabiano, definitely. Bathe and enjoy yourself, for one only lives once, to be sure. Barberina is still not very well, not to say worse than usual. She sends her kind regards and returns your kiss. Corticelli, too, is not always in the best of health, and seems to me to have aged a lot; perhaps that's why he's not getting on very well with his new tasks. You have no need of news of Verdi, because he gives it to you himself. I still have my pains in the knees and my liverish spots, which will pass away, if they do pass away, even without bathing. For the rest, good or bad health matters little to me.

This is not a cheerful letter, and becomes a good deal less so when one adds at the end what she wrote in the draft and then cancelled: 'and I would like to have made my peace with God, so as to go to rest and take a cure in another world'. Poor Giuseppina! 'You have no need of news of Verdi, because he gives it to you himself.' Did that mean only that he was writing separately? Or was he visiting the singer at Tabiano?

[1] *Carteggi verdiani*, II, p. 298.

In the event Giuseppina and Maria did go to Tabiano for a time and Verdi fetched them back to Sant' Agata on 4th September. And with them came Teresa Stolz. A letter from Verdi to Maria Waldmann on 22nd September said: 'I passed on your message to Signora Stolz, who has been here for about a fortnight; I don't know how much longer she will be staying.' Giuseppina had therefore to play the hostess for several weeks to the woman she had objected to Verdi visiting daily in Paris.

In October (the precise date is not given in the letter-book) she sat down, probably in her sister Barberina's house at Cremona, to draft another letter to Verdi. It began:

> Since fate has willed that that which was my whole happiness in this life [*cancelled:* and embellished it with eternal youth] should now be irreparably lost, there may serve to alleviate the sufferings of my spirit the good that, through my suggestion and your natural generosity, you can do and will do, I am sure, especially to those who are your blood relations and bear, or bore, your name.

The rest is difficult to decipher fully from the draft, but the sense is clear. A former friend, probably Du Locle, through whom Verdi had lost a considerable sum of money, had offered to repay him, in whole or in part, or had suggested ways and means whereby the money might be recovered. Giuseppina wished part of the interest on this money to be given to the heads of six poor families in the vicinity. The details of these charitable dispensations, however, are unimportant. But look again at that opening sentence: 'Since fate has willed that that which was my whole happiness in this life should now be irreparably lost . . .' These are terrible words.

This seems the best place to mention a few scraps of information given to me personally, by different people and at wide intervals of time. Shortly after the war, on my first visit to Sant' Agata, long before I ever thought I should become so deeply involved in the problems of Verdian biography, I was being shown over the house and garden by a servant who, with no prompting on my part, volunteered the statement that 'the old gardener used to say that la Stolz once came to Sant' Agata and stayed two months, and la Strepponi went away—she was jealous'. The 'old gardener' would be Basilio Pizzola, who was left 3,000 lire in Verdi's will, in recognition of his many years' service at Sant' Agata. He died in 1951, aged over ninety, and could have been already employed there in 1876. Or he could have been told things by others, perhaps not quite accurately—'two months' may be an exaggeration. This story links up most curiously with something I learned ten years later. A person of undoubted integrity told me that Giulio Ricordi had told him personally that there was a time when Giuseppina said to Verdi:

'Either this woman leaves the house, or I leave it' and received the reply: 'This woman stays, or I blow my brains out.' Some people, no doubt, will dismiss this as a piece of ridiculous melodrama. I am not prepared to do that myself, since my informant, a universally respected scholar, had it directly from Ricordi, and since a passage in the letter from Illica to Mascagni's wife, already referred to, goes some way towards corroborating it. Lina Mascagni's jealousy had been aroused by some escapade of her husband and Illica was intent on persuading her not to make scenes about it. In a similar situation, he said: 'La Strepponi, so good and so much in love, led Giuseppe Verdi to the verge of suicide! Campanari is alive and can confirm it!' Life sometimes *is* ridiculously melodramatic, and the documents published in this chapter must surely persuade everybody that a tense and dangerous situation existed at Sant' Agata in the early autumn of 1876. Is this what lies behind Verdi's impassive statements, to Maria Waldmann on 22nd September: 'Signora Stolz . . . has been here for about a fortnight; I don't know how much longer she will be staying,' and to Clarina Maffei on 18th October: 'Peppina has been at Cremona for a few days'? If she did walk out of the house, the most natural thing for her to do would have been to go to her sister at Cremona.

Teresa Stolz meanwhile had gone again to Russia. 'A hundred and forty thousand francs in gold, with little exertion, *amour-propre* satisfied, etc.,' Verdi told Clarina. 'She couldn't refuse.' Nevertheless it seems likely that the singer, whose retirement had already been announced in the *Gazzetta Musicale* on 2nd July, changed her mind and accepted an engagement she had previously rejected because it enabled her to escape from an impossible position. She did well to take herself off to Russia for six months.

On 18th October Giuseppina wrote to her at St Petersburg:

> I hope you may never have to struggle with the sorrows of life, and especially the disillusions and sorrows of the heart.

And again on 16th December:

> Here is Christmas. The Man-God appears to redeem humanity and to teach by his example the greatest of virtues: that of not only forgiving offences, but also of loving the offender.

This is almost superhuman. Only a truly extraordinary woman could, in such circumstances, have written such words. Giuseppina was remarkably clever at inserting in her letters veiled allusions, little hints and warnings that said nothing very much but implied a great deal. This is the nearest she ever came to suggesting that there *was* an offence to be forgiven. But the same letter contains also these words: 'I wish you all that you yourself desire, certain that you will desire only things that are honest, good and worthy of you.' This sentence, in Cenzato's quotation from the letter, follows directly after the other; in the letter-book it is separated from it by a long, rambling passage about the joys of Christmas and the memories of childhood it evoked. Did she cancel all this in rewriting the letter, or did Cenzato pick out these sentences and silently omit the rest? I cannot feel sure.

There are numerous uncopied letters recorded at this time and among them the following:

21st December: 'Wrote to Filippo P[agliai]. Send 50 francs' [in English].
29th December: 'To Montebruno.'
17th January: 'Wrote to la Stolz.'
20th January: 'Wrote to la Ravina.'
20th March: 'Wrote to Giovannina Strepponi, and send the hundred' [the last four words in English].
20th March: 'Stolz.'

Charity, in every sense of the word, Giuseppina possessed.

The surviving letters to her friend Nina Ravina, when they become available, may tell us much more about the relations between Verdi and Teresa Stolz. Or they may do no more than amplify our documentation of Giuseppina's anguished doubts. The owner of these letters told me that in them she relieves her feelings; he quoted one sentence: 'I can't stand it any longer!' Everything, however, depends on the dates, and precisely what she said.

After Giuseppina's death the newspaper *La Fanfulla*, drawing information from the letters to Lanari, recalled her suicidal tendencies at the time of her early misfortunes.[1] This drew a reply from an anonymous writer in *Il Cittadino di Lodi* who quoted two brief passages from letters to Don Montebruno (genuine ones, not the forgeries of Lorenzo Alpino). In a letter of 1877 she said: 'I thank God a thousand times that I went, though with trepidation, to such a Father.' This sentence, surviving almost by a miracle, is of extraordinary interest in the light of what we now know about the events of 1876. It indicates, surely, that after the removal to Genoa for the winter she had taken her troubles to Don Montebruno. His influence was behind the eminently Christian sentiments of the marvellous Christmas letter to Teresa Stolz at St Petersburg. It may be that it was only at this time that she entered into personal relations with Don Montebruno,[2] who became her confessor and led her back to orthodox Catholic beliefs. His spiritual support was of immense value in the latter part of her life. The other quotation in *Il Cittadino di*

[1] 'La Moglie del M. Verdi,' 27th November 1897.
[2] I found in the letter-books only one entry concerning Montebruno between 27th February 1872, when she had not yet met him, and 29th December 1876. This entry, of 29th March 1875, says only: 'Montebruno hundred.'

Lodi, from a letter of three years later, says: 'I believe in God, I believe in and adore Jesus Christ, and the reading of the Gospels moves me always. . . . I am not worth much, but I have wished to become better. . . . Recommend me to God.'

What happened next? There was a gradual relaxation of tension, and return to normal conditions in Verdi's household. Time, absence, advancing age and, one hopes, reason played their parts in restoring calm, after this year of agitation. It seems to have been tacitly accepted by everyone concerned that a period of less close relations was necessary. Teresa Stolz had made this possible by her withdrawal to Russia for six months. She did not reply to Giuseppina's Christmas letter. On her return to Milan in March 1877 she publicly announced her retirement from the stage. Unwell and not very happy, she was touched to receive another letter from Giuseppina and correspondence was resumed. 'My dearest Peppina,' she wrote on 19th March, 'God keep you always in perfect health, happy and beloved by your friends, among whom I flatter myself I too have a tiny place. . . . Accept an affectionate kiss from your poor Teresa, who loves you very much and begs you to love her a little in return.' Can anyone believe this was hypocrisy? And on 22nd March, with reference to the common name-day: 'You know, dear Peppina, that I very much wished to pay you a visit and bring in person all my good wishes for Saints Giuseppe and Giuseppina, but after having thought it over I decided not to give you one of those surprises that too often turn out importunate!' And again on 3rd May, to Verdi: 'It's not a century since you wrote to me, nor is it two centuries since I wrote to you. If I do not reply at once, it's only for fear of being importunate.' It seems evident that she was doing her best to avoid causing further trouble. Verdi was to conduct the *Requiem* at Cologne later in this month and she suggested that if they were passing through Milan they should meet and dine together at her house. 'Dear Peppina, what do you think of my idea, expressed in my letter to the Maestro? I don't dare insist, but if you decided to come to Milan for twenty-four hours I assure you it would really make me happy.' They did pass through Milan, as a letter to Clarina Maffei shows, and they probably saw each other again, briefly, after an interval of nearly eight months. A much longer interval followed, during which they did not meet, nor, it seems, very often correspond. On 7th March 1878 Teresa wrote that she had not had any direct news from Verdi for 'a century'. On 18th March she wrote again, for the name-day:

I am not a woman of empty phrases and compliments, so that I express myself badly, but I would like to find words eloquent enough to express all the affection I feel for you both. You are for me persons absolutely to be revered; every word of yours is to me an oracle, so you can imagine all my good wishes for your happiness.

In May she sang in public again, in performances of the *Requiem* at Bologna, under Faccio.

Verdi wrote to Clarina Maffei on 18th June:

Let me know what our distinguished friend Signora Teresa is doing. It's a century since I heard anything of her. Since the Mass at Bologna I haven't received a word from her! I can quite understand how, living in a great city, in fine apartments, paying and receiving calls, going to theatres and concerts, as I often read in the papers, she doesn't think any more about the old Maestro. (La Waldmann, though, writes to me fairly often.) Give her my regards and abuse her a bit too, and if she pulls a face take no notice: it means to say she knows she's in the wrong. It could be, however, that I am in the wrong, and haven't replied to her last letter. Alas! arguing on those lines I am lost!

This produced a reply from Teresa on 27th June: 'Dear Maestro, your kind reproach gave me great pleasure. I have not forgotten you and never shall forget you, as long as I live. I abstained from writing only from fear of being a nuisance'. In the next month she declined an invitation to Sant' Agata, being confined to bed with a heavy cold, and suggested the visit should be put off until the autumn, perhaps, after she had been to see her relatives in Bohemia.

Giuseppina on 11th August had good news to convey:

Maria is going to marry the son of our friend the lawyer, Dr Angiolo Carrara. He's a young man of about twenty-seven, without the brilliant qualities that allure at first sight, but of upright mind, severe honesty, and with a very good heart. He, like his father, his uncles, like all that family, will make an excellent companion to the wife of his choice, and his affection will certainly be returned by Maria who, as you know, has a heart of gold. Maria, for her part, is glad to lean on the arm of this honourable man, and to enter a family who await her with open arms, and to be able to look forward without trepidation to the serene and calm life she will pass with her life-companion. She will not have, certainly, the alluring and dangerous joys of dances and balls, of vain display and vanity satisfied of the great city world, but in compensation will have the peace of the heart, the chaste and blessed joys of wife and mother, joys undisturbed by tempestuous passions, happy in her modest position with the affection and the esteem with which she will be surrounded always. Verdi is very pleased with this event and we all most sincerely wish for the happiness of this young couple, who soon will be indissolubly united before God and before men. Add your own good wishes to ours, keep well, retain a bit of affection for your old friends, and we'll see you again after your trip to Bohemia.

To Don Montebruno on 5th September she wrote:

Allow me to thank you for your letters, which Maria and I read with profound emotion. I read too, and made her read, your beautiful printed letter. How just and true! What knowledge of the human heart, of the realities of life and the necessity of higher aspirations! For God made us with souls and bodies, and if the soul, by God's grace, raises us up to pure and holy aspirations, the body remains in contact with the earth and is subject to its imperious claims, its inevitable and sometimes invincible weaknesses. Always, and especially at certain solemn moments of life, the mission of God's ministers should be to point out and illuminate, by wise and charitable advice, the road to be taken in order to reach the end ordained by Divine Providence, and to act so that the gates are opened of our Eternal Home, where the sorrows and the struggles of life cease for ever!

On her sixty-third birthday, three days later, she gave Verdi an inscribed photograph: 'To my Verdi, with my former affection and veneration! Peppina.' Gatti, in his second edition,[1] remarks of this: 'Why with her "former" and not her "constant" affection? One should remember that la Strepponi was a woman of the subtlest intelligence and of singular acumen in expressing herself.' One can only agree. But another comment, in Gatti's first edition,[2] is also worth recalling: 'Veneration, after decades of married life!'

Teresa Stolz came again to Sant' Agata, after two years, in a calmer atmosphere. She did not stay for the wedding, which is charmingly described by Giuseppina in a letter of 18th October to Daniele Morchio at Genoa:

Maria, who for some time had the honour of being your pupil, last Thursday gave her hand in marriage to Alberto Carrara. When I saw her walk to the altar, in her white bridal veil, shyly leaning on Verdi's arm, I was profoundly moved and she seemed to me a true symbol of virginity, with a beauty *wholly chaste and innocent, full of modesty and virginal grace.* The religious part of this touching ceremony took place in our new oratory, where at the same time the first Mass was celebrated. Our old friend Canon Avanzi, who knew Maria as a child and who was always her confessor and thus able to follow her spiritual and intellectual development up to this moment, gave the Nuptial Benediction, in the presence of a restricted number of near relations. Afterwards he read a short discourse fitted to the occasion, full of elevation and tenderness. When he came to the last sentences that venerable old man could not restrain his tears and we all surrounded him, weeping together and blessing him, and blessing a thousand times the bridal pair, who left on their honeymoon amid the tears of relations and the smile of the first kiss.

Two passages from letters to Teresa Stolz:

26th December 1878:

Thank you for remembering me always and for the good wishes you send for the future. Although, as you know, I am *sceptical,* and completely

[1] p. 635. [2] II, pp. 447–8.

distrustful of the world, yet I ought to believe, and I do believe, your protestations; for truly, truly, [*erased:* if I have not been able to do you any good; *also erased:* if I have never done you any harm] you would have no reason at all not to wish me well, sincerely and cordially. For my part, I wish you every good thing, material and moral, that an honest person can desire, not only for 1879, but for many years to come.

20th March 1879:

If you say 'I hope you live long and happily' I believe you say it for us both. If that were not the case, you would not be what you are, a fine woman and a loyal friend.

Maria Waldmann and Teresa Stolz made their last public appearances in a performance of the *Requiem* at La Scala, for the benefit of flood victims, conducted by Verdi on 30th June 1879.

Verdi and Giuseppina were in Paris again in February and March of the following year, for the first performances of *Aida* in French. Teresa Stolz joined them there. She afterwards wrote: 'What am I to say to you, my dear friends, about the delicious month I spent in your dear company in Paris? I ask your pardon for having perhaps too much abused your cordiality; my presence was perhaps sometimes inopportune; the pleasure of being with you made me exceed the limits, did it not? Well then, when you come here you can thoroughly abuse me, and I'll love you (if that's possible) even more.'

Giuseppina, writing to her sister Barberina of Verdi's renewed triumphs in Paris, had described herself as being 'moved to the point of being ill from it'. A month later, on 21st April, she wrote a most beautiful letter to Verdi, like something from twenty or more years earlier:

MY DEAREST VERDI,

I am writing a few lines to accompany a note from Perosio and a telegram from Rome that, in parenthesis, cost over five francs!

These posthumous enthusiasms for *Aida* and the Mass must lead you to strange reflections on human nature and at the same time to exclamations of 'Enough! Enough!' Such is the world! And yet, not only are you the same man of genius as six months ago, but you are what you appeared to me at the time of *Nabucco* and the old artistic struggles. The difference lies in this: then, good glasses were needed to see the star that was rising in the sky; now, that star illuminates wherever it shines—they all want to be lit up by it in order to be seen, and everyone would like to catch more light than the others, in order to attract more attention, and so that he can say: 'I am the first!' Vanity of vanities, all is vanity!

You can call me what you like, but I am a bit different from the common crowd. One must take off one's sandals before entering the tabernacle and must contemplate the Highest prostrate on the ground! To shout out hosannas at the top of one's voice is a profanation and deprives the deepest feelings of that mystic tint that transports us to the infinite. But perhaps I am wrong, and that is a mistake to be added to my many mistakes concerning God and his creatures! So let's allow the scale of ovations to mount up to heaven, as long as you take me with you. You will see that I shall not disturb you, but only tell you, *sotto voce*, how much I love and esteem you, when the others are silent . . . in order to get their breath back and blow their noses! God! . . . *et des petits pois*, as poor Maggioni would say if he were alive!

I got up less tired than yesterday and absolutely without any desire to speak a word. I am however content that, apart from the donkeys which are braying at this moment, today at least no one will come to disturb the profound quiet of this Wednesday, 21st April. If the weather is fine I shall occupy myself tomorrow with the furs and winter clothes that have to be put in pepper and camphor. . . .

Don't work too hard, my dear Pasticcio, and consider how, however little is left, it will always be too much for the merits of the heirs! In your art, in the matter of glory (except for an *opéra comique*) you can rise no higher. Try then to arrange things so that you live as long as Methuselah (966 years), if only to give pleasure to those who love you, in despite of the French composers, not excluding the best! If Fetid, i.e. Fétis, were still alive, he would die of jaundice, seeing the colour of things today!

Now I salute you, I kiss and embrace you. I wish you a good appetite and hope to see you arrive soon, very soon, because I still love you with a crazy affection and sometimes when I am in a bad mood it's a sort of *loving fever*, unknown to the doctors, Todeschini included!

What stupid things I have written! I'll be seeing you soon then.

PEPPINA.

The draft of another, very different, letter to Verdi is found on a loose sheet inserted in Giuseppina's letter-book. It is briefly mentioned by Luzio,[1] and published almost in full by Abbiati.[2] Both these writers attribute it to the end of 1875, a date corresponding to the point at which it is found in the letter-book, but, as its content shows, it is certainly later than this. It was written at Genoa, after Verdi had left on one of his trips to Sant' Agata:

I'm glad to hear, and not surprised, that your indisposition cleared up as soon as you were past the mountains. You will perhaps remember that I have pointed out several times recently the necessity of a talk between us on certain matters which concern us both, and which it would be well to settle without delay, since time for us is getting short. The opportunity presents itself and I seize it, since quiet permits me to write a letter instead of talking.

It is certain that the climate of Genoa doesn't suit you. The coal smoke that, with the new commercial developments, now reaches us, has worsened, so to speak, the atmospheric conditions of this locality and made a move, sooner or later, almost inevitable. It is true that you haven't moved a step

[1] *Carteggi*, II, p. 45.

[2] III, pp. 783–4.

to get to know it, but instinctively you don't like Genoese society. So we shall have the bother of a removal, we shall be forced to move away from the sea, light and air, without any compensation from society for these sacrifices. Now listen carefully, my Verdi, hear me out with a little patience, and believe that what I am going to say is the result of long reflection, and set forth in all sincerity. You love Milan and its climate is not harmful to you. You like its society, you have in that city your old friends, memories of your first successes and, to use a modern term, there is at Milan the *milieu* suited to an artist. I suggest we go to Milan. The climate cannot harm me, since it's almost my native climate. You will be able to have, at least in the evenings, a bit of company and, should there be none, will be able to go to the theatre or a café, to pass an agreeable hour or so. As you know, I have no need of society, but only of one or two good people, now and then, with whom to exchange a few words. I ask only for an apartment with light and air, and that you don't abandon me completely in these last years of life. By that I mean: don't be always out of the house.

In the level streets of that city I shall be able to walk more, to pay a few calls and shall have occasion to spend a little money, on myself even, which at Genoa I never have either occasion or wish to do. If this project suits you we'll come to agreement together about the apartment, etc. If it doesn't suit you, then I propose another arrangement. With the addition of the two rooms at Sant' Agata we shall be able to put there the best of our furniture now at Genoa. We'll sell what we can of the inferior stuff and if we can't sell it profitably we'll distribute it among relatives, who are all in need and will be glad to have a better bed, table or chair. With just the one house we shall be able to spend the winter at Milan, Rome, Naples or any other town that attracts us, without cares and responsibilities. Think it over and choose. But it's a continual vexation to me to stay at Genoa, and of no benefit to you, physically or morally.

It is difficult to decide precisely when this was written. Other resigned references to the brief space of time remaining to her are found in letters of 1876, when she actually had another twenty-one years to live. Her troubles with her knees, which made walking difficult, are also mentioned in that year. The pollution of the atmosphere by coal smoke must refer to conditions at Palazzo Doria, where they lived after Palazzo Sauli was given up in the autumn of 1874. Palazzo Doria is near the docks. They moved from the top floor to the first floor, to a magnificent suite of rooms opening on to the terrace with the clock-tower, in 1877. The above letter was clearly written after they had been living for some considerable time in Palazzo Doria. The addition of two rooms at Sant' Agata is mentioned, and this probably refers to the results of rebuilding that took place in 1878 and 1879. It seems likely that the letter was written about 1880, not long after the alterations at Sant' Agata, and while some of Verdi's old friends at Milan (Clarina Maffei, Tenca, Carcano, Tito Ricordi) were still living.

Nothing came of Giuseppina's suggestion. The pattern of the rest of their lives was now set—Sant' Agata for the greater part of the year, Genoa for the winter, with occasional visits to Milan and, in the early summer, to Montecatini to take the waters. Relations with Teresa Stolz continued unchanged; she was a regular visitor on birthdays and name-days, and nearly always at Genoa for the new year. She often accompanied them to Montecatini.

Verdi's creative life seemed to be over. If it had closed with *Aida* and the *Requiem* it would still have been a great life. His triumphs, however, had not brought him happiness. His letters of this period breathe despondency and pessimism. The realities of Italian unity seemed the mockery of his old dreams; in artistic spheres the young were turning towards ideals that were not his, and acute resentment and indignation burned within him at what he considered the surrender of Italy's musical heritage to the Germans.

A leading figure among the younger writers and composers in this movement to widen the basis of Italian musical culture was Arrigo Boito. Without him, Verdi's last great Shakespearian operas would never have been written. But before their wonderful late friendship and collaboration could take root and flourish, before Verdi himself, as it were, could be enlisted in the ranks of the progressive party and Boito's ideals find their fulfilment through the older man's tremendous creative genius, tenaciously held erroneous ideas and intense suspicion had to be overcome, and years that must have seemed endless to those, like Faccio and Giulio Ricordi, who watched and hoped, had to pass by.

As one studies the documents from the dark period following *Aida* and the *Requiem*, one feels the absolute *necessity* of Boito's advent, by which Verdi's art and life moved on to a higher plane. The story of the relations of these two men is a magnificent subject in itself. Before we turn to it, in our last chapter, we must look again at Giuseppina's correspondence, in its sad late phase.

Verdi's greatest achievements were still in the future, but Giuseppina was growing old before her time. When there was company she could still seem gay, as the reminiscences of Edmondo De Amicis show. Too often, when she was alone with Verdi, silence descended on the house. She had suffered further disillusionment towards the end of 1879, when it was found that Corticelli, her old friend and former ally against Mariani, had been misusing the savings of the cook and another person of the *entourage* at Sant' Agata, with whom he had apparently been having a love affair. This 'Maddalena', mentioned in some of Verdi's letters to Piroli, may have been another servant, or may have been Barezzi's widow. Corticelli was dismissed, and six months later tried to drown himself in the canal at Milan. When she read about this in the paper Giuseppina at once wrote to Teresa Stolz:

In view of the catastrophe, which could end in the death of that unfortunate man, any comment or recrimination would be out of place. Compassion is all one can feel in such grave circumstances, and it is compassion that impels me to ask you to go to him in my name.

I don't know of anybody at Milan who is intimate with Corticelli except, I think, Signor Brosovich, whom I don't know but you know personally. Send for him in that case and ask him to go to Mauro in my name and ask if I can do anything for him, and what, for I'll do it to the limit of my resources. Let him reply without reticence.

Maria Carrara Verdi was a mother before she was twenty, and soon found herself again pregnant. She seems to have lamented the passing of her youth. Giuseppina comforted her: 'Let life go by for you as it does for us all; it's the destiny of all who are born and no one can escape it. What matters is to be able to repair, as you can so far, to your woman's heart as to a blessed and chaste sanctuary! That has been my constant thought, my ardent desire, ever since I agreed to direct your education. It would not have been difficult, perhaps, to settle you in a richer family, to give you a more brilliant position. Impossible, however, to assign you to a more affectionate and honest man, or to a better family, for kindness of heart and rectitude of feelings. Verdi and I are happy to see you where you are and hope that we shall be so until the last days of our lives.' In Marietta Calvi Carrara, Maria's husband's stepmother, the third wife of Angiolo Carrara, Giuseppina had found a friend. To her are addressed some of the most intimate late letters: 'It's so rare to be able to rest secure in the friendship of anyone that I, a jester sometimes but always at bottom full of melancholy and suspicion, feel a blessed warmth in my heart and my blood that makes me young again, makes me love life and thank God for having given it to me!' Again: 'Natures like yours and mine have moments of, I should say, almost excessive energy and merriment, succeeded by other moments of depression, or moral sadness, of the need for solitude and silence. Sometimes one seeks the reason of these apparent oddities; one prays then to God to give strength to the oppressed spirit, or one institutes a dialogue between the two personalities that exist in every human creature, and if that creature is of good faith and reasonable, little by little one feels calm return in the struggles of the heart and light in the obscurity of the spirit; the veil is rent, one breathes freely again, the crisis is over!'

Verdi's comments on Wagner's death are well known. Giuseppina's are interesting too. They occur in a letter to Vigna of 3rd March 1883. She began: 'Verdi, who is in the country at the moment, never knew or even saw Wagner. This great individuality, now departed, if he had had to be shut up in a lunatic asylum, would not have been so . . .' She broke off and started again: 'This great individuality, now departed, was never afflicted with the little itch of vanity, but devoured by an incandescent, measureless pride, like Satan or Lucifer, the most beautiful of fallen angels!' The following passage is cancelled in the letter-book: 'Alas! for great and small a few feet of earth suffice, to shut him up for ever and give him that peace which, I think, he never enjoyed, even when he was glorified by kings, by his country, and overwhelmed with riches.'

Three last quotations:

To Canon Avanzi, April 1884:

In truth, with the retired life I lead, my letters would be small resource in your solitude. No news, except what you can read in the papers. Changes of ministers; the good faith of the few; the bad faith of the many, who hymn in every tone of voice the patriotism they do not feel. In almost all a hypocrisy, a dishonesty, a growing corruption, which threatens to inundate, like a torrent in flood, the little of good, of the elect, that still remains to humanity.

I live in solitude and, returning in thought to early years, I wish I had lived always in that time, on account both of the sentence I pass on myself and of that I pass on the world, which I know *all too well*! To cancel out the past is not given even to the Almighty—who, however, assuredly can see that the future is better! That is what all must do and desire who know and seek to nourish themselves on the Gospel. God's mercy on us; our mercy on all others! . . . I'll stop, for, in spite of a splendid day, and the immense sea, which on the horizon seems to unite itself smilingly to the heavens in a divine kiss, my heart is sad and my mind full of gloomy thoughts.

To the same, 5th February 1886:

Alas! I have nothing new or agreeable to tell you. I've been indoors all the time but haven't been able, even, to receive the very few people who come sometimes to see us. La Stolz was here the last few days, full of health and merriment. She left yesterday for Milan, where she will certainly not dedicate herself to meditation on the miseries of humanity, or the world to come! If she attains happiness in that way, God preserve it for her for another hundred years!

To Teresa Stolz, 24th December 1886:

Verdi is well, and it is with joy full of tenderness that I say it!

CHAPTER

9

Boito and Verdi

WE HAVE to look back to 1862 to trace the beginnings of a relationship that was to reach its glorious culmination in the creation of *Otello* and *Falstaff*. Early in that year Verdi, after his first visit to Russia, was staying in Paris, thinking over his plans for the work commissioned from him, as the representative of Italy, for the opening of the International Exhibition in London in the following spring. Towards the end of February two young musicians called to see him, armed with a letter of introduction from Clarina Maffei. They were Arrigo Boito and Franco Faccio, bosom friends.

Boito, born at Padua in 1842, was the younger son of a disreputable Italian miniature painter and an impoverished Polish countess. Faccio, born at Verona in 1840, was the son of an innkeeper. The two friends had made their mark as fellow students of the Milan Conservatorio by two patriotic cantatas, *Il quattro giugno* (1860) and *Le sorelle d'Italia* (1861), which they had written in collaboration, on texts by Boito. They had been awarded a grant by the Government, which had enabled them to go abroad, and they had made for Paris.

On 3rd March Verdi was still talking of 'this stupid march for the London Exhibition' but on learning from Auber that he, too, as the representative of France, had been asked to write a march, he decided to contribute a cantata instead and commissioned Boito, who was conveniently on the spot, to provide the text. Thus the *Inno delle Nazioni*, first fruit of this historic partnership, came into existence. The text was completed by 29th March, when its receipt was acknowledged by Verdi:

> In thanking you for the fine work written for me, I permit myself to offer you, as a token of esteem, this modest watch. Accept it in the friendly

spirit in which it is offered. May it recall to you my name, and the value of time!

My regards to Faccio, and Glory and Fortune to you both!

'The value of time!' By what miracle of insight did Verdi at once put his finger on what was to become Boito's lifelong preoccupation and torment?

Letters from Camillo Boito, the architect, Arrigo's elder brother, show that the latter was already occupied with the two great themes of his life's work. 'Have you progressed with the scoring of *Faust*?' Camillo asked in February. 'Have you formed the idea of *Nerone*?' And in March: 'Hurry on with the composition of *Faust*; I think it's not impossible to arrange for it to be given at La Scala in the next Carnival season.' [1] That was in 1862. Boito's *Mefistofele*, based on Goethe's *Faust*, was to be heard at La Scala only in 1868; the four acts that were all he ever completed of *Nerone* were to be given in the same theatre only in 1924, six years after their composer's death.

From Paris, Faccio went to London, where on 24th May, at Her Majesty's Theatre, he heard the first performance of the *Inno delle Nazioni*, from Verdi's box. Boito went to Poland to visit his many relatives. During the summer he completed a libretto, *Amleto*, after Shakespeare, for Faccio, wrote poems, worked on *Faust* and brooded over *Nerone*. In November the two friends were together again at Milan.

A copy of Boito's collected poems, the *Libro dei versi*, bears an inscription to Francesco Novati according to which the poems were written 'in the time of my blessed and insane and most ignorant youth'. It was the period of 'Scapigliatura', of wild bohemianism, of experiments with hashish and absinth, of intoxication with wine and the poetry of Baudelaire and Victor Hugo, of iconoclastic challenge and dreams of a renewal and regeneration of the arts. A close companion was Emilio Praga, poet and painter, in collaboration with whom Boito wrote a play, *Le madri galanti*, which had one performance at Turin in March 1863 and was hissed off the stage. If Boito had been a man of weaker fibre, association with Praga, who destroyed himself and his talent with drink and drugs, might have been disastrous. But though he hymned a generation of pallid, suicidal poets, several of whom did indeed take their own lives in despair, Boito survived. He explored the artificial paradises, but found his way back to reality. He sought every experience before rejecting all that was foreign to his nature.

Camillo Boito's letters to Arrigo from the winter of 1861–2 include remarks about *Un ballo in maschera*, which, for him, was 'an ugly opera, written unconscientiously, without wisdom, without loftiness

[1] Piero Nardi, *Vita di Arrigo Boito* (Milan, 1942), p. 92.

of concept and means . . . it's a fragmentary work, stolen from here and there, fruit of a talent worn out and buried'. One has the feeling that Camillo had little musical understanding, especially since he compares *Un ballo in maschera* unfavourably with *I vespri siciliani.* It is no wonder that when he declared, in the *salon* of the Countess Maffei, that *Un ballo in maschera* was the most wretched music Verdi had ever written, he was thought to be joking. But Camillo was a good brother to Arrigo and it was he who had obtained from Clarina Maffei the letter of introduction to Verdi.

On 18th July 1863, Clarina told Verdi that Faccio and Boito were among those who came every evening to see her. 'Faccio will soon be giving his first opera. . . . What do you think of his ability? Boito has talent, but vacillates still between poetry and music, and to succeed in both would be almost a miracle. In the last few evenings these two young men let me hear the whole of *La forza del destino* and *Un ballo in maschera.*' Verdi replied on 31st July: [1]

> In Paris last year I often saw Boito and Faccio, and they are certainly two young men of much talent, but I can't say anything about their musical gifts because I've never heard anything by Boito and only a few things by Faccio that he came one day to play me. For the rest, if Faccio presents an opera the public will pass sentence on it. These two young men are accused of being very warm admirers of Wagner. No harm in that, as long as admiration doesn't degenerate into imitation. . . . Let Faccio put his hand on his heart and, without paying attention to anything else, write as his heart dictates. Let him be *bold* to try new paths, and *courageous* in face of opposition.

The opera awaited was not *Amleto*, but *I profughi fiamminghi*, with libretto by Praga. It was first performed at La Scala on 11th November, and repeated four times during the season, with moderate success. The text was curiously old-fashioned, and Faccio, in reality, was far from being a revolutionary musical innovator. Still, it was much for the twenty-three-year-old composer to have made his *début* at La Scala. His friends gave a banquet in his honour, in the course of which Boito rose to recite a curious ode, *All' Arte italiana*, expressing in drastic form his views on the debased state of Italian music since the days of the 'holy harmonics of Pergolesi and Marcello', and his hopes that it would be reformed and revivified by a younger generation of composers. 'Perhaps the man is already born', he declared, 'who will restore art in its purity, on the altar now defiled like the wall of a brothel':

> Forse già nacque chi sovra l'altare
> Rizzerà l'arte, verecondo e puro,
> Su quell'altar bruttato come un muro
> Di lupanare.

[1] *Carteggi verdiani*, IV, pp. 83–4.

This ode, published a few days later in a periodical, was read by Verdi and taken by him as a personal insult.

Five days after the first performance of the opera, and six days before the publication of the ode, Faccio, at the instigation of Clarina Maffei, who had taken him very much under her wing, sent an obsequious letter to Sant' Agata, attributing what success he had had to Verdi's encouragement. This letter, which conveyed also the homage of Boito, went unanswered for a month. Then on 13th December Verdi wrote to Clarina Maffei, stating frankly that Faccio's letter had embarrassed him:

> What can I reply? 'A word of encouragement,' you say; but what need is there of such a word, to one who has presented himself before the public, and made the public his judge? It's an affair, now, to be settled between them, and every word is useless. I know there has been much talk about this opera—too much talk, in my opinion—and I have read some articles in the newspapers, where I've found big words about *Art, Aesthetics, Revelations*, the *Past* and the *Future*, etc., etc., and I confess that (great ignoramus that I am) I understood nothing of all that. On the other hand, I don't know Faccio's talent, nor his opera, and I don't want to know it, so as not to have to discuss it, or give an opinion on it—things I detest because they're utterly useless. *Discussions* never persuade anyone; *opinions* are generally fallacious. Finally, if Faccio, as his friends say, has found new paths, if Faccio is destined to restore art, on the altar now *defiled with the filth of the brothel*, all the better for him, and for the public. If he has gone astray, as others assert, let him get back on the right path, if he thinks fit.

On the following day Giuseppina drafted for Verdi a short note to Faccio, suggesting that if the public had received his work with favour, he should continue his career 'and add to the great names of Pergolesi and Marcello another glorious name—your own'. The much-altered draft of this note is followed in Giuseppina's letter-book by a copy of Verdi's letter to Clarina and by a letter of 23rd December to Piave:

> Verdi can't answer you, one of his eyes being inflamed and half closed, but it came wide open on hearing from you that Faccio, the countess and others were thrilled by certain replies which, as you know, had to be waited for some little time! Goodwill was shown in interpreting them—that's all I can say!

To Tito Ricordi, who tried to excuse the poet's excesses, Verdi replied: 'If I too, among the others, have soiled the altar, as Boito says, let him clean it and I shall be the first to come and light a candle.'

Nardi has shown [1] that an unsigned article about *I profughi fiamminghi* in *La Perseveranza*, reprinted by De Rensis and quoted

[1] op. cit., pp. 127–8.

by Gatti,[1] was not by Boito at all. Judicious in praise and blame of composer and librettist, it was probably by Filippi, the regular music critic of that paper. An earlier article in *La Perseveranza*, however, published two months before the production of *I profughi fiamminghi*, is definitely Boito's; it includes an important statement of his views on the operatic situation:

> There are in the language of men words and meanings which are easily confused, and which, especially in aesthetic matters, it is useful to disentangle; two of these words are *form* and *formula*. The Latins, who knew what's what, made of the second the diminutive of the first; but the Latins also knew how to talk and to think more clearly than we. *Form*, the extrinsic manifestation, the fine clay of art, has as much in common with *formula* as an ode of Horace has with Ruscelli's rhyming dictionary, or the shining rays of Moses with the ears of an ass. And here it is necessary to state at once that since opera has existed in Italy, down to our own times, we have never had true operatic form, but always only the diminutive, the *formula*. Born with Monteverdi, the operatic formula passed to Peri, to Cesti, to Sacchini, to Paisiello, to Rossini, to Bellini, to Verdi, acquiring force, development, variety (and acquiring much with these last great figures), yet remaining still *formula*, as *formula* it was born. The designations: aria, rondo, cabaletta, stretto, ritornello, *pezzo concertato*, are all there, drawn up for inspection, to confirm the truth of this assertion. The hour has come for a change of style, form, largely attained in the other arts, must develop, too, in our own; its time of maturity must have arrived; let it take off the *toga praetexta* and assume the *toga virilis*, let it change name and construction, and instead of saying *libretto*, the term of conventional art, say and write *tragedy*, as did the Greeks.
>
> All this discussion . . . leads naturally to the conclusion that today it is impossible to write good or beautiful music, not only on a bad *libretto*, but on any sort of a *libretto*.

For the propagation of their ideas, Boito and Praga founded a weekly periodical, *Figaro*, which survived for three months in 1864. All the contributors took pseudonyms from Beaumarchais, and Boito, as 'Almaviva', wrote on music and drama. If his opinions seemed excessively bold and strange, readers were told, they could attribute this to the fact that, in his first youth, he had travelled abroad and seen things that were great and new. Boito's writings are, indeed, full of reminiscences of his experiences in Paris. The articles contributed to *Figaro* sparkle with wit and bristle with erudition. There are several passages which help to clarify his attitude towards Verdi. He restated, concisely, the views expressed earlier in *La Perseveranza*:

> The opera of today, to have life and glory, and to fulfil the high destiny prescribed for it, must attain, in our opinion:
>
> I The complete obliteration of *formula*.

[1] First edition, II, pp. 93–6; second edition, pp. 443–5; together with quotations from articles really by Boito, of various dates.

II The creation of *form*.
III The actualization of the most vast tonal and rhythmic development possible today.
IV The supreme incarnation of the drama.

La Scala, instead of *Der Freischütz*, *Oberon*, *Orfeo*, *Don Giovanni* or *La Juive*, had put on a bad performance of *I Lombardi*, an opera which, even if well sung, was beginning to show its age:

> Time has covered it with a first layer of dust, and the later discoveries of Verdi himself, and of others, have revealed to the public the existence of an art more serious, more complete, more true.
>
> There are certainly here and there marvellous traces of eternal beauty, but in general these Lombards have grown old and rather grey. Portentous and marvellous truth! In no art, in no science, is the march of time and progress so rapid, resolute and vertiginous as in music.
>
> In the space of a few years—ten, twenty, thirty at most—what overturnings, what conquests, what falls of geniuses before other geniuses, and how many destroyed by themselves, to rise again more powerful from their own ruins! Meyerbeer, who repudiates *Il Crociato* with *Les Huguenots*, Rossini, who repudiates *Otello* with *William Tell*, Wagner, who repudiates *Rienzi* with *Lohengrin*! Verdi, who repudiates *I Lombardi* with *Rigoletto*!

When Verdi wrote *I Lombardi* he had one eye on the public and one on his art, and that was already much, when many composers kept both eyes only on the public. But now the time had come to gaze straight ahead, in the face of art, serene and confident. 'That is why *I Lombardi* shows its age; that is why *Rigoletto* is still young, and sends the Parisian public into ecstasies at the Théâtre Lyrique.'

A performance of *Un ballo in maschera* at La Scala was better sung, and better received, than performances two years earlier. Boito made no comment on the music. The only other opera by Verdi discussed, *I vespri siciliani*, was decidedly overpraised: 'It would take a long time to enumerate all the graces and the strength of this solemn opera, for one would have to stop and admire every piece.' Boito only regretted that a grand subject had been ruined by a poor libretto. Verdi, 'a very bold genius, creator, innovator', had won the battle of art without the aid of poetry.

Perhaps it was the strong Meyerbeerian element in the music of *I vespri siciliani* that Boito liked. Apropos of *Les Huguenots* he wrote that when Meyerbeer began to be understood by the public of La Scala 'there collapsed, like the bricks of the walls of Jericho, hundreds of Italian operas: a great part of those of Bellini, a greater part of those of Donizetti, almost all those of Rossini (except those two marvellously and eternally youthful ones) and a few of Verdi's'.

Boito found a new platform with the establishment, in the summer of 1864, of the Società del Quartetto, the aim of which was to introduce the classics of chamber music to the almost exclusively operatic-minded public of Milan. The society published a journal, edited by Alberto Mazzucato, Boito's teacher at the Conservatorio, and published by Ricordi. Giulio Ricordi, now friendly with Boito and Faccio, in the musical vanguard of Milan, was the secretary of the Società del Quartetto.

A long, rambling discourse, *Mendelssohn in Italia*, by Boito, appeared serially in the *Giornale della Società del Quartetto* between 20th July and 31st December 1864. This took as its starting point the publication of a French translation of the *Reisebriefe*, sketched the life and character of the composer, attacked Fétis for the errors and erroneous opinions of his *Biographic universelle*, and discussed Mendelssohn's impressions, agreeable and otherwise, of the Italy of thirty years earlier. Here Boito found texts for his own sermons; indeed, a kind of self-identification with his subject ('more than a musician, a thinker, a contemplative, a poet') becomes apparent. In Italy, reverence for high art was lacking. 'Compared with the Germans, we are a race of improvisers, of more or less fortunate empiricists of the Muses, of somnambulists assiduously oppressed by the succubus "do nothing" and the incubus "do it quickly".' 'Ask Shakespeare why he thought about *Hamlet* for more than twenty years; ask Goethe why he worked all his life on *Faust*, you who write a hundred operas in ten years!' Boito passed to 'Mendelssohn's castle in the air, that dream of all his life, that ideal opera he cherished in his heart: Shakespeare's *Tempest*'. The dream never became reality because the poet-collaborator was never found. 'He carried his conception into the tomb, free still from the weight of form, immaterial, white, ethereal, virginal, sublime, as when he knew it for the first time, in his heart.' Is this a characterization of Mendelssohn, or of Boito himself?

One of the letters written by Camillo Boito to Arrigo at Paris includes the sentence: 'Tell me whether Rossini has heard your Wagnerian music.' *Mendelssohn in Italia*, rather less than three years later, ends surprisingly with an anti-Wagnerian diatribe:

> Mendelssohn died, and the poet has not yet appeared in Germany.
>
> There appeared instead a false apostle of this poet, a false precursor, one of those dangerous propagators of truths ill said, ill thought, ill heard; one of those madmen who, with their thoughts on the light, diffuse darkness; pompous disseminators of clamorous confusion; spoilers of theories by their practice and of practice by their theories; talents more swollen with vanity than nourished with knowledge: Richard Wagner.

Wagner had understood the operatic situation in Germany after the death of Weber and the musical naturalization of Meyerbeer in France:

> That new development of tragic form implored by Mendelssohn . . .

Wagner perceived it, understood it, but formulated it badly, with his crooked theorizing; he led it to a worse end in his poems.

Richard Wagner was the Bar-Jesus of art in his day. But his day, by great good fortune, is over. The confiding crowd of young men who followed him closely in Germany, and from afar in Italy, is today falling away, with disillusion on their faces, with indifference in their hearts.

We confess that the first words of Wagner moved us; we all understood, better than an obscure explanation permitted, his courageous idea. Wagner destroyed the *operatic formula*; Wagner promised to widen the bounds of rhythm and melody; Wagner, poet-composer-aesthete, in his triple aspect seemed the man born and predestined to fulfil the innovatory mission.

It was false.... His dramas are inept, shallow, ridiculous, in face of the supreme task they were called upon to undertake. The great problem remains unsolved.

There were signs that 'the high poem, tragic and epic, mimic and rhapsodic, that grand restoration of *Greek tragedy* and the *medieval mystery play*, which will be the opera of the not distant future' would arise soon in Germany. He would have liked to predict its advent in Italy but, 'in the matter of poetry much more than in that of music', lacked faith to do so.

In the first half of 1865 Boito contributed four articles to the *Giornale della Società del Quartetto*, reviews of concerts of classical chamber music. He was never at a loss for a literary image to convey his idea of the character of a composer: 'Haydn proceeds from Bach as the flowering laburnum from the terrible rock'; 'Schumann is the sail of a ship before the wind, thrust forward, swollen, battered; Mendelssohn is the wing of an eagle, stronger than any gust, immobile above the whirlwinds.' 'Beethoven, a solar intelligence, a nature almost divine, amphibian of sky and earth, is Mendelssohn and Schumann in one.' Beethoven was the greatest of all: 'Bach comes up to his chest, Mendelssohn to his heart, Schumann to his elbow, Haydn to his knee, Wagner to the clavicle of his foot.' But if Beethoven was supreme, it was Mendelssohn to whom were devoted most space and the most extravagant epithets. A concert on 7th May 1865, which included Mozart's string Quartet in G, K. 387, and Mendelssohn's string Quintet in B flat, Op. 87, evoked the following musical hashish-dream:

We have heard Mendelssohn's Adagio in D minor; we have drunk the essence of the Ideal from the amphora of the Beautiful and we are intoxicated.... At the last page of the Adagio, where the rays of the paradisiacal melody seem all to concentrate into one focal point in an indefinable incandescence which the mind's eye can scarcely bear, at certain bars of this last page we heard a sob, the cry of a multitude, rise from the pit and we gazed at each other with a wild surmise. Who had emitted that sound? *We* had. All of us.... Omnipotence of music! Our faces were pale with anguish, our arteries beat violently, as if we had witnessed some startling catastrophe; there were some who wept. Oh, the sovereign power of this art of ours! Yes, we assert it with affectionate pride and with the most complete conviction: music is the Queen of all the arts—more than the Queen, the Goddess. . . .

The Sublime is more simple than the Beautiful. The Beautiful can incarnate itself in all sorts of forms, the most strange, the most multiple, the most disparate; but for the Sublime only the one great form is fitting, the divine form, universal, eternal—the *spherical* form. The horizon is sublime, the sea is sublime, the sun is sublime. Shakespeare is spherical, Dante is spherical, Beethoven is spherical; the sun is more simple than a carnation, the sea is more simple than a brook; Mendelssohn's Adagio is spherical and more simple than Mozart's Andante.

A week later, in the last of these articles, Boito announced that, after all, the days of the symphony and of chamber music were over; the renewal of opera, the tragedy in music, was the task of contemporary composers. A string Quartet by Faccio, a meritorious work, had been performed on 14th May, but, said Boito, 'the opera is his dream, his battlefield; an ineluctable current of the heart draws him to the theatre'. While his Quartet was being played at Milan, Faccio was at Genoa, preparing for the performance of his second opera, *Amleto*, on Boito's libretto, under Mariani. 'The musical epoch is about to change; a great amplification of the art is imminent; music is about to suffer a displacement of centre and an extension of circumference.'

The production of *Amleto* on 30th May, if it did not mark the beginning of a new musical epoch, brought a *succès d'estime*, for both poet and composer. The opera was much talked about, and much discussed in print. A congratulatory open letter about it, from Mazzucato to Stefano Ronchetti-Monteviti, Faccio's teacher, was published in the *Giornale della Società del Quartetto*. Ghislanzoni, in his *Rivista minima*, mocked the propagandists, the 'mobile *claque*', who according to him had secured the success of the opera, and advised the composer to save himself from his friends.

Piero Nardi discovered at Sant' Agata a copy of *Re Orso*, Boito's fantastic fable in verse, with the inscription: 'To Giuseppe Verdi, that he may recall my name. Milan, 20th December 1864.' This shows that Boito was not conscious of having irreparably offended.

But Verdi did not forgive or forget easily, and his comments on Boito's articles and the production of Faccio's opera were bitter:

To Piave, 21st May 1865:[1]

Don't be frightened by the Babel of the Music of the Future! This too is quite in order—it had to be so. These so-called apostles of the future are instigators of a grand, sublime thing. It was necessary to *wash the altar, soiled by the swine of the past*. They want music that is pure, virginal, *holy*,

[1] *Carteggi verdiani*, II, p. 355.

spherical. I look upwards and I await the star that shall show me where the new Messiah is born, so that, like the Magi, I may go to adore him. *Hosanna in excelsis!*

To Arrivabene, 14th June 1865:

You will have heard about Faccio's opera. Who can understand a thing in all that uproar, and with all that *entourage*? Couldn't they do things a little more quietly? I believe, however, that if Faccio really has talent it will be necessary, if anything is to come of it, for him to get away from Professors, Conservatorists, Aesthetes and Critics, and neither study nor listen to music for ten years.

Recent events had conspired to confirm Verdi in his attitude of resentment and unmistakable hostility.

A mysterious inscription is found in one of Giuseppina's letter-books: 'Sr Ihganrot Onalim Euqnic Oiggam 1865.' When the words are read backwards this becomes: 'Sr Tornaghi, Milano, Cinque Maggio 1865', and what follows is a copy of a letter from Giuseppina to Tornaghi that was published by Luzio from another draft.[1] It concerns the young Giulio Ricordi, now associated, as we have seen, through the Società del Quartetto and by close personal friendship, with Faccio and Boito:

I received your letter yesterday morning and from that which arrived today for Verdi I have ground for hope that you have been able to prevent Giulio from carrying out his unspeakable idea of writing in a way that could offend Verdi!

I don't know whether my husband wrote to Tito, and if so whether he made reference to a côterie and those who may form part of it. If he did, for a joke, amen; and if he spoke seriously he will have had good reason and will have done so, certainly, with all due seemliness.

It is not necessary to assume, as Luzio does, that Giulio was on the point of bursting out into 'direct epistolary insolence' to Verdi. But we can take it that he wanted to defend himself and his friends from charges made or implied in recent letters to his father. Alarmed at the possible consequences, Tornaghi had asked Giuseppina to try to intercept any letter from Giulio to Verdi. In this very long reply, Giuseppina underlined the dangers of the situation. For many years now, criticism of Verdi's operas in Ricordi's own *Gazzetta Musicale* had come 'wonderfully close to hostility'. Yet he had laughed at this anomaly:

All these things I know, and I know besides that Giulio is the son and grandson of these publishers! Whence you can imagine how astonished and sorry I was about the threatened *incartade*. . . . I waited on the bridge and in the road to prevent the man from going directly into the house and, God be thanked, that ill-omened missive not having arrived, I breathed

[1] *Carteggi*, IV, pp. 183–4, misdated 8th May.

again! The consequences could have been very serious and, whatever the scandal and the result that would have followed from it, it is certain that the shame and perhaps also the loss would have fallen on Giulio and the House of Ricordi.

Giulio, who is very gifted, should begin to think that he has a wife and children, that two and two make four, and that however much elasticity one possesses a miscalculated leap can lead to a broken neck.

Your letter, dear Tornaghi, reached the hands of Peppina Verdi, and from me there is no indiscretion to be feared.

Just at this time Emilio Praga was elected to a newly created chair of Poetic and Dramatic Literature at the Milan Conservatorio, for which Verdi, through Piroli, had recommended Piave. The letter to Piave of 21st May, with its sarcastic references to Boito's ode and articles, begins: 'Everyone has his troubles. Don't despair, and send the Conservatorio to Hell! It was a dream of yours, impossible of realization.' An earlier letter [1] had prophesied this result: 'The affair of the Conservatorio is lost, if the nomination depends on that commission.' And among the members of the commission was Boito's teacher: 'Ah! So you too know Mazzucato at last? That's a man with enough talent to recognize that he hasn't any genius. *Inde ira* (1) against the Eternal Father who didn't give him any, and (2) against all the others who have more than he.' Piave's letters at this time, recently published by Abbiati,[2] reveal a thoroughly unpleasant side of his personality and show that no one more than he stoked the fires of Verdi's resentment against 'the musical Camorra of the future'. He retailed unworthy gossip even about Clarina Maffei, who had used her influence to help Praga to secure the position at the Conservatorio. This explains a surprising reference to her in another passage of Verdi's letter of 21st May: 'I have been, and am, very friendly with that person, but I don't want to be made a fool of, and I wish to be friendly with people who are worth the trouble.'

It was not going to be easy to bring Boito and Verdi together again.

Giuseppina wrote truly of Clarina Maffei that she had made of friendship her temple, her God and all her joys. Nardi rightly refers to the countess's genius for reconciling opposites. She revered Manzoni, her 'Saint', of whom Praga had written in blasphemous terms:

> Casto poeta che l'Italia adora,
> Vegliardo in sante visioni assorto,
> Tu puoi morir! . . . degli antecristi è l'ora!
> Cristo è rimorto!

Yet she went out of her way to help Praga and his family. Knowledge

[1] *Carteggi*, IV, p. 231, wrongly dated 1869.
[2] II, pp. 823–4; III, pp. 19–21, 27–8.

of the strained relations between her old friend Verdi and the younger group of composers who frequented her *salon* only made her eager to heal the breach. For Faccio, in particular, her affection was immense, becoming a sort of spiritual adoption, so that she called him her 'son' and signed her letters 'your Mother'. The most benevolent feelings for Boito, too, are apparent in her correspondence, but it would seem that his attitude towards her was more reserved. The letters of Camillo Boito to Arrigo include some disparaging references to the company in the famous *salon*, now beginning to seem stuffy and outmoded to a younger generation.

The essence of the Boito of the years of 'Scapigliatura' is found in this note to Praga from April 1866, inspired by a false report of the death of Baudelaire:

DEAR EMILIO,

We shall see Baudelaire no more. I send you the funereal news that I have just read with distress.

Realism is dying, Brother, dying the double death of the soul and the body. The realists are in their agony, with no priest at the bedside, and depart with no glory.

Praga, how are you?

Let us feel each other's pulse and, if it still beats, God and Victor Hugo help us!

J'ai plus de souvenirs que si j'avais mille ans!

!!!!!

Your ARRIGO.

Blessed and insane, but by no means ignorant youth!

The war of 1866 saw them all volunteers with Garibaldi. Faccio and Boito, inseparable through the whole campaign, marched long distances, got very dusty and dirty, and once saw the Austrians in the distance from the top of a mountain. Just when it seemed as if they might get a whiff of gunpowder there came the armistice.

Soon after this their ways diverged for a while. Faccio, launched on his career as conductor, left to direct seasons of Italian opera in Berlin and Copenhagen. Boito resumed his life at Milan, writing dramatic criticism for *Il Politecnico* and the first of his few remarkable short stories. Clarina Maffei's letters to Faccio depict Boito, sometimes negligent, sometimes assiduous in attendance at her *salon*: 'I'm afraid he's not doing much work, but is always the excellent and noble character you know.' Praga was going rapidly downhill: 'He's always in despair at being constrained, with his genius, to give lessons at the Conservatorio, and his pupils are more desperate than he.' Giulio Ricordi, with Donna Vittoria Cima, had played the Funeral March from *Amleto* for Clarina and her guests; then he had gone to Paris, for the last weeks of preparation of *Don Carlos*: 'Giulio says it's stupendous, but rather difficult music.'

In the spring of 1867 Boito was again in Poland. His brother's letters make it clear that it was at this time that he decided to enlarge the scope and scale of his opera, now already called *Mefistofele*, to incorporate the substance of both parts of Goethe's *Faust*, which he had originally intended to treat in two separate operas. It seems certain that Boito went to Poland via Paris, and that he heard *Don Carlos* there; the idea of condensing both parts of *Faust* into one vast opera, in five acts and a long prologue, may well have been suggested by acquaintance with Verdi's five-act French grand opera. But Boito did not approve of everything in *Don Carlos*, as is clear from a letter of Camillo's of 23rd April:[1]

If your score can be finished before the Carnival season, I am sure you can get it performed at La Scala, all the more as the management doesn't know where to turn. Mazzucato's influence is increasing, I think, and you would do well to write to him, since, you having left it to me to judge whether it was opportune to give him the letter about *Don Carlos*, it didn't seem to me, or to Mancini to whom I read it, helpful to send it on to his address. Mazzucato, who is rather a gossip, would perhaps have mentioned it to Ricordi or others, and people would have attacked you, although your letter was very soberly written and the criticisms seemed true and measured.

Mefistofele was in fact to be performed at La Scala in the next Carnival season, together with *Don Carlos*, so that Boito this year must really have worked hard.

A letter from Clarina Maffei to Faccio of 15th May 1867[2] describes Giuseppina's surprise visit to her, and allows us to see it from another angle:

I ran to meet her, with one of those impulses of the heart which you know. I pressed her to my bosom, lovingly kissed her and, both of us deeply moved, we introduced ourselves to each other. I can't tell you how good she was, how expansive, and how blissful at having visited me at last. It was most welcome and evident proof of the benevolence that Verdi feels for me still. How many dear and consoling things she told me, of what Verdi had repeatedly told her about me! Oh, old age has most sweet compensations, when such old affections are found constant and most cordial! I spoke to her about you (we were together for hours, and I am expecting her again at any moment), I convinced her of the truth, and I believe I dissipated every trace of that stupid gossip. Luckily I had your last letter, in which you write of your artistic longings and of *Rigoletto* with such admiration. We went together to visit Tito Ricordi, and so I formed a connection with him, which, I think, pleased Giulio and Giuditta, whom I saw last night more affectionate than ever.

This was a turning point, clearly, if Giuseppina was really convinced

[1] Nardi, p. 237.
[2] De Rensis, *Franco Faccio e Verdi*, pp. 62–3. De Rensis quotes some of these letters at greater length than does Nardi.

of Faccio's sincere admiration for Verdi. But Clarina underestimated the difficulties of her conciliatory mission. On 14th June Giuseppina had to admit that she had failed to obtain a portrait of Verdi for the critic Filippi, which Clarina had asked for:

> I tried several times to bring up the subject, without success; when your letter came I hoped I was armed at every point and returned to the assault. Being unable to escape by evasion, he said brusquely: 'I gladly give my portrait to my friends if they want it. If my enemies want it they can go and buy it.' And he turned his back on me.

Filippi was no enemy of Verdi's. He was a critic of independent mind, an admirer of Verdi, and also of Meyerbeer and Wagner.

The draft of another letter from Giuseppina to Clarina, dated 21st June in her letter-book, refers to one of Faccio's; Giuseppina had not shown this letter to Verdi, she said; however, in the draft, the precise phrase about 'Faccio and Co.' that he wished to be used in Giuseppina's letter to Clarina is in *his* hand! They could be his enemies if they liked, for all he cared. 'He says: "I have always tried to avoid useless things, things I don't like and men I don't completely trust." And after these words his mouth shuts, and there's no way of going on.'

The production of *Mefistofele* at La Scala, 5th March 1868, was preceded and followed by press campaigns, for or against the work, far exceeding in intensity anything aroused by either of Faccio's operas. The composer, at Filippi's suggestion, unwisely agreed to conduct, in place of Mazzucato. The initial goodwill of a large part of the audience was lost through the excesses of Boito's supporters, as well as those of his enemies, the singers lost heart and intonation, and the opera ended at half past one in a storm of hissing and whistling, a disastrous fiasco. A second performance followed on 7th–8th March, the Prologue and the first three acts being given on one day, and the Prologue, again, and the last two acts on the next. There were increasingly hostile demonstrations, especially during the fourth and fifth acts, and *Mefistofele* disappeared from the placards of La Scala.

On the day after the first performance of Boito's opera Verdi wrote to Arrivabene about the artists and the musicians of the day, the latter even crazier than the former: 'They don't know what they want nor where they are going. A fine novelty! I know myself that there is a *Music of the Future* but I think at present, and I shall think next year, too, that to make a shoe one needs *leather* and some *skins*! What do you think of this stupid comparison, which means to say that to write an opera one needs to have in one, in the first place, some music!? I declare that I am and shall be an enthusiastic admirer of the futurists, on condition that they produce some music no matter what the system, as long as it's music!' Arrivabene always echoed Verdi's own opinions in musical matters; if his mind had been more independent he might have suggested that in order to pass judgment on a shoe or an opera it is necessary first to examine it.

This was the year of the controversy over Broglio's letter to Rossini, which had caused Verdi to return his decoration. Broglio had also referred to 'musical mastodons', 'interminable operas that last five hours' and 'Mephistophelian presumptions', and this brought Boito into the fray. In a long 'Letter in four paragraphs', the most brilliant and amusing thing in all his prose writings, published in *Il Pungolo* for 21st May, he held Broglio up to ridicule before all Italy. In another letter, to Manzoni, Broglio had advocated the thorough-going Tuscanization of the Italian language and the earlier part of Boito's reply concerns this. It is written in a style that is a parody of the minister's intentions, is quite untranslatable and need not concern us here. The latter part of the reply concerns the letter to Rossini and includes an outspoken tribute to Verdi:

> God save me from thinking of belittling the august figure of Rossini, but not even for him is it permissible to belittle the history of Italian opera.
>
> 'Since Rossini what have we had?' Your Excellency asks. Eh! nothing; since '29 only trifles! *nugaeque canorae!*
>
> In '31, for example, there was *Norma*, a trifle which made Rossini say: 'I'll write no more'—and he kept his word.
>
> Then in '35 *I Puritani*, another trifle! Then in '40 *La Favorita* and in '43 *Don Sebastiano: nugaeque canorae*!
>
> In '51 *Rigoletto* and in '53 *Il Trovatore*, and all the Verdian theatre, fascinating, glorious and fecund! And since you had the grace to mention Meyerbeer, why didn't you also mention Halévy, Gounod, Weber, Wag . . . (don't be frightened!)? Your Excellency sees that there is something here for all tastes. But Your Excellency calls such history sterility. . . .
>
> Yesterday you got a mocking reply from Rossini; today a rebuff from Verdi, who refuses the Order of the Crown of Italy. . . .
>
> All Your Excellency's ideas about language and music are frivolous and fantastic.
>
> The language has no need of Your Excellency, and neither has music.
>
> The young composers have no need of your Rossinian Society, and neither has Rossini. . . .
>
> With regard to the question of musical decadence, I am in a position, Signor Ministro, to reassure you.
>
> Your Excellency should know, first of all, that Verdi is alive and well and still writing. Further, Your Excellency should know that there are in Italy a number of young men who think and study and work intrepidly, and I can also assure you that this incessant work will bear good fruit, such as derives from a firm faith and severe conscience.

So now the musical action at law is not between us and Your Excellency the Minister, but rather between us and His Excellency the Public.

Let us settle it then without your ministerial assistance.

These musical Mastodons don't at all 'crush' the young composers and don't in the least 'alarm the impresarios'.

I know a young composer who, as soon as he had finished writing a certain musical Mastodon of his, found at once an impresario to perform it, and it was not the composer who sought out the impresario, but *vice versa*, and the first performance of the said Mastodon not only covered all the expenses of the undertaking, but even brought in a profit.

These extracts from the *Lettera in quattro paragrafi* complete the evidence available concerning the young Boito's attitude towards Verdi. What justification is there for the assumption, frequently encountered, that he was hostile, and disliked and despised the music of the older composer? The answer, unless Verdi's whole output is held to be utterly beyond criticism, must surely be: 'None at all, apart from the Ode of 1863.' And the Ode is of dubious interpretation. There is nothing in the articles that could be considered hostile or disrespectful, and there are a number of passages indicative of high admiration. It is true that there are also things not calculated to please Verdi, such as the reference to the effect of the introduction of Meyerbeer's music into Italy. But that is another matter altogether.

The position of Boito, a true poet and a man of high literary ideals, was that he saw Verdi heedlessly expending his great gifts in the debased medium of the Italian operatic melodrama, on librettos that were a by-word for absurdity and banality of language. He had a vision of the possibility of a new marriage of poetry and music, such as he imagined to have existed in Greek tragedy. He worked consistently towards this ideal. It was Boito's tragedy that he and his friends were incapable of the tremendous tasks they set themselves; it was his glory that he was eventually able to achieve his aims in collaboration with Verdi.

Before that could happen a deep and rankling wound had to be healed. About the Ode one can only say that, as a high-spirited challenge to the established order, as the extravagant expression of youthful ambitions, it was in place at the banquet in Faccio's honour, among friends. But it should never have been published.

Verdi, for his part, thought he had been publicly insulted by this pupil of Mazzucato, whom he deeply distrusted. In addition, he had a general dislike of all critics and of the sort of preliminary fuss that had been made over *Amleto* and *Mefistofele*, and a firm belief that the activities of the Società del Quartetto could only be harmful to the cause of Italian music. He could not foresee how important his relationship with Boito was to become in the future and knew no reason why he should concern himself further with him: 'I have always tried to avoid useless things, things I don't like and men I don't completely trust.'

A distinct change in the atmosphere is discernible early in 1869. Faccio had returned to Milan in July 1868; in the autumn he conducted a season of opera at the Teatro Carcano which was so successful that he was at once engaged as assistant conductor at La Scala for the Carnival season of 1869. Verdi was thus brought into direct contact with him when he came to Milan to direct the rehearsals of the revised *Forza del destino*. As a result he conceived a great liking and admiration for Faccio, and every trace of suspicion was banished from his mind. After the production of the opera a pact of peace and mutual assistance was signed and sealed in a letter from Giuseppina to Faccio of 23rd March. She and Verdi considered him 'a true friend', she told him, and would like to spend a few days together with him 'of the sort that illuminate life for years and years'. Giulio Ricordi's goodwill and loyalty had been recognized at the same time; Giuseppina wrote to him on 4th March: 'You express yourself in a manner so warm and sincere that I must believe, and am happy to believe, everything you say. I feel a sweet contentment of mind in believing that Verdi, in associating with you, has been able to appreciate and love your talents. It is the purest joy to me that I have succeeded in dissipating that light cloud which obscured the truth about your heart and character.'

We have no evidence as to whether the amnesty extended also to Boito. No similar letter to him is recorded by Gixseppina, nor is he mentioned, as Faccio is, in her letters to Clarina Maffei at this time. Not even Nardi can tell us anything at all about what he was doing, or even where he was, in 1869. But it was not long before Giulio Ricordi, with mingled commercial and artistic motives such as characterized all his actions, was seeking to bring the two men together.

A letter from Verdi to Du Locle of 23rd January 1870 mentions the possibility of an opera on the subject of Nero. Ricordi, who had also heard Verdi discuss this possibility, seems to have undertaken to find out something more about the opera Boito was known to be working on. He sent in his report on 10th February 1870: [1]

Today, by artful interrogation, I succeeded in discovering that Boito has not yet begun to set to music *Nerone*, of which indeed he has not even finished the libretto.

Now a way must be found of discovering what ideas he has about it: whether he is absolutely relying wholly on that subject—and that without letting out what it's all about.

From the few words said to me by a third person, I think he has treated the subject from a point of view *different from that which you outlined to*

[1] *Carteggi*, IV, p. 186.

me. Certainly *Nerone* is a splendid, grandiose and interesting subject and before setting it aside don't you think, Maestro, it's worth trying something in this direction? Little was said about that because, from what Boito himself told me, it seemed that not only was the libretto finished, but that he had begun to set it to music. Now, according to recent information, that is not the case. Please let me know what you think about this.

There was no immediate reply, and Ricordi then sought Giuseppina's aid. The following letter, ascribed to 1875 by Nardi,[1] is found under the date of 24th February 1870 in Giuseppina's letter-book. It therefore concerns the *Nerone* project:

You explain yourself very well always, in Italian, in Milanese dialect and in God knows how many other languages. You know, too, how to apply the appropriate sauces—hot, cold, sweet, piquant, artistic or diplomatic. Your talent, one must agree, is great, fine, multiform. But however my feminine vanity is tickled by a master hand, and however much I wish, as artist and Italian, that Verdi should be persuaded to take up his pen again, I yet retain enough common sense to understand and declare that no pressure on my part will weigh anything in the balance of *yes* or *no*, whatever you and many other people may believe to the contrary. What I am anxious to assure you, dear Giulio, is that nobody will ever find me in opposition, when it's a matter of national glory and the good of the art that shed lustre on our poor name, even when the whole world tried to bury it in mud and oblivion.

The idea of *Nerone* was driven out of Verdi's head when he decided to write *Aida* for Cairo. But this opera was hardly completed before Giulio Ricordi returned to the charge, employing all his skill in both diplomacy and musical power politics. The diplomacy was reserved for Verdi, the power politics for Boito. Faccio's *Amleto* was to be performed at La Scala during the Carnival season. So Ricordi opened his campaign by sending a copy of the libretto to Verdi. Then he turned his attention to the librettist. While in 1870 he had been careful to conceal the true reason for his interest in the progress of *Nerone*, in 1871 he made use of the fact that Verdi was tempted by this subject to extort from Boito a promise to give it up. This is what he wrote to Verdi on 26th January:

I sent you the libretto of *Amleto* and appropriately I enter at once on a Great Project!! . . . over which you know I ruminate worse than an ox!! Well then; two or three times you mentioned *Nerone* to me . . . and I saw that this subject did not displease you. . . .

Yesterday Boito came to see me and *boom*! I fired off the cannonade. Boito asked for a night to think it over and this morning was here, and stayed a long time with me discussing this affair. The conclusion is that Boito would consider himself the *happiest*, the most *fortunate* of men, if

[1] p. 460.

he could write the libretto of *Nerone* for you; and would renounce at once, and with pleasure, the idea of writing the music. Boito told me frankly that he would feel able to satisfy all your requirements, and that never would he address himself with such zeal and such enthusiasm as to this undertaking, the *very rare* combination presenting itself of a poet and a composer both convinced of the beauty of the subject, and he considers that no subject was ever found, so vast, so beautiful, so well adapted to the genius of Verdi, as this *Nerone*.

I am perhaps too much an interested party, and too unimportant a person, to be able to risk a few words about this! . . . but if I had the courage I would persist in begging you, with all the strength of my mind, to give this proposal serious consideration and to keep alive this idea, which would give to Italian art a new musical masterpiece, and perhaps one of its greatest masterpieces! I know by this time what your part is in the preparation of a libretto, and Boito under your direction would do well, very well! . . . it would be hard to find a versifier more splendid and more elegant than he, in form and substance.

For the rest, this is a matter to be dealt with in all tranquillity, and whenever it seems to you that the time is ripe: meanwhile, however, it would be well for you to write me something about it, so that Boito too may know what he is to do: needless to say, the most scrupulous silence is necessary.

I *dare* (I'm not mad for nothing) to hope! . . . and in all conscientiousness I can send a word of recommendation of this young man, endowed with talents of a truly superior nature, and deserving of good fortune. It's a pity I can't write at greater length, for I should have a lot to tell you about the many precious confessions that Boito, in a moment of enthusiasm at the idea of writing *Nerone* for you, made to me this morning about its musical possibilities.

But no more about that. I wait anxiously to hear from you; if necessary I'm ready always to come to see you, even at the risk of the journey lasting twenty hours. There would be ample compensation in the pleasure of seeing you and Signora Peppina again.

Verdi wrote briefly from Genoa on 28th January: 'I can't reply now about the *Nerone* affair. I haven't a minute to lose. A Great Project, you say! . . . Very true, but is it capable of realization? We'll see! As soon as I have an hour to spare, tomorrow or the next day, I'll write at length. Meanwhile be patient. . . .' On or just before the receipt of this, on 29th January, Ricordi could not refrain from exerting further his powers of blandishment and persuasion:

The *Nerone* affair is so important that it must be seriously considered; then *Aida* is still in the field, so, as I very well understand, it's not an affair to be settled *à tambour battant*, and even when it's once decided on, time will be needed before it's brought to an end. However, I thought it opportune to speak of it straight away, because if by good fortune it can be arranged, it's useless for Boito to continue his work, and it would have been an irreparable, immense, incommensurable loss if you, liking the subject, should have given up the idea out of a more than kind consideration for Boito.

I have done nothing but keep the idea alive, and there are time and means of cherishing it and studying it, and I am sure, if you write this *Nerone*, it will be a thing to astonish the world, for truly I cannot imagine a more beautiful subject, nor situations nor passions more apt to make shine resplendently your portentous genius!

It is impossible not to admire Ricordi's adroitness—the way he touches, in these two letters, on all the chords most calculated to awaken a response in Verdi. It was perhaps necessary, if the plot was to succeed, to anticipate and stifle the most serious of Verdi's possible objections by obtaining Boito's consent in advance. But still, there is something monstrous about Ricordi's ready sacrifice of his friend's cherished ambition. After the performance of *Mefistofele* he had published in the *Gazzetta Musicale di Milano* one of the best and most judicious of all the articles on that opera. He had ended by weighing good qualities against defects. If the latter were the result of inexperience, Ricordi said, there were grounds for hope that Boito would become one of Italy's best composers. If, however, the defects were the consequence of a preconceived system, of an unshakeable artistic belief, then in all frankness he could only say: 'You will be a poet, a distinguished man of letters, but never a successful composer of operas.' This implied a scepticism, an incomplete conviction about the musical side of Boito's double gifts; it was logical, in this case, for Giulio to act as he did over the *Nerone* project. It was logical, it was to the probable great advantage of art and the House of Ricordi, but the decision forced on Boito was cruel in the extreme.

No praise could be too high for Boito's own conduct on this occasion. The fact that nothing came of the project in the end does not detract from the magnanimity of his renunciation in Verdi's favour of his long-cherished dream.

The production of *Aida* having been delayed by the Franco-Prussian War and its aftermath, Verdi temporized about *Nerone*:

It is unnecessary to tell you again how much I love this subject. It is equally unnecessary for me to say how glad I should be to have as collaborator a young poet, whose very great talents I have recently had occasion to admire in *Amleto*.

But you know my affairs and my commitments well enough to understand what a serious business it would be for me to take on this new obligation. I find myself in a most unusual situation. I lack the courage to say: 'Let's do it', and yet I don't dare give up such a fine project.

But tell me, dear Giulio, couldn't we leave the matter open for a while, and return to it later? . . .

I don't ask Boito to remain at my disposition. God forbid! I shouldn't want that at any cost. Let him continue his own opera, as if we had never spoken of this. Later on, if it's still practicable, and convenient to both, we'll take the matter up again and settle it in two words.

Verdi in 1871 could not know all that *Nerone* meant to Boito. And he certainly showed more consideration for him than Ricordi did. But how could Boito continue working on his own opera, while there existed the possibility of one by Verdi on the same subject? The very idea must have paralysed him. Did he have long to wait for a clarification of the situation? We do not know; we have no more documents concerning this episode. But it is surely significant that later in this year he wrote for himself a new libretto, *Ero e Leandro*, and began to set it to music.[1]

Verdi had now accepted the possibility of collaboration with Boito.

Yet another suspicion was overcome when Mazzucato, a member of the commission for the organization of the collective Requiem Mass for Rossini, expressed by letter his astonishment and admiration, after examining the score of Verdi's contribution, the *Libera me*. When Mazzucato died some years later, an extract from his manuscript memoirs or diary was sent to Verdi on the back of a photograph:[2]

Monday, 6th February 1871:

I had written to Verdi about the profound, immense impression made on me by the reading of his *Libera me, Domine*. He replied in an expansive letter—extraordinarily expansive when one considers his usual reluctance to speak of his own things or to embrace a critic.

Verdi awoke great surprise in me with his *Nabucco* and *I Lombardi*. I saw him then descend to popular passions in *Ernani*, *Il Trovatore*, etc. I saw him raise himself again in *Macbeth*, and continually increase his stature with *Luisa Miller* and *Stiffelio*. He became insuperable with *Rigoletto*, with *Boccanegra*, etc.

I adore this composer, and I want him to know it, and thus to know the truth, hidden from him by interested persons for a good twenty-five years.

Verdi's mistrust derived from the very early days when *Ernani* had driven from the stage an opera on the same subject by Mazzucato. Even before this, in a private letter, he had written in terms of great crudity and violence about Mazzucato's *I due sergenti*.[3] But the operatic jungle warfare of the first half of the century could now be forgotten.

It used to be thought that Verdi had deliberately excluded Boito's name from the list of composers invited to contribute to the Requiem

[1] The true date of composition of *Ero e Leandro*, believed by De Rensis and, following him, Gatti to have preceded *Mefistofele*, is established by Nardi (pp. 337–41, 366–7) from letters of Camillo Boito and Luigi Chialiva.

[2] Reproduced in Gatti's *Verdi nelle Immagini*, p. 197. The letters exchanged over the *Libera me* are in the *Copialettere*.

[3] *Carteggi*, IV, p. 78.

for Rossini. We have seen that Scalaberni mentioned the exclusion of the younger composers, such as Boito, Dall' Argine, Faccio and Marchetti, as one of the grounds for his refusal to allow the artists under contract to him to take part. But the choice of composers was actually left, at Verdi's own suggestion, to the commission formed at Milan, and the commission, consisting of Lauro Rossi, Mazzucato and Ronchetti-Monteviti, with Giulio Ricordi as secretary, was anything but hostile to Boito and Faccio. As composer of a single opera that had failed completely and been withdrawn after two performances, Boito had really little claim to inclusion.

Now poor Faccio's opera, too, was a dismal failure on its revival at La Scala on 12th February 1871, largely because the tenor, Mario Tiberini, almost entirely lost his voice—it was, truly, a case of *Amleto* without the Prince of Denmark. This gave the final death blow to Faccio's creative ambitions in the operatic field. Within a year, with the first performances in Italy of *Aida*, he was to establish himself as the leading conductor of Verdi's operas, the successor of Mariani.

Both Faccio and Boito meanwhile had again revised their opinions about Wagner, and reached, finally, something like a just estimate, after hearing in actual performance the works they had first judged only from the vocal scores. Faccio had heard *Lohengrin* and *Tannhäuser* in Berlin in February 1867; Boito attended more than one of the famous performances of *Lohengrin* under Mariani, at Bologna in November 1871. It was to him that, six days after the first performance, Wagner addressed his *Brief an einen italienischen Freund* beginning: 'I must take advantage of your knowledge of German to beg you to convey my heartfelt thanks to your honoured countrymen in your mother tongue.' This was almost certainly at the suggestion of Giovannina Lucca. It does not appear to be true, as Nardi states,[1] that Boito first wrote congratulating Wagner on the triumph of *Lohengrin*. He had earlier translated *Rienzi* for Lucca, and was later to translate *Tristan*, *Das Liebesmahl der Apostel* and the *Wesendonklieder*. These translations were among many pieces of hack work undertaken both for Lucca and Ricordi, irrespective of his personal sympathies. In translating Wagner's letter and publishing it in *La Perseveranza*, whence it was widely reprinted, he was merely doing what Wagner had asked him to do. These actions do not imply any betrayal or weakening of his allegiance to Verdi. But it was perhaps unfortunate that he had anything at all to do with the events at Bologna, in view of the challenging character imparted to them by circumstances and the commercial rivalry of the publishers.

It so happened that Boito attended the same performance of *Lohengrin* as did Verdi, on 19th November. He was seen in the

[1] Probably following Gatti in his first edition. In Gatti's second edition the statement is deleted, though it remains in the analytical index.

theatre and the Bolognese newspaper *Il Monitore* published a report that he had visited Verdi in his box and highly praised some of the music of *Aida* which he had seen: 'In this opera Verdi is rejuvenated; it's the Verdi of *Rigoletto*.' Verdi was stated to have replied: 'Before praising it, let's await the verdict of the public.' The whole story was denied in the *Gazzetta Musicale di Milano* on 26th November. The truth was that Boito and Verdi had talked together in the waiting-room on Bologna station at three in the morning: 'The conversation turned principally on the difficulty of sleeping in a railway carriage.'

Nearly eight years were to pass, after this encounter in the waiting-room of Bologna railway station, before the two men met again.

As time went by it became apparent that Verdi was not to be tempted by *Nerone* nor, it seemed, ever again by any other operatic project. He was entering one of his most difficult periods. The enormous success of *Aida* at Cairo, Milan and elsewhere seemed to mean nothing to him.

To Giulio Ricordi, 31st March 1872:

> This evening, then, the last performance of *Aida*!! I breathe again!! They won't talk about it any more, or at any rate, they'll only say a few last words. Perhaps some new insult, accusing me of Wagnerism, and then . . . *Requiescat in pacem*!

To Tito Ricordi, 2nd January 1873:

> Look how I've been treated by the press during this year in which I've gone to such trouble and expended money and hard labour! Stupid criticism and praise more stupid still! Not a single elevated or artistic idea! No one has wished to point out my intentions; absurdities and stupidities all the time, and at bottom a sort of spite against me, as if I had committed a crime in writing *Aida* and having it well performed. Nobody, finally, has wished to point out even the material fact of a performance and *mise en scène* out of the ordinary! No one has said to me: '*Thanks, dog!*'—recall how I parted from the mayor and the theatre management.

Again and again in his letters of this period he deplores the increasing Germanic influence in politics and the sciences and arts. In music, of course, this was found in its most potent and, to Verdi's way of thinking, most pernicious form in the influence of Wagner on the younger Italian composers.

Boito's name occurs again in a letter to Giulio Ricordi of April 1875,[1] after an angry outburst about what Verdi considered the massacre of *Aida* in Rome:

> Then you talk of the results obtained!!!!!!!!! What results? I'll tell you. After twenty-five years' absence from La Scala I was hissed after the first act of *La forza del destino*. After *Aida* endless chatter: that I was no

[1] G. Cesari, 'L'Arte superstite del Maestro' (*Corriere della Sera*, 27th Jan. 1926).

more the Verdi of *Un ballo in maschera* (that *Ballo* that was hissed the first time it was performed at La Scala); that it was saved by the fourth act (so D'Arcais); that I *didn't know how to write* for the singers; that there were only a few tolerable things in the second and fourth acts (nothing in the third); and that, finally, I was an imitator of Wagner!!! A fine result, after a career of thirty-five years, to end up as an *imitator*!!!

It is certain that chatter like this won't make me, any more than it has done in the past, deviate in the least from what I want to do, for I have always known what I *wanted* to do; but having reached my present position, be it high, be it low, I am well able to say: 'If that's how it is, you can help yourselves,' and when I want to make music I can make it in my own room, without hearing the verdicts of the learned or the imbeciles.

I can't take as anything but a joke your sentence: '*The whole salvation of the theatre and of art is in your hands!!*' Oh no! Never fear, composers will never be lacking, and I will myself repeat what Boito said in a toast to Faccio after his first opera: '. . . and perhaps the man is born who will sweep the altar' . . . Amen!

The Ode was unforgotten, after nearly twelve years. Verdi never quotes it accurately, but finds always an interesting variant. Was there ever a composer so sensitive to criticism, so tenacious in rancour? He often declared that people could say and write what they liked about his operas, that it was a matter of indifference to him. It was far from true; he was vulnerable in the highest degree. A few hisses or whistles amid storms of applause after the first act of *La forza del destino* at La Scala in January 1869 were unforgotten and unforgiven; and what the critics did write about his operas became exaggerated and distorted in his memory.

A great change came over Boito's life with the successful revival of *Mefistofele* after drastic revision at Bologna in 1875. The subsequent career of the opera lifted him out of the round of journalism, hack translation and the writing of librettos for others. *Ero e Leandro* had been abandoned, apparently after completion of the music, and all that survives of it, apart from the libretto, is the beautiful duet 'Lontano, lontano, lontano', incorporated in the revised *Mefistofele*, and a chorus, 'La notte diffonde', published separately as a barcarole.

On 15th February 1876, little more than four months after the revival of *Mefistofele*, Boito wrote to Count Agostino Salina that he lived 'immersed in the blood and perfumes of Roman decadence' and thought it possible that *Nerone* could be produced within a year. On 22nd November he wrote to Salina's son: 'Your father has a right to know what I am doing and if I am working. Please tell him that my new opera puts out almost every day a new leaf and if I hadn't to go to Turin and Rome to watch over the fate of *Mefistofele*, and thus lose a couple of precious months, I could perhaps have completed *Nerone* for next year.' Verdi's first comment on *Mefistofele*, which he had not yet heard, occurs in a letter to Arrivabene of 21st March 1877, after the latter had sent news of the success of the opera in Rome:

It is difficult just now to say whether Boito will be able to give Italy any masterpieces. He has much talent, aspires to originality but succeeds only in being strange. He lacks spontaneity and he lacks invention; many musical qualities. With these tendencies one can succeed more or less well in a subject as strange and theatrical as *Mefistofele*, but less easily in *Nerone*.

According to *Opinione*, the newspaper of which D'Arcais was music critic, two acts and a half of *Nerone* were already written at this time.

Giulio Ricordi, meanwhile, continued to hope for Verdi's return to the theatre and lost no chance of coaxing and persuading, soothing and cajoling him. Knowing Verdi's great admiration for Adelina Patti, he suggested a new opera should be written for her. Meeting with a refusal, he renewed the assault through Giuseppina, to whom he sent a long, reasoned letter to be passed on to Verdi at an opportune moment. But on 14th November 1877 she had to confess defeat: 'I presented, then, with the best grace I could summon, the long letter of which you know to the celebrated composer in question: he read it calmly and said to me: "When you write, tell Giulio that I regret I am unable to give a reply different from that I have given already."' Clarina Maffei also pleaded with him, but with the same result, and any mention of the subject touched on the same wounds, aroused the same exacerbation. 'What?' he exclaimed on 19th March 1878, apropos of a revival of *Aida*, 'They miss the *power* and *passion* of la Stolz?!! But if then she *couldn't sing* that part . . . if then she was *sacrificed* . . . if then I *didn't know how to write*, etc.! And five years later!!! . . . You see? Time's little jokes! . . . You, even you, advise me to write? But let's talk seriously. Why on earth should I write music? What should I succeed in doing? What have I to gain from it? The result would be wretched. I should be told all over again that I *don't know how to write*, and that I have become a *follower of Wagner*. A fine sort of glory! After a career of almost forty years to end up as an *imitator*!' He was in his sixty-sixth year, his creative life apparently over. Pessimistic of the future of the Italian opera houses, in the prevailing conditions, he was hard to persuade that *Don Carlos*, revived at La Scala in the Carnival season of 1879, was a success, and told Faccio:

What is important now is to watch attentively the state of our theatre. It is sick unto death and it is necessary to keep it alive at all costs. And let you and Giulio, who are omnipotent, see that you don't have any failures. Find operas good or bad (for the moment, you understand); it suffices if they attract the crowds. You will say that that is unworthy, inartistic and *defiles the altar*; never mind, you can clean it afterwards. Meanwhile it is necessary to live. If the theatres close, they will never reopen. And if *Don Carlos* doesn't make money, set it aside and put on *Le Roi de Lahore* with all speed. . . .

He contrasted Massenet's reception with his own, seven years before. He told Clarina Maffei:

All this fuss about an opera, this praise and adulation, makes me recall the time (you know the old always praise their own times) when without advertisement, almost without knowing anybody, we presented our faces to the public, and if they applauded us we said, or didn't say, 'Thanks'; if they hissed: 'See you another time.' I don't know if this was beautiful, but it was certainly more dignified. Among those cuttings Corticelli made me read one which gave me a good laugh. That paper proposed to have a tablet made, to be affixed to La Scala: 'In the year 1879 a foreign composer came here who was greatly fêted, and a banquet was given, attended by the Mayor and Corporation. In 1872 a certain Verdi came in person to produce *Aida* and he was not even offered a glass of water.' 'A glass of water indeed!' I then said. 'They almost beat me up.' Don't take this phrase literally; I only mean to say that for *Aida* I had battles of words with everybody, and they all looked at me in surly fashion as though I were a wild beast. I hasten to add that it was my fault, because to tell the truth I am not very gracious in the theatre—or outside it.

Mefistofele was performed at Genoa in March 1879 and from a later letter of Giulio Ricordi's we know that Boito called to see Verdi at Palazzo Doria. He was kindly received, but did not venture to discuss what was nearest his heart. As far as is known, this was the only meeting he had had with Verdi, apart from that chance encounter in the waiting-room of Bologna station in 1871, since he had first made his acquaintance in Paris in 1862. Relations between Verdi and Faccio and Ricordi had become so cordial that it is very surprising that Boito remained so long a comparative stranger. His own diffidence, as well as Verdi's *diffidenza*, undoubtedly contributed to this.

At Genoa, Verdi and Giuseppina attended an unsatisfactory performance of *Mefistofele* and we have some unenthusiastic comments on it by both of them.

Giuseppina to Teresa Stolz, 20th March 1879:[1]

We saw Mephistopheles in company with Faust. The latter seemed to me seriously indisposed, for which reason I could not properly understand what they said to each other, and all the more as behind those big clouds in the Prologue in Heaven there was a Hellish uproar. When they receive again, and I pay another call, I'll be able to say something about it. So much on my own account. Verdi, who has a keener ear than I, will perhaps have understood everything.

[1] From her letter-book.

Verdi to Arrivabene, on the same day:

I had always heard tell, and always read, that the Prologue in Heaven was cast in a single piece, a thing of genius . . . and I, listening to the harmonies of that piece, based almost always on dissonances, seemed to be . . . not in *heaven* certainly! You see what it is not to be any longer *dans le mouvement*!

The origins of *Otello* date from Verdi's visit to Milan in June of this year to conduct a performance of the *Requiem* for the benefit of the victims of the recent floods. This was the occasion on which Teresa Stolz and Maria Waldmann emerged from retirement to sing together for the last time. The performance, on 30th June, brought in no less than 37,000 lire, and Verdi was delighted. He had a tremendous reception from the Milanese, at La Scala and in the streets. At the end of the performance flowers rained on to the stage from the boxes. The Albergo Milano, where he was staying, welcomed him back with 'Viva Verdi' in flowers across the hall. Via Manzoni was blocked by cheering crowds and he had to appear on the balcony to acknowledge their homage. Then the orchestra of La Scala arrived to serenade him, under Faccio's direction, with performances of the overture to *Nabucco*, the prelude to the third act of *La Traviata* and other pieces. It was a nice combination of heart-warming spontaneity, on the part of the public and, one suspects, the most careful organization by Giulio Ricordi aided by Faccio. And surely it had some effect in persuading Verdi that he was not a forgotten man, that it was not only for foreigners that enthusiasm was shown. When Ricordi made his next attempt to induce Verdi to return to the theatre, to consider the possibility of a new opera, conditions proved more favourable.

Ricordi told Giuseppe Adami: [1] 'The idea of the opera arose during a dinner among friends, when I turned the conversation, by chance, on Shakespeare and on Boito. At the mention of *Othello* I saw Verdi fix his eyes on me, with suspicion, but with interest. He had certainly understood; he had certainly reacted. I believed the time was ripe.' Faccio took Boito to see Verdi and three days later Boito returned with the plan for a libretto and was encouraged to complete it. He at once dropped everything else and set to work, at first at Milan and then at Venice, where he was to take a cure. Ricordi urged him on by every means at his disposal, hoping to have the libretto completely finished by the end of August or the beginning of September.

While Boito was labouring over the libretto at Venice, Verdi, back at Sant' Agata, picked up the latest number of the *Gazzetta Musicale di Milano* and read there an extract from the memoirs of the sculptor

[1] *Giulio Ricordi e i suoi musicisti* (Milan, 1933), p. 64.

Duprè, whom he had met at Florence in 1847. Duprè recalled a pronouncement of Rossini's to the effect that he esteemed Verdi highly as a composer of dark, melancholy, serious character, but was sure he would never write an *opera semi-seria* like Donizetti's *Linda di Chamounix*, much less an *opera buffa* like *L'Elisir d'amore*. This touched on one of Verdi's old wounds, the fiasco of *Un giorno di regno* in 1840. He sat up as if he had been stung and indited the well-known protest, which he carefully entered in his *Copialettere*:

I have read in your paper Duprè's words on our meeting, and the sentence of Jove Rossini (as Meyerbeer called him). But look here! For twenty years now I have been searching for a libretto for an *opera buffa* and now that I have, one can say, found it, you, by that article, put in the public's head a crazy desire to hiss the opera even before it is written, thus prejudicing your interests and mine.

But have no fear! If by chance, by misfortune, by fatality, in spite of the Great Sentence, my evil genius leads me to write this *opera buffa*, have no fear, I say . . . I'll ruin another publisher!

Poor Ricordi, astonished at this talk of an *opera buffa* when he thought he had set Verdi's mind working on *Otello*, and startled at the threat of it going to another publisher, said everything in his reply that could possibly be said in extenuation and excuse. He poured out the soothing syrup, and Verdi was mollified. It is not certainly known what was the subject for an *opera buffa* discovered at this time. Nothing more was heard of it.

Ricordi, in his reply, had mentioned his hope of being able to visit Sant' Agata 'with a friend' in the first half of September. Verdi warily countered this move:

A visit from you in company with a friend—who would of course be Boito—will always be agreeable. Permit me, however, to speak on this subject very clearly and frankly. A visit from him would commit me too much, and I wish absolutely to avoid committing myself. You know how this chocolate project came into being. You dined with me, together with a few friends. We spoke about *Othello*, about Shakespeare and about Boito. The next day Faccio brought Boito to see me at the hotel. Three days later Boito brought me the sketch of *Otello*, which I read and found good. 'Write the libretto,' I told him. 'It will come in handy for yourself, for me, or for someone else.' Now if you come here with Boito, I shall necessarily be obliged to read the finished libretto which he will bring with him. If I completely approve of it, I find myself to some extent committed. If I approve of it but suggest modifications, which Boito accepts, I find myself committed to an even greater degree. If, however beautiful it is, I don't like it, it would be difficult to say that to his face. No, no, you have gone too far and must stop before unpleasantness arises. In my view, the best thing (if you agree and if it suits Boito) is for him to send me the finished poem so that I can read it and give my opinion calmly, without committing either party. Once these somewhat prickly difficulties have been overcome, I shall be most happy to see you arrive here with Boito.

He was still very far from capitulation. But he had at least admitted that the libretto could possibly be of use to him, and that was something.

Boito wrote the libretto of *Otello*, in its original form, in the intervals of bouts of facial neuralgia and toothache, culminating in a most painful abscess. Ill health and over-anxiety led to delays which occasioned, up to mid October, an anguished three-sided correspondence between poet, publisher and composer. Ricordi bombarded Boito with exhortations, pleas, conjurations, warnings; Boito replied with explanations, excuses and assurances, the substance of which was passed on to Verdi by Ricordi, with lengthy commentaries of his own. Only Verdi, behind his protective barrier of reserve, remained apparently calm. But the 'chocolate project' certainly attracted him.

Ricordi seems to have decided that the occasion called for a certain amount of rather fulsome flattery or, at least, a most pronouncedly respectful attitude on his part and on Boito's, as of fear and trembling before the throne of a powerful and notoriously short-tempered deity. One cannot feel sure that he was altogether wrong. But, much more than the many thousands of words contributed by Ricordi, it was the transparent sincerity and selfless dedication of Boito that were decisive in the end. Among letters passed on by Ricordi to Verdi was this one:

DEAR GIULIO,

I am in much greater anguish than you. Today I was up at half past seven and at my table. I am working as hard as I can, but until yesterday afternoon the abscess that torments me had not burst, and with that inferno in my mouth I could not work. I hope the abscess will prove to be definitely the end of my troubles. I think only of completing my work, as best I can, and as soon as I can. No other undertaking in all my life has caused me the inquietude and agitation experienced in these months of intellectual and physical struggle.

Don't imagine that the libretto can be finished by the day after tomorrow. The abscess lost me three days and I only resumed work again this morning. You must therefore add three days on to Thursday. The fatal influence hostile to this work shall be overcome.

For the rest, whatever happens, even if Verdi won't have me any more as collaborator, I shall finish the work as best I can, so that he may have proof that I, though physically tormented, have dedicated to him, with all the affection he inspires in me, four months of my time. By that I would not wish, heaven forbid, to claim any material reward, either from him or from you, if the thing does not turn out well. It would be enough for me to have given Verdi proof that I am very much more truly devoted to him than he believes.

He finished the libretto, but was not entirely satisfied and wished to revise it. Ricordi seems to have insisted on sending at least part of it at once to Sant' Agata. Anxiously they awaited Verdi's reaction, and invoked the aid of Giuseppina. She replied on 7th November:

> I don't know Boito at all well, but I believe I have divined his character. A nervous nature, highly excitable! When overcome with admiration, capable of limitless enthusiasm and perhaps also sometimes, *by effect of contrast*, of excessive antipathies! All that, however, in brief paroxysms and only when there is a struggle within him between mind and heart, or rather between opposing passions or powers. The loyalty and justice of his character soon gain the upper hand and bring all his faculties again into equilibrium. Constant in friendship and at the same time mild and docile, like a boy, except when his fibre is, so to speak, *plucked*. I say all this to show that I believe I have *understood* the man, so that his feverish state at the present time does not surprise me.

In about a fortnight's time, she went on, they would be coming to Milan, and then Boito could talk the matter over quietly with Verdi. 'Between ourselves, what Boito has so far written of the African seems to please him, and is very well done.' He was to finish the libretto and send it to Verdi before he came to Milan. 'I repeat, the impression is good: modifications and polishing will come later.' The end of this letter is very fine:

> I want us to be able to say: 'All's well that ends well.' Don't write or speak to Verdi, then, of fears, desires or hesitations; and I add: Don't even tell Verdi that I have written to you on this subject. I believe that is the best way to avoid arousing in his mind the idea of even the slightest pressure. Let us allow the stream to find its own way, down to the sea. It's in the wide open spaces that certain men are destined to meet and to understand one another.

On 18th November Verdi told Ricordi: 'I have just received the chocolate'; a few days later he and Giuseppina went to Milan. On 18th December, replying to a probably unwelcome inquiry from an old friend of Verdi's, Giuseppina admitted that the libretto was complete: 'Verdi must have liked it, for after reading it he bought it, but . . . he put it beside Somma's *Re Lear*, which has slept profoundly and without disturbance for thirty years in its portfolio. What will become of this *Otello*? No one knows. I would like Verdi to be able to let it sleep like *Re Lear* for another thirty years and then find sufficient strength and courage to set it to music, to his own glory and the glory of art.'

Not thirty, but another five years, almost, were to go by before he began to compose *Otello*.

The year 1880 brought, for Verdi, the triumph of *Aida* in Paris in March, and for Boito the success of *Mefistofele* in London in June.

It does not appear that, so far, Boito had ever written directly to Verdi. Ricordi, the intermediary and arch-plotter, thought the time had come for another move. 'It's necessary to wake our Verdi up a bit,' he wrote to Boito on 24th July. 'You will recall that at your request I wrote to him to say that on your return you would occupy yourself with the finale. . . . By now the fumes of the English beer will have dispersed and your nerves recovered their calm. I have the feeling that Verdi has put the Moor to sleep for a bit! An electric shock from your verses would work wonders! Do me the favour then of sending this blessed finale of yours to Busseto.' The finale was that of the third act of *Otello*, which had not satisfied Verdi in its original form. The arrival of Boito's second version, about a fortnight later, brought a reply showing that the Moor was far from inactive in the composer's imagination. This letter, the first from Verdi to Boito since 1862, marks the real beginning of their correspondence as collaborators:

Sant' Agata, 15th August 1880.

DEAR SIG. BOITO,

Giulio will have told you that I received your verses a few days ago and wanted to read and study them carefully before replying.

They are certainly better than the first, but to my way of thinking it's still not a dramatically effective piece, because the possibility of that does not exist. After Othello has insulted Desdemona there's nothing more to say—at the most a phrase, a reproach, a curse on the *barbarian* who has insulted a woman! And here either bring down the curtain, or *invent* something that's not in Shakespeare! For example, after the words: 'Silence, Devil!' Lodovico, with all the pride of a patrician and the dignity of an ambassador, could apostrophize Othello: 'Unworthy Moor, you dare to insult a Venetian patrician, my relative, and do not fear the wrath of the senate?' (a stanza of 4 or 6 lines);

Iago gloats over his work (a similar stanza);
Desdemona laments (a similar stanza);
Roderigo (a stanza);
Emilia and chorus (a stanza);
Othello mute, immobile, terrible, says nothing. . . .

Suddenly distant drums, trumpets, cannon fire, etc., are heard. The Turks! The Turks! The stage is invaded by soldiers and the populace; general surprise and terror. Othello shakes himself like a lion and draws himself erect; he brandishes his sword. 'Come on; I will lead you again to victory.' They all leave the stage except Desdemona. Meanwhile the women, gathering from all sides, fall on their knees in terror while offstage are heard the cries of the soldiers, cannon fire, drums, trumpets and all the tumult of the battle. Desdemona, isolated and immobile in the centre of the stage, her eyes turned to Heaven, prays for Othello. The curtain falls.

The musical piece would be there, and a composer could be content. The critic would have much to say. For example: If the Turks were defeated (as is said at the beginning) how could they now fight? This however is not a serious criticism because one could suppose, and state in a few words, that the Turks suffered damage and were dispersed by the storm, but not destroyed. There would be a more serious objection: Can Othello, crushed with sorrow, gnawed by jealousy, discouraged, physically and morally sick—can he suddenly pull himself together and become again the hero that he was? And if he can, if glory can still fascinate him, and he can forget love, sorrow and jealousy, why should he kill Desdemona and then himself?

Are these needless scruples, or are they serious objections? I wanted to tell you what's going through my head. Who knows? Perhaps you'll find among these stupidities a germ from which something could be made! Think it over, write to me and believe me,

Yours sincerely,

G. VERDI.

PS. Allow me most sincerely to congratulate you on the success of *Mefistofele* in London.

There is a brief lacuna in our documents at this point; from those that follow, one can only suppose that Boito was disconcerted by Verdi's suggestion, of which he could not approve, and that Ricordi then proposed a verbal discussion to clear up the difficulty. On 7th September we find Giuseppina again politely discouraging Giulio from paying a visit, in company with Boito, on the grounds that the newspapers would be sure to hear of it, and to make a fuss. 'As a result, a stronger tie, a deeper commitment, to the writing of this *Otello*, on which Verdi's ideas are not yet clear, in spite of the very beautiful verses. And without clear ideas, now or later, Verdi will never write.' The substance of this letter was dictated by Verdi himself; a draft in his hand is found on a loose sheet inserted in Giuseppina's letter-book. It includes the passage: 'Several times I've heard him say: *I'm becoming too deeply involved; things are going too far and I don't want to be constrained to do what I don't wish to do*.'

This was a step backwards, clearly. What was to be done? Boito worked out the whole new finale, exactly as envisaged by Verdi, and sent it to Sant' Agata, without commentary. 'Dear Boito,' the composer wrote on 14th October, 'I received today the finale of the third act. Divinely well done! . . . And now what do you think of the scruples manifested in my last letter? What do you think of the character of Othello?' Boito was forced to reply:

When you ask me, or rather ask yourself: Are these needless scruples, or are they serious objections? I reply: They are serious objections. Othello is like a man moving in circles under an incubus, and under the fatal and growing domination of that incubus he thinks, he acts, he suffers and commits his tremendous crime. Now if we invent something which must necessarily excite and distract Othello from this tenacious incubus, we destroy all the sinister enchantment created by Shakespeare and we cannot logically reach the climax of the action. That attack by the Turks is like a fist breaking the window of a room where two persons were on the point of dying of asphyxiation. That intimate atmosphere of death, so carefully built up by Shakespeare, is suddenly dispelled. Vital air circulates again in our tragedy and Othello and Desdemona are saved. In order to set them again on the way to death we must enclose them again in the lethal chamber, reconstruct the incubus, patiently reconduct Iago to his prey, and there is only one act left for us to begin the tragedy over again. In other words: *We have found the end of an act, but at the cost of the effect of the final catastrophe.*

This was absolutely convincing, and the idea was abandoned. The episode gives a clear idea of the unique nature of this collaboration. Rather too much has been made, by Luzio [1] and others, of Verdi's share in the final shaping of these librettos. He drew his pen through half a page, at the conclusion of the tragedy, and found what seems now the inevitably right form of that scene. But he did not dominate Boito as he had dominated his earlier librettists, like poor Piave; sometimes he got on the wrong track and had to be very gently led back, as in this instance. There was as yet no certainty that Verdi would ever set this libretto to music. The great thing was to encourage his interest in it in every possible way. When Verdi conceived this non-Shakespearian finale to the third act, Boito gave him exactly what he wanted, without argument; when pressed for his opinion, he argued against it and carried the day.

One of Ricordi's earlier attempts to coax Verdi back to the theatre involved the revision of *Simon Boccanegra*, a score full of fine music which had never had much success. The composer's initial reaction had not been encouraging: 'I received yesterday a large parcel containing, I suppose, the score of *Simon*. If you come to Sant' Agata in six months' time, or in a year, two years, three, etc., you will find it intact, just as you sent it. I told you at Genoa that I detest all useless things.' But then he began to find the idea attractive, and made it his own. The trouble with the old score, he decided, lay principally in the 'second' act (he now counted what is actually the prologue as the first act), and when he asked: 'Who could revise it?' the answer was easy. Ricordi assured him that Boito was ready to do anything and everything he wished.

No reply had come to Boito's letter setting out the objections to the suggested departure from Shakespeare, and he did not know, for about six weeks, whether he had indeed succeeded in convincing Verdi. But meanwhile he had devised another version of the finale, and at Ricordi's urging sent it to Verdi at Genoa.

[1] Luzio was so anxious to show that Verdi was always right that he omitted Boito's long and splendid reply from the *Carteggi*. It was first published by Nardi (pp. 469–71).

Genoa, 2nd December 1880.

DEAR BOITO,

Well contrived, this third finale! I like Othello's fainting fit better in this finale than in the place where it was first. Only I don't find, or feel, the big *ensemble*! But one could do without that. We'll talk about it later; for at present, as Giulio will have told you, there's something else to think about.

I thought there would be a lot to do in this *Boccanegra*, but now I see that if we can find a *good beginning* to a finale, which gives variety, plenty of variety, to the too uniform substance of this drama, the rest would amount to no more than a line or two here and there, in order to alter a few musical phrases, etc.

Think it over a bit, then, and write to me as soon as you have found something.

A warm handshake in haste from your affectionate

G. VERDI.

Boito's first three letters on *Simon Boccanegra* seem to be lost, so that we have no details of his first plan, for a whole new act, in the church of San Siro. He compared the old libretto to a rickety table, one of the legs of which would have to be renewed to make it stand firmly on the floor. But Verdi was not prepared for such extensive revision.

Genoa, 11th December 1880.

DEAR BOITO,

'Either the Council Chamber . . . or the church of San Siro . . . or do nothing. . . .'

To *do nothing* would be best, but there are reasons, not commercial but, let me say, *professional*, which prevent me giving up the idea of putting this *Boccanegra* in order without at least having first tried to make something of it.

In parenthesis, it's in everyone's interest that La Scala should survive! The programmes for this year are deplorable. Ponchielli's opera is an excellent choice, but the rest? . . . There is one opera which would arouse great interest in the public and I don't understand why its composer and publisher persist in refusing it! I mean *Mefistofele*. The moment would be opportune, and you would be rendering a service to art and to us all.

The act conceived by you in the church of San Siro is stupendous in every respect—for novelty, historical colour, and from the scenico-musical standpoint—but it would involve me in too much work and I could not undertake it.

Having, unfortunately, to renounce this act, we must stick to the scene in the Council Chamber which, written by you, will be effective, I do not doubt. Your criticisms are justified, but you, immersed in more elevated works, and with *Otello* in mind, are aiming at a perfection impossible here. I aim lower and, more optimistic than you, I don't despair. I agree that the table rocks, but, adjusting the legs a bit, I believe it will stand up. I agree also that there are none of those characters (always very rare!) which make one exclaim: 'How monumental!' Nevertheless it seems to me that there is something in the characters of Fiesco and Simone which could be put to good use.

Let's try, then, and do this finale, with the Tartar Ambassador and Petrarch's letters, etc., etc., etc.

Let's try, I say; we are not so inexpert as not to understand, even beforehand, whether it promises to succeed in the theatre.

If it's not a burden to you, and if you have time, set to work at once. Meanwhile I'll try to straighten here and there the many crooked legs of my notes, and then we'll see.

Yours affectionately,

G. VERDI.

Genoa, 28th December 1880.

DEAR BOITO,

This scene in the Council Chamber is most beautiful, full of movement, of local colour, with your usual very elegant and forceful verses. I agree about the verses to be altered at the beginning of the third act, and the poisoning of the Doge in that way will do very well. But to my misfortune the piece is vast in the extreme, difficult to set to music, and I don't know whether, now that I am no longer *dans le mouvement*, I shall be able to get back in practice in time to do this, and patch up all the rest.

Allow me now a few remarks, simply to clarify things to myself:

1 Do you think it necessary to let it be known in the beginning that Amelia is safe, and is *calling for justice*?

2 Do you think that the affair of Tartary is alone sufficient to call the Council together? Could one not add some other affairs of state, a Corsair raid, for example, or even the war with Venice, cursed by the poet? All that, of course, in passing, in a few lines?

3 If Adorno says: 'I killed Lorenzino because he carried off my betrothed' and Amelia: 'Save my betrothed!' we spoil the scene in the third act between the Doge and Amelia—a scene not very important in itself but which prepares very well for the Doge's sleep and the terzetto. It seems to me that the action would lose nothing if when the Doge says: 'Why did you take up arms?' Gabriele replied: 'You had Amelia Grimaldi carried off. Vile crowned Corsair, die!'

Doge: 'Strike, then!'

Gabriele: 'Amelia!'

All: 'Amelia!'

Doge: 'Adorno, you protected this maiden; I admire you and absolve you. . . . Amelia, tell us how you were carried off,' etc., etc.

The rest will do very well. Stupendous from 'Plebeians! Patricians! People!' to the end, which we will close with 'Be accursed!'

Reply as soon as possible.

Sincere good wishes,

G. VERDI.

Genoa, 8th January 1881.

DEAR BOITO,

Don't blame yourself for having wasted my time. So far I have done nothing about the music. Now however I am thinking about it, indeed I have been thinking all day about this *Boccanegra*, and this is what it seems to me could be done:

I pass over the Prologue, of which I'll perhaps alter the first recitative and a few bars here and there in the orchestra.

In the first act I should take out the cabaletta of the first piece, not because it's a cabaletta but because it's very ugly. I should alter the prelude, to which I should link Amelia's *cantabile*, changing the scoring, and making them *one single piece*. At the end I should take up again an orchestral movement from the prelude, over which Amelia would say 'Day has dawned . . . he's not coming!' or something similar. So patch me up a couple of short lines in broken phrases. I should not want that expression of jealousy on Amelia's part!

The tenor's offstage romanza would stay as it is.

In the following duet I should alter the line: 'You agree to our marriage.' If the audience doesn't catch the word 'humble' it would not understand anything further. If he said, for example, 'Listen . . . a deep secret!' etc., etc.—these are words that always make an audience prick up its ears. And therefore, if you think fit, add a couple of lines—or don't, just as you wish. What really matters to me is to alter the duet between Fiesco and Gabriele: 'Tremble, O Doge!' It's too ferocious, and says nothing at all. Instead I should like Fiesco, who is almost Amelia's father, to bless bride and bridegroom to be. A pathetic moment could result which would be a ray of light amid so much gloom. To maintain the atmosphere introduce too a bit of local patriotic feeling. Fiesco can say: 'Love this angel . . but after God . . . our country,' etc. All good words to make the ears prick up. . . .

Eight lines then for Fiesco and as many for Gabriele, simple, touching, affectionate, on which to write a bit of melody, or something that at least resembles it. Ah, if one could bring Amelia back into the scene, and write an unaccompanied terzettino! How delightful to write for three voices! Amelia and Gabriele kneeling, Fiesco, above, blessing them! But I can understand that, apart from the difficulty of bringing Amelia back, we should have an almost identical final scene in the last act.

Have I made myself clear? I'm not quite sure. Try to guess at what I haven't been able to say and send me meanwhile those few verses as soon as possible, and tomorrow or the next day I'll tell you about the rest. Meanwhile I shall set to work on the first piece of this first act, to get myself in practice before I come to the finale.

I would like to do everything in order, as if a new opera were concerned.

I await your reply. Believe me,

Your

G. VERDI.

Genoa, 10th January 1881.

DEAR BOITO,

Your two registered letters with the variants arrive just at the right moment. With the four lines: '*S'inalba il ciel . . .*' etc., I shall end the first piece, which indeed can be said to be already finished. The few lines added to the following scene for Andrea and Gabriele will do well. I'm afraid the little duet will turn out too long and too loud. I would like just at this moment something calm, solemn, religious. It concerns a marriage. It's a father blessing his adopted children.

I don't much like the octosyllabic rhythm owing to those two cursed notes to be taken out . . . but I shall avoid them, and so as not to lose time I am setting about this duet at once, on Andrea's four lines:

Vieni a me ti benedico
. . . .
. . . .
. . . .

I shall patch up meanwhile four other words for Gabriele, so as to get on with the work, until your lines arrive. Four lines for each of them are enough. To make myself clearer: I would like Gabriele to be able to sing his verse kneeling; something religious then. Besides the fact that this, as it seems to me, does no harm, this calm, and that of the following scene, would help to throw into greater prominence the tumult of the finale.

You say that the little duet would start after the *blank verse*. All of it? It seems to me that this little duet should start after 'In terra e in ciel.' Or after

Ma non rallenti amore
La foga in te dei cittadini affetti

adapting, of course, the rhymes and the lines as you think fit. If you agree, then, we can put

Il Doge vien. . . . Andiam
. . . .
. . . .

after the little duet, during the sounding of the trumpets or the huntsmen's chorus.

All the other variants will do very well, and the *poison* recitative is very fine. Perhaps we shall find ourselves a bit embarrassed, as far as the stage is concerned, at Amelia's words:

O Doge (*o Padre*)
Salva l'Adorno tu

How will she say these words? *Sotto voce* to the Doge? That would not be very effective. But these are trifles that can be got over by a word or two, or by a stage gesture.

Courage then, my dear Boito. Do me these four octosyllabic lines for Gabriele. Not more than four lines each. That is enough. Send them as soon as possible. Meanwhile I am working. . . .

Kind regards, from my wife as well,

G. VERDI.

He was probably not consciously submitting Boito to the practical test of collaboration on *Simon Boccanegra* before finally making up his mind about *Otello*. But in effect this revision was an exploration of the possibilities of working together, and some of the results, such as the magnificent scene in the Council Chamber and the villainous Paolo's Iago-like recitatives, foreshadow the later opera. Boito's intelligence and the way he tackled the difficulties presented by the old libretto made a very favourable impression on Verdi. We cannot follow here all the rather voluminous correspondence over the revision of *Simon Boccanegra*. For the history of the relations of these two men, however, it is important to note the increasing cordiality; a sense of humour, on both sides, greatly helped to overcome the difficulties.

Verdi to Boito, 15th January:

You imagine you've finished, dear Boito? Anything but! We shall have finished after the dress rehearsal—if we get that far. Meanwhile in the duet between father and daughter there is something to which greater relief must be given. . . .

17th January:

Just a line to say that I received your verses this morning and that they'll do very well. That's all for now. . . . About the future I'm not so sure. . . .

24th January:

I need another drop of your ink. I say *another*. . . . I don't say it'll be the *last*!

2nd February:

If only we had finished!

5th February:

We haven't finished!!!!

and

After this perhaps we shall have finished!

Then Boito, every bit as conscientious as Verdi, began himself to suggest further changes: 'I return to my old comparison with the table; now it's the fourth leg that wobbles. It must be mended, and the operation performed with such care that, when this is put right, the other three don't begin to limp again. For two days now I've been thinking and thinking about this fourth act.'

And Verdi, 6th February:

We'll adjust the fourth leg too, then. . . .

15th February:

We haven't finished yet! . . . The beautiful, most beautiful finale you have written for me has rather adversely affected the scene in the last act between Fiesco and the Doge. . . .

At length they really had finished and the revised *Boccanegra* was warmly received at La Scala on 24th March. The Gabriele was Tamagno, the Boccanegra Maurel, with whose interpretation Verdi was so pleased that at one of the rehearsals he said, in an expansive moment: 'If God gives me strength, I'll write *Iago* for you!'

Two months after the revised *Simon Boccanegra*, the revised *Mefistofele* was produced at La Scala. Verdi sent a telegram: 'Delighted with the success, I send my most cordial, sincere congratulations, and let's have *Nerone* soon.' There had been further conversation between them about *Otello*, for on the day of the first performance of *Mefistofele* at La Scala Boito had written to Verdi: 'Don't think that I've forgotten the *Moor of Venice*. I have thought about it, but so far I have lacked the necessary tranquillity to work on it at my table.' The outstanding problems of the libretto were the introduction of the chorus of homage to Desdemona in the second act, the big ensemble in the third act and some cuts to be made in Othello's part. After three weeks of lionization following the success of *Mefistofele*, Boito shut himself in his rooms and soon resolved the first of the problems to Verdi's satisfaction.

Sant' Agata, 23rd June 1881.

DEAR BOITO,

Don't be angry if I haven't replied before now to your most welcome and important letter.

I think the chorus you have sent me will do very well. I say 'I think' because, not having before my eyes the second act, I'm not really clear about the position the chorus will occupy. At all events that chorus could not be more graceful, more elegant or beautiful. And then, what a splash of light, amid so much gloom! Get busy then on the finale, and make it a well-developed piece, a piece *on a big scale*, I should say. The theatre demands it; but more than the theatre the colossal power of the drama demands it. The idea (which I still like) of setting *Otello* to music without a chorus was and is, perhaps, a crazy one!

As for the cuts in Othello's part, all right, we'll make them together.

Kind regards from my wife, and I affectionately press your hand.

G. VERDI.

Then at last the first visit to Sant' Agata, in Ricordi's company, took place, and Boito on 10th July was able to tell Tornaghi: 'We have settled with the Maestro the last dubious point of the work, and I am now occupied in giving form to the result of that exchange of ideas.'

It seems obvious that 'the last dubious point of the work' was the great concerted finale. But according to Nardi [1] the text of this finale was not provided by Boito until 1885. It is not often that one can disagree with Nardi, but here he is definitely mistaken. The letter of 10th July to Tornaghi was written at Monticello, near Monza.[2] An undated letter of 'Wednesday' to Verdi, beginning: 'You had begun to think I had forgotten, along with the hat, the sponge and the brush, the big finale of *Otello*,' assigned by Nardi to 1885, says: 'I leave again for Monticello tomorrow.' It is only in 1881 that we find Boito at Monticello. Nardi was misled by Luzio, who presented these letters out of order in the *Carteggi* because he failed to consult Verdi's side of the correspondence. The letter of 'Wednesday' about the concerted finale appears in the *Carteggi* [3] between two others respectively of April 1884 and July 1886, and Luzio connects it with a note dated '12th June, Milan', which says: 'I must say that I was still half asleep when, in the morning of the day before yesterday, I made my preparations for departure. I laughed when I read the list of objects forgotten at Sant' Agata.' But Boito made quite a habit of leaving things behind him and this note has nothing to do with the letter about the finale; it is from *1895*, as Verdi's side of the correspondence shows (11th June 1895. 'Dear Boito. You left here: 4 handkerchiefs, 1 vest, 1 note case, 1 button'). It was in the second half of July or in August of 1881, and not in June of 1885, that the text of the finale was completed and sent off to Sant' Agata with the long accompanying letter of 'Wednesday'.

This is shown also by Verdi's reply, which is among the others in possession of the Albertini family at Parella, but which is not mentioned or quoted either by Gatti or by Nardi.[4] Verdi's letter, unusually for him, is also undated, but can be confidently assigned to the latter half of August 1881, when he was on a visit to Milan to see the exhibition of that year. It employs the formal, third-person mode of address ('Ella' and 'Lei'), as do the other letters of this period; all the later letters, from 1884–5 onwards, use the second person ('voi').

DEAR BOITO,

I am at Milan and your two letters were sent on to me here from Busseto. The finale is very well done indeed. What a difference between this one and the first!

I shall add the four lines for Roderigo.

Perhaps the other four for Desdemona will not be needed.

[1] pp. 471 and 499. Nardi is followed by Abbiati (IV, pp. 174 and 256).

[2] *Lettere di Arrigo Boito* (Rome, 1932), p. 87.

[3] II, pp. 112–15.

[4] It was missing from the copies of Verdi's letters used by Nardi, which he so kindly gave me for use in this book.

It's so true that a silent Othello is grander and more terrible that my opinion would be not to have him speak at all during the whole *ensemble*. It seems to me that Iago alone can say, and more briefly, everything that must be said for the spectator's understanding, without Othello replying.

Iago: Hurry! Time is flying! Concentrate on your task, and on that alone! I'll see to Cassio. I'll pluck out his infamous, guilty soul. I swear it. You shall have news of him at midnight.

(Altering the verses, of course.)

After the *ensemble* and after the words: *Tutti fuggite Otello* it seems to me that Othello does not speak or cry out enough. He is silent for four lines and it seems to me that (scenically speaking) after *Che d'ogni senso il priva* Othello ought to bellow one or two lines: 'Away! I detest you . . . myself . . . the whole world!'

And it seems to me, too, that a few lines could be spared when Othello and Iago remain together:

[Othello]: *Fuggirmi io sol non so. . . . Ah l'idra!*
[Iago]: *Signor!*
[Othello]: *Vederli insieme avvinti . . . Ah maledetto*
Pensiero . . . Sangue, sangue . . .
(a cry and he faints) *Il fazzoletto!*
[Iago]: *Il mio velen lavora.*
(Cries offstage]: *Viva l'eroe di Cipro!*
[Iago]: *Chi può vietar che questa fronte io prema*
Col mio tallone?
[Cries offstage]: *Gloria*
Al Leon di Venezia!
[Iago]: *Ecco il Leone!*

A strangled cry on the word *fazzoletto* seems to me more terrible than a commonplace exclamation like *Oh Satana!* The words *svenuto . . . immobil . . . muto* somewhat hold up the action. One stops to think and here it's a case of hurrying on to the end. Let me have your opinion.

I haven't finished!! The chorus has little or nothing to do. Could one not find a way of moving it about a bit? For example, after the words *In Cipro elegge mio successor. . . . Cassio!*:

Chorus, with four lines, not of revolt, but of protest: 'No, no, we want Othello!'

I know perfectly well that you will reply at once: 'Dear Signor Maestro, don't you know that nobody dared to breathe after a decree of the *Serenissima*, and that sometimes the mere presence of the *Messer Grande* sufficed to disperse the crowd, and subdue the tumult?'

I would dare to rejoin that the action takes place in Cyprus, the *Serenissimi* were far away and perhaps for that reason the Cypriots were bolder than the Venetians.

If you come to Milan I hope to see you. I'm not sure, but I think you have all the poetry of the third act.

In haste, farewell, farewell.

G. VERDI.

Hotel Milan.

It is probable that Boito came to Milan from Monticello, and that, after further discussion, the finale was given its definitive form at this time. There are no more letters about it. Nothing came of Verdi's suggestion of a popular protest against Othello's recall; he must again have been dissuaded by Boito.

Two years and more went by. Verdi continued to correspond, from time to time, with Domenico Morelli, the Neapolitan painter, about the characters, the costumes and settings of *Otello*. Ricordi dropped hints in the form of Christmas cakes decorated with the figure of the Moor in chocolate and sugar. The French critic Baron Blaze de Bury inquired about the possibility of his being entrusted with the French translation of the libretto. Verdi's only letter to Boito of 1882 refers to this: '"*Un jour ou l'autre Iago* [1] . . . *existera*". . . . I am surprised that the Baron is so sure, because I personally do not know whether it will ever *exist*.' After discussion of the difficulties of a French translation the letter continues: 'But why talk now of an opera that does not exist? Of an opera that will have Italian proportions and who knows how many other things that are Italian? Perhaps a few melodies (if I can find some). And melody is always Italian, essentially Italian, and cannot be anything but Italian. . . .'

From 1883 there is only one short letter to Boito. It is however very cordial. He had begun to spend part of the winter at Nervi, and was a welcome visitor at Palazzo Doria, whenever he came to Genoa: 'If I had imagined that you would still be at Nervi on San Giuseppe's day,' Verdi wrote on 7th April, 'I should have come in person to take you by the leg. . . .'

In the succeeding winter they had several meetings at Genoa, and a few further small alterations were made in the libretto. And then at length, early in 1884, at the age of seventy, Verdi began the composition of *Otello*. Boito on 20th March wrote to Giulio Ricordi: 'I have good news for you, but for charity's sake don't tell anyone, don't tell even your family, don't tell even yourself; I fear I have already committed an indiscretion. The Maestro is writing, indeed he has already written a good part of the opening of the first act and seems to be working with fervour.'

And almost at once an incident occurred that was nearly fatal. *Mefistofele* was performed with success at Naples, a banquet was given in Boito's honour, and he was questioned by some of those present about *Otello*. A misleading account of what he said appeared in some of the newspapers and was read by Verdi. It was strangely like the earlier episode of the ode *All'Arte italiana* after Faccio's *Profughi fiamminghi*. According to the newspapers, Boito had said that he had written his *Otello* libretto against his will, but that when it was finished he had regretted not being able to set it to music

[1] The original title of the projected opera.

himself. Verdi stiffened; the pen dropped from his hand. But he acted in the most generous and delicate way possible. He wrote to Faccio a noble letter:

> The worst of it is that Boito's regret that he cannot set it to music himself leads naturally to the supposition that he has no hope of seeing it set to music by me in the way he would like. I admit this possibility, I admit it completely; and that is why I turn to you, the oldest and closest of Boito's friends, to ask that, when he returns to Milan, you tell him—not in writing, but by word of mouth—that I give him back his manuscript intact, without a shadow of resentment, without rancour of any kind. More, as that manuscript is my property, I offer it to him as a gift if he wishes to set it to music.

Boito, who had seen the statements attributed to him by the newspapers, but had hoped they had not come to Verdi's notice, was horrified. His reply is one of the most deeply moving and revealing things he ever wrote. His only desire, he said, had been to have his libretto set to music by Verdi; he had written it solely for the joy of seeing Verdi resume composition, and for the glory of becoming his working associate:

> This theme and my libretto are yours by right of conquest. You alone can set *Othello* to music—all the dramatic creations you have given us proclaim this truth. If I have been able to divine the inherent powerful musicality of the Shakespearian tragedy, which at first I did not feel, and if I have been able to demonstrate it in fact with my libretto, that is because I put myself at the viewpoint of Verdian art, because I felt in writing those verses what you would feel in representing them in that other language, a thousand times more intimate and strong, the language of sound. . . . What you cannot suspect is the irony that, through no fault of yours, appeared to me to be contained in that offer. Look! Already for seven or eight years, perhaps, I have been working on *Nerone* (put the *perhaps* where you like, attached to the word *years*, or to the word *working*). I live under that incubus; on the days when I don't work I pass the hours in reproaching myself for laziness; on the days when I do work I pass the hours in reproaching myself for stupidity; and thus life runs away and I am slowly asphyxiated by an ideal too exalted for my powers. To my misfortune, I have studied my period—that is, the period of my subject—too intently, and I am terribly in love with it, and no other subject in the world, not even Shakespeare's *Othello*, could distract me from my theme. It responds in everything to my character as an artist and to the conception I have formed of opera. I shall finish *Nerone*, or I shall not finish it, but it is certain that I shall never abandon it for another work, and if I haven't the strength to finish it I shall not complain, but shall pass my life, neither sorry nor glad, with that dream in my mind. Now judge for yourself whether, with this obstinate disposition, I could accept your offer? But for charity's sake, don't abandon *Otello*, don't abandon it! It is predestined for you. Create it. You had begun work upon it and I was all

encouraged and was hoping already to see it finished at some not distant date. You are sounder than I, stronger than I; we tested our strength and my arm bent beneath yours. Your life is tranquil and serene; take up your pen again and write to me soon: Dear Boito, do me the favour of altering these verses, etc., etc. I will change them at once, with joy, and I shall know how to work for you, I who do not know how to work for myself, for you live in the true and real world of art, and I in the world of hallucinations.

Verdi's reply, on 26th April said: 'It's useless now to talk any more about this, if you absolutely don't wish to accept the offer I made you (and, believe me, without a trace of irony). You say: "*I shall finish Nerone, or I shall not finish it.*" I say the same thing about *Otello*. There's been too much talk about it! Too much time has gone by! I'm too old! My *years of service* are too many!!!! I don't wish the public to have to say to me too evidently: *Enough!* The conclusion is that all this has cast a chill over this *Otello*, and stiffened the hand that had begun to trace out a few bars! What will happen in the future? I don't know!'

The situation was still perilous, and a false step would have led to disaster. But Boito's next move was most beautifully judged:

Your letter, though wise and kind, yet left me, I don't know why, somewhat disquieted, and I had no peace until I set to work for you again. I remembered that you were not satisfied with a scene for Iago in the second act, in double five-syllabled lines, and that you wanted a freer form, less lyrical; I proposed a sort of *evil Credo*, and I have tried to write one, in broken metre, unsymmetrical.

The link is missing between this extract and the preceding recitative, but I haven't the manuscript here and so haven't been able to do it, but the lacuna will be of two lines, or three at most.

If this attempt has turned out badly, put it down to haste and agitation; I'll do it again better whenever you wish. Meanwhile, if you don't think it absolutely a failure, please put this fragment together with the other pages of *Otello*. I did it for my own comfort and personal satisfaction, because I felt the need of doing it. You can interpret this need how you like—as puerility, sentimentality or superstition—it doesn't matter. All I ask is that you do not reply, even to say 'Thank you' (that page is not worth it); if you do, I shall become disquieted all over again.

Verdi could not leave this unanswered:

Genoa, 3rd May 1884.

DEAR BOITO,

Since you don't wish it, I won't say 'Thank you'; but I will say 'Bravo'.

Most beautiful, this Credo; most powerful and wholly Shakespearian. You'll have naturally to link it by a line or two with the preceding scene between Cassio and Iago; but you can think about that later. Meanwhile it would be well to leave this *Otello* in peace for a bit, for he, too, is nervous, as we are—you perhaps more than I.

If later on you come to Sant' Agata, as you've given me reason to hope, we shall be able to talk it over again, and by then with the necessary calm.

So get rid of all disquietude. With kind regards from Peppina, I am always

Yours affectionately,

G. VERDI.

PS. I am late in replying because I have been to Sant' Agata.

Boito did visit Sant' Agata, with his friend Giacosa, for three days at the end of September. Then on 9th December, once again from Genoa, he received the news he was waiting for: 'It seems impossible, and yet it is true!! I am busy, I am writing!!' Verdi asked for four more lines each for Iago and Emilia in the quartet in the second act. Boito, highly elated, supplied the want at once: 'Your letter was for me a joy I have kept entirely to myself, but which did not surprise me. One can't escape one's destiny, and by a law of intellectual affinity that tragedy of Shakespeare's is predestined for you.'

All was well again.

Further revision of the accepted history of the composition of the opera is necessary at this point.

Gatti, Nardi and Abbiati are all in agreement about the course of events in 1885. According to Gatti:[1] 'All the winter from 1884 to 1885 and the spring and summer of the latter year passed in the composition of *Otello*. . . . Almost the whole of 1885 was needed by the composer to rough out the entire composition of *Otello*. . . .' According to Nardi:[2] 'The remainder of 1884 and all 1885 Boito can be said to have been at Verdi's disposition. . . . A good part of the literary variants for *Otello* must have been settled verbally, in meetings at Genoa and Sant' Agata. The concerted piece for the finale of the third act, left imperfect four years earlier, began to take on its definitive form at Sant' Agata in the first ten days of June 1885.' We have already seen that this date is incorrect, deriving from a rare oversight on Nardi's part and the erroneous juxtaposition by Luzio of two letters of 1881 and 1895. Abbiati[3] at this point transcribes the whole of Boito's long letter of 1881, attributing it for reasons best known to himself to the *end* of June 1885. Otherwise he follows the earlier writers, though elaborating the background in his usual way. He depicts Verdi, possessed by a tragic demon, sweating over the score in the dog-days of 1885 'while the sun of July, in the still, almost stagnant air, split the tiles and cracked the terraces of the villa'.

The facts, however, are quite different.

Here is a short letter from Boito, together with Verdi's reply:

[1] First edition, II, pp. 375, 379; second edition, pp. 687, 691.
[2] pp. 498–9.
[3] IV, pp. 256–8, 263.

Milan, Wednesday.

My desire to see you again is great, but my fear of disturbing you is equally great.

If you assure me that I shan't be a nuisance I'll make up my mind to descend on Sant' Agata next Sunday, but if my coming could in the least disturb the beautiful tranquillity of your house or, what would be worse, the course of your work, you must tell me so, with that frankness I so much like in you, and I shall be just as happy about your frank words as about your courteous hospitality.

And I recommend Signora Giuseppina to do the same.

Cordial greetings to both of you from your affectionate

ARRIGO BOITO.

Sant' Agata, 10th September 1885.

DEAR BOITO,

You can never disturb! Come, and you will give such great pleasure both to me and to Peppina. And have no fear of interrupting the course of my work, as you say! Alas! Since I've been here (I blush to say it) I've done nothing! The country, to some extent, the baths, the excessive heat and, let us add, my unimaginable laziness have prevented it. Until Sunday, then. If you leave Milan by the 11.40 train, you get out at two o'clock in the afternoon at Fiorenzuola, where you will find a Bucephalus of mine to bring you here.

We'll see you soon, then. Peppina sends her regards, and I press your hands. Farewell.

Affectionately,

G. VERDI.

Now Verdi's letter is assigned to *1883* by both Gatti and Nardi. The autographs at Parella are numbered, not impossibly by Boito himself in later years, and according to this numeration, too, this letter would be of 1883. Nevertheless, the badly written last figure in the date more resembles a Verdian 5 than a 3. And Boito's letter, not considered by Gatti and Nardi, bears the postmark of 9th September 1885, according to Luzio. This time Luzio was not mistaken—9th September was indeed a Wednesday in 1885; in 1883 it was a *Sunday*. So both letters are from 1885.

The importance of this is that it gives us quite a different view of the course of the composition of *Otello*. Verdi probably left Genoa at the end of April; on 2nd May he was at Milan, where he saw his dentist; he announced his safe arrival at Sant' Agata to Clarina Maffei on 6th May. Letters from this year are very scarce—I know of none at all from June or July. There was a visit to Montecatini, probably in July, and to Tabiano ('the baths' in the above letter to Boito), probably in August. But during all this time—four and a half months, from the end of April to mid September—he did nothing to *Otello*.

Boito's conversation seems to have had an immensely stimulating effect, for on 5th October, only three weeks after his visit, Verdi announced: 'I have finished the fourth act, and I breathe again!'

We see now that *Otello*, in essentials, was completed in three comparatively short bouts of composition: the first, very brief, was at Genoa in March 1884; the second, the principal one, at Genoa from December 1884 to April 1885; the third at Sant' Agata from the middle of September to early October 1885. The scoring of the opera occupied another year, with intervals, and during this time there was some revision, particularly of the first act, and working out of details left unsettled in the composition sketch.

Nardi says: 'Boito's labours on account of *Otello* occupied, one can say, also the whole of 1886. . . . Letters asking for changes in the libretto recommenced, from 11th January onwards. In July that blessed *ensemble* for the concerted finale of the third act was still under discussion.' Boito certainly had plenty to do in this year, looking for a possible Desdemona, discussing scenery and costumes with the stage designer Edel and in the autumn most courageously embarking on a French translation of the third and fourth acts (while Du Locle worked on the first and second). But judging from the letters the revision of the Italian text after completion of the composition sketch amounted to very little. On 11th January Verdi asked whether Montano ought not to have a part in the great finale; he was glad to accept Boito's humorous explanation that Montano was confined to bed, as the result of his wounding in the first act, and so could not be present. Verdi also asked for four lines to be compressed into two, in the exchanges in recitative preceding the finale proper. According to a letter from Muzio to Ricordi,[1] the love duet at the end of the first act was finished in March, when it was played to Boito by Verdi in Muzio's presence. In May Verdi conceived the magnificently effective entry of Othello in the first act, with the 'Esultate' sung from the top of the bulwarks. He made a cut here of four lines, with Boito's enthusiastic approval. In July Boito himself proposed two brief additions, again in the exchanges in recitative preceding the finale of the third act, to explain better Desdemona's presence, but, in spite of what Nardi says, there is no evidence of changes in the *ensemble* itself. In September Verdi decided to replace four lines which had earlier been deleted, in the duet between Othello and Desdemona in the third act. On 9th September he reported: 'Tomorrow I shall send to Casa Ricordi, completely finished, all the first act and all scene vi of the third; and thus with the fourth, already sent, perhaps three-fifths of the Moor are ready.' On 1st November he announced: 'It's finished!' but then, it seems, found something further to do. Boito sent a two-line variant for Iago's part at the end of the serenade in the second act. Verdi acknowledged this on 18th

[1] Abbiati, IV, p. 279.

December: 'Thank you for the two lines. I have just consigned to Garignani (of Ricordi's staff) the last acts of *Otello*! Poor Othello! . . . He won't come back here any more!!!' Boito replied: 'The Moor will come no more to knock on the door of Palazzo Doria, but you will go to meet the Moor at La Scala. *Otello* exists. The great dream has become reality.'

When, after the first performance, under Faccio, on 5th February 1887, Verdi took Boito's hand and drew him on to the stage of La Scala to share one of the most tremendous ovations that theatre had ever seen, the ode *All'Arte italiana* of nearly twenty-four years earlier was finally atoned for, buried and forgotten. Verdi was seventy-three; in the past few years he had lost, one by one, most of his oldest friends. Giulio Carcano had died in 1884, Maffei in 1885; Clarina Maffei's death from meningitis on 13th July 1886 had been a bitter blow; another old and trusted friend who just failed to see the production of *Otello* was Arrivabene. Before long others were to follow—Tito Ricordi in September 1888, Florimo in December of the same year, and within a fortnight of each other Piroli and Muzio in November 1890. To people the growing void around him there was Giuseppina still, growing old and frail, with her sister Barberina, a perpetual invalid; there was Teresa Stolz, garrulous, jolly and fat; there was Maria Carrara Verdi and her growing family; there was Giulio Ricordi, De Amicis at Genoa, and a few others; but above all there was Boito, who had won for himself by now a truly paternal affection. It was fortunate for us, and for Verdi, that among the younger generation there was this companion, so subtly intelligent, so unselfishly devoted. The more one learns of Boito the more he appears one of the noblest and purest spirits of the whole romantic movement.

The material rewards of *Otello*—a fee of 150,000 lire, with the usual percentages of the receipts from the hire and sale of the scores—enabled Verdi to proceed with the notable works of charity he had long contemplated but only partly executed. In recent years he had built a hospital for the commune of Villanova d'Arda, in which Sant' Agata lies. Villanova is just over the border of the province of Parma, so that sick peasants were not admitted to the nearby hospital at Busseto, but taken over twenty miles by road to Piacenza. From 6th November 1888, when the new hospital was inaugurated, they were saved this long and sometimes fatal journey. Verdi and the commune shared the expenses of the upkeep of this hospital. Then in January 1889 negotiations were in progress for the purchase of a site at Milan for the last great work at all, the Casa di Riposo per Musicisti. The architect of this home for aged musicians was to be Boito's brother Camillo, with whom Verdi was already in communication in January 1889, although the building was not begun until about ten years later.

The story of *Falstaff* has little of the dramatic tension of the story of the creation of *Otello*. There was now perfect mutual confidence between composer and poet and it was comparatively easy to persuade Verdi to embark, in all secrecy and for his own amusement and delight, on the comic opera. Boito seems to have envisaged the whole thing from the start; he *knew* Verdi, at the age of nearly eighty, still had it in him to create that scintillating score. The project had first been discussed between them at Milan, on visits in connection with the purchase of the site for the Casa di Riposo. Then Verdi had left for his annual summer cure at Montecatini, where, apparently, he received Boito's sketch for the libretto of *Falstaff*. A lively correspondence began at once.

Montecatini, 6th July 1889.

DEAR BOITO,

Excellent! Excellent!

Before reading your sketch I wanted to re-read the *Merry Wives*, the two parts of *Henry IV* and *Henry V*, and I can only repeat: *Excellent*, for one could not do better than you have done.

A pity that the interest (it's not your fault) does not go on increasing to the end. The culminating point is the finale of the second act; and the appearance of Falstaff's face amid the linen, etc., is a true comic invention.

I'm afraid, too, that the last act, in spite of its touch of fantasy, will be trivial, with all those little pieces, songs, ariettas, etc., etc. You bring back Bardolph—and why not *Pistol* too, both of them, to get up to some prank or other?

You reduce the weddings to two! All the better, for they are only loosely connected with the principal plot.

The two trials by water and fire suffice to punish Falstaff; nevertheless, I should have liked to see him thoroughly well beaten as well.

I am talking for the sake of talking—take no notice. We have now very different matters to discuss, so that this *Falstaff*, or *Merry Wives*, which two days ago was in the world of dreams, now takes shape and becomes reality! When? How? . . . Who knows? I'll write to you tomorrow or the next day.

Greetings from Peppina. Farewell.

Affectionately,

G. VERDI.

Montecatini, 7th July 1889.

I said yesterday that I would write to you today, and I am keeping my word, even at the risk of vexing you. . . .

As long as one wanders in the realm of ideas, every prospect pleases, but when one comes down to earth, to practical matters, doubts and discouragement arise.

In outlining *Falstaff* did you never think of the enormous number of my years?

I know you will reply exaggerating the state of my health, which is good, excellent, robust. . . . So be it, but in spite of that you must agree that I could be taxed with great rashness in taking on so much! Supposing I couldn't stand the strain? And failed to finish it? You would then have uselessly wasted your time and trouble! For all the gold in the world I would not wish that. This idea is insupportable to me; and all the more insupportable if you, in writing *Falstaff*, had, I won't say to abandon, but to distract your attention from *Nerone*, or delay its production. I should be blamed for this delay and the thunderbolts of malignity would fall about my head.

How are we to overcome these obstacles? Have you a sound argument to oppose to mine? I hope so, but I don't believe it. Still, let's think it over (and be careful to do nothing that could be harmful to your career) and if you can find one for me, and I some way of throwing off ten years or so, then . . . what joy, to be able to say to the public:

Here we are again!!

Farewell, farewell. Affectionately,

G. VERDI.

Boito replied that he never thought of Verdi's age, in speaking or writing to him, or working for him. In his view the only thing that should cause them to pause before deciding to embark on a new opera was the sublimity of the achievement of two years earlier. 'It is rare indeed to see a life of artistic endeavour concluded with a world triumph. *Otello* is such a triumph. All the other arguments—*age, strength, hard work for you, hard work for me*, etc., etc.—are not valid and are not obstacles to a new work.' He was optimistic even about *Nerone*: 'Since you oblige me to speak of myself, I shall say that notwithstanding the engagement I should assume with *Falstaff* I shall be able to finish my own work within the term promised. I am sure of it.' He had much more to say, but Verdi really needed little persuading:

Montecatini, 10th July 1889.

DEAR BOITO,

Amen. So be it!

We'll write this *Falstaff* then! We won't think for the moment of obstacles, of age, of illness!

I too wish to conserve the profoundest *secrecy*—a word that I too underline three times, to tell you that no one must know anything about it! But wait . . . Peppina knew it, I believe, before we did! Be sure, however, she will keep the secret; when women have this quality they have it in greater measure than we.

I take note of your phrase: '*Notwithstanding the engagement I should assume with Falstaff I shall be able to finish my own work within the term promised.*'

And now a last word. A very prosaic word, yet, especially for me, necessary and due. But no, no. . . .

Today *Falstaff* is too much in my mind and I could not talk to you of anything else. I'll talk to you about this something else tomorrow.

Meanwhile, if you feel in the mood, make a start at once. In the two first acts there is nothing to alter, apart, perhaps, from the monologue of the jealous husband, which would be better at the end of the First Part than at the beginning of the Second. It would have more warmth and efficacy.

Until tomorrow, then, with regards from Peppina. Farewell, farewell.

Affectionately,

G. VERDI.

Montecatini, 11th July 1889.

DEAR BOITO,

. . . I continue yesterday's letter. When you have finished your work you will cede the rights to me for the sum of . . . (to be fixed). And if ever, through age or disability, or for any other reason, I cannot finish the music, you will recover your *Falstaff*; I myself offer it to you, to remember me by, and you will make whatever use of it you think fit. . . .

Boito wrote beautifully about the new project:

This love between Nannetta and Fenton must appear suddenly at very frequent intervals; in all the scenes in which they take part they will keep on kissing by stealth in corners, astutely, boldly, without letting themselves be discovered, with fresh little phrases and brief, very rapid little dialogues, from the beginning to the end of the comedy; it will be a most lively, merry love, always disturbed and interrupted and always ready to recommence. . . . I should like, as one sprinkles sugar on a tart, to sprinkle the whole comedy with that gay love, without collecting it together at any one point.

During the first few days I was in despair. To sketch the characters in a few strokes, to weave the plot, to extract all the juice from that enormous Shakespearian orange, without letting the useless pips slip into the little glass, to write with colour and clarity and brevity, to delineate the musical plan of the scene, so that there results an organic unity that is a *piece of music* and yet is not, to make the joyous comedy live from beginning to end, to make it live with a natural and communicative gaiety, is difficult, difficult, difficult; and yet must seem simple, simple, simple.

He promised to bring 'at least the first two acts' to Sant' Agata in October. He needed the rest of July, he said, to settle a few details of his own work. On 1st August he sent a note: 'I'm ready. Please return me the sketch of *Falstaff*; re-reading it and thinking it over again, I shall work more easily.' He said nothing about *Nerone*, allowing Verdi, it seems, to presume it was finished: 'Bravo, bravo, bravo three times over! How punctual you were!!! Here is the sketch of . . . and get to work. It seems like a dream.' On 18th August Verdi wrote again: 'You are working, I hope? The strangest thing of all is that I am working too! I'm amusing myself by writing fugues! Yes, sir; a fugue . . . and a *comic fugue*, which would be in place in *Falstaff*!

You will say: "But how do you mean, a comic fugue? Why comic?" I don't know *how* or *why*, but it's a *comic fugue*!' It thus seems likely that the concluding fugue, 'Tutto nel mondo è burla', was the very first part of the opera to be written, before he even had the words.

By the end of October the first two acts of the libretto were almost ready and early in November Boito took them to Sant' Agata, where he stayed a week. The third act was finished in the first week of March 1890. On the 8th of that month Verdi sent the librettist the agreed sum of money, 'not as payment, but as a mark of gratitude for your having written for me this stupendous *Falstaff*'. Meanwhile he had not been idle. On 17th March he announced: 'The first act is finished, without any alteration at all to the poetry—just as you gave it me. I believe the same thing will happen with the second act, apart from a few cuts in the concerted piece, such as you yourself suggested. We won't talk of the third, but I don't think there will be much to do in that either.'

A shadow fell over this joyous collaboration with the illness and death of Faccio, who if all had gone well would probably have conducted the first performance of the new opera. Faccio's health had already given cause for concern; his position at La Scala was no longer secure and he had many rivals; Verdi had strongly recommended him to accept the position of director of the Conservatorio at Parma. For a time he resisted, but then gave in to the combined urging of all his friends. But it was already too late; the onset of general paralysis was suspected and he was sent to Graz to consult Krafft-Ebing. A large part of the cares and responsibilities resulting from this tragedy fell on Boito's shoulders. 'Sad days, dear Maestro,' he wrote, after Faccio had left. 'He was so good, so genuinely honourable. We were fellow students. . . .'

Krafft-Ebing refused to accept the case, and Faccio returned to Milan, already out of his mind. 'Our poor friend is lost,' Boito told Verdi on 12th April. 'There is no hope of saving him. He would be better dead. I'll spare you the details of his condition, so as not to renew the anguish in talking of it. . . . In a few days' time we shall move him to a house in the country, near Monza, very well chosen, isolated and quiet. Let us hope he stays there until the end, and that the end comes quickly.' A delicate question now arose as to Faccio's position at Parma. Could he continue to draw his salary, of which his family had need, in these circumstances? Boito consulted Verdi, whose opinion, though sympathetic, was that poor Faccio, condemned by the doctors, had no further claim. And Boito, who valued his liberty above all else, sacrificed part of it for his friend, accepting an appointment as honorary director. The intrigues of the Neapolitan Paolo Serrao, who aspired to the post, and was pulling all the strings within his reach, were thus frustrated, and Faccio's salary continued to be paid.

All this was in the course of Boito's long love affair with Eleonora Duse, and the agony of mind he largely concealed from others is revealed in some of his letters to her, published by Nardi: 'If you knew in what sorrow and horror I live, you would spare me your harsh words and your suspicions. My sick friend has returned insane. There is no more hope. It is terrifying to see him. I spend my days, all my hours, beside him. . . . There where he hoped for healing, they would not have him. There is no more hope for the poor fellow. It's a horrible thing. I shall stay beside him as much as I can; I hope to be able to accustom myself to this torment.'

Circumstances such as these were far from favourable for work on a comic opera, but on 21st May Boito sent Verdi a variant of the text for the final fugue. He would be coming to Sant' Agata after a visit to Parma, he said, and hoped to hear some new music. But Verdi had to tell him: 'Alas! I have done nothing more . . . except for a few full stops or commas added or altered in what was already written.'

Announcing another visit from Parma, later in the year, Boito wrote: 'This world is full of sorrows; our friend's condition grows continually worse, his old father's life is in danger—he is very ill. Let us try to keep well, dear Maestro, as long as we can, and forget life in working.' This time Verdi had better news about the opera:

I have not worked much, but something I have done.

The sonnet in the third act tormented me, and to get it out of my head I put aside the second act and, beginning at that sonnet, on and on, one note after another, I got right to the end. . . .

It's only a sketch! And who knows how much of it will have to be rewritten! We'll see later on. *Mondo ladro, mondo ribaldo, reo mondo!*—says Falstaff!

I know, and I knew it, indeed, thirty years before you.

That poor Faccio!

It's not a year since he came here and, walking late in the garden, I spoke to him in frank, sincere, and perhaps also rather harsh words, for which I now reproach myself. . . .

Mondo ladro! . . .

Replying to outside inquiries he always emphasized that he was merely amusing himself in writing this music; he generally minimized the progress that had been made. He told the journalist Eugenio Checchi on 30th December that little or almost nothing of the music was written; two days later he told Ricordi that about half of it was sketched; he did not expect to finish it in 1891, he said.

Nothing at all was done in the early months of that year. 'I have not been able to warm up the engine,' he told Boito. But then the wheels began slowly to turn again. '*Falstaff* after his four months' illness is thin, very thin! Let's hope we find some fat capon to fill up his belly! Everything depends on the doctor! Who knows? Who knows?' Boito's visits were always stimulating. At Sant' Agata in May he read aloud the libretto of *Nerone*, which Verdi found 'splendid' and about which he wrote enthusiastically to Ricordi. And then in June came this:

> Big Belly is going crazy. There are days when he doesn't move, but sleeps and is in a bad humour. At other times he shouts, runs, jumps, causes a devil of a rumpus. I let him indulge his whims a bit; if he continues I'll put on a muzzle and a strait jacket.

And Boito:

> Three cheers! Let him go, let him run, he will break all the windows and all the furniture of your room—it doesn't matter, you will buy some more. He will smash the piano—it doesn't matter, you will buy another. Let everything be turned upside down, as long as the great scene is finished. Three cheers! Give it him! Give it him! What pandemonium! But pandemonium as clear as sunlight and as vertiginous as a madhouse!

Faccio died on 21st July. 'It's all over,' Boito wrote. 'Death alone could cure him and death has truly cured him. On his face, after life had departed, there reappeared the noble expression of human reason.'

Two acts and a half were completed by September, and Verdi decided to push on with the scoring. 'Dear Boito,' he wrote on 10th September, 'just one word: I have a correction to make. It is not true that I have finished *Falstaff*. I am putting into full score all I have done, because I'm afraid of forgetting some passages and instrumental combinations. Afterwards I'll do the first part of the third act, and then amen! This part is shorter and less difficult than the others.'

The winter again brought an interruption of work, both poet and composer being laid low by influenza. The scoring of the first act was completed in April 1892. Boito, as in the case of *Otello*, was thinking of the casting, the costumes and scenery; he was also to undertake the extremely difficult task of translating the libretto into French, in collaboration this time with Paul Solanges. But in May 1892 Verdi was still refusing to be hurried: 'It's too early, too early, to be thinking of the costumes and scenery for *Falstaff*. First of all, will it be performed? And where? With what singers? In what theatre? And with what impresario? And then . . . shall I finish what remains to be done? At this moment I feel so tired, so listless, that it seems impossible that I shall be able to finish it! When Giulio returns we'll talk it over.'

In August he tried hard to stimulate Boito. A Genoese newspaper had published statements made by Mascagni in the course of a gathering in a restaurant. He was reported to have said that his *I Rantzau* and the one-act *Zanetto* were both finished, that he had in mind a Roman subject, *Vestilia*, and was studying Hamerling's writings, because he was thinking also of a *Nerone*; and to his startled listeners he added: 'Yes, *Nerone*, for which Maestro Boito still gives me so much time.' Verdi read this, and wrote at once:

Sant' Agata, 6th August 1892.

DEAR BOITO,

I don't think I've ever been as indiscreet as others, in speaking to you too often of *Nerone*. But after the enclosed article from *Il Secolo XIX*, of Genoa, I think it my duty, on account of our friendship and the esteem in which I hold you, to say that now you must hesitate no longer. You must work night and day, if need be, so that *Nerone* is ready next year. Indeed, it would be well to have published at once: 'This year *Falstaff* at La Scala, next year *Nerone*.' This will seem to you like replying to the impertinent remarks quoted in the Genoese paper. True! But it can't be helped and, to my way of thinking, there's nothing else to be done.

If I've expressed myself badly, if I've said too much . . . consider my words unspoken! You know that the old are gossips and grumblers. . . .

Farewell. Farewell.

Affectionately,

G. VERDI.

Boito replied that the article left him completely indifferent, that on account of Mascagni's words he would not hurry on the completion of his work by a single day, but that Verdi's kind and forcible letter had been such an incitement that if now he did not make progress he would never do so. 'I promise you, by the great love I bear you, that I will make every effort to finish the work in time for performance the year after *Falstaff*.'

The first act of Verdi's opera, fully scored, had been sent to Ricordi in August; the third act followed in September. It is not clear when the music of the first part of the second act, the last to be composed, was written, nor precisely when this act too was completely scored and thus the whole work finished. Early in October Ricordi and Boito took to Sant' Agata a model theatre, to settle all the details of the staging. In November and December, at Genoa, Verdi was coaching some of the singers in their roles.

After the triumphal first performance of *Falstaff*, under Edoardo Mascheroni, at La Scala on 9th February 1893, Verdi again drew Boito on to the stage to share the acclamations. Later that night he led him on to the balcony of his rooms at the Albergo Milano, besieged by cheering crowds. Boito's own first impressions are given in a letter to his friend Camille Bellaigue, the French critic:

> What am I to say? Where am I to begin? In your letter, with admirable clairvoyance, you touch with the tip of your finger on the very essence of the work. You say: This is the true modern and Latin lyric drama (or lyric comedy). But what you cannot imagine is the immense intellectual joy that this Latin lyric comedy produces on the stage. It's a real outpouring of grace, of strength and gaiety. Shakespeare's sparkling farce is led back by the miracle of sound to its clear Tuscan source, to 'Ser Giovanni Fiorentino'. Come, come, dear friend, to hear this masterpiece; come to spend two hours in the gardens of the Decameron. . . . If you come soon, perhaps Verdi will still be here; he is not leaving until about the middle of next week. You will hear a performance that still retains all the freshness and charm of things newly born.

After *Falstaff* there was one persistent question in his mind: did any possibility exist of further collaboration? After the first performance of *Falstaff* in Rome, a little later in this year, Boito suggested *Antony and Cleopatra*, which he had translated for Eleonora Duse, as the subject of a new opera. There were persistent rumours, too, about *King Lear*, and he certainly did some work on this subject. Nardi found the plan of a libretto in three acts, and a fragment of the opening scene; there are annotations, too, in Boito's hand in his copy of the play, like those in his copies of *Othello* and the various sources of *Falstaff*. But nothing came of all this, after Giuseppina gave the anxious warning: 'Verdi is too old, too tired.'

The last works were the very concise and beautiful *Te Deum* (1895–6) and the *Stabat Mater* (1896–7), which, together with the *Ave Maria* on an 'enigmatic scale' (1889) and the *Laudi alla Vergine Maria* (composed at an uncertain date between *Otello* and *Falstaff*) make up the *Quattro Pezzi Sacri.*

Verdi was particularly attached to his *Te Deum*; he is said to have wished it to be buried with him. He had been struck by the contrast between the text of the canticle and the jubilant, festal strains to which it had often been set. 'The opening lends itself to that,' he told Giovanni Tebaldini, 'for Heaven and Earth rejoice: *Sanctus, Sanctus, Deus Sabaoth*; but towards the middle it changes tone and expression. *Tu ad liberandum*—it is Christ born of the Virgin, who opens to humanity *Regnum coelorum*. Humanity believes in the *Judex venturus*, invokes Him in *Salvum fac*, and ends with a prayer, *Dignare Domine die isto*, moving, sad, to the point of terror. All that has nothing to do with victories and coronations. . . .' For a time he was interested in discovering whether other settings existed which interpreted the text in his way. Tebaldini helped to find some for him, in print and manuscript.

Several letters to Boito mention these last compositions:

Genoa, 18th February 1896.

DEAR BOITO,

Eureka!

I have found a *Te Deum*! Nothing less! Composed by Padre Vallotti, whom, as you know, I greatly admire.

I have written to Tebaldini to have a copy made for me.

I tell you all this so that you may remember that on 14th February 1896 you saw a *Te Deum* of mine, in case they accuse me . . . but no, no, there's no danger, for I shall never publish it.

I know that Gallignani is at Milan; give him my regards.

Here everything is as usual.

L'Eclair asks for my opinion of poor Thomas. . . . I'm not replying at all, and don't you reply to this either. Farewell.

G. VERDI.

Sant' Agata, 11th June 1896.

DEAR BOITO,

Peppina is out of bed; she's not ill, but eats nothing, so her strength is returning with difficulty.

As for Montecatini, it's not to be thought of now; if she can undertake that journey we'll see each other first at Milan.

Thank Tebaldini for the trouble he has taken over the *Te Deum*; but now what is done is done, nor could I give a different interpretation to that canticle, even if the reading of the *Te Deums* of Purcell and Vittoria showed me I was wrong. Once it's finished, for only a few passages of the scoring are lacking, I'll put it together with the *Ave Marias* and they'll sleep without ever seeing the light of day. Amen.

Until we meet again then!

When?

Perhaps at Milan! . . . But certainly at Sant' Agata.

Thanks and greetings from Peppina; I affectionately clasp your hand.

Your

G. VERDI.

Genoa, 17th April 1897.

DEAR BOITO,

. . . I haven't thought any more about the *Stabat*, the orchestration of which is *in statu quo*. I haven't thought any more about it, nor am I thinking about it! . . . and if I do think about it, the idea of exposing myself before the public again is repugnant to me. In fact, why should I affront judgments, useless chatter, criticism, praise, hatred, affection in which I don't believe?

Just now I don't know what I want to do!

Everything I could do seems useless! I can't settle anything now! In case I finish the scoring I'll write to you about it!

Thank you for everything and farewell.

Yours affectionately,

G. VERDI.

Boito's task now was to persuade Verdi to allow the *Pezzi Sacri* to be performed and published. He had undertaken the greater part of the preliminary negotiations before the first performances in Paris of *Falstaff* and *Otello*, respectively in the spring and autumn of 1894—both attended by Verdi. Duse had written to him: 'That old magician makes the fairies sing, and makes you dance, too.' One reads in the biographies that Boito made arrangements in secret for the performance of the *Pezzi Sacri* in Paris in Holy Week, 1898, disclosing this to Verdi only after everything was settled. This sounds improbable, though he may well have made provisional arrangements, while Verdi was still uncertain what he wanted to do. The remark in the above letter, 'In case I finish the scoring I'll write to you about it,' suggests that Boito had already broached the subject of performance. There is correspondence with Ricordi about these works in the succeeding months: Verdi hesitated a long time before allowing himself to be persuaded to publish them; he finally sent them to Ricordi in October.

Boito was invited to pay his usual autumn visit:

Sant' Agata, 10th October 1897.

DEAR BOITO,

You usually come to Sant' Agata when there's no one else here. Now we are alone; and if you come you'll find Sant' Agata even more boring than usual.

Peppina has been ill, confined to bed for several weeks. Now her cough is almost gone, but she doesn't take nourishment and is extremely weak; she is not happy, speaks very little, and it's almost as though it vexes her to hear others speak. As for myself, without being very ill, I have a thousand troubles. My legs barely support me and I can hardly walk any more; my eyes are weak and I can't read for long; furthermore I'm also a bit deaf. In short, a thousand troubles!

You will understand that if Sant' Agata was boring in the past, now it is very gloomy indeed! If you come and have the courage to face so many troubles you will always be welcome and will perform a Work of Mercy:

No. 6: *Visit the sick*.

Farewell. Farewell.

Affectionately,

G. VERDI.

In case you come, you must let me know in advance, because this year too Peppina wants to drag herself to Cremona for a few days with her sister.

Giuseppina's strength, and with it her life, was slowly ebbing away. Her last known letter is this to her sister: [1]

[1] In the Scala Museum.

Sant' Agata, 1st November 1897.

DEAR BARBERINA,

I haven't written to you for some time, being always in and out of bed, owing to this catarrhal cough I can't get rid of. I have thought of you, however, and am always thinking of you, and I am glad of the good news received through Maria. May God at least concede you a bit of better health than mine! I can barely bring myself to swallow an occasional mouthful, and in consequence am becoming continually weaker. But one must resign oneself, and God's will be done!

You will have received the 100 lire, which will cover your expenses. Today is All Saints Day, but every day to me seems a day of mourning! You, at least, take every care of yourself, so that you can enjoy a few days of sunshine, and excuse me if weakness obliges me to write infrequently. Give my regards to Maria.

To you, from the depths of my heart a kiss and an embrace from your affectionate sister.

PEPPINA VERDI.

Pneumonia supervened and the end came on 14th November.

Boito was in Paris, probably in connection with arrangements for the projected performance of the *Pezzi Sacri*, and came hurrying back when he heard the news. Maria Carrara and her family, Teresa Stolz, the Ricordis and Boito did what they could for the stricken composer. For a time he was quite silent, erect, refusing to sit down, unable to trust himself to speak, like a great oak, still standing after a lightning flash.

He opened Giuseppina's will.

Sound in mind and body, I invoke Divine Justice, that my last will, the ultimate act of my life, may respond to justice and equity.

Having already provided during my lifetime for the benefit of other persons dear to me, I institute and nominate as universal legatee of all my remaining private property my beloved husband Giuseppe Verdi, praying the Almighty to protect him in life and in death and to reunite him to me for eternity in a better world.

The will is dated from Cremona, 24th May 1897, with a list of personal legacies of jewellery and clothes, dated from Sant' Agata, 18th–20th June 1897. These personal legacies include:

To Teresa Stolz:

(1) A watch covered in brilliants and
(2) a chatelaine of gold and green enamel;
(3) a bracelet of Roman work, with the word *Souvenir* in brilliants.

After the series of legacies comes this:

One sole object I beg him, with tears in my eyes, to keep by him until his death and then to leave to my sister Barberina, if she is still living, or to Maria Carrara Verdi, who will keep it as a sacred memory!—that is my gold bracelet, given me at Naples, bearing the inscription: 'To my dear Peppina, 1872,' and the wedding ring.

And in conclusion:

To relieve my beloved husband and universal legatee of the greater part of the trouble and legal duties concerning the execution of this my last will and testament, I nominate as my executors the advocate Amilcare Martinelli and the notary Lino Carrara.

And now: Farewell, my Verdi! . . . As we were united in life, may God lead our spirits together again in Heaven!

What did Verdi feel, as he read it? Had she led him, as some people think, to Christian beliefs again? Was it significant that his last creative strength was given to religious works? Boito did not think so, as his celebrated later letter to Bellaigue shows:

This is the day, of all the days of the year, that he loved the best. Christmas Eve recalled to him the holy marvels of childhood, the enchantments of faith, which is only truly celestial when it mounts as far as belief in miracles. That belief, alas, he had early lost, like all of us, but he retained, more than the rest of us, perhaps, a poignant regret for it all his life.

He gave the example of Christian faith by the moving beauty of his religious works, by the observance of rites (you must recall his handsome head bowed in the chapel of Sant' Agata), by his homage to Manzoni, by the ordering of his funeral, found in his will: *one priest, one candle, one cross*. He knew that faith is the sustenance of the heart. To the workers in the fields, to the unhappy, to the afflicted around him, he offered himself as example, without ostentation, humbly, severely, to be useful to their consciences.

And here one must arrest the inquiry: to proceed further would take me far in the meanderings of psychological research, where his great personality would have nothing to lose, but where I myself would fear to miss my way. In the ideal, moral and social sense he was a great Christian, but one must be very careful not to present him as a Catholic in the political and strictly theological sense of the word: *nothing could be further from the truth.*

This letter has been misused in the most amazing way, by Don Botti and Luzio among others, to 'prove' the very opposite of what Boito meant.

The arrangements for the performance of the *Pezzi Sacri* (except for the *Ave Maria* on the 'enigmatic scale' which he called a mere 'charade') were providential in distracting Verdi in the months after Giuseppina's death. He agreed to go to Paris himself, but in the end, on medical advice, he decided that Boito should go instead. During the rehearsals he wrote long letters almost daily, about the soloists, the chorus, the orchestra and all the most important points of interpretation. When everything went off well he was profoundly relieved, and thankful.

Genoa, 8th April 1898.

DEAR BOITO,

In going to Paris in my place you have rendered me a service for which I shall always be grateful. But if you reject any form of recognition I remain crushed by a burden I cannot and ought not to support. Well then, my dear Boito, let's talk frankly, without reticence, like the true friends we are.

To show you my gratitude, I could offer you some trifle or other, but what use would it be? It would be embarrassing for me, and useless to you.

Permit me therefore, when you are back from Paris, to clasp your hand here. And for this handclasp you will not say a word, not even 'Thank you'. Further, absolute silence on the present letter. Amen. So be it.

Affectionately,

G. VERDI.

Boito paid that visit. Nothing was said about Verdi's gratitude, but much was understood. Nothing was said either about the serious illness of Camillo Boito's wife. Arrigo only learned of this when he reached Milan.

Genoa, 14th April 1898.

DEAR ARRIGO,

It's all too true that I was aware of poor Madonnina's condition.

I did not wish to mention it to you here, so as not to anticipate by a few hours an inevitable sorrow.

I can imagine poor Camillo's anguish! How I can imagine it!!

And you, my poor Arrigo!!!

All I can find to say to you is an unnecessary word—*Courage!*

If I can do anything I am at your service. Farewell.

Affectionately,

G. VERDI.

Here for the first and only time in this correspondence he uses Boito's Christian name.

Two months later Madonnina Boito died:

Sant' Agata, 24th June 1898.

DEAR BOITO,

I have just read the terrible news!

I weep with Camillo and with you in this fatal loss!

If my poor house of Sant' Agata can be any relief to both of you, come. I await you with open arms. Farewell.

G. VERDI.

PS. La Stolz has just arrived from Salsomaggiore.

Sant' Agata, 4th August 1898.

DEAR BOITO,

You will both be always welcome at Sant' Agata at any time. I am very glad your brother is able to occupy himself. Occupation, study, the exertions of the journey will be a first relief for him.

About myself I can tell you no more than that I am about the same as before I went to Montecatini. But now for nearly a year I have been feeling the burden of age! Life is departing!

Good night.

Farewell. Farewell.

G. VERDI.

He spent more time in these last years at Milan, where Boito and his friends were constant in attendance. His letters are full of complaints about his health, but to others he seemed, at eighty-five, still full of life. 'Verdi is marvellously well,' Boito told Bellaigue. 'He plays the piano, sings, eats as he pleases, walks, argues with juvenile vivacity. He is as merry as a lark. I shall see him this evening. I'll tell him I have written to you; he will say: "You must give him my regards." I shall reply: "It's already done."'

This is the last dated letter to Boito:

Sant' Agata, 20th October 1900.

DEAR BOITO,

I shall be brief because writing tires me; and be it said once and for all, whenever you please and your engagements permit you to come to Sant' Agata, it will always be a joy to me and to us all.

I am as God wills! I'm not really ill, but my legs barely support me, and my strength diminishes from day to day. The doctor comes twice daily for the massage but I don't feel any improvement.

I don't know when I shall be able to come to Milan. I have need of Winderling, but I don't know yet whether he is at Milan.

We are in agreement then. With a warm handclasp I am

Yours affectionately,

G. VERDI.

He moved to Milan in December, to his usual apartments in the Albergo Milano. There, in the morning of 21st January 1901, he had a stroke, while dressing himself; he lay unconscious for nearly a week and died on 27th January.

The pious say he smiled and even squeezed the hand of the priest when extreme unction was administered on 24th January. Boito told Giovanni Cenzato, however, that on that same day the only momentary return to consciousness came when the doctor, Pietro Grocco, put his gold watch, which struck the hours with a brief musical phrase, to the ear of the dying composer. He opened his eyes, smiled, and lost consciousness again.

The death of Verdi is described by Boito in a wonderful letter to Bellaigue:

Today is Easter Day, day of forgiveness; you must forgive me then. I used to spend this day with him at Genoa, every year; I arrived on Good Friday (he kept in his heart the great Christian festivals, Christmas and Easter); I stayed until Monday. The tranquil charm of that annual visit comes back to my mind, with the Maestro's conversation, the patriarchal table with the customary dishes, strictly according to ritual, the piercing sweetness of the air and of that great Palazzo Doria, of which he was the Doge.

This is the first time I have dared to write of him in a letter. You see that you must forgive me. I was victim of a kind of partial *abulia*; my thoughts, in the form of true remorse, were with you almost every day. You write me such kind letters; I had read your beautiful words in *Le Temps*, so deeply moved and so nobly moving; my will was powerless to reply, for it would have been necessary to say something about this great loss, and I could not do it. I suffered over it; I was ill.

I threw myself into my work, as if into the sea, to save myself, to enter into another element, to reach I know not what shore or to be engulfed with my burden in exertions (pity me, my dear friend) too great for my limited prowess.

Verdi is dead; he has carried away with him an enormous measure of light and vital warmth. We had all basked in the sunshine of that Olympian old age.

He died magnificently, like a fighter, formidable and mute. The silence of death had fallen over him a week before he died.

Do you know the admirable bust by Gemito? M. Cain (the composer you know) has it in his house. That bust, made forty years ago, is the exact image of the Maestro, as he was on the fourth day before the end. With head bowed on his breast and knitted brows he looked downwards and seemed to weigh with his glance an unknown and formidable adversary and to calculate mentally the forces needed to oppose him.

His resistance was heroic. The breathing of his great chest sustained him for four days and three nights. On the fourth night the sound of his breathing still filled the room, but the fatigue. . . . Poor Maestro, how brave and handsome he was, up to the last moment! No matter; the old reaper went off with his scythe well battered.

My dear friend, in the course of my life I have lost those I have idolized, and grief has outlasted resignation. But never have I experienced such a feeling of hatred against death, of contempt for that mysterious, blind, stupid, triumphant and craven power. It needed the death of this octogenarian to arouse those feelings in me.

He too hated it, for he was the most powerful expression of life that it is possible to imagine. He hated it as he hated laziness, enigmas and doubt.

Now all is over. He sleeps like a King of Spain in his Escurial, under a bronze slab that completely covers him.

My dear Bellaigue, imagine what consolation it would be for me to collaborate with you in a work on Verdi! At the moment it is impossible.

When my own cruel labour is ended I shall reclaim that great joy—be sure of that. Meanwhile do something yourself.

Bellaigue's *Verdi* was published in 1913, the centenary year, in French and Italian; it includes a few extracts from these letters and is dedicated to Boito: 'En souvenir du maître que nous avons aimé.' They wrote nothing together, for Boito's own 'cruel labour' was never ended. After Verdi's death, an infinitely touching and lovable figure, he went forward into the new century, under the Atlas-burden of his unfinished, unfinishable opera. 'I have forged with my own hands the instrument of my torture,' he said. The rest of his life was spent in ineffectual struggles to complete *Nerone*, in despite of melancholia, neurasthenia and the graphophobia which for long periods made it impossible for him to write so much as a letter. The memory of his work for Verdi, of his intimacy with that titanic creative figure, the embodiment of everything he himself was not, became almost his sole consolation. 'I feel the need to thank you for having found a place for my name beside his,' he told Bellaigue. 'Nothing moves me so profoundly as to hear myself named when he is spoken of.' There are many such echoes in his late letters. 'The *voluntary servitude* I consecrated to that just, most noble and truly great man is the act of my life that gives me most satisfaction.' And again: 'Dear, dear friend! That man was a prodigious artist! A genius! A genius of music and the theatre! In a month and a half's time, ten years will have passed since I watched him die!' . . . 'To be the faithful servant of Verdi, and of that other, born on the Avon—I ask no more.' In his last illness, in 1918, he wept on hearing the name of Toscanini, already chosen to conduct the first performance of his opera. 'No one can help me,' he said. But he had really fulfilled his destiny in causing the 'bronze colossus', as he called Verdi, to resound twice. He lives still, less as a composer than as a personality, an influence, a letter-writer, and as Verdi's incomparable librettist.

Index

Index